PENGUIN BOOKS

SERGIO

Samantha Power serves in the Obama administration as the Special Assistant to the President for Multilateral Affairs and Human Rights. She is on leave from Harvard Kennedy School, where she is the Anna Lindh Professor of the Practice of Global Leadership. Her book *A Problem from Hell: America and the Age of Genocide* won the 2003 National Book Critics Circle Award for Nonfiction and the Pulitzer Prize for nonfiction. She began her career covering the wars in the former Yugoslavia from 1993 to 1996, writing for the *Boston Globe*, *U.S. News and World Report*, and the *New Republic*. Before joining the administration, she was an active journalist, reporting from Cambodia, East Timor, Kosovo, Rwanda, Sudan, Zimbabwe, and elsewhere. She is a contributor to *The New Yorker* and a foreign policy columnist for *Time* magazine. She was the founding executive director of the Carr Center for Human Rights at the Kennedy School (1998–2002). A graduate of Yale University and Harvard Law School, Power moved to the United States from Ireland in 1979, at the age of nine. She is married to Cass Sunstein.

Praise for *Sergio* by Samantha Power

"Surely the life and death of Sergio Vieira de Mello is a good place to begin a serious debate about the proper way to manage world order in the future."
—Francis Fukuyama, *The New York Times Book Review*

"The strength of the book lies in Power's use of Vieira de Mello's life (and death) as a well-placed window on the international community's successes and failures. . . . An ambitious effort . . . [that] succeeds brilliantly." —James Mann, *The Washington Post*

"Her book [has] the dramatic quality of a leaked memo. . . . Sergio Vieira de Mello, with his flaws and heroism, represents us at our best and at our most helpless."
—Paul Berman, *Slate*

"[A] detailed and sympathetic biography. . . . Thoughtful." —*The Economist*

"Power presents a fiercely precise, extraordinary dramatic biography. . . . Strongly argued, lacerating, and utterly human, this invaluable history will be the catalyst for soul searching and debate." —*Booklist*

"Power's writing is . . . excellent, and the story is told with forceful analysis and an open mind." —*Seattle Post-Intelligencer*

"*Sergio* is an impressively researched book. Power's notes include references to more than four hundred interviews, and she cites everything from interoffice e-mails to Vieira de Mello's high school term papers. Casting a wide net provides Power with memorable details that capture Vieira de Mello's charisma and complexity: a bottle of Johnny Walker hidden in his desk, a plastic bag full of foreign coins for pay-phones . . . she nimbly excavates colorful artifacts from Vieira de Mello's life."

—*San Francisco Chronicle*

"[*Sergio*] is fascinating on several levels: how a person immersed in horror keeps moving toward the goal of peace, making compromises along the way; how the United Nations works and, quite often, doesn't work; and how passive most of the world remains in the face of humanitarian disasters. . . . A gripping heartbreaking story."

—*The Dallas Morning News*

"Power incorporates the moral indignation into her account that readers will be accustomed to from her previous book, '*A Problem from Hell*,' about genocide in the twentieth century. She is unequivocal in condemning injustice and demanding more-effective policies from the UN and various nations, especially the U.S. She brings Vieira de Mello to life as a mirror for the tragedies of our contemporary world—filled with idealistic effort and little delivery on that promise. . . . Power's insightful book should remind us how much our world needs new international institutions. Building these institutions—and perhaps restructuring the UN in the process—should be a priority for the next American president." —*Chicago Tribune*

"Samantha Power has written a stirring biography of Sergio Vieira de Mello. . . . Yet Power . . . doesn't stop there. Her new book examines the travails of the United Nations itself during Vieira de Mello's decades with the organization."

—*Milwaukee Journal Sentinel*

"A masterful biography." —*Marie Claire*

"In meticulous, unsentimental prose, Power portrays Vieira de Mello not as a martyr but as a man who knew too much, a tragic emblem of squandered opportunities in Iraq. . . . In eloquently asking who will keep [the flame] alive, Power proves herself a worthy candidate." —*Vogue*

"Fact, observation, analysis—these are Samantha Power's strong suits, as *Sergio* demonstrates. Power is a romantic, a person of unebbing passion and in *Sergio* she has undertaken to save Viera de Mello's legacy through a relentless sorting of the rubble of his many postings during a thirty-year UN career." —*02138*

"Samantha Power offers an ambitious, comprehensive biography of Vieira de Mello, and in the process disassembles questions about how the whole international community should respond to civil wars and genocide." —*The Santa Barbara Independent*

"If Joan of Arc were alive today, she'd be Samantha Power. . . . Power breaks the frame of what a hero is." —*Contribute New York*

"Riveting." —*Bloomberg.com*

"Compelling." —*men.style.com*

"[A] rich life story." —*Deseret Morning News*

"[Power] tackles policy and personality with equal deftness, comprehensively depicting the paradoxical elements of Vieira de Mello's character.... We need these maxims on the page." —*Stop Smiling*

"Power's new book provides a finely etched, brutally honest yet reverential portrait of perhaps the most talented diplomat the UN ever produced." —*The Globe and Mail*

"*Sergio* is a brilliantly researched biography about an extraordinary man." —*The Times* (London)

"Power, who combines humanitarian passion and a girlish capacity for hero worship with analytical rigor, a clear prose style, and a gift for narrative, has written a remarkable book. It is not only a gripping story, which takes on the awful fascination of a Greek tragedy as it approaches the catastrophic ending.... It also forces the reader to think about some of the most uncomfortable issues in contemporary politics, without offering an easy or simple solution." —*The Guardian* (London)

"Power brilliantly reconstructs the horror of the blast." —*The Telegraph* (London)

"Inspirational, wise in its rueful acknowledgment of the limitations placed on humanitarian action by the powerful, Power's book is a fitting memorial to a great and generously flawed life. It is also one of the most engrossing and frightening accounts of our troubled, conflicted century." —*The Observer* (London)

"A compelling work, culminating in a brilliant and moving reconstruction of Vieira de Mello's doomed last mission in Iraq, and the frantic, disorganized rescue efforts to pull survivors from the bombed-out Canal Hotel as his life seeped away in the rubble." —*The Times Literary Supplement* (London)

"With her compelling and insightful biography, Power has done something marvelous—and, considering the spirit of the times, urgent and bold.... What Power has done is to narrate a life of the UN itself through the story of one of its most distinguished and heroic officials.... An illustrative tale and a way to move forward." —*National Post* (Canada)

"Samantha Power's new book is a tribute to an important man, and beyond that a tribute to the idea of possibility and optimism in the world today, which is a rare enough thing to merit mention.... [An] excellent new book." —*The Walrus* (Canada)

"While Vieira de Mello's story is compelling in itself, the real value of this book is Power's ability to use the UN diplomat as a symbol for the trials and tribulations of the organization he so proudly served. By viewing the myriad issues facing the UN through the experiences of one individual, the reader gains unique insight into challenges that continue to test the institution." —*Winnipeg Free Press* (Canada)

"Power has brought to life . . . a complex figure who dared to take on the greatest challenges, always seeking to reach even higher." —*Library Journal*

"Her description of failed attempts to rescue Sergio from the rubble of the UN's quarters in Baghdad, where he was Secretary General Kofi Annan's special representative, is both riveting and heartbreaking." —*Kirkus Reviews*

"This majestic, profoundly important book deserves to reach the widest possible audience. As a biography of an endlessly fascinating man, it is beautifully written, enthralling from start to finish and as a study of leadership, it ranks with the very best. As an analysis of how to respond to the struggles of the new era in which we find ourselves, it is the defining work for our generation."
—Doris Kearns Goodwin, author of *Team of Rivals*

"The best way to understand today's messy world is to appreciate the inspiring life and diplomatic genius of Vieira de Mello. Samantha Power has done a brilliant job. This is a compelling biography of a fascinating man but also more: through his life and tragic death we get a better feel for how to deal with the challenges of religious extremism, refugees, terrorism, and ethnic struggle. If only he were still alive! Read this book and weep, read it and understand, read it and cheer."
—Walter Isaacson, president of the Aspen Institute and author
of *Einstein: His Life and Universe*

"Samantha Power has mined the tragic 2003 death of UN High Commissioner Sergio Vieira de Mello in Iraq to tell an even bigger story. For three decades Vieira de Mello courageously embodied the oft-maligned and seemingly hopeless UN mission to bring kindness, sanity, and peace to a cruel and war-torn world. He ultimately was martyred to it, struggling to salvage order out of the mess the U.S. invasion had made in Iraq. In this captivating life story, the charming Brazilian internationalist emerges as a wry, Scotch-loving, womanizing philosopher, a kind of secular saint who wedded his considerable personal ambition to the best hopes of mankind. It is a stirring portrait of courage and tenaciously pragmatic idealism."
—Mark Bowden, author of *Guests of the Ayatollah* and
national correspondent for *The Atlantic*

"This book fascinates, both because of its subject, Sergio Vieira de Mello, the urbane UN troubleshooter who was regarded by many as the Secretary-General-in-Waiting, and because of the infinite complexity of the issues Vieira de Mello faced in places like Lebanon, Kosovo, and Iraq, where he ultimately met his death. Samantha Power has engaged in a work of vivid reportage that also contemplates with subtlety and depth the pivotal question that preoccupied Vieira de Mello: how the international community could intervene effectively in the many places that threaten to engulf the world in flames." —Scott Turow, author of *Presumed Innocent*

SERGIO

One Man's Fight to Save the World

SAMANTHA POWER

Penguin Books

Previously published as *Chasing the Flame*

PENGUIN BOOKS

Published by the Penguin Group

Penguin Group (USA) Inc., 375 Hudson Street, New York, New York 10014, U.S.A.

Penguin Group (Canada), 90 Eglinton Avenue East, Suite 700, Toronto,
Ontario, Canada M4P 2Y3 (a division of Pearson Penguin Canada Inc.)

Penguin Books Ltd, 80 Strand, London WC2R 0RL, England

Penguin Ireland, 25 St Stephen's Green, Dublin 2, Ireland (a division of Penguin Books Ltd)

Penguin Group (Australia), 250 Camberwell Road, Camberwell,
Victoria 3124, Australia (a division of Pearson Australia Group Pty Ltd)

Penguin Books India Pvt Ltd, 11 Community Centre, Panchsheel Park, New Delhi – 110 017, India

Penguin Group (NZ), 67 Apollo Drive, Rosedale, North Shore 0632,
New Zealand (a division of Pearson New Zealand Ltd)

Penguin Books (South Africa) (Pty) Ltd, 24 Sturdee Avenue,
Rosebank, Johannesburg 2196, South Africa

Penguin Books Ltd, Registered Offices:
80 Strand, London WC2R 0RL, England

First published in the United States of America as *Chasing the Flame* by The Penguin Press,
a member of Penguin Group (USA) Inc. 2008
Published in Penguin Books 2008
This edition with the title *Sergio* published 2010

1   3   5   7   9   10   8   6   4   2

Photograph credits appear on pages 595–96.

THE LIBRARY OF CONGRESS HAS CATALOGED THE HARDCOVER EDITION AS FOLLOWS:
Power, Samantha.
Chasing the flame : Sergio Vieira de Mello and the fight to save the world / Samantha Power.
p.   cm.
Includes bibliographical references and index.
ISBN 978-1-59420-128-8 (hc.)
ISBN 978-0-14-311777-3 (this pbk.)
1. Mello, Sergio Vieira de, 1948–2003.   2. United Nations. High Commission for Human Rights.
3. War relief.   4. Peace building.   5. Iraq War, 2003—Casualities.   6. United Nations—Biography.
7. Diplomats—Brazil—Biography.   I. Title.
D839.7.M45P68   2008   2007030978
341.4'8092—dc22

Printed in the United States of America
Designed by Meighan Cavanaugh

For Morton Abramowitz,

Stephen Power, and

Frederick Zollo

CONTENTS

PART II

PART III

CHRONOLOGY

January 1942   In Washington, D.C., representatives of twenty-six countries fighting against the Axis Powers sign a "Declaration by United Nations" in support of the Atlantic Charter, which was signed by President Franklin Roosevelt and Prime Minister Winston Churchill the previous August. This is the first official use of the term "United Nations," a phrase suggested by Roosevelt.

1945   Germany surrenders on May 7, and Japan surrenders on August 15, ending World War II. More than six million Jews and five million others were exterminated in the Holocaust.

1946   The first UN General Assembly, gathering fifty-one nations, meets in Westminster, London. The UN takes up residence in New York later in the year.

The Nuremberg tribunal convicts twenty-two of the twenty-four leading Nazi suspects on charges of war crimes, crimes against humanity, and crimes against peace.

March 15, 1948   *Sergio Vieira de Mello is born in Rio de Janeiro, Brazil.*

June 1950   With the Soviets boycotting the Security Council, the Council calls on member states to send troops to protect Korea from a northern invasion. President Harry Truman declares, "We can't

let the UN down," and sends 50,000 troops into the Korean
War, which ends in an armistice in 1953.

November 1956   The First Emergency Special Session of the UN General
Assembly responds to the British and French seizure of the
Suez Canal by sending the first-ever UN peacekeeping force
to Egypt.

September 1960   In the UN's biggest increase in membership in a single year,
seventeen newly independent states, sixteen from Africa, join
the organization.

March 1964   The military stages a coup in Brazil, ushering in twenty-one
years of military rule.

1966–1969   *After graduation from a Franco-Brazilian high school in Rio
and a short stint at the University of Rio, Vieira de Mello
moves to Europe, where he studies philosophy at the University
of Fribourg and then at the Sorbonne in Paris.*

May 1968   *Students and workers stage mass demonstrations in Paris,
where Vieira de Mello is badly beaten.*

1969   *Vieira de Mello's father, Arnaldo, is forced to retire from the
Brazilian foreign service.*

*After graduating from the Sorbonne, Vieira de Mello joins the office
of the UN High Commissioner for Refugees (UNHCR) in
Geneva, becoming an assistant editor at the agency's headquarters.*

1970–1974   *While working at UNHCR, Vieira de Mello completes
his doctorate in philosophy (Doctorat de Troisième Cycle en
Philosophie) at the Sorbonne.*

1971–1972   *Vieira de Mello serves as a UNHCR field officer in Dhaka,
East Pakistan/Bangladesh.*

June 2, 1973   *Vieira de Mello marries Annie Personnaz near her parents'
home in France.*

June 12, 1973   *Arnaldo Vieira de Mello dies suddenly in Rio de Janeiro.*

1973–1974   *Vieira de Mello works as a UNHCR associate program officer
                  in Khartoum and Juba, Sudan.*

December 1974   *Thomas Jamieson, former UNHCR director of operations,
                  dies suddenly in Geneva.*

1974–1975   *Vieira de Mello serves as a UNHCR program officer and
                  assistant representative in Nicosia, Cyprus.*

April 1975   The brutal Khmer Rouge take power in Cambodia. The last
                  U.S. forces depart from Vietnam.

1975–1977   *Vieira de Mello serves as UNHCR deputy representative
                  in Maputo, Mozambique.*

1978–1980   *Annie Vieira de Mello gives birth to two sons, Laurent (1978)
                  and Adrien (1980).*

                  *Vieira de Mello works as UNHCR regional representative
                  in northern South America, in Lima, Peru.*

1978–1985   *Vieira de Mello completes the prestigious state doctorate
                  (Doctorat d'État ès Lettres et Sciences Humaines) at the
                  Sorbonne.*

1981–1983   *Vieira de Mello takes leave from UNHCR to serve as
                  the senior political adviser to the UN Interim Force in
                  Lebanon (UNIFIL) in Naqoura, Lebanon.*

June 1982   Complaining of Palestinian raids into northern Israel,
                  Israeli forces invade Lebanon, where they will remain
                  until 2000.

October 1983   In Beirut, Lebanon, Islamic suicide bombers drive trucks
                  into the U.S. Marine and French army barracks, killing
                  241 American and 58 French soldiers.

1983–1985   *Vieira de Mello works under Kofi Annan as UNHCR's deputy head of personnel services in Geneva.*

1986–1988   Mikhail Gorbachev, who became Soviet premier in 1985, introduces *glasnost* ("opening up") and *perestroika* ("reconstruction").

Vieira de Mello serves as chief of staff for UN High Commissioner for Refugees Jean-Pierre Hocké.

1988–1990   *Vieira de Mello directs UNHCR's Asia Bureau while also serving as chairman of the steering committee of the International Conference on Indochinese Refugees.*

June 1989   Some seventy governments gather in Geneva to sign the Comprehensive Plan of Action, facilitating the return and resettlement of Indochinese refugees.

November 1989   The Berlin Wall falls, marking the beginning of the end of the cold war.

1990–1993   *Vieira de Mello serves as director of external relations at UNHCR, helping to raise funds and overseeing communications.*

1991   The Soviet Union collapses under the weight of dire economic straits and surging nationalism. In January 1992, Russia will take over the Soviet seat at the UN Security Council.

A U.S.-led, UN-backed coalition defeats Iraqi forces in the Persian Gulf War, forcing Saddam Hussein to leave Kuwait. With the encouragement of President George H. W. Bush, Iraqi Kurds and Shiites rebel against the Iraqi regime, but are crushed. In April the United States, the U.K., and France launch Operation Provide Comfort in northern Iraq, facilitating the return of half a million Kurds to their homes.

June 1991	Croatia and Slovenia declare their independence, unleashing war in Yugoslavia.
October 1991	Cambodia's four main factions sign the Paris peace agreement, agreeing to demilitarize, allow the return of refugees, and hold free elections. In March 1992 the UN Transitional Authority in Cambodia (UNTAC), a peacekeeping mission of 22,000 UN soldiers and civilians, will be sent to Cambodia to enforce the peace.
1991–1993	*Vieira de Mello serves as UNHCR special envoy for Cambodia and UNTAC director of repatriation. He also takes on the role of interim director of the Cambodian Mine Action Center.*
April 1992	After Bosnia follows Croatia and Slovenia in seceding from Yugoslavia, Serb nationalists launch a war to create a "Greater Serbia" that will unite Serbs across the region. A vicious three-and-a-half-year conflict in Bosnia ensues.
1993	UNHCR completes the repatriation of some 360,000 Cambodian refugees, and UNTAC holds relatively peaceful elections in Cambodia. In 1997, Hun Sen, who finished second in the elections, will seize power in a coup.
1993–1994	*Vieira de Mello takes leave from UNHCR to join the United Nations Protection Force (UNPROFOR) in Bosnia. Initially he serves as the top UN civilian official in Sarajevo and then becomes the head of civil affairs, based in Zagreb.*
October 1993	A firefight in Mogadishu, Somalia, erupts between U.S. forces assisting a UN peacekeeping mission and militants loyal to the Somali warlord Mohammed Farah Aideed. Eighteen Americans are left dead, along with more than a thousand Somalis. President Bill Clinton announces a U.S. withdrawal, and he urges the UN to "learn to say no" to some peacekeeping missions.

April 1994 The plane carrying the Rwandan and Burundian presidents is shot down, sparking a one-hundred-day genocide in which Hutu extremists exterminate some 800,000 Rwandan Tutsi and moderate Hutu.

In Bosnia, after the UN-declared "safe area" of Gorazde comes under Serb attack, Vieira de Mello leads a small team into the enclave to gauge Serb compliance with a NATO ultimatum.

June 1994 Nelson Mandela is elected president of South Africa. After a twenty-four-year absence, South Africa once again takes its seat in the UN General Assembly.

July 1994 Some two million Rwandan Hutu flee to neighboring Congo and Tanzania, where UNHCR sets up camps that both keep civilians alive and keep Rwandan *génocidaires* fed and clothed, enabling them to rearm for future battle.

1995–1996 *Vieira de Mello serves as UNHCR director of policy planning and operations, based in Geneva.*

July 1995 In Bosnia, the UN "safe area" of Srebrenica is overrun by Serb forces, who systematically murder eight thousand Bosnian men and boys. The largest massacre in Europe in fifty years sparks international outrage, which gives rise to a NATO bombing campaign that helps end the Bosnian war and bring about the Dayton Peace Agreement.

November 1996 Rwandan government forces team up with Zairean rebels to wipe out the Rwandan Hutu refugee camps in Zaire and, in May 1997, to overthrow Zairean dictator Mobutu Sese Seko.

Vieira de Mello serves as UN humanitarian coordinator for the Great Lakes region of Africa, a post he will hold for two months.

December 1996 *Vieira de Mello and the Tanzanian government negotiate an agreement to close the UNHCR camps housing Hutu*

*refugees along the Rwandan border. The announcement results in an
exodus of more than 450,000 people from the camps.*

Kofi Annan is named the seventh secretary-general of the
UN, replacing Boutros Boutros-Ghali, whose second term
was vetoed by the United States. Annan will serve two terms
and step down in December 2006.

1998–1999   *Vieira de Mello leaves UNHCR and moves to UN Headquarters
in New York, where he serves as under-secretary-general for
humanitarian affairs and emergency relief coordinator.*

March 1999   NATO launches what will be a seventy-eight-day bombing
campaign in Serbia, aimed at securing autonomy for Kosovo.

May 1999   *Vieira de Mello leads a small interagency UN team on an
assessment mission into Kosovo to assess NATO collateral
damage and Serb ethnic cleansing.*

June–July 1999   *After Serbia surrenders, Vieira de Mello is named interim
Special Representative of the Secretary-General in Kosovo,
governing the province before handing off to the permanent
UN administrator, Bernard Kouchner of France.*

September 1999   The people of East Timor vote overwhelmingly for
independence, and Indonesian-backed militia respond with
a rampage of arson and murder. An Australian-led
Multinational Force of 11,500 intervenes to help restore
stability to the island.

November 1999–   *Vieira de Mello serves as Special Representative of the
May 2002   Secretary-General and UN transitional administrator in
East Timor.*

September 11,   Al-Qaeda operatives use civilian airliners to attack the
2001   World Trade Center and the Pentagon, resulting in the deaths
of more than three thousand Americans. President George W.
Bush soon announces the launch of a "global war on terror."

October 2001   The United States leads a coalition of forces to war in Afghanistan, ousting the Taliban in December.

June 2002   The UN helps convene a *loya jirga,* which chooses Hamid Karzai as the new president of Afghanistan.

September 2002   *Vieira de Mello becomes United Nations High Commissioner for Human Rights in Geneva.*

March 5, 2003   *Vieira de Mello meets with President Bush and National Security Adviser Condoleezza Rice at the White House.*

March 20, 2003   The United States and the U.K. lead an invasion of Iraq.

April 2003   Iraqis celebrate the overthrow of Saddam Hussein by tearing down statues of him throughout Iraq. Widespread looting begins.

June 2003   *Vieira de Mello becomes Special Representative of the Secretary-General in Iraq and leads a small political team to Baghdad.*

August 19, 2003   *A suicide bomber drives a truck into the UN headquarters in Baghdad, killing Vieira de Mello and twenty-one others.*

INTRODUCTION

A t 8:45 a.m., on Tuesday, August 19, 2003, five months after the American-led invasion of Iraq, Sergio Vieira de Mello arrived by car at the headquarters of the United Nations in Baghdad. He had been unusually quiet on the drive over, and his bodyguards thought that he was showing signs of the strain of an ever less relevant UN presence and a collapsing security situation.

Having worked his entire adult life for the UN, Vieira de Mello, a fifty-five-year-old Brazilian, had plenty of experience with frustration. In his thirty-four years of service, he had moved with the headlines, working in Bangladesh, Sudan, Cyprus, Mozambique, Lebanon, Cambodia, Bosnia, Rwanda, Congo, Kosovo, and East Timor. He spoke Portuguese, English, French, Italian, and Spanish fluently and dabbled in several other languages. He had been rewarded for his talents with the toughest assignment of his career: UN envoy to Iraq.

He was suited for the job not because he knew Iraq—he didn't—but because he had amassed so much experience working in violent places. He could perhaps show the Americans what to do—and what not to do. He had long ago stopped believing that he brought the solutions to a place's woes, but he had grown masterful at asking the questions that helped reveal constructive ideas.

Work had always been a place of refuge, and when he entered the UN's Baghdad base at the Canal Hotel he took the stairs up to his third-floor office, greeting staff members along the way. He spent the morning reading the latest cable traffic from UN Headquarters in New York and responding to e-mails.

In the late morning his security guards prepared a convoy to take him to the Green Zone, the fortified district where the American and British Coalition administrators had set up their base in Saddam Hussein's abandoned palaces. He was scheduled to meet with L. Paul Bremer, the American administrator of Iraq, and a delegation of U.S. lawmakers from Washington.

By noon his armored sedan was ready to go, but just then Bremer's office called. The flight bringing the U.S. congressional delegation to Baghdad from Kuwait had been delayed, and the lunch meeting would have to be canceled. He telephoned Carolina Larriera, his fiancée, who was an economic officer in the mission. "I've been spared," he said. "Do you want to grab a sandwich?" Larriera said she couldn't because she had to send out invitations for an upcoming conference by 5 p.m. He told her he was counting the days—forty-two remaining—before they would fly to Brazil for a month's holiday.

UN officials had not expected to play a significant political role in Iraq. In the run-up to the war, the White House had scorned the UN, likening it to the ineffectual League of Nations. Vice President Dick Cheney had said that the UN had proven itself "incapable of dealing with the threat that Saddam Hussein represents, incapable of enforcing its own resolutions, incapable of meeting the challenge we face in the twenty-first century."[1]

But in the weeks following the toppling of Saddam Hussein's statue in Baghdad, it had become clear that U.S. soldiers were going to need help. Suicide bombings had not yet begun, but widespread looting had, and those who had so easily dislodged the Iraqi dictator seemed increasingly lost when it came to managing the turbulent aftermath of his reign. European leaders who felt they had been snubbed back in March, when the United States and Britain had chosen to go to war, now agreed with Washington on one issue: Kofi Annan, the UN secretary-general, should deploy a team of specialists to help speed the day that Iraqis regained control of their country.

Vieira de Mello was chosen to head that team because of his vast experience, but also because a few weeks before the U.S. invasion of Iraq, he had done something few UN officials before him had managed: He charmed George W. Bush. In a meeting in the Oval Office, Vieira de Mello had criticized U.S. detention policies in Guantánamo and Afghanistan and pressed the president to renounce torture; yet Bush had warmed to him as a man. When the day came to choose an envoy, Annan appointed Vieira de Mello, believing he was the one man whose advice the Bush administration might heed. Annan also knew that his charismatic colleague was the rare troubleshooter who could secure the simultaneous backing of the American, European, and Arab governments.

During the eleven weeks he had spent in Iraq, Vieira de Mello had tried to find and expand the space where the UN could make a difference. Under Saddam Hussein, Sunnis had been the favored sect, but Vieira de Mello saw the danger of a new Shiite tyranny of the majority. He attempted to forestall it by pressing for the inclusion of Sunni leaders in the transition process and by enlisting the support of the leading Shiite clerics who were refusing to meet with Bremer. And he pressed Coalition officials to end their dependence on Ahmad Chalabi and other exiles who had a greater following in Washington than in Iraq.

But Bremer resisted implementing the UN's most important suggestions. Vieira de Mello had tried and failed to gain greater UN and Red Cross access to Iraqi detainees in U.S. custody. He had tried and failed to persuade Bremer to devise concrete timelines for a constitution, for elections, and for the exit of U.S. troops. And he had tried and failed to get the Coalition to rescind or scale back its two most destabilizing decrees—the wholesale de-Ba'athification of Iraqi institutions and the disbanding of the Iraqi army. By late July he had grown depressed. He told colleagues that Bremer and the Iraqis had stopped returning his phone calls.

Now, with two hours unexpectedly freed up, he returned to his cluttered to-do list. Up to then he had never publicly criticized the Coalition's excessive use of force, but he decided to change course, instructing an aide to draft a press release criticizing the Coalition's recent shooting of civilians. The more obstruction he met in Baghdad, the more his mind drifted forward to September 30, the day he would return to his full-time job in Geneva as UN High Commissioner for Human Rights. His time in Iraq had filled him with ideas about how to make a UN backwater—a sponsor of costly reports and seminars—matter in the lives of real people.

At 3 p.m. he met with two officials from the International Monetary Fund to discuss the Coalition's rush to privatize Iraqi state enterprises. Around 4:25 p.m. he started his last meeting of the day, warmly greeting Gil Loescher and

Arthur Helton, two American researchers who were in Iraq to examine the humanitarian costs of the war. He ushered them to a coffee table in an alcove near his office window. Two members of his UN team—Fiona Watson, a Scottish political affairs officer, and Nadia Younes, his wisecracking Egyptian chief of staff, rounded out the circle.

Just after the group had taken their seats, a deafening explosion sounded, and the sky flashed white. One person present likened the light to "one million flashbulbs going off all at once." The windows shattered, sending thousands of glass spears flying across the office. The roof, the walls, and the floor beneath the office caved in, then crashed down, pancake style, onto the floors below. The last words uttered, a split-second after the explosion, belonged to Vieira de Mello. "Oh shit," he said, seemingly more in resignation than in surprise.

"HE'S LIKE A cross between James Bond and Bobby Kennedy." This was how a journalist colleague described Sergio Vieira de Mello to me on the eve of my first meeting with him. It was April 1994, I was a novice reporter in the former Yugoslavia, and he was reputed to be the most dynamic and politically savvy figure in the UN mission there. We had friends in common, and he agreed to brief me on the conflict over a meal on April 15 in the Croatian capital of Zagreb.

The UN peacekeeping mission in neighboring Bosnia, which had been in a state of steady crisis for two years, was on the brink of collapse. On April 10, NATO had staged the first bombing raid in its entire forty-five-year history, attacking Serbs who were besieging the UN "safe area" of Gorazde. Yet in the face of what proved a tame show of Western force, the Serbs defiantly continued their assault. I had been told that Vieira de Mello was a true believer in the UN. I did not expect him to keep our appointment for dinner.

But when I telephoned to give him the opportunity to cancel, he was remarkably calm. "The sky is falling here," he said, "but a man has got to eat, hasn't he? If World War Three starts while we're at dinner, we won't order a second bottle of wine."

The UN had been established in 1945—in the words of its founding Charter—to "save succeeding generations from the scourge of war."

The Security Council, the UN's most powerful organ, was responsible for maintaining international peace and security. Because each of its five permanent members—Britain, China, France, the Soviet Union, and the United States—could veto the resolutions of the others, the Council had been paralyzed by U.S.-Soviet tensions during the cold war. But for a brief period after the fall of the Berlin Wall, the major powers at last seemed prepared to work together through the UN to keep peace. In 1991, in keeping with his promise of promoting a "new world order," President George H. W. Bush had obtained UN support to oust Saddam Hussein's Iraqi forces from occupied Kuwait.

Within a year of the U.S.-led coalition's triumph in Kuwait, however, it had become clear that many governments did not believe their national interests were imperiled by the carnage in the Balkans. They spent hundreds of millions of dollars on humanitarian aid, which prevented Bosnians from starving, but they did not stop the slaughter. They sent peacekeepers into a live war zone, causing critics to chide UN officials like Vieira de Mello for simply "passing out sandwiches at the gates of Auschwitz."[2]

We met at 8 p.m. at a seafood restaurant on the outskirts of town. He carried a cell phone, then still a fairly exotic device. While living in Cambodia in 1992, he told me, he had one of the earliest available models. The size of a quart of milk, it had lengthy antennae and could work only outdoors. By the time of his posting to the Balkans, the phones had slimmed down to the size of walkie-talkies.

No sooner had we been seated than the phone rang. Lieutenant General Sir Michael Rose, the UN commander, was telephoning from Sarajevo to brief him on the evening's tumultuous events. I made a motion to move away in order to give him his privacy. He insistently waved me back to my seat and pointed to the wine that the waiter had just brought to the table. He did not seem to be the type of international diplomat who spent his time scheming about how to plant self-serving stories in the press. But if he happened to have an audience for his high-stakes activities, he also wouldn't shoo it away.

He winced throughout Rose's update, which lasted around five minutes. When he hung up, he told me what he had learned: Bosnian defenses around Gorazde had collapsed, exposing British soldiers to attack. One of Rose's men had been shot and badly injured. The UN was attempting to manage a medical evacuation, and NATO bombers were standing by in case they were needed again. Gorazde, which was home to 65,000 Bosnians, looked poised to fall. "It's going to be a long night," Vieira de Mello said wearily, though no part of him seemed to mind. I could see how he had gained a reputation for workaholism, unflappability, and a commitment to enjoying life despite the despair around him.

In the breaks between calls, I asked him how he had ended up at the United Nations. "Nobody else would take me," he said, implausibly. "I was a child of 1968," he explained, proudly recounting how, when he was studying philosophy at the Sorbonne in Paris in 1968, he had joined his fellow students in revolt. He was beaten so badly by the police that he had required hospitalization. He pointed to the scar above his right eye—a monument to his rebellious youth.

I asked if he had been tempted to follow in the footsteps of his father, who had worked for the Brazilian foreign service. He shook his head violently. "The Brazilian government ruined my father's life," he said. A few years after the military regime seized power in 1964, the generals had forced his father into early retirement. "I would never work for Brazil," he said.

As he rattled off the various war zones he had worked in, I wondered how a man of his adventurous tastes was managing to endure the staid pace of life in peaceful Zagreb. When I asked him if he missed Sarajevo, where he had lived for five months, he groaned. "You have no idea," he said. "I would take life under siege any day over endless staff meetings and paperwork. I was born to be in the field."

Again his phone rang, transforming this man of hearty laughter and animated tales into a sober diplomat, deliberate and exceedingly self-conscious about his choice of words and even his grave facial expressions. His eyes narrowed in concentration as General Rose told him that Serb shelling had abated long enough for the UN to evacuate the wounded British officer to Sarajevo. But soon after the young soldier arrived, he died. "I'm so sorry, Mike," Vieira de Mello said. When he ended the call, I asked him what the UN would do. He said he was certain of only one thing. "In the UN, we cannot surrender our impartiality. It is perhaps our greatest asset."

I asked him what he would do if he were in charge. "In charge of the world?" he asked. "Or in charge of the UN mission?" The distinction was essential, he insisted. While the peacekeepers had become global symbols of cowardice, they were following instructions from powerful capitals. "The one thing you have to remember," he said, "is that the major powers will kick the UN. They'll scream at the UN. But at the end of the day they are getting the UN that they want and deserve. If the United States and Europe wanted a muscular peacekeeping operation here, they would insist on adding muscle. If they really wanted to stop the Serbs, they would have done so long ago."

As our meal wound down, he reached into the breast pocket of his elegantly tailored blazer and pulled out a battered piece of paper—a single page—that constituted the only formal instructions the Security Council had ever offered him or the peacekeepers there in the Balkans. It was the third page of UN Security Council Resolution 836, which had set up the six "safe areas," including Gorazde. He had underlined and double-underlined the important passages and made notes to himself in the margins in blue pen, red pen, black pen, and pencil. He had refolded the resolution so many times that when he held it up to the table lamp, its creases made it virtually see-through.

He pointed to the key paragraph, which said the UN peacekeepers were in Bosnia "to deter attacks against the safe areas." "But what is required for 'deterrence'?" he asked. "What constitutes an 'attack'?" he continued. "And what in the hell—no, where in the hell—are the 'safe areas'?" The countries on the Security Council had passed the resolution, he said, but they had never bothered to delineate the boundaries of the safe zones. "That's not a coincidence," he insisted. "If nobody knows what is officially protected, then nobody can be called upon to do the protecting."

He focused on a pivotal comma. "Look at this," he said. "The resolution says we should 'comma—*acting in self-defense*—comma—take the necessary measures—comma—including the use of force' to respond to attacks against civilians!" No matter how many times he had studied the UN mandate, its vagueness continued to enrage him. "What are the commas supposed to mean?" he asked. "Does it mean the UN should only use force in self-defense? Or does it mean we should use force in self-defense and also to protect the Bosnians?" I was flabbergasted by his intimacy with the text. I had never even thought to read the text of UN resolutions, which seemed of little relevance to the tragedy unfolding.

At the end of our dinner, he was driven back to the operations room at UN headquarters. As we parted, he told me somewhat melodramatically that

Western countries were on the verge of deciding more than the future of a troubled region. They were defining their approach to the post–cold war global order and determining the future of the United Nations, which had been waiting almost a half century for its chance to civilize the world. He seemed to believe the UN was up to the task. Judging from what I had seen in Bosnia, I was skeptical.

IN THE DECADE that separated the war in Bosnia from that in Iraq, Vieira de Mello became a global figure. In 1999 the UN got into the governing business for the first time, and he was the one tapped to run two small statelets—Kosovo, where he deployed on seventy-two hours' notice, and then the tiny half-island nation of East Timor, which he administered for two and a half years. Suddenly a man who had practiced his leftism "loudly" back in 1968 was walking around in a safari suit and being teased by his staff for taking on the absolute powers of a colonial "viceroy." After years of critiquing governments, he found himself struggling to balance fiscal discipline and social welfare, liberty and security, and peace and justice. In the eyes of powerful governments, he had become the "go-to guy"—handed one mission impossible after another. By the time he shepherded East Timor to independence in 2002, colleagues and international diplomats had begun placing wagers on when—not whether—he would become UN secretary-general.

Vieira de Mello carried a leather-bound copy of the UN Charter with him when he traveled, and he suffered when the UN suffered. In his long career he saw religious extremists and militants take shelter in UN refugee camps, where they sold UN food for money to buy arms. He saw warlords transform themselves into used-car salesmen by selling stolen UN Land Cruisers (repainted but still bearing UN license plates). He saw proud French and British peacekeepers stripped of their weapons, handcuffed to lampposts, and turned into human shields. But he was more stung by the UN's self-inflicted wounds. While the bad guys in war zones were predictably bad, he was sometimes more frustrated by the sins of the nominal "good guys" who carried UN passports or wore UN berets. Senior officials, including himself, were often so eager to tell the major powers what they wanted to hear that they had covered up deadly facts or exaggerated their own successes. In Rwanda and Srebrenica, another UN "safe area" in Bosnia, UN peacekeepers had turned their backs on civilians who had sought the protection of the UN flag, paving the way for some of the largest massacres since the Second World War.

And yet. For all the indignities, he didn't believe countries acting outside the UN would fare much better. He knew that there was no other forum where all countries gathered to try to stop the planet's bleeding. Even while the debate over Iraq had shown that diplomacy would not always prevent war, many countries still tried to settle their differences through the UN. The organization had helped colonized peoples in the developing world achieve their independence, causing UN membership to nearly quadruple from 51 at the founding to 192. The UN had offered shelter, food, and medicine to civilians neglected or persecuted by their governments. For all of the UN's high-profile peacekeeping failures in the 1990s, blue helmets had been found to be more reliable and less expensive preventers of conflict than states acting alone. Most of the war zones in which Vieira de Mello had worked over the years had stumbled toward shaky peace, and UN officials had played essential roles in demobilizing combatants, punishing war criminals, rebuilding schools and health clinics, organizing elections, and returning refugees to their homes.

The organization had also paid him to see the world. In the UN he had made his closest friends—a multilingual and multicultural group of "ne'er-do-wells," as he described them—some idealistic and some cynical, but all, in his words, "bloody fascinating." The UN constituted his family. When he was asked how, with all of his intellectual and diplomatic gifts, he could tolerate the headaches that came with working for such a terrible bureaucracy, he would say, "Where else would I go?" But in unguarded, more freely sentimental moments, he confided, "Just look at everything the UN has given me." He also believed—initially as a function of his idealism, but later in keeping with his ruthless pragmatism—that the only way to bring about lasting global stability was to press countries to play by international rules—by UN rules.

Our paths intersected only occasionally after the Balkans, but whenever I ran into him, I was struck by his intellectual and cultural range. In conversation he would dart from the likely results of the next midterm election in the United States to the arrest of an opposition leader in Egypt to the favorites in the next World Cup soccer championship to his considered view of the latest R.E.M. album. In September 2002 I was surprised to learn that he had been named UN High Commissioner for Human Rights. He had always seemed more comfortable negotiating with wrongdoers than denouncing them from a distant platform. It didn't surprise me when I heard that he was the first human rights commissioner to meet with a sitting U.S. president. "Typical Sergio timing," I thought. "He becomes human rights czar at just the time George Bush decides to start talking about freedom and democracy."

I found the subsequent news of his appointment to Iraq both infuriating and encouraging. After deriding the UN in the run-up to war, Washington was now using it for its own purposes. But if Iraq had a prayer—and at that point it still seemed to—Vieira de Mello and his handpicked UN "A team" seemed to have the highest odds of answering it.

In the course of exploring Vieira de Mello's life, work, and ideas,* I have caught glimpses of the person I met on April 15, 1994. The contradictions that I encountered at our first dinner remain evident. He was somehow both the worldly realist who understood the interests of states and the motives of politicians and the UN acolyte who clung to his mauled copy of the latest Security Council resolution. He was a bon vivant who could drink and socialize into the wee hours of the morning and a fiercely disciplined official who was at his most content holed up in his office at 11 p.m. making phone calls to his UN colleagues several time zones away.

This is a dual biography. It is the life story of a brave and enigmatic man who saw the world very differently in 2003 than he had when he joined the UN in 1969. At the start of his career he advocated strict adherence to a binding set of principles. Like a good anti-imperialist, he was deeply mistrustful of state power and of military force. But as he moved from Sudan to Lebanon to Cambodia to Bosnia to Congo to Kosovo to East Timor to Iraq, he tailored his tactics to the troubles around him and tried to enlist the powerful. He brought a gritty pragmatism to negotiations, yet no amount of exposure to brutality seemed to dislodge his ideals. Unusually, he managed simultaneously to perform high-stakes peacemaking and nation-building tasks *and* to reflect critically on them. He thought a lot about legitimacy—about who had it and how they could keep it. He thought about competence and wondered, with all the ingenuity that fueled progress in the developed world,

---

*Quotations that are not sourced in the Notes are taken from my interviews, conducted between January 2004 and November 2007.

why so little of it was ever made available to assist what he called "convalesc-ing states." He thought about dignity, noting, "a wounded soul may hurt as much as a wounded body."[3] He thought, naturally, about how to work with a United States that was deeply ambivalent about—and often hostile to—inter-national institutions and laws. And long before they became catchphrases in the White House, he thought about the nature of evil and the roots of terror. By 2003 he had begun to worry that powerful countries were pursuing their own security in ways that aggravated their peril.

He had blind spots and made many mistakes, but he never stopped ques-tioning his own decisions or those of the world's governments. Thus, at the very time he was arranging food deliveries, organizing refugee returns, or negotiating with warlords, he was also pressing colleagues to join him in grappling with such questions as: When should killers be engaged, and when should they be shunned? Can peace be lasting without justice? Can hu-manitarian aid do more harm than good? Are the UN's singular virtues—impartiality, independence, and integrity—viable in an age of terror? When is military force necessary? How can its inevitably harmful effects be mitigated? He did not have the luxury of simply posing these questions. He had to find answers, apply them, and live with the consequences.

The biography of Sergio Vieira de Mello is also the biography of a dan-gerous world whose ills are too big to ignore but too complex to manage quickly or cheaply. Although the types of conflict—and the loci of Western attention—have shifted over the last four decades, every generation has had to deal with broken lives and broken societies. Because of the terrible costs of the U.S.-led war in Iraq, Americans today seem torn between two impulses. The first is to retreat from global engagement altogether. We do not feel sure that our government or we ourselves know what we are doing. The second is to go abroad to stamp out threats in the hopes of achieving full security. Vieira de Mello's life reminds us of the impossibility of either course. The United States can no more pack up and turn away from today's global threats than it can remake the world to its own liking. Vieira de Mello understood that just because he couldn't cure all ills didn't mean he should not do what he could to ameliorate some.

The question, for him and us, is not whether to engage in the world but how to engage. Although he did not have time to formulate a guiding doc-trine, he did have a thirty-four-year head start in thinking about the plagues that preoccupy us today: civil war, refugee flows, religious extremism, suppressed national and religious identity, genocide, and terrorism. He started out as a humanitarian, but by 2003 he had become a diplomat and politician, comfortable weighing lesser evils. His professional journey led him to believe the world's leaders needed to do three big things. First, they had to invest far greater resources in trying to ensure that people enjoyed law and order. Second, they had to engage even the most unsavory militants. Even if they did not find common ground with rogue states or rebels, at least they might acquire a better sense of how to outmaneuver them. And third, they would be wise to orient their activities less around democracy than around individual dignity. And the best way for outsiders to make a dent in enhancing that dignity would be to improve their linguistic and cultural knowledge base, to remind themselves of their own fallibility, to empower those who know their societies best, and to be resilient and adaptable in the face of inevitable setbacks.

Sergio Vieira de Mello spent more than three decades attempting to save and improve lives—lives that today continue to hang in the balance. As the war drums roll, and as cultural and religious fissures widen into canyons, there is no better time to turn for guidance to a man whose long journey under fire helps to reveal the roots of our current predicament—and perhaps the remedies.

Part I

Sergio Vieira de Mello in what would become
Bangladesh, November 1971.

One

DISPLACED

Sergio Vieira de Mello's youth left him with the impression that politics disrupted lives more than it improved them. In March 1964, around the time of his sixteenth birthday, a group of military officers decided to unseat João Goulart, Brazil's democratically elected president. Under Goulart the rural poor had begun seizing farmland, and the urban poor were staging food riots. The generals accused Goulart of allowing Communists to take over the country. Just five years after the Communist victory in Cuba, U.S. president Lyndon Johnson had similar concerns. The U.S. ambassador in Rio de Janeiro warned that if Washington did not act against Brazil's "radical left revolutionaries," the country could become "the China of the 1960s."[1] In an operation code-named "Brother Sam," four U.S. Navy oil tankers and one U.S. aircraft carrier sailed toward the Brazilian coast in case the generals needed help.[2]

They didn't. President Goulart had some support in the countryside, but much of the public had tired of him. On March 29 the front-page headline of the Rio newspaper *Correio da Manhã* declared "ENOUGH!" The next day it proclaimed "OUT!"[3] A force of ten thousand mutinous Brazilian troops marched from the state of Minas Gerais toward Rio. Goulart ordered his infantry to suppress the revolt, but they chose instead to join the coup, and Goulart fled with his wife and two children to Uruguay.

Young Sergio was no more political than most teenagers. His focus was on keeping up with his studies (he would finish first in his high school class), following the Botafogo soccer team (which that year would share the prestigious Rio–São Paulo Championship), and chasing girls on the Ipanema beach, just two blocks from his home. But his relatives and schoolteachers had led him to believe that Communism would be bad for Brazil and the military could be trusted to restore order. Brazil's generals had taken power in 1945, 1954, and 1961 and had ruled benignly and only briefly each time. Since the leaders of the coup promised to hold elections the following year, he joined his family and friends in initially cheering the military takeover.

"Their Tranquillity Has Disintegrated"

Arnaldo Vieira de Mello, Sergio's father, had grown up in a farming family in the agricultural hinterland of Bahia, Brazil's northeastern province.[4] Arnaldo and his four siblings had been sent away to a Jesuit boarding school in Salvador, the province's capital. After attending university in Rio, Arnaldo worked as an editor and war commentator at *A Noite* ("The Night"), a leading newspaper at the time. He was determined to pass the entrance exams for the Brazilian foreign ministry, which he did in 1941. So poor that he could afford neither books nor notebooks, Arnaldo did all of his reading at the Rio public library, squeezing his notes onto the palm-sized forms used to order library books. He carried around plastic bags filled with stacks of such forms and arranged the bags by subject area.

In 1935 Arnaldo met Gilda Dos Santos, a seventeen-year-old Rio beauty. He quickly befriended her mother, Isabelle Dacosta Santos, an accomplished painter, and her father, Miguel Antonio Dos Santos, a man of many talents who was well known in Rio as a writer of musical theater, a French and German translator, and a poet who ran a jewelry store with his brothers. "Arnaldo is getting engaged to my father," Gilda joked to friends. The young couple married in 1940 in Rio, and Gilda gave birth to a daughter, Sonia, in 1943 and then to Sergio on March 15, 1948.

The Vieira de Mellos lived a peripatetic existence typical of diplomatic families. In 1950 Arnaldo, then thirty-six, moved his wife and two children from Argentina, where young Sergio had spent his first two years, to Genoa, Italy. In 1952 Arnaldo was posted back to Brazil, where Sergio lived until he was nearly six. Arnaldo was next sent back to Italy to work at the con-

sulate in Milan, where Sergio and Sonia were enrolled in the local French
school. In 1956, the year of the Suez crisis, the family lived in Beirut, and
in 1958 they finally settled in Rome, where they lived for four years, one
of the longest consecutive stints Sergio would spend in a single city in his
entire life.

Arnaldo Vieira de Mello was a charismatic and highly cultured man.
"Audacity is the winner's gift," he liked to say, as he urged his son to be bold
in his intellectual and personal pursuits. But his own career stalled, and he
never earned the rank of ambassador. Frustrated by this professional plateau,
he became an increasingly heavy scotch drinker. When he brought the family back to Rio in 1962, he became a regular on the trendy nightclub circuit
there, keeping up with the current fashions and socializing late into the evenings. On the nights he stayed at home, he disappeared into his study, where
he immersed himself in a world of books and maps. While he maintained his
day job as a diplomat, he managed to write a history of nineteenth-century
Brazilian foreign policy, which was published in 1963 and became part of
the curriculum for aspiring Brazilian civil servants. He also embarked upon
an ambitious history of Latin American navies.[5] It was Gilda who kept close

The Vieira de Mello family (left to right: Sergio, Arnaldo, Gilda,
and Sonia) *in Cairo, December 28, 1956.*

watch on Sergio's studies, promising to buy him gifts in return for high marks
and taking him shopping the very day he received his grades.

When Arnaldo was assigned to the Brazilian consulate in Naples in late
1963, Gilda, who had learned to live a life that revolved around her children
more than her husband, thought it best to remain in Brazil. Their daughter,
Sonia, had gotten married and was expecting a child, while Sergio was attending the Franco-Brazilian lycée, a Rio school popular with the children
of diplomats. Arnaldo was afraid of flying, and since the steamer from Europe
took more than a week, he returned to Brazil just once a year.

The Brazilian military, which ended up running the country until 1985,
would rule more mildly than other Latin American martial regimes. Still,
the generals muzzled the press, suspended basic civil liberties, and ended up
killing more than three thousand people.[6] The military's reign was neither as
benign nor as temporary as Brazilians had expected.

Some of the ruling generals proved especially ruthless. In 1965, the year
after the coup, a group of hard-liners held sway. Sergio, who was by then
seventeen, spent several afternoons each week volunteering at the Rio de
Janeiro campaign headquarters of Carlos Lacerda, a charismatic local governor and anticorruption crusader who hoped to become Brazil's president
in the next election. But the generals turned on Lacerda, barring him from
political office and dissolving all major political parties. Sergio's uncle Tarcilo,
Arnaldo's youngest brother, was a brilliant congressman and orator who had
gained fame as the leading proponent of legalizing divorce. As the generals
tightened their grip, Tarcilo called on diverse political players, including Lacerda and the deposed president Goulart, to join forces in a Frente Ampla, or
"Broad Front," devoted to ending military rule and restoring democracy. But
after he ran unsuccessfully for governor of Bahia in 1967, he dropped out of
politics, and the generals maintained their grip on power.[7]

Sergio had studied philosophy in high school, and in an essay in his final
year, he reflected on the foundations of a just world, which, he argued, were
rooted not in religious morality but in the "more objective notions of justice
and respect." International politics were no different from social intercourse,
he wrote, in that the key to amicable ties was what he called "individual and
collective self-esteem." Only then could stability be built "on peace and understanding and not on terror."[8]

Later that year he enrolled in the philosophy faculty at the Federal University of Rio de Janeiro, which was plagued by teacher strikes. After one frustrating semester in the classroom, he asked his father, who had left Naples and become Brazil's consul-general in Stuttgart, Germany, if he could travel to Europe for a proper university education. Arnaldo granted his son's request, and Gilda traveled by ship with Sergio across the Atlantic in order to help him get settled. In Switzerland he met up with Flavio da Silveira, a Brazilian friend from childhood whose family lived in Geneva. The two friends enrolled at the University of Fribourg, in the picturesque medieval town an hour's drive from Geneva. They spent a year studying the writings of Sartre, Camus, Aristotle, and Kant, with a faculty composed largely of Dominican priests. Their appetites whetted, they applied for admission to the Sorbonne in Paris. Sergio, who had been educated in French schools his whole life, was admitted, while da Silveira was not and went instead to the University of Paris at Nanterre. It was at the Sorbonne, studying under the legendary moral philosopher Vladimir Jankélévitch, that Sergio received an in-depth introduction to Marx and Hegel and proclaimed himself a student revolutionary.

In May 1968 he was one of some 20,000 students who took to the streets against the de Gaulle government, demanding greater say in the national university system and calling for the abolition of the "capitalist establishment." In the worst fighting Paris had seen since 1945, riot police stormed student barricades with tear gas, water cannons, and truncheons, arresting Vieira de Mello and nearly six hundred other student protesters. The gash he received above his right eye was so severe that he would require corrective surgery thirty-five years later. Arnaldo drove in an official car from the Brazilian consulate in Stuttgart to Paris to see his son. When Sergio learned that his father had parked in the Latin Quarter, he exclaimed, "Run back there and move the car! The students are burning all the cars there today!" The standoff would become so violent that the rector of the Sorbonne would close the university for the first time in its seven-hundred-year history.

After a few weeks the French public began to turn against the protests, and workers who had joined the students in striking returned to work out of fear they would lose their jobs. After the student revolt had fizzled, Sergio penned a lengthy letter to the editor of the French leftist daily newspaper *Combat* complaining that the mainstream press was delighting in denigrating the student revolt. In his first published writing, he commended the violence as "salutary," noting that if the students had staged only peaceful rallies on the university campus, the French public would have looked the other way. Street fighting had been necessary in order to get the attention of an indifferent public. "One can awaken the masses from their lethargy only with the sound of animal struggle," he wrote.[9] But unless the struggle became "global, irreversible, and permanent" and brought about the "demise of fossilized thought," he argued, the students would go down in the French annals as "the organizers of a huge and laughable folkloric bazaar." He closed his letter with a raging salvo against the "old scum." "Let them cry over their repugnant past, let them worship their lost pettiness, let them fatten themselves at will," he wrote. "One thing is now certain: their tranquillity has disintegrated. We may be walking toward our most resounding failure, but their victory will also be their hell."[10] Sergio was so proud of his irate debut that he passed around copies of the article to friends. Although he could not have imagined it then, May 1968 would prove the apex of his antiestablishment activism.

Word of his contribution to *Combat* quickly reached his family in Brazil. His sister, Sonia, spotted a news item in one of the Rio newspapers describing a Brazilian student involved in the Paris clashes who had returned home and been abducted and murdered, presumably by the military regime. She panicked and passed the article along to a friend who was traveling to Europe. When Arnaldo saw it, he told his son that he should not risk returning to Brazil anytime soon. The French government had granted amnesty to foreign students arrested in the riots, but it required them to check in with the authorities at the police station on a weekly basis. This seemed a small price to pay for continuing his education at the Sorbonne, and Sergio went back to class in the fall of 1968 in the hopes of combining his credits from Rio, Fribourg, and Paris to graduate in 1969.

Although he relished the educational rigors of the Sorbonne, he was lonely in Paris and nostalgic for Rio. "People don't exist here," he wrote to a girlfriend in Geneva in March 1969. "I spend my time with books."[11] His letters grew increasingly mournful as he noted that "for two years nothing has changed except myself. Complaining of the crowds, cars, noise, and "an uninformed mass that I'm tired of, " he wrote that he missed "the days where I could walk alone with my sea birds."[12]

But back in Brazil the military dictatorship was growing more repressive. Paramilitary forces roamed the country arresting and often torturing those suspected of subversive activity. Well-known Brazilian diplomats such as Vinicius de Moraes, who in his spare time had helped launch the bossa nova genre by writing the lyrics for such songs as "The Girl from Ipanema," were dismissed from the foreign diplomatic corps. In the spring of 1969, five years after the initial coup, Arnaldo Vieira de Mello, who was neither well known nor openly critical of the military regime, was sitting at the breakfast table of his residence in Stuttgart, sipping his morning coffee, reading the morning papers, and flipping through Brazil's diplomatic digest. As he scanned the list of civil servants whom the military regime had forced into retirement, his eyes fixed suddenly upon a name he had not expected to find: his own. He had been sacked by a government he had served for twenty-eight years.

Sergio was in Paris when he learned the news. He raged at the Brazilian government for hurting his family and complained that his father had been fired for his political views. But Arnaldo's colleagues and relatives speculated that his worsening drinking habit may also have been a factor. The military regime offered no explanation.

As Arnaldo packed up his life in Europe, he told his son that he would not be able to pay for his graduate studies at the Sorbonne. In May, just two months before graduation, Sergio wrote again to the young woman he had dated when he was in Geneva. Sounding depressed and confused about his future, he informed her that his father had been fired. "The dictatorship is a reality," he wrote. "I will be obliged to earn my bread starting in August." He would try to find work but had "no idea" where. "My future is more than up in the air."[13]

In June he wrote to her that he expected to receive high marks in his philosophy exams. (He would in fact dazzle the Sorbonne faculty, finishing first out of 198 candidates in metaphysics.) "But for what?" he wrote sarcastically. If he had studied economics or marketing instead, "some American company would have assured me a 'happy' future strewn with dollars." He would never sell out, he told her, and "just short of dying of hunger," he would "never abandon philosophy." The philosopher, he wrote, could become either "the most just man" or "the most radical bandit." Either way, he insisted, "to do philosophy is to have it in your blood and to do what very few will do—to both be a man and to think everywhere and always."[14]

After trying briefly to find a philosophy teaching job, Sergio made his way to Geneva, where the da Silveira home had become his European base.

He decided to try to find work with one of the many international organizations there. Knowing Sergio's gift with languages (he already spoke flawless Portuguese, Spanish, Italian, and French), an acquaintance of his father's put him in touch with Jean Halpérin, the forty-eight-year-old Swiss director of the language division at the United Nations. Halpérin had hesitated to take the meeting because he knew of no available jobs, but when they met, he was immediately taken in by the young man's passion for philosophy. Halpérin offered to call the United Nations Educational, Scientific and Cultural Organization (UNESCO), which often needed ushers for large conferences on the preservation of cultural monuments. "Thank you very much," Sergio said, smiling politely. "I know UNESCO, and it is not my cup of tea. My sense is that it is a lot of 'blah, blah, blah.'" Surprised that someone unemployed would be so picky, Halpérin explained that his academic background would not leave him many options within the United Nations. "I'm very sorry, Sergio," he said, "but the UN deals with everything under the sun except philosophy."

A few days later Halpérin received a call from a colleague at the office of the United Nations High Commissioner for Refugees (UNHCR), which was looking for a French editor. UNHCR performed two main tasks—it gave people fleeing political persecution the material assistance they needed to survive in exile, and it tried to ensure that the displaced were not forced back to the countries that had driven them out. The United Nations required fluent English and two years of professional experience. Sergio spoke little English and had never held a full-time job, but he interviewed better than any of his fellow applicants and was given a temporary contract. He started his career at UNHCR in November 1969 and would spend the next thirty-four years working under the UN flag.

"WHAT WOULD JAMIE DO?"

Almost as soon as he took up his post at UNHCR, he began hearing tales of a man who was every bit his opposite. Vieira de Mello was a twenty-one-year-old Sorbonne-educated, multilingual Brazilian with a lean physique and a movie-star smile. Thomas Jamieson, UNHCR's director of field operations, was a fifty-eight-year-old pale, balding, rotund, bespectacled Scotsman who had never graduated from secondary school. And although Jamieson had lived in and out of French-speaking countries since the Second World War, he prided himself on having never bothered to master French. Despite these cosmetic differences, Vieira de Mello quickly found a mentor in the man known as "Jamie."

Jamieson had joined UNHCR in 1959 after working with UN and nongovernmental groups to resettle German, Korean, and Palestinian war refugees. Vieira de Mello actively sought him out, peppering him with questions about his experiences. Warm and instantly accessible to those he liked, Jamieson was not an intellectual like Vieira de Mello's father, but he placed a similar emphasis on audacity, and he shared Arnaldo's taste for scotch. First-time visitors to Jamieson's home near Geneva knew they had reached their destination when they saw the trash cans outside overflowing with empty whiskey bottles. Whether he was in his office at UNHCR or roaming around some dusty outpost in Nigeria, Jamieson always invited colleagues to join him for his close-of-business drink of Johnnie Walker Red Label. More than five thousand miles from his family and discouraged from returning to Brazil, Vieira de Mello seemed to prize the new bond.

Jamieson explained that his overarching aim—and that of the UN—was simple: "Children should have a better and happier life than their parents." He decried the refugee camps that had clogged the European continent after World War II. "If there is a way to avoid setting up a camp, find it," he would say. "If there is a way to close a camp, take it." His central message, conveyed to all who encountered him, was that "UNHCR ought to endeavor to eliminate itself."[15] Over long lunches in Geneva he warned Vieira de Mello that charitable enterprises could quickly grow more concerned with their own self-perpetuation than with helping the needy. Jamieson urged him to be sure to distinguish the interests of the UN, his place of employment, from the interests of refugees, his reason for working.

Jamieson generally managed field operations from afar, spending most of his time at UNHCR headquarters in Geneva. But when he ventured overseas, he made the most of it, ostentatiously arriving back, in the words of one colleague, "with the red dust of the Sahara still on his safari suit." He used slide shows and stirring oral accounts of the suffering of refugees to spice up the sterile and impersonal chambers of the Palais des Nations, where UN staff and ambassadors from donor countries gathered. Jamieson often sounded contemptuous of diplomats. "You're all sitting here in comfort," he would say after a trip. "I've come from the real world where the action is and where the answers are." He was never shy about voicing his impatience with legal hairsplitting, UN red tape, or diplomatic pomposity, and he despised the incessant and interminable array of meetings his job required. It was not uncommon for him to stroll fifteen minutes late into a coordination session that he was supposed to chair. "Ohhhh so I see we are having a meeting. How charming," he would say. "If there's one thing in the world I like, it is meetings. Tell you what we are going to do: I'll tell you what I have decided, then we can meet for as long as you wish!" Undemocratic in his approach, Jamieson got his way by relying upon his personal relationship with Prince Sadruddin Aga Khan, the powerful and visionary high commissioner who ran UNHCR.* Although Sadruddin could find Jamieson taxing, he valued his ability, in the words of a colleague, to "kick bean-counters with such finesse." While Vieira de Mello had none of Jamieson's willingness to make enemies, he shared his mentor's distaste for bureaucracy.

Vieira de Mello had joined UNHCR at an electrifying time. Under the leadership of Sadruddin, UNHCR shifted its emphasis from Europe, where refugees from World War II and the Soviet Union had commanded attention in the 1940s and 1950s, to Africa and Asia, where decolonization wars had created new refugee flows in the 1960s and 1970s. Of all the UN agencies, UNHCR had the best reputation among aid workers and donor governments. The U.S.-Soviet rivalry had neutered the Security Council, but UNHCR, which had its own governing board, or executive committee, had managed to thrive. It had already won one Nobel Prize—in 1954, for resettling European refugees after the Second World War—and was on its way to another in 1981, for managing the flight of refugees from Southeast Asia. As UNHCR expanded its work from Europe to Latin America, Africa, and Asia, staff members who spoke multiple languages or hailed from the developing world were put to use. Vieira de Mello, who had been UNHCR's youngest professional staff member when he joined at twenty-one, rose more quickly than most of his peers.

---

*Prince Sadruddin was the second son of Sultan Mohamed Shah Aga Khan III, imam of the Ismaili Shi-ites. He spent much of his youth in India, but he had French, Iranian, and Swiss nationalities. Educated at Harvard, he became the publisher of the *Paris Review* in the early 1950s and then joined the UN as a civil servant. He was appointed UN High Commissioner for Refugees in 1965 at the age of thirty-two, a post he held until 1977.

His leftist ideals still brewed close to the surface. Although he did not romanticize Communism as it was being practiced in the Soviet Union, China, or Cuba, he slammed the United States for its war in Vietnam and its support for repressive right-wing regimes like Brazil's. When he spotted an American-made car while walking down the streets of Geneva with friends, he would bend down as if picking up a stone and make the motion of hurling it at the passing vehicle. "Imperialists!" he would exclaim. In restaurants too when he heard an American accent, he occasionally made a show of getting up and moving out of earshot. "You can just hear the capitalism in their voices," he would say with disdain.

Although he had stopped attending classes at the Sorbonne after receiving his basic degree in philosophy in 1969, he had continued to work toward his master's from afar, reading and writing mainly at night and on the weekends. In 1970 he used up his UN vacation days studying for his oral exams and earned a master's from the Sorbonne in moral philosophy. He still viewed the UN as a place of temporary employment. Although Jamieson had captured his imagination, the UN's byzantine procedural requirements had not. He wrote to his former girlfriend in July 1970 that the UN had not changed: "From the sludge, I have only been able to learn one thing: the inanity of a life filled with forms of imaginary content."[16]

Jamieson never asked about his protégé's philosophical pursuits, which he found excessively abstract, but Vieira de Mello did not mind. He laughed whenever Jamieson contrasted his own self-made path with that of his over-credentialed, privileged colleagues. "If I had a formal education," Jamieson liked to say impishly, "I wouldn't be working in this office. I'd be prime minister of England!"

A few of Vieira de Mello's colleagues felt that he was too forgiving of Jamieson's condescension. "Jamie was friendly," recalls one, "but his friendliness was like that of a colonial sahib who treated his Indian valet nicely." Jamieson sounded like many Western visitors to Africa when he spoke admiringly of its people, telling a UNHCR newsletter of "their great sense of humour; their happy spirit even in great difficulties."[17] Vieira de Mello saw those colonial tendencies as forgivable by-products of Jamieson's age and upbringing.

In 1971, two years into his time at UNHCR, Vieira de Mello was transformed by his first-ever field mission. The agency had taken on its largest challenge to date, managing the entire UN emergency response to the staggering influx into India of some ten million Bengalis. Pakistan had forced them out of their homes in the eastern part of the country, which would soon become Bangladesh. UNHCR's global budget was then only $7 million, but High Commissioner Sadruddin raised nearly $200 million to contribute to an operation that would cost more than $430 million.[18] Operating under fierce pressure, Jamieson brought his favorite staff to the region—first to India to manage the refugee arrivals, and then to newly independent Bangladesh to help lay the ground for the massive return. He shuttled around as if he owned the region, even calling Indian prime minister Indira Gandhi "my dear girl." Vieira de Mello, who was only twenty-three, was based in Dhaka, Bangladesh, where he helped organize the distribution of food aid and shelter to Bengalis as they returned home. When he disagreed with his boss, Jamieson would tell him, "My dear boy, you are completely and utterly wrong."

For the first time in his life, Vieira de Mello felt he was doing something practical to operationalize his philosophical commitment to elevating individual and collective self-esteem. Human suffering—starvation, disease, displacement—would never be abstractions for him again. "Bangladesh was a revelation for Sergio," recalls his Brazilian friend da Silveira. "By being in the field, he recognized a part of himself he had never seen before. He understood he was a man of action. He was made for it."

Around the same time that Vieira de Mello had fallen under Jamieson's spell, he met Annie Personnaz, a French secretary at UNHCR. The two began dating, and just as Arnaldo had done with Gilda's family, Vieira de Mello grew close to Annie's parents, who owned a family hotel and spa in Thonon, France.

In May 1972 Jamieson, who was sixty, retired in accordance with UN rules. He was miserable and kept his eyes glued to the newspapers for a chance to return to duty. When the government of Sudan signed a peace agreement with southern rebels, seemingly ending a seventeen-year civil war and paving the way for the return of some 650,000 Sudanese refugees and displaced persons, Jamieson saw his opportunity and persuaded the high commissioner to ask him to come out of retirement to lead the effort. Just as Vieira de Mello's courtship with Annie was intensifying, Jamieson asked him to join a small team helping organize the return of the Sudanese refugees. Vieira de Mello wrote Annie letters while he was in southern Sudan, and she even visited him in the capital, Juba. He soon pro-

Vieira de Mello (in a light-colored suit, third from left) walking in Dhaka, Bangladesh, with a delegation that included UNHCR's high commissioner Sadruddin Aga Khan (far right), November 1972.

posed, and they scheduled their wedding for June 2, 1973. Flavio da Silveira would be his best man.

The Sudan mission afforded Vieira de Mello the chance to work more closely with Jamieson than he ever had before. Rotating between Geneva, Khartoum, and Juba, he helped his mentor establish an airlift that transported food, medicine, farming tools, and the returning refugees themselves. Jamieson could be an ingenious problem-solver. When he saw that an antiquated barge was the only means of carrying commercial traffic across the Nile River, he declared, "If we're going to bring these people home, we need a bridge." But UNHCR passed out food; it didn't build bridges. So Jamieson began appealing to Western governments. When he made the case on charity grounds alone, he got nowhere. But in discussions with the Dutch government, he found an argument that worked. "This will be a training exercise," Jamieson said. "The Dutch military engineers can use this as a drill to see how quickly they can build a bridge in difficult circumstances." Initially Jamieson's scheme looked doomed because the Sudanese rejected the presence of Western soldiers on their soil, and the Dutch military refused to perform the task out of uniform. But Jamieson quickly devised a compromise formula by which the Dutch would wear their uniforms without Dutch insignia. The all-steel Bailey bridge, which was completed in the spring of 1974, opened up southern Sudan to Kenya and Uganda, vastly increasing the flow of people and goods into the area.

Vieira de Mello watched Jamieson take what he had seen in the field and turn it into a fund-raising pitch at headquarters. At a press conference in Geneva in July 1972, decked out in a suit and tie, with a matching handkerchief and prominent cuff links, Jamieson argued that what the Sudanese wanted was not emergency relief but development assistance. "I found they are more interested in seeing something long-range done for their children, than in food," he said. "Strange. I'd like to see *us* in similar circumstances. I'd ask for fish-and-chips first and then talk about education second."[19] Vieira de Mello saw that while UNHCR had become skilled at feeding people in flight, governments were far less adept at preventing crises in the first place, or at rebuilding societies after emergencies so they could become self-sufficient.

Jamieson carried his taste for scotch with him on the road, and Vieira de

High Commissioner Sadruddin presenting Thomas Jamieson with the Sudanese Order of the Two Niles on behalf of Sudanese president Jaafar Nimeiri, 1973.

Mello eagerly joined in. "Don't bother with antimalaria pills," Jamieson told a young Iranian colleague Jamshid Anvar. "Whiskey is the best vaccine for everything." But the drinking took its toll. Jamieson's complexion grew ruddier, and in May 1973 he suffered a mild heart attack. The doctor told him to ease his workload.

Vieira de Mello juggled his own duties in Sudan with the planning of his wedding in the French countryside. He had invited both of his parents to attend the ceremony, but Arnaldo declined. Back in Brazil, without work, he had retreated further into himself. His drinking picked up, and his health grew worse. His depression had deepened in 1970 when his youngest brother, Tarcilo, was killed by a passing car as he exited a taxi in Rio. Gilda urged her husband to reconsider their son's wedding invitation, but Arnaldo said that he was only halfway through his second book and needed to finish. Gilda was upset. "How am I going to attend my son's wedding ceremony by myself?" she asked. "I want to go with my husband. I am not a widow." But Arnaldo insisted that on his small pension he could not afford to buy new suits for both the religious and the civil ceremonies, and he would not appear in the same suit at the two events. In all likelihood he was not feeling well enough to travel.

Gilda, Sonia, and André, Sonia's six-year-old son and Vieira de Mello's godson, flew to France for the wedding. On June 12, 1973, ten days after the couple had wed, Sonia, who had traveled on to Rome, received a telephone call from a friend in Rio: Arnaldo, fifty-nine, had suffered a stroke and pulmonary edema and died. Gilda, who was reached in London, was devastated. Vieira de Mello had driven with Annie across Europe to Greece. The couple had just arrived at the hotel to start their honeymoon when he got the news. Vieira de Mello had worried about his father's health for years and was not surprised, but he was deeply saddened. He put the couple's luggage back into the car, drove back to France, and flew alone to Brazil, where he arrived in time for the memorial service. In 1992, after years of trying to find a publisher for his father's incomplete manuscript, Sergio would himself pay to have it published in Brazil.[20]

With the sudden death of his father, Vieira de Mello grew even closer to his mother. For the rest of his life, no matter where he went in the world, he made a point of speaking to her at least once—but usually several times—each week. She also became a one-woman clipping service, tearing out articles from the Brazilian press that pertained to the places her son had worked. Vieira de Mello's ties to Jamieson also grew more intense. Jamieson had taken one lesson from his heart attack: Work was a "blessing," and he needed to get back to it. He had always been dismissive of physical hazards of any kind. When two of his colleagues were badly injured in an attack in Ethiopia, High Commissioner Sadruddin had considered withdrawing UN staff, but Jamieson had ridiculed the idea. "Prince, look," he had said, "if you don't want to take any risks, you might as well go out and sell ice cream."

Jamieson maintained an indefatigable pace, ignoring his doctor's orders to avoid the scorching equatorial sun. Often with Vieira de Mello by his side, he crisscrossed the vast Sudan, personally visiting camps and villages to ascertain whether returning refugees would have the water and fertile soil they needed in order to survive. In late 1973, while Jamieson was visiting refugee camps in the eastern part of the country, he collapsed and was rushed by plane back to Khartoum. The doctors told him his heart condition was severe but released him so that he could spend the night back in his room at the Hilton Hotel. A panicked Vieira de Mello helped to arrange the medical evacuation to Geneva and volunteered to remain by Jamieson's bedside throughout the night.

Anvar, the Iranian UNHCR official, had been with Jamieson when he collapsed. When he spotted Vieira de Mello at the hotel, he said, "Sergio, you must be crazy to want to stay up all night with him."

"He might need help," Vieira de Mello said.

"He is in absolutely no danger," Anvar said. "The hospital would not have released him if there was a risk."

"I will not be able to sleep," Vieira de Mello said. "And I don't trust doctors anyway."

"I don't understand you," Anvar countered. "Jamie is condescending and patronizing toward anybody who isn't British. He is everything that you are not and you are everything that he isn't. What do you see in him that I can't see?"

"He's like a father to me," Vieira de Mello said simply. "I love the man."

The following day Vieira de Mello flew with Jamieson back to Geneva. Jamieson survived the incident but never returned to the field or recovered his health. He died in December 1974 at the age of sixty-three.

Vieira de Mello turned back to developing his philosophical theories, which had taken a practical turn. On returning to Geneva from Bangladesh, he had reached out to Robert Misrahi, a philosophy professor who specialized in Spinoza at the Sorbonne and whom he had studied with in the past. "He was a young student settling down intellectually," Misrahi remembers. "He was extremely intelligent and dynamic, but he was without a doctrine. Fueled by painful personal experiences—his father's firing, his own exile, and what he had witnessed in Bangladesh—he wanted to be a man of generous action or a man of active generosity."[21] Under Misrahi's supervision, Vieira de Mello completed a 250-page doctoral thesis in 1974, entitled "The Role of Philosophy in Contemporary Society." He took several months of special leave without pay to finish up, relying upon Annie's UNHCR salary. Forgiving of her new husband's relentless work habits, she threw herself into the process, typing up his manuscript for submission.

The thesis took aim at philosophy itself, which he deemed too apolitical and abstract to shape human affairs. "Not only has history ceased to feed philosophy," he wrote, "but philosophy no longer feeds history." He credited Marxism with being the rare theory that attempted to play a role in real-life human betterment. By defining the contours of a social utopia, Vieira de Mello argued, Marxism at least laid out benchmarks that could inspire political action. Although he was pleading for a more relevant and political philosophy, Vieira de Mello wrote in the dense, jargon-filled style of Paris in the 1970s. He argued that the core philosophical principle that should drive human and interstate relations was "intersubjectivity," or an ability to step into the shoes of others—even into the shoes of wrongdoers. If philosophers could help broaden each individual's ability to adopt another's perspective, he argued, they could help usher in what Misrahi called a "conversion."[22]

UNHCR continued to offer assignments that kept pace with his growing appetite for adventure and learning. In 1974, still just twenty-six, he helped manage the mechanics of aid deliveries to Cypriots displaced in the Greek-Turkish war. "Leave all the logistics to me," the young man told Ghassan Arnaout, his Syrian supervisor in Geneva. "You keep your mind on the political and the strategic picture, and I'll handle the groceries." Vieira de Mello already seemed to view the assistance that UNHCR gave refugees—or "grocery delivery"—as a routine household chore. He had a lot to learn about protecting and feeding refugees, but if he remained within the UN system, he told Arnaout, he hoped to eventually involve himself in high-stakes political negotiations.

He and Annie lived in an apartment near her parents' home in the French town of Thonon. After a few years they built a permanent home for themselves in the French village of Massongy, a twenty-minute drive from Thonon and a half hour from his workplace in Geneva. In 1975 the couple moved to Mozambique, where he joined a UNHCR staff that was caring for the 26,000 refugees who had fled white supremacist rule and civil war in neighboring Rhodesia (now Zimbabwe). He had been named the deputy head of the office, but owing to an absent boss he ended up effectively running the mission, an enormous responsibility for one just twenty-eight years old. Initially the novelty of new tasks and a new region sustained him. He particularly enjoyed getting to know independence fighters and leaders from Rhodesia, South Africa, and East Timor, the tiny former Portuguese colony that had just been brutally annexed by Indonesia. Yet after a year in the job he began mailing long, restless letters to his senior UN colleagues in Geneva, inquiring about other job postings. It was as if, as soon as he settled into a routine by helping develop systems to house and feed the refugees, he was eager to move on. When word of these ambitions began circulating around UNHCR headquarters, Franz-Josef Homann-Herimberg, an Austrian UN official whom Vieira de Mello had often approached for career advice, warned him, "Sergio, you've got to cool it. It is natural that you don't want to wait until jobs are offered to you, but you are starting to get a reputation for being one who spends his time plotting his next move."

In 1978 Vieira de Mello and Annie returned to France, where she gave birth to a son, Laurent. Then they moved to Peru, where Vieira de Mello became UNHCR's regional representative for northern South America and attempted to help asylum-seekers who were fleeing the Latin American military dictatorships. This assignment moved him closer to home, allowing him to spend more time in Brazil than he had in the previous decade. In 1980 he and Annie had a second son, Adrien.

Vieira de Mello kept a permanent stash of Johnnie Walker Black Label—an upgrade from Jamieson's Red Label—in his desk drawer at his UNHCR office or in his suitcase while on the road. He also kept a framed photograph of his mentor on his desk at UNHCR. He took it with him on most field assignments and sometimes placed it on hotel nightstands during short over-seas trips. A decade or so after Jamieson's death, Vieira de Mello called Maria Therese Emery, Jamieson's longtime secretary, and apologetically asked if she might be able to give him another photograph of Jamieson. "I've been in too many hot places," he said. "The photo I have has faded in the sun."

Two

"I WILL NEVER USE THE WORD 'UNACCEPTABLE' AGAIN"

*Vieira de Mello holding his six-day-old
son Laurent, June 8, 1978.*

It was in Lebanon that Vieira de Mello first encountered terrorism. Although he knew that many promising careers were torpedoed in the Middle East, for him the region's most damning qualities—its contested geography, political turmoil, and religious extremism—were what enticed him. By 1981 he had been performing purely humanitarian tasks at UNHCR for twelve years, and he felt his learning curve had leveled off. When he heard from a colleague that a UN job had opened up in Lebanon, which he judged the most challenging of all UN assignments, he submitted his résumé and was selected to become political adviser to the commander of peacekeeping forces in the UN Interim Force in Lebanon (UNIFIL). Just thirty-three years old, he took leave of UNHCR, his home agency, with strong convictions about the indispensability of the UN's role as an "honest broker" in conflict areas. But over the next eighteen months he would see for the first time how little the UN flag could mean to those consumed with their own grievances and fears. Lebanon was the place where Vieira de Mello's youthful absolutism began to give way to the pragmatism for which he would later be known.

"A Series of Difficult and Sometimes Homicidal Clients"

In 1978, after a Palestinian terrorist attack on the road north of Tel Aviv left thirty-six Israelis dead, some 25,000 Israeli forces had invaded southern Lebanon. Israeli leaders said the invasion was aimed at eradicating strongholds of the Palestine Liberation Organization (PLO), which was staging ever-deadlier cross-border attacks from southern Lebanon into northern Israel with the aim of forcing Israelis to end the occupation of Palestinian territories in the West Bank and Gaza. In its weeklong offensive, Israel captured a fifteen-mile-deep belt of Lebanese territory.[1]

Only the large coastal city of Tyre, and a two-by-eight-mile sliver of territory north of the Litani River, had remained in Palestinian hands. Although the United States and the Soviet Union then agreed on little at the UN Security Council, they did agree that Israeli forces should withdraw from Lebanon and that UN peacekeepers should be sent to monitor their exit.*[2] In an editorial that reflected what would prove to be a fleeting optimism about the UN, the *Washington Post* hailed the decision to send the blue helmets. "Peacekeeping is the one activity in the Mideast," the editors noted, that "the world organization has learned to do well."[3]

Peacekeeping was then loosely defined as the interpositioning of neutral, lightly armed multinational forces between warring factions that had agreed to a truce or political settlement. It was a relatively new practice, initiated in 1956 by Lester Pearson, Canada's foreign minister, who helped organize the deployment of international troops to supervise the withdrawal of British,

---

* U.S. officials were normally unwilling to criticize Israel, but in 1978 President Jimmy Carter was closing in on his landmark Camp David peace deal between Israel and Egypt, and he feared that an Israeli occupation of Lebanon could derail it. Carter decided that the best way to secure an Israeli withdrawal while also saving Israeli face was to authorize the dispatch of UN peacekeepers. The United States drove a resolution through the Council, taking Israel by surprise, and the Soviets abstained from the vote.

French, and Israeli troops from the Suez region of Egypt.[4] Soon afterward the UN Security Council had sent some 20,000 UN peacekeepers to the Congo, where from 1960 to 1964 they oversaw the withdrawal of Belgian colonial forces and attempted (unsuccessfully) to stabilize the newly independent country. Smaller UN missions in West New Guinea, Yemen, Cyprus, the Dominican Republic, and India/Pakistan had followed.[5] The UNIFIL mission in southern Lebanon was given an annual budget of around $180 million. Its 4,000 troops—later increased to 6,000—made it the largest UN mission then in existence.[6]

In the three and a half years that had elapsed since UNIFIL's initial deployment in 1978, Israeli forces had refused to comply with the spirit of international demands to withdraw, handing their positions to their proxy forces, while Palestinian forces had failed to disarm. The resolution establishing the mission had given PLO guerrillas the right to remain where they were.[*] The UN mission's flaws were thus obvious. The major powers on the Security Council were not prepared to deal with the gnarly issues that had sparked the Israeli invasion in the first place: dispossessed Palestinians and Israeli insecurity. And the Council had given the peacekeepers no instructions as to what to do if the parties continued to attack one another, as they would inevitably do.

By the time of Vieira de Mello's arrival in southern Lebanon, command of UNIFIL troops had passed to a second UN force commander: General William Callaghan, a sixty-year-old three-star Irish general who had done UN tours in Congo, Cyprus, and Israel. Vieira de Mello's main task was to provide Callaghan with the political lay of the land. Because he had lived in Beirut for nearly two years as a boy, Vieira de Mello had long followed events in the region. But once he moved there, he set out to acquaint himself with Lebanese, Israeli, and Western diplomatic officialdom and with the region's various subterranean militia groups.

He shared an office with Timur Goksel, a thirty-eight-year-old Turkish spokesperson who had been with the mission from the beginning. Goksel

---

[*] In 2006, after Hezbollah rocket attacks on northern Israel prompted another Israeli invasion, the Security Council authorized a 12,000-person UN force for southern Lebanon. Israel criticized the resolution because again Hezbollah fighters were permitted to remain in the south.

gravitated toward what he termed the "gray zones." "You've got to reach out to the men with guns in their hands," Goksel told his new colleague. "We'll learn much more from the coffee shops and the mosques than we will from governments." He brought Vieira de Mello with him to his unofficial meetings. "I have only one requirement," he said. "You must take off your damn coat and tie!" Vieira de Mello came to understand how essential it was to get to know armed groups such as the Shiite militia Amal, which grew in strength during the early 1980s and would later be largely supplanted by Hezbollah, and the breakaway factions from the PLO, such as the Popular Front for the Liberation of Palestine, which often fired on UNIFIL peacekeepers. He preferred his informal meetings to those with state officials. He marveled to Goksel, "The UN is such a statist organization. If we played by UN rules, we wouldn't have a clue what the people with power and guns were plotting."

Vieira de Mello was amazed at the degree of disrespect accorded to the UN by all parties. UNIFIL had set up observation posts and checkpoints throughout the mission area in the hope of preventing PLO fighters from moving closer to Israel. But the fighters simply stayed off the main roads and used dirt trails to transport arms and men. And because the central Lebanese authorities did not control southern Lebanon, when UNIFIL picked up a PLO infiltrator on patrol, no local Lebanese civil administration existed to press charges. The demoralized UN soldiers simply escorted Palestinian fighters out of the border area and released them. Some found themselves arresting the same raiders again and again.[7] UN peacekeepers who challenged armed Palestinians were regularly taken hostage. On November 30, 1981, just after Vieira de Mello arrived, PLO fighters stopped two UN staff officers, fired shots at their feet, and ridiculed them as "spies for Israel."

The Israelis were equally brazen. They made no attempt to conceal their residual presence. They laid mines, manned checkpoints, built asphalt roads, transported supplies, and constructed new positions on the Lebanese side of the border.[8] Still, because UN officials did not want to offend the most powerful military in the region, they chose not to refer to Israel's control of the area as "annexation" or "occupation" and complained instead of "permanent border violations."[9]

The Israeli authorities did not return the favor. They threatened the peacekeepers and regularly denigrated them.[10] Back in 1975 the Israeli public had

turned against the UN when the General Assembly—the one UN body that
gave equal votes to all countries, rich and poor, large and small—had passed
a resolution equating Zionism with racism.* Callaghan and Vieira de Mello
pleaded with their Israeli interlocutors to cease their anti-UN propaganda,
arguing that it was endangering the lives of UN blue helmets, more than
seventy of whom had already been killed.

Israel had handed many of its positions to Lebanese proxy forces under
a Christian renegade leader named Major Saad Haddad, who delighted in
sending Callaghan insolent demands.† "I want you to know that tomorrow
at 10 a.m., I am intending to send a patrol," he wrote in a typical message. "I
ask for a positive answer."[11] Whenever the UN peacekeepers got in his way,
Haddad simply sealed off the roads in his area, preventing the movement of
UN personnel and vehicles. When UN equipment was stolen, which was
often, neither Callaghan nor Vieira de Mello could secure its return.

The PLO had amassed long-range weapons and continued to fire them
into Israel; the Israeli army and its Christian proxies regularly retaliated with
raids against PLO camps and bases in southern Lebanon. Vieira de Mello's letters and in-person protestations over the next eighteen months would convey
"surprise," "dismay," and "condemnation"; they would insist that bad behavior
by the Israelis, the Christian proxy forces, and the Palestinians would "not be
tolerated"; and they would remind the parties that their transgressions would
be "brought before the Security Council." But because the peacekeepers had
neither sticks nor carrots to bring to bear, his protests were generally ignored.
Vieira de Mello quickly deduced that the Security Council had placed peacekeepers in an environment in which there was no real peace to keep. As
was typical during the cold war, influential governments seemed to be more
interested in freezing a conflict in place than they were in trying to solve it.
Until the Israelis and Palestinians resolved their differences, or the powerful
countries in the UN decided to impose peace, there would be little that a
small peacekeeping force could do.

Powerless to deter violence, Vieira de Mello tried to do what he did

---

* In December 1991 the UN General Assembly voted to revoke the 1975 resolution.
† Haddad's army, which he called the South Lebanese Army, was made up largely of poor Shi'a from the
border villages.

best: learn. As a boy, he had been obsessed with naval warfare and had harbored dreams of joining the Brazilian armed forces. "If I hadn't become a humanitarian," he liked to joke, "I would have become an admiral." Although he detested the Brazilian military regime, he never looked down upon the military as an institution, which often surprised some of his antiwar progressive colleagues in Geneva. In his early months in Lebanon, he spent nearly as much time asking General Callaghan questions on military matters as he did dispensing political advice. "It took him a while to understand the nuances associated with military people," recalls Callaghan. "He had to get oriented around rankings, structures, equipment, deployments, communication systems, and the camaraderie that the military brings to a job." He pressed Callaghan for tales of previous peacekeeping missions. Callaghan, an animated Irish storyteller, was eager to oblige the impatient young man. "He wanted to do the job today and now," Callaghan recalls. "He didn't appreciate that in this kind of situation you have to learn to count to ten as well."

Vieira de Mello went out on foot on back trails, and he joined motorized patrols along key highways and into Lebanese villages. He knew that UNIFIL soldiers were stuck in the middle of a conflict where all the parties were more committed to their aims than the peacekeepers serving temporarily under a UN flag would ever be to theirs. "This is their land and their war," Vieira de Mello told Goksel. "Of course they are going to outmaneuver us."

Any single Western military force would have had its hands full stabilizing southern Lebanon, but the mishmash of countries that constituted UNIFIL was particularly disadvantaged. Callaghan's forces came from all over the world and were of wildly different quality. In 1945 the key founders of the UN—the United States, the U.K., and the Soviet Union—had hoped that governments would place forces on standby that the Security Council could call upon when one UN member state threatened to invade another. But after the establishment of the UN, those same major powers, along with most UN member states, insisted that they needed to keep their forces on call to meet national crises as they arose, and no standby force was ever assembled. Brian Urquhart, a highly respected British intelligence officer during World War II, had been with the UN since its founding, advising each of its secretaries-general and setting up what was then a small office for peacekeeping operations at UN Headquarters. When in 1978 the Security Council had called for monitors and peacekeepers for Lebanon, Urquhart had, as usual, raised troops on the fly.[12] He borrowed units from existing UN missions elsewhere in the world, relocating an Iranian rifle company from the small observer mission in the Golan Heights and a Swedish rifle company from the UN squad in the Suez Canal zone. France, Nepal, and Norway volunteered contingents, as did Fiji, Ireland, Nigeria, and Senegal, but the forces trickled in, arriving from different entry points.

"You don't have any say in who you get," Callaghan said. "It's an advantage to be multinational because you can bring to bear the political support of all the different nations. But from a military point of view, if you had a choice, this would not be the way you would go about planning and running an operation." UNIFIL relied on fifty-three different types of vehicles—from German, Austrian, British, French, and Scandinavian manufacturers, which made it almost impossible for the vehicles to be maintained because of the vast array of spare parts needed.[13] Vieira de Mello would pick up a phrase that would become a mantra in future peacekeeping missions: "Beggars can't be choosers."

Most soldiers who were asked to become neutral peacekeepers had been trained in their national armies as war fighters. They often had difficulty adjusting to being inserted into volatile environments in which they were told to maintain neutrality and to use force only in self-defense. The commander of UNIFIL's French parachute battalion constantly referred to the rival armed factions as "the enemy." When Urquhart traveled from UN Headquarters in New York to southern Lebanon, he had to take the officer aside to explain that, unlike a soldier fighting under his national flag, a peacekeeper had no "enemies." He had only "a series of difficult and sometimes homicidal clients."[14]

Vieira de Mello had never seen the UN operate with so little clout. While working as a humanitarian for UNHCR in Bangladesh, Sudan, Cyprus, and Mozambique, he had found it frustrating merely to address the symptoms of violence—feeding and sheltering refugees in exile or preparing to welcome them home—while doing nothing to stop the violence or redress the insecurity that had caused people to flee their homes in the first place. But at least as an aid worker he had generally been able to bring tangible succor to those in need. Because he and other humanitarians were unarmed, they did not raise expectations among civilians who, when they saw UN soldiers, expected them to fight back against their attackers.

UNIFIL headquarters had been established in Naqoura, a desolate Lebanese village on a bluff overlooking the sea just two miles north of the Israeli border. When the UN had first arrived in 1978, the village had only two permanent buildings—a border customs house and an old Turkish cemetery—but it had since turned into a lively beach town that catered to the foreign soldiers and civilians.[15] Most evenings Vieira de Mello drove across the border to the Israeli town of Nahariya, where he lived with Annie and their two young sons. Because Palestinian Katyusha rockets sometimes landed near Nahariya, Annie grew practiced at bringing Laurent and Adrien into the local bomb shelter. Vieira de Mello remained in close contact with his mother, Gilda, who was in a state of such perpetual anxiety about her son's safety that she developed acute insomnia, a condition that would not abate even after he left the Middle East.

When he first began traveling from southern Lebanon to Beirut, which still experienced violent flare-ups despite the truce in the civil war, he too was skittish. Once, while he was attending a meeting with the speaker of the Lebanese parliament, the sound of a heavy exchange of fire drew near. Unsure of what was occurring in this, his first live combat zone, he passed a note to Samir Sanbar, a UN colleague based in Beirut. "Are we finished?" his note read. "Is this our end?" Sanbar assured him that they were not in immediate danger, and the meeting concluded uneventfully. "At the start Sergio was new to war," recalls Sanbar. "After a few more trips to Beirut, he learned that gunfire was as natural a background noise as the sound of passing cars."

On most of his trips to the Lebanese capital, Vieira de Mello stopped into Western embassies to urge the Irish, Dutch, French, and other diplomatic staff to persuade their governments to extend or expand their troop contributions to UNIFIL. He had a sense of foreboding and knew reinforcements were needed. Vieira de Mello also made a point of stopping in to see Ryan Crocker, the thirty-two-year-old head of the political section at the U.S. embassy and a fluent Arabic speaker. The two men would cross paths again in 2003 in Iraq, where Crocker would serve as a senior administrator in

Paul Bremer's Coalition Provisional Authority.* Vieira de Mello immediately won over the U.S. diplomat by telling him, "People say you know your way around. I could really use your help." As Crocker remembers, "Nothing quite succeeds so well as carefully constructed flattery. He had me."

In fact, each man had something to offer the other. U.S. diplomats, unlike their European counterparts, were prohibited from making contact with terrorist groups. Thus Crocker came to rely on Vieira de Mello for his insights into the PLO and other armed groups. He also valued his read on southern Lebanon. "I was wild with jealousy that he could talk to people I couldn't," Crocker recalls. "Whenever I thought, 'Oh my God, are we falling off the edge here?' or 'What does this mean?' he'd be the guy to bounce things off of."

Falling off the Edge

In February 1982, sensing mounting Israeli hostility toward the PLO, Vieira de Mello met with Yassir Arafat in Beirut and warned him that if he did not remove PLO fighters from the UN area, the Israelis would likely take matters into their own hands.[16] Abu Walid, Arafat's chief of staff, gave his "word of honor" that "not one single violation" of the cease-fire was the fault of the PLO.[17] Met with such lies, Vieira de Mello knew the UN's efforts at mediation were hopeless.

UN officials and Western governments began to fear a second, all-out Israeli invasion. In April 1982 Urquhart, in New York, wrote to General Callaghan in Lebanon: "There is great concern in virtually all quarters here tonight about immediate future Israeli intentions. We have no firm facts to go on but I felt you should be aware of mood here."[18] The two men drew up contingency plans. They agreed that since the Security Council had neither equipped nor mandated the peacekeepers to make war, the blue helmets would stand aside in the event of an Israeli attack. Urquhart was so firm a believer that peacekeepers should avoid using force that when asked once why UN soldiers did not fight back, he said: "Jesus Christ is universally remembered after 2,000 years, but the same cannot be said about his con-

---

* In 2007 President George W. Bush would name Crocker U.S. ambassador to Iraq.

temporaries who did *not* turn the other cheek."[19] All UN units in southern Lebanon were informed that the Israelis might soon launch "an airborne, airmobile, amphibious or ground operation, or a combination of these." In the event of an invasion, Callaghan cabled his troops, the UN radio code signal would be "RUBICON."[20]

The tenuous cease-fire was falling apart and the propaganda war was escalating. On April 21 Israel launched massive air raids against PLO targets in southern Lebanon. It did the same on May 9, and PLO fighters in Tyre fired rockets into northern Israel for the first time in nearly a year. UNIFIL's chief medical officer in Naqoura began to investigate hospital facilities in Israel, Lebanon, and Cyprus in the event that the UN took mass casualties in a new war.[21]

On June 3, 1982, a gunman with the Abu Nidal organization, which the Israelis accused of being linked to the PLO, shot Shlomo Argov, the Israeli ambassador to the United Kingdom, outside the Dorchester Hotel in London.[22] On the morning of June 6, General Rafael Eitan, the chief of staff of the Israeli army, summoned Callaghan to Zefat in Israel, some twenty miles from UNIFIL headquarters. Vieira de Mello accompanied his boss and took notes. As soon as the UN team sat down, Eitan told Callaghan that the Israeli army was about to "initiate an operation" to ensure that PLO artillery would no longer reach Israel. Eitan said he "expected" that UN troops would not interfere with the Israeli advance.[23]

Callaghan was enraged both by the invasion and by Eitan's ploy to pull him away from the UN base just as the attack was being staged. "Israel's behavior is totally unacceptable!" the Irish general exclaimed. Eitan was unmoved. "Our sole targets are the terrorists," he said. "We shall accomplish our mission as assigned to us by our government." He told Callaghan that UN resolutions were "a political matter for politicians to deal with," and that twenty-eight minutes hence Israel would embark on its military operation.[24] Callaghan knew that he had to alert his troops immediately. Out of radio range, he had no choice but to deliver the coded message—RUBICON—on an Israeli army phone.[25] And remarkably the real humiliation had not yet begun.

At 11:00 a.m. Israel launched Operation Peace in Galilee and reinvaded Lebanon. It attacked with some 90,000 troops in 1,200 tanks and 4,000 armored vehicles, backed by aircraft and offshore naval units. Israeli troops poured into the country across a flimsy wire fence at the border, and they cut through UN lines—"like a warm knife through butter," as Urquhart later described it.

The invasion did not come as a shock. In recent days all UN personnel had heard the sonic boom of Israeli war planes overhead and had seen the Israeli fleet line up in hostile formation off the coast. Vieira de Mello's mind raced to Annie and their two sons, who were nearby. When he got back to Naqoura and reached her on the telephone, she was frantic with worry. "Sergio, I have never seen so many tanks in my life. The street is packed with them. What is going on?" He said, "They're coming here." He assured her that the Israelis would not dare to target the UN itself, but he told her to take the boys to the nearby shelter, where they would be safe in the event that the Palestinians fired their rockets from Tyre. He told her that as soon as Israeli troops allowed UN officials to cross into northern Israel, he would evacuate them back to France, which he did within several days.

UNIFIL peacekeepers were armed only with light defensive weapons, and one Norwegian soldier was killed by shrapnel the day of the invasion. Most got out of the way of the Israeli assault.[26] However, a few mounted resistance. On the coastal road leading north to Tyre, Dutch soldiers planted iron beams in front of an Israeli tank column, ruining the tracks of two oncoming tanks. Elsewhere a French sergeant armed only with a pistol stopped an Israeli tank as it rounded a curve. Thinking the tank was traveling alone, the peacekeeper told the Israeli driver that he had no business entering the UN zone. The tank driver pointed to the curve behind him and said, "Well, you might stop me, but there are 149 tanks just like this one behind me. What are you going to do about them?"

The Israelis had initially invaded to push the PLO out of rocket range, but once deep inside Lebanon, they kept going. On June 10 they reached the outskirts of Beirut, from where they encircled the city and cut off PLO exit routes. A week later they laid siege to West Beirut, where some 6,000 PLO fighters were cloistered, causing heavy damage to the town and killing more than 5,000 Lebanese.[27]

Though he knew he was living through one of the lowest moments in UN history, Vieira de Mello was initially exhilarated. He had never before found himself at the center of such high-stakes political drama. Overnight UN statements made in the sleepy town of Naqoura were suddenly capturing global headlines. Once Annie and the boys had flown back to Europe, he based himself at UNIFIL headquarters full-time.

Vieira de Mello's main diplomatic task in the weeks after the invasion was convincing the PLO that the UN was not in cahoots with Israel. Leading Palestinian officials pointed to Callaghan's meeting with Eitan the day of the invasion as evidence of collusion. Arafat accused UNIFIL of helping the Israelis "stab the Palestinians in the back."[28] The Palestinian deputy representative at the UN in New York denounced the entire institution and said, "We feel this action by the United Nations and by the Israeli invading force has dealt a serious blow to the whole concept of peace-keeping and credibility of the UN."[29]

Vieira de Mello defended the UN's honor. He drafted a cable to PLO leaders on Callaghan's behalf, angrily pointing the finger back at the Palestinians for provoking the Israeli invasion. In light of their "unwarranted accusations of collaboration," he reminded them that the Palestinians had infiltrated the UN area, hijacked UN vehicles, and attacked UN personnel. Since the Palestinians had ignored UN warnings and egged on the Israelis, they should "accept full responsibility" for the invasion.[30] Although both Callaghan and Vieira de Mello were even angrier with the Israelis, they knew the invaders controlled the area. Callaghan requested that UN officials in New York "avoid any open criticism of the Israelis as this will surely be counterproductive."[31]

As soon as the whirlwind of the initial invasion had passed, the morale of UN peacekeepers—Vieira de Mello included—plummeted. Israel had thumbed its nose at the Security Council resolutions that demanded that Israel stay out of Lebanon, and in the course of invading a neighbor, its forces had trampled on the UN peacekeepers in their way. "We were never going to stop a determined Israeli offensive," Vieira de Mello wistfully told Goksel, "but do you think we could have made it just a little harder for these bastards? The UN looks pathetic." The troops serving the UN had been humiliated, but they would return home to their national armed services. Vieira de Mello had come to cherish the UN flag almost as much as he did Brazil's, and the sting of the invasion would linger.

Callaghan was adamant that, however humiliating it might have felt, peacekeepers had been right not to contest the Israelis. "Soldiers don't like to be marched through, no matter where they come from," Callaghan said.

"But I am the man answerable for these soldiers' lives. What if I launch an operation against this invasion and twenty of my soldiers are killed? I do not have a mandate to risk the lives of soldiers equipped for self-defense." He agreed with Urquhart that lightly armed UN peacekeepers could succeed only if the heavily armed warring parties kept their promises.

After witnessing Callaghan's sputtering protests on the day of the invasion, Vieira de Mello told colleagues he was sure of one thing: "I will never use the word 'unacceptable' again." There seemed little point in issuing shrill denunciations with nothing more than moral outrage behind them.

"Sorry State of Affairs"

UNIFIL had been sent to Lebanon to monitor Israeli troop withdrawals and restore Lebanese sovereignty in the south. Now that Israel had reinvaded and occupied Lebanon outright, Vieira de Mello did not see how UNIFIL could continue. If the blue helmets attempted to remain during a full-scale Israeli occupation, he believed the neutrality of the peacekeepers would end up compromised. "We know that the Americans aren't going to force Israel out of Lebanon this time," he told Jean-Claude Aimé, a Haitian UN political officer who worked for the UN in Jerusalem. "Are we to watch Israeli troops mop up?" Aimé favored a UN withdrawal, and Vieira de Mello said he agreed. "If we stay and pretend nothing has happened," he said, "it's as if we are condoning their invasion." He expected the Security Council to shut down the mission, and he began planning his return to Geneva.

Callaghan pointed to the good that the UN mission was doing in humanitarian terms. "Pulling out would mean conceding totally," he argued. "The local people depend on us. We can't leave them on their own." Since UNIFIL had set up base in southern Lebanon in 1978, some 250,000 civilians had returned to the area. The UN peacekeepers supplied water and electricity, maintained a hospital in Naqoura (run by the Swedes), repaired public buildings and roads, and cleared the area of explosive devices. Instead of throwing out used typewriters, photocopiers, desks, or chairs, the UN donated them to local schools. The peacekeepers also staged what became known as "harvest patrols," escorting Lebanese civilians whose farms or olive plantations were located along the front lines.[32] When he was with Callaghan,

Vieira de Mello acted as though he agreed with the general. "Sergio never said, 'I think UNIFIL should withdraw.' Never," recalls Callaghan. "And if that was his opinion he would have said so."

Irrespective of whether Vieira de Mello was testing out his ideas or simply telling both men what he thought they most wanted to hear, he knew that UNIFIL officers and civilian officials would have little say in what happened next. The powerful countries on the Security Council would decide whether the UN peacekeepers would pack up and go home.

And decide they did. On June 18 the Security Council extended UNIFIL's mandate.[33] Four years after the blue helmets had been sent in to monitor Israel's withdrawal, they were now being asked, temporarily, to submit to an Israeli occupation and restrict their role to delivering humanitarian aid. "The Security Council told us to stay," recalls Goksel, "but they basically told us there was nothing for us to do. The signal we got was, 'Do what you can to justify your salaries.' We felt useless. We hid in Naqoura and tried to become invisible. After that, even Sergio didn't want to go around saying, 'I'm a UN guy.'"

Vieira de Mello repeatedly telephoned UN Headquarters in New York in search of consolation. It was the first time in his life that he was part of something that was being publicly condemned and ridiculed. He insisted on replaying June 6, the day of the invasion, again and again. "Is there something else I could have done?" he asked Virendra Dayal, the UN secretary-general's chief of staff with whom he had worked in Bangladesh. Dayal tried to soothe his colleague. "Sergio, what could you as a young man have done all by yourself in the face of a massive land, air, and naval invasion?" Dayal wanted him to pass through New York on his way to Brazil for home leave in July. He thought a debriefing might help. But when he reached New York, Vieira de Mello just kept up his second-guessing. "Stop lacerating yourself," Dayal urged. But his junior colleague was adamant: "We should have made more of a show," Vieira de Mello said.

However degrading it had been to be part of the UNIFIL mission before the Israeli invasion, it felt far worse afterward. When Vieira de Mello returned to Lebanon after his leave, he found that Israeli forces were keeping UN officials largely pinned down to the UN base in Naqoura. The Israelis seemed to hope that their invasion would cause the peacekeepers to leave. They closed the Lebanese-Israeli border to UN personnel and vehicles at will, blocking resupply and personnel rotation convoys, and they denied UN personnel flight permission except for rare medical emergencies. The Israeli press suggested that the UN was passing information to Palestinian terrorists about Israeli military positions. In a cable to Urquhart, Callaghan criticized Israel's "official smear campaign" against UNIFIL and begged UN officials in New York to approach the Israeli delegation so as "to put a firm stop to this sorry state of affairs."[34]

Vieira de Mello staged small acts of civil disobedience, refusing to submit requests for travel permits to the Israeli authorities, moving around without escorts, and often sitting in his vehicle at Israeli checkpoints in the hot sun for entire afternoons, refusing to allow the Israelis to search his car. "We are the United Nations," he would fume, sometimes astonishing Goksel. "Can't you see the flag? We will not submit to the will of an illegal occupying force." When he briefed incoming units of peacekeepers, he gave them the same advice he himself would receive from friends before leaving for Iraq in 2003, urging them to avoid close association with the occupiers, so as to maintain the faith of the populace.

After Vieira de Mello received his doctorate in 1974, Robert Misrahi, his adviser, had persuaded him to pursue a "state doctorate," the highest and most competitive degree offered by the French university system. Vieira de Mello had done so, working intermittently but intensely on what he considered to be his most ambitious philosophical work. The only bright side to the paralysis of the UN mission in Lebanon was that he had time to dive more deeply into his thesis in a region where many of his ideas were being tested. When he corresponded with Misrahi, he lamented the inadequacy of philosophical tools. "Things are much more complicated in practice," he told his professor. "Philosophical ideas must be applicable on the ground, and the field should be their only judge, their only criteria."[35] When Misrahi visited Israel on personal business, he met with his pupil and applauded his attempts to apply philosophy to his humanitarian and diplomatic work. But he thought Vieira de Mello could not expect mere reason and dialogue to yield conversion when little mutual understanding existed among the factions. "Just going and meeting with the enemy is not enough to establish reciprocal respect," Misrahi insisted, urging him to take a longer view of human progress. "History is slow," Misrahi says. "Vieira de Mello thought it could be quick."[36]

The Israeli invasion had chased the PLO and Yassir Arafat north to Beirut. The Palestinians were encircled. Fearing a massacre and hoping to end the siege peacefully, the United States, France, and Italy decided to deploy a Multinational Force, totally separate from the UN peacekeeping mission that was based in the southern part of the country. In August 1982, 800 U.S. troops, 800 French, and 400 Italians assisted with the evacuation of besieged Palestinian fighters and fanned out to the outskirts of Beirut to protect the sprawling settlements filled with Palestinian refugees.[37] After some 15,000 Palestinians and Syrians left West Beirut, Arafat himself made his way to Greece, and then went on to Tunisia.

The Western forces departed almost as quickly as they had arrived, retreating from Beirut on September 10, 1982, under banners of MISSION ACCOMPLISHED.[38] With their exit the responsibility for ensuring the safety of the remaining half-million Palestinian civilians in Lebanon passed to the Lebanese government, which was weak and divided. When Bashir Gemayel, the newly elected Christian president of Lebanon, was assassinated on September 14, Israeli-backed Christian militia intent on exacting revenge closed in on the Palestinian camps. Speaking from Rome, Yassir Arafat pleaded for the Multinational Force to return: "I ask Italy, France and the United States: What of your promise to protect the inhabitants of Beirut?"[39] On September 16, as Israeli soldiers looked on, the militia forces entered the undefended Palestinian camps of Sabra and Shatila in Beirut. In the two days that followed, in the name of flushing out Palestinian terrorists, the militia murdered more than seven hundred men, women, and children.[40]

On September 20, 1982, largely in response to the massacres, President Ronald Reagan announced his intention to redeploy U.S. Marines to Beirut. "Millions of us have seen pictures of the Palestinian victims of this tragedy," Reagan said. "There is little that words can add, but there are actions we can and must take."[41] The Western countries that had sent armed contingents in August now offered larger forces: 1,400 American soldiers, 1,400 Italians, and 1,500 French (including 500 who were reassigned from UNIFIL) returned to Lebanon, accompanied by armored vehicles, mortars, and heavy artillery.[42] Initially, their presence seemed to calm tensions.

Israel's fight, up until that point, had been with the Palestinians. But with their occupation of Lebanon, Israeli forces began to meet new resistance—that of Lebanese Shiites. In January 1983, with the UNIFIL mandate in

southern Lebanon up for renewal again, Urquhart flew to Jerusalem and met
with the Israelis, whose occupying forces were suffering a growing number
of casualties. In his notes on the trip, he wrote that he observed "a genuine
desire amongst intelligent Israelis to get out of Lebanon before it overwhelms
them. They have certainly bitten off more than they can chew."[43] The Israelis
would not withdraw from Lebanon for eighteen years. They would lose 675
soldiers there.

Urquhart's visit to Lebanon gave Vieira de Mello his first chance to spend
time with a legendary UN figure. For once he made a terrible impression.
After they had dinner together in a Turkish restaurant, Urquhart wrote in his
diary that Vieira de Mello had

> a very severe case of localitis and constantly lecture[d] and boom[ed] at one
> about the iniquities of the Israelis, the humiliating position in which UNIFIL
> finds itself, etc., etc. I got rather annoyed at this and pointed out to de Mello
> that since he had been in UNIFIL nothing has happened to compare with
> all the things that had happened before, not to mention the experiences that
> some of us had had in other parts of the world, and that humiliation was in
> the eye of the observer.

Urquhart concluded his entry with a stinging verdict on his ambitious young
colleague. "He has become a great prima donna and cry-baby, and I think
he should be sent back to the High Commissioner for Refugees as soon as
possible."[44]

TAKING SIDES

For all of his frustrations as a UN official, Vieira de Mello knew that the
Multinational Force in Beirut wasn't faring much better. On his periodic
trips to the capital, he continued to see Ryan Crocker at the U.S. embassy.
Entering an American embassy in the 1980s was nowhere near as challenging as it would later become. Like any visitor, he could walk right past a
Lebanese army checkpoint, up the driveway, and into the main lobby of the
eight-story building. Only then would he present his ID card and make his
business known to U.S. guards.

At 1:05 p.m. on April 18, 1983, when Vieira de Mello was back in south-ern Lebanon, a man in a leather jacket drove a black delivery van with five hundred pounds of explosives through the embassy's front entrance. The blast, which destroyed the van and all traces of its driver, killed fifty people, includ-ing seventeen Americans. It was the first-ever suicide bomb attack against a U.S. target, the opening salvo in an unconventional battle that would not command significant high-level attention until the al-Qaeda attacks on U.S. soil on September 11, 2001.

When Vieira de Mello next saw Crocker, who had narrowly escaped the blast, the two men commiserated on the impossible task of putting Lebanon back together again. "This is a hopeless mess," said Vieira de Mello. "I see no way out that is going to be good for anyone—not the UN, the Lebanese, the U.S., nor Israel. No way out whatsoever." Crocker agreed. "There is a new player on the court out there," the U.S. diplomat noted, "and this player is definitely changing the rules of the game." They wondered aloud how this new breed of Islamic fighter willing to die for his cause would be sup-pressed.

Vieira de Mello's tour in Lebanon was winding down, and in his last weeks he tried to ensure that a small incident would not ignite a far larger one. On March 30, 1983, a jumpy Fijian soldier manning a UN checkpoint had shot and killed a highly respected forty-year-old Lebanese doctor named Khalil Kaloush. Upon learning of the incident, Vieira de Mello, Goksel, and a small UN delegation proceeded to Kaloush's hometown to meet with the village chiefs, who demanded compensation, or "blood money."[45]

When the grieving family rejected Vieira de Mello's request to attend the funeral, he had UNIFIL send a floral wreath, which the family also turned away. But he didn't give up, visiting the Kaloush family multiple times and telling them that he understood that the UN had to pay up. Dr. Kaloush's widow asked that the couple's four children, who ranged in age from four to ten, be educated. Over a ten-year period this would cost around $150,000.

Vieira de Mello knew that the New York bureaucracy was no match for a tribal culture prone to exacting swift revenge. UN administrative staff ini-tially told him that the hurdles would be insurmountable. But after weeks of badgering, he finally received permission to dispense the funds.[46] In one of his few victories in eighteen months in Lebanon, on June 23, he delivered the payment to Mrs. Kaloush. A week later his Lebanon mission came to an end, and he returned to Geneva.

Back at a desk at UNHCR, Vieira de Mello watched, horrified, as the Western troops in the Multinational Force in Beirut ratcheted up their firepower against the Lebanese armed groups. U.S. warships off the coast of Beirut and U.S. Marines in the city offered military backing for the beleaguered Lebanese army, which was at war with other Lebanese armed groups. In September and October six U.S. servicemen were killed in action and fifty were wounded. In a lengthy analysis in October 1983, *New York Times* Beirut correspondent Thomas Friedman described the shift: "Without anyone really noticing it at first, the Marines here have been transformed during the last month of fighting from a largely symbolic peacekeeping force—welcomed by all—to just one more faction in the internal Lebanese conflict."[47] Vieira de Mello disapproved of what was occurring. "They have taken sides," he noted to a colleague. "They've lost any appearance of neutrality. And when you throw neutrality away, you better hope you've chosen the right side."

On October 19, 1983, at a televised press conference in Washington, D.C., a *Washington Times* reporter and former U.S. Marine named Jeremiah O'Leary asked President Reagan why U.S. troops had set up their base at Beirut airport on flat terrain instead of finding high ground elsewhere in the city. Reagan said that since the Marines in Lebanon were not performing a traditional combat role, they observed different rules. U.S. forces were peacekeepers, he said, not war fighters.

Four days later, at around 6:20 a.m., a yellow Mercedes truck carrying 2,500 pounds of TNT entered an empty public airport parking lot, circled the parking lot twice so as to pick up speed, and plowed through a six-foot-high iron fence around the U.S. Marine barracks. By the time the U.S. sentry guarding the compound had installed a bullet clip into his previously unloaded gun, the truck had already barreled past. A fourteen-foot-long, foot-and-a-half-thick black barrier usually helped block the building entrance, but Marines had removed it the previous day for a Saturday-afternoon country-western concert and pizza party.[48] Although one Marine fired on the oncoming vehicle and another threw himself in front of it, the truck easily plowed into the lobby of the four-story building. When the driver detonated his explosives, the blast blew bodies out of the building as far as fifty yards away and left a crater thirty feet deep and forty feet wide.[49] A total of 241

American servicemen were killed in what was at that time the deadliest terrorist attack that had ever been carried out against Americans.[50]

Initially President Reagan was defiant. Appearing with his wife, Nancy, his voice trembling, the president decried the "bestial nature" of the attack and stressed that such people "cannot take over that vital and strategic area of the earth or for that matter any other part of the earth."[51] He quickly dispatched three hundred more U.S. troops. "Many Americans are wondering why we must keep our forces in Lebanon," Reagan said. "We cannot pick and choose where we will support freedom."[52] Defense Secretary Caspar Weinberger suggested that Moscow might be behind the suicide attack. "The Soviets love to fish in troubled waters," he said.[53] In a formal address to the nation Reagan described the good that U.S. forces were doing, staving off Soviet influence, stabilizing a "powder-keg" region, safeguarding energy resources, and protecting Israel. "Would the terrorists have launched their suicide attacks against the Multinational Force if it were not doing its job?" he asked.[54] Reagan appointed a new Middle East envoy. He chose a man who had served as secretary of defense under President Gerald Ford and who would again serve as secretary of defense under George W. Bush: the fifty-one-year-old Donald Rumsfeld.

The U.S. public was angered by the death toll, the continued sniper and shelling attacks against Americans, and the confusion about what U.S. troops were doing in Lebanon.[55] Although Reagan initially ignored the public unrest, by February 1984 he had announced that he was "re-concentrating" U.S. forces. The last of the Marines had left by the end of the month. With Congress crying, "Bring our men home," Reagan complained, "All this can do is stimulate the terrorists and urge them on to further attacks."[56]

In 2003, on the twentieth anniversary of the attack on the Marine barracks, Defense Secretary Rumsfeld would say that his experience as Reagan's envoy in Lebanon had shaped his approach to fighting twenty-first-century terrorism. When U.S. forces left Beirut in 1984, Rumsfeld said, the United States had mistakenly shown extremists that "terrorism works." In the wake of the 9/11 attacks, by contrast, Washington would "take the war to them, to go after them where they are, where they live, where they plan, where they hide."[57] He noted, "We can't simply defend. We can't hunker down and hope they'll go away."[58] That, for Rumsfeld, was the "lesson of Lebanon."

Vieira de Mello drew a different lesson. Any doubts he had about whether

UNIFIL should have fought back in the face of the Israeli invasion were dispelled. If UN peacekeepers were to surrender their neutrality, as the troops in the Multinational Force had done, they would be viewed as combatants. He had come to appreciate the tangible virtues of the UN's commitment to impartiality. More than a decade would pass before—in a peacekeeping mission in the Balkans—he would realize that impartiality too carried grave risks.

Three

BLOOD RUNNING BLUE

COMMITMENTS FOR LIFE

Vieira de Mello had joined the UN in 1969 by happenstance, but he gradually came to see the UN not merely as his place of employment but as his family and the embodiment of his evolving political ideals. By the 1980s he had grown used to the red tape and had committed the UN Charter's provisions to memory with the same zeal with which he had once memorized the teachings of Karl Marx. His colleagues saw that he had a fiercely pragmatic side, but they also began teasing him that his blood had begun to run, not red, but "UN blue."

In August 1983, after returning from Lebanon, Vieira de Mello was named UNHCR deputy head of personnel services. He would work directly under Kofi Annan, who in 1996 would become the first UN official ever to work his way up the UN ranks to become secretary-general. Vieira de Mello helped Annan restructure the personnel office, which oversaw recruitment, hiring, promotions, and overseas postings. Annan made him the first head of training. "Sergio liked to explain, he liked to teach, he liked to talk about the organization, where he had been, what he had done, what he had learned," Annan recalls. The two men became friends, but Annan, who was divorced, left the office every day at 5 p.m. to meet his son after school, so they rarely socialized.

The UNHCR of 1983 was very different from the agency Vieira de Mello had joined in 1969. Its regular budget had grown sixtyfold, from

$6 million to $400 million, and its staff had exploded from 140 to more than 700 in some 80 offices around the globe. What had been a European organization had become truly international. He no longer knew the names of most of his colleagues.

Vieira de Mello adorned his new office with the plaques and ribbons given to him by the battalions that had served in Lebanon. "What is this, Sergio? You've started playing with guns?" Jamshid Anvar, his Iranian colleague, said playfully. "Well, well, Lebanon has turned our resident Marxist into a bourgeois militarist!" Vieira de Mello laughed good-naturedly and then said seriously that the soldiers who served the UN were not militarists.

Yet whatever his boyish pride at his newfound experience working with the military, he also confessed his sense of shame over the humiliations that the UN force had suffered in Lebanon. Even though the suicide attacks against the American and French units in Lebanon had convinced him that UN peacekeepers should not become combatants, he described the mission as a "black chapter" in his life. "The UN was powerless," he told colleagues. "It was awful."

Sometimes, when he spoke about the UN's aspirations, he could sound credulous. He said he strove to observe the Hammarskjöld principles—"independence, integrity, impartiality"—a reference to the UN's legendary Swedish secretary-general who was killed in a plane crash in Congo in 1961. Once when he and Jahanshah Assadi, a close colleague from Iran, were working all night to prepare a report in time for a meeting of UNHCR's governing executive committee, Vieira de Mello burst into their shared office with tears in his eyes. The Tanzanian ambassador, who was chairing the executive committee, had read over his summary of the day's events and accused him of giving a biased rendition of the discussion. "He thinks I'm being partial here, that I'm not being objective, that I'm playing favorites," Vieira de Mello said almost desperately. Assadi tried to console him. "Aw, Sergio, every government has its own agenda, just forget about it, let it go." But he couldn't. "I am partial," he said. "But I am partial to the mission of the United Nations." Assadi, who was taken aback by his agitation, recalls, "For Sergio, the worst insult someone could hurl at you was that you were not behaving like a proper UN person." He carried his UN passport proudly and treated it as though it constituted a nationality of its own. "I'm not Latin American," he would tell non-UN people. "I'm not Brazilian."[1]

Often after work, instead of driving immediately back to his home just across the French-Swiss border in Massongy, he would head out with Antonio Carlos Diegues Santana, a fellow Brazilian who ran UNHCR's field support unit. They would speak in Portuguese about Brazilian politics, play pinball, and drink beer. Vieira de Mello prided himself on his ties to Brazil, and even his insistence that everyone call him "Sergio" was a relic from his country, where public figures go by familiar names (Pelé, Lula, etc.). Still, he was not nearly as politically active as his friend. His leftist rage had by then largely evaporated, and he saw no harm in stopping by the Brazilian mission in Geneva to pick up that week's Brazilian newspapers and magazines. Diegues Santana refused to set foot inside the building because it represented the military regime. He told Vieira de Mello that the day the generals stepped down would be the day he returned to his homeland.

When that day finally came, in March 1985, and Diegues Santana announced that he intended to leave the UN and return to Brazil, Vieira de Mello initially didn't believe him. "If I am still stuck here in Geneva in three months' time," Diegues Santana said to a small circle of friends gathered for a drink, "I will take a knife to my guts and commit suicide." Vieira de Mello laughed and said dramatically, "No, no, if you are still here in three months, I promise, with all of our friends here as witnesses, I will take a knife to your guts!" Diegues Santana could tell that his friend had not understood that he was serious about leaving. When he submitted his resignation a few weeks later, he and Vieira de Mello ended up out on the bar's terrace in an hour-long heated argument, both men gesturing wildly with their hands and swearing at each other in their native tongue. "Sergio didn't believe I would leave," Diegues Santana recalls. "It was not because of me. It was because of the organization. He thought it was the most important thing in the whole world."

Vieira de Mello offset his seeming priggishness about UN principles by flamboyantly playing up his love of women. He would be known throughout his career for treating cafeteria workers, security guards, and maintenance staff with unusual respect, prompting Omar Bakhet, an Eritrean colleague, to compliment him on his egalitarianism. "But, Omar, I am not a true egalitarian," he said. "I don't see class, race, or religion, but I most definitely see gender!" Once, as he entered La Glycine, his favorite restaurant in Geneva, with his Italian colleague Salvatore Lombardo, he exclaimed in Italian, "Look around you.

What has happened?" Lombardo wasn't sure what he meant. *"Come è possibile che ci non è una donna in questo ristorante?"* Vieira de Mello asked, openmouthed. "How is it possible that there is not a single woman in this restaurant?" After the two men sat down and began to discuss refugee matters, the door to the restaurant opened, and he cut Lombardo off midsentence. "Finally!" he exclaimed, leaping out of his seat and beginning a slow, rhythmic clap. Initially the patrons in the restaurant did not know what he was applauding, but one by one, as they looked around, they realized the significance of the woman's arrival and joined in. In under a minute the unsuspecting woman had roused a thunderous standing ovation from the male-only lunchtime crowd.

His reputation as a ladies' man followed him throughout his career, and he seemed to relish the rumors of his exploits. In 1982 Mark Malloch Brown, a twenty-nine-year-old unmarried British aid worker who a quarter-century later would become deputy secretary-general of the UN under Annan, had spent several months pursuing an attractive British UNHCR official. After finally spending the night in her apartment, Malloch Brown awoke buoyantly the next morning, only to notice that beside her alarm clock was a framed photograph of the woman with her parents—and Vieira de Mello. "If it was just Sergio, that wouldn't have been so bad," Malloch Brown recalls. "But it was clear Sergio had already insinuated himself in the deepest quarters of this woman's life. I didn't stand a chance!"

Vieira de Mello claimed a huge amount of freedom in his marriage. Early on Annie complained about the phone calls from women and his late-night arrivals, but eventually she grew resigned. "Nothing I said was going to change him," she remembers, "and when I complained, it just made him angry." He would tell his friends, "Everybody has a cross to bear in life, and I am Annie's cross."

Over the years he would have several significant relationships with women, but he was unwilling to give up his home life, which anchored him. In the mid-1980s he told a UN friend, Fabienne Morisset, "I will never get divorced—neither from my marriage nor from the UN." When his sons were young, he brought his family back to Brazil every two years on UN home leave. He also took them on a skiing holiday every winter, and in periods when he was based in Geneva, he drove the boys to school every morning on his way to work. Even though he often worked late during the week, he and Annie were known for hosting barbecues and dinner parties on the weekends. When guests came to the house, he wandered around in his bedroom slippers, boasting about his one culinary specialty, *feijoada*, the Brazilian national stew that is a potpourri of pork, ham, sausage, spices, and carefully soaked beans.

He likely would not have been able to work in the places he did—or rise at the pace he did—if his chief priority had been raising his sons. As his career progressed, he never stopped accepting the most challenging assignments, no matter how dangerous or remote they were. His willingness to go wherever he was needed—whenever—was unique. Many of his peers who embraced jobs in Geneva and New York did not like desk jobs, but they understood that being in the office would enable them to stay close to home while their children grew up. Vieira de Mello lived a daily zero-sum game: The more he traveled, the more skilled a UN troubleshooter he became, and the less he met the daily needs of his family.

He maintained close ties with a few of his childhood Brazilian friends, including Flavio da Silveira, who still lived in Geneva. But he spent most of his after-hours time with his colleagues from work. Curiously, he often sought out the company of the more cynical UN staffers. Alexander "Sacha" Casella, an Italian-Czech who was twenty-two years his senior, was one UN official who believed life was nasty, brutish, and short and could hardly contain his skepticism about the motives of UN member states, senior officials, and human beings in general. To any colleague bordering on earnest, Casella would offer one of his maxims. "Living is a prelude to death," he would say. "Marriage is a prelude to divorce." Exhibiting ethical behavior within an unethical system was unwise. "You should never tell the truth," Casella said. "People will take you for granted. Even if you see someone in the hall and you're going to a meeting, tell them you are going to the bathroom." And he liked to recite a parable that he believed summed up humanitarianism:

> A bird gets stuck in the mud. The bird makes noises to try to get the attention of those who might come to his rescue. A farmer hears the noises, arrives at the scene, chops the head off the bird, and eats it for dinner. The moral of this story is, "If you get stuck, don't make noises; if you make noises, it will not necessarily be your friend who comes to help; and in the end whoever saves you will likely eat you."

Vieira de Mello frequently asked Casella to accompany him on his missions overseas. "You are so cynical that having you around helps me understand the mind-set of the killers and crooks," he told his friend. Casella urged him to stop taking UN life so seriously and once handed him an envelope: "Sergio, the only thing that should anger you is when this doesn't come." Vieira de Mello opened the envelope, and inside the envelope he found another envelope. Inside that was a third. And finally in a tiny envelope, he found Casella's intended pick-me-up device: a UNHCR pay stub.

But while the UN offered its professional employees good salaries and generous benefits, Vieira de Mello did not stay with the UN for the money. He saw it as the place a person of his nationality and background could best make a difference in the world. While European academia had no place for him, the UN valued what he had to offer. He imagined himself soaring to great heights within the organization. "When I die, I will have a state funeral," he told Heidi Cervantes, a Swiss girlfriend. "I would like every one of my girlfriends to come to my funeral and walk behind my coffin. You'll come, right?"

Cervantes could not tell if he was serious. "How do you know you will be so important as to deserve a state funeral?" she asked.

"I will be an important man," he said. "You will see."

"Do you want to become an ambassador?" she asked.

He was aghast. "No way," he said. "Any Swiss jerk can become an ambassador. I want to become the UN secretary-general."

Cervantes laughed. "At your funeral, Sergio, they will say your only fault was your modesty."

RULES OF THE GAME

Vieira de Mello had come to understand that devotion to the UN meant serving at the whim of his supervisors and being prepared to pack up and move to a new region on a moment's notice. In 1986, at thirty-eight, he eagerly took up a position as UNHCR regional representative for South America with responsibility for a dozen countries. He rented a home in Buenos Aires, where he expected Annie and their two sons, seven and five, to join him. He was elated, as the assignment would enable him to visit his mother more often than he had been able to do since he left Rio in 1966. It would also allow him to leave his desk job. "The restless part of Sergio would come to you and say, 'I need another challenge.' Then you would know he was bored," Annan remembers. "He felt there was nothing more he could bring to a job or he didn't have the space to do what he wanted to do. Being in the field gave him room for creativity. He knew himself and the environment in which he did best."

No sooner had he arrived in Buenos Aires than UN secretary-general Javier Pérez de Cuéllar announced that Jean-Pierre Hocké, a forty-seven-year-old Swiss national, would take over as the new UN High Commissioner for Refugees.[2] Having pledged to reinvigorate the agency by drawing on its youth, Hocké summoned Vieira de Mello back to Geneva to serve as his chief of staff.* Annie, who had just boxed up their life in Massongy, was forced to adjust to yet another life-changing promotion. "Let's just say I had stopped cracking open the bottles of champagne," she says. Though Vieira de Mello was returning to Geneva to take up a senior position, he was uncharacteristically melancholy. "I have broken my promise to my mother yet again," he told an Argentinian friend. "She will be devastated." The demands of the UN had come to take precedence over all others.

The United States had aggressively pushed for Hocké's appointment. In UNHCR's early decades Washington had prized the agency as a vehicle for resettling refugees fleeing Communism. But by the 1980s U.S. impatience with wastefulness in the UN system was spilling over into its dealings even with UNHCR. In 1985 the U.S. Congress passed a law for the first time requiring that America's annual dues to the UN be reduced pending major UN reform. The Reagan administration expected Hocké to run a lean shop.

Vieira de Mello was excited by the little he knew about his new boss. Hocké came from the International Committee of the Red Cross (ICRC), a well-regarded humanitarian organization that tried to ensure that in wartime the rights of civilians and prisoners were respected. He had managed all of ICRC's field operations and had personally headed missions in Nigeria, Lebanon, Jordan, and Vietnam. When Hocké learned that the Somalian govern-

---

*Vieira de Mello was also named secretary of the executive committee.

ment had claimed double the number of refugees in its camps, so as to feed its army with the extra aid, the high commissioner temporarily suspended relief. He vowed to tackle the chronic refugee crises, or the "Palestinization" of refugee populations like the Afghans in Pakistan. He reminded UN staff and donor countries that the long-term care the UN offered refugees was nothing to boast about: It simply showed that conditions in the refugees' home countries were not improving. And he took the radical step of arguing that it wasn't enough to press neighboring countries to grant asylum to those fleeing persecution; UNHCR had to work with the other UN bodies to end poverty and persecution in their countries of origin. Vieira de Mello, who admired his new boss's energy and ideas, supplied the scotch for early-evening gossip and brainstorming sessions in Hocké's office. He kept the Black Label hidden in the hard-file folder marked "Organization of American States" and the Red Label disguised in the "Organization of African Unity" folder.

But Hocké's relations with other staff members quickly deteriorated, as he was seen to micromanage field operations from afar and to dismiss alternative viewpoints. He also raised less money than UNHCR was spending, and the agency fell into debt for the first time in its history.[3] Détente had set in between the Soviet Union and the United States, and Washington stopped treating refugees as pawns in the larger ideological struggle and reduced its contribution to UNHCR accordingly. After a year serving as chief of staff and another year as director of UNHCR's Asia Bureau, Vieira de Mello started to believe that the discontent among staff and the decisions by donor countries to cut back their contributions were harming his home agency. He came to the conclusion that his colleagues had reached months before: for the good of the UN, Hocké had to go. "He has lost the plot," Vieira de Mello told Morisset.

In the fall of 1989 a group of disgruntled UNHCR staff members (not including Vieira de Mello) sent a dossier on Hocké to donor governments and to a Swiss television crew. They charged, accurately, that Hocké had dipped into a special Danish fund for his personal use, spending some $300,000 to fly himself and his wife on the Concorde and regularly upgrading his business-class flights to first class, which, at a time of U.S.-driven fiscal belt-tightening, only the UN secretary-general was permitted to do.[4] Although Washington had backed Hocké's candidacy, U.S. support dried up.

In late October 1989 Dennis McNamara, a New Zealander who was one of Vieira de Mello's closest friends at UNHCR, jubilantly told his friend, "Sergio, he's resigned." "Who?" Vieira de Mello asked. "Who?! Hocké, you ass," said McNamara. "That's bullshit," Vieira de Mello said. The two men scrambled around agency headquarters to confirm the high commissioner's departure. The headline in *Le Monde* the next day summed up his aborted tenure: RESIGNATION OF MR. J-P HOCKÉ: GOOD MANAGER BUT TOO AUTHORITARIAN.[5] Although Hocké had given him the biggest promotion of his career, Vieira de Mello did not stop by his office as he boxed up his belongings. Nor did he send Hocké a farewell note. "Other people I didn't give a damn about," Hocké recalls, "but from Sergio, a friend, I expected more."

A year later Vieira de Mello arranged a meeting with the fallen high commissioner, who was working in downtown Geneva. "Jean-Pierre, you look so well," Vieira de Mello said, cheerily inquiring after his family and new line of work but making no mention of what had happened and offering no apology for his silence. "He seemed to want to clear the air without clearing the air," says Hocké. "He wanted to be admired by everyone, to be on good terms with everyone. He was basically a seducer. He tried to pretend like nothing had happened, but I wasn't prepared to go along with that." When Hocké heard that Vieira de Mello had returned to UNHCR headquarters and told colleagues that they had resolved their differences, he wrote his former chief of staff a bitter letter in which he informed him that he would not forget his disloyalty. Vieira de Mello made no further attempts at rapprochement.

Thorvald Stoltenberg, who had been Norway's foreign minister, succeeded Hocké but quit after ten months to reclaim his old job in Oslo. "Politicians come here to build their careers but not to serve refugees," Vieira de Mello fumed, making a mental note that former elected officials who were appointed to senior UN posts would bring Rolodexes and fund-raising savvy but would usually lack fealty to the UN itself.

Vieira de Mello's own loyalty to the UN deepened by the day, even as the organization's flaws continued to reveal themselves. One of his main annoyances was that no matter how fast he found himself rising in the UN system, his nationality would ultimately matter as much as, if not more than, his performance. He saw this on countless occasions, but in 1990, after Stoltenberg's exit, he witnessed a rare occasion where a friend of his, Virendra Dayal, fought back. Secretary-General Pérez de Cuéllar asked Dayal, his chief of staff, to become the high commissioner. Dayal, a fifty-five-year-old Oxford-educated Indian national, had worked at UNHCR from 1965 to 1972, serving under Jamieson during the Bangladesh emergency. He understood that the agency was struggling and was eager to bail it out. But no sooner had Pérez de Cuéllar publicly revealed his intention to appoint Dayal than an unnamed U.S. official—suspected to be John Bolton, who was then President Reagan's assistant secretary of state for international organizations and would later become George W. Bush's controversial ambassador to the UN—was quoted in the *New York Times* slamming the secretary-general's choice and saying that the United States wanted to see a prominent politician from a rich country in the job rather than a UN bureaucrat from the developing world.

Dayal was livid. He gathered the press in the secretary-general's conference room on the thirty-eighth floor of UN Headquarters and let loose. He said he felt "great pain" that certain people were "more comfortable with second-level politicians from the first world rather than with first-rate international civil servants from the third world."[6] He'd had enough. "To hell with this," he said. "I'm going back to India to tend to my garden." With Dayal's exit, Bolton triumphantly hailed the fact that donor countries could now "get control of this process." A nominee's experience working on refugee issues was a plus, he stressed, but should not be "a determining factor."[7]

Vieira de Mello, who had been unhappy about the turmoil at UNHCR, delightedly passed photocopies of Dayal's angry press briefing around UNHCR headquarters. "Thank god somebody has spoken about the ridiculous tradition of reserving certain posts for certain nationalities," he told Dayal. He revered the UN's commitment to multinationality but hated being reminded, as he was on a near-daily basis, that "some nations were more equal than others."

In December 1990 Pérez de Cuéllar nominated Sadako Ogata, a sixty-three-year-old Japanese political science professor, to become high commissioner. Educated at Georgetown University and the University of California–Berkeley, she was the first woman and the first academic to fill the post. In lobbying on Ogata's behalf, the Japanese government had promised to increase its contribution to the refugee agency were she selected. And so it did, doubling its contribution from $52 million in 1990 to $113 million the following year.

The Hour of the United Nations:
The Comprehensive Plan of Action

What Vieira de Mello found most frustrating about UNHCR's leadership setbacks was that they coincided with heady times at the United Nations as a whole. In the late 1980s, with the waning of U.S.-Soviet tensions, the entire organization had a prominence and a sense of possibility that it had not had since its founding in 1945. The president of the UN General Assembly, Dante Caputo of Argentina, reflected the spirit of the moment when he noted, "This, more than any earlier time, is the hour of the United Nations."[8]

The UN's "hour," as far as Vieira de Mello was concerned, was long over-due. In a world of conflict, repression, and extreme poverty, he had come to see the UN as the only body that could serve both as a humanitarian actor in its own right and as a platform for governments to identify common interests and pool their resources to meet global challenges. The end of the cold war meant that more countries could use the UN as the forum in which to debate their differences. He thought it would also mean that the powerful countries with permanent seats on the UN Security Council would be more prone to act collectively to defuse threats to international peace and security.

Hopes that once had sounded impossibly naïve suddenly became mainstream. And in 1988 and 1989, as director of UNHCR's Asia Bureau, responsible for overseeing agency policy throughout the region, Vieira de Mello saw firsthand how salutary the new climate could be, as he worked to help resolve one of the messiest chapters of the cold war: the displacement of the Vietnamese "boat people." It was his role in these negotiations that would begin to give him a name outside the UN.

Remarkably, more than a decade after the end of the Vietnam War, thousands of Vietnamese were still washing up on the shores of Malaysia, Hong Kong, Indonesia, and Thailand. Indeed, in Hong Kong, for instance, where 3,395 boat people had arrived in 1987, a whopping 8,900 arrived in May 1989 alone.[9] Most of them were likely fleeing not political persecution but economic hardship.[10] Compounding the challenge, Western countries that had once been generous in resettling the Vietnamese had stiffened their entry criteria.[11] This meant that Vietnam's neighbors were stuck sheltering boat people whom the United States refused to resettle but whom Washington also insisted not be sent back to Vietnam. The countries bordering Vietnam were fed up and started denying the Vietnamese access to their shores—deputizing fishermen to ram the boat people so they would not be able to land and herding those who arrived into squalid, overcrowded camps.[12]

Vieira de Mello inherited a multiyear effort by UNHCR staff and by Western diplomats to resolve the matter. Each person who fled Vietnam had a different story. Neighboring countries could not treat all of them as economic migrants. Some individuals would in fact face violent reprisals if they were sent back to Vietnam. As the guardian of refugee law, UNHCR had to help find a way to ensure that Vietnamese civilians who faced genuine political threats would continue to be admitted. Vieira de Mello had to try to persuade key governments to allow case-by-case screenings.

He spent thirteen months shuttling between the major Western capitals and the East Asian countries where the refugees were being crammed into camps. He stroked the egos of ambassadors and tried to convince them that a multifaceted compromise was in their long-term interest. He developed a habit that would never leave him. On the road constantly, he would scribble notes from his meetings onto hotel stationery pads. On these tiny slips of paper—probably no larger than the library request slips his father had amassed—he would spell out the key talking points for everything from meetings with minor consular officials to major plenary addresses. His colleagues marveled at how one so fastidious could end up delivering pivotal remarks while reading from a Hilton Hotel note pad. "Is that the best you can do?" Assadi ribbed him. "Look, I'm always moving so these pads are convenient," Vieira de Mello replied. "But I've also learned over the years that if I can't fit my argument on a hotel note pad, I probably don't know what I'm trying to say!" Just as his mother, Gilda, had helped organize his father's library scraps, Vieira de Mello's secretary at UNHCR grew accustomed to unusual piles turning up in her in-box. "Would you mind typing this up for the files?" he would ask, handing her palm-sized shards of paper covered in his miniature handwriting in felt-tip pen, held together by a paper clip or stuffed into a hotel stationery envelope.

The key concessions had been made in the months before he got involved: Vietnam had shown a desire to improve its regional and international ties at a time of diminished Soviet support, and Washington had finally begun to rethink its long-standing policy that every fleeing Vietnamese should be considered an automatic legal refugee. With Vieira de Mello's coaxing, and themselves already ripe to reach an agreement, Western countries agreed to open up additional resettlement slots for Vietnamese who had been languishing in neighboring countries. These countries in turn agreed to grant asylum to those whom UNHCR's new screening policies determined to be genuine refugees.[13] Border officials would be trained to discern, on a case-by-case basis, which Vietnamese were actually fleeing for their lives and which could be fairly sent back to Vietnam. After a preliminary meeting in Kuala Lumpur, Malaysia, in March 1989, some seventy governments gathered in Geneva that June and signed this compromise package, known as the Comprehensive Plan of Action—the first-ever three-way agreement among countries of origin, asylum, and resettlement.[14] A *New York Times* editorial hailed the compromise as "A Cure for Compassion Fatigue."[15]

The plan was controversial. Arthur Helton, the refugee advocate who fourteen years later would be killed in Iraq in the attack on the UN, was perhaps the most vocal American critic. He documented the flaws in the screening process. The screeners and immigration officials who classified whether or not a person was a refugee were often ignorant of conditions in Vietnam, vulnerable to bribes, and hasty in their review of the cases before them. The average interview lasted twenty minutes.[16] In addition, too few UNHCR staff were in place to monitor the sessions. In Hong Kong many of the Vietnamese felt physically manhandled or emotionally browbeaten into declaring themselves "economic migrants." Helton quoted one Vietnamese boat person as saying, "The major aim of this policy is not to select the real refugee but to stop the flow of refugees."[17]

But Vieira de Mello did not see a viable alternative. "If we don't find a compromise," he told his critics, "we will permanently kill asylum." The status quo was simply not an option. Although Vietnam might be an inhospitable place to return to, he agreed with Thomas Jamieson's old adage: "If there is a way to close a camp, take it." The only hope for deterring the outflow of economic migrants and saving those fleeing political oppression was to develop a mechanism for sending nonrefugees back.

Securing the agreement proved easy compared with implementing it. Vieira de Mello instructed UNHCR staff to suspend medical and counseling services and scale back education and employment programs for screened-out boat people in the camps in neighboring countries.[18] More controversially, he defied the spirit of a key UNHCR principle, which was that the agency would only assist in *voluntarily* returning refugees to their countries of origin. Technically, those being sent back were not "refugees," but UNHCR would still have to help return terrified Vietnamese to their homeland against their will. Vieira de Mello traveled to Hong Kong, and accompanied by Casella, he spoke with Vietnamese community leaders who had been denied refugee status in the screening process but were refusing to return to Vietnam. One man told Vieira de Mello that he intended to commit suicide if the UN tried to force him home. Vieira de Mello's face grew dark and solemn. "How could you say such a thing?" he asked. "Your wife and your children rely upon you. You cannot abandon them when you have survived all you have together." When the man insisted he would prefer to die than face the Communists in Vietnam, Vieira de Mello grew even more emotional and delivered a sweeping oration on the value of life and the importance of returning to one's own soil and providing for one's family. Casella could take his colleague's melodrama no longer. "Listen, if you are going to kill yourself," he said, "make sure you use a knife and sever the vein properly because we'd hate for you to have to try twice. And since this will make an enormous mess, we'd appreciate it if you did it outside, so that we don't have to clean up after you." Vieira de Mello was astonished, but he later conceded that Casella's bluntness may have been more effective. The Comprehensive Plan of Action would fail unless nonrefugees left the camps and went back to Vietnam.

Although Vieira de Mello believed UNHCR would have to compel some refugees to return, he knew that many of the UNHCR staff who worked under him in the region would object to doing anything that hinted of forced return, even to those who had not qualified as refugees. In December 1989, on the occasion of the first return operation, he planned the transport of those classed as illegal migrants with the Hong Kong authorities, deliberately bypassing his own staff. Hong Kong police and prison guards in riot gear arrived at 3 a.m., roughly shepherded fifty-one Vietnamese onto buses, and then flew them to Hanoi. In later repatriations the Hong Kong guards even went so far as to inject refugees with sedatives in order to get them to board the transport planes.[19]

As word of the new screening process made its way back to Vietnam, refugee flows declined considerably. In 1989 some 70,000 Vietnamese had sought asylum in Southeast Asia. In 1992, by contrast, only forty-one Vietnamese landed in neighboring countries.[20] Although other factors, such as the start of Vietnam's economic boom, played a role in the reduced flows, the agreement proved pivotal. Some 70,000 illegal migrants were sent back to Vietnam from the camps, and although UNHCR did not have the staff to monitor them on return, they were generally not mistreated by the Vietnamese authorities. All the boat people had been cleared out of camps by 1996, with the United States resettling some 40 percent of the refugees.[21]

For a person who recited UN ideals with near-romantic reverence, Vieira de Mello had proven himself remarkably willing to compromise those principles. He argued that such pragmatic concessions served the long-term interests of both the refugees and the UN. In this case he may have been correct that he had extracted the most humane outcome he could from the governments involved. But he could have gone to greater lengths to use his pulpit at UNHCR to try to ensure that the Vietnamese were more fairly screened in the camps and were better treated en route back to Vietnam. This was the first of several prominent instances in his career in which he would downplay his and the UN's obligation to try to *shape* the preferences of governments. By the 1980s he had come to see himself as a UN man, but since the organization was both a body of self-interested governments and a body of ideals, he did not seem sure yet whether serving the UN meant doing what states demanded or pressing for what refugees needed.

The demands on the United Nations were multiplying. In 1991 the UN Security Council authorized the Persian Gulf War, and the U.S.-led coalition swiftly removed Saddam Hussein's Iraqi forces from Kuwait. Sadako Ogata, the newly crowned UN High Commissioner for Refugees, was immediately thrust into UNHCR's most complex mission to date—working with Western armies to care for and repatriate some 1.5 million Kurds displaced inside and outside Iraq.[22]

On April 5, 1991, in a radical break with the Security Council's traditional deference to state sovereignty, the Council demanded that international humanitarian organizations like UNHCR be granted immediate access to Iraq. In Operation Provide Comfort, U.S., French, and British planes began dropping food packages to the Kurds from the air and then expanded the operation by sending ground troops inside northern Iraq to set up and protect temporary UNHCR camps.[23] It was the first military intervention in history carried out in the name of displaced persons. And it marked the beginning of an era in which borders seemed less sacred and the traditional line separating humanitarian matters from political and military affairs became blurred.

Just before the Gulf War, Vieira de Mello had been promoted to UNHCR director of external relations, responsible for managing the agency's ties with governments and fund-raising. With the UN breaking new legal and geopolitical ground each day, he found himself desk-bound in Geneva. But while he played little role in the Gulf crisis, the UN was being handed two other challenges that would soon pull him in: the end of war in Cambodia and the start of conflict in the former Yugoslavia.

In September 1991 Vietnam announced that, after a twelve-year occupation of Cambodia, it was withdrawing its soldiers. And on October 23, 1991, after twenty-two years of continuous conflict and more than a decade of tortured negotiations, Cambodia's four factions signed the momentous Paris peace agreement. The same country that for decades had been at the epicenter of decolonization struggles and U.S. and Soviet proxy wars now seemed destined to become a laboratory for post–cold war transition. The newfound unity among the five permanent members of the Security Council—China, France, the Soviet Union, the U.K., and the United States—was almost unprecedented in the history of the Council, and it had produced results. The belligerents promised to lay down their guns, to submit to a UN transitional authority, and to participate in the country's first free elections. The Council informed UN officials in New York in the small Department of Peacekeeping Operations, which had just been set up because of heightened demand, that they would need to field 16,000 troops and 3,600 police to serve in the new mission. And they told Ogata's UNHCR that it would be responsible for facilitating the return of 360,000 Cambodian refugees from border camps into a volatile "postwar" environment.

Just when UN agencies were reeling under the strain of managing a huge refugee operation in northern Iraq and launching one in Cambodia, war broke out in the Balkans. In 1991 Ogata dispatched dozens of aid workers to Croatia to try to feed and shelter those on the run, and in December the Security Council called for some 14,000 peacekeepers to be sent to Croatia to patrol a shaky cease-fire there. UN staff in New York could not keep up.

An office that had fielded a total of 11,000 peacekeepers the previous year was being called upon to find five times that many, and the phone would keep ringing. In addition, unarmed humanitarian aid workers were suddenly being called upon to operate in the midst of live and deadly conflict, assuming risks traditionally taken only by soldiers.

Initially removed from "the action" as it unfolded, Vieira de Mello used his spare time to theorize about the geopolitical and humanitarian implications of the end of the cold war. After Saddam Hussein's seizure of Kuwait and his monstrous attacks on the Shiites and the Kurds, the decision by the most powerful governments in the UN to bypass a sovereign government in order to assist civilians in need impressed Vieira de Mello. Like many, he understood this to be the harbinger of a "new world order" in which citizens might be rescued from their abusive governments. He did not yet appreciate how unprepared the UN system was to tackle these complex new challenges.

INVENTING THE FUTURE

Cheered on by Robert Misrahi, Vieira de Mello had completed the French system's most demanding and competitive "state doctorate" (*doctorat d'état*) back in 1985. At night, after eating dinner with Annie and the boys at their home, he had disappeared into his large study lined with wall-to-wall bookcases. Typed again by Annie, the thesis was entitled *Civitas Maxima: Origins, Foundations, and Philosophical and Practical Significance of the Supranationality Concept.*[24] His colleagues marveled at his productivity. Omar Bakhet recalls, "I was shocked when he told me one day, 'I'm going to go and defend my thesis." I said, "Thesis? What thesis?"

In his 1974 doctorate Vieira de Mello had credited Marxism with defining a social utopia by which civilization could measure its progress. In *Civitas Maxima,* a more mature six-hundred-page conceptual work of philosophy, he defined his own version of a utopian egalitarian society. He no longer vented against philosophy's irrelevance but instead tried to introduce an affirmative theory of universalism rooted in reciprocal respect. Clearly influenced by the cold war détente, he had begun to see such universality as possible, but he asked, "Does universality carry within itself the germs of its own annihilation?" Although what would later be called "globalization" was already tearing down barriers among peoples, states were also acquiring ever greater powers of destruction, and man's inhumanity to man seemed not to be abating. He tried to define a social order that would curb those tendencies, and he moved away from the historical determinism of Marxism, toward the aspirational philosophy of Misrahi and of the German philosopher Ernst Bloch, whose main work, *The Principle of Hope,* argued that individuals had to first define and wish into being the utopia that they sought to create. Only man would pull history toward a more just future.

Vieira de Mello took immense satisfaction in seeing through the grueling doctorate process, and he hoped that his thesis might find a wider audience. He sent a copy of it to Sonia, his multilingual sister in Brazil, in the hopes that she might help him translate it into Portuguese for possible publication in Brazil. "Sergio, this is not French. It is some language other than French," she teased her brother. "How can I translate what I can't understand?"

In December 1991 Vieira de Mello drew upon his dissertation in order to deliver a lecture at the Geneva International Peace Research Institute entitled "Philosophical History and Real History: The Relevance of Kant's Political Thought in Current Times." He used his remarks to respond to American political scientist Francis Fukuyama's argument that the end of the cold war signified the triumph of political and economic liberalism and the "end of history." He criticized Fukuyama and others for "a combination of naïve optimism and supreme arrogance." "No," Vieira de Mello declared, "history is not finished."[25] But it was, he argued, changing course.

His lecture offered an ambitious and vivid—if dense—articulation of his worldview. Writing around the time of the French Revolution, Vieira de Mello noted, Immanuel Kant had been conscious that he was living through a turning point both in philosophical history and in real-world history. In the aftermath of Communism's demise, he now argued, the world had reached an analogous juncture. International law, which was being fortified by the day, offered evidence of humanity's "long march" toward reason. But "history's schizophrenia" was on full display, as he was struck by the enormous "distance separating institutional progress from ethical progress, law from morals." Whatever laws had been placed on the books, one could not rely upon governments to respect, promote, or enforce those strictures. With a "fascinating persistence," sovereign states showed that they would be overtaken by the "impulse to not reason," he argued. The same "childlike madness, vanity, meanness, and thirst for destruction" that Kant observed among political leaders in his day still ensured that, in the coming century, "history" would stubbornly live on.

But this did not deter Vieira de Mello from urging individuals and governments to strive toward a new Ideal. He argued that generating constructive change required a "synthesis of utopia and realism." "The persistent tendency to fail represents equally persistent encouragement to shape such a system," he insisted. What would the ideal system entail? Governments needed to accept that their interests would be best advanced if they united in a community based on laws. Kant's proposals for a federation of states, which had been taken up by Simón Bolívar in 1826 and by European statesmen with renewed vigor in the 1990s, needed to be resurrected globally. Kant was calling not for a supranational federal state, Vieira de Mello stressed, but for a "federation of peoples" that did not require individuals, groups, or countries to abandon their identities.

Vieira de Mello did not believe a federation of peoples or a corresponding "perpetual peace" was close at hand, but other Kantian ideas could be embraced in the present. If countries insisted on resorting to violence, for instance, they needed to play by certain rules. "War," he argued, "must not stain the state of peace with infamy." If atrocities committed in battle went unpunished, the warring factions would find it impossible to trust one another after they had stopped fighting. Peace deals simultaneously had to provide for accountability and somehow show empathy for a war's losers. He returned to a theme he had emphasized in his high school essay in Brazil. "How many wars could have been avoided," he wrote, "if statesmen had not shown contempt for nations' sense of self-esteem!"

For Vieira de Mello, the most challenging and timely aspect of Kant's political thought centered on the right of intervention—a debate that the UN-sponsored incursion on behalf of the Kurds in northern Iraq had revived. Kant was adamant that a state should not interfere in the internal affairs of another. But he made an exception that Vieira de Mello endorsed: When a state fell into anarchy and threatened the stability of its neighbors, other countries had to step up. Since the circumstances in northern Iraq met these criteria, he believed Kant "would have applauded" the UN-authorized operation there.

Vieira de Mello did not believe that it was enough for philosophers, or even statesmen, to declare the Ideal; the world's citizenry had to make it real.

Yet it seemed to him that democratic voters in the West had grown complacent because of their enhanced material well-being. And he worried that now, thanks to the cold war's end, "messianic" ideas about the "end of history" were further seducing them. Vieira de Mello argued that citizens could not afford to "wash our hands of the construction of a real peace" and leave the important decisions to statesmen. Regular people simply had to participate. "Are we to abdicate this responsibility?" he asked. "We are all—you and me, affluent and destitute peoples—jointly responsible for the opportunity, which is a right, to fully participate in the formation of progress." He closed out his lecture with words that would foreshadow his approach to negotiating in conflict zones. "We must act as if perpetual peace is something real, though perhaps it is not," Vieira de Mello said, quoting Kant. Then he added his own coda: "The future is to be invented."

Vieira de Mello was the rare UN official who had the background in philosophy to prepare such a lecture. Yet while he seemed to have infinite patience for ideas, his greatest ambition was to bring "the Ideal" to life in practice. And he did not feel that this was something he was achieving in Geneva. "I studied philosophy a long time, but I need to look for confirmation of philosophy and of values in the real world," he once told an interviewer. "I'm restless. I like challenges, changes. I look for trouble, it's true. Because in trouble I find truth and reality."[26]

Ever since he had returned from Lebanon eight years before, he had kept his eye out for an opportunity to participate in another UN peacekeeping mission. "Sergio had caught the political bug," Kofi Annan recalls. Vieira de Mello's experience chairing talks aimed at resettling the Vietnamese boat people only whetted his appetite for political negotiations, which were likely to be rare at a humanitarian agency like UNHCR. He began phoning colleagues elsewhere in the UN system, inquiring as to whether they knew of any openings. He wanted a job in the field that would allow him to help refugees and sharpen his understanding of the political challenges likely to emerge in the new era.

An opportunity soon presented itself in Cambodia.

Four

HITTING THE
GROUND RUNNING

B y 1991 Vieira de Mello, at forty-three, had helped care for refugees in Bangladesh, Sudan, Mozambique, and South America. He had helped advise the commander of a UN military peacekeeping mission in Lebanon. And he had helped negotiate a political compromise among UN member states over the fate of refugees and migrants from Vietnam. But in Cambodia the Security Council was for the first time making the UN responsible for all three sets of tasks at once: humanitarian, military, and political. And Vieira de Mello was convinced that stability in the post–cold war era would turn on whether the UN system succeeded in managing such complex challenges.

After Cambodia's four factions signed the Paris peace agreement in October 1991, the Security Council countries made clear their intention to authorize a large UN peacekeeping mission known as the UN Transitional Authority in Cambodia (UNTAC).* While UN peacekeepers in Lebanon had generally avoided involvement in regional politics and simply attempted

---

* The four Cambodian parties that signed the Paris agreement were FUNCINPEC, the anti-Communist royalist party of Prince Sihanouk, led by his son, Prince Norodom Ranariddh; the somewhat marginal Khmer People's National Liberation Front (KPNLF) of former prime minister Son Sann; the Khmer Rouge (KR), formally under Khieu Samphan (but with Pol Pot still in fact in charge); and the State of Cambodia (SOC), controlled by Prime Minister Hun Sen.

to serve as a buffer along the border between Israel and Lebanon, UNTAC was given responsibility for seven pillars—one for each of the vital sectors that the country would need in order to move from dictatorship to democracy: human rights, elections, military (demobilization), civil administration, civilian police, refugee repatriation, and rehabilitation. The mission was oriented around elections, which were likely to be held in the spring of 1993. Vieira de Mello convinced Sadako Ogata, his boss, that he was the person best suited to manage the repatriation pillar—helping return some 360,000 Cambodian refugees who had long been marooned on the Thai border.*

His team would have to ensure that Cambodians who had been living outside their country for more than a decade would return in time to vote. This would be no easy task. His friend Dennis McNamara was put in charge of the UN human rights pillar. "You got the better job," Vieira de Mello told him. "What?" McNamara exclaimed. "You've got refugees to bring home. They would come home even without you, but you'll be able to take the credit!"

Vieira de Mello would wear two hats in Cambodia. As Ogata's special envoy, he would answer to UNHCR in Geneva and manage his own budget of $120 million to oversee the return of the refugees. But as the head of one pillar in the larger UNTAC peacekeeping mission, he would also answer to a Japanese diplomat named Yasushi Akashi, who had been named the head of the overall UNTAC operation.[1] Akashi was a fairly typical UN bureaucrat who seemed unlikely to inspire; yet what he lacked in charisma, UN planners hoped he would bring in funds. And in fact the Japanese government would contribute hundreds of millions of dollars to Cambodia's reconstruction in the coming years. It would also become the second-largest funder of peacekeeping in the world, behind only the United States.

On December 5, 1991, Vieira de Mello departed Geneva to take up his new post in the Cambodian capital, Phnom Penh. Because the countries on the UN Security Council were haggling over the terms of the new UNTAC mission, he was the only senior UN official present in Cambodia for several months. He liked the idea of arriving ahead of the peacekeepers and spoke, as he always did, of the need to "hit the ground running." But after some

---

* The KR controlled three camps—Site 8, O'Trao, and Site K. The KPNLF, Son Sann's faction, controlled two—Sok Sann and Site 2. FUNCINPEC controlled one—Site B. And the final site, Khao-I-Dang, was controlled not by any faction but by UNHCR.

seventeen new embassies and consulates had already opened shop, he grew impatient. "What the hell is taking the Council so long?" he asked, knowing that, even after the Council finally gave the UN peacekeeping mission the green light, it would need months to deploy some 22,000 UN peacekeepers and civilians.* From the moment he set foot in Cambodia, he felt the clock ticking.

Cambodia was a small country of nine million, wedged between sixty million Thais to the west and seventy million Vietnamese to the east. Vieira de Mello was enraptured by the country's mix of tradition and modernity. Peasants rowed their boats along the Mekong, carrying rice and chickens to market, while students rode their mopeds and bicycles, their mouths wrapped in *kharma,* the traditional Cambodian checkered scarf made notorious by the Khmer Rouge. The country's infrastructure was shattered by war and neglect. Roads that would be essential for moving refugees had long ago been washed away by the rains. The rice paddy fields were sown with land mines. Some 80 percent of the bridges had been destroyed, replaced with rickety wooden planks or not at all. The wide boulevards in Phnom Penh were lined with crumbling relics of the ornate mansions that French colonizers had once occupied.

Cambodians still seemed shell-shocked by the violence that had engulfed them for almost a quarter of a century. As he delved into the country's history, Vieira de Mello was struck by the remarkably diverse forms of terror and repression that Cambodia had suffered since it won its independence from France in 1953. In the early 1970s the Nixon administration had targeted the country in a secret bombing campaign. A five-year civil war then raged between the corrupt U.S.-backed government of Lon Nol and a band of notoriously brutal Maoist guerrillas known as the Khmer Rouge. And in April 1975 the Khmer Rouge victory ushered in a totalitarian terror that left more than two million Cambodians dead—a terror that was brought to an end only in 1978, when Vietnam invaded Cambodia and installed the Vietnamese puppet regime that still held power.

Foreigners had not really been present in Cambodia in significant numbers since the Khmer Rouge had run them out of the country. Yet already by the time of Vieira de Mello's early arrival, herds of Cambodian *cyclos,* or bicycle-

---

* The UN Security Council authorized a core of 15,900 military troops, along with 3,600 police monitors and 2,400 civilian administrators.

powered sedan chairs, were being overwhelmed on the roads by gleaming white Toyota Land Cruisers belonging to UN agencies or humanitarian aid groups. He knew that the trickiest part of any postconflict environment was managing local expectations, and he hoped that foreigners would bring real resources that could be used to deliver tangible change.

In his early months in Cambodia, Vieira de Mello did three things that would become hallmarks of his subsequent missions in Bosnia, Kosovo, East Timor, and Iraq: He assembled a trustworthy, "no bullshit" UN team around him; he cultivated ties with the country's most influential players; and he contrasted the plans and resources he had been handed by UN Headquarters with the ground reality, attempting to adapt the plans to fit what he (like Jamieson before him) called "the real world."

ASSEMBLING THE TEAM

UNHCR, Vieira de Mello's home agency, was more limber than UN Head-quarters, which managed peacekeeping missions. While the Department of Peacekeeping Operations at UN Headquarters in New York took months to screen job applicants, UNHCR was able to send staff to Cambodia almost immediately. Since he would have only a small team under him to manage the massive repatriation operation, he knew that the quality and commitment of the staff he assembled would be essential. Even the most coherent UN mandate could be bungled if he hired the wrong people.

Over the course of 1991, one of Vieira de Mello's primary functions in Geneva had been to interact with UNHCR's governing board, or executive committee. In that capacity he had encountered the Dutch government's representative to the committee, a razor-sharp twenty-nine-year-old brunette named Mieke Bos. Vieira de Mello was quickly smitten, and the two became romantically involved before he was appointed UNHCR special envoy. Bos had joined the Dutch government in the hopes of working on human rights issues, but she had never worked in the field. "How can you sit behind a desk in an office when there is so much work to be done in the world?" he pressed her. "Come with me to Cambodia. I need a special assistant." He was offering a path she had long considered but had never known how to pursue. Within weeks the Dutch government had agreed to loan Bos to the United Nations, and she joined Vieira de Mello in Phnom Penh in February 1992.

He had taken a room in the Hotel Cambodiana, a newly opened luxury hotel on the Mekong that was home to dozens of foreign embassies and residences. He rarely sat still, but when he did, he liked to retire to comfortable living quarters. In his hotel room he ended the day by dipping into an extensive classical music CD collection, as well as his trademark stash of Johnnie Walker Black Label imported from Thailand. On weekends when he and Bos were in Phnom Penh, they got their exercise in the hotel pool.

The couple worked day and night and traveled the country together. As their relationship deepened, she moved into his suite at the hotel. Although he remained in close telephone contact with Annie and his thirteen- and eleven-year-old sons back in France, he made no effort to hide his romance from his colleagues. It was the most open relationship he had had since he got married almost two decades before. "Annie and I have an understanding," he told friends. He never talked with Bos about a future together, but he behaved as if he were unattached, accompanying her on a trip to Europe to meet her family. "Somehow, because Sergio was so open, it took the stigma away," recalls one UN colleague. "We'd often have to remind ourselves, 'Wait, this guy has a wife back home. I wonder what she makes of this?'" On the rare occasions Vieira de Mello discussed his marriage, he spoke sympathetically and respectfully about Annie. "She is doing a wonderful job raising the boys," he said. "Without her sacrifices, I would never be able to do what I do." Only when Annie, Laurent, and Adrien traveled to Cambodia for a visit did Bos move out of their shared hotel room, temporarily taking up quarters elsewhere in the hotel.

In most professional hierarchies, a relationship between a senior manager and a special assistant would require the end of the romantic relationship or the dismissal of the supervisor. But for Vieira de Mello, who worked eighteen-hour days, special assistants made natural partners. Throughout his career he often became involved with colleagues with whom he could discuss the day's challenges. "The UN then was still like a third-world country," says one UN senior official. "Nobody thought twice when the boss slept with the assistant. Today not even a person as popular as Sergio would be able to get away with a relationship like that."

Because of the routine he and Bos had established, he rarely socialized with his other colleagues after hours. One evening he had planned to have dinner with Sten Bronee, a friend from UNHCR who was passing through

Phnom Penh. But at the last minute he sent Bronee an apologetic note saying he had to cancel owing to an "urgent, unexpected meeting." Bronee decided to take up the recommendation of the hotel concierge to try a newly opened restaurant. When he entered the restaurant, he did a double-take. Vieira de Mello was sitting with Bos at a secluded table in the corner. When he spotted Bronee, he looked a bit embarrassed and waved sheepishly. Bronee smiled. "If I had the choice of having dinner with me or with her," he recalls thinking, "I would have chosen her too."

Jamshid Anvar, Vieira de Mello's Iranian colleague who held a senior post in Geneva, advised Vieira de Mello not to bring Bos with him when he flew overseas to meet with donors. "Sergio, it doesn't look right," Anvar said. "You are at a wholly different level now." Vieira de Mello was defensive. "I'm not bringing her to sleep with her," he said. "I'm bringing her because she's brilliant and I need her." Anvar said he knew that, but others did not. "You are a man known for your integrity," he continued. "You should bend over backward to protect your reputation." Vieira de Mello told Anvar that he believed his reputation would rise or fall on whether he successfully brought home the refugees, and for that he needed Bos.

In assembling the rest of his team, Vieira de Mello generally relied upon staff with whom he had worked before. Newcomers found their way into his orbit in roundabout ways. Andrew Thomson, a doctor from New Zealand, ended up in Cambodia by happenstance. As a medical student in the mid-1980s, he had been dissecting frogs in his lab when he met a Cambodian refugee who was getting recertified as a surgeon. The man, a survivor of the Khmer Rouge horrors, told Thomson about the last operation he had performed in Phnom Penh before Pol Pot's bloody takeover: He had removed the diamond from his wife's engagement ring, sterilized it, and camouflaged it by sewing it into the flesh of her arm, beneath her vaccination scar. One of only sixty Cambodian doctors (out of six hundred) to survive the terror, the man eventually escaped to Thailand, then was resettled to Auckland, where he operated again on his wife to remove the diamond, which he sold in order to begin their new life. Thomson had been so mesmerized by the man's descriptions of Cambodia that as soon as he finished medical school, he had made his way to the Thai-Cambodian border, where he worked for two years as a Red Cross medic.

In 1991, unsure where he would go after Thailand, Thomson, twenty-

seven, had visited Geneva to attend a monthlong course on health emergencies. At lunchtime after the final class, he joined a group of his classmates for
a beer in a café beside Lake Geneva. One of them mentioned that UNHCR
would soon be managing the return of Cambodia's refugees. Although he
had never worked for the UN before, Thomson spoke Khmer and knew
the medical hazards the returnees would face. "Does anybody know where
UNHCR is?" he asked the other students. Nobody did, but somebody pulled
out a small tourist map, which bore the agency's tiny emblem. Slightly tipsy,
Thomson marched over to UNHCR headquarters and wandered the halls
until he found a door marked CAMBODIA. He knocked and began chatting
with an official who was helping to plan the repatriation operation from
afar and who seemed thoroughly overwhelmed. Thomson soon finagled a
consultant's contract to join Vieira de Mello's team.

Once in Cambodia, UN officials were most likely to earn Vieira de
Mello's trust if they worked with him one-on-one. One day Giuseppe de
Vincentis, a junior UNHCR official from Italy, ran into his boss in the lobby
of the Hotel Cambodiana. Vieira de Mello told him to be prepared to attend a meeting with him that afternoon. De Vincentis, thirty-one, asked if he
should wear a jacket and tie, and Vieira de Mello, who himself usually wore
one of his "lucky suits"—unflattering pale blue and gray Asian matching tu-
nics and trousers, similar to those donned by Cambodia's politicians—said he
should, elaborating no further. As an overdressed de Vincentis sat stiffly near
the hotel's front desk, his UN colleagues who wandered by teased him about
his appearance. When Vieira de Mello finally arrived, he explained that he
wanted de Vincentis to accompany him to a meeting with one of the opposition factions. He said that in Lebanon, General Callaghan had occasionally
made the mistake of meeting on his own with the Israelis and Palestinians and
thus had later lacked corroboration when the parties broke their promises.
"Ever since then one of my rules is 'never discuss sensitive issues without a
witness,'" Vieira de Mello said. "You are my witness." As they drove outside
Phnom Penh and passed into opposition territory that UN officials had never
visited before, he said, "Here's where we make the sign of the cross, Peppe. I
have no idea what lies ahead." Vieira de Mello did not believe in God, but
he remained superstitious and made a habit of appealing, usually playfully, for
whatever help he could get.

Those like de Vincentis who gained entrée to his close inner circle felt privileged to be part of a lithe and dynamic team. Others felt the chill of their boss's indifference. "If you weren't charmed by him," recalls Norah Niland, a thirty-nine-year-old Irish aid worker with UNHCR, "he loved you less." But most UN officials who knew him were drawn to him. Even Sylvana Foa, a UNHCR spokesperson with whom he frequently sparred, recalls: "When you were with Sergio, he made you feel that you were more beautiful and more interesting than you had ever felt before. When he left you to go and talk to someone else, he'd make you feel that it was a terrible burden for him to have to leave."

BEFRIENDING THE POWERFUL

Of all the Cambodian leaders, Vieira de Mello was most intent on befriending Prince Norodom Sihanouk, the most influential person in Cambodia and perhaps the most colorful character in all of Asia. He knew that the sixty-nine-year-old prince was the only person capable of fostering reconciliation among Cambodia's warring factions. A gourmand, a womanizer, and a movie director, Sihanouk had been Cambodia's king and, on ten separate occasions, its prime minister. Pol Pot's Khmer Rouge had put the royal leader under house arrest and killed three of Sihanouk's daughters, two of his sons, and fifteen of his grandchildren. Although Sihanouk later maintained lavish palaces in China and North Korea, Cambodian survivors of the Khmer Rouge's terror felt that he too had suffered. Without Sihanouk's mediation, the Paris negotiations would likely not have produced the October 1991 deal.[2]

The agreement had also assigned the UN—not Prime Minister Hun Sen—the task of exercising "direct control" over ministries whose performance could have bearing on the outcome of the future elections: defense, foreign affairs, finance, public security, and information. Because Sihanouk was revered by Cambodians, the Paris agreement had named him the chairman of a new quasi-governing body called the Supreme National Council, which included representatives of all four of Cambodia's main factions, including the Hun Sen government.[3] As chairman, it would be his job to prod the factions into sticking to the terms of the deal they had struck in Paris and settling their differences through dialogue. Vieira de Mello saw that the UN would not be able to exercise its ambitious mandate if it did not keep the old man on its side.

Instead of criticizing Sihanouk for his long absences from Cambodia, as some of his UN colleagues did, Vieira de Mello wrote him lengthy letters by hand and attempted to keep him in the loop even when the prince was at his home in Beijing. In January 1993 Sihanouk would write in French to Vieira de Mello from the Chinese capital in order to thank him for his letters, which, Sihanouk wrote, "reflect your understanding, your goodwill, your concern and, above all, your compassion for our most unfortunate grassroot people." Sihanouk continued: "You who are so kind to always keep me well informed of your benevolent activities through your letters and documents which all reach me."[4]

Unfortunately, while the Hun Sen government and the Khmer Rouge had managed to come together to sign the Paris agreement, their underlying hatred for each other had not diminished. Indeed, each side had cooperated in the negotiations because it thought that the final agreement would destroy the other—the Khmer Rouge believed that a powerful UN administration would set up shop in Cambodia and run the country, stripping Prime Minister Hun Sen of his power; Hun Sen, for his part, believed that the UN would disarm the Khmer Rouge, thereby defanging his main opponent. Vieira de Mello worried about what might happen if Hun Sen refused to surrender power or if the Khmer Rouge refused to relinquish their weapons. UN planners in New York were so busy scrambling to round up 22,000 UN military and civilian staff that they had no time to undertake worst-case contingency planning.[5] In fact, UN Headquarters did not even have a strategic planning unit. Thus, in Cambodia and elsewhere, once the Security Council decided on the contours of a UN mission, UN personnel on the ground often felt they lacked the freedom—not to mention the wherewithal—to change course.

Vieira de Mello did not like what he saw of Hun Sen, whose regime was taking advantage of the security vacuum that existed in advance of the arrival of UN blue helmets. In the months preceding the official launch of the UNTAC mission, he received daily disturbing reports of government-backed thugs carrying out revenge killings and other violent acts. Officials in Hun Sen's government who assumed that they would soon be replaced by UN officials sold off government office desks, chairs, and light fixtures and pocketed the money. Fearing the UN would soon take their guns away, many Cambodian soldiers took to armed banditry.[6] "Security cannot wait,"

Vieira de Mello said. "If the peacekeepers don't get here soon," he told Bos, "they will have to *make* peace."

In Cambodia Vieira de Mello saw that the twin UN values of peace and human rights clashed. From a human rights perspective, the Khmer Rouge deserved to be punished or, at the very least, shunned. Yet the letter of the Paris agreement required UN officials—and Cambodians—to treat the Khmer Rouge as one faction among many. He could understand why traumatized Cambodians might find this difficult, and he was surprised when the president of the Khmer Rouge, Khieu Samphan, who had not set foot in Phnom Penh since his notorious regime had been overthrown in 1978, was able to slip quietly into town a few days after Sihanouk. Khieu moved into a downtown office, tried not to draw attention to himself, and seemed open to the idea of participating in the transitional Supreme National Council—an audaciously trusting approach for one so senior in one of the bloodiest regimes in modern memory. "I'm going to live here for a very long time," Khieu declared. "I am very happy to be back."[7] It was a scene that would have been unthinkable just a year before.

But the calm did not last. No sooner had Khieu and his Maoist associates taken up their new offices in Phnom Penh than they were greeted by thousands of angry demonstrators. As Khieu and Son Sen, the Khmer Rouge minister of defense, huddled inside, protesters charged the building with hatchets, rocks, and sticks, breaking the windows and chanting "Kill, kill, kill!" Lightly armed Cambodian troops who were loyal to Hun Sen stood by as the mob kicked in the front gate and barged into the house, stealing $200,000 of the Khmer Rouge's money and setting much of the cash ablaze. Hun Sen arrived at the scene, but he did not order the mob to disperse. When the demonstrators finally reached Khieu, they beat him with their fists and sticks and attempted to choke him with electric wire. By the time government soldiers actually intervened—four hours into the ordeal—Khieu, who had put on a steel helmet, was badly bruised and cut, bleeding heavily from a gash to his head.[8] John Sanderson, the Australian general who would soon become the commander of the UNTAC peacekeeping force, happened to be in Phnom Penh on a UN planning mission. When Sanderson went to Hun Sen to complain about the attack, the Cambodian premier denied responsibility. "The people turned out to protest the Khmer Rouge," Hun Sen said. "It would have been wrong of me in this new democracy to deny them their right of free expression." Vieira de Mello trusted neither the genocidal Khmer Rouge nor the tyrannical Hun Sen. He thought only Sihanouk had Cambodia's interests at heart, but the prince said he was powerless to stop the violence. "I am only a figurehead," he admitted publicly.[9] This was a disturbing confession. If Sihanouk, the father of modern Cambodia, could not exert control over Hun Sen, Vieira de Mello wondered, how would the UN?

"Getting Real"

Vieira de Mello and his staff discussed the many things that could go wrong once they began returning refugees to Cambodia. Six of the seven Cambodian refugee camps in Thailand were effectively controlled by one of the three opposition factions, each of whom could rescind its support for repatriation at any time. The Khmer Rouge housed more than 77,000 Cambodians in their camps, and they had never before permitted camp inhabitants to move freely.

Even if the refugees were not coerced outright, Vieira de Mello knew that they might prove too terrified to budge. Those Cambodians who had been born and raised in border camps had been reared on a steady diet of propaganda, mostly about the bloodthirstiness of Hun Sen. Vieira de Mello also had concerns about the refugees' self-sufficiency after years of receiving clean water, medical services, and food aid from relief groups.[10] The camps had become like small towns. The Site 2 camp, for instance, had a population of 216,000, the second-largest gathering of Cambodians in the world, after Phnom Penh. It contained hospitals, pharmacies, Buddhist temples, factories, a newspaper, courts, a prison, gambling dens, an alcohol treatment center, and a red-light district.[11] "International generosity may have gone too far in terms of the care and maintenance, even the spoon-feeding, of Cambodians in exile in the Thai border camps," Vieira de Mello told a reporter. "So we wonder if the refugees are now capable of reacquiring initiative and independence."[12] The mortality rate in the camps was three times lower than in Cambodia. The poverty-stricken country had the world's lowest life expectancy of 49.7 years. And it was unclear how conditions would improve, as fewer than three thousand Cambodians had been educated beyond secondary school.[13]

Vieira de Mello inherited a detailed plan for repatriation. The French government had spent $675,000 hiring a satellite company, Spot Image, to survey the country.[14] The satellite photographs showed some 571,000 acres of "potentially available arable land" in western Cambodia. On the basis of this finding, the Cambodia experts at UNHCR had prepared an elaborate, 242-page repatriation "Blue Book."[15] UN officials had announced that each refugee family would receive five acres of this arable land, as well as agricultural implements to till it. UNHCR staff in the camps showed videos and distributed flyers showcasing the farmland. It seemed that all that remained for Vieira de Mello to do was to execute a well-mapped formula for return.

But as he and his staff began traveling to territory in Cambodia that had previously been off-limits, the scheme began to sit badly with them. By their very definition, the satellite photographs were not able to detect two features of the land that would necessarily topple the best-laid plans: land mines and malaria-ridden mosquitoes.

Vieira de Mello had been told that Cambodia possessed nearly one mine for every two Cambodians and that the country had the highest proportion of amputees in the world.[16] Still, it was not until he contracted HALO Trust, a British charity, to conduct on-the-ground surveys of possible resettlement areas that he understood how deadly the terrain was. Out of 173,000 acres it surveyed, HALO Trust found that only 76,000 were "probably clear of mines," 69,000 were "probably mined," and 28,000 were "heavily mined." Desperate for land so as to be able to fulfill the promise UNHCR had made to refugees, he asked which UN peacekeeping units had been assigned to do the de-mining and learned that none of the countries sending troops to Cambodia were prepared to volunteer them for such a risky assignment. As another UNHCR official put it: "The only de-mining going on now is when people tread on them."[17] Because the fate of refugees would depend in large measure on the removal of the country's mines, Vieira de Mello was made head of the Cambodia Mine Action Center. By the time of his departure in the spring of 1993, however, the UN had helped clear only 15,000 out of an estimated eight million mines and other unexploded ordnance.[18]

Andrew Thomson, who had more experience working in Cambodia than other UN personnel, was the bearer of bad news on malaria. Soon after arriving he got his hands on a recent malaria survey and superimposed the results on a land map of Cambodia, marking Xs through those districts that were too infested to responsibly resettle refugees. He brought the map to Vieira de Mello and told him UNHCR had to declare "no-go" areas. "If we send people back to these areas," Thomson said, "we'll be sending them into a death trap." Vieira de Mello looked at the map and observed that most of the areas that Thomson had marked off-limits were areas that had traditionally been strongholds of the Khmer Rouge. If the Khmer Rouge leaders were told that Cambodian refugees in Thailand could go to territory Hun Sen controlled, but not to theirs, the guerrillas would likely abandon the peace process. The repatriation operation had not even begun, and already the immediate safety of the refugees was colliding with the long-term stability of the peace process. Vieira de Mello waved off Thomson. "We can't wait for perfect conditions before we bring people back," he said. "But these aren't imperfect conditions," Thomson countered. "These are *deadly* conditions. Do you want to be responsible for mass death?" Vieira de Mello conceded part of the point, saying that UNHCR would begin by resettling people to areas where malaria was less prevalent and decide later about the rest of the country. Every decision seemed to be one that carried with it necessary benefits and potentially catastrophic costs.[19]

From his trips into the hinterland and his conversations with refugees and his own staff, Vieira de Mello had reluctantly concluded that UNHCR stood no chance of delivering the land that it had promised. He would have to throw out the detailed Blue Book that he had received on arrival. He lamented the stark "contradiction between allowing free choice and the impossibility of satisfying it" and set out to find an alternative to what he called the "silly, irresponsible offer of five acres of free land."[20]

Vieira de Mello summoned a cross section of his field staff to Phnom Penh to discuss the way forward. On the day of the minisummit, the UN generators, which functioned only intermittently, were not working, and without air-conditioning UN staffers wilted in the heat. "I'm not allowing any of you to leave this room until we come up with a solution," he said, only half joking, as sweat saturated his clothes.

Determined to extract ideas from his team, and sensitive to the need to secure staff buy-in, he had a habit of allowing discussions to descend into angry free-for-alls in which junior officials felt free to talk back to him. He was less concerned with the rank of a colleague than he was with laying the foundation for a smooth return operation. If a twenty-eight-year-old rookie aid worker had a useful suggestion to make, he was all ears. He saw no inconsistency in soliciting that person's views alongside those of key ambassadors in Phnom Penh. To that end, he hosted a wine-and-cheese cocktail hour most Sundays in his room at the Hotel Cambodiana, with Charles Twining, the U.S. ambassador.

Vieira de Mello instinctively relied for feedback not only on international staff and diplomats but also on the Cambodians who worked with the UN—the drivers, translators, security guards, and messengers. He learned their names and their life stories and regularly inquired after their families. "He made the clerks and drivers feel like they were quite somebody, like they were indispensable to this grand mission," recalls Jahanshah Assadi, the UNHCR field representative in Aranyaprathet, Thailand. Once, in rural Cambodia, Vieira de Mello's own driver faltered as he attempted to drive across an irrigation canal on a narrow two-plank "bridge." If the vehicle's tires strayed an inch in either direction, the car would have tumbled ten feet down into the canal below. Seeing his driver sweat at the prospect of endangering UN officials' lives, Vieira de Mello intervened. "Allow me," he said, taking the wheel and adding a white lie so as not to undermine the driver's authority. "This is my favorite part of the drive."

In a meeting in Phnom Penh, a senior UNHCR official was laying into the local staff for their poor bookkeeping habits when Vieira de Mello cut him off midsentence. "Have you stopped for one second to think about what our local staff have gone through?" he asked. "Do you expect them to have developed perfect bookkeeping habits when their families were being slaughtered by the Khmer Rouge?" He grew angrier as he continued. "Instead of criticizing them, why don't you take the time to show them how to keep proper financial records?" he asked. "After everything they have survived, I don't think they'll have trouble improving their accounting."

His deputy François Fouinat suggested that UNHCR replace the offer of land with that of cash. In desperate need of a new plan, Vieira de Mello leaped at the idea, even though his bosses in New York and Geneva had already rejected it. For many in the refugee-advocacy community, the idea of providing each refugee with a lump sum of hard currency was sacrilege. Large amounts of money would suddenly be circulating in communities that had never seen such sums before. It could lead to theft, violent crime, and simple profligacy. It could also cause a wholesale demographic transformation—instead of moving back to rural areas, where they might farm, refugees might move en masse to Cambodia's major cities. This would clog the towns with temporary big spenders who would have no means of supporting themselves after the money ran out.

Many UN staffers shared Vieira de Mello's belief (instilled in him by Thomas Jamieson) that almost any life in one's home is preferable to life in a refugee camp. Although the feeding times in the camps were predictable and the water was reliably clean, most refugees found the life of dependence intolerable. Norah Niland, the Irish UNHCR official, was responsible for looking out for extremely vulnerable refugees—the elderly, the sick, and the very young. At the staff summit, when Vieira de Mello raised the cash option, she felt as though her peers were speaking unwittingly condescendingly toward poor people. "Underlying all the arguments against cash was 'Poor people can't manage money,'" she recalls. But she, who had grown up poor in County Mayo, argued that poor people were just as likely to save their money—and to waste it—as rich people. Her boss took her side. "If you place your trust in people, they tend to act responsibly," Vieira de Mello said, echoing her view. "And they have a far better sense of what they need money for than we ever will."

UNHCR staff admired Vieira de Mello's decisiveness, but some criticized his haste. Normally, refugees returned to their homes after elections and the establishment of more stable governing bodies; but in Cambodia repatriation was preceding the vote. Dennis McNamara, who ran the UN human rights branch of the mission, believed his friend was neglecting the safety of refugees, who would be returning to districts where UN troops and police were not yet present to provide security. Whenever Vieira de Mello saw McNamara approaching in the hallway of UN headquarters in Phnom Penh, he groaned audibly, "Uh-oh, here comes McNamara, the pope of principle!"

Vieira de Mello believed UNHCR had reason to rush. He was deeply affected by the tongue-lashing he received when he visited one of the Khmer Rouge–controlled camps along the Thai border. The refugees he spoke with were adamant that Cambodia was where they belonged. Sensing their impatience in the camps, he feared that, in their eagerness to get home, the refugees might flood across the border without UNHCR assistance, endangering themselves and increasing the likelihood of mine amputations, violent clashes, and dashed expectations. With the elections a year away, he did not feel UNHCR could afford to wait until more UN peacekeepers were in place to begin moving the refugees home. "If you have any objections, raise them now," he told staff. "If you have alternatives, suggest them now." However imperfect the cash option was, nobody offered a better idea as to how to bring the refugees home and launch them on their new lives, and he decided to press on. "I will take full responsibility if something goes wrong," he assured uneasy colleagues.

A few UN officials speculated that Vieira de Mello's obsessive punctuality in his personal life was dictating his thinking. It was as if he could not conceive of arriving late for a political appointment. "Sergio had made a commitment to the UN, to Cambodia, and to the refugees," recalls Nici Dahrendorf, a British UNHCR official with the mission. "He wouldn't turn up late for repatriation any more than he would arrive late for dinner."

Having made the decision, Vieira de Mello hung the expensive aerial photos, commissioned before his time, on the walls of the UNHCR office in Phnom Penh. These monuments to useless planning resembled abstract paintings. Whenever he ushered visitors into the office, he drew attention to the UN artwork. "I prefer the UN satellite artists to Jackson Pollock myself," he would say.

While the original plan had put the onus on UNHCR to track down tracts of land to resettle refugees, the introduction of the cash option put Cambodians in charge of their own destinies. All returnees would get a domestic kit that included utensils, tools, a large water bucket, reinforced plastic sheeting, chemically impregnated mosquito nets to protect against malaria, and coupons for four hundred days' worth of food rations (two hundred days for those who moved to the Phnom Penh area). A refugee family could still decide to wait for the UN to find them a small plot of land. Or they could choose the cash option (Option C), which critics nicknamed "Option Catastrophe." Refugee families who chose this option would receive a modest cash grant of $50 per adult and $25 per child. The cash would pay for the returnees to plant seeds in a small garden or to pay relatives in exchange for accommodation.[21] Vieira de Mello believed it was essential for UNHCR to stop micromanaging the repatriation. "We can't dictate the return," he told his colleagues. "We have to follow the people."

Because he encouraged debate at UNHCR, the staff often unearthed ideas that might otherwise have remained buried in the bureaucracy. As UNHCR officials in Battambang attempted to map a schedule for refugee returns, they wondered what they would do during monsoon season (May–August), when the roads from the camps at the border into Cambodia would be too flooded to traverse. "What about the train that Cambodians used before the war?" Vieira de Mello asked. Others had proposed this same idea of repairing the wagons and tracks, but UNHCR staff had written it off as too expensive. This time he asked, "Has anybody talked to the former railway managers to see what it would take to repair?" Nobody had. And after a short investigation, it emerged that the rickety train and tracks could be restored for $100,000. Remarkably, the antiquated train with its blue UN flag, dubbed the Sisophon Express, would reduce the duration of the 210-mile trip from Sisophon, the town where refugees would be dropped off just inside Cambodia, all the way to Phnom Penh, from three days to twelve hours.[22]

FOLLOWING THE PEOPLE

On March 21, 1992, five days after Akashi, the UN head of mission, finally moved to Cambodia, he gave Vieira de Mello the green light to start repatriation. Vieira de Mello sent a fax to Ogata on Hotel Cambodiana stationery, apologizing for contacting her at home but jubilant. "Yet another week-end interference!" he wrote. "You'll end up calling me Special Pain rather than Envoy." He told Ogata that the first batch of refugees would return to their country on March 30 and that the dignitaries who would greet them in Cambodia would likely constitute a "crowd larger than the number of actual returnees!"[23]

As he counted down the days, he saw that tensions in the camps were building. On March 25 in the Site 8 camp, gunmen presumed to belong to the Khmer Rouge asked for two refugees by name and executed them. On March 29, the eve of the scheduled repatriation launch, Khmer Rouge forces seized part of a key roadway in Cambodia between Kompong Thom and the northern province of Preah Vihear, and then Hun Sen retaliated by attacking them.[24] It felt as though all-out war could resume at any time.

Although the UNTAC political and military mission had only technically come into existence on March 15, and only 2,000 of the anticipated 16,000 peacekeepers had yet deployed, Cambodians looked to the UN blue helmets to quell the fighting. But General Sanderson, who had taken over the military side of the mission (while Akashi ran the political), stressed that he had no intention of forcing the parties to comply with the terms of the Paris agreement. UN peacekeepers would in fact steer clear of violent areas. "We are in Cambodia as peacekeepers, not peace enforcers," Sanderson said. "I will not put UN forces in the middle of a confused environment and no cease-fire, where the roads are mined."[25]

Vieira de Mello knew that every UN political and military mission got one chance to make a formidable first impression, and he worried that the blue helmets were missing this opportunity. As he had seen in Lebanon, the troops that made up UN forces varied in quality and attitude. The well-equipped Dutch units that General Sanderson sent to northwestern Cambodia fired back decisively in defense of civilians and their soldiers. The Malaysian forces in western Cambodia learned Khmer and attempted to secure the cooperation of the Khmer Rouge. By contrast, some of the African units, in Sanderson's words, "came with their backsides hanging out of their trousers." The Tunisians and the Cameroonians were participating simply because in the Security Council, France had been so intent on offsetting Anglo influence in the region that it had insisted that a large number of French-speaking troops be sent. Cambodians developed a saying about how a typical UNTAC soldier filled his days. Set to rhyme in Khmer, it translated as "In the morning he jogs, in the afternoon he drives, in the evening he drinks."[26] Sanderson worked with what he was given but recalls, "I wouldn't have taken many of the troops if I had a choice."

Perhaps owing to his own youthful run-in with the Paris police in 1968, Vieira de Mello had never warmed to law enforcement officials as he had to soldiers. But in Cambodia he understood that, in order for refugees to feel secure once they returned to Cambodia, policing would have to be a vital component of the UN mission. But he also knew that in its forty-seven-year history the UN had never really done policing. Unsurprisingly, almost none of the expected 3,600 police arrived in time for the first refugee returns on March 30, and only 800 would arrive before May. Many lacked driver's licenses and spoke neither English nor French, UNTAC's two official languages.[27]

As hard as it was to quickly rally soldiers to participate in peacekeeping missions, soldiers were at least always on standby in their countries and rarely engaged in actual combat. Police officers, by contrast, tended to be busy doing police work at home and thus could rarely be spared. Police work also relied upon the officers' links with the local population, and it would be hard to find trained police who had the necessary language skills, the knowledge of local law, and the confidence of the population. The "policing gap" would undermine this and every one of Vieira de Mello's subsequent UN missions.

Nonetheless, despite the mounting violence and the thinness of UN security forces, he stuck to his plan to go ahead and begin helping refugees return on March 30. He understood the gamble he was taking: If a returning refugee was murdered or stepped on a mine, it would send a chill through the refugee camps in Thailand and possibly torpedo the repatriation operation. This, in turn, could ruin the chances of holding elections the following year. Still, he opposed delaying the launch because he thought it would send a signal to both the spoilers and the refugees that the UN could be cowed. His deputy Fouinat asked Thomson, the public health specialist, "Doc, can you assure us that there will be no deaths in the first convoys?" Thomson was incredulous. "Listen, François, I'm not Jesus Christ," he said. "People die no matter where they live. People die in Paris. They aren't going to start not dying just because they are put on UNHCR convoys."

On March 30 Vieira de Mello traveled to Site 2, the largest camp on the Thai border, and spoke to the 527 refugees who had volunteered to be part of the first returning group. Looking out at men and women who were clinging to their blue departure passes and green nylon UN travel bags containing noodles, sugar, soap, and a toothbrush, he said that the UN had no intention of telling Cambodians—"an independent and proud people"—what to do. The organization would try to create conditions that would enable them "to regain control of their fate and to shape their own future." "Today, we are, at long last, gathered to make a dream come true: that of breaking the spiral of violence in Cambodia and of witnessing the emergence of a reunited, reconciled and pacified society," he said. "We are betting on peace. We will, as from this morning and with deep emotion, escort you home."[28]

A small contingent of Malaysian peacekeepers would escort the first seventy families who bravely volunteered to return to Cambodia. Beneath signs that read GRATITUDE TO THAILAND in Khmer, Thai, and English, some of the departing refugees wept with fear or anticipation, others smiled and waved, and most filed stoically onto the buses. None had any idea what lay in store for them in their homeland or whether the shaky peace would last.

In his send-off speech Vieira de Mello had sounded more confident than he felt. He had many outstanding questions that only time would answer: Would those who had survived the war inside Cambodia welcome the exiles back? Would Hun Sen's government treat the refugees as traitors? If they moved in with their extended families, how long would the generosity of their relatives last? Would the returnees' desperation to return to land they owned before the war lead them to ignore land-mine warnings? Would they give up on rural areas altogether and pour into the cities?

Before the convoy departed Site 2, Vieira de Mello briefly dropped out of sight. He made a short pilgrimage to a shrine in front of the Hotel Sarin, where in front of a three-foot-high statue of the Buddha he burned incense and lit candles, issuing a prayer to the gods—again born more of superstition than faith—that nothing would go wrong.

A firm asphalt road dotted with houses and well-groomed gardens ran from the Thai refugee camp to the border. But once the UN convoy crossed the narrow bridge that marked the crossing into Cambodia, the terrain changed. Sturdy houses gave way to bamboo and leaf shacks, and water wells and pipes were replaced by shallow pools of stagnant water. Abandoned military posts offered reminders of the fighting that had recently raged in the area. In the weeks leading up to the return, some 428 mines had been removed from the road between the border and the UNHCR reception center in Sisophon. The refugees had been warned that just six feet on either side of the road had been cleared, but beyond that mines were omnipresent. In March alone thirteen Cambodian villagers had been killed or maimed by mines in the nearby fields.[29]

Vieira de Mello traveled in the second vehicle in a refugee convoy of several dozen buses. He maintained radio contact with Dahrendorf of UNHCR, who drove in the lead vehicle. He was so tense that she could hardly recognize his voice. The convoy had left later than he had planned, and he was afraid of being tardy to the welcoming reception in Sisophon, which he had scripted minute by minute. "Nici, can you please tell your driver to go faster," he thundered over the radio. Dahrendorf explained that if they sped up, they would lose the busloads of refugees behind them. He was insistent. "I said, 'Drive faster,'" he snapped. When she again refused, he ordered her to stop the car and leaped out of the passenger seat. "This is ridiculous," he blared. "My car will drive in front." He succeeded in spurring on his driver, but as

Dahrendorf had warned, his vehicle outpaced the convoy and ended up having to stop to wait for the buses filled with refugees to catch up.

As the buses wended their way into Sisophon, schoolchildren lined the road waving Cambodian flags, pop music blared, and Cambodian musicians performed traditional song. After a two-hour drive, the refugees disembarked, looking dazed. Some had never set foot outside a refugee camp. In conversations with journalists, they explained their fears. "I'm worried about the Khmer Rouge because they haven't settled down yet," said So Koemsan, twenty-eight, whose parents and four siblings had died of starvation during the Maoists' bloody reign. "If they fail in their objectives, they might take it out on people like us . . . but I hope the UN will protect us."[30] Eng Peo, thirty-seven, had raised two children in the camp. "I have not been a farmer for many years, and my children have never seen a farm," he said. "How do I start again?"[31]

Vieira de Mello had a keen eye for symbolism. He had invited UN blue helmets to intersperse themselves in the convoy so that the peacekeepers would begin to feel ownership over the repatriation operation. But just before he left Thailand—a country that had often treated the Cambodian refugees brutally—the head of the Thai army had told him that he intended to travel to Cambodia to be a part of the welcoming delegation. Throughout the drive Vieira de Mello complained that the general's very presence would send a paternalistic message from Thailand and would possibly upstage Prince Sihanouk. As his UN car approached the Sisophon reception center, he saw the Thai general standing smugly on the podium with his arms folded. "What the hell does that bastard think he's doing?" Vieira de Mello fumed to Assadi. "This is not the message we want to send. This is Sihanouk's show."

Prince Sihanouk quickly made that clear. He swooped down dramatically in a Russian-made helicopter, along with his wife, Monique, to give the homecoming his blessing, and the Thai general disappeared. As Cambodian officials presented the refugees with orchids onstage, Vieira de Mello spoke into a megaphone, his comments translated into Khmer. "Welcome home," he said. "We were there for you in Thailand and, I promise you, we will be here to help you resettle in your homeland."[32]

Iain Guest, the UNHCR spokesman, watched his boss standing at the dais in the hot sun. Vieira de Mello's pale blue Asian suit was soaked through with perspiration, and the look on his face was grim, resolute, and triumphant.

"For Sergio, that was a moment of fierce vindication," Guest remembers. "It was a look that said, 'I told you this would work and by god it did, and I'm going to stand in the sun longer than any of you sons of bitches.'"

When asked by a journalist about the recent upsurge in fighting, Vieira de Mello said, "Don't expect peace to be instantaneous after 20 years of war. The refugees' return is a strong message to those who are tempted to violate the ceasefire."[33] But whether the return of refugees would deter the violent—or incite them—remained an open question. And nearly 360,000 Cambodians remained on the Thai-Cambodian border, awaiting UN help.

Five

"BLACK BOXING"

*Cambodian refugees returning to their country on
the UN-renovated Sisophon Express.*

As a student of philosophy Vieira de Mello had often pondered the
nature of evil. But in Cambodia he actually got to know some
of the world's most feared mass murderers. Soon after arriving in
Phnom Penh, he had visited the Tuol Sleng torture and execution center,
where the Khmer Rouge had murdered as many as 20,000 alleged opponents and which Hun Sen's government kept open as a museum. Although
he was thoroughly revolted by the photos of executed men and women of
all ages, he was absolutely convinced that he and other UN officials had to
engage potential spoilers. He was convinced that peace hinged upon whether

the UN could secure the Khmer Rouge's cooperation. For many humanitarians the prospect of working with the Khmer Rouge was loathsome. Human rights advocates had criticized international mediators for glossing over Khmer Rouge crimes—deliberately avoiding the word "genocide" in the Paris agreement, for instance, and stipulating euphemistically that the signatories wished to avoid a return to "past practices." But Vieira de Mello believed in what he called "black boxing." "Sometimes you have to black box past behavior and black box future intentions," he told colleagues. "You just have to take people at their word in the present." He returned to Kant's admonition, "We should act *as if* the thing that perhaps does not exist, does exist."[1]

The Khmer Rouge were bitterly disappointed by UNTAC's performance. They had expected Akashi and the UN Transitional Authority to take charge of Cambodia and end Vietnamese influence in the country. But while the Paris agreement had authorized the UN to take direct control of the key ministries, a mere 218 UN professionals—95 in Phnom Penh and 123 in the provinces—had been tasked to supervise the activities of some 140,000 Cambodian civil servants in Hun Sen's government, and almost none of the UN officials spoke Khmer.[2] UNTAC's role was thus inevitably more advisory than supervisory.

Akashi had also proven reluctant to exercise the authority and capacity that he had actually been given by the Paris agreement. Although he was supposed to take "appropriate corrective steps" when Cambodian officials misbehaved, he rarely reassigned Cambodian personnel. He told colleagues that because the Japanese constitution had been imposed by Douglas MacArthur and the American occupiers after World War II, it had lacked legitimacy with many Japanese. He believed that the UN would alienate Cambodians if it tried to impose its vision. When the Khmer Rouge saw that Akashi intended to take a minimalist approach to his job, they began to renege on the commitments they had made in Paris. If Hun Sen would not relinquish control of the key ministries or purge the Vietnamese, the Khmer Rouge would in turn deny UNTAC access to its territory. None of the factions that had been at war since the early 1970s agreed to disarm.

CHARMING THE KHMER ROUGE

Vieira de Mello set out to get to know the Khmer Rouge leadership. While UN officials who worked in the camps at the Thai border had met with mid-level Khmer Rouge officials over the years, no international official had yet met with senior Khmer Rouge leaders on their turf. He was determined to become the first. "Part of him thought, 'What kind of feat would it be if I could be the one to bring the Khmer Rouge to heel?'" recalls Courtland Robinson, a longtime analyst of Cambodian affairs.

But Vieira de Mello had other motives. He had always been intrigued by the question of how Khmer Rouge revolutionaries like Ieng Sary, Pol Pot, and Khieu Samphan could have studied in Paris, even reading the same philosophy tracts as he had at university. "I want to look into Ieng Sary's eyes," he told Nici Dahrendorf. "I want to see if they are still burning with ideological fire." At this stage in his career, mulling the roots of evil was more stimulating than managing the logistics of easing the suffering that resulted from that evil. Late at night, as he sat in his hotel suite with McNamara, Bos, and a bottle of Black Label, he could debate the Khmer Rouge's history into the early-morning hours. "How did they go astray?" he asked. "Was there a moment where they turned down the wrong path, or was the ideology destined to be carried to its extreme? And if it was going to be carried to the extreme, was the extreme destined to be murderous?" McNamara did not believe the Khmer Rouge could change their ways. He was known around the mission for declaring, "Let's give 'em hell." By contrast, Vieira de Mello rarely pushed the parties to go much beyond where they had proven themselves inclined to go. "Will you for once think of the morning after we give them hell, Dennis?" he asked. "I give them hell, but what happens then? They won't return my calls ever again." William Shawcross, the British journalist, teased Vieira de Mello that his eventual autobiography would be aptly titled *My Friends, the War Criminals.*

One day Salvatore Lombardo, the Italian UNHCR official, entered the dusty UN office in Battambang to find his boss Vieira de Mello sprawled out on the couch reading Kant's *Critique of Practical Reason* in French. "Sergio, what the hell are you doing?" Lombardo asked. Vieira de Mello replied without raising his eyes from the text: "This is the only kind of reading I can do that enables me to actually escape this place." Kant was fresh in his mind because he had recently delivered his lecture at the Geneva International Peace Research Institute. He brought the paper to Cambodia and excitedly shared it with Bos, who made a valiant effort to navigate his prose but could never follow the argument. "No matter how I tried, I would either fall asleep after two pages, or put it down in frustration at my inability to understand it," she recalls. He pretended as though it didn't matter, but she noticed that he kept leaving it lying around their hotel room in the not-so-subtle hope that she might get a second wind.

In some sense, Vieira de Mello's desire to charm the Khmer Rouge was rooted in his general desire to keep everyone on his side. A few years before, when he had been UNHCR's director of the Asia Bureau in Geneva, he had asked Douglas Stafford, the deputy high commissioner, to replace a country director in Indonesia who was terrorizing the staff, and one in Hong Kong who was drinking too much. But when Stafford reviewed the personnel files, he saw that Vieira de Mello had given both employees "outstanding" reviews. "Without a paper record of incompetence or abusiveness, how am I supposed to help you get rid of these people?" Stafford asked. "Why did you mark them 'outstanding'?" Vieira de Mello was unapologetic. "You never know where you are going to end up," he said. "One day you could be that person's boss. The next day you could be working for them. Why make an enemy when you don't have to?" Stafford commented to a colleague, "You know what Sergio's biggest problem is? He refuses to make enemies."

While ambition, intellectual curiosity, and this refusal to make enemies certainly played a role in steering Vieira de Mello toward the Khmer Rouge, he also knew that the Paris agreement was hanging in the balance. If the Khmer Rouge stopped cooperating with the UN altogether, war could restart. Since the Maoist guerrillas controlled several refugee camps on the Thai border, they could refuse to allow "their" 77,000-plus refugees to return to Cambodia. Or they could sabotage the UN-sponsored elections less than a year away by shooting at Cambodians who headed out to vote.

It was never clear exactly who was in charge of the Khmer Rouge. Neither Brother Number One (Pol Pot) nor Brother Number Three (Ieng Sary), the group's best-known leaders, showed their faces in Phnom Penh. Khieu

Samphan, the public face of the Khmer Rouge, tape-recorded his meetings with UN officials, giving rise to speculation that he was sending the tapes to Pol Pot. For insight on the Khmer Rouge, Vieira de Mello relied most closely upon a thirty-four-year-old American named James Lynch. A former corporate lawyer from Connecticut, Lynch had helped Cambodian refugees resettle in the United States as a pro bono service for his law firm and then moved to Thailand in order to take up a job processing refugee asylum requests. Lynch had spent half a decade negotiating with Khmer Rouge officials at the Thai border, and Vieira de Mello asked him to arrange for him to travel deep into the bush to meet them.

On April 6, 1992, Vieira de Mello, Bos, and Andrew Thomson headed out with a de-mining expert, an agricultural engineer, and Udo Janz, the head of the UNHCR office in Battambang, Cambodia's second-largest town. Lynch and Jahanshah Assadi were to drive from Thai territory and join Vieira de Mello and the others at the Khmer Rouge base camp. Heading into dangerous territory, the UN team did not spell out their plans to their Cambodian army escorts. But as they approached the Mongkol Borei River, one of the escorts Hun Sen's government had provided exclaimed, "We aren't going any further. This is suicide!" They had never before skirted Khmer Rouge territory, and they hurriedly abandoned the UN group.

The bridge that the UN team had been instructed to cross had been blown out. Perched atop a riverbank at the edge of Khmer Rouge territory, the staff looked to Vieira de Mello for guidance. His plan began to look simultaneously wildly ambitious and shockingly amateurish. But suddenly he pointed across the river. "Look!" he proclaimed gleefully. "They're here!" Standing atop the opposite riverbank were three Khmer Rouge soldiers, carrying Kalashnikovs and wearing Mao caps, khakis, and their trademark kerchiefs. "Go talk to them, Doc," he instructed Thomson, the group's only Khmer speaker. "See if they are our guides."

Thomson stared at Vieira de Mello in disbelief. Ever since he had moved to Cambodia in 1989, the New Zealander had experienced a recurrent nightmare, influenced by the Academy Award–winning film *The Killing Fields*. In the dream, while he slept in his tent in an Australian Red Cross hospital, a Khmer Rouge cadre in black pajamas waded through a field of rice paddies, entered the back of the tent, dragged Thomson outside, and executed him.

In the two years he had spent in Cambodia before joining the UN, he had never met a Khmer Rouge soldier and had sworn to himself that he never would. Although the Paris agreement stipulated that UN officials were to work with the Maoists, Thomson had lived among Cambodians too long to be able to overlook the guerrillas' bloody past. "We were supposed to treat the Khmer Rouge like the other parties," he recalls, "but they weren't like the others. They were mass murderers." Nonetheless, Vieira de Mello's enthusiasm for the adventure had been so infectious and the case he made to Thomson about his indispensability had been so persuasive that the young doctor suddenly found himself being summoned to begin chatting with a member of a militia known to shoot without asking questions.

Thomson made his way down a twenty-foot-high sloping mud riverbank toward the shallow river below. He walked halfway across the river and changed his mind, freezing in his tracks. "Shit," he said to himself. "I can keep going and get a bullet in the chest, or I can turn around now and get shot in the back." The soldier on the opposite bank peered down at him, but because the sun was behind his head, Thomson could only make out the soldier's silhouette and not his facial expression.

"Hi," Thomson said in Khmer, quaking with fear. "Are you the Khmer Rouge?"

The soldier nodded.

"Where's the bridge?" Thomson asked.

The soldier gazed down and answered listlessly, "There's no bridge. You must walk across." The UN officials would have to trust that there were no mines on the river floor if they wanted to continue their journey.

If the UN team members were to leave their vehicles behind, they would be entirely dependent on the Khmer Rouge. Without the Land Cruisers' long-range antennas, they would not be able to maintain radio contact with the UN base. A few of the officials carried handheld radios, but the radios had neither the range nor the battery life to be of use for long. Vieira de Mello shrugged, rolled up his trousers, and headed down to where Thomson was standing. The others followed, knowing that once they crossed the river, they would be heading into the unknown.

As the single-file line of UN officials walked through the water, carrying their day packs of mosquito nets, notebooks, and bottled water, the tension and the absurdity of the encounter were such that somebody in the group

Vieira de Mello and Mieke Bos crossing the Mongkol Borei River
en route to Khmer Rouge territory, April 6, 1992.

began giggling, and within seconds the others had joined in. By the time they had crossed the narrow river, the entire crew was howling with laughter. The expression on the faces of their dour Khmer Rouge guides did not change.

The soldiers led the UN team into the forest on a two-mile walk, warning them not to step off the trail because the woods were smothered with mines. Alongside the path the UN officials saw rocket launchers, piles of ammunition, and bunkers. "So much for UN disarmament!" Vieira de Mello exclaimed. He produced a camera and began snapping photos of the soldiers beside their weaponry. Thomson, who remained rattled, said, "Sergio, I just know you don't want to be taking photos. They are, after all, *the Khmer Rouge!*" Vieira de Mello was amused. "You bet I do, Doc. I may not get the chance again."

The group came upon a Chinese flatbed truck, which they were told to board. As the truck traveled through ever-denser brush, Vieira de Mello used sanitary wipes to keep himself clean. After around two hours of driving amid bamboo that was three stories high, the truck entered a field where two hundred Khmer Rouge soldiers were lined up as if for inspection. The UN team had reached the Khmer Rouge camp.

Lynch and Assadi had arrived several hours earlier from Thailand and had grown alarmed when they were unable to reach their colleagues on the radio.

When their boss arrived all smiles, however, the two men feigned coolness. "What took you so long?" Assadi asked. Lynch was the person who had mapped out the itinerary. "How exactly did you expect us to cross that river in our car?" Vieira de Mello ribbed him.

The Khmer Rouge treated the visiting UN delegation like royalty. General Ny Korn, the Khmer Rouge military commander for the region, ushered them into a small hut, offering beer, Coca-Cola, and the most precious commodity of all—ice cubes, which had been driven in that afternoon from Thailand. Vieira de Mello had behaved much like a giddy boy on a school field trip on the journey into the jungle, but as soon as the negotiations began, he was all business. Instead of ignoring or marginalizing the Khmer Rouge, as Akashi and Sanderson were doing, he tried to convince them that in order to remain a significant political force, they would need to entice refugees to return to land under their control in Cambodia. If nobody returned to their former strongholds, they would not score well in the 1993 vote.

He told General Ny Korn that as long as the returns were genuinely voluntary, UNHCR would help Cambodians move to Khmer Rouge–held lands. And the general made it easy, quickly agreeing with the UN principle that every Cambodian refugee had the right to return to whichever area he or she chose. This meant that refugees in the Khmer Rouge–controlled camps would have the freedom to choose to leave the cultish Maoist organization and settle anywhere in Cambodia. But it also meant that those refugees who chose to move to Cambodian lands under Khmer Rouge control would get UNHCR assistance. Yet for Vieira de Mello to offer this, he told the general, the reclusive Khmer Rouge would have to grant the UN unfettered access to the area, so that experts could conduct full health, water, and mine assessments. The Khmer Rouge took the UN officials around the area and pointed to the lush vegetation and the fertile land. "The best farming land in the country," said one. "You must tell the people in the camps."

As the afternoon wore on, mosquitoes began to take aim at the UN visitors. Udo Janz applied roll-on mosquito repellent, and the Khmer Rouge officials at the table pointed to his device with openmouthed wonder. Janz told them that the repellent would keep mosquitoes and malaria away. One of the bolder soldiers grabbed the stick, took a whiff, and exclaimed in Khmer, "Lemon, lemon!" He then did as Janz had done, dispensing the repellent the length of his arm. On his map Thomson had placed an enormous X through the territory they were sitting in because it was known to be laden with malaria-infested mosquitoes. But when he raised the matter, a Khmer Rouge public health official said, "We don't have malaria here. We cut down all the forests, and the malaria went away." Thomson did a double take. "You're trying to tell me that none of you has malaria?" he asked. "Don't insult me by lying to me." The Khmer Rouge official grew angry. "What do you know about my country?" he asked. Suddenly Vieira de Mello, the diplomat, broke from his conversation with General Ny Korn and placed himself between the two sparring health professionals. "I think we can all agree that malaria is a serious problem," he said. "And of course it warrants careful consideration. You two can follow up at a later date."

Aid workers and diplomats in war-torn areas often have to weigh offers of hospitality against potentially life-threatening consequences. In the late afternoon a Khmer Rouge soldier suggested that the UN team ward off the heat by taking a swim in the river. "We're fine," said Vieira de Mello, on behalf of the others. But the soldiers were insistent. "We don't have bathing suits," Vieira de Mello tried. General Ny Korn delivered a stern order in Khmer. Within minutes a Khmer Rouge cadre had returned with sarongs for the UN officials to wear. With trepidation, Vieira de Mello and the others eased themselves into the water, which proved immensely refreshing. The Khmer Rouge soldiers stood beaming on the banks of the river. "You see how clean the river is now," one shouted. "When the Vietnamese ruled Cambodia, the rivers were filled with body parts and corpses." The UN swimmers cringed at the thought of what lay beneath them. The young Khmer Rouge soldiers, most of them still teenagers, took special delight in gawking at Bos, the lone woman in the group, as she swam. "She's torturing these poor lads," Assadi said to Lynch. "It just isn't fair."

Before dinner the UN visitors heard the sound of gunfire in the distance. Thomson, who had still not relaxed, took it as a bad omen. But his fears were quickly soothed when rifle-wielding Khmer Rouge soldiers entered the camp carrying their bounty: a deer that they had shot for dinner. After the feast, the group retired to simple wooden huts, where they stayed the night sleeping on sheets that still bore the creases from having just been removed from their store wrapping.

After a final meeting over breakfast the next morning, Vieira de Mello's UN team parted, retracing its steps. When photos from the trip made the rounds at UN headquarters in Phnom Penh, most UN officials were stunned that their colleagues had dared to make such a trip. Vieira de Mello's cable to Geneva noted proudly that theirs was "the first official visit by international staff to the Khmer Rouge area." [3]

Ever since his stint in Lebanon, he had bristled under the label of "humanitarian." But after his trip into Khmer Rouge territory, he made the case to Akashi that a humanitarian could play a role with profound political importance. If he could use refugee returns to open up a channel of communication to the one warring faction that no one else in the UN could reach, he could be the wedge for other parts of UNTAC to gain access and eventual cooperation. He knew his strategy was risky. The Khmer Rouge could shut down as quickly as they opened up. He wrote to Ogata that rather than trusting General Ny Korn's assurances, UN officials had to "put this sudden forthcomingness to repeated tests in the weeks to come." [4]

In fact, the Khmer Rouge "forthcomingness" did not last, as they denied access to UN peacekeepers, de-miners, and public health officials. On May 8, a month after his meeting with General Ny Korn, Vieira de Mello traveled back to forbidden territory to meet with Ieng Sary, the second-most important Khmer Rouge official, in Ieng's villa. The journey was as adventurous as the first, involving tractors, donkey carts, and Chinese trucks. Again, upon arrival Vieira de Mello bore no signs of the stress. Accompanied by Bos, Assadi, and Lynch, he managed to remain immaculate, even as their vehicle sailed from one deep puddle to another. Lynch and Assadi were covered in mud by the time they arrived. Vieira de Mello, who once again used his wipes to remain spotless, gave his colleagues a once-over on arrival and shook his head. "I've wondered this my whole life," he said, smiling, "but now I finally know what it means to look like shit."

Ieng Sary served an even more elaborate meal than General Ny Korn had, complete with French wines and cheeses. Although Ieng spoke through a Khmer-French translator, he frequently corrected the translations. The meeting broke no new ground. Vieira de Mello urged Ieng Sary to use his clout to improve Khmer Rouge cooperation with the UN, and Ieng Sary urged Vieira de Mello to use his clout to strip Hun Sen of his power. Impressed by Ieng's cultured ways, Vieira de Mello was again flummoxed by the disconnect between the man he met and the crimes for which he was responsible.

"When you are drinking Ieng Sary's cold Thai beer and eating filet mignon like that," he whispered to Assadi as they departed, "it is easy to forget that the man is a killer." Whenever Vieira de Mello met with Khmer Rouge officials, he avoided mention of the crimes of the past. As Bos recalls, "Sergio's focus was always on the future. He was not confrontational and didn't see the point of asking, 'How much blood do you have on your hands?'"

TRANSITIONAL AUTHORITY WITHOUT THE AUTHORITY

Vieira de Mello's inroads earned him respect from his colleagues, but they did not appear to be changing Khmer Rouge behavior. On May 30, just three weeks after he shared his banquet lunch with Ieng Sary, UNTAC suffered its lowest moment. Akashi and General Sanderson had traveled to the Khmer Rouge self-styled headquarters in the town of Pailin, where they had met with several Khmer Rouge leaders. Afterward, instead of heading back to Phnom Penh, Akashi decided that he would try to exercise the free movement promised the UN by the Paris agreement. Akashi's convoy drove along a bumpy dirt road until it reached a checkpoint in an area where the Khmer Rouge were known to be smuggling precious gems and timber into Thailand. Two bone-thin Khmer Rouge soldiers manned the single bamboo pole that blocked the road. When Akashi asked the soldiers to lift the pole, they refused.

Akashi initially acted as though he would not be denied. He angrily demanded that the soldiers go and fetch their commander.[5] But when a more senior Khmer Rouge officer turned up, he too refused to allow the UN to proceed. Akashi did not have a backup plan and simply instructed the UN drivers to turn around. Sanderson, who had thought it ill advised to attempt to penetrate forbidden Khmer Rouge territory in the first place, defended the retreat, noting that a large machine-gun post abutted the checkpoint. But the Cambodian and Western media, who were traveling in tow, exploited the incident to ridicule UN passivity.

Cambodians had hoped that UN soldiers would enforce the terms of the Paris agreement, but that expectation was slowly giving way to a fear that the UN would bow in the face of resistance from any of the factions. "We are the United Nations Transitional Authority, without the authority," ob-

served one British peacekeeper. "The Cambodians are contemptuous of us."[6]
Hun Sen's military attacks on the Khmer Rouge rose steadily from 1992 into
1993, as did the occurrences of banditry in the countryside.

Akashi and Sanderson had both made it plain that they had no intention
of getting their way by using force. This was a clear-cut peace*keeping* mission,
and they intended to keep it that way. "Many of our troop-contributing
countries were sending their soldiers on their first-ever UN missions," Sanderson recalls. "Some hadn't even arrived yet. How many of them would
have signed on if the mission had been advertised as 'Come to Cambodia
to make war with the Khmer Rouge!'" Akashi blamed the factions for the
stalemate—not the UN. "Blithe proponents of 'enforcement' seem to overlook the fact that the Vietnamese occupied Cambodia for a decade with
200,000 troops without managing to bring the country fully under their
control," he said.[7]

UN officials were divided on the question of how tough Akashi and
Sanderson should get with those who were sabotaging the peace. McNamara
thought human rights abuses would continue to increase if Akashi allowed
the UN—and, by definition, its principles—to be walked over. "I don't see
the point of having thousands of soldiers and police if one bamboo pole can
stop us," McNamara argued. Sanderson's deputy, a French general named
Michel Loridon, went further, urging UNTAC to "call the Khmer Rouge's
bluff."[8] Loridon believed a UN mission was no different from any military
mission: It demanded risk taking. "It is not a question of troop strength. I
have done a lot more with 300 troops than is now being done with 14,000,"
Loridon told journalists. If the Khmer Rouge fought back against UN troops,
he argued, "one may lose 200 men—and that could include myself—but the
Khmer Rouge problem would be solved for good."[9] Sanderson called Loridon into his office when he saw the press reports. "Did you actually say these
things?" Sanderson asked, incredulous. "*Oui, mon général,*" Loridon answered,
"but of course my loyalty is to you."

Vieira de Mello did not believe that Akashi and Sanderson should have
barreled through the bamboo pole. Having spent endless hours meeting with
key ambassadors, he knew troop-contributing countries were not prepared
to risk their soldiers' lives to do battle with the genocidal Khmer Rouge.
Vieira de Mello deemed Loridon a loose cannon, and for the rest of his career he cautioned against crossing "the Loridon line." "Give me a few French

paratroopers," Vieira de Mello would say, mimicking Loridon, "and I'll take care of the Khmer Rouge!" But he agreed with McNamara that the incident made the UN look spineless and that it highlighted Akashi's weakness as a diplomat. "This is a major loss of face and blow to the credibility of the UN," he told Bos. "The art of diplomacy is to avoid placing yourself in a position where you can be humiliated."

Vieira de Mello got along well with General Sanderson, as he did with most senior military officers. But occasionally tensions flared up between the two men, as Sanderson faulted him for legitimating the Khmer Rouge. "You're playing right into their hands," the general said. But Vieira de Mello stood his ground. "Look, I have them cooperating with the UN on something. Nothing else is moving. How else are we going to keep them in the game?"

Vieira de Mello's ties with Akashi grew strained. Akashi was obsequious toward influential diplomats in Phnom Penh, but he treated top UN officials within the mission as mere technicians. Vieira de Mello was in constant contact with UNHCR's field offices throughout the country, and he believed he had his finger nearer the country's political pulse than Akashi, who interacted mainly with other foreigners in the Cambodian capital.

On June 15, 1992, just as Akashi departed for a donors' conference in Tokyo, Vieira de Mello, McNamara, and Reginald Austin, the senior UN official in charge of planning elections, authored a joint memo urging Akashi to adopt a more "participatory" management style and to overhaul UNTAC's approach to Hun Sen and the Khmer Rouge. Because UNTAC had failed to assert control over Cambodia's five key ministries, Hun Sen's faction retained power it was supposed to have surrendered, and it lorded that power over the others. Whatever Akashi's reluctance to act like a MacArthur-style occupier, the UN directors argued that he needed to take on greater authority himself so that Hun Sen would not continue to dictate events. He also needed to make use of Vieira de Mello's back channel to the Khmer Rouge.[10]

When Vieira de Mello joined Akashi in Tokyo later in the week, he asked to discuss the memo. But the Japanese diplomat waved off the criticisms. "I was of the feeling that they didn't have the breadth of information and intelligence that I had," Akashi recalls. "So I didn't think they were in the position to join me in decision making. They were a little overambitious, I thought."

Akashi convinced himself that the men took the brush-off in good faith. "They did not have enduring grudges," he remembers, inaccurately. "They saw I appreciated their work and their ideas but that they were somewhat limited."

A Dangerous Experiment

Vieira de Mello continued to believe that constructive engagement with the Khmer Rouge was the only way to save the faltering Cambodian peace process. In an internal July 1992 memo he instructed UNHCR officials to refrain—"in accordance with their humanitarian and non-political mandate"—from criticizing the Khmer Rouge in the press.[11] In September 1992 he chastised UN official Christophe Peschoux for telling *Le Monde* that the guerrillas were falling apart.[12] He faxed the clipping to Peschoux with a handwritten note: "I need hardly point out that interviews of this kind are most unhelpful and embarrassing, particularly at a time when I am doing my best to keep channels of communication with the [Khmer Rouge] open."[13] Denunciation and isolation had offered Akashi fleeting satisfaction, but the approach was not sustainable. "By slamming the Khmer Rouge in public, what are we gaining?" Vieira de Mello vented to Assadi. "We'll be one voice in a million criticizing them. To them we'll be just another enemy."

Ever since his meeting with Ieng Sary in May, he had been lobbying Khmer Rouge officials in Phnom Penh to grant him a return visit to their rural territory. Finally, in August he got his opening after a Cambodian refugee couple, whom UNHCR had just brought back from Thailand, were killed by a group of Khmer Rouge soldiers.[14] Although the Khmer Rouge leadership denied involvement in the murders, they tried to counteract the public relations blow by inviting Vieira de Mello back for a visit.

On September 30, 1992, he and Bos retraced the journey they had taken in April. The transformation since their last visit was staggering. An entire town had sprung up, as the Khmer Rouge had made good on their promise to give returning refugees land for rice cultivation and gardening. UNHCR had not yet assisted in the returns, but refugees had started finding their way to the area on their own.

In a meeting with General Ny Korn's civilian representative, Vieira de

Mello spelled out the contents of a "pragmatic package" he hoped the guerrillas could accept. "It has been six months since we were last here," he told the official. "Many more refugees in the camps would like to come back, but we can't give them assurances that they should do so unless you open up your territory." Even if the Khmer Rouge continued to refuse to deal with Akashi at a political level, Vieira de Mello urged that the general allow unhindered access for UNHCR staff, for UNTAC de-miners, and for UN civilian police who would help ensure the safety of returnees. "Time is running out," Vieira de Mello said.[15]

The Khmer Rouge official nodded. "The door is open," he said, adding, "if you come in, start doing something." He asked for food, medical assistance, and diesel for bulldozers to improve the access road, but he said UN police were unnecessary because the Khmer Rouge would keep returnees safe. UNTAC de-miners would be allowed, but only those "of the right nationality." Vieira de Mello understood this to mean the Thais, who were the longtime backers of the Khmer Rouge. He had an imperfect deal, but a deal at last.[16] "I know that they were using us," he said later, "but we were using them too."[17]

The UN investigated the murder of the two returnees. In October 1992 Son Sen, the commander of the Khmer Rouge forces, wrote to Vieira de Mello denying responsibility. Instead of responding by presenting the UN's evidence of Khmer Rouge guilt, Vieira de Mello wrote:

Excellency,

I have the honour to acknowledge receipt of your telegram dated 11 October in which you informed me that, according to your investigation, the [Khmer Rouge] was not involved in the alleged murders of two returnees that are said to have occurred in Siem Reap Province on 22 and 23 August. It proves that caution in the handling of and publicity on alleged incidents such as the one mentioned above, without a proper investigation having been conducted, is the correct approach.

Conversely, your message reinforces the request I made in my letter to you of 3 September, as repeated in my message of 16 September, that UNHCR/

UNTAC Repatriation Component, in particular, be granted access to the village in order to allow the investigation.

Yours sincerely,
Sergio Vieira de Mello

His unfailing politeness with the Khmer Rouge had earned him their respect—and at times it seemed even their affection. In 1992 Ieng Sary and Khieu Samphan sent Vieira de Mello identical New Year's cards, each bearing a grainy photo of the remains of a majestic twelfth-century temple in Angkor Wat.

McNamara thought his friend was going too far. He believed it would be madness to place civilians back in the custody of mass murderers. At a minimum he believed the UN had a duty to advertise to the refugees the fact that they would be entrusting their fates to the same men who were responsible for two million deaths when they governed Cambodia from 1975 to 1978.

But Vieira de Mello plowed ahead. A November 1992 UNHCR leaflet distributed in Site 8 said nonchalantly: "UNHCR is about to start movements to some new areas where previously UNHCR had no access. Before deciding that it was safe to send you, UNHCR visited these areas a number of times." The leaflet did not mention that the sites in question would be governed by the Khmer Rouge.[18] Reporters who journeyed to Khmer Rouge lands and spoke to returnees found widespread ignorance about the bloody past of local officials.[19] "We do not believe the stories about the Khmer Rouge genocide," Eum Suem, a forty-three-year-old teacher who had spent seven years in a refugee camp, told the *New York Times*.[20] Many, like Eum, had fled the Vietnamese invasion in 1978 and found it more chilling to entertain the idea of settling in land controlled by Hun Sen, whom they still saw as a Vietnamese puppet.

In January 1993 Vieira de Mello bucked the complaints of his peers, whom he wrote off as purists, and for the first time involved UNHCR in returning refugees to a Khmer Rouge–controlled area, known as Yeah Ath, or "Grandmother Ath." On January 13, 1993, UNHCR helped 252 Cambodians in the Site 8 camp move to Yeah Ath, which he considered a pilot return village.[21] The Khmer Rouge managed to deliver unmined, fertile land, and the returnees used the UNHCR household kits to build houses, a pagoda, and a small school. UNHCR built a new access road, bridges, and seven wells. In the coming weeks some 2,714 Cambodians came directly from the border camps, while another 3,729 people made their way to Yeah Ath from other locations. "I do believe," Vieira de Mello told an interviewer, "that Yeah Ath may be recognized in a few years as having been what I always had in mind: that is, a bridge—a very experimental, social bridge between the [Khmer Rouge] and the rest of the world."[22]

He defended the risks by citing Cambodian self-determination. "It is the choice of these people to come here, and we must respect that choice," he told Philip Shenon of the *New York Times*. When Shenon mentioned the savagery of the Khmer Rouge, Vieira de Mello snapped, "I don't need anybody to tell me about that history. The Cambodians who are returning here are Ph.D.s in that history."[23] But sometimes he did in fact make it sound as though he had lost sight of the bloodshed. After he left Cambodia, he would recall bringing journalists to Khmer Rouge lands so that "they could show to the world, to the international media that they were not the monsters that everybody believed they were." Even though the monstrosity of the Khmer Rouge leadership had long been proven, Vieira de Mello simply did not keep it foremost in his mind.

He asked Lynch to base himself with the returnees in Yeah Ath so as to give UNHCR a pair of "eyes and ears" on the ground. Lynch agreed without hesitating. He made clear that Lynch should stay in Yeah Ath around the clock. "I don't want to hear about you driving back to the Thai border to sleep," Vieira de Mello said.

Initially Lynch had company, as Vieira de Mello had prevailed upon the Khmer Rouge authorities to allow an UNTAC civil police presence. But the American lawyer had watched in amusement as the UNTAC police attempted to set up shop in the inaccessible village. As a UN helicopter delivered a portable toilet, the wire snapped and the toilet tumbled into the Tonle Sap River. When the UN police tried to lower their housing containers into the area, the Khmer Rouge began shooting at them, and they fled in panic. Only later did they learn that the guerrillas had not been firing aggressively but had in fact been trying to alert the strangers that they were on the verge of making house in a minefield. Unsurprisingly, the UNTAC police did not last long in Yeah Ath. When Hun Sen's forces attacked the village, the Fijian police voluntarily handed their vehicles to the Khmer Rouge, and soon packed up and left.

Even though reaching Yeah Ath posed enormous challenges, Vieira de Mello loved making the journey. He appreciated Lynch's dedication. "I hear you're living in a hammock," he teased. "The returnees have already built houses for themselves, and look at the example you are setting!" Always one who prized languages, he urged Lynch, who already spoke Thai, to work on improving his Khmer. "All you do is sit under a tree," he said playfully, "at least learn the damn language!" Lynch found it intensely annoying that, although Vieira de Mello knew only a few dozen words of Khmer, he pronounced them so flawlessly that Cambodians often mistook him for one of their own.

Vieira de Mello's long-range radio call sign was TIN MINE, and he gave Lynch the moniker TIN MINE ONE. Months later Lynch inquired of his colleague Assadi about the origins of the strange moniker, and Assadi told him that it had nothing to do with Cambodia's mining potential. Rather, it derived from Vieira de Mello's favorite disco in Malaysia, which was called Tin Mine and which he remembered fondly from his days chairing the negotiations over the return of the Vietnamese boat people.

Vieira de Mello respected the risks that Lynch was taking by living on his own among the Khmer Rouge, but he did not cut the American any slack. Lynch had received two gifts from his Khmer Rouge hosts—the hammock and a pair of their light military boots. In presenting Lynch with the boots, the Khmer Rouge soldiers told him that if he stepped on a mine in the boots, he would lose a foot instead of an entire leg. Lynch, naturally, wore the boots everywhere. But Vieira de Mello spotted Lynch's footwear on one of his visits. "What are you wearing?" he asked, enraged. "Take those off. You are here as an employee of the United Nations. Don't you go native on me!" But his pique passed quickly. Several months later, when UNHCR rotated Lynch to Kenya, Vieira de Mello called Lynch's boss in order to pay the highest compliment he could. "Put Jamie to good use," he said. "He really knows how to work with thugs."

Six

WHITE CAR SYNDROME

Vieira de Mello was bringing the refugees home, but he could not save the UN mission as a whole. Nor could he preserve the exuberance that he had felt after the fall of the Berlin Wall. He saw that while the UN system could manage humanitarian tasks like the one he had been handed, it could not yet deliver either economic or physical security, the two ingredients crucial for a country's long-term stability. Irrespective of how many refugees the UN helped return, he knew the standing of the UNTAC mission would continue to plunge.

EXPECTATION GAPS

The major donor countries were willing to spend enormous sums on highly visible tasks like bringing refugees home and holding elections, but they were not willing to rebuild Cambodian infrastructure or spur economic development until they were sure that the country would not return to war. And since the Soviet Union, Cambodia's former benefactor, had slashed its assistance, Cambodia's health, education, and civil administration sectors were starved for funds.

In a phenomenon that would become known as the White Car Syndrome, prices in Cambodia had soared with the arrival of 30,000 foreigners. The UN spent some $300,000 per day for bed and board for mission staff.[1] For living expenses UN staff received an extra allowance of $140 per day—equal to the average Cambodian's yearly salary in 1991, and twice the monthly wage of a Cambodian de-miner.[2] Because of these high UN salaries, the price of gas and pork doubled. Cambodians had salivated at word that UNTAC would bring a whopping $2 billion budget to Cambodia. But in practice the bulk of UN funds were spent outside the country on the purchase of equipment and supplies, or on salary payments to foreign UNTAC peacekeepers and civilians. And indeed, while the UN boasted of the jobs it was creating, the $2 million spent on the salaries of Cambodian staff in 1992 was less than that spent on UN vehicle repair.[3] Those jobs that the UN did create for Cambodians would not exist beyond UNTAC's departure in 1993.

Vieira de Mello worried for Cambodia's future but also for its present, as a "rejection syndrome" could take hold if Cambodians believed that returning refugees were being treated better than those who had remained in Cambodia during the civil war.[4] By late 1992 a French businessman named Jean-Marie Bertron, who had opened the hugely successful Café No Problem in Phnom Penh, had packed his bags and returned to Europe. "The UN," Bertron told the *Washington Post,* "has turned a princess into a hooker."[5]

Some thirty donor countries had combined to pledge some $880 million to Cambodia, but a year into the UNTAC mission they had disbursed only $100 million.[6] Roger Lawrence, the head of UNTAC's rehabilitation pillar, described the caution of rich countries: "We are in a vicious circle here in which the peace process founders in part because the economic component isn't working—and the economic part is not working because the peace process is perceived as foundering. Whole regions of Cambodia haven't seen any tangible evidence of reconstruction."[7] Rural areas were especially slighted.

UN officials on the ground in Cambodia were largely powerless to break the cycle because resources for development had to come from governments. Vieira de Mello embraced what were called Quick Impact Projects (QIPs), which were executed by private aid organizations but paid for by UNHCR. The first was a two-week project employing Cambodians to repair a bridge in Siem Reap province. Other QIPs improved access to clean water and set up mobile health units, or distributed rice seeds and fertilizer, along with fishery equipment, water jars, and mosquito nets. A few offered start-up loans for farmers or gave assistance to vulnerable elderly persons, orphans, or amputees. Projects would eventually be undertaken in all of Cambodia's twenty-one provinces. At a time when instability deterred investors, he hoped the QIPs would serve as an essential bridge between emergency relief and longer-term development. Unfortunately, by the end of 1993, UNHCR had spent only $3.5 million on QIPs, a pittance of what was needed.[8]

For all the country's divisions—between rich and poor, urban and rural, capitalist and Communist—Cambodians seemed virtually united in their conviction that the Paris agreement was unraveling. Vieira de Mello had succeeded in maintaining humanitarian ties to the Khmer Rouge, but this approach had not yielded the political dividend he had anticipated. UN peacekeepers were not seen as providing security, and they were increasingly despised. Between July and November 1992 UNTAC repatriated eighty-one military personnel for disciplinary reasons, including fifty-six Bulgarians. Some blue helmets were involved in smuggling, sexual harassment, and reckless driving that resulted in the deaths of Cambodians. General Sanderson could investigate incidents, but only a soldier's own national military superiors could ship a transgressor home or garnish his wages.[9] Just as Vieira de Mello had seen in Lebanon, Sanderson saw that the price of operating under a UN flag was that you lacked unified command and control of your troops.

HIV/AIDS, which had not been discussed much in Cambodia before the arrival of the peacekeepers, was raging, and Cambodians blamed the UN soldiers for their frequent dalliances with prostitutes.[10] The acronym UNTAC became ridiculed as "UN Transmission of AIDS to Cambodians."[11] The mission's reputation for sexual predation became so pronounced that even the Khmer Rouge, in their isolation, used radio broadcasts to accuse French troops of being "too busy with prostitutes to check on the presence of Vietnamese soldiers."[12] Instead of publicly condemning prostitution, Akashi, the head of the mission, astonished civil society leaders when he told them, "I am not a puritan. Eighteen-year-old hot-blooded soldiers who come in from the field after working hard should be able to chase after young, beautiful beings of the opposite sex."[13] Akashi's comments unleashed a public firestorm, and French paratroopers felt compelled to dismantle the rickety brothels that had sprung up beside their base. UN doctors ordered 800,000 condoms for distribution among soldiers, and UN officers allegedly told their soldiers not to park their vehicles in front of brothels where they could be spotted.

It was not just UN soldiers who were raising eyebrows. Some UN civilian officials developed relationships with Cambodian women who did not speak English. The power differential made it hard to gauge how consensual the relationships were. With his "boys will be boys" comments, Akashi had disqualified himself from speaking out on gender-related matters, and other senior managers said that they did not have the right to interfere in the aid workers' relationships with autonomous adults. Vieira de Mello steered clear of the issue. "Because Sergio played fast and loose in his own relationships with women," recalls a female UN employee, "it would have been very hard for him to take the moral high ground, so he just kept his mouth shut."

SECURITY MELTDOWN

Since the Khmer Rouge had refused to disarm, and since Akashi's UN administration had opted not to assert meaningful "direct control" over the key ministries, the only parts of the Paris agreement that seemed salvageable were the repatriation operation, which had picked up pace, and the elections, which had been scheduled for May 1993. Hun Sen saw that Prince Sihanouk's son Ranariddh was his main opposition and began physically assaulting candidates in his party. UN police continued to trickle into Cambodia, but they were spread too thin to investigate human rights complaints, protect voter registration sites, or guard political party offices.[14] Lacking the power to make arrests, they could not stop Hun Sen's hit squads from assaulting political opponents or Khmer Rouge forces from attacking ethnic Vietnamese with impunity.

Prince Sihanouk denounced UNTAC's failure to punish Hun Sen's attacks. He said that while he and the Cambodian people had initially welcomed the UN, they had come to realize that "UNTAC is a terrible cocktail of races who do not even understand each other." Sihanouk said that thanks to the arrival of thousands of Vietnamese prostitutes, and the tremendous spike in prices caused by the peacekeepers' arrival, "UNTAC is detested, hated."[15] He criticized the UN's decision to proceed with the elections. "In order to be able to tell the UN and the world that they have succeeded in their mission, UNTAC is going to have an election despite the fact none of the conditions for the election have been met. None. It is a hideous comedy."[16]

In January 1993 Akashi reacted to the criticism—which had initially come only from the Khmer Rouge but was now emanating from all sides—by creating, for the first time in the history of the UN, a UN special prosecutor's office with the power to arrest and punish those suspected of committing political crimes and human rights violations. The very first UN arrest was made on January 11, when a Cambodian government official was apprehended while he was destroying an opposition party office with an ax. However, because the UN did not itself have the facilities or the personnel to prosecute suspects, it handed the man over to the Cambodian police, who promptly released him.[17]

With Cambodia increasingly resembling the Wild West, the Khmer Rouge too grew yet more brazen. In December 1992 they took some sixty-seven UNTAC peacekeepers hostage, charging them with spying on behalf of Hun Sen and the Vietnamese.[18] On December 27, 1992, they massacred thirteen ethnic Vietnamese, including four children, in a river village. The killers scattered leaflets that demanded that Akashi rid the country of Vietnamese. A month later the Khmer Rouge killed eight people, including three local policemen and an eight-year-old girl.[19]

In his correspondence with UN Headquarters, Vieira de Mello noted a "clear trend" in the Khmer Rouge ranks toward "isolationism, introversion and pathological suspiciousness." But while his boss Akashi favored sanctions, he continued to believe that further punitive measures would only cause the Khmer Rouge to opt out of the political process altogether.[20] On March 10, 1993, in another fishing village in Siem Reap province, the Khmer Rouge killed thirty-three ethnic Vietnamese and wounded another twenty-nine. Among those killed were eight children and a baby.[21] It was the worst massacre of the postwar period. On March 27, 1993, a Bangladeshi soldier was killed in the first deliberate murder of UNTAC personnel. By May, the month of the vote, eleven UNTAC civilians and soldiers had been killed.

"One in Many Unknown Stories"

Remarkably, amid all the massacres and military skirmishes, Vieira de Mello's repatriation effort proceeded smoothly. The operation that filled him with the most pride involved a weary and malaria-infected group of displaced Montagnards (French for "mountain people") whom UNTAC soldiers had encountered on patrol in the dense forests of northeastern Cambodia. The Montagnards had lived in the central highlands of Vietnam and teamed up with U.S. Special Forces to fight the Vietcong during the Vietnam War. In 1979, facing persecution for their pro-American allegiances, they had fled from Vietnam to Cambodia, where they were also shunned by Cambodians hostile to anybody associated with Vietnam.

Throughout long bouts of fighting and hardship, the Montagnards had relied on shortwave radio sermons and a few worn Bibles translated into their dialect in order to maintain their Christian faith.[22] The Montagnards had attracted some interest in the United States in 1985, when Lutheran missionaries in Raleigh, North Carolina, helped resettle some two hundred there. But until Vieira de Mello and UNHCR took interest in them, the rest of their group had languished in the Cambodian bush.

The Security Council had tasked UNTAC with demobilizing and disarming all military elements, but when the Montagnards were discovered, their commander, Colonel Y-Pen Ayun, was reluctant to comply for fear his people would be forced back to Vietnam. He said his men could turn over their arms only if they got instructions to do so from their leader, a general whom they had been waiting to hear from since 1975. UN officials had the unfortunate task of breaking the bad news to Ayun that their leader had been executed by the Khmer Rouge almost as soon as he had traveled to Phnom Penh nearly two decades before. When Ayun was told the news, he and his men protested, asking the UN for proof of the general's murder, but eventually their eyes filled with tears and they realized that their long journey in the wilderness was over. Ayun's deputy, Lieutenant Colonel Y-Hinnie, told Nate Thayer of the *Far Eastern Economic Review*, "I am not angry, but very sad that the Americans forgot us. The Americans are like our elder brother, so it is very sad when your brother forgets you."[23] Ayun told UN officials that since his people were unwelcome in both Vietnam and Cambodia, they wanted to join their kin in North Carolina.

Vieira de Mello knew that responding to the plight of the Montagnards would consume sizable staff resources and would have scant bearing on Cambodia's future. But he saw an opportunity to close one of the many doors the cold war had left ajar, to personally guarantee the safety of a forgotten ethnic minority, and, not incidentally, to cater to a useful and vocal Christian constituency in the United States. On September 28, 1992, he paid the Montagnards an incognito visit and, in a meeting with Colonel Ayun, produced a pen and a notebook and declared, "Put your disarmament in writing!" After more than thirty years as a fighting force, Ayun wrote in cursive handwriting, "We the Montagnard people . . . have today put down our arms and have agreed to dismantle our military and political movement and stop and never start again any hostile activities of any kinds. We agreed to do all this so that we can become refugees and be resettled in the U.S. where we want to live in peace."[24]

Vieira de Mello presided over a brief ceremony in the middle of the jungle, where Ayun's men solemnly handed over 144 old but well-maintained AK-47 assault rifles and 2,557 rounds of ammunition. The Montagnards lowered their flag and handed it to Vieira de Mello, who later hung it in his UN office in Geneva.

On October 10, 1992, he faxed a note to Lionel Rosenblatt, one of the group's long-standing advocates in the United States:

> Dear Lionel,
>
> Operation concluded!
> They were disarmed between last night and this morning (144 weapons), dissolved as a political/military organization and were relocated* . . .
> The ball is in your court.
> Please help with expedited processing.
>
> All the best and thanks,
> Sergio

---

*238 men, 58 women and 102 children (and dogs and monkeys and even a hen)[25]

Pushed by Rosenblatt and other refugee advocates, President George H. W. Bush's administration sent immigration officers to Cambodia in record speed. Within six weeks all the Montagnards had been resettled in North Carolina, the home state of Republican senator Jesse Helms, who had taken a personal interest in this persecuted Christian group.

Early on in his career Vieira de Mello had observed military commanders routinely take note of the achievements of their soldiers in written letters of thanks and commendation. He brought this practice to the world of UN civilian performance and became famous among UN staff for his thank-you letters. After this operation he quickly wrote to General Sanderson, expressing his personal thanks to the Uruguayan colonel, the Ghanaian major, the Malian captain, the Australian private, and the American navy major who provided invaluable assistance in the repatriation operation. In a memo back to UNHCR headquarters, Vieira de Mello also handwrote a note crediting Giuseppe de Vincentis, the young UNHCR field officer, for his leadership on the issue. "Peppe can be proud of what he did," Vieira de Mello wrote. "One of the last pages of [the] IndoChinese tragedy was resolved peacefully. Only one in many unknown stories in the careers of HCR staff and small humanitarian achievements that give us pride in serving UNHCR."[26]

While the return of the Montagnards earned Vieira de Mello friends in the United States, his reputation was solidified globally because the larger repatriation operation never suffered the calamities that Cambodians or international experts had predicted. Although the returns had started slowly, as the election approached UNHCR was meeting its target of sending home some 40,000 Cambodians each month. Refugees relied upon the UN for bus and train transit, for protection against banditry and extortion en route, for assistance in tracking down family members, and of course for food, land, building materials, and cash. By the time of the elections in May 1993 a total of 362,209 Cambodians had returned, 90,000 of whom took the refurbished train from Sisophon to Phnom Penh. Most of them rushed back to the places where they had grown up. And to the surprise of outside experts, those refugees who had lived in a camp controlled by one of the three opposition factions showed great independence in their choices, often choosing to return to land that was under the grip of Hun Sen. Only one returnee died en route—in a bus accident in Thailand.[27]

"Our mistake was being too paternalistic," Vieira de Mello told a journalist, decrying the "imbecilic notion" of "telling people where to go."[28] He observed that he had been wrong to assume that the refugees in the camps "had lost any initiative, any freedom of judgment, any freedom of thought; had become totally dependent and might follow the instructions of their leaders like sheep." He had found the opposite. "The moment you removed the lid," he recalled, "they were quite capable of deciding for themselves."[29] Like Thomas Jamieson, he would henceforth be a fierce advocate of relying on refugees for planning guidance.

In March 1993 the last convoy of 199 returnees left Khao-I-Dang, the oldest of the refugee camps and the backdrop for the final scene in the film *The Killing Fields*. In his remarks at the closing ceremony, Vieira de Mello reported that since 1979 nearly 235,000 Cambodian refugees had been resettled from camps in Thailand to the United States and elsewhere overseas. But the international community should not treat this as a source of pride, he said. "I cannot but share the misgivings of a former colleague," he declared, "when he said many years ago that he could never quite see how we were contributing to the solution of Cambodia's problem by flying its few remaining qualified people to new homes thousands of miles away."[30] Having managed the repatriation and stuck to deadlines that others had faulted, Vieira de Mello was proud of having "proved wrong all the prophecies of doom."[31]

Exit

The previous April, when Secretary-General Boutros Boutros-Ghali had visited Cambodia, Vieira de Mello had personally escorted him around. Having laid out the risks of renewed civil war, he explained to the secretary-general how each challenge could be overcome. "I am optimistic like you," Boutros-Ghali had said.[32] Vieira de Mello had never before had the opportunity to perform before a UN secretary-general, and he made a memorable impression. Jean-Claude Aimé, whom Vieira de Mello had worked with in Bangladesh and Lebanon, and who was Boutros-Ghali's chief of staff, told him that the secretary-general had big plans for him.

Boutros-Ghali returned to Phnom Penh in April 1993, a year after his first visit, to usher in Cambodia's election season. Some twenty political parties had registered, and they faced serious risks. He got a taste of the violence on his second day in the country when four Cambodian gunmen shot dead a twenty-five-year-old Japanese volunteer election supervisor, the sixth UN worker killed in two weeks. In the wake of the murder, UN security officials held emergency meetings aimed at enhancing security for staff. Armed UN troops and barbed-wire barricades blocked the roads around UNTAC headquarters. But Boutros-Ghali took a tough line, declaring in a speech: "The UN will not be intimidated by violence. The election will take place."[33] In mid-April, however, Khieu Samphan cast further doubt on this proclamation when he announced that he and other Khmer Rouge leaders were leaving

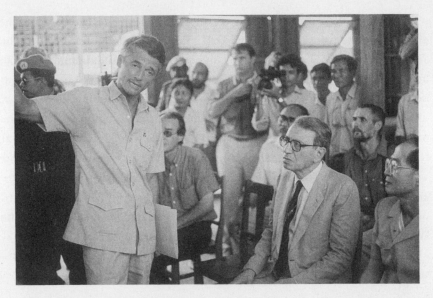

Secretary-General Boutros Boutros-Ghali and his special representative Yasushi Akashi being briefed by Vieira de Mello on his repatriation plan, April 19, 1992.

Phnom Penh and formally withdrawing from the Paris peace process. They would not participate in the elections.

With violence flaring and UNTAC foundering, many UN officials had assumed that Vieira de Mello would find a way to remain in Cambodia through the landmark elections. But to his delight Boutros-Ghali asked him to serve as his envoy to Angola. Although he had been separated from his family for a year and a half, he did not hesitate before accepting the promotion. While Akashi had pointedly excluded him from strategic decision making in Cambodia, in Angola he would be the boss. He would answer only to the secretary-general and to the countries on the Security Council. He would no longer have to use humanitarian successes to pursue political ends. He could tackle political and diplomatic challenges head-on, while leaving the delivery of the "groceries" to others.

Angola had been at war almost nonstop since its Portuguese colonizers had departed in 1975. It had held its first free elections in September 1992, but Jonas Savimbi, the leader of the rebel movement, had lost the vote and again taken up arms. It would be up to Vieira de Mello to try to end the civil

war for good. Although the challenge was enormous, after nearly a quarter
century in the UN, he believed he was up to it. He would be returning to
a neighborhood he knew well from his time in Mozambique in the 1970s,
he would be able to speak his native Portuguese, and he would draw on the
negotiation skills he had honed with the Khmer Rouge and others.

He informed his UN colleagues that he would be leaving Cambodia before the elections. "I would stay if I could," he said, "but the secretary-general
has asked me to go." When he invoked the UN's highest authority, he could
sound alternately pompous and self-parodying. His colleagues were disappointed. "Things felt like they were going to hell," recalls Michael Williams,
who worked as Dennis McNamara's deputy in UNTAC's Human Rights
Division. "Sergio was this dynamic and commanding figure in UNTAC, and
UNTAC didn't have commanding figures. We were worried that Cambodia
would descend into civil war, and the best we had was leaving. We were
stunned."

At Vieira de Mello's going-away party Andrew Thomson made the mistake of asking Mieke Bos if she, too, was moving to Angola. "No," she said
tersely, "I'm staying here." Vieira de Mello flew from Phnom Penh to Brazil,
where he took his family on a ten-day vacation. He left knowing that his
job had been well done but that the UN mission as a whole still hung in
the balance.

Once he got back to Geneva, he busily assembled his Angola team. Squat-
ting in a temporary office in an annex building near the main UNHCR
headquarters, he began telephoning colleagues to try to persuade them to
join him. Many turned him down because it was a hardship post to which
they could not bring their families, or because they spoke only French and
English and not Portuguese. When Annick Roulet, Vieira de Mello's communications officer in Cambodia, refused on linguistic grounds, he waved off
her worries. "Come on," he said. "You have a month to learn, and Portuguese
is a very easy language." Roulet shook her head. "Sergio," she said, "you have
no credibility: Every language is easy for you." But he prevailed, and Roulet
again agreed to accompany him.

Vieira de Mello's giddy scheming proved short-lived. On May 11, 1993,
the UN leaked unofficial word that he was to be named the UN Special
Representative of the Secretary-General in Angola.[34] Several days later he

received a call from Boutros-Ghali's office in New York informing him that his candidacy had been nixed. UN officials had cleared his appointment with the Angolan government, but they had somehow failed to consult with Savimbi, and the rebels were furious. They had "nothing against" Vieira de Mello personally, a rebel spokesman said, but under no circumstances would they work with a Brazilian national.[35] Savimbi had never forgiven Brazil for having been the first Western nation to recognize Angolan independence under his rival Agostinho Neto in 1975. And he even accused Brazil of helping rig the country's recent elections in favor of the ruling party.[36] "How can a Brazilian citizen claim to be neutral when they actively helped President dos Santos to be elected?" a rebel official asked.[37]

Vieira de Mello was crushed. His paychecks at UNHCR had already been suspended—his salary was to be paid by the UN Secretariat in New York—and he had practically booked his flight to Angola. "Ogata has already given me farewell presents," he complained to friends, referring to the high commissioner for refugees. "Now what?" He was furious with Boutros-Ghali and his staff for mishandling the appointment. Also, although he was a proud Brazilian, he had not lived in Brazil since he was a teenager and had no connection with the government there. Yet he was being held responsible for Brazil's policies. He had grown so devoted to the transnational ideals of the United Nations that it infuriated him when others pigeonholed him on the basis of nationality. "How could they saddle me with the sins of a government I can't control?" he asked sympathetic colleagues, though he knew full well that such lumping was commonplace in the UN.

He kept busy in Geneva by reading press reports and UN cables from Cambodia. But the news from the country he had left was grim. Between March 1 and May 14 more than a hundred violent incidents had been recorded, causing 200 deaths, 338 injuries, and 114 abductions.[38] UN Headquarters had ordered the families of UN officials to evacuate Cambodia. Some three hundred polling sites had been closed because of the violence. UNTAC's goal, when it arrived fourteen months before, had been to preside over "free and fair" elections. By the time of the vote, though, UNTAC's electoral director Reginald Austin was saying that the UN would content itself with establishing whatever "neutral political acreages" it could. The main goal was to stage a vote without igniting another civil war. On the eve of the vote Akashi, who had consistently attempted to claim the peace process was on track, could only muster: "I can say with every confidence that this election will be the freest and fairest in Cambodia's recent history."[39] This was not saying much, as each of Cambodia's previous elections had been marred by coercion and terror.

Miraculously, the elections proved a calm and inspiring success. On May 23, the first day of voting, Vieira de Mello read reports of jubilant and defiant Cambodians queuing up for hours to vote. By the end of the six-day process, nearly 90 percent of Cambodia's 4.7 million registered voters had cast ballots. One of the great mysteries of the vote was why the Khmer Rouge, who had pulled out of the Paris agreement, did not sabotage it. "All they had to do was kill a bunch of foreigners," recalls Austin, "and that would have shut the whole thing down." Every UN official had a theory as to why the Khmer Rouge did not act up. Clearly, the revolutionaries were divided among themselves, and their organizational structure had broken down. But, Austin speculates, "partly it was because Sergio had softened them up somewhat. He ensured that 'foreigners' or 'UN officials' were no longer abstractions to the senior Khmer Rouge command."

Prince Norodom Ranariddh, Sihanouk's son, won a near majority in the vote, taking 58 seats out of the 120 in the constituent assembly. Hun Sen's ruling party came in second, scoring 51 seats. Initially Hun Sen contested the results, persuading seven provinces to announce they would secede from Cambodia. But the elder Sihanouk soon persuaded him to join the new government. As the UNTAC mandate expired, Prince Sihanouk was crowned Cambodia's king, Ranariddh became first prime minister, and Hun Sen became second prime minister.

The negotiations on the shape of Cambodia's coalition government proved far more important than the voting itself. Yet at precisely the time international attention was needed, UN officials were declaring successful elections and preparing to head home. "The distinct message from the Security Council and from Boutros-Ghali was 'hold the elections and get the hell out,'" McNamara remembers.

By the end of 1993 all UNTAC staff had vanished from the country. The mission had cost $2.5 billion, by far the most expensive in UN history, but it left little tangible behind it—besides a fragile, divided government.[40]

The following year Vieira de Mello got word that the Cambodian army had attacked and completely destroyed the Khmer Rouge's "model village" settlement of Yeah Ath, sending several thousand people fleeing yet again. He later described the event as "one of the saddest moments in my career, in my life, to realize that something that we had been working on so carefully, so prudently, and that we had hoped would be like a crack in the wall, in the impenetrable wall that surrounded the Khmer Rouge areas, and that we hoped would also serve as a model inside, it went literally down the drain."[41] He sent a note to James Lynch in Kenya, in which he confessed he had been "naïve" to think that Hun Sen would allow a utopian Khmer Rouge farming village to flourish right under his nose." The news from Cambodia would only get worse. In July 1997 Hun Sen deposed Ranariddh in a coup, disavowing the results of the UN election.

STALLED

Vieira de Mello was out of a job. Ogata was grateful for his services, but she had filled all of her senior positions assuming that he was heading to Angola. He tried to make a virtue out of necessity. "I've always said I wanted time to reflect and write," he told colleagues. "Well, now I have all the time in the world. Be careful what you wish for."

Cooped up at a borrowed desk in the UNHCR annex—Dennis McNamara teased his friend that he was being housed in a "cupboard"—Vieira de Mello read and commented on a lengthy manuscript by researcher Courtland Robinson on the repatriation operation. He had opened up UNHCR's files to Robinson and felt a little stung by the critique. He wrote to Robinson, "Never forget that what may be obvious *after* the fact requires a great deal of soul-searching and debate and involves a lot of anxiety and uncertainty before the fact, especially when a decision affecting the lives of people is about to be taken." Robinson criticized UNHCR's decision to return refugees to unsafe areas. Here Vieira de Mello accepted the charge but wrote, "It is difficult to imagine how one could spell out conditions under which return may be deemed safe. Should, for instance, returnees require higher standards than those enjoyed by the majority that never left?" He urged Robinson to take on UNTAC's most serious weakness: the absence of a meaningful economic rehabilitation strategy, which undermined Cambodia's long-term prospects.[42]

He spent the summer of 1993 in Geneva on the telephone to UN Headquarters in New York attempting to scrounge up a useful job, contemplating his future, and drafting a book proposal, which he tentatively titled "Deceit and Estrangement: The Aborted Relationship Between the Khmer Rouge and the Cambodian Peace Process (1989–1993)." At the heart of his proposal, which would examine whether the Khmer Rouge could have been kept engaged, was an implicit question: Which approach was more fruitful—his or Akashi's? In terms of outcomes, he knew that he had the edge, as 360,000 Cambodian refugees had returned safely, including 77,000-plus who had been trapped in Khmer Rouge–controlled camps. But he also knew that lessons from the humanitarian sphere could not always be applied to the political realm. Still, he believed Akashi had been wrong to push the already-mistrustful Maoist guerrillas into an even darker and more suspicious vortex of isolation than the one they had inhabited when the UN first arrived. What was required, there and elsewhere, Vieira de Mello wrote, was "a dynamic even-handed diplomacy open to all the parties to the conflict."[43]

His pitch to Ogata was endearing. It was that of a man determined to remain a student all of his life. "As you know," he wrote to her, "I have followed Cambodian affairs since University." He did not request a study leave but said he intended to use his spare time and annual leave to conduct the research. He did not seem to mind much that any project tacked on to his normal seventy- or eighty-hour workweek would further reduce the time he spent with his family. He argued that his study would help strengthen the UN capacity "to resolve internal conflicts in the turbulent times ahead."

A UN man to his core, he knew that the organization frowned upon those officials who drew upon their field and diplomatic experiences to produce public manifestos. He wrote to Ogata, "I trust that my nearly twenty-four years of service with the Organization and my academic record will suffice as a guarantee of my ability to use the information at my disposal in the interest and not the detriment of the United Nations."[44]

But his credentials did not suffice. Christine Dodson, director of personnel at UN Headquarters in New York, responded to his request. "Mr. Vieira de Mello is of course at liberty to engage in personal research in his own time on any topic. However he should bear in mind that any manuscript that emerges would have to be submitted to the Secretary-General for approval. . . . Such approval seems unlikely to be granted."[45]

Vieira de Mello spent the summer of 1993 overcome by the most severe wave of professional self-doubt he had ever experienced. "I'm not going anywhere in the UN," he told Irene Khan, a UNHCR colleague who would later become secretary-general of Amnesty International. "What are you talking about?" she said. "You're not even forty-five!" "Yes," he said, "but at fifty I could be dead." Because of his father's death at fifty-nine, he carried with him a persistent fear of heart attack. Famously fond of his whiskey, he had cut back significantly in his thirties. He told friends, "I don't want to end up like my father." He exercised obsessively and kept vigilant tabs on his cholesterol and blood pressure. After one doctor's appointment in Geneva, he returned to the office, and his assistant inquired after his results. "Everything is fine except there is a little fluctuation in my cardia," he said. "Just like my father." While in Cambodia, Vieira de Mello had received a letter from a Canadian researcher requesting an interview. He had jotted a note at the bottom of her letter in black pen, "Ok for mid-Dec if still around or alive."[46]

His colleagues in UNHCR saw that he had outgrown the humanitarian agency that had been his home for twenty-four years. They were stunned that Boutros-Ghali had not found a place for him. "Sergio, they have no idea what they are missing," Jahanshah Assadi said to his friend. "You are this diamond in the rough, and they will find you." Vieira de Mello shook his head. "You know how it is, Jahanshah," he said. "We are the lowly humanitarians. We're the guys who pass out food and fix roads. They look down on us elsewhere in the UN. They don't see us as capable of handling high politics." Assadi agreed. "That's all true, Sergio, but once they get their hands on you, they will not let you go." Many UN officials were already speculating that he would be the first person to scale the rungs of UNHCR to succeed Ogata as the high commissioner, or even move beyond to do what no lifelong UN civil servant to that point had ever done—become secretary-general of the whole United Nations. Alluding to the top floor of UN Headquarters where the secretary-general kept his office, Omar Bakhet reassured his friend that the pause was only temporary, saying, "Sergio, you will ride the escalator from Cambodia all the way up to the thirty-eighth floor."

While in Cambodia, Vieira de Mello had read the bloody news from the former Yugoslavia. An Italian UN colleague of his, Staffan de Mistura, had even called him in Phnom Penh from a guesthouse in Serb territory for advice on how to get a convoy of 80,000 blankets past an angry throng of

Serb women who were blocking the only roads to Bosnian territory. Vieira de Mello urged him to think laterally. "When there is a wall in front of you," he said by phone, "you either break it, you jump over it if you are tall enough, or you bypass it." When de Mistura said he couldn't bypass five hundred women, Vieira de Mello asked why he didn't hire Serb smugglers. "The trick will be the carrot," he said. "Money may not be enough. Give them something morally different from what they get in their lives. Give them a sense of dignity." Vieira de Mello suggested de Mistura match the pay the black marketeers got for smuggling cigarettes but also provide a certificate that said "UN consultant." The "Sergio solution" worked, as the smugglers got the blankets through, and when de Mistura visited one of them in his home months later, he saw the UN certificate hanging above his fireplace.

But while Vieira de Mello was always willing to don his thinking cap for a colleague, he had no particular attachment to the former Yugoslavia and generally found himself resenting the amount of staff and press attention it consumed relative to Cambodia. Bosnia's war was unfortunate, of course, but Cambodia, which received far less political attention, had seemed to have a genuine chance at peace. Yet donor countries spent twenty-four times more per capita in Bosnia than they did in Cambodia. He had quietly applauded when in July 1992, at the height of the siege of Sarajevo, Secretary-General Boutros-Ghali had outraged sensibilities in the Western world by defiantly dubbing the Bosnia conflict "a rich man's war" and later saying on a visit to Bosnia, "You have a situation that is better than ten other places in the world. I can give you a list."[47]

Perhaps because he felt his personal clock ticking, Vieira de Mello seemed to be in a great hurry to register his professional achievements. On the few occasions when he felt his career was stalled—and this was one—he fell into a fearsome funk. But even in such a low period, his wide smile and humor shielded most of his colleagues from his insecurities. "It's ok," he said, "as long as they don't send me to the former Yugoslavia!"[48] Having expressed misgivings about working in the Balkans, however, he promptly turned his attention to securing the most high-level job there that he could find.

After six months of limbo in Geneva, Vieira de Mello was named the Bosnia-based political adviser to Thorvald Stoltenberg, the Special Representative of the Secretary-General in the former Yugoslavia. Stoltenberg was the same man whom Vieira de Mello blamed for hastily jumping ship as high commissioner three years before.

In one sense the Bosnia job compounded Vieira de Mello's sense of professional stagnation. Despite all of his feats—serving as High Commissioner Hocké's chief of staff, negotiating the Comprehensive Plan of Action for Vietnamese boat people, and overseeing the massive repatriation operation in Cambodia—he was returning to a job similar to the one he had held a decade before when he advised General Callaghan in Lebanon. In order to serve Stoltenberg, he would again work at the right hand of the generals who commanded the peacekeepers. He would assess the political climate in Bosnia and identify humanitarian and diplomatic targets of opportunity for what was known as the UN Protection Force, or UNPROFOR.

While in Lebanon, Vieira de Mello had signed up for a relatively peaceful mission that had turned violent with the Israeli invasion in 1982, in the Balkans he knew from the outset that he was entering a raging war zone. U.S. and European statesmen would continue to try to broker a political settlement, and he and the UN peacekeepers would try to build local confidence by easing civilian suffering on the ground. "I'm heading into Dante's inferno," he told friends.

The optimism that had followed the fall of the Berlin Wall had faded. Indeed, by the time of his posting to Sarajevo, the eruption of ethnic violence across the globe had begun to stir a nostalgia among pundits for the stability of the mutually assured destruction of the cold war. The democracies that had triumphed against Communism seemed outmatched by a new generation of brazen ethnic and religious nationalists and warlords. And whatever hopes existed for a UN renaissance seemed to die the very week of his departure for the Balkans.

On October 4, 1993, three days before he would fly to the former Yugoslavia, he watched chilling television footage from Mogadishu, Somalia.[49] Over the course of the street battle, Somali fighters loyal to Mohammed Farah Aideed shot down two U.S. Black Hawk helicopters and killed eighteen U.S. soldiers. More than a thousand Somalis were also thought to have died. The evening news depicted jubilant Somalis dragging the mutilated corpse of a naked U.S. soldier along the streets of Mogadishu. The Somalia fiasco would prove to be one of the pivotal events of the 1990s. Because U.S. soldiers had gone to Somalia to assist a beleaguered UN mission, the incident solidified the anti-UN prejudice of many in the U.S. Congress and deepened the Pentagon's distrust of the Clinton administration, which it blamed for sending U.S. troops into harm's way without a proper plan.

At a news conference after the firefight, President Clinton said, "I still believe that UN peacekeeping is important. And I still believe that America can play a role in that." But he urged the UN to learn from its recent struggles. "The UN went into Cambodia first of all with this theory about what they had to do to or with the Khmer Rouge, and then moved away from any kind of military approach . . . in effect, creating a process in which the local people had to take responsibility for their own future. If we are going to do that kind of work, we ought to take the Cambodian model in Somalia and everyplace else."[50]Vieira de Mello was proud of his achievements in Cambodia, but he knew the flaws of the UNTAC mission, and he knew that the key predictor of any UN mission's success was its clarity of purpose and the backing it got from the major powers. He initially thought that what the Balkan mission lacked in clarity, it gained in support from the major powers. But he did not realize how divided those powers were over what should be done, and he did not foresee how he, the UN he cherished, and Bosnia itself would suffer the consequences.

Seven

"SANDWICHES AT
THE GATES"

If the UN's Cambodia mission had put a dent in Vieira de Mello's hopes
for a "new world order," his time in Bosnia would temporarily extin-
guish them. On October 7, 1993, unaware of just how dark a pall Somalia would cast over UN operations around the world, he said good-bye to his
wife and sons, fifteen and thirteen, and made his way to the familiar Geneva
airport to embark upon yet another journey into the unknown.

Although UN Headquarters in New York had kept him waiting for
months before offering him the Bosnia posting, his bosses now wanted him
in place immediately. Amid the craze of his departure, Annick Roulet, his
friend and former press officer in Cambodia, had been unable to steal time to
discuss how she might support him from Geneva. They had agreed to meet
at the airport for a cup of coffee before his flight.

Roulet was on time, but he burst through the doors of the airport
just forty-five minutes before his plane was to depart. "I'm sorry, Annick,"
he said, breathlessly. "I think we'll only manage a quick hello." She proceeded to the nearest ticket desk and purchased a business-class ticket to
London. "What have you done?" he asked when she rejoined him in the
security line. "Working for you," she said, "one learns to innovate." He
glanced at the ticket she was holding. "Why London?" he asked. "Why not
London?" she answered. After clearing security, the two shared a relaxed cup
of coffee in the business-class lounge in the departures area. When it was
time for him to board, Roulet walked him to his gate and then retraced her

steps, exiting the terminal and apologetically informing the Swissair agent that her boss had just called canceling her London meeting. She received a full refund.

Vieira de Mello knew the basics of the crisis. Slovenia and Croatia had seceded from Serb-dominated Yugoslavia in 1991, and a bloody war had ensued. At just the time he had been complaining about the slow deployment of UN peacekeepers to Cambodia in 1992, the UN's tiny Department of Peacekeeping Operations in New York had been attempting to find an additional 14,000 peacekeepers to send to Croatia to patrol a shaky cease-fire there. Then in April 1992, with the peacekeeping office stretched to its breaking point, Bosnia too had declared independence from Yugoslavia, and Serb nationalists had declared war. Bosnia's population (43 percent Bosnian, 35 percent Serb, and 18 percent Croat) lived so intermingled that the violence instantly turned savage.* Serb paramilitary forces herded Bosnian and Croat men into concentration camps, burned down non-Serb villages, and besieged a number of heavily populated towns that the UN Security Council eventually declared "safe areas."

With the murder of European civilians captured on television, the pressure mounted on President Bush to intervene in the Balkans as he had done over Kuwait in 1991. But the circumstances in the Gulf had been very different from those in the former Yugoslavia. Saddam Hussein had invaded a neighbor and threatened U.S. oil supplies. Bosnia was home to a messy civil war that the Bush administration did not feel threatened "vital U.S. interests."

But because the Western media covered the Bosnian conflict incessantly, the major powers could not afford to look away entirely. The United States joined European countries in funding UN humanitarian agencies that fed the war's victims. The Security Council voted to send UN peacekeepers to the war-torn country in order to escort the aid workers who were delivering relief, and a number of European countries contributed soldiers to the dangerous mission. By the time of Vieira de Mello's posting, the French had put more than 3,000 troops in Bosnia, the British nearly 2,300, and the Spanish

---

*I use the word "Bosnian" to describe those who remained in territory under Bosnian government control and who, for much of the war, clung to the ideal of a multiethnic, unitary state. At the outset the "Bosnians" were Muslim, Croat, and Serb, but by the end of the war "Bosnian" and "Muslim" had become almost synonymous. After the war the term "Bosniak" was introduced to describe this mainly Muslim population.

over 1,200.[1] But Western governments told their soldiers with the UN to avoid risk, and the blue helmets rarely fought back against marauding militia. Each country on the Security Council framed the crisis differently: the Bush and later Clinton administrations, which refused to put boots on the ground, blamed the Serbs for their "war of aggression"; Britain and France, which had troops in harm's way, wanted to stay neutral in the conflict and played up a "tragic civil war"; and the Russians, out of solidarity with their fellow Orthodox Christian Slavs, sided with the Serbs. These divisions among the UN's most powerful countries would paralyze the mission Vieira de Mello was joining.

For all of the shortcomings of the UN mission in Cambodia, its two concrete achievements—the return of 360,000 refugees and the elections—had earned it a fairly glowing reputation outside Asia. By contrast, UNPROFOR was already seen as a "loser." Few Bosnians read the fine print of UN mandates and inevitably saw the peacekeepers in their flak jackets, blue helmets, and armored personnel carriers as protectors. They were thus crushed to realize that most peacekeepers saw themselves as mere monitors.

FORCE PROTECTION

Vieira de Mello spent October 7 in Zagreb, the peaceful capital of Croatia where UNPROFOR kept its headquarters, then flew to Sarajevo. One of the UN's most significant achievements in the region had been the establishment of a humanitarian airlift into the Bosnian capital, which was encircled by Bosnian Serb gunners. The UN relied on the airport, which it controlled, to transport its peacekeepers and supplies, to fly in journalists who were essential for maintaining public support and funding for the mission, and to deliver humanitarian relief to trapped civilians. The cargo planes were flown by American, French, British, German, and Canadian pilots, who operated what they called "Maybe Airlines."[2]

By the time of Vieira de Mello's arrival, the daredevil pilots had grown quite practiced at evading Serb attacks, but it meant a roller coaster of a ride. He had been warned that Serb gunfire could pierce the base of the plane and penetrate his seat from below, so he sat atop his flak jacket and braced for what he knew would be a rapid and unwieldy descent. Starting at 18,000 feet, the plane took a steep and unforgiving dive, leveled for a short stretch, and then plunged again, this time twisting to and fro in order to prevent Serb ground missile sites from locking on. At the last minute the nose of the plane jerked upward, and the wheels crashed into the runway, jolting him and the other passengers forward. After the plane had skidded to a halt, he disembarked carrying a light suitcase and a briefcase.

The journey from the airport offered him his first in-person glimpse of the Bosnian war. Sarajevo had hosted the 1984 Winter Olympics, and he was told that the identical rectangular gray concrete apartment buildings around the airport had housed the athletes. The complex was so gutted by shell and sniper fire that he assumed it had been deserted. But a closer inspection revealed flowerpots on the window ledges, laundry hanging between telephone poles outside, and children kicking soccer balls against entranceways. Plastic sheeting affixed with the UNHCR logo had replaced glass in almost all the windows. Rusted hulks of cars had been propped on their sides along the road in a largely futile effort to shield pedestrians.

Vieira de Mello's UN driver brought him to the bunkered compound where he would work and live for the next several months. The "UN residency" was located in the former Delegates' Club of the Yugoslav Communist Party, and it was a frequent target of Serb sniper and shell fire. He was shown a tiny office next to the briefing room, which would double as his sleeping quarters. Because he could speak with nearly all of the UNPROFOR officers in their native tongues, he quickly became a popular presence. But the soldiers teased him for his primness. The Belgian who commanded UN forces in Bosnia, Francis Briquemont, marveled at the number of times during the day that he spotted Vieira de Mello shuttling to and from the bathroom with his toothbrush and toothpaste.[3]

Vieira de Mello and his UN colleagues kept attuned to events in Somalia. Initially, in the wake of the October 4 firefight, the Clinton administration did just what the Reagan administration had done after the attack on the U.S. Marine barracks in Beirut in 1983—it pledged it would remain until the job was done. "We came to Somalia to rescue innocent people in a burning house," President Clinton said in an address from the Oval Office, the day of Vieira de Mello's arrival in Sarajevo. By remaining, Clinton said, "we've got a reasonable chance of cooling off the embers and getting other firefighters to take our place. So now we face a choice. Do we leave when the job gets tough, or when the job is well done?" Clinton announced that he was sending some 1,700 reinforcements, 104 additional armored vehicles, an aircraft carrier, and 3,600 offshore Marines.[4]

But as Vieira de Mello adjusted to life under siege in Sarajevo, Clinton changed his mind. On October 19 the president backtracked—again as the Reagan administration had done almost exactly a decade before—announcing that U.S. forces in Somalia would "stand down."[5] The United States would not attempt to apprehend General Aideed. Indeed, the man whom Clinton officials had so recently branded a "thug" was now described by a Clinton spokesperson as "a clan leader with a substantial constituency in Somalia."[6]

Vieira de Mello and his UN colleagues in Bosnia saw that the fates of the two missions were intertwined. In Somalia U.S. troops henceforth rarely ventured out of their compounds. "Force protection" became the American mantra. One U.S. officer was quoted in the *Washington Post* on the eve of his departure. "We're not cops and we're having to adopt war-fighting technology for a fugitive hunt in a city of about a million," he said.[7]

Bosnia was similar to Somalia, Vieira de Mello understood, in that non-combatants in both places were the prime victims of the violence and the prime pawns of political leaders. Once-bustling cities were held under siege by Serb gunners, and snipers fired upon civilians carrying water or UN rations. The Bosnian army, which was much weaker than its Serb opponent, often positioned its weapons in civilian neighborhoods, despite knowing that the Serbs would retaliate disproportionately. They did so in part because the front lines ran close to the center of town and also in order to camouflage the few heavy weapons they had in their possession. The UN estimated that more than 90 percent of the 100,000 people eventually killed in the conflict were civilians. These "unconventional wars" would be the wars of the future.

CONSTRUCTIVE ENGAGEMENT

Vieira de Mello loved being back with the military. He settled into a routine in Sarajevo, offering his political advice to Stoltenberg in Zagreb and counseling General Briquemont in Sarajevo, while building close ties with the key

Vieira de Mello (right) *and UN Bosnia Force
Commander Francis Briquemont* (center)
scouring the Bosnian hills.

Serb and Bosnian personalities. He was told his time in Bosnia would entail negotiating prisoner exchange agreements, cease-fires, and access for UN aid convoys. Prominent Western diplomats would be the ones to try to craft a lasting political settlement.

Stoltenberg was a career Norwegian politician, not a UN veteran. This led him to make choices that his new aide did not like. Vieira de Mello believed that the UN drew legitimacy and strength from the geographical diversity of its field staff. He was thus aghast when Stoltenberg decided to hire one Norwegian as his adviser and another as his deputy chief of mission. "He can't do what he's doing," Vieira de Mello fumed to colleagues. "He's not establishing a Norwegian foreign ministry in exile. He's working now for the United Nations." Stoltenberg, for his part, valued efficiency above what he saw as the UN's overly romantic commitment to multinationality. He also did not think that his staffing choices were unusual. "It is common to have thirty French or fifty Americans in a mission," he says, "but when you have three Norwegians, people start to talk." Vieira de Mello, who rarely picked losing battles, avoided raising the matter with Stoltenberg directly.

Since the Serbs frequently obstructed the movement of UN relief deliveries, he purposefully cultivated a warm relationship with Bosnian Serb political leader Radovan Karadžić, who before the war had worked as a psychiatrist in Sarajevo and fancied himself a poet. Vieira de Mello was repulsed by the Bosnian Serb leader's anti-Muslim fervor and unimpressed by his poetry, but he was determined—just as he had been with the Khmer Rouge's Ieng Sary—to do what it took to butter up the Bosnian Serbs' most influential politician. On one occasion, when he visited Bosnian Serb headquarters in the town of Pale, he brought a copy of *The New York Review of Books* as a gift to Karadžić, because it featured a cover story on psychiatry.[8] Whenever the Serb leader saw fit to go on long rants about how Serbs were saving Christian civilization from a Muslim jihad, Vieira de Mello gave Karadžić his full attention. The only hint of his impatience with the Serb was the incessant jittering of his leg beneath the table. Alone with friends or colleagues, he complained about Karadžić's bloviating and his incessant references to Serb grievances dating back to the fourteenth century. He said that he was tempted to open every meeting in the Balkans with the proviso "Today we are going to begin this meeting in 1945." But in practice he never dared to alienate his interlocutors.

His closest friend in the Balkans was Haris Silajdžić, the dashing forty-eight-year-old prime minister of Bosnia. The two men talked about philosophy, music, and women. While Vieira de Mello's graciousness toward Karadžić was contrived, his affection toward Silajdžić was genuine. Each man delighted in being known as a lady-killer. On one occasion Silajdžić was half an hour late for one of their meetings. As the minutes ticked by, a Bosnian official suggested that since the prime minister had proven unreachable at his home and office, somebody might telephone a woman in the Bosnian government with whom he was said to be involved. When Vieira de Mello heard the name of the woman in question, he reached into his pocket and produced a crumpled piece of paper with a telephone number scrawled upon it. "Perhaps I can help," he said, smiling.

Silajdžić and Vieira de Mello both functioned on little sleep, so they frequently met for drinks or dinner in generator-powered restaurants, and they spoke by telephone at all hours. "Sergio came to breakfast with new ideas," Silajdžić recalls. "That meant he had been thinking through the night."

Not content to remain cooped up inside the secure but stuffy UN compound, Vieira de Mello tried to establish a connection with the "Bosnian street." He explored the majestic, battered capital city with Lola Urošević, his twenty-eight-year-old translator, accompanying her on walks through the town, visiting her home, and getting to know her family. Urošević felt calmed by her boss's presence. As sniper and shell fire crackled in the winter afternoons, he seemed unflustered and rarely wore his UN-issued flak jacket. "How could I wear that thing," he asked her, "when you, your family, and neighbors walk around with nothing?" Back in the UN bunker with international staff, he explained his disavowal of the flak jacket in a more self-parodying way. "Do you have any idea how fat those things make you look?" he said.

Before the war Urošević had been a full-time medical student at the University of Sarajevo. But when the violence erupted, because she spoke French and English, she had gone to work for the UN, where she earned ten times the pay that she would have received had she practiced medicine. Vieira de Mello made a point of inquiring about Urošević's studies, which she continued at night. One day when she hurried back to UN headquarters after a low-key ceremony celebrating her graduation, she found him smiling ear-to-ear in her office, along with several other colleagues. "Congratulations, Dr. Urošević," he said. Reaching beneath his desk, he produced a bottle of champagne, an exotic commodity in the besieged capital. "I managed to track down a little something for the occasion!"

The suffering of Sarajevans made a deep impression on him. The city was filled with men and women of high culture and learning. As the temperature dropped and the frigid winter set in, proud Europeans who had run out of firewood began burning their books in order to cook UN humanitarian aid. And when the cemeteries quickly filled up, he watched Sarajevan families use once-placid city parks to bury their dead. He worked with General Briquemont to help smuggle gasoline for generators to a resistance organization called the Sarajevo Group of Authors, a gathering of Sarajevo's leading filmmakers, artists, and students who composed eye-catching graphic art and films and exported them to Western capitals in the hopes of mobilizing a Western rescue operation.

AFFIRMATIVE ACTION

On December 24, 1993, while most UN officials around the world celebrated Christmas with their families, Vieira de Mello's sympathy for the
Bosnians prompted him to undertake one of his boldest schemes as a UN
official. He summoned his new forty-four-year-old military aide, a Canadian
major named John Russell, to his office. "John," he said, "we're going to break
the siege of Sarajevo." Russell was flummoxed. The Serbs had the city surrounded, and unless Russell had failed to notice a radical change of heart in
Western capitals, the outside world had no intention of forcibly removing
Serb forces from the deadly hills ringing the city. "I want you to find a way
to get people out," Vieira de Mello explained. "People who don't fit within
the UN rules, but who need to get out—because they can't get the medical
care they need here, because they are separated from a loved one, or because
they can do more good on the outside than they are doing inside." Russell
nodded but, afraid he might not be up to the task, cautioned, "Okay, sir, but
keep in mind that it was just two days ago that I learned where Sarajevo
airport was."

Vieira de Mello spent the next three days shuttling Russell around the city,
introducing him to Bosnian officials as well as key international actors, such
as the head of the French battalion in Sarajevo and the logistics and customs
officials who ran the airlift at the airport. The pair also traveled to Pale, where
they met with the Bosnian Serb authorities. Vieira de Mello's introduction
was the same in each instance. "This is John Russell. He is my new military
aide. In my absence he speaks for me and for the United Nations." Russell
was taken aback by the gravity of his new responsibilities. "I was thinking,
'What's going on here?'" he recalls. "Overnight I found myself operating at
the highest level."

Russell would manage what Vieira de Mello dubbed "the train," a UN
convoy that transported Bosnian civilians out of the city. The Canadian began
timing trial runs to the airport. He clocked his trips down Sarajevo's main
boulevard, which had become known as "Sniper's Alley." In order to smuggle
civilians out of the city, he would have to first pass through a checkpoint at
the airport manned by armed Bosnians, then get by a Serb checkpoint, and
finally get UN authorization.

Russell led the convoy in one of two cars—either Vieira de Mello's personal car, a bullet-proof American Chevrolet, which the Bosnian and UN guards already recognized, or a standard-issue UN Nissan Pathfinder. Often the shell and sniper fire on Sniper's Alley forced him to drive at a hundred miles per hour. The most perilous part of the journey came when the "train" reached the airport itself. In January 1993 the forty-seven-year-old Bosnian vice president Hakija Turajlic had been riding in the back of a French UN armored personnel carrier when Serb soldiers outside the airport stopped the vehicle, yanked Turajlic out, and killed him by firing seven bullets over the shoulder of his UN escort.[9] In order to ensure that Vieira de Mello's human cargo did not meet the same fate, Russell made sure that the door of each APC harboring Bosnian civilians was shuttered and locked from the inside.

In allowing the UN humanitarian airlift, the Serbs had granted a one-hour block of time to UN Hercules or Ilyushin cargo planes to fly in the morning and a second slot in the afternoon. Russell tried to ensure that every flight that left the city carried Bosnian civilians. Once the Bosnians under his charge had cleared the military checkpoints, he waited with them at the airport in the VIP lounge, away from aid workers, journalists, and diplomats. UN airport officials were under instructions to load Russell's passengers onto the airplane before the others.

Vieira de Mello would cheerily check in every now and then ("Is the train running on time today, John?") or would pass his aide a list of names of people to be evacuated ("Take care of this family, will you, John?"). He told Russell to select the most "deserving" cases but did not stipulate precise criteria. Deciding who was eligible to leave the city was by far the worst part of Russell's job, and Vieira de Mello was glad it was a task he could delegate. "It's a balancing act," he said, instructing Russell to maximize the good they were doing but to be sure the train was not publicized. The more individuals the UN helped, the more likely it was that somebody would blurt out the details of the operation to the media, and either the Bosnian Serb authorities or the Bosnian government would shut it down. Russell usually took no more than a half-dozen civilians at a time.

The roster of those evacuated included a delegation of Bosnian athletes who Vieira de Mello thought would ably publicize the country's suffering at the Winter Olympics in Lillehammer, Norway; the Roman Catholic archbishop of Sarajevo, who had been granted an audience with the pope; a Bosnian doctor who enrolled in a specialized course in treating bullet wounds; and a man whose wife was dying of cancer in France.

As word began to spread across the capital that Russell was the man playing God at the UN, the Canadian grew edgy. One woman asked if she could bring her dog on the flight. He exploded. "I'm not going to waste my resources moving a fucking poodle around." Another tried to bring a huge suitcase filled with books. "The UN is not Lufthansa," Russell snapped. One woman had terminal cancer and wanted to seek treatment in Western Europe. Russell made a cold calculation in turning down her request. "There are only so many seats," he said to himself, "and she's going to die anyway. It's sad, but I have to spend my time focusing on the living." The only persons he automatically rejected were those who attempted to bribe him with sex or money, or Bosnian men of fighting age who he believed might be deserting. "I had people who kissed my hand like I was royalty," Russell recalls. "But I also saw people I turned down, lying dead on the street. They died at my hands, indirectly." All told, in the 110 days that he ran the train for Vieira de Mello, Russell rescued 298 people. Pat Dray, the Canadian captain who replaced him, evacuated several hundred more. Vieira de Mello did not discuss the operation, or his role in launching it, with his friends, colleagues, or critics.

In addition to getting certain Bosnians out of Sarajevo, he also worked on bringing important visitors in. The same week he initiated "the train," he helped arrange for the American soprano Barbara Hendricks, a UNHCR goodwill ambassador, to perform a New Year's concert in Sarajevo. At midnight on December 31, 1993, in one of the few glimmers of hope the city had enjoyed in nearly two years, Hendricks sang with a much-shrunken Bosnian Symphony Orchestra. Many of its members had fled, been conscripted, or been killed, including a trombone player who had been shot the week before. Yet Vieira de Mello and some two hundred local and foreign dignitaries savored the sounds of Mozart's Mass in C Minor, Gabriel Fauré's *Requiem,* and Schubert's *Ave Maria.* The concert was broadcast live on local television, but because the city lacked electricity, few Bosnians could watch. The concert's main effect was to make Sarajevans who heard about the performance feel slightly less alone. In the forty-five minutes in which Hendricks sang and Vieira de Mello listened, half a dozen shells landed within a hundred yards of the TV studio that had been converted into a concert hall for the occasion. Over the course of New Year's Day, five people were killed and forty-six wounded in the capital.[10]

General Briquemont had been away from Sarajevo visiting his troops while Hendricks delivered her midnight performance. The next day, at a formal lunch in her honor in the officers' mess, Briquemont asked whether she would mind singing something a cappella. No sooner had the soprano cleared her throat and begun to sing than a shell crashed down beside the building, causing the lights to flicker and the silverware to clatter. Hendricks kept on singing through the din. When Vieira de Mello asked her afterward how she had managed to remain so calm, she said, "If I die, I know I want to go out singing." He had always been skeptical about goodwill ambassadors, believing that the logistics of arranging celebrity visits brought more headaches than benefits. But after the incident, Hendricks recalls, "I could tell I went up several notches in his estimation." The following evening Vieira de Mello played a CD of Brazilian music and attempted to teach her and the French officers to dance the samba. Hendricks told him that no matter how many ravaged cities she had visited for the UN, nothing had prepared her to see a European city in such a state. "I feel like I have walked into a Kafka novel," she said. "If I see giant cockroaches on the wall, I won't be surprised." He agreed, saying, "This kind of savagery probably lies buried within us all."

They discussed their respective personal lives. He reflected on how much he missed his sons during the holidays. He and Annie were together so rarely that Hendricks asked why they had not formalized their separation. "Don't wait too long," she advised. "You need to give Annie a chance to start another life of her own. She should get to live without waiting for you. The longer you postpone dealing with this, the harder it will be." He deflected the question. "We've grown apart," he said, "but that's no reason to end a marriage."

"We Must Not Be Partial"

Vieira de Mello was an expert compartmentalizer and concentrated on the work at hand. The singular dilemma that he and his colleagues faced was that the very UN humanitarian airlift that had loosened the Serb noose around the necks of Bosnian civilians had evolved into something of a noose around UNPROFOR itself. He was of the view that if UN peace-keepers fought back against Serbs who were targeting civilians, Serb gunners would retaliate by firing several well-placed, shoulder-launched missiles at a UN cargo plane, closing down the whole feeding operation and endangering several million lives. The countries that had sent soldiers to serve in the peacekeeping mission cared enough about Bosnia to try to prevent mass starvation, but he did not believe that they cared enough to fight the Serbs in a war. The blue helmets were thus in a bind.[11] They were passing out food, but not preventing those fed from being felled by sniper or shell fire, causing critics to accuse the UN of "passing out sandwiches at the gates of Auschwitz."[12]

Vieira de Mello defended UNPROFOR's approach. He argued that the blue helmets played a vital humanitarian role and cautioned against using force. "There are 95% fewer casualties in Bosnia now than there were a year ago," he argued. "We are buying time for the Bosnians until a peace agreement can be signed." For that to happen the major powers—not the UN peacekeepers—would have to ratchet up their diplomatic involvement. "Expecting UNPROFOR to bring about a political solution," he told an interviewer, "is, at the very least, absurd. It's a conceptual mistake."[13] UN officials had to resist the impulse to be trigger-happy. "If we opt for force," he insisted, "we have chosen war."[14]

Impartiality was so central to his understanding of the essence of UN peacekeeping that he refused journalists' requests to state which party bore the greatest responsibility for the carnage. "We must not be partial," he explained. "I understand it is hard for you to understand, but it is the only way for us to help stop the war in Bosnia."[15] He hailed the virtues of what he called "affirmative action"—humanitarian work that made life a little more bearable for civilians in war. "We may not be able to change the world here," he told his demoralized staff, "but we can change individual worlds, one at a time." If UN peacekeepers could simply freeze the battle lines in place, and UN aid agencies could keep civilians alive, the UN mission was doing its part. From his perspective, Western negotiators would have to be the ones to use their considerable resources to negotiate a permanent peace.

But many UN officials saw the situation differently. Some argued that the peacekeepers should challenge the Serbs militarily. More junior UN officials—often on their first field missions—were outraged just as he had been on his first peacekeeping mission in Lebanon. They believed that the blue helmets were too timid, and that UN officials who had been in the system too long were so interested in protecting their own reputations that they were downplaying carnage that they should have been denouncing. They were treating a stopgap feeding operation as an end in itself. They had made themselves complicit by not vocally urging Western governments to rescue civilians. "The system is broken," David Harland, a thirty-two-year-old political officer from New Zealand, argued. "We are being used. We aren't going to get a peace agreement by simply hanging around."

Bosnia was one of the few missions Vieira de Mello undertook in the absence of Dennis McNamara, who was back in Geneva as UNHCR's director of external relations. Still, McNamara kept up his role jabbing at his friend's conscience, teasing over the telephone, "That's not peacekeeping you are doing, Sergio. It's war monitoring." *The Economist* chided the UN as "an armour-plated meals-on-wheels service."[16] More stinging to him, the Bosnians themselves jeered the blue helmets as either the UN *Self*-Protection Force or "SERBPROFOR." He kept some of the hate mail he received while on mission. One letter, entitled "War Criminals and Their Supporters," included cut-out photographs of Slobodan Milošević and Karadžić alongside Boutros-Ghali and Stoltenberg.

In late January 1994, however, Bosnian civilians began to believe that UNPROFOR might at last defend them. Lieutenant General Sir Michael Rose, a fifty-three-year-old former British SAS officer who had served in Northern Ireland and fought in the Falklands War, took over as commander of UN forces in Bosnia, replacing General Briquemont. Rose, the general whom Vieira de Mello spoke with the night of our first meeting, arrived in Sarajevo citing the SAS motto: "Who dares, wins." Peace had to be pushed; Serb harassment of civilians and peacekeepers had to stop. "If they shoot at us, we'll shoot back," Rose said, "and I have no hesitation about that whatsoever."[17] In some places the Serbs were blocking or siphoning 80 percent of humanitarian supplies. "We've got to lean on the door harder, and if we keep leaning in a very, very concerted way," the general said, "then that door is going to open further, and more aid will go through."[18] This spirit was infectious, as UN civil servants and peacekeepers who had grown fatalistic were inspired by their new commander.

Just as Rose arrived, UN Headquarters in New York informed Vieira de

Mello that he was being promoted. He would no longer be based in Sarajevo as a roaming adviser to Stoltenberg and the generals. Instead he would be relocated to UNPROFOR headquarters in Zagreb and would run the Department of Civil Affairs, managing a team of fifty international political analysts spread out throughout the former Yugoslavia and retaining the function of top political adviser to the head of the mission. He groaned when he heard the rest of the news—instead of answering to Stoltenberg, whom he at least saw as a political heavyweight, he would serve under the new UN Special Representative of the Secretary-General: his former boss in Cambodia, Yasushi Akashi.

Vieira de Mello joked privately that in order for him to earn the title of "adviser," he needed to work for somebody who was interested in taking advice. Akashi was not that person. Boutros-Ghali later admitted that he had peevishly chosen a Japanese (rather than a European) diplomat "as a rebuke to the Europeans for their failure to deal with this conflict on their own continent."[19] Undoubtedly, Japan's heavy share of the UN peacekeeping budget was again a factor. Even though he had known his new boss for more than two years, Vieira de Mello continued to call him "Mr. Akashi" and "sir." "For somebody who cut such a dashing figure," recalls Michael Williams, who worked with Vieira de Mello in Cambodia and again in UNPROFOR, "Sergio was remarkably *protocolaire*."

Vieira de Mello overlapped with General Rose in Sarajevo for just thirteen days. But the two men took an instant liking to each other. Rose had been educated at Oxford and the Sorbonne and spoke fluent French, which endeared him to Vieira de Mello and to the French soldiers in Sarajevo who might otherwise have been suspicious of a British commander. Rose respected the relationships Vieira de Mello had already managed to build with Balkan leaders and his vast experience living and working in conflict areas. Rose later noted that he admired Vieira de Mello "above anyone else I worked with in Bosnia."[20]

One of their first encounters was telling. Rose, who was readying himself for his first trip to meet Bosnian president Alija Izetbegović, was donning a flak jacket and helmet and preparing to board an armored UN convoy. He saw Vieira de Mello exiting the residency for the same meeting. "How are you getting down there?" Rose asked. Vieira de Mello said he was walking because the people of Sarajevo resented UN peacekeepers who zoomed past them in armored vehicles. Ignoring the UN security protocol, Rose ripped off his protective layers and ambled down the dangerous street with his colleague, stopping to talk to Sarajevans along the way. When the men arrived at the pockmarked Austro-Hungarian–era building that served as the Presidency, they entered a dark and subfreezing tomb where Bosnian waiters in white gloves served orange juice and UN aid biscuits off silver trays. When a shell struck nearby, the ceiling sent a shower of light dust down upon them. The men struggled to suppress their giggles at what Rose remembered as "a mad hatter's tea party."[21]

For a person who had just arrived in the Balkans, Rose was remarkably sure of himself, which impressed Vieira de Mello and thrilled Bosnian civilians who were desperate to see a more aggressive UN. But in private meetings Rose's self-assuredness began to take a turn that some of his UN colleagues found disturbing. As a professional officer, he seemed to look down upon the ragtag Bosnian army, which was disorganized and poorly equipped, and to respect Serb forces who made use of officers and heavy weapons they inherited from the Yugoslav National Army. Rose was also suspicious of the Western media, whose sympathies lay with the Bosnians, the war's main victims. He later called the Sarajevo press corps "a pair of jackals circling the decaying corpse of Bosnia."[22]

In late January 1994 Aryeh Neier, the head of Helsinki Watch (the precursor to Human Rights Watch), visited Sarajevo and met with both men. Neier urged Rose to have his peacekeepers take a tougher stand with the Serbs. Rose counseled against doing what Washington had pressed peacekeepers to do in Somalia—cross what he called the "Mogadishu line," which for him meant surrendering their neutrality and "making war out of white-painted vehicles." While Vieira de Mello looked on silently, Rose argued that Sarajevo was not technically under siege, since UN aid deliveries were reaching civilians. "A lot of the shooting," Rose said, "is done to create the impression of major battles when there is no real fighting. They are trying to look good on CNN." Neier, who believed that Rose was downplaying the Serbs' culpability in order to justify UN neutrality, angrily relayed Rose's claim to the Sarajevo media.[23]

Vieira de Mello knew that Sarajevo was very much under siege. Indeed, with some twelve hundred shells falling per day, the Bosnian capital was then probably the most dangerous city on earth. He sent a cable to UN Headquarters three days after Rose's arrival, in which he wrote: "Sarajevo is definitely not a town where civil—or, for that matter, military—personnel of UNPROFOR should be allowed to expose themselves to undue risk, in particular by driving in soft-skin vehicles. [My] own cars have been repeatedly shot at. A simple ballistic analysis would show that the only reason both of us are able to respond to your fax is that such vehicles were armoured."[24]

He had survived two close calls in Bosnia. In December 1993, when on his way to the airport, he saw that the car driving in front of his, which was marked PRESS, had been hit by two Serb snipers firing from a nearby building. "Stop the car!" he shouted, instructing his driver to move his armored car into a position that would allow it to shield the journalist, who had been shot in the arm, and the driver, who had been hit in the leg. Felix Faix, a former French paratrooper who was his bodyguard, shoved Vieira de Mello into the backseat of the car, pulled out his gun, and fired at the two snipers, who were apparently hit and collapsed out of view. On a second occasion, when driving along Sniper's Alley, Vieira de Mello's own armored car was hit three times by a sniper but managed to limp back to headquarters, as Faix again kept his boss pinned down in the backseat. But while Vieira de Mello clearly appreciated the dangers posed by Serb gunners, he never stood up to Rose or challenged his public portrayal of Sarajevo as a city that was not in fact besieged. Rose remembers no disagreement of any kind. "We were absolutely hand and glove," he recalls. "Instinctively we felt the same way about things."

MARKET MASSACRE

Saturday, February 5, 1994, was scheduled to be Vieira de Mello's last day in Sarajevo. But at 12:10 p.m. a shell landed in a crowded downtown Sarajevo market on the busiest shopping day of the week, blowing sixty-eight Bosnian shoppers and vendors to bits. It took him time to reach Akashi by phone because the special representative had chosen that weekend to take his closest advisers to his favorite Japanese restaurant in Graz, Austria. When he finally got through, Akashi told him to remain in Sarajevo and offer his political judgment on what seemed to be a shrinking number of options for preventing the war's escalation.

The scene at the market was ghastly. The green awnings and corrugated tin roofs that covered the market stalls had been converted into stretchers to carry the injured, or tarps on which to lay out the dead. Somebody had drawn a chalk ring around the spot where the deadly mortar shell had landed. The crater formed the base of a paw mark, with the toes offering evidence of the spray of hot metal, which had done most of the damage. Severed body parts were intermingled with cigarettes, daily newspapers, Coca-Cola cans, clothing, household goods, and homegrown vegetables.

Many of the dead were transported to the local morgue in a dump truck. Eight of the victims were so badly mangled that hospital staff could not determine whether they were men or women.[25] More than 150 people had been wounded, and the hospitals, short-staffed and underresourced on the best of days, could not keep up with the deluge. Doctors in the emergency room, their white coats stained with blood, yelled instructions to one another as they rushed to grab gauze, medicines, and bandages delivered by international relief groups. Family members waited outside to get word of the fate of their loved ones, and they let out shrieks of agony when doctors emerged with bad news. The wounded simply lay in the halls moaning for attention. The following day the main Sarajevo daily newspaper, *Oslobodjenje*, ran six full pages of black-bordered death notices.[26] Virtually every person Vieira de Mello knew in the city had a relative, neighbor, or friend affected by the massacre.

Even though powerful governments had dictated the international response to Serb aggression, Sarajevans directed their anger at UNPROFOR, which was present in a way that the United States and Europe were not. "Boutros-Ghali just watches all this and he does nothing," said one woman interviewed near the market. "He's worse than Milošević and Karadžić. He's their accomplice."[27] It was not a good weekend to be seen driving in a white UN vehicle. Vieira de Mello was sickened by the incident. "Bastards!" he exclaimed, referring to those who had fired the shell. "How do they call themselves soldiers?" But after what he later called "the worst day of my life, where I cried with anger," he buried his emotions.[28] He believed that Bosnia's most tragic day could also be its most transformative. The world's major powers might now focus their attention and their resources long enough on Bosnia to bring peace.

The Serbs had made a habit of trying to cover their tracks by accusing the Bosnians of attacking themselves. Just a month earlier Bosnian Serb leader Karadžić had told Vieira de Mello and Rose, "The Muslims would kill Allah himself in order to discredit the Serbs!"[29] The Bosnian war was the first twentieth-century conflict in which the parties used CNN to argue their cases. The day of the attack Karadžić told the network, "This is a cold-blooded murder and I would demand the strongest sentence against those who are responsible for this."[30] He threatened to block all air and land relief deliveries to Sarajevo if the UN did not exonerate them. A visibly shattered Bosnian prime minister Silajdžić was interviewed as well. "This is defacing the international community and our civilization," he countered. "Please, let's forget about my being the prime minister for a minute. I'm talking as a man, now. Please remember these scenes; if we don't stop it, it is going to come to your doorstep."[31]

In the past, when the Serbs refused UN demands, UNPROFOR officials had lacked leverage and simply scaled back their requests. This time, though, the public outcry in capitals over the market massacre gave Western leaders little choice but to throw the weight of NATO, the most powerful military alliance in history, behind UN diplomacy. The German government, which just two weeks before had said it opposed military action, reversed its position, saying it now supported NATO air strikes against the Serbs. The French demanded an emergency NATO summit to discuss an immediate military response. Only the British remained reluctant to use force against the Serbs. "The rest of the world cannot send armies into what is a cruel and vicious civil war," British foreign secretary Malcolm Rifkind said.[32]

On February 9, four days after the market attack, NATO's sixteen foreign ministers haggled for more than twelve hours to produce an unprecedented ultimatum: The Serbs had until midnight GMT on February 20 to withdraw their heavy weapons from a twelve-mile "exclusion zone" around Sarajevo. Any weapons that remained after that time would be placed in the custody of UN peacekeepers or bombed by NATO. The alliance had never before made such an explicit threat. And Sarajevo civilians had never felt so close to being rescued. "Nobody should doubt NATO's resolve," President Clinton warned from Washington. "NATO is now ready to act."[33] But after so many false promises in the past, skeptics abounded. One cartoon summed up the Western track record. A survivor peered out from behind the ruins of Sarajevo, shouting, "The rhetoric is coming! The rhetoric is coming!"[34]

NATO and the UN had much in common. The most influential countries in NATO—the United States, Britain, and France—held permanent seats and vetoes on the UN Security Council. But many in Russia, which also held a UN Security Council seat, continued to see NATO as the enemy it had been during the cold war.[35] In addition, as the Serbs' benefactor, Russia staunchly opposed the idea of air strikes.

UN officials like Vieira de Mello and Rose favored only what was called NATO "close air support"—the limited, surgical use of air power against the Serbs on the rare occasions when blue helmets came under serious attack. In aiding the peacekeepers' self-defense, NATO pilots were allowed to hit only the offending weapon. Vieira de Mello opposed the kind of strikes that the Clinton administration favored, NATO offensive "air strikes," which he saw as incompatible with impartial peacekeeping. If NATO wanted to make war, he reasoned, the major powers should withdraw the UN peacekeepers and the United States should ensure success by putting its own troops on the ground and joining a NATO ground force. Short of that unlikely turn of events, he argued, the Clinton administration should stop pushing the lightly armed blue helmets to absorb the physical risks that would flow from NATO bombing from the air.

Secretary-General Boutros-Ghali held the same view. He liked to quote Elliot Cohen, the U.S. military analyst, who said, "Air power is an unusually seductive form of military strength because, like modern courtship, it appears to offer gratification without commitment."[36] Vieira de Mello and Rose agreed: A NATO air campaign that was not backed by a larger plan to protect Bosnian civilians would do more harm than good. Defenseless citizens would be better off if NATO did not bomb. UNPROFOR would be able to continue to deliver relief and buy time for negotiators to hatch a political settlement. "You don't stand on the moral high ground with other nations' soldiers," Rose said, echoing Vieira de Mello's view. "The logic of war is not the logic of peacekeeping. Do one or the other, but don't try to conflate the two." Their UN team set out to use the threat of NATO air strikes against Serb positions to persuade the Serbs to remove their heavy weapons from the hills around Sarajevo. No matter how much carnage he had seen in Bosnia or elsewhere, Vieira de Mello could not shake his belief that patient dialogue could eventually bring about the kind of "conversion" that his philosophy mentor, Robert Misrahi, had advocated.

Because Western leaders were fearful that bombing might lead the Serbs to take UN hostages, and because French and British soldiers might be the first to be rounded up, the NATO ultimatum left it to UN officials in the field to decide whether to call for NATO bombing. Akashi, the same man who had been turned back by a few scrawny Khmer Rouge soldiers at a bamboo pole two years before, would decide whether air power would be employed. And Akashi had already made up his mind. "If Serb guns are silent and a significant number of them have been placed under UNPROFOR control," he wrote in an internal note to Headquarters days before the ultimatum was to expire, "I have no intention of agreeing to NATO air strikes."[37]

Sensing the reluctance of UNPROFOR officials and the British government to bomb, and knowing the disdain Russians felt toward NATO, the Serbs were initially defiant. The Bosnian Serb deputy force commander, Major General Manojlo Milovanovic, wrote to Rose: "I would like you to understand that the Serbs have never and will never accept anybody's ultimatum, even at the price of being wiped off the planet."[38]

But Vieira de Mello spent hours driving back and forth to the Bosnian Serb stronghold of Pale and on the phone with Bosnian Serb leaders in an effort to persuade them to pull back their forces. "Since there were large elements in NATO that wanted to bomb," recalls Simon Shadbolt, Rose's military assistant, "Sergio was able to portray NATO as the bad cop and the UN as good cop. He urged the Serbs to move to do the minimum of what NATO would accept."[39]

With the February 20 deadline for Serb cooperation fast approaching, the Serbs still had not removed many of their heavy weapons. Bosnians were in great suspense over the expiration of the NATO deadline, but Vieira de Mello was not. He knew that Akashi, the man with his finger on the trigger, had never viewed NATO air strikes as a real option. He traveled with Akashi to Pale on the eve of the NATO deadline, and when they attempted to return to Sarajevo, the narrow mountain road back to the capital was so clogged with Serb tanks and heavy weapons attempting to scurry out of range that they had to spend a cold and snowy night together in their vehicle.[40] Akashi was elated, as some progress was better than none. Vieira de Mello told the press, "If in the coming hours things continue as they have been for the past 48 hours, then there is no reason for concern."[41] When a journalist asked Rose where he would be when the deadline passed, the general said, "Asleep, in bed."[42]

As the deadline expired, Akashi admitted to UN Headquarters that the exclusion zone was not entirely clear of heavy weapons. Nonetheless, he declared the Serbs in "substantial compliance" with the terms of the ultimatum.[43] He told CNN, "There's no need to resort to air strikes."[44] As soon as the announcement was made, a relieved Vieira de Mello joined a group of military officers for a late-night whiskey toast at the residency. "Živeli," he exclaimed in Serbo-Croatian, amid the sound of clinking glasses. "To life!"

"The Path to a Normal Life"

Bosnian officials and civilians had hoped that a NATO intervention would eliminate the Serb heavy weapons that had taken some ten thousand lives in the city. They worried that when Western attention drifted elsewhere, the Serbs would simply reclaim guns that they had placed under UN supervision and reimpose the siege. Vieira de Mello, the UN official whom the Bosnians trusted most, attempted to allay their fears. The day after the deadline passed, he met with President Izetbegović, explaining that he had personally toured by Puma helicopter the most remote places where Serb heavy weapons were being gathered under UN watch. While he said there was naturally "room for improvement" in the UN's control system, which consisted of thirty-six land inspection and helicopter patrols, he appealed to the Bosnians "to appreciate that snow, ice, mud and mountainous terrain were making UNPROFOR's task unenviable." The Serb weapons that remained in range, he insisted, were "unimpressive."[45] He urged President Izetbegović to publicly praise developments, which Izetbegović agreed to do on Bosnian television. "I believe this is a great victory for us although it might not be quite clear, and not without shortcomings," Izetbegović said. "You can let your children out to play and not be afraid for their lives; you can go to the market place without being afraid and wondering whether you will come back or not. After twenty-three months of killing this is something important indeed."[46]

But most Bosnians were conflicted. Sarajevans still could not leave the city, and Serbs were still attacking Bosnians in the rest of the country—sometimes using the very heavy weapons that they had relocated from the hills surrounding the capital. Gordana Knežević, the editor of *Oslobodjenje* in Sarajevo, remarked: "It is as though our death sentence has been commuted to life imprisonment."[47]

The lessons of the Sarajevo experience seemed obvious. Tasked to deliver food aid but not to fight ethnic cleansing, UNPROFOR had lost both the trust of the Bosnians and the respect of the Serbs. But when the United States brought the weight of NATO to bear on the crisis, it conveyed a resolve that had been absent before. The ghastly carnage of February 5, 1994, had caused the Clinton administration to invest its clout in ending civilian suffering. Diplomacy backed by the threat of force had yielded concessions. As a result, starting on February 21, the people of Sarajevo savored the first quiet days they had enjoyed in nearly two years. Vieira de Mello telephoned Annick Roulet in Geneva: "Annick, the trams are running again in Sarajevo!!"

He knew from Lebanon and Cambodia how quickly Western leaders would again forget Bosnia. In the brief window they had, UNPROFOR officials had to try to turn the cease-fire around Sarajevo into a countrywide peace.[48] Vieira de Mello swiftly set out to do what he had done in Cambodia: use humanitarian progress to try to forge common ground among the bitter foes. If people in the region could become reacquainted with the creature comforts of peace—electricity, running water, and markets brimming with commercial goods—they might be less willing to return to violence. If in Cambodia Vieira de Mello had persuaded the Khmer Rouge to cooperate with the UN repatriation operation because they too wanted refugees to return to lands under their control, in Bosnia he hoped that the taste of normalcy might prompt citizens to press their leaders to concede territory in political negotiations.

From the beginning of the war in 1992, the Serbs had cut off utilities and food supplies to Sarajevo. Most of the old roads into the city were mined or booby-trapped, and the only link that Bosnian civilians had to the outside world was a tunnel under the airport runway. But by maintaining this stranglehold, the Serb authorities were also besieging their own kin, as the Serb suburbs around Sarajevo got their electricity and water from sources inside the Bosnian capital. In addition, in order for Serbs to move between two of the suburbs, they had to circumnavigate the entire city, which took almost a full day.

On Thursday, March 17, 1994, after an all-night negotiation session, Vieira de Mello sealed a landmark deal. Four so-called Blue Routes would be opened. From 9 a.m. to 2 p.m. daily, the Bosnians would open the Brotherhood and Unity Bridge connecting Sarajevo with one of the Serb suburbs. The roads linking the two main Serb suburbs would also be opened for two hours in the morning and the afternoon. In return the Serbs would open the road linking two Bosnian suburbs and the road between Sarajevo and central Bosnia, enabling humanitarian relief and civilian bus traffic to pass into the capital. Thanks to Vieira de Mello's Blue Routes accord, civilians in Sarajevo would be able to travel openly to the outside world for the first time since the outbreak of war in 1992. It started to look as though their sentence of life imprisonment too would be lifted.

Vieira de Mello's beaming visage appeared in news broadcasts around the world. Even though he was flushed with excitement, he also tried to manage the expectations of the local population. "Much to our regret this country is still technically at war," he reminded people. "So don't expect the opening of the city overnight."[49] In announcing the terms of the accord, he nudged the Serb and Bosnian negotiators into a handshake, which was the first public handshake between senior officials from the two sides since the war began. Almost a decade later, notwithstanding all his other achievements, he would tell a Brazilian journalist that this 1994 agreement constituted the proudest act in his career as a UN official.[50]

On the day that the bridge into Sarajevo actually opened for the first time, Bosnians and Serbs who had not seen their family members for more than two years crossed into lands held by their battlefield rivals. Hundreds of people gathered to see if their relatives or friends would appear.[51] One sixty-seven-year-old Bosnian man, Hasan Begic, whom the Serbs had evicted from his Sarajevo apartment with ten minutes' notice back in September 1992, made the trek across the bridge to the Serb neighborhood so as to find his disabled son Edhem. An hour after he crossed the bridge, he returned, horrified. "They told me my son was killed by a sniper on January 11 in front of the house," Begic told a reporter. "I have nothing more to do over there."[52]

Despite the trauma and loss that Bosnian civilians continued to endure, a tidal wave of optimism swept through the country and through the UN mission. A cease-fire was holding for a fifth straight week. Cafés in Sarajevo were reopening. With commercial traffic entering the city at last, prices tumbled.

On March 20 some 20,000 Sarajevans signaled their trust in the new calm by pouring into Sarajevo's open-air Olympic stadium to cheer the city football team in its 4–0 victory over a UN squad composed of one Egyptian, five British, three French, and two Ukrainian soldiers.

On March 22 a UN Ilyushin 76 landed at the airport in the besieged Bosnian city of Tuzla, providing the first food airlift of the war to more than a million people living there. Akashi said, "This is a very happy day for all of us. There's a new positive momentum for a cease-fire, disengagement, the establishment of a durable peace and the improvement of the life of the people in Bosnia and Herzegovina. I think the dark days are almost over."[53]

Eight

"SERBIO"

The dark days in Bosnia were in fact far from over. Even though the NATO ultimatum had halted fighting around Sarajevo, the rest of the country remained at war. And the more determined Vieira de Mello became to defend the impotent UN mission, the more morally compromised he became.

He did not warm to his new post in Zagreb, Croatia. Although the Bosnian capital had been deadly dangerous, it had brimmed with life; Zagreb, with its large luxury hotels and visible sector of war profiteers, was hard to get used to. The tensions inherent in helping run a peacekeeping mission in a country not at peace had not abated. But what made matters worse was that he now had a "field job" away from the field. In a meeting with his new team on February 25, 1994, he told them that he looked forward to once-a-week staff meetings. A Canadian military lawyer raised her hand and said she would prefer it if the staff met three times per week. This was only a hint of the office atmosphere that would smother him in the coming months.

As the head of UNPROFOR's civil affairs department, he inherited a slew of personnel who had been hired before his time and whom he couldn't unload. He was quickly overwhelmed by the paperwork, the phone calls, the meetings, and the staff-management issues, and he asked Elisabeth Naucler, a Finnish lawyer, to become his chief of staff so that he could spend more time troubleshooting back in Bosnia. "The most difficult thing in a peacekeeping mission is the internal peacekeeping," he told her. "His mind and heart were in Bosnia while his body was stuck in Zagreb dealing with staff infighting," Naucler remembers. "It must have been torture."

THE BLUFF THAT FAILED

But he soon got a reprieve from his desk job. Having escaped NATO bombing in the wake of the gruesome market massacre, Serb forces began attacking Bosnia's eastern enclave of Gorazde in late March. Another of the six UN-declared "safe areas," Gorazde was perched strategically on the main thruway connecting Belgrade and the Serb-held regions of Bosnia. Although the Gorazde enclave was quite large—it ran twelve miles from north to south and nineteen miles from west to east—only a handful of unarmed UN military observers and four UN aid workers were based there, which left its 65,000 inhabitants especially vulnerable. On April 6, the UN observers reported that the Serb offensive had left 67 people dead, including 10 children and 19 women and elderly men. Some 325 Bosnians had been injured. The food in the area would not last longer than two weeks.[1]

That same day Vieira de Mello, who was visiting Sarajevo, set off with General Rose on a fact-finding trip to Gorazde. As the men entered Serb territory, they passed Serb trenches along the front line, and they saw an Orthodox priest in black robes giving communion to the soldiers. They got only as far as the Serb stronghold of Pale and were turned back. Vieira de Mello tried to convince the Bosnian Serb military commander Ratko Mladić that if the Serbs blocked passage, it would only prove their hostile designs. Mladić knew that the one thing few UN officials could resist was the promise of a cease-fire. He told the UN duo that if they returned to Sarajevo, he would negotiate a halt in fighting with the Bosnian army. True to form, the UN delegation agreed to return to the Bosnian capital. "If the Serbs say the situation is such that they don't want us to go there now, we have to accept that," Rose told the press.[2] Nonetheless, before returning to Sarajevo, Rose did persuade Mladić to allow a dozen mainly British elite officers to proceed to Gorazde to have a look around.

After his failed effort to reach Gorazde, Vieira de Mello took a preplanned trip back to Geneva and France. While he was away, the Serbs pressed ahead with their offensive, seizing a crucial 3,400-foot-high ridge overlooking Gorazde and setting fire to neighboring villages. U.S. intelligence, which had been monitoring the situation, intercepted a message from Mladić to one of his field commanders in which he said he did not want "a single lavatory left standing in the town."[3]

Just two months after NATO had threatened to bomb the Bosnian Serbs around Sarajevo, the lives of Bosnians hung in the balance yet again. While in February the mere threat of force had caused the Serbs to pull back most of their weapons from around Sarajevo, in Gorazde it looked as though threats would not suffice; NATO would actually have to use air power if the Serbs were to be stopped. If Rose and Akashi did not call for help from NATO pilots, Gorazde and its large civilian populace looked certain to fall into Serb hands.

On April 10 General Rose did something few expected him to do: He summoned NATO bombers to give the peacekeepers he had sent into Gorazde "close air support." Rose and Akashi had long said they were more comfortable with limited close air support (a defensive measure) than with air strikes (which they considered an act of war). And they believed a surgical defensive strike against Serbs firing on UN troops would deter the Serbs without squandering the momentum toward peace. Since the founding of NATO in 1949, the alliance had never before placed itself at the disposal of UN blue helmets. And it would not soon do so again. First Rose had to sign off on air request forms; then Akashi (who was in Paris) had to give political clearance; and finally NATO had to agree. By the time all three approvals had been received, more than an hour had passed. The cloud cover and rain were so thick that two NATO A-10 aircraft had to fly low through Bosnia's valleys, which made them vulnerable to Serb ground fire. They were initially unable to find the offending Serb tanks and ran out of fuel. Two U.S. Air Force F-16C Fighting Falcons picked up where they left off, and at 6:26 p.m., two hours after Rose initiated the request, NATO struck, eliminating a Serb artillery command post four miles from town and reportedly killing nine Serb officers. This was the alliance's first attack on a ground target in its history.

UN and NATO officials understood that a threshold had been crossed— for the UN, for NATO, and for Bosnia. The people of Gorazde were elated. They gathered in the streets and gave thumbs-up signs to the members of the small UN team encamped in the central bank building. Serbian president Slobodan Milošević predictably denounced the attack, which he said "heavily harms the reputation of the UN in its role as mediator of the peace process."[4] By calling on NATO to bomb one faction, he said, UNPROFOR had taken sides. The following day, when the Serbs kept up their shelling, NATO struck again, destroying two Serb APCs and damaging one tank.

At his home in Massongy, France, Vieira de Mello was not where he wanted to be. After twenty-four years of service to the United Nations, he had happened to leave his mission area during one of the most important crises in UN history. Indeed, while NATO's first-ever air operation was under way on April 10, he had the surreal experience of receiving a phone call from Charles Kirudja, Akashi's chief of staff, who complained about personnel infighting in the office. Vieira de Mello rushed back to Zagreb on April 11, the day of the second strike, and found that the Serb offensive had not abated.

NATO's sparing use of air power—critics quickly branded the two attacks "pin-pricks"—revealed just how constrained NATO was by UN concerns about retaliation against peacekeepers. It also showed the limits, in mountain areas, of the gleaming laser-guided technology that had seemed invincible in the Persian Gulf War. Western commentators noted that, with its tepid uses of force, NATO resembled the proverbial elephant that had given birth to a mouse.[5] On April 12 the Serbs raided three of seven weapons-collection points that had been established outside Sarajevo in February, taking back heavy weapons from a cantonment as a result of NATO's ultimatum. By April 14, sensing that the UN and NATO were paralyzed, the Serbs had detained, placed under house arrest, or blocked the movement of 150 UN soldiers across Bosnia.[6] A New York Times headline summed up the letdown: "THE BLUFF THAT FAILED; SERBS AROUND GORAZDE ARE UNDETERRED BY NATO'S POLICY OF LIMITED AIR STRIKES."[7]

Having pushed for air power to be used, President Clinton tried to claim that international forces remained neutral. "I would remind the Serbs that we have taken no action, none, through NATO and with the support of the UN, to try to win a military victory for their adversaries," he said.[8] But Vieira de Mello saw that Clinton was trying to have it both ways: feeling good by standing up for the Bosnians but feeling safe by placating the Serbs. "This is Clinton's 'I didn't inhale' moment," he told me at our first dinner meeting. "He wants to please everyone at once."

At around 3 p.m. on April 15, the Bosnian defenses to the north and southeast of the town collapsed. The Serbs overran a UN observation post, pummeling a UN Land Rover north of Gorazde with machine-gun fire and seriously wounding two members of the elite squad of British officers that Rose had sent into Gorazde the previous week.

At just the time NATO might have struck back in retaliation for the attack on the British soldiers, Akashi was in the midst of a seven-hour meeting with Karadžić in his Pale headquarters.[9] John Almstrom, Akashi's Canadian military adviser, set up the secure satellite phone to NATO in the parking lot and carried the military maps of potential targets in his briefcase. "This was a bad dream," recalls Almstrom. "You are in Karadžić's office and you know you are probably going to bomb Karadžić." But unsurprisingly Akashi chose not to do so, opting instead to work with the Serbs to evacuate the wounded British soldiers.

Vieira de Mello had seen UN resolutions and observation posts trampled in Lebanon, but this time around he was the second-highest-ranking political official in the mission, beneath only Akashi. He could try to use his clout to alter UNPROFOR's course. But as he confessed to me that evening, he did not see a way out.

The following day, with the Serbs continuing their stampede toward Gorazde, Rose called for NATO air power for a third time, but on this occasion, in order to avoid inflaming Serb tempers, he informed Mladić that he had done so. At the sight of NATO planes, the forewarned Serb tanks shot down a British Sea Harrier with a shoulder-fired missile. Even though the pilot safely ejected and reunited with Rose's men in Gorazde, this was the first time in NATO history that it had ever lost a plane in a combat operation, and Admiral Leighton Smith, the American who commanded NATO forces, was furious. Smith said he was fed up with the restrictive rules of engagement insisted upon by Akashi and Rose. The tactical constraints and the UN's advance warnings to the Serbs were endangering his pilots.

Inside the UN safe area Bosnian military resistance had evaporated, and artillery rounds were falling in the town once every twenty seconds.[10] In Washington, U.S. national security adviser Anthony Lake said that the possibility of saving Gorazde was "very limited."[11] Back in New York the Bosnian representative to the UN, Muhamed Sacirbey, released a statement that said that the UN, the "most noble of institutions," had been "usurped into a chamber of false promises and rationalizations for inaction."[12]

No matter how aggressive the Serbs became, Vieira de Mello clung to the belief that full-on NATO air strikes were not compatible with UN neutrality, and that UN neutrality was the cornerstone of the UN system. He did what he could to defend UNPROFOR's dwindling reputation. In Zagreb he met with a delegation of Bosnian government officials who slammed the UN. He explained that UN Security Council Resolution 836, which created the six safe areas, had been "badly drafted" by the Council, "probably on purpose." But he spoke as though he lacked free will of his own. Since he and the peacekeepers had been told they could use military force only in self-defense, they were not to blame for their passivity. It never seemed to dawn on him that he might help shape the views of governments from within the system. Perhaps knowing that he was shirking responsibility and uncomfortable in doing so, he lashed out, repeating Serb accusations that the Bosnians kept weapons in the safe areas and adding, in an uncharacteristically hectoring tone, "You know it is true!" At the end of the meeting Bosnia's secretary for foreign affairs, Esad Suljić, issued a prophecy: If the UN did not step up immediately to protect Bosnians in Gorazde, the Serbs would attack the two other nearby safe areas. "Srebrenica and Zepa will be next," the Bosnian official said.[13]

While the Bosnians were desperate, the Serbs were flush with confidence. In Belgrade they stripped CNN, AFP, SKY, *Le Monde, Die Presse,* Radio Free Europe, and the *Christian Science Monitor* of their media accreditation.[14] Outside Sarajevo they overran a UN weapons-collection site under French guard and seized an additional eighteen antiaircraft guns. They fired four shells at the central bank in Gorazde, where UN officials slept and worked. The strike knocked out the UN telex system that the small UN team was using to file their reports.[15]

With the safe area seemingly written off, an Irish UNHCR doctor named Mary McLaughlin wrote a letter to UNHCR headquarters in Geneva that was leaked to the press. It read in part:

> Greetings from a city where only the dead are lucky. The last two days here are a living hell. Both residents and refugees have crowded into crumbling buildings, waiting for the next shell. When it hits, many are killed, as there are such crowds in each building.

The wounded lie for hours in the debris, as it is suicidal to try and bring them to the hospital.... The Serb excuse for targeting [the hospital] is that it is a military institution. I've been in all parts of the hospital 100 times in the last month and can assure the outside world that it's a lie.

... Presidents Clinton and Yeltsin want to hold talks about the future of Bosnia next month. There will be little left in Gorazde by then but corpses and rubble.[16]

Aid workers and peacekeepers throughout Bosnia understood that they were at a turning point. "Clearly it is a very sad week for the world," Rose admitted to the press.[17]

"THESE GUYS HAVE BALLS"

But just when all appeared lost, the United States and Russia conspired to preserve what was left of the Gorazde enclave. In the United States public criticism of the Clinton administration had been fierce. It was not merely civilians in Gorazde who were at stake. NATO, which had acted for the first time in its history, had suffered a major blow to its prestige. At a White House press conference President Clinton felt he had no choice but to ratchet up the threat of NATO air power.

But U.S. threats alone carried little clout. Luckily for Gorazde, Vitaly Churkin, Russia's envoy in the region, turned on the Serbs. He had spent a week shuttling between Pale and Belgrade and was fed up: "I have heard more broken promises in the past 48 hours [than] I have heard probably in the rest of my life." Upon returning to Moscow, he was even more emphatic. "The time for talking is over," he said. "The Bosnian Serbs must understand that by dealing with Russia, they are dealing with a great power and not a banana republic."[18] On April 19 President Yeltsin called on the Serbs to fulfill the promises they made to Russia. "Stop the attacks," he said. "Withdraw from Gorazde."[19] "Our professional patriots always talk about 'special relations with Serbia,'" an editorial in the Russian newspaper *Izvestia* said. "What does that mean? Approval of everything the Serbs do, even if they commit a crime?"[20] Vieira de Mello saw Russia's shift as a diplomatic breakthrough. "At last, perhaps, it will not be divided nations attempting to make peace," he told me, "but the *United* Nations." With Russia now standing behind NATO's hard-line condemnations, the Serbs would no longer be able to play the major powers off one another.

On April 22 the sixteen Western ambassadors to NATO issued an ultimatum in Brussels meant to rescue Gorazde. The Serbs were told that they had to cease firing around Gorazde immediately. By one minute after midnight GMT (2:01 a.m. Bosnia time) on April 24, Serb troops had to withdraw to two miles outside the town center and allow UN peacekeepers, relief convoys, and medical teams to enter. And by one minute after midnight GMT on April 27, they had to pull their heavy weapons (including tanks, artillery pieces, mortars, rocket launchers, missiles, and antiaircraft weapons) out of a twelve-mile exclusion zone similar to that which had been established around Sarajevo. If the Serbs did not comply with these terms, they would be bombed, and this time the air attacks would leave no doubt about NATO's seriousness. NATO pilots no longer had to find the offending weapons; they would be unleashed to strike at a range of military targets. NATO generals said they had picked out two dozen ammunition sites, fuel dumps, command bunkers, and gun posts around the area. Washington withdrew nonessential personnel and diplomats' families from Belgrade. "The plan is to bomb the crap out of them," one NATO official said.[21]

Because the UN still had peacekeepers on the ground, however, NATO would still not be able to bomb without getting the request from Rose and Akashi, who continued to worry about crossing the "Mogadishu line" and jeopardizing the safety of peacekeepers. Vieira de Mello and Akashi received permission from the Serbs to travel to Belgrade, where they hoped to negotiate a way out with—and for—Karadžić and Mladić. The UN officials preferred agreements to ultimatums, and irrespective of any NATO threats, they remained convinced that they could talk the Serbs out of taking Gorazde.

At the talks in Belgrade, the same day as the ultimatum, the UN delegation lined up on one side of the table, the Bosnian Serbs took seats opposite them, and Serbian president Slobodan Milošević, who was thought to be responsible for the war, served as the chair. On one occasion when General Mladić spoke up, Milošević snapped at him in English. "Will you shut the fuck up?!" Milošević's every gesture and statement seemed designed to show the UN who was boss but also to create the illusion that he was estranged from the field commander known to be bombarding Gorazde's civilians.

Instead of repenting, the Bosnian Serbs were more brazen than ever. Since NATO had carried out two air strikes, Karadžić said, "it will take us time to trust the UN again." When Akashi said he understood, his aide Izumi Nakamitsu passed a note to her colleague David Harland, saying, "This makes me sick."

Toward the end of the Serb-UN negotiations, which lasted from 1 p.m. to the late evening, Akashi asked how the UN might verify Serb compliance. Suddenly the Bosnian Serb vice president Nikola Koljevic spoke up: "Why doesn't Sergio go to Gorazde?" Vieira de Mello leaped to agree. "Sure," he said, "I'll go." The rest of the UN team was stunned. "It happened so fast and it was so last minute that we didn't see it coming," Almstrom, Akashi's military adviser, recalls. "I used to call him 'Sergio the gunfighter,' but this was ridiculous. I thought either he's got huge courage or he doesn't realize the implications of this. What if the Serbs don't pull their weapons back? Or what if they do and NATO bombs anyway?" The Serbs had a more cunning agenda. If Vieira de Mello led a UN team into Gorazde, NATO countries would be even more reluctant to bomb. Milošević adjourned the meeting with the deal nearly finalized. He urged both sides to shore up the remaining details in the morning. Delays were costly, the Serb leader said insincerely, "while people are dying."[22]

As the UN officials staggered out of the negotiations, Almstrom asked, "Sergio, what if the ultimatum fails and you get bombed?" Vieira de Mello shrugged. "The United Nations will just have to make sure the ultimatum doesn't fail, won't we?" Rose was thrilled when he learned that his friend would be the one with his finger on the UN trigger. He lent him a sleeping bag and a pair of British army boots for the trip.[23] In a classic testament to the lack of synchronization between UNPROFOR and NATO, the UN's agreement with the Serbs was drafted using local time, creating a two-hour time difference between it and the deadlines in the NATO ultimatum, which were issued in Greenwich mean time.

Remarkably, at the very time the Belgrade negotiations were under way, the Serbs had gone right on shelling Gorazde. A UN observer wrote from Gorazde: "Team leader's assessment: These guys have balls." The UN team had recorded fifty-five shell explosions in Gorazde in one ten-minute period. "They have blatantly increased their aggressive activities in the face of the NATO ultimatum," the UN observer noted.[24] Major Pat Stogran, the thirty-six-year-old head of the UN military observer team in Gorazde, sent several consecutive panicked messages to headquarters and heard nothing back. He finally threatened to stop sending reports. "If you had any idea of the situation on the ground here you would understand the futility of the messages that we are sending off into the dark expanse," he wrote. "It is embarrassing that I, as the senior representative of UNPROFOR, cannot advise the local civilian and military authorities of the activities of UNPROFOR except that which we glean from BBC."[25]

More than twenty people in Gorazde would be killed the day of Vieira de Mello's trip to Belgrade.[26]

BREAKING THE SIEGE, BLOCKING AIR STRIKES

Critics pounced on the UN deal. Vieira de Mello's verification team seemed to be walking into a trap with their eyes open, as if they were willfully placing themselves in harm's way in order to supply the Serbs with potential hostages and foil any potential NATO attack. He ignored the grumblings and focused on the task he had been assigned. From the airport in Belgrade, he telephoned UNPROFOR headquarters in Zagreb and put out the word that he was looking for UN volunteers. When he received phone calls back, he did not try to sugarcoat the mission. "I warn you," he told interested staff, "you might end up trapped in Gorazde or NATO might bomb." He flew to Zagreb for a few hours in order to pack, then flew to Sarajevo, where he stopped into the Bosnian Presidency to explain the mission to Prime Minister Silajdžić, who had broken off contact with Akashi and Rose. "You know that by going you are ensuring NATO does not use force again?" Silajdžić said. Vieira de Mello did not respond. "Good luck anyway, my friend," Silajdžić said. "Be careful."

Around 8 p.m. on Saturday, April 23, Vieira de Mello met up with a large UN convoy at Sarajevo airport. The convoy included 40 medical personnel, 100 Ukrainians who reported to a French general, and 15 political officers and civilian police who reported to him. Anthony Banbury, who had been with the UN in Cambodia, had arrived in Bosnia earlier in the month. When he heard that Vieira de Mello had issued the call for volunteers, he made his way to the snowy airport in hopes of earning a spot on the team. Banbury

Vieira de Mello and UN General André Soubirou planning to enter Gorazde.

walked to the lead vehicle in the convoy, where Vieira de Mello was seated with his French bodyguard, and tapped on the glass of the armored personnel carrier. The French soldier opened the door and raised his machine gun as a barrier to keep Banbury away. "It's okay, it's okay," Vieira de Mello said, smiling broadly at the young American, whom he had not seen since Cambodia. "Tony, what are you doing here?!" Although he had been impatient to depart, he stepped out of his vehicle and inquired about Banbury's recent posting in Haiti and his plans with UNPROFOR. "There we were in the dark, at the Sarajevo airport with gunfire going off in the background, the UN mission crumbling, and the NATO threat of air strikes hanging over us," recalls Banbury. "And Sergio calmly emerged from the armored personnel carrier and made me feel, for those few minutes, like nothing in the world was more important than me." Vieira de Mello instructed the French soldier to make room for Banbury in one of the vehicles, and the convoy set off in the dark.

They arrived on the outskirts of Gorazde just after midnight. Vieira de Mello saw houses still burning, dead animals on the roadside, and crowds of refugees crammed into the roofless hulks of charred houses. He drove into town and headed to the central bank, where he found Stogran and the other UN observers looking exhausted and unshaven. "The only food left here is what is left of UNHCR rations," the Canadian told him.

The next morning, Vieira de Mello gathered his small political team for a morning meeting. Groggy UN officials found their boss looking meticulously groomed. "What did you do?" Banbury asked. "Pack a shower in your suitcase?" "If we look our best," he replied, "we will remind people here of the dignity they used to have. And we will show them that the siege has been broken." When Mark Baskin, a forty-one-year-old American, asked, "What should we do?" Vieira de Mello answered, "Walk around." "Walk around for what?" Baskin asked. "Show the flag," Vieira de Mello said. "Then the people will know that the UN has come to town."

Although the shooting had largely stopped, team members saw bullet casings, shrapnel, pockmarks, and bloodstains on the buildings. Vieira de Mello was determined to make the UN as visible as possible, and he was intrepid in that pursuit. Surrounded by UNPROFOR soldiers decked out in helmets and Kevlar, he strode around town in slacks and a winter parka, crossing the downtown bridge that had been the scene of fierce battles. The sound of gunfire and the presence of Serb militiamen hardly seemed to register with him. "We were completely surrounded," recalls Nick Costello, a Serbian-speaking British UN officer. "We were vulnerable from all the high ground, and as we drove around in our shiny white vehicles, we made ripe targets." Vieira de Mello's nonchalance was strategic. "Normalcy is returning to Gorazde," he told his aides. "If we show the people that we are not afraid, we can ease their own fears. If we act as though life is normal, life will become more normal."

Stogran, who had felt ignored by his UN superiors when it mattered, was suddenly overwhelmed by UN officials who had not suffered through the siege and yet who now overran his team's meager resources. He had used diesel containers to store water from the local river in case of emergencies, but he found the newcomers unthinkingly pouring the river water into the generator, believing it was fuel. "This is classic UN," Vieira de Mello said to Stogran, acknowledging the strain he must have felt. "So many chefs, we can't even find the kitchen!"

Stogran found the self-styled "UN saviors" uncurious about the past and sanctimonious about how the Serbs and Bosnians could be brought into line in the future. Though they had never set foot in Gorazde before, they had their maps and their preexisting assumptions and asked few questions. But Vieira de Mello was different. "You were the voice of this place," he told Stogran. "You made it far harder for the politicians to look away." The beleaguered major was touched. "After every conversation with Sergio," he recalls, "I walked away feeling a deep and totally novel sense of calm."

At around 5 p.m. on Vieira de Mello's first full day in Gorazde, the Serbs began to leave the town in accordance with the ultimatum. But as they retreated, they adopted a scorched-earth policy, blowing up houses and the sole water-pumping station in the area. Vieira de Mello was incensed. "This was the most outraged I had ever seen him," recalls Costello. "He was full of passion, his voice was trembling, but at the same time he was trying to maintain his charm with the Serbs."

At midnight he and Costello drove in their Land Rover to a village called Kopaci on the outskirts of town. The Serbs were blocking the entry of a second UN supply convoy, and he hoped to negotiate its release. A line of UNHCR relief trucks stood stalled roadside, while the surrounding hills blazed with fire. Suddenly, in the headlights, he spotted the burly figure of General Mladić, who was yelling about the desecration of the town's old Serbian Orthodox church. When Mladić saw him, he seemed pleased and beckoned him. Mladić used Costello's flashlight to steer them to the graveyard behind the church, where he directed Vieira de Mello's attention to the smashed headstones and to the freshly dug graves of Serb soldiers who had died in recent fighting. Vieira de Mello, who was not entirely comfortable being led into the pitch black by this suspected war criminal, noticed that Mladić was weeping. "Don't ever forget what you have seen here," Mladić said. He shook Vieira de Mello's hand and said he would at last allow the stalled UN relief convoy to proceed into Gorazde. It was 2 a.m.[27]

Vieira de Mello did not have a big enough team or enough time to thoroughly certify whether the Serbs had withdrawn all their heavy weapons from the twelve-mile exclusion zone. As he told the press, "In these hills and forests, we don't have the means to tell you they are clear."[28] But this was somewhat disingenuous. He knew that he did not want to see NATO air strikes, and as the person who would determine whether the Serbs were in violation of NATO's terms, he had the power to prevent them. Costello remembers the exchange that preceded Vieira de Mello's final communication with Akashi before he announced his verdict: "Sergio asked us, nudge nudge, wink wink, 'Have you verified the weapons are out of the exclusion zone?' and we said, 'Yes, we have.' We lied to NATO," recalls Costello. "We knew NATO was itching to do air strikes and we knew it would have been the wrong thing to do. We physically couldn't check all the sites—we had run out of time—but we also knew that confirming Serb compliance was what was best for everyone."

Vieira de Mello even compromised on the two-mile area in the center of town that was meant to be free of soldiers. As early as April 25 Serb militia were found there. The Serbs said these police had remained so as to protect Serb civilians, but the "policemen" were obviously soldiers who had just changed from green army to blue police uniforms. Vieira de Mello opted to let the matter rest.

On April 27 Akashi declared publicly that the Serbs were in "effective compliance" with the ultimatum. Thus, for a second time in two months, he announced that he would not call for NATO air power.[29]

The Bosnians were crushed, as they knew that their only lasting reprieve would come if NATO stopped the Serbs militarily, and UNPROFOR seemed intent on preventing that from happening. But Vieira de Mello made the implausible claim that he had acted in accordance with the will of the Bosnian people. "I was in Gorazde. I spoke with the inhabitants," he told a Croatian journalist. "The majority of them agreed with me, because if we had struck from the air, they would have been worse off."[30]

MUDDLING ALONG

Although Vieira de Mello had spent only four days in Gorazde, he returned to Zagreb with a new mystique. Izumi Nakamitsu, Akashi's special assistant, saw him back at headquarters and inquired, "Weren't you frightened about being bombed?" He smiled. "Izumi, please, you know they would never bomb while I was there." Most people recalled his grace under pressure. The tales of his brushing his teeth with Italian mineral water fed his increasingly hallowed persona.

Akashi contentedly took credit for the apparent calming of tensions. He responded to a congratulatory message from Secretary-General Boutros-Ghali with a letter of his own:

Mr. Secretary-General,

I am touched by your kind message. I am proud that UNPROFOR has again proved its ability to control a dangerous situation. Under your wise guidance I will continue to serve the cause of our Organization by combining firmness with flexibility and by harnessing power with diplomacy.

Kindest regards,
Yasushi Akashi[31]

But flush with confidence, Akashi then sparked a minidrama at UN Headquarters in New York, causing already substantial fissures between the United States and the UN to widen. Washington, the UN's largest funder, had always been hard on the organization for its financial laxity. But as the isolationist wing of the Republican Party gained strength in the post–cold war world, some members of Congress had started calling for outright withdrawal from the UN, and both Republicans and Democrats had begun invoking UN peacekeeping failures in Somalia and Bosnia as grounds for cutting off vital U.S. funds. The normally reserved Akashi gave an interview to the *New York Times* in which he suggested that since Somalia, the United States had lost its nerve, becoming "somewhat reticent, somewhat afraid, timid and tentative," avoiding putting its own troops where they were needed to help in "situations like Gorazde."[32] Akashi, who was himself extremely timid, wanted U.S. troops on the ground because he felt U.S. officials would then share his opposition to using air power. But Madeleine Albright, the U.S. ambassador to the UN, lit into Akashi, calling it "totally counterproductive for an international civil servant to be criticizing any government" and adding that UN officials "should remember where their salaries are paid." Appearing before the UN Security Council, Albright warned, "Statements such as these cannot help but call into question the utility of further U.S. contributions, financial or otherwise, to UN peacekeeping. It is no secret that at present UN peacekeeping is not popular among either the American people or the U.S. Congress."[33]

While Akashi's statement had been manifestly accurate, Albright's rebuttal made it clear who buttered Akashi's bread. There was simply no way, structurally, that a senior official in the UN could get away with publicly criticizing the wealthiest and most powerful country in the organization.

And the hole Akashi was digging for himself grew deeper. In early May he crossed a line that stunned even his harshest critics: He instructed UNPROFOR peacekeepers to escort Serb tanks through the heavy weapons exclusion zone ringing Sarajevo, effectively using blue helmets to shield offensive weapons that were being transferred for use at another battlefront. Vieira de Mello could not believe his ears when he received news of Akashi's blunder. "Here was Sergio, who spent hours every day cultivating these relationships, and finessing these incredibly intricate deals, and suddenly Akashi offers to help the Serbs move their weapons," recalls Simon Shadbolt, Rose's military assistant. "He was horrified." So was Prime Minister Silajdžić, who declared, "Whatever credibility the UN and the international community had has been ruined . . . by the behavior of UN representatives here."[34] U.S. Senate minority leader Bob Dole called for Akashi's resignation. "Akashi's approach is one of appeasement," Dole said in a statement:

> He meets with war criminals and calls them friends. And when the United States refuses to send soldiers under UN command, he calls us timid. Akashi should be sent packing to a post far away where his weakness and indecisiveness will not cost lives . . . UN officials speak of the need for neutrality as though they are referees in a sports match. The problem is that this game is aggression.[35]

When I saw Vieira de Mello in Zagreb and asked him what he thought of what became known as "tank-gate," he was unwilling as ever to break ranks. He went as far as he could, answering, "Not ideal."

With Akashi discredited, Vieira de Mello became the only senior UN official whom the Bosnian government would see. Although he had supported the approach taken by Akashi and Rose, he somehow escaped criticism. "He was a man first, a UN official second," explains Silajdžić. "He always made us feel he understood our point of view and was brainstorming constantly to help us get what we needed. He didn't hide behind the usual UN excuses." Although Gorazde was no longer being shelled, the enclave was still racked by violence. UN troops were being shot at by both sides, and Serb troops returned inside the two-mile zone. "It is tense," Mark Baskin, the UN political officer, wrote from Gorazde. "We seek direction."[36]

Vieira de Mello felt as though he had little to offer. UN peacekeepers were back in a situation much like that in southern Lebanon, where they had been bossed about by Israeli troops and their Christian proxies. Just as he had done then for General Callaghan, he drafted letters of protest on his boss's behalf. As then, he could only warn Karadžić that if he didn't remove Serb gunmen from Gorazde, "I shall have no alternative but to report to the Secretary-General of the United Nations and, through him, to the Security Council."[37] The Serbs knew that they could do as they pleased. A Karadžić aide wrote back mischievously that the armed Serbs in the Gorazde exclusion zone were not in fact soldiers—they just could not find "anything to wear" other than uniforms.[38] Vieira de Mello knew that the UN could not keep traveling to the brink and back. "We must get away from this succession of exclusion zones, violations, cease-fires which go nowhere," he told reporters at a press conference. "We need a political solution."[39]

He wondered if a Cyprus-like stalemate was the best that the former Yugoslavia could hope for. At a May 10 meeting with a delegation of potential donors, he exclaimed dogmatically that in the Balkans "hatred is the bottom line!"[40] He saw that the UN brand could end up permanently soiled if it remained implicated in a mission that was no more achievable than Somalia had been. The countries on the Security Council that had sent the peacekeepers to Bosnia with an ambiguous mandate and insufficient means were the ones letting the Bosnians down. But it was the "UN," and not the responsible individual governments, that would take the blame. "Americans are justifiably wary about putting troops at the United Nations' disposal," said a *New York Times* editorial. "UN troops in Bosnia are empowered to do little more than flash their blue berets and count the Serb shells obliterating Gorazde." The editorial hailed a new U.S. presidential directive that placed strict limits on U.S. funding and participation in UN peacekeeping missions.[41]

When Rose first arrived in Bosnia, he had been eager to push the boundaries of the UN mandate. But he had grown similarly resigned. "The guns could be heading for their next offensive," he said. "If somebody wants to fight a war here, a peacekeeping force cannot stop it."[42] Under his command UNPROFOR would not call in NATO air strikes to protect civilians. "We took peacekeeping as far as it could go," Rose said. "We took it right to the line."[43] The Serbs, who carefully tracked all international statements, took heed. With no threat of NATO air power hanging overhead, the Serbs treated UNPROFOR as a nuisance that they could manipulate or ignore.

While Vieira de Mello had hoped to use humanitarian achievements to bring about political change, by the late summer of 1994 it was clear that international heavyweights like the United States, Russia, and Europe would have to step up their commitments if they were to negotiate a peace to save civilians. UNPROFOR was increasingly unable even to deliver food to hungry civilians. In July the Serbs suspended UN aid convoys into Sarajevo. On July 20, after several UN planes were hit by Serb gunfire, the UN stopped sending in relief by air. And on July 27 Bosnian Serb leader Karadžić sent a letter to UN authorities announcing the closure of Vieira de Mello's precious Blue Routes, which had done so much to restore life in the Bosnian capital. Some 160,000 civilians and 32,000 vehicles had made use of the open roads.[44] But after a four-month reprieve, the Serbs were strangling Sarajevo once again. What Vieira de Mello did not seem to recognize was that by covering up Serb violations rather than appealing to Western countries for sustained help, UNPROFOR was actually reducing the odds of a stronger Western stand. He, Akashi, and Rose were making it easier for powerful governments to look away.

He plodded ahead, attempting to negotiate a large prisoner exchange. Bosnian vice president Ejup Ganic asked how Vieira de Mello could trust the Serbs to free prisoners when in the previous two months they had deported some two thousand elderly Bosnians from the town of Bjeljina. "I appreciate Mr. Vieira de Mello's optimism," Ganic said at a press conference. "But for God's sake, they are expelling thousands of people from their homes, putting them into labour and concentration camps."[45] Vieira de Mello relayed the statements made by Bosnian Serb leader Karadžić as if they were reliable. "[Karadžić] assured us this was not his policy, that this was obviously contrary to the interests and the reputation of the Bosnian Serbs and that he was taking every possible measure, including the replacement of the police chief of Bjeljina, so as to bring these practices to an end," he said credulously.[46] The longer he remained a part of the flawed UNPROFOR mission, the more he sounded as though he had stopped seeing the facts as they were. For the first time in his career, he seemed to be valuing the UN's interest in looking good over civilians' interest in being safe.

He had been a consistent supporter of the nascent UN war crimes tribunal that had been set up in The Hague in 1993 to punish crimes carried out in the former Yugoslavia. Even if he was willing to "black box" the brutal deeds of suspected war criminals in his negotiations, he believed it was important that the UN system as a whole find a way to punish the perpetrators of atrocity. He had argued this position over Akashi's objections. Yet by the fall of 1994 he was so dispirited that he started contradicting his own beliefs. He sat down with the *Washington Post's* John Pomfret and discussed the role that grievances from the Second World War were playing in fueling the Balkan crisis. "These people should just forget," he said sharply. He compared the military rule in Argentina with that in Brazil and argued that the reason Brazil had managed to move on, while Argentina still seemed mired in recriminations over its past, was that Brazilians had decided to let go of their pain. Pomfret challenged him, arguing that it was precisely the failure to reckon with previous crimes that had made it easier for Serb extremists to rally their people to pursue long-sought revenge. This time around, when the wars ended, some form of accountability for the atrocities and some attempt at closure were essential. Vieira de Mello said he disagreed, calling the idea "very American." When Pomfret, a China expert, said that in fact he had learned these lessons in China, where the crimes of the Great Leap Forward and Cultural Revolution had been covered up at considerable cost, Vieira de Mello shook his head. "China is on the right track," he argued. "Remembering history will only slow them down."

In September he traveled to Pale to attempt to defuse tensions between UNPROFOR and the Serbs. When Karadžić lectured him about the UN's "intolerable" pro-Muslim bias, he said he understood the Serbs' bitterness but rejected their allegations. "The UN *is* impartial," he said. "Our efforts to seek peace in the Balkans are benefiting all sides equally." And then to underscore the point he admitted, "NATO intervention might have been far more serious if not for UNPROFOR's restraint." Karadžić knew this to be true, but he countered that "UNPROFOR's presence had prevented the total defeat of the Muslims."[47] Here Karadžić too was correct.

Despite the mounting indications that he and UNPROFOR were ad-

dressing symptoms and not causes, Vieira de Mello kept his focus on tactical
humanitarian gains. He began his final negotiations on prisoner exchanges on
September 30, 1994. The talks began in the morning, and the parties spent
the entire day feuding. As the discussions dragged on past midnight, French
UN officials began serving whiskey and plum brandy. Several people drank so
much that they passed out in their chairs. Vieira de Mello, who was returning
to UNHCR in Geneva the following week, would not be denied. As dawn
broke, after twenty hours of negotiation, the Bosnians and the Serbs settled
on the terms of the lengthy agreement, which would allow for the release
of more than three hundred prisoners. All that was left was for him to add
his official signature.

However, when Darko Mocibob, a Bosnian UN official, began translating the annexes to the agreement, Vieira de Mello realized that, during the
bathroom breaks, the parties had struck a number of side deals benefiting
their friends and families. As Mocibob translated the handwritten side texts,
he watched a frown come over his boss's face. "I could hardly suppress my
laughter as I read him the additional terms, which none of us had expected,"
Mocibob recalls. "It was 'when Mehmed is released to the other side, he can
carry 400 deutsch marks and 5 kilos of tobacco. Milos will be allowed to
bring his pistol. And all the returnees will all be able to carry shoe glue.'"
Vieira de Mello was desperate to close the deal, but not at the expense of the
UN's prestige. He refused to affix his signature to the private bargains. "I'm
very happy for you that you have reached this agreement," he said, too tired
to be amused. "But you'll have to find somebody else to be a witness. I am
a senior official with the United Nations." Only when the parties removed
their side annexes did he agree to sign.

The UNPROFOR mission was neither effective nor respected. Vieira de
Mello had been away from UNHCR for a year and was due back. In one
of his final interviews, he said he was leaving the region with a "bitter taste
in my mouth."[48] Yet while he would not miss the humiliations, he would
miss the people, the drama, and the global stakes. At a farewell reception at
UN headquarters in Zagreb, his colleagues presented him with a parting
gift of a framed photograph of the trams running along Sniper's Alley in
Sarajevo, with children running nearby. One UN official joked, "Just think,
Sergio, one of those children might be yours." Vieira de Mello smiled po-

litely, but as Elisabeth Naucler, his Finnish aide, recalls, "He could have done without it."

He conducted a mini–farewell tour of the former Yugoslavia. In Zagreb he bade a stiff farewell to Croatian president Franjo Tudjman, whom he had never liked. In Belgrade he pounded the pavement of the old city, looking for a gift for Serbian president Slobodan Milošević. In the end he settled on a painting, which he presented at a warm final meeting in the Presidential Palace in downtown Belgrade. In Sarajevo, the city that had stolen his heart, he said good-bye to President Izetbegović, and Prime Minister Silajdžić, whom he now considered a close friend.

What was most remarkable about his departure was that each of the feuding factions had come to believe he was their ally. "How many UN officials do you think would be sent off like that by all sides?" asks Vladislav Guerassev, who headed the UN office in Belgrade. "It shows you what a remarkable diplomat he was." But during a bloody and morally fraught conflict in which the Serb side committed the bulk of the atrocities, his popularity with wrongdoers stemmed in part from his moral relativism. Even though he was unfailingly kind to Bosnian *individuals,* he had lost sight of the big picture. He seemed more interested in being liked and in maintaining access than in standing up for those who were suffering. He had brought a traditional approach to peacekeeping to a radically novel set of circumstances. And uncharacteristically, he had failed to adapt. Although Vieira de Mello was unaware of it, his seeming eagerness to side with strength had caused some of his critical UN colleagues to nickname him "Serbio." It would take a massacre in another of the UN's "safe areas" to jolt him into the belated recognition that impartial peacekeeping between two unequal sides was its own form of side-taking.

Nine

IN RETROSPECT

Vieira de Mello was demoralized by his time in the Balkans, but he was not yet ashamed. Impartiality was such a bedrock UN principle and his daily activities had so consumed him that he had not yet questioned his or the UN's performance.

When he returned to Geneva in October 1994 he also had more prosaic matters on his mind. For starters, he was not sure whether High Commissioner Ogata would welcome him back. Ogata had qualities that Vieira de Mello admired. New to the UN, she disdained organizational habits that had been reflexively passed from one generation of UN officials and aid workers to the next. She was unafraid to speak her mind. UN staff in Geneva joked that in the male-dominated UN, Ogata kept a box outside her office, accompanied by a sign that read: PLEASE BE SURE TO DEPOSIT YOUR BALLS IN THE BOX BEFORE ENTERING. Vieira de Mello referred to Ogata as "La Vieille" (the Old Lady) and the "Diminutive Giant," terms of both endearment and respect.

But no matter how long he interacted with her, he never felt as though he knew her. She did not have the personal warmth that he most valued in people. Her eagerness to "put UNHCR on the map" had caused UNHCR to compete with agencies with which it had once collaborated. He still ventured into their one-on-one lunches with apprehension, sometimes dramatically grabbing his stomach and feigning physical cramps to show his amused colleagues the physical toll of his anxiety. Before entering her office, he would sigh, shake his head, and mockingly offer one of his favorite expressions: "Ahhh, the things I must do in service of humanity!"

Having been away from UNHCR headquarters in Geneva for three years while in Cambodia and the former Yugoslavia, Vieira de Mello expected to undergo an uncomfortable period of hazing, and it duly followed. He saw the UN holistically, as a system with many complementary parts, but Ogata saw other branches of the UN—such as the Department of Peacekeeping Operations for which he had worked in Bosnia—as competition. Toward the end of his time in the Balkans, she had grudgingly written to Kofi Annan, who was running the peacekeeping department in New York, that UNHCR was "under extreme strain" and that she wished Vieira de Mello "could have been around to help me tackle these crises." The absence of staff of his caliber, she had written, "was jeopardizing the capacity of my Office to answer adequately to emergencies."[1]

But since Annan was closer to Boutros-Ghali, the boss, he had gotten Vieira de Mello's leave from UNHCR extended three times. "For Ogata if you work at Toyota, you stay at Toyota until the end," recalls Kamel Morjane, then director of the Africa Division at UNHCR. "Sergio decided to leave Toyota and work at Honda. When he returned, he had to be subjected to a new test. He had to prove his loyalty." Ogata now denies that she was testing him and claims she had no objection to his lengthy leave. "What Sergio was doing in Bosnia was rather limited compared to what we in UNHCR were doing," she says. "There were many brilliant officials in UNHCR that I could call upon in his absence." She could often sound as though his emerging public profile was a threat to her own.

For all of her downplaying of Vieira de Mello's assets, Ogata was very fond of him. When she was invited to meet the queen of England, she told her aides that she was tempted to invite him rather than her own husband. Ogata also understood that she would not be able to keep him by her side at UNHCR if she did not reward his manifest talents. The repatriation of 360,000 refugees to Cambodia, followed so swiftly by his high-profile trip into Gorazde, had earned him praise far beyond the humanitarian community. She valued his Rolodex and his pragmatic and creative approach to crises, as well as the fact that he did not get bogged down in ideology. "Sergio was a problem-solver," she recalls. "I got the impression he agreed with my way of doing things." Ogata told him that she would create a new post of director of policy planning and operations just for him. This made him the number three official at UNHCR, an agency that then employed five thousand sta The position of director of operations had not been refilled at UNH since Thomas Jamieson had left it to retire in 1972, so history had come full circle. Ogata also promised him that she would work to get his new position bumped up to assistant secretary-general, which was the third-highest rank in the UN system. This would happen in January 1996.

Ogata asked him to organize what she hoped would be a pathbreaking intergovernmental summit to address the problems of displacement and migration in the former Soviet Union. Russia wanted to use the conference to earn international sympathy and money to support the twenty-five million ethnic Russians who were being discriminated against in and sometimes even expelled from Ukraine, Estonia, Lithuania, and the other former Soviet republics.* UNHCR hoped to gather leaders to get them to agree to broader legislation that would protect minorities and guarantee freedom of movement across boundaries.[2]

He enlisted a twenty-seven-year-old Italian named Claire Messina, who had written her Ph.D. on Russian migration, to help manage the process. "Most senior people pretend they know things," Messina recalls. "Sergio saw no shame in saying, 'I don't know anything about the region. Tell me what to do and I'll do it.'" He also persuaded Viktor Andreev, the Russian with whom he had worked closely in Bosnia, to move to Geneva to join his team. Although Andreev was notoriously lazy and Messina did most of the work herself, Vieira de Mello did not seem to mind. He explained the hire by saying, "First, we need a Russian in this process. And second, Viktor is very loyal. He never played games with me in Bosnia. He was straight. And for a Russian in the Balkans that was very rare." In fact, hiring a Russian national for such a politically sensitive conference was more likely to alienate non-Russians. But for Vieira de Mello, loyalty and personal history more than compensated.

The conference, which would be held in May 1996, would prove something of a bust, as the governments that attended would largely limit themselves to reciting old complaints rather than devising new guidelines to meet the challenges of discrimination and migration. Nonetheless Vieira de Mello enjoyed the groundwork. In 1995 he traveled to Armenia, Azerbaijan, Belarus, Georgia, Kazakhstan, Kyrgyzstan, Moldova, Russia, Tajikistan, Turkmenistan, Ukraine, and Uzbekistan, where he briefed senior officials and heard their concerns. The combination of his new UN rank, the contacts he had amassed

---

*Between 1992 and 1996 some three million Russians had fled the other republics for Russia.

over the years, and the public profile he had established for himself in Bosnia
meant that, on his visits to the former Soviet Union, he gained entrée at an
entirely new level: with heads of state and foreign ministers. "Are you not
impressed that prime ministers drop everything to see me?" he asked his new
special assistant Izumi Nakamitsu, who had been Akashi's aide in the Balkans.
"Don't get carried away," she reminded him. "These are prime ministers from
very small countries." He stuck his tongue out at her in pretend offense.

His steady climb through the ranks of the UN had not stripped him of
his unusual regard for the individuals in whose name UN programs were run.
On one trip in September 1996 to Azerbaijan, a country that had been at war
with Armenia over the province of Nagorno Karabakh, the deputy foreign
minister escorted him around a sprawling refugee camp. The country was
teeming with refugees, as one in eight Azerbaijanis had been displaced by the
conflict. The fetid camp was starting to acquire the air of permanence that
Jamieson had so despised. Individual refugees approached him to share their
grievances. He told them he was meeting with the president of the country
later in the day and asked, "Is there a message that I can deliver on your behalf?" At the start of his tour of the camp, he chatted at length with an elderly
woman, probably in her late seventies, who described the melancholy she felt
at being unable to return to her rural home. He continued speaking with
other camp residents, with Azerbaijani officials, and with UN field workers.
After an hour the deputy foreign minister steered him toward the camp exit,
where his official limousine waited. Suddenly, just as he was about to enter
the vehicle, he stopped. "I need to find that old lady again," he said.

The delegation made its way back to the woman's battered tent, where she
remained standing outside. "What do you miss the most?" Vieira de Mello
asked the woman. "I am a proud person," she said through a translator. "My
whole life I have lived alone, and I have worked the land myself. I have never
depended on anybody for anything. And now here I am for three years dependent on handouts from the UN. It is very hard." She looked down at the
ground. "And what do you want for yourself?" he asked. She looked straight
at him and said simply: "I want to go up into the sky and become a cloud.
And then as a cloud, I want to travel through the sky many miles to where
my home is, and when I see my land, I want to turn into rain, and fall from
the sky, landing in the soil so I can remain forever in the place that I belong."
He shook his head in wonder. He knew how unlikely it was that the crisis

in Nagorno Karabakh would be resolved in her lifetime, but he promised he would do what he could. "A wounded soul may hurt as much as a wounded body," he often told colleagues.[3]

He moved naturally between refugee camps and the capital cities where he made his appeals for diplomatic interventions or financial resources. He was increasingly popular in Washington. Many of those he had encountered over the years at U.S. embassies or in the refugee world had amassed power in the Clinton administration. Still, when he visited town, he would feign irritation with Dawn Calabia, the UNHCR official who managed his schedule. "These people are too low level. Why can't you get me a meeting with the secretary of state, the vice president, or the president?" he said. "Just wait," Calabia replied. "When the president actually needs you for something, then you'll get that meeting."

He did not like the ritual of paying homage to midlevel officialdom. "These people should come to me," he would say, pointing to the schedule, sometimes with genuine indignation and sometimes with contrived pomposity: "That way, I can wear my jeans, and you can supply the cold beer." There were only two categories of people he really wanted to meet with: old friends and people who could be useful to him in tackling the crises of the day. "Why do I have to meet him?" he would groan. "Why does it have to be me? I only have eight hours in this town and no time to breathe and you want me to waste my time with him?"

He was most comfortable in Southeast Asia. Six years after helping to negotiate the plan to resettle Vietnamese boat people, he was able to personally oversee the closure of the refugee camps in the region. Although he took pride in his role, his mind was drifting to the political sphere. On the plane ride to Hanoi, where once he would have consumed situation reports on refugee housing and education needs, he instead read Robert McNamara's *In Retrospect,* the former U.S. secretary of defense's reckoning with the Vietnam War. When Nakamitsu asked him his view of the book, he shook his head. "Some people can't say 'in retrospect,'" he said. "It's too late."

Whenever he was in Geneva for more than a month, he grew restless. On the wall of his office, he had hung his framed photograph of the Sarajevo tram, alongside the bronze plaques given to him by UN peacekeeping units in Lebanon and Bosnia, and the flag of the Montagnards whom he had helped resettle from Cambodia to North Carolina. On his desk he kept the framed photograph of Jamieson. Beside his computer he kept a shoebox.

One day Nakamitsu inquired about the contents of the box. "That is the box of possibilities," he told her. "Inside are the names of people who have impressed me over the years. Someday when I run my own mission, I will call upon those people, and we will put together a dream team." He opened up the box, and she peered inside to see Vieira de Mello's professional confetti: hundreds of business cards and handwritten names and numbers scribbled onto napkins, hotel stationery, and fragments of bar coasters. She marveled at the variety of names he had gathered—government officials, unheralded UN field officers, soldiers, journalists, bodyguards, even the salesperson who had sold him his home air conditioner.

He retained the names of others as well—those who he felt had let him down. As sensitive to impingements on his own dignity as he was to those on others', he was not one to forget even imagined slights. A small piece of paper with the name "Tim Wirth" remained pinned beneath his stapler on his desk for more than a year. Once, when he had traveled to Washington for meetings, Wirth, who was undersecretary of state for global affairs in the Clinton administration, had been unable to receive him. "One day Tim Wirth will ask me for a meeting," he told Nakamitsu, "and I will turn it down." It wasn't just the lack of access that got to him. As she recalls, "Sergio took the snub as one more sign that the United States didn't take the UN seriously." Even though Wirth was perhaps the biggest backer of the UN in the Clinton administration—so big that after he left office he would take over the UN Foundation, funded by Ted Turner, and would lead the effort to improve the UN's standing in the eyes of Americans—Vieira de Mello carried the grudge.

Since he and Nakamitsu had worked in the Balkans at the same time, they spent a lot of time discussing UNPROFOR, the Balkan mission that continued to founder in their absence. He always defended the mission, believing the peacekeepers were doing more good than harm for civilians. He also refrained from publicly jabbing the major powers on the UN Security Council, who continued to bring great bombast but insufficient resolve to the conflict. In Geneva, where UNHCR civilian relief workers were seen to be outperforming the UNPROFOR peacekeepers, he insisted that the blue helmets were getting a bad rap: UNHCR food convoys would not be able to reach civilians amid such violence were they not escorted by UN soldiers. In addition, he said, the peacekeepers were guarding heavy-weapons collection points around Sarajevo, and they had helped end the siege of Gorazde.

But as the months wore on and he acquired the distance to reflect on UNPROFOR's performance, he changed his mind. He suddenly became plagued by memories of the UN's timidity and, he feared, its complicity. He reflected critically on the way he and other UNPROFOR officials had downplayed Serb brutality in order to stop NATO from using air power. UNPROFOR was the first peacekeeping force to be given a humanitarian mandate in the context of "an all-out and merciless war," he wrote. "A greater contradiction in terms and, indeed, on the ground, would have been difficult to achieve."[4] He wrote of the "senselessness of providing relief where there was no security, where shelling and sniper fire took their daily toll on those recently 'assisted.'"[5] Absent political remedies, the humanitarian aid deliveries were a "frustrating palliative." He worried privately that he had become what critic David Rieff called a "cultist of the small victory"—so consumed by small humanitarian tasks that he had lost sight of how best to make a meaningful difference.[6]

He finally stopped treating the UN Security Council's Resolution 836, which had established Sarajevo, Gorazde, and Srebrenica as "safe areas," as worth probing for guidance, later referring to it simply as a "museum piece of irresponsible political and military behavior." He confessed to one reporter that "you would get up in Sarajevo during that fucking winter and look at yourself in the mirror and wonder whether we were not the wardens of a huge concentration camp."[7] By failing to protect the "safe areas" and effectively forcing civilians to remain in their squalor, he said, Western countries and international institutions had exposed "the limits of our own moral conscience." He finally even felt comfortable joking about Akashi. "Akashi is amoral and inhumane," he told colleagues. "But apart from that he is a good guy!"

No longer weighted down by the day-to-day crisis management of the Balkans, and at a safe remove from the fighting, the philosopher who had argued for melding utopia and realism began to reemerge. The same man who had insisted to John Pomfret that the parties in the Balkans negotiate peace and give up on legal prosecutions now tacked a Hague MOST WANTED poster of the war's prime suspects on his office wall. The poster bore the names and faces of many he had wined and dined, almost all of whom remained at large. If the UN had failed to protect civilians in need, the organization now had a duty to punish the guilty. As he had argued back in 1991 in his lecture on Kant, fair judicial processes were needed to halt cycles of violence.

He saw that the progress he had made in easing the siege of Sarajevo had been fully reversed. In the spring of 1995 the Bosnian Serbs sealed the roads into the city, recommenced sniper and shelling attacks on the capital, and began shutting down the airport and the trams at whim. "The Serbs have seen what NATO air power looks like," he told Nakamitsu, "and they aren't terribly impressed." Serb forces brazenly fired upon the safe areas, blocked the delivery of humanitarian aid to trapped civilians in them, and with little to fear from UN peacekeepers, even obstructed the passage of supplies to the blue helmets, who by the summer of 1995 had so little fuel that they were forced to conduct patrols on mules.

He did not see a way out. But he also did not foresee the catastrophic events of July 1995. On July 11 he was in Tbilisi, Georgia, preparing for the UNHCR conference on migration in the former Soviet Union. He turned on CNN in his hotel room and saw that the safe area of Srebrenica, which was just sixty-two miles northeast of the enclave of Gorazde, was being pounded by the Bosnian Serb army. Television images depicted tens of thousands of Bosnian refugees fleeing along the main road in the enclave and gathering at the Dutch UN base. He did not believe that the major powers were prepared to employ serious NATO military force in order to protect the fleeing civilians. Some 400 Dutch troops were in the enclave, tasked with protecting some 40,000 Bosnian civilians.

He grew even more pessimistic when CNN showed the broad, ruddy face of General Mladić, the Serb general who fifteen months before had taken him on the morbid tour of the desecrated Serb cemetery outside Gorazde. If Mladić viewed NATO as a "paper tiger" in 1994, Vieira de Mello could only imagine how emboldened he had become after marching uncontested into Srebrenica. By the middle of the day the UN announced that the Srebrenica safe area had officially fallen. Mladić was shown passing out candy to small, terrified Bosnian children and telling the men and women gathered at the UNPROFOR base that they had nothing to fear. "No one will do you any harm," the general said. "First women and children are to be taken. . . . Don't be afraid."[8] All males over sixteen, he said nonchalantly, would be "screened for war crimes." Even though the footage of Mladić rounding up Bosnian men aired on CNN and the BBC, Western leaders did not publicly demand that the male detainees be released.

That night at dinner Vieira de Mello and Nakamitsu discussed the capture of the safe area. "This is the biggest blow to the UN yet," he said. "I'm not sure we will recover. It is one thing for the UN to fail to protect civilians. But it is another thing for the UN to promise to protect people and then to open its gates to those intent on harming them." Bosnian civilians had flocked to the Dutch UN base in Srebrenica, trusting that there they would be safe, but the Dutch had turned them away. With a dark sense of foreboding, the two former UNPROFOR officials drank a bad bottle of Georgian red wine and resumed the familiar debate as to whether Akashi should have called for the bombing of the Serbs outside Sarajevo after the market massacre of February 1994 or whether Vieira de Mello himself should have requested all-out air strikes when the Serbs had not complied properly with the Gorazde ultimatum. For the first time he suggested aloud that the choices he and others had made in Bosnia may have cost lives. "I'm glad I'm not there now," he confessed. "I'm not sure what I would have done." It was an admission that seemed to reflect both moral insecurity and professional relief.

He understood that night that the fall of a UN safe area had damaged the UN's standing and that civilians would forever be traumatized by the ordeal. But over the next several weeks he would learn that the Serb seizure of the territory of Srebrenica was only part of the catastrophe. The real tragedy involved the fate of the Bosnian men and boys whom Mladić had hauled away to undisclosed locations. Over the next five days, while Vieira de Mello and Nakamitsu continued their tour of the former Soviet Union, Mladić presided over the systematic slaughter of every Bosnian man and boy in his custody, some eight thousand in all. When the Serb mass graves were discovered six weeks later, Vieira de Mello was stunned. "I never thought Mladić was this stupid," he said, projecting his own reverence for reason onto one who clearly observed different norms. "The massacre was totally unnecessary." The safe-area concept that Vieira de Mello had himself helped to preserve had brought ruin and death to those who mistakenly believed that the UN flag represented an international promise of protection.

When Vieira de Mello lived in the Balkans, he had deduced that NATO countries were not willing to make war to protect civilians. And he had believed that NATO air power would have caused Serbs to retaliate against UN peacekeepers and UNHCR aid workers. But with revelations about the Srebrenica massacre, public pressure on Western governments suddenly rose to an unprecedented pitch. UNPROFOR peacekeepers had been exposed as unable or unwilling to protect civilians who relied upon them. And cries for the withdrawal of the blue helmets—by those who cared about saving lives in Bosnia and by those who cared about the future of the UN—were heard around the world.

Finally, in late August 1995 the UNPROFOR mission in Bosnia collapsed under the weight of its own contradictions. On August 28 a second massacre occurred around the corner from the infamous bloodied market that Vieira de Mello had visited eighteen months before. This shell killed thirty-seven people. This time UN peacekeepers were withdrawn from Serb territory so that NATO could strike from the air without worrying about the safety of the blue helmets. Acting through NATO, the United States and Europe began a two-week heavy bombing campaign. NATO replaced the "pin-prick" air strikes seen around Gorazde with systematic attacks on Serb bunkers, ammunitions depots, and airstrips.

Vieira de Mello welcomed the NATO onslaught he had once opposed. He saw the air attacks as the only way to break a deadly stalemate. And indeed with their intervention Western governments finally altered the balance of power on the ground, reversed Serb gains, and enabled negotiators to press all three sides into signing the Dayton Peace Agreement, which divided Bosnia into two roughly equal halves, one controlled by the Serbs, the other by an uneasy alliance of Bosnians and Croats. Some 198 peacekeepers and aid workers had been killed in the war in Bosnia, along with more than 100,000 Bosnian civilians. The approach favored by General Rose, which Vieira de Mello had strongly favored, was judged harshly by history. A UN report, issued in 2000, noted that when one party to a conflict repeatedly attacked civilians, the UN's "continued equal treatment" of all sides "can in the best case result in ineffectiveness and in the worst may amount to complicity with evil."[9]

The Bosnia peacekeeping failure, combined with the experience of UN blue helmets who were bystanders to genocide in Rwanda in 1994, dealt devastating blows to the reputation of the United Nations. Released from the cold war stalemate, the Security Council of the 1990s had been liberated to enforce international peace and security. But the back-to-back calamities had made it clear that, if civilians were not pawns in a larger ideological struggle, as they had been in the cold war, their welfare would command hardly any attention at all. Instead of using the Security Council to establish and enforce a new global order, the major powers sent lightly armed peacekeepers into harm's way simply to monitor the carnage. The results were devastating in two regards. First, civilians were murdered en masse. And second, the UN peacekeepers took far more of the blame than the politicians who had handed them an assignment that was, Vieira de Mello liked to say, "mission impossible."

He returned to Bosnia only once. On January 9, 1996, as 60,000 NATO troops were arriving to enforce the new Dayton peace, Ogata sent him to mark the end of the Sarajevo humanitarian airlift. With the war over, the checkpoints were gone and the roads that Vieira de Mello had worked so hard to open were now cluttered with traffic. At the airport ceremony he smashed a champagne bottle against a large food crate and declared, "Our efforts helped keep the city alive, but now we are no longer needed."[10] He credited Sarajevo civilians for their "resilience, courage and pride," acknowledging, "We know we only partially mitigated their suffering." The airlift, Operation Provide Promise, which had run from July 2, 1992, to January 4, 1996, had outlasted the fifteen-month Berlin airlift.[11] Twenty-one countries had flown nearly 13,000 missions and delivered 160,677 metric tons of food, medicines, and other supplies.[12] Vieira de Mello let the occasion pass without mentioning the hundreds of Bosnians whom he had helped smuggle out of Sarajevo on the UN "train" that he had run from his office. Never one to pause long in a sentimental moment, he smiled to the assembled dignitaries and muttered under his breath to Nakamitsu, "I can't believe we just wasted a good bottle of Dom Pérignon!"

Even though UNHCR had been criticized in the former Yugoslavia for overextending itself, unlike the peacekeepers', its presumptive virtue had not been challenged. In fact, it was the rare UN agency that (with the exception of the crisis over deposed high commissioner Jean-Pierre Hocké) had escaped serious scandal during its forty-five-year history. Because he had departed the Balkans long before Srebrenica's fall, Vieira de Mello too managed to avoid being blamed by the media or by critics of the UN. But all of that changed as a result of the humanitarian crisis brought about by the genocide in Rwanda. UNHCR would be attacked with vitriol, and for the first time in Vieira de Mello's unblemished career, he would find himself personally tarred by an international moral and humanitarian calamity.

Ten

DAMNED IF YOU DO

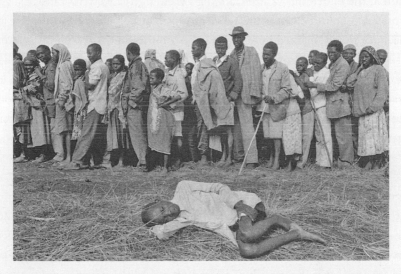

Rwandan refugees in the Ngara camp in Tanzania, 1994.

Vieira de Mello had never been one to expend his energy on hopeless places. Thus, although he was earning a deserved reputation as one of the UN system's elite troubleshooters, he wanted nothing to do with the part of the world that in 1996 presented the most trouble of all: the Great Lakes region of Africa, which included Rwanda, Zaire, and Tanzania.

In April 1994, at the very time he was leading a UN convoy into the Bosnian safe area of Gorazde, Hutu extremists in Rwanda were in the process of butchering 800,000 Tutsi and moderate Hutu. After one hundred days of slaughter, the *génocidaires* were finally driven out of Rwanda by the Rwandan

Patriotic Front (RPF), headed by Paul Kagame, the country's future president.* The killers fled into neighboring Tanzania and Zaire, hidden amid a fifteen-mile-long river of humanity. Some two million Hutu civilians, who had been led to believe by their leaders that they would be harmed if they stayed in Rwanda, were on the move.

In the first month of the exodus, cholera and dysentery epidemics killed at least 50,000 of the Hutu refugees who crossed into Zaire, and UNHCR, along with a wide variety of international aid groups, quickly sprang into action in the enormous (Zaire's landmass is as large as Western Europe's) and inhospitable country. Once the relief groups had helped control the disease epidemics, they remained in order to maintain the camps, which lay in Zaire and Tanzania not far from the Rwandan border.[1] At these sprawling camps, which contained a mix of Hutu gunmen and legitimate Hutu refugees, international aid agencies doled out between 6,000 and 7,000 tons of food a week, at a cost of approximately $1 million per day, paid for by Western governments.

QUAGMIRE

In the quarter century since Vieira de Mello first joined UNHCR, humanitarian agencies had developed speedy and sophisticated mechanisms to deliver medicine, food, sanitation, and shelter to refugees in crisis. But aid workers knew that the care they offered often had the adverse consequence of leaving men in the camps free to concentrate on their military pursuits.[2] Indeed, the international relief community had become so reliable that by the mid-1990s armed groups around the world had started factoring in the presence of donated relief as they plotted their military strategies. The Hutu *génocidaires* in Zaire had already proven themselves master planners.

Unsurprisingly, the same Hutu government officials who had orchestrated the fastest killing spree in recorded history quickly asserted control in their new environment. A UN team estimated that some 21 former ministers, 54 former members of parliament, and 126 ex-mayors resided in the camps.[3] These former regime officials retained their weapons and access to their well-

---

*Between 1994 and 2000 Kagame was the country's vice president and minister of defense. He became president in the spring of 2000.

stocked foreign bank accounts. In many camps they quickly reconstituted the structures they had used to govern Rwanda, dividing the camps among prefectures and communes or, in some, establishing formal "ministries" for security, social welfare, finance, and communications. Camp leaders beat, or in some cases murdered, Hutu whom they suspected of wanting to head back to Rwanda. UNHCR aid workers regularly discovered fresh corpses in the camps, but they felt they had no choice but to work with the suspected killers. "The UNHCR emergency field manual said, 'Find the natural leaders and get them to help you distribute relief,'" recalls Caroll Faubert, UNHCR's special envoy to the Great Lakes region. "We didn't think this through, but it meant: Give the genocidal leaders more power." The Hutu militia in the Zairean camps soon began attacking Tutsi in Rwanda, and the Tutsi-led Rwandan government started staging small retaliatory strikes into Zaire. The location of several of the UNHCR camps within two miles of Rwanda made it easier for the *génocidaires* to stage their attacks and for the Rwandan army to strike back.[4]

As UNHCR's director of policy planning and operations in Geneva, Vieira de Mello should have been heavily involved in the agency's pivotal decision making concerning this controversial aid operation. But while others in Ogata's inner circle had been involved in Rwanda since the genocide itself, he had been in the former Yugoslavia when the 1994 slaughter occurred, and he was initially content to stay largely removed from managing its messy aftermath. "Sergio didn't want to get deeply involved in a problem that he knew had no solution," recalls Izumi Nakamitsu, his special assistant at the time. Kamel Morjane, the director of UNHCR's Africa Division, had a difficult time getting his colleague to focus on the region. Vieira de Mello stuck to his comfort areas: Asia, the Balkans, and the former Soviet Union. "Sergio," Morjane said, "if you're not interested in Africa, that's okay. But at least give me a time and I can come and brief you!" Morjane managed to impose one fixed meeting each week.[5]

Vieira de Mello had still been in the Balkans when Ogata made her most important choices. She had considered closing the camps in the hopes that the Hutu exiles would go back to Rwanda, but she decided not to because she did not believe conditions there were safe. If the camps were to remain in place, she knew, they would have to be demilitarized. But UNHCR, a civilian agency, did not by itself have either the mandate or the security forces needed to neutralize the Hutu militants. The agency's field officers and logisticians were unarmed and intended to stay that way. On Ogata's pleading, Secretary-General Boutros-Ghali had tried to persuade powerful countries in the UN to send troops or police to the camps in Zaire to arrest the *génocidaires* and ship them off to the newly established UN war crimes tribunal for Rwanda in Arusha, Tanzania. But when Boutros-Ghali attempted to round up international troops for the task, he had struck out. On January 10, 1995, he telephoned Ogata with the bad news: He had asked thirty-nine countries to send troops, and only one country, Bangladesh, had agreed. The world had turned its back on Rwanda during the genocide, so it was not surprising that, in its aftermath, countries were not leaping to deploy troops to arrest the *génocidaires* who were still armed and dangerous.[6] The shadow of Somalia loomed large in many countries, and few were sympathetic to Rwandan Hutu, who as a collective were blamed for the genocide. Ogata and UNHCR had been told they would have to find a way to manage the genocidal gunmen on their own.

Vieira de Mello naturally got dragged into tortured in-house discussions about how to proceed. Several aid agencies, including Médecins Sans Frontières (MSF)–France and the International Rescue Committee (IRC), the largest U.S. aid agency, decided to pull out of the camps. In the IRC's sixty-four-year history, this marked the first time that it had terminated its feeding programs out of repugnance for its clientele. "It was a terrible decision to have to make," IRC vice president Roy Williams said later, but "sometimes we just shouldn't show up for a disaster."[7] Vieira de Mello did not consider recommending that Ogata end UN aid to the Hutu camps as a sign of protest against the *génocidaires*. "There is no justification for the suspension of UNHCR assistance," he wrote in one report.[8] He often argued that UNHCR had a special responsibility because it was the last frontier for refugees. Nongovernmental organizations could leave knowing UNHCR would be there to back them up. "We could have made ourselves feel good by saying, 'We're leaving,'" Ogata recalls. "But while principles are important, real life is more important." In a statement to her staff Ogata cautioned against confusing a human rights mandate and a humanitarian mandate. "Unlike human rights actors," she said, "UNHCR's role is not judgmental but humanitarian. UNHCR is there not to expose the perpetrators but to help the victims."[9] She would not think of pulling out. "There were also innocent refugees in the camps; more than half were women and children," she said later. "Should we have said: you are related to murderers, so you are guilty too?"*[10] Although she felt UNHCR had been abandoned by the world's governments, she also never considered stepping down as high commissioner.[11]

Fresh out of options and desperate for help, Ogata took the hugely controversial step of using UN funds to rent out part of President Mobutu Sese Seko's notoriously abusive Zairean army to do what no other country would do: provide security in the camps. On February 12, 1995, in a surreal scene, she traveled to Goma and presided over a ceremony in which the Zairean deputy prime minister, Admiral Mavua Mudima, turned over 150 soldiers from the Zairean presidential guard to UNHCR, the first installment of what others would call "Ogata's troops." UNHCR issued mustard-colored uniforms to the Zairean soldiers to distinguish them from the multitude of armed groups in the region, and the agency paid each of the soldiers three dollars per day, giving them vehicles, radios, and office equipment.[12] At the cost of $10 million per year, some 1,500 of these subcontracted Zairean soldiers would offer security for UNHCR staff and for refugees at the camps in Zaire.[13] "The troops are not going to divide the perpetrators from the innocent, only maintain law and order," she said. "That is as far as my office can go."[14] She was already going further than any UN civilian official had dared go before. When reporters railed against UNHCR for continuing to feed the *génocidaires,* she pressed back. "Who would separate them?" she asked. "Who would pay for all this? The international community never came up with an answer."[15]

Vieira de Mello did not personally visit the camps until July 1996, when he traveled to the Zairean border with Nakamitsu. If he had been skeptical that UNHCR could help resolve the mess in the Great Lakes region before his trip, he was downright despondent afterward. Militant camp leaders anointed by UNHCR lorded it over their fellow citizens. They sat beside stacks of UN flour and blankets with fists full of bills. They kept their guns

---

*Critics believed that Ogata created a false dichotomy between withdrawing and remaining, instead of creatively responding to the bind in which UNHCR found itself. They say UNHCR should have insisted on moving the camps deeper into Zaire to cut down on violent cross-border raids, or it should have cut off aid in certain camps to see whether this might prompt those who had committed no crimes during the genocide to return to their homes, leaving the guilty in Zaire to fend for themselves.

visible and strutted around in new track suits, ordering each household to pay a monthly tax and press-ganging men into joining the genocidal militia that patrolled the camps and plotted for a future war in Rwanda. Instead of dispersing the free UN humanitarian aid, they often sold it. The profits allowed them to amass huge stashes of firearms and grenades.[16]

As he toured the camps with Nakamitsu, Vieira de Mello described Zaire as the "armpit of the world" and predicted that the country's weak governing structures would soon crumble, causing the sprawling multiethnic nation to disintegrate. He found the experience of navigating the camps a chilling one. "There's one," he said to Nakamitsu, singling out a man he thought was a *génocidaire* crouching beside the blue UNHCR tents or bossing villagers around. "And there, there's another one." "How can you tell?" she asked him. "Look in their eyes," he said. "There is nothing left in them." He was disgusted by the scene. "The people here are being controlled by sheer terror, and there's not a damn thing we can do about it."

He had been told ahead of his trip that in just two years the camps had come to seem permanent, but he was unprepared for what he saw: a structured, seemingly permanent city life very similar to that in the Cambodian camps in Thailand before he had helped empty them. Indeed, a late-1995 survey of the four main camps in Goma, which housed 650,000 refugees, found 2,324 bars, 450 restaurants, 589 shops, 62 hairdressers, 51 pharmacies, 30 tailors, 25 butchers, 5 ironsmiths, 4 photographic studios, 3 cinemas, 2 hotels, and 1 animal slaughterhouse.[17]

In both Cambodia and Zaire the major powers were willing to spend hundreds of millions of dollars feeding the refugees, but they were not willing to insert their forces into the camps to ensure that the perpetrators of genocide were punished or removed. The crucial difference between the two circumstances, he saw, was that in the 1980s Western governments had spent millions aiding the Cambodian refugees as a way of destabilizing the Vietnam-installed regime in Phnom Penh. But in the Great Lakes area, a region of marginal strategic value, Western governments were not using aid as a tool for promoting their national interests. Rather, they were using aid as a substitute for meaningful foreign policy engagement of any kind.

Upon his return to Geneva, Vieira de Mello warned in his trip report, "Our camps serve as transit, rest [and] recruitment bases in support of incursions into Rwanda."[18] He made three sets of recommendations for how

UNHCR might disentangle itself from the moral and logistic quagmire. He recommended that UNHCR move its camps back from the Zairean-Rwandan border. To avoid border clashes, the agency's rules required camps to be erected a "reasonable distance" from any international border, which was usually interpreted to mean at least thirty miles. But once the camps had been established near the border in 1994, Ogata had not pursued relocating them farther into Zaire because the move would have cost between $90 million and $125 million, and she would still have likely needed military force to move recalcitrant Hutu.[19] She had also worried that moving the camps deeper into Zaire would signal to the refugees that the UN intended to offer them permanent care, and it would give the *génocidaires* in the camps a more spacious sanctuary in which to arm and train for future battle.[20] Vieira de Mello now weighed in, arguing that even by just starting to plan to move the camps, UNHCR would at least show Hutu civilians and soldiers that they could not remain in limbo indefinitely.

Unsurprisingly, the Zairean troops who had been hired by Ogata were not proving reliable. They did not protect the refugees, and in many camps they constituted a threat in their own right. They took bribes from the Hutu militants, and some were reported to be involved in sexually exploiting young female refugees.[21] Yet despite their worrying track record, Vieira de Mello's second recommendation was to increase the force size of what he called "Mrs. Ogata's contingent" from 1,500 to 2,500. Boxed in by impossible circumstances, he was desperate enough to tell himself that the Zairean forces could change. Since the morale of the Zairean contingent had sunk, he even drew on his memories of UN peacekeepers' pride in Lebanon and Bosnia and urged UNHCR to host medal ceremonies for the Zairean soldiers.

After speaking to some of the Hutu refugees in Zaire, Vieira de Mello realized that they were staying for more complicated reasons than he had understood before visiting. Yes, he wrote, there was intimidation in the camps, but many of the refugees were also being deterred by the signals emanating from Rwanda. The Rwandan authorities denounced the UNHCR camps in Zaire and Tanzania, but they also made clear that they did not want all Hutu in the camps to return. As Emmanuel Ndahiro, Vice President Paul Kagame's closest adviser, declared publicly, "Not even powerful America can afford to take in one million people at once."[22] Rwandan officials did not visit the camps or use media to encourage the Hutu to return. Nor did they release a list of "wanted" war crime suspects, which might have soothed the concerns of Hutu refugees who had not murdered their Tutsi neighbors but who worried that they would nonetheless be caught up in a dragnet. On July 13, just two weeks before Vieira de Mello's trip to Zaire, Rwandan government troops in the northwestern province of Gisenyi, Rwanda, retaliated for the death of a Tutsi soldier at the hands of Hutu infiltrators by massacring sixty-two local Hutu residents, including women with infants strapped to their backs.[23] Tit-for-tat ethnic massacres were occurring regularly in the border areas. Therefore, Vieira de Mello's third recommendation was that UNHCR officials stop "distracting ourselves in a futile search for 'intimidators'"—the camps were stuck with them—and instead concentrate on pressing the Rwandan authorities to do more than they had yet done to assure the Hutu that they would be safe on return.[24]

Rwandan government officials were contemptuous of his viewpoint. They were trying to manage the social and economic consequences of the extermination of 800,000 people and were tired of hearing about the plight of Hutu refugees in Zaire. "What is this nonsense about refugees?" Kagame said on the two-year anniversary of the genocide. "This is their home and they should return. I was a refugee myself for over 30 years and nobody made a fuss about it. Personally, I think this question of refugees is being overplayed at the expense of all our other problems. We no longer talk about orphans, widows, victims. We're only talking about refugees, refugees, refugees. . . . If the refugees say 'we're not returning,' that stops being my problem. It is their problem."[25]

But Kagame knew the refugees were in fact his problem because the Hutu *génocidaires* in the camps in Zaire were still determined to exterminate Tutsi and retake power in Rwanda. In a visit to Washington, Kagame informed Clinton administration officials that if UNHCR did not dismantle its camps in Zaire, his forces would do so. He later recalled, "I delivered a veiled warning: The failure of the international community to take action would mean Rwanda would take action." Kagame, who had studied at the U.S. Army Command and General Staff College at Fort Leavenworth, Kansas, was pleased by the U.S. reaction. "Their response was really no response," he said.[26]

In offering his recommendations to Ogata, Vieira de Mello knew all the options were bad. He was acutely conscious of the damage the crisis was doing to the standing of the United Nations locally and internationally. "UNHCR's passivity," he wrote in his trip report, "is untenable and is exposing the office to criticism and cheap accusations." UNHCR could take the small steps he proposed, but what was really needed to resolve the situation were large steps by the governments of Rwanda and Zaire and concerted involvement by the major powers, who were claiming credit for generously supplying humanitarian aid but who were allowing the crisis to fester and deteriorate. "The prevailing *status quo* is not tenable without potentially disastrous consequences for the Office," he concluded. "Unless UNHCR displays vision and sustained action, it is likely to become increasingly part of the problem and unable to preempt or effectively respond to looming ominous threats, over which it is losing any control."[27]

Ogata was pleased that Vieira de Mello's trip to the region had finally caused him to apply himself to finding a way out for UNHCR. It had only been when he toured the camps that the costs of the catastrophe—to the refugees and to the UN—fully registered with him. He paid his second visit to Zaire later in the summer and found UNHCR staff even more frustrated and helpless. On this trip he stopped in Rwanda. A few hours after arriving in Kigali he told Nakamitsu, "People don't know how to smile here." Only two and a half years after the slaughter of 1994, it was the gloomiest place he had ever visited. His formal meetings were unpleasant. The Rwandan chairman for refugee return, Ephraim Kabaija, railed against the UN for first doing nothing about the genocide and then for feeding war criminals in the camps across the border. The Rwandan president delivered a two-hour harangue on Belgium's responsibility for the genocide. Leaving the meeting, Vieira de Mello muttered to Nakamitsu, "That's the problem with Africans: They blame everything on colonialism." Every official he met with echoed Kagame's warning that Rwanda would not tolerate the existence of the camps for much longer. Vieira de Mello warned Ogata that the Rwandans were on the verge of invading Zaire.

He blocked out half a day to spend with his old friend Omar Bakhet, who had left UNHCR and was running the UN Development Program office in Rwanda, helping build a new legal system. Bakhet brought him to a church in Nyamata, where ten thousand Rwandans had been butchered on April 8, 1994. The Hutu *génocidaires* had sprayed the inside of the church with machine-gun fire, lobbed in grenades, and then used machetes to finish off any survivors. Vieira de Mello wandered around the church interior, which contained row upon row of shelves lined with skulls, and examined its bullet holes and shrapnel marks. He looked up at a sculpture of the Virgin Mary. Her serene visage smiled down upon him, but the wall beside her was still stained in blood.

Bakhet next brought him to the Don Bosco school, which UN peacekeepers from Belgium had used as a base in 1994. Some two thousand desperate Rwandan Tutsi had huddled with the blue helmets until April 11, 1994, when the Belgian UN commander at the school had been ordered to withdraw his forces. With the *génocidaires* outside the school drinking banana beer, brandishing their machetes, and chanting "Hutu power," the Rwandan Tutsi inside had thrown themselves at the feet of the Belgians, begging them not to abandon the school. But the UN soldiers had shooed the helpless Tutsi away, even firing over their heads so as to ensure that they did not block the passage of UN vehicles. As soon as the Belgian peacekeepers departed, the militia had entered, butchering all those Rwandans who had made the mistake of seeking shelter beneath the UN flag. Vieira de Mello had already thought a great deal about the UN failure to protect Bosnian civilians in Srebrenica, but henceforth he described the Rwanda massacre as the gravest single act of betrayal ever committed by the United Nations.

In the car ride back to Kigali, Vieira de Mello stared out the window, lost in his own thoughts. When the car reached the Hotel Mille Collines, he disembarked quietly and retired to his room. By the next day he had returned to his garrulous self, but he was focused on the future. "I just feel this thing is about to blow open," he told Bakhet. The tension in the air was similar to that he had felt in Lebanon before the Israeli invasion in 1982.

War in Zaire: "The West Means Death!"

A month later, Kagame's forces invaded Zaire in order to close the camps and eliminate the Hutu threat once and for all. "People who want to continue exterminating others have got to be resisted," the Rwandan vice president said.[28] His soldiers teamed up with an unheralded fifty-six-year-old former Marxist warlord named Laurent-Désiré Kabila and his newly formed Zairean rebel movement, which aspired to overthrow Zairean president Mobutu.

Kabila's rebels and Kagame's regular Rwandan army forces launched a combined assault on the southernmost Hutu refugee camps along Zaire's border
with Rwanda. Some 220,000 refugees from the camps, along with some
30,000 local Zaireans, took flight. Under fire, Ogata's contingent of Zairean
soldiers proved a mixed bag. Some helped to evacuate UNHCR's international staff, but many simply joined Mobutu's defense against the joint
Zairean rebel–Rwandan attack. Some of these units were even reported
to have used UNHCR planes to transport war matériel into battle against
Kabila's rebels.[29]

At the sight of the Kabila-Rwandan attackers, most of the frantic Hutu
refugees fled northward away from Rwanda, toward the UN camps in Bukavu. But Bukavu was next on the attackers' target list. On October 25 the
UNHCR representative there telephoned Ogata in Geneva and passed the
telephone to the local archbishop, Monsignor Christophe Munzihirwa, who
begged Ogata to secure international military intervention to save the people
in the camp from the joint rebel-Rwandan assault. Four days later Bukavu
fell and UNHCR and other aid organizations suspended operations. Amid
the slaughter that ensued, the attacking forces murdered Archbishop Munzihirwa.[30]

Many of the 1994 *génocidaires* were undoubtedly killed in the offensive.
But testimonies of survivors revealed that thousands of Hutu civilians also
likely died. One Hutu refugee told Amnesty International that when five
Zairean rebels entered a church compound where Hutu were hiding, one
of the foreign priests in charge went to speak to the gunmen. The Hutu
survivor remembered:

> [The priest] then called one of us, Pascal Murwirano, a 22-year-old Rwandese,
> to help, as he did not speak Kinyarwanda. The conversation went like this:
> "Are you from Rwanda?"
> "Yes."
> "Are you Hutu?"
> "Yes."
> "When did you leave Rwanda?"
> "1994."
> "Take off your clothes."

Pascal crossed himself. I remember it so well. He unbuttoned the first but-
ton of his shirt and before he could unbutton the second one, he was shot. He
took one bullet in the heart, four in the stomach and one in the head.[31]

The battle lines were drawn. On one side were Mobutu's Zairean government forces and armed Rwandan Hutu refugees, mostly *génocidaires*, while on
the other were the Kabila-led Zairean rebels and the mainly Tutsi Rwandan
army forces. A UNHCR spokesperson in Geneva warned of "a humanitarian catastrophe of greater dimensions than the one in 1994."[32]

With tens of thousands of Hutu refugees now fleeing westward into the
Zairean jungle, Ogata and Vieira de Mello no longer had any ambivalence
about where the refugees belonged. Civilians would undoubtedly be safer
in Rwanda than trapped between warring armies in Zaire. He telephoned
Lionel Rosenblatt, with whom he had helped organize the resettlement of
the Montagnards from Cambodia. He now begged Rosenblatt, who ran
Refugees International, a leading advocacy group in Washington, to alert
the Clinton administration to the fact that the Hutu were moving away
from food and shelter. "The west means death!" Vieira de Mello exclaimed.
If Hutu families headed west into the deep jungle with the militants, they
would be pursued and killed, or they would die of starvation or disease. Aid
workers and diplomats had to find a way to persuade the refugees at long last
to head back to their former homes in Rwanda.

On October 30, as another bloody crisis engulfed the region and the
Western media descended again on Rwanda and Zaire, Secretary-General
Boutros-Ghali appointed as his special political envoy to the region Raymond Chrétien, Canada's ambassador to the United States.[33] A week later,
in another boon to Vieira de Mello's résumé, Boutros-Ghali named him
humanitarian coordinator, answering not to Ogata but to the Department of
Humanitarian Affairs (DHA), a newly created division at UN Headquarters
in New York. Improbably, he would once again answer to Yasushi Akashi,
who, despite his mediocre performances in Cambodia and Bosnia, had been
promoted to run DHA, once again out of deference to Japan, the UN's
second-largest donor. Chrétien and Vieira de Mello were meant to coordinate their efforts, with Chrétien managing the political negotiations and
Vieira de Mello relegated to the humanitarian.

Vieira de Mello immediately made his way to Kinshasa, Zaire. On November 7 he was told that Chrétien, his political counterpart, was already en route to the region. Chrétien would arrive in Kigali the following morning for his first meetings with the Rwandan authorities. Vieira de Mello knew that political envoys tended to view humanitarians as expendable "grocery deliverers" who would play no important role in high-stakes political talks. Already Chrétien had stopped to see Mobutu in France, where the Zairean president was receiving cancer treatment. Vieira de Mello did not want Chrétien to hold any further high-level meetings without him. But when he telephoned the UNHCR office in Kinshasa, he was told that no commercial or UN flight would be able to fly him a thousand miles from Kinshasa to Kigali in time to greet Chrétien. If he was to make it, he would have to charter a private jet to fly him to an airport in Entebbe, Uganda, where he could then catch a regular UN flight to Kigali. He reflexively accepted, and when he and his UNHCR colleague Chefike Desalegn arrived at the Kinshasa airport, he gasped at the sight of the jet on the runway. "Chefike," he exclaimed, delighted, "it's Mobutu's personal Learjet!" Seated on the plane, he shouted up to his colleague: "Tell them to take their time getting to Entebbe. If they make a few laps, we can get a full night's sleep!" The two men reached Kigali several hours ahead of Chrétien.

Months later, when Vieira de Mello returned to Geneva, he was informed that the three-hour charter leg had cost UNHCR $50,000. In 1998 the *Financial Times* would publish an exposé on UN corruption, making Vieira de Mello's extravagance a prime example of the organization's excesses.[34] This would be the first such charge ever lodged against him, but while he worried that the UN's critics would use it to tarnish his entire career, the scandal did not stick.

Having managed to insinuate himself into Chrétien's small negotiating team, Vieira de Mello got to hear the Rwandans again lambaste the UN. "They just vomited all over the organization," recalls Chrétien. "I mean it was savage. I didn't take the hatred personally. I was the UN special envoy for a month or two, but for Sergio it was his lifelong employer. They looked right at him when they attacked the organization. He seemed very uncomfortable."

Events in Zaire made him even more uncomfortable. International aid workers had been largely evacuated from refugee camps in eastern Zaire, so he had no idea how many Hutu refugees were in pain or dying out of view.

The rare eyewitness reports indicated that the newly displaced were sleeping in the forests without food or blankets and were sucking on tree roots to quench their thirst. As the coordinator of all humanitarian activities in the region, Vieira de Mello had to find a way to enable aid workers to go behind the front lines to reach the refugees. He knew from his past missions that although the UN system frowned upon contact with nonstate actors (like Shiite militia in Lebanon or the Khmer Rouge in Cambodia), somebody in the UN had to reach out to Kabila, the Zairean rebel leader. Without Kabila's authorization, it would be too dangerous for aid workers to reenter Zaire in order to feed and clothe Hutu refugees on the run.

On the evening of November 8, Omar Bakhet saw a face outside the window of his home in Kigali. It was a Rwandan government official who asked Bakhet if he would like to meet Kabila at the rebel leader's new head-quarters in Zaire. The Rwandans were adamant that Bakhet not bring any-body from UNHCR, which they blamed for feeding the *génocidaires* in the refugee camps. Bakhet suggested Daniel Toole, a forty-year-old American colleague from UNICEF. The Rwandan official agreed, saying, "He is the right nationality."

The following morning Bakhet and Toole drove to the Rwandan border town of Gisenyi and seated themselves in the lobby of a local hotel, as they had been instructed to do. The place was teeming with journalists, who were themselves hoping to get the Rwandan government's permission to cross into Zaire so they could cover the war there. By the late afternoon, after hours of idle waiting and far too many cups of coffee, Bakhet and Toole were poised to give up. But just as they were preparing to pay their bill, a Rwandan of-ficer approached and told them to follow him. They did so, exiting through the back of the hotel, then driving a circuitous route to the border so as to elude the press.

As the sun was setting, the officer led Bakhet and Toole into rebel-held Zaire. Both men knew that what they were doing was risky, physically and professionally. UN peacekeepers and UN civilians were supposed to respect national boundaries. Aware that UN Headquarters in New York would not have granted him permission to cross from Rwanda into Zaire, Bakhet had not asked his superiors for clearance, which Toole did not know. Their Rwandan driver seemed terrified.

When the men reached one of Mobutu's darkened old villas, they found

Laurent Kabila sitting at a coffee table in a heavily starched tan officer's uniform. Over the course of several hours of discussion, the men succeeded in negotiating an informal humanitarian agreement, whereby the rebel leader promised to allow the unimpeded delivery of aid to civilians. It was only when Kabila excused himself to go to the restroom that Bakhet and Toole simultaneously noticed, to their amazement, that along with his crisp new uniform, the rebel leader was wearing white socks and high-heeled, lizard-skin disco dancing shoes.

When Toole himself headed to the bathroom a short while later, Kabila leaned over to Bakhet and confessed that he had one need above all others: a satellite telephone. Bakhet promised that if Kabila allowed vital relief to pass into Goma, he would place his personal phone in the first truck of the first UN convoy of relief. The two men shook hands, and six trucks filled with hospital supplies, along with Bakhet's satellite phone, soon rumbled across the border into Zaire.

As Bakhet and Toole drove back to Rwanda after the meeting, they felt triumphant. They had taken a significant risk, and in so doing they had managed to open up a discreet channel of UN communication with the rebels. However, Bakhet's satisfaction at having scored a diplomatic coup faded almost as soon as he was back in cell phone range. Vieira de Mello telephoned him and raged, "Omar, where the hell have you been? Christiane Amanpour has been on CNN claiming that the UN is holding secret talks with Kabila in Zaire. Mobutu is furious, and in New York, Headquarters is going out of its mind!"

Bakhet started to explain, but his friend interrupted, asking, "So you met with Kabila in no-man's-land, right?" Bakhet answered, "No, I—" But Vieira de Mello cut him off again. "Listen, Omar," he said, "I told New York you met Kabila on the Rwandan side of no-man's-land. Now where did you meet Kabila?" Bakhet understood. Vieira de Mello knew how to work the system in a way he knew he never would.

Benon Sevan, who ran the UN security department in New York and a decade later would be indicted for his involvement in the UN's oil-for-food scandal in Iraq, reprimanded Bakhet for violating UN rules. But Vieira de Mello stuck to his contrived story, lying outright in a cable to Sevan: "It is my understanding that Mr. Bakhet did not cross the border into Zaire. The meeting he held was at the border, i.e., in the no-man's-land separating the two border posts. The mission was authorized by me on that basis. Mr. Bakhet, therefore, did not violate standing instructions. Warm regards, Sergio."[35]

"MULTINATIONAL FARCE"

Vieira de Mello believed neither the aid workers nor the refugees would be safe unless international forces were sent to create and protect safe routes through rebel-held territory. The safe corridors would simultaneously allow the delivery of relief in one direction, and the secure passage of refugees back to Rwanda in the other.[*]

Although he knew what was required, he was highly skeptical that Western countries would agree to put their troops in harm's way to protect civilians. The UN Security Council had not only done nothing to stop the 1994 genocide, but had left UNHCR alone to manage the camps in the Great Lakes region for more than two years. Whenever U.S. officials had pressed Mobutu's Zaire to do more to persuade the refugees to go home, France had interfered on Mobutu's and the Hutu's behalf. Whenever France had turned up the heat on the Rwandan government, Washington had taken Kagame's side. Vieira de Mello also knew from the tragic failure to defend the safe areas in Bosnia how easy it was to declare land "safe," yet how difficult it was to persuade the major powers in fact to secure civilians. As the violence in Zaire escalated, UN member states began debating sending troops. The negotiations proceeded so slowly that Emma Bonino, the feisty European commissioner for humanitarian aid, slammed the ambassadors in New York, saying, "UN Security Council representatives should keep in mind that the thousands of refugees dying every day in [Zaire] cannot spend the weekend in Long Island, as they do."[36]

However, on November 11, Vieira de Mello got the shocking and welcome news that Canada had agreed to head a large UN-authorized force to secure the humanitarian corridors that UNHCR had proposed. During the 1994 genocide the commander of UN forces in Rwanda had been Canadian lieutenant-general Roméo Dallaire, and because of Dallaire's awareness-raising, many Canadians felt they had a debt to repay the region. General

---

[*]The corridors UNHCR proposed would run from Goma to Gisenyi, Rwanda; Bukavu to Cyangugu, Rwanda; and Uvira to Bujumbura, Burundi.

Maurice Baril, the head of Canada's armed forces who had previously worked as a senior UN military adviser to Boutros-Ghali, would command the Multinational Force (MNF), which was expected to consist of 10,000 to 12,000 troops.

Because of the bloodshed, Western governments finally seemed willing to offer the armed assistance UNHCR had been seeking since 1994. Even U.S. officials pledged a thousand troops, though U.S. defense secretary William Perry cautioned that the forces would not "be used to disarm militants."[37] With the countries on the Security Council at last serious about intervening in the region, Søren Jessen-Petersen, a mild-mannered Danish bureaucrat who ran UNHCR's office in New York, sent a jubilant cable that reached Vieira de Mello in Zaire. "We are on board and the train is moving fast," he wrote. "FINALLY!!"[38]

But Kabila's rebels and the Rwandan government wanted the train to head back to the station. They were convinced that any international force would foil their offensive and benefit the Hutu militants. They decided to strike a knockout blow before the international troops had time to assemble. On November 14 the Kabila-Rwandan forces fired artillery and rockets into the Mugunga camp, the last stronghold for Rwandan Hutu in Zaire. Mugunga had been home to 200,000 Rwandan refugees, and that number had reached 500,000 after the attacks on the other camps. This time the joint forces attacked the camp from the west, and the only place that refugees could run was toward Rwanda. Some 12,000 Hutu refugees fled across the border per hour, and by nightfall on November 15, UNHCR estimated that 200,000 had returned to Rwanda in the previous two days. Another 300,000 were on the road. That same day, after days of haggling, the UN Security Council passed a resolution authorizing the deployment of the Multinational Force to Zaire.

No matter how removed he was from the capitals in which decisions were being made, Vieira de Mello stayed plugged in. In the 1980s, before the era of phone cards and cell phones, he was known for carrying plastic bags filled with coins from all over the world, which he used in public pay phones. By the mid-1990s he had less cumbersome ways of staying in touch with headquarters. Martin Griffiths, a forty-five-year-old from Wales whom New York had assigned to be his deputy, found his new senior colleague businesslike to the point of being brusque. "After a long day of meetings, we would come back to our hotels exhausted, and the general rule on missions is that the team will convene for dinner to drink and remember—or try to forget—the day," recalls Griffiths. "But not Sergio. He would go straight back to his hotel room, order room service, read the faxes from Geneva and New York, and make dozens and dozens of phone calls."

Vieira de Mello was attempting to follow the progress of the international force. Initially, Western countries acted as though the joint rebel-Rwandan offensive would not affect their plans. The countries that had offered troops went through the motions of preparing to deploy, and a Canadian reconnaissance team under General Baril flew to the region. But the first sign of wavering enthusiasm for the Multinational Force came when the U.S. aerial search teams said they had spotted only 165,000 Hutu refugees in the forest—far fewer than the 700,000 or so UNHCR thought were still on the run. If most refugees had returned safely to Rwanda, as the Americans were suggesting, countries that had promised to send troops to Zaire would have the excuse they needed to back out.

In New York, Jessen-Petersen of UNHCR pleaded with Western ambassadors to appreciate the "chicken and egg" bind in which UNHCR found itself. Governments wanted information on the number, whereabouts, and conditions of the Hutu refugees in the Zairean jungle before sending forces. But a few dozen UNHCR aid workers would by themselves be unable to obtain that information. Only national militaries could supply the mobility, security, and intelligence to stage such a hunt.[39]

If Jessen-Petersen was exasperated in New York, Vieira de Mello was practically numb from the deception and obstruction he was encountering in his official meetings in the region. On one occasion an army colonel known to be responsible for waging a scorched-earth policy rattled off a string of denials and then asked credulously, "Why would the army deliberately attack civilian populations?"[40] After the meeting, as Vieira de Mello and Griffiths walked to their car, Griffiths remarked: "It's extraordinary, isn't it? Every time we go into meetings with these war criminals, I come out—and I'm sure it's the same for you—absolutely convinced of the plausibility of their arguments. What is it? Why does this happen?" Vieira de Mello stopped, turned to look at Griffiths, and said, "It's because you're extraordinarily stupid."[41] The two men burst into laughter, struck by the absurdity of their seemingly fruitless negotiations. They would become close friends in the months and years ahead.

Oppressed by officialdom, Vieira de Mello tried to find ways to remain connected to the human drama under way, relying upon Filippo Grandi, a thirty-six-year-old Italian who was UNHCR's Goma representative. In 1994, when Grandi had returned to Geneva from Congo after the cholera outbreak, he had prepared to deliver remarks to a group of outside dignitaries and had run his remarks by Vieira de Mello, who was a legend to young staff. "No, Filippo, when you speak with important people, you have to convey a visceral sense of the dramatic experiences you have been through," Vieira de Mello had said. "I'm not asking you to say anything wrong or fake, but you have to be very graphic because that is how you grab people's attention. And our success at UNHCR depends on our ability to get and hold people's attention." When Grandi replied that he doubted he had comparable powers of persuasion, Vieira de Mello had exclaimed, "Nonsense! We are Latin, both of us. It is in the blood."

In late November, now in the region together, Vieira de Mello told Grandi that he would like to visit rebel territory so that he could get an up-close feel for the displacement. He knew that he would be a more effective advocate if he had witnessed firsthand the terror and squalor of the refugees' new circumstances, but he also knew that carrying out such a visit would be frowned upon by New York. He could get caught up in the crossfire of the joint rebel-Rwandan offensive, or, given anti UN feeling among the Rwandans, he might even be targeted. But the bigger risks were political. It had been one thing for his friend Bakhet to slip into eastern Zaire, but it would be quite another thing for a UN official of his stature to make the trek. He would be seen to be legitimating Kabila's rule, and Mobutu's government would be incensed. "The Zaireans are only willing to endure me here because I'm junior," Grandi told his senior colleague. "They will erupt if you come." But Vieira de Mello had made up his mind. "We will be discreet," he said, "and we will not meet with the rebels. I will just look around." In the end Grandi prepared a travel manifest that listed the assistant secretary-general as a lowly field officer, and on November 25 Vieira de Mello slipped anonymously across the border to spend a few hours in the Goma, Mugunga, and Lake Vert camps, where he could meet with shell-shocked refugees who had survived the attacks. What he saw in Zaire only deepened his conviction that the Multinational Force was urgently needed. "The people we can see are by definition the lucky ones," he said to Grandi. "Where the hell are the rest?"

On November 27 Vieira de Mello traveled to Entebbe, where General Baril was setting up MNF advance headquarters. He eagerly told Baril that the MNF could do everything from airlifting groups of refugees out of the forest to arresting the *génocidaires* and turning them over to the UN war crimes tribunal. Baril nodded politely, but on his way to Entebbe he had stopped in Stuttgart, Germany, to consult with troop contributors, and he knew that Western enthusiasm for the mission was evaporating. He explained that the troop contributors had discussed four levels of MNF engagement:

- Level A: ascertaining the location and condition of the refugees;
- Level B: establishing airlift capacity for delivering humanitarian aid;
- Level C: helping return the refugees to Rwanda in a permissive environment; and
- Level D: helping return the refugees to Rwanda in a dangerous environment.

Baril told Vieira de Mello that the MNF would go no further than Level A. Under no circumstances would it separate out the *génocidaires* or protect aid workers.[42] Vieira de Mello, who was crestfallen, battled, in Baril's words, "like a bulldog." "If we can save a hundred refugees," he pleaded, "let's save a hundred!" But Baril shook his head. "Sergio, the machinery I have isn't meant to save a hundred. Militaries are big, cumbersome, slow, and expensive." He suggested that UNHCR charter its own commercial planes to retrieve the refugees from the jungle. When Vieira de Mello said that was a military's job, Baril put his foot down. "Look, Sergio, your plan is limited only by your imagination. Mine is limited by the countries who have sent troops to serve under me." Vieira de Mello never ceased to wonder how political and military leaders saw nothing unseemly about asking unarmed aid workers to enter areas into which they would not dare send their soldiers.

Having hoped fleetingly that UN member states were prepared to step in to help the desperate refugees, he saw now that the plans had collapsed. His own mission had come to feel like a failure on every front. In his entire career he could not recall a field job where he spent so much time in motion and achieved so little. "In Bosnia, we humanitarians may have been fig leaves for Western powers," he told a colleague later, "but in Zaire we were invisible and irrelevant. I'm not sure which was more pathetic."

On December 23 the UN Security Council decided to disband the nascent MNF. The United States called off the search for refugees, claiming that UNHCR had exaggerated the number of missing refugees and blaming the agency for failing to separate out the "intimidators." Vieira de Mello was furious. "They think it would have been so easy to say, '*Génocidaires* to the left, civilians to the right,'" he fumed. "Well, if it was so easy, why didn't they come and help when we asked them?" Henceforth he would borrow European humanitarian commissioner Bonino's description of the Multinational Force: "Multinational Farce."

REPATRIATION FROM TANZANIA: SIDING WITH POWER

Having felt powerless to address the humanitarian debacle in Zaire, Vieira de Mello decided to take charge of the less threatening but equally untenable situation in the refugee camps in neighboring Tanzania. In the aftermath of the Rwandan genocide, Tanzania had absorbed 535,000 Rwandan exiles, and now, after more than two years of playing host, the Tanzanian government wanted to expel the Hutu refugees in the camps whom they blamed for deforestation, theft, and violence.[43] Tanzania had the backing of the United States and the U.K., which were urging Ogata to scale back food aid in the camps as a precursor to closing them.[44] UNHCR was dependent on voluntary contributions and took such demands from donor governments seriously.

Vieira de Mello had last visited the Tanzanian refugee camps in September. They were not nearly as militarized as those he had seen in Zaire because the Tanzanian authorities had been more effective in keeping heavy armaments out of the camps and even in arresting a few high-profile *génocidaires*. But these actions had the unintended effect of making the camps more comfortable for the Rwandan exiles. Tanzania's largest camp, Benaco, which was home to 160,000 refugees, bore street signs named for such people as Nelson Mandela and even Sadako Ogata. Beside row upon row of small mud-brick huts, the Rwandan Hutu grew maize and vegetables in their well-groomed gardens.[45] Having witnessed the violence in Zaire and fearful it would spread next to Tanzania, Vieira de Mello was prepared to urge Ogata to pull the plug on assistance.

But on November 27, 1996, the Tanzanian authorities beat him to it, officially informing UNHCR that they intended to close the camps and send the refugees home. The Tanzanians asked Vieira de Mello if UNHCR would help fund the $1.7 million operation. If UNHCR was squeamish about cooperating, they said, they would proceed on their own and would not hesitate to employ their "own methods."[46] Vieira de Mello agreed to team up.

His decision put him on a collision course with his old friend Dennis McNamara, who had become UNHCR's director of protection.[47] McNamara adamantly opposed UNHCR's complicity in any plan that would force refugees to return to Rwanda, where many had genuine reasons to fear persecution. The two friends engaged in tense, pitched battles by phone and in person.[48] "We don't have a choice," Vieira de Mello argued. "The Tanzanians are going to send them back anyway." McNamara thought the Tanzanians might be bluffing, but regardless he did not believe that their threats should dictate UNHCR's stance. "Let them do it anyway," he said. "Just don't let UNHCR be a part of pushing people back." Vieira de Mello said he was committed to a voluntary and orderly return, but he could not afford to be a purist. In camps controlled by *génocidaires,* the whole notion of voluntariness, a cornerstone of UNHCR's existence, had been thrown on its head. Could anybody really claim that the refugees were voluntarily remaining in the border camps of Tanzania or voluntarily serving as human shields for Hutu gunmen fleeing deeper into the jungles in Zaire? In addition, Tanzania was receiving a flood of new refugees from Burundi, and he worried that a testy Tanzania might seal its borders, keeping out people who were fleeing for their lives.[49] "Get real, Dennis," he said. "You can't just come riding in on that great white horse of moral principle; you have to solve the problem."

On Friday, November 29, Vieira de Mello flew to the Tanzanian capital, Dar-es-Salaam, where he held a three-hour meeting that would decide the fates of the refugees. He appealed to the Tanzanians "as far as possible" to carry out the repatriation "consistent with established principles."[50] At the start of the meeting he said that force should not be used to move the refugees. But since he doubted that the refugees would budge without some form of coercion, he did not object when the Tanzanians said they would send police and security forces to the camps. In a testament to his desire to solve the refugee problem once and for all, he even offered UNHCR funds to transport and pay the forces. Griffiths, his deputy, was struck by the speed and ease with which he accepted the Tanzanian arguments. "Sergio had been briefed before the meeting about all the arguments on each side, but when we got into the meeting, he seemed to have made up his mind," Griffiths recalls. "He effectively said, 'Do it, do it quickly, and if you have to use the police to do it, do your best to keep them out of sight.'" The Tanzanians said they wanted the matter resolved by December 31.[51] This gave Vieira de Mello and UNHCR almost no time to try to ensure that the operation would be carried out humanely. Nonetheless, he insisted that an imperfect refugee return operation was preferable to the status quo. "We have to choose the least bad option here," he told his critics.

Repatriating more than half a million Hutu from Tanzania was bound to be messy. In Cambodia he had managed the return of 360,000 Cambodians over thirteen months, making use of huge financial resources and a large peacekeeping presence. In Tanzania, UNHCR would have just three weeks, and once the Hutu refugees returned to Rwanda, they would not receive international protection. The most crucial difference was one of mind-set: The refugees on the Thai-Cambodian border had been impatient to go home, while the refugees in Tanzania were so frightened of returning to Rwanda that some would likely take up arms to stay where they were.

On December 5, 1996, Vieira de Mello signed off on a joint UNHCR-Tanzanian "Message to all Rwandese Refugees in Tanzania." Remarkably, even though he had growing concerns about human rights conditions in Rwanda and could by no means guarantee the refugees' safety, he put UNHCR's stamp on the assurance that "all Rwandese refugees can now return to their country in safety."[52] UNHCR arranged for leaflets to be printed and distributed in the camps and for loudspeakers to broadcast the joint communiqué in Kinyarwanda. The statement did not inform the refugees that, under the 1951 Refugee Convention, any person who feared persecution had the legal right to remain in Tanzania and apply for asylum.

By the evening of December 11, rumors began circulating among aid workers that some refugees had begun to leave the Tanzanian camps voluntarily. The refugees had harvested crops from their small gardens, waited to receive their biweekly ration of red beans, corn, and cooking oil, and taken off on foot.[53] At first the aid workers were hopeful that the commotion signaled the end of the spell the *génocidaires* had cast over the refugees. But by the morning of December 12, UNHCR officials were aghast to learn that the refugees were in fact trudging toward Kenya and Zambia, away from the border and thus away from their former homes in Rwanda. Camps that just twenty-four hours before had teemed with life were being completely vacated.

Rwandan Hutu militiamen had gone hut-to-hut ordering the refugees to move east across the plains of northwestern Tanzania. Some headed into the hills of the Burigi Game Reserve, the home of lions, zebras, elephants, and giraffes. Many of the women carried children strapped to their backs. Refugees told the few aid workers and journalists they encountered that Kagame's Rwandan troops were waiting to arrest or kill them if they returned to Rwanda. The horror stories were vivid: Babies would be snatched from their mothers, and the hands and feet of returning Hutu would be chopped off.[54] "Is it true that they will castrate all the men and boys at the border?" one refugee asked a reporter.[55]

Vieira de Mello had already left Tanzania for Rwanda when all hell broke loose. Ogata consulted with him by phone and issued instructions from Geneva: UNHCR should support the Tanzanian government's attempt to redirect the refugees toward Rwanda. Ten thousand Tanzanian soldiers carrying clubs and AK-47s had already set up roadblocks and begun forcing the refugees to do an about-face. The "orderly and humane" return promised by UNHCR had turned into a military push-back, as McNamara had feared.

By December 16 the rate of return was staggering. More than 10,000 people crossed per hour, 51,000 by midday, and more than 100,000 by the time the border crossing was closed for the night.[56] The refugees, who were herded over a narrow concrete bridge over the Kagera River into Rusumo, Rwanda, were exhausted and terrified. The farther they had walked, the more swollen were their feet. Draped in rags and plastic bags, they had braved heavy rains. The wealthier ones carried their belongings piled high on bicycles or in wheelbarrows. An estimated twenty-five babies were born each day along the way.[57] So many children were getting separated from their parents—134 children had gotten lost on December 15 alone—that Red Cross workers began tying children to their mothers with yellow string.[58]

The operation grew increasingly violent. The refugees described systematic beatings, demands for bribes, theft of their Tanzanian currency (under the ruse that the refugees were not permitted to take currency out of the country), strip searches, and the looting of personal property such as bicycles, blankets, jerry cans, and even UNHCR plastic sheeting. A few refugees were found raped or beaten to death.[59] The Tanzanians were so determined to rid their country of the Rwandan Hutu exiles that they fired guns into the air, used tear gas, and beat the refugees with sticks in order to keep them moving. Several refugees attempted suicide. One man used a blunt knife to cut his neck but survived, while another drowned himself in a shallow puddle of water.[60] In less than two weeks more than 450,000 refugees returned to Rwanda from Tanzania.[61] And these on the heels of the 700,000 who had arrived back after fleeing the camps in Zaire.

Ogata and UNHCR were so afraid of jeopardizing their relationship with the Tanzanian government that they said little in response to the forceful push-back. On January 10, 1997, Ogata finally signed a relatively tame letter of protest over the "reported use of force." But when Vieira de Mello telephoned Elly Mtango, a leading official in the Tanzanian foreign ministry, to inform him that the protest would be sent to the president the following day, Mtango warned him that UNHCR would have to "live with the consequences" of such a hostile act.[62] Knowing that UNHCR needed Tanzania to keep its borders open to refugees from other countries, Vieira de Mello agreed not to send the letter.[63]

UNHCR had been complicit in this forced repatriation, and both the agency and Vieira de Mello came under attack. Human rights groups speculated that the agency had simply bowed before the whims of its largest donors, who had made no secret of their desire to see the camps closed. Since the end of the cold war, UNHCR had seemed to internalize the impatience of host countries and donors who wanted to rush repatriation. "UNHCR may not have been able to stop the repatriation from Tanzania," says Gil Loescher, a refugee expert who in 2003 would be meeting with Vieira de Mello in Iraq on the day of the attack on the UN base. "But it should have made clear it opposed it, and it should have publicized what Tanzania was planning. It should have used its leverage with donor governments. And at the very least it should not have sanctioned forced repatriation." Human Rights Watch accused the agency of having "shamefully abandoned its responsibility to protect refugees."[64]

Ogata had been every bit as eager as Vieira de Mello to rid UNHCR of the albatross of the Rwandan refugee problem. But seeing the price UNHCR was paying for the bungled Tanzania repatriation, she distanced herself from the operation and pointed the finger at Vieira de Mello. "The return of refugees from Tanzania cost UNHCR a lot," she says. "Sergio knew Tanzania well. But in choosing the lesser evil you can make a mistake. And it is not just Sergio who suffers the consequences. It is me as well."

ENDGAME

In Zaire, Kabila had effectively broken off all contact with the UN after a UN human rights rapporteur had accused his rebels of committing massacres. By the spring of 1997, with Kabila's army closing in on Kinshasa, it was essential that UNHCR restore its relations with the man who was now seemingly destined to become president of Zaire. Ogata asked Vieira de Mello to head back to the region in order to try to charm the warlord.

By the time he was able to meet with Kabila personally for the first time, Kabila's rebel forces were perched just sixty miles east of Kinshasa, and Mobutu was on the verge of surrendering. On May 12, 1997, upon arriving at Kabila's temporary base, Vieira de Mello was told he would have to wait. Grandi, the Italian UNHCR official who had arranged the visit and who knew that his boss had a packed schedule, was crestfallen. He apologized for the mix-up. "No problem," Vieira de Mello said. "You live out in the jungle the whole time. We bourgeois diplomats from Geneva can rough it occasionally. We will wait here until we are summoned."

He took advantage of the delay by holding meetings with individual members of Kabila's entourage and by plotting strategy. "I will use my usual tactics," he told Grandi. "I will build a bond up front by telling Kabila, 'I am not an American. I am not a Frenchman. I am a Brazilian, from the third world just like you.'" When the rebel leader finally turned up for the meeting the following day, Vieira de Mello did as he forecast, capitalizing on their shared third-world pedigree. "Sergio could mingle in all possible worlds. With Kabila he was a man from a poor former colony in the developing world," recalls Grandi. "And with European diplomats he was a Sorbonne-educated dignitary."

Vieira de Mello told Kabila that he hoped that he and UNHCR could "abandon polemic" and make a "fresh start" in repatriating all Hutu refugees remaining in Zaire to Rwanda. True to form, he said that while he was concerned about Kabila's alleged massacres, he saw no point in embarrassing the rebels by denouncing them publicly. Kabila was delighted. He told Vieira de Mello that he had been "beginning to despair" about working with UNHCR but found himself "encouraged" by their discussion. As the two men parted, Vieira de Mello wished him luck in his negotiations with Mobutu, which were scheduled for the following day. "This is going to be rapid," said Kabila.[65]

Indeed, Kabila brought his seven-month rebellion to a triumphant end just five days later. On May 17, 1997, he marched his forces into Kinshasa, declared the end of Mobutu's reign of nearly thirty-two years, and announced the birth of the Democratic Republic of Congo.[66] Kinshasa's residents poured into the streets to greet the rebels. They sang, chanted, and waved anything they could find that was white in order to signal peace: flags, paper, shirts, socks, and even plastic chairs. Mobutu flew that night to Morocco, while his ministers hightailed it by speedboat across the Congo River to Brazzaville, Congo, carrying their designer luggage.[67]

By July 1997 some 834,000 Hutu refugees who had once lived in the UNHCR camps had returned to Rwanda. Some 52,000 were known to still be living in Zaire and neighboring countries. This meant that 213,000 refugees who had at one point resided in the camps remained unaccounted for. Most were presumed to have been killed in battle or massacres, or to have died of disease, dehydration, or starvation in flight.[68] It was impossible to know how many of the deceased were killers and how many were civilians who had played no role in the 1994 genocide.

Rwandan vice president Paul Kagame said he had no remorse about the deaths of Hutu civilians. "It is my strong belief that the United Nations people are trying to deflect the blame for failures of their own making onto us," he said. "Their failure to act in eastern Zaire directly caused these problems, and when things blew up in their faces they blamed us. These are people who want to be judges and nobody can judge them."[69]

The Rwandan government had been brutal, yes; it had been deceitful, yes; but by joining forces with Kabila, it had also managed to destroy the hostile Hutuland at its border when nobody else would.

Back in Geneva, Vieira de Mello found himself attacked by colleagues and close friends for the decisions he had made in the field. He brushed off his critics, telling them, "You can't be involved in an operation this messy and expect to come out clean." He and McNamara picked up their argument where it had left off. "Sergio wanted to be friends with everyone," McNamara recalls. "But in this case he could not be friends both with Tanzania and the U.S. government, which wanted to force return, and with human rights advocates, who wanted any return to be voluntary." He had to choose a side, and, his friend remembers, "he sided with power." The heated battles took their toll. "It's hard enough to fight with friends professionally," McNamara says, "but when you fight with friends about principle, it is especially rough."

Vieira de Mello used the occasion of a gathering of the agency's governing board to strike back at those who were attacking him. The philosopher in him emerged in his defense of UNHCR. "Voluntariness is based on the execution of free will—freedom is the basis of will—and that is precisely what these [refugee] populations had been deprived of since the genocide." He closed his remarks defiantly:

> I request, therefore, those who so impulsively criticize us, including friends and institutions we deeply respect, those who have the privilege of distance and responsibility, to place events in their chronology and in their overall context, and not to use their memory in a selective manner.... To my knowledge, our critics had no better formula to offer. Damned if you do, damned if you don't! That, Mr. Chairman, is the frustration many of us felt.[70]

He was worn out. Having once believed that UNHCR should remain apolitical, he had grown exasperated by UNHCR's dependence on governments that themselves avoided exercising political leadership. He had never seen the UN's reputation so tattered by its performance, or relief to refugees carry such perverse side effects. "Would Rwanda, Zaire, and the UN all be better off if we had never set foot in those camps?" he wrote in an article for a book on peacekeeping. In instances in which proper security conditions did not exist, he asked provocatively, "Should humanitarian agencies refuse to intervene?"[71]

As a young man in UNHCR, Vieira de Mello had believed in a pure humanitarian ideal. He had believed that aid agencies could and should perform apolitical lifesaving tasks, and that peacekeepers could and should remain impartial and avoid the use of force. But Bosnia and Rwanda had taught him that sometimes when UN humanitarians tried to be neutral, they abetted criminal acts. If Bosnia had exposed for Vieira de Mello the shortcomings of UN peacekeeping, the Great Lakes crises exposed the limits of offering humanitarian care. He was now convinced that UN officials would better serve the powerless if they could find a way to enlist the power of the world's largest countries. His transformation from student revolutionary was complete.

What UN aid agencies had been missing in Bosnia had not been plastic sheeting to replace windows in wintertime but a determination by Western governments to halt aggression. What they had been missing in the Zaire crisis were not tents or high-protein biscuits but a willingness among the major powers to send police to Zaire to arrest the *génocidaires*. In his public remarks Vieira de Mello began exhorting his colleagues to stop hiding behind their allegedly apolitical, humanitarian roles. The Great Lakes ordeal showed that the innocent victim was "often a fictitious concept." He urged UN officials to accept "that humanitarian crises are almost always political crises, that humanitarian action always has political consequences, both perceived and real." Since everybody else was playing politics with humanitarian aid, he wrote, "we can hardly afford to be apolitical."[72]

Vieira de Mello needed to find a political job in a hurry. Ever since Lebanon, he had been keeping his eye on UN Headquarters in New York. In November the United States had vetoed Boutros-Ghali's nomination for a second term in office. The vote was 14–1, and U.S. officials had quickly tried to appease disgruntled African countries by choosing another African as the UN's seventh secretary-general: Kofi Annan, Vieira de Mello's friend and former colleague.[73] Vieira de Mello was thrilled. "I think Kofi will be able to bring me to New York at some point," he told Nakamitsu. "I am ready to make a move."

His ties with Ogata had stiffened. The year that had just passed was the darkest and most challenging in UNHCR's history. The plight of refugees and the trade-offs inherent in negotiating on their behalf no longer engaged him as they once had. The problems were too familiar, and the solutions to those problems resided not in Geneva and not in the field but in Washington, Paris, London, Moscow, and Beijing. "We are so remarkably ill informed," he told Griffiths. "We go into a place, we have no intelligence, we don't understand the politics, and we can't identify the points of leverage. I don't know why we are surprised that right now we are failing at almost everything. We can't protect refugees, and we can't protect the UN reputation."

His personal life too was changing. Laurent, his eighteen-year-old son, had entered university in Lausanne, Switzerland. And when Vieira de Mello returned from his posting in the Great Lakes, he took a step he had not taken before, renting his own apartment in Geneva. Although he did not consider filing for a legal separation, he lived more like a bachelor than he had since his early twenties.

But he was biding his time. His ambitions were professional, and he felt he was being wasted where he was. Maybe, he thought, if Annan brought him to New York, where global leaders converged, he might be able to lobby the major powers. But there were only so many political jobs suitable for a person of his rank. It was obvious that his next move would be to the prestigious rank of under-secretary-general, the hierarchical equivalent of earning his second star. The UN system had only twenty-one such slots.

If ascent in the UN were strictly merit-based, by 1997 Vieira de Mello would have been vying for one of several prominent jobs at UN Headquarters. With all of his proven gifts negotiating with governments, he might have been named under-secretary-general for political affairs. Or with his extensive experience working with and within UN peacekeeping missions, he could have been chosen under-secretary-general for peacekeeping operations.

But the UN could never be confused with a meritocracy. The permanent five Security Council countries got to vet who would fill key positions in the UN Secretariat. In the 1990s, the Department of Political Affairs generally went to a Brit, the Department of Peacekeeping Operations was slated for the French, both the Department of Management and the UN Development Program went to Americans, and the Secretariat's satellite office in Geneva was run by a Russian.[74] China, the only permanent member of the Security Council not looked after, did not yet complain about being under-represented.[75]

The one UN department in New York that had not been earmarked for a particular nationality was the small Department of Humanitarian Affairs, under which he had just served. DHA, which had been created after the Gulf

War to coordinate the UN's emergency-relief activities, had been run by a Swede, a Dane, and most recently by Akashi.

DHA had achieved little in its six years of existence. The heads of the agencies it was meant to coordinate—UNHCR, the World Food Program, and other UN relief organizations—had not warmed to a body that they saw as a nuisance. Ogata, who had dramatically expanded UNHCR's budget and global reach, resisted any efforts to give up the turf she had acquired.[76] But Vieira de Mello told Nakamitsu, who knew DHA well and advised him against taking the job, that he viewed the post as a "stepping stone" to a more political job in New York. "The main attraction is that I will be exposed to the Security Council," he said.

Normally, he was reluctant to campaign for himself. "I'm not like Shashi," he told colleagues, referring to Shashi Tharoor, an Indian national who had a reputation for wining and dining powerful diplomats. Vieira de Mello marveled at how, in his tenure at the UN, Tharoor had also managed to publish four nonfiction books, three novels, a collection of short stories, and a collection of essays.[77] While India would name Tharoor as its candidate for secretary-general in 2006, Vieira de Mello took it as a point of pride that his home country would never pull strings for him. "I have never asked Brazil for favors," he liked to say. But he had so impressed ambassadors from Western countries in recent years that he had their backing instead. In November 1997 Annan announced that Vieira de Mello would take over the department as under-secretary-general for humanitarian affairs.

People worked backward from Vieira de Mello's rapid rise in the UN and assumed he had a Machiavellian lust for power. They had started to interpret his every move as proof of an elaborate plan to earn the top job, that of UN secretary-general. Vieira de Mello had held this ambition early on in his career, but other factors had since crept into his thinking. "People thought Sergio plotted his life like in a chess game," recalls Fabrizio Hochschild, a Chilean Brit, then thirty-two, who succeeded Nakamitsu as his special assistant. "But he didn't think long-term. What he thought was, 'I'm bored now. It's time to move on. Where can I go? What can I learn?'" When a colleague in Geneva offered him congratulations on his promotion to under-secretary-general, he replied, "Big deal. Big fucking deal." But one aspect of the move was a big deal. Having worked at UNHCR for twenty-eight years, bowing out only twice to serve in peacekeeping missions in Lebanon and Bosnia, he was leaving his mother ship for good.

Several hundred people gathered for his farewell party in Geneva. He gave a very short speech in which he said, "I have gotten a lot from this place. I hope I have given something back. If I have any gift, it is that I am aware of my weaknesses." With Ogata away on leave, her deputy Gerald Walzer presented him with a UN flak jacket in its singular baby blue. "You'll need this to protect you against all the backstabbing in New York," Walzer said. One junior UNHCR official asked Vieira de Mello whether he had any recommendations for young staff who aspired to follow in his footsteps. "Be in the field," he replied. "That is it. That's what I built my career on. That's what's relevant. Nothing else matters."

He would keep the flak jacket hanging on a coatrack in his New York office.

Part II

Vieira de Mello with General Michael Jackson (center) in Kosovo.

Eleven

"GIVING WAR A CHANCE"

BECOMING A BUREAUCRAT

Working at UN Headquarters in New York for the first time in his career, Vieira de Mello sometimes felt as though he were suffering death by a thousand paper cuts. His first public appearance came on November 14, 1997. After Secretary-General Annan introduced him to the media as the new under-secretary-general for humanitarian affairs, responsible for coordinating all the humanitarian efforts in the UN system, he offered characteristically understated remarks. "I hope to contribute my modest field experience in humanitarian and peacekeeping operations to the strengthening of the office," he said. "Since solutions to humanitarian problems cannot be humanitarian," he continued, he intended to enlist the support of political, military, human rights, and economic development experts.

At the press conference he stood beside Annan in order to field journalists' questions. But the media had more pressing issues on their minds. The Republican-controlled U.S. Congress had torpedoed a spending bill that would have turned over to the UN nearly $1 billion of the $1.4 billion that the United States owed in back dues.[1] Annan warned that the UN could not keep borrowing from its peacekeeping budget in order to meet its obligations around the world.[2]

But the main topic of the day was the one that would define Annan's tenure as secretary-general: Iraq. Since the end of the Gulf War in 1991, UN inspectors had been mandated to dismantle Iraq's long-range ballistic missiles and its biological and chemical weapons programs. But two days before the press conference, Saddam Hussein had expelled the American weapons inspectors, and the Clinton administration had responded by threatening to bomb Iraq. Asked during the press conference whether he planned to evacuate UN staff there, Annan said he still hoped a diplomatic solution could be found. "We would definitely not put our staff in harm's way," he said. "And the moment we feel their lives are in danger, we will pull them out."[3]

When Vieira de Mello was at UNHCR, his colleagues could be roughly divided between two camps. On one side were the rights "fundamentalists" like Dennis McNamara who believed refugee law permitted few compromises with governments. On the other were the "pragmatists" like himself who were prepared to make deals that appeased the powerful in the belief that such compromises served the long-term interest of civilians. Having generally failed to persuade the UNHCR fundamentalists of his views, he had taken a good deal of heat and was glad by 1997 to strike out in a new place.

But no sooner had he arrived at the intensely pragmatic Secretariat in New York than he grew nostalgic for what he had left behind. The countries in the UN General Assembly had established UNHCR in 1951 as an office distinct from the UN as a whole. Because it raised its own funds and answered to its own governing board, it had a high degree of autonomy. By contrast, senior officials at UN Headquarters knew that their salaries were paid by the annual dues of UN member states. While UNHCR officials thought of themselves as servants of the refugees, UN officials in the Secretariat saw themselves as servants of governments. "There is the UN that meets and the UN that does," his UNHCR colleague Nicholas Morris told him. "Now you are joining the UN that meets."

Kofi Annan had been elected secretary-general the previous year by promising sweeping UN reform and by pledging to meet the demands of Republican senators Jesse Helms and Bob Dole to cut the bloated UN down to size. In announcing his plans, Annan said that the changes he proposed were the "most extensive and far-reaching reforms in the fifty-two-year history of the Organization."[4] One of the first targets for Annan's scalpel was the branch of the UN that Vieira de Mello had been tapped to run.

Annan tasked Vieira de Mello with downgrading the Department of Humanitarian Affairs into a smaller Office for the Coordination of Humanitarian Affairs (OCHA). Vieira de Mello did as asked, restructuring the office. Strongly partial to field experience over desk jobs, he filled vacancies by borrowing staff from the humanitarian field agencies. Joe Connor, the under-secretary-general for management who would have to approve any structural changes, raised no objections. But when Vieira de Mello sent a written version of his restructuring plan up to Annan's office, Connor summoned his colleague to see him. Connor and his team lined up on one side of the table, while Vieira de Mello and his closest associates stacked the other. In what Vieira de Mello took to be a patronizing lecture, Connor told him that New York was not Geneva, UN Headquarters was not UNHCR, and he would spare himself and the UN great inconvenience if he would put plans in writing and receive formal clearance before sending anything to the secretary-general. Vieira de Mello was so angry that he could not even speak. His tapped his leg under the table, and he took no notes. As soon as he got back to his office, he exploded in rage, telling Fabrizio Hochschild, his special assistant, "Who do they think I am? Some unknowing little humanitarian child who doesn't know the wise ways of the adults in New York!"

Since he hated being disliked, he was the wrong person to manage shrinking an office. As a field person accustomed to making do with very few people around him, he reviewed the posts within his department and wondered, "What the hell do all these people do every day?" He cut the staff size by half, which naturally demoralized officials who had predated him.

But the hostility of his immediate staff paled beside that of the powerful UN agencies that OCHA was supposed to coordinate. The heads of agencies more often came to meetings to protect their own interests than to develop common strategies. Hochschild remembers, "The attitude among the agencies toward Sergio then was, 'You can pretend to coordinate us if you want, but we're going to go right ahead with what we are doing, thank you.'" Vieira de Mello knew he lacked the one thing that might help him secure cooperation: money. Indeed, he had no operational budget at all.

He was miserable. For the first time in his long career, the wars he spent his days fighting were several thousand miles from any battlefield or refugee camp. He turned on his charm for number crunchers, not warlords. And while he had always found the paperwork at UNHCR tiresome, he had never had to fill out as many forms as he did at Headquarters. A man whose strongest asset was his charisma was reduced to making his appeals on paper—and in service not of action, but of mere coordination. "I'm not sure I believe in what we're doing," he confessed to an aide. "Do we really need this place?"

Once he had completed the restructuring of OCHA, he did what he had always done. Rather than bowing to fixed hierarchies, he identified and relied upon those who could get the job done and largely excluded those he considered deadweight. In his inner circle were those he trusted; in a more distant circle, those he respected; and in the outermost circle, those he deemed mediocre. The more junior staff flocked to him. "Young people at Headquarters trailed him around as if he were the Pied Piper," recalls John Ruggie, an assistant secretary-general.

Annie had remained in Europe with Laurent and Adrien, now nineteen and seventeen. Laurent was studying in Lausanne, while Adrien would enroll at the university in Lyon, France. Vieira de Mello bought an apartment for himself in the Manhattan Place complex on First Avenue between East Thirty-sixth and Thirty-seventh streets.

The building lobby was marbled and manned by a doorman with white gloves. The apartment itself was a drab, 1970s-style two-bedroom, lined with mirrors, but it had a stunning 180-degree view of the New York skyline, spanning from the East River to the World Trade Center towers at the southern tip of Manhattan. He loved the view and cherished finally having his own permanent base.

He had long appreciated wine, fine food, music, and the arts. But in New York, the world's cultural capital, he remained in "mission mode." With the exception of the runs he took several times each week in Central Park, his routine was indistinguishable from that in remote southern Lebanon. He remained in the office later than almost anybody on his staff, and he seemed perfectly content at night being one of the only officials in the entire UN system who read all the code cables from the field. On the occasions he took advantage of New York's culinary or cultural assets, he did so with friends from the UN, rarely reaching beyond his work circle. "For Sergio there was never a clear division between his personal life and his professional life," recalls Hochschild. "There was no such thing as 'after hours.'"

Each day he was in New York, his appetite for management shrank further.

By late 1998 he had delegated much of the bookkeeping and coordination to Martin Griffiths, his deputy whom he had come to nickname "the one-and-only Martin Griffiths." The bureaucratic battles were dull, degrading, and time-consuming. "Sergio had endless patience for everything else," says Hochschild, "but no patience for administration."

But parts of the job did suit Vieira de Mello: diplomacy, big-picture reflection, and speaking up on behalf of endangered civilians. In the multiple calls he paid to ambassadors with seats on the Security Council, he framed issues in language they would understand—both by speaking their languages and by relating the natural disasters, refugee flows, and civil wars to crises that their countries had endured. He knew that the more they trusted him, the more funds he would be able to extract from them during emergencies. Yet there were certain lines he would not cross: he despised diplomatic receptions and avoided them with vehemence.

One of the few people that Vieira de Mello failed to woo was the under-secretary-general for political affairs, Kieran Prendergast, a knighted former British ambassador.[5] Prendergast found Vieira de Mello's charm "studied" and his overall persona "obsequious." And Vieira de Mello could not stand Prendergast's prefacing his own name with "Sir" in his UN correspondence, as he thought it sent a message of class division ill suited to the UN's egalitarian ideal. The two men often sparred over minutiae. On one occasion Vieira de Mello argued that the term "hegemon" should be used in a public speech to describe the United States. Prendergast told him in his posh English accent that the word had pejorative overtones. Vieira de Mello believed that the term neutrally described U.S. predominance and telephoned Prendergast later in the day to happily inform him that the Oxford English Dictionary indeed defined "hegemon" neutrally as "leadership, predominance, preponderance." Prendergast dismissed him again. "I'm a native English speaker," he said coolly. "You'll have to trust me."

Vieira de Mello had hoped that being based in New York would afford him the time to branch out intellectually. He blocked out two or three hours each morning so that he could get reading done. But these reading slots were usually eaten up by unavoidable meetings or by the unexpected arrival of an old acquaintance from places as far-flung as Mozambique or Mongolia, for whom Vieira de Mello would always make time. Still, he did manage

to offer philosophical guidance on nettlesome intellectual and moral challenges to UN officials who did not themselves have the luxury of time to
reflect. To nonexperts, humanitarian action and human rights sounded like
synonyms or, at the very least, complements. But he knew that, in the real
world, feeding people was often incompatible with speaking out. "How do
we reconcile the need for humanitarian access and thus discretion, with the
need, sometimes the obligation, for human rights?" he asked a gathering of
diplomats from donor countries in Geneva, undoubtedly with the events of
Zaire and Tanzania on his mind. "In the face of overwhelming human rights
abuses, when do humanitarian agencies withdraw? Does the so-called humanitarian imperative have its limits?" Aid workers were generally so reactive
that they could seem unprofessional. "In each situation we have to invent
a new set of ground rules," he argued. "This in turn has led to accusations
that we are inconsistent and promote different standards in different situations."[6] When he laid out these fundamental questions, he sounded almost
embarrassed for having introduced theory into practice. "I have grown a bit
abstract," he told diplomats at the gathering, "a symptom that the remoteness
of New York is beginning to have an effect on me!"[7] But if he didn't devise
principles to guide humanitarian action, he worried that the aid organizations his office coordinated would continue to drift haphazardly from one
crisis to the next.

He excelled at serving as an emissary in New York for afflicted peoples
and regions. Nobody in the UN system was more persuasive about why a
place or a cause mattered morally or strategically. In November 1998 he visited the Central American countries (El Salvador, Honduras, Nicaragua, and
Guatemala) that had been devastated by Hurricane Mitch. In December 1998
he traveled to North Korea and returned to launch an appeal for $260 mil-
lion in UN food aid. The UN officials who accompanied him on his various
trips gaped at the ease with which he rattled off the names of officials from a
rural Chinese province or from the obscure Russian republic of Ingushetia,
pronouncing each name as if he were a local. His recall was photographic. Yet
no matter how compelling his presentations, donors were often uninterested
in contributing. After visiting Ukraine, for instance, he tried to draw attention to the needs of the survivors of Chernobyl, but his office raised just $1.5
million out of the $100 million it requested.[8]

AFGHANISTAN: "THE HUMANITARIAN TRAP"

Afghanistan was his hardest sell. He visited the country soon after he started in New York. An earthquake had killed 4,500 and displaced another 30,000, which only compounded the poverty and cruelty in a country that had suffered nineteen years of war. "In my 28 years with the UN, I have seen few places that gather as many nightmarish conditions as Afghanistan," he told the press. "Kabul looked to me like an immense Sarajevo. There is every reason to feel outraged."[9]

Since the Taliban took over in September 1996, the country had become what he called "the most difficult place to work on earth."[10] Taliban leaders said that they would not accept UN aid if the organization delivered relief directly to women. As the nominal coordinator of aid agencies, Vieira de Mello had to decide whether the UN agencies should accept the Taliban's discriminatory dispersal of aid, when he was sure that suspending aid on principled grounds would, in his words, "sentence civilian populations to death or greater suffering."[11] Asked by a reporter whether women still had access to humanitarian aid, he answered: "Yes. But if you ask me if they have access to a number of more important things than immediate food aid for survival, such as education, work, sanitary services, and medical professions, where women were previously in the majority, the answer is no. Or rather, they have access that is extremely limited to an unacceptable and revolting degree."[12]

As he usually did, he chose the path of negotiation. He treated the Taliban as rational actors, meeting with them in Kabul and creating what he called "a test of sincerity." In order to receive UN aid, they had to allow five schools for girls to be built along with five for boys.[13] But when he returned to New York, he received a letter from the Taliban informing him that they had no intention of educating girls and that foreign female UN employees would no longer be permitted to work in the country unless they were accompanied by their male relatives. Unsurprisingly, the Taliban had flunked his sincerity test.

Vieira de Mello protested the new regulations, but he also urged the UN agencies to send Muslim women to replace non-Muslims in the hopes of smoothing ties. The Taliban just grew more brazen. On March 23, 1998, the

Taliban governor of Kandahar slapped the locally hired head of one UN agency in the face. The governor previously had struck an official from the International Committee of the Red Cross and thrown a thermos at a UN regional coordinator. Vieira de Mello felt he had no choice but to recommend that the UN pull its international staff out of Kandahar and that it suspend its aid programs in southern Afghanistan.

Yet still he bowed to the humanitarian imperative. Not long after the face-slap, he appealed to UN agencies to return to the region. Before long, most evacuated staff had in fact resumed aid deliveries. No matter how many lines the Taliban crossed, relief groups brought the same attitude to bear that they had with the Serbs and the Rwandan Hutu: They believed their primary duty was to provide food, medicine, and educational services to civilians. They were willing to swallow an awful lot if it meant continuing to deliver aid. Vieira de Mello had taken to calling this the "humanitarian trap." In May 1998, when Griffiths helped negotiate a twenty-three-point memorandum of understanding between the UN and the Taliban, human rights groups denounced the UN for accepting the Taliban's rules. "The UN endorsement of Taliban restrictions on women's basic rights to education and health care," Physicians for Human Rights said in a press release, "is a betrayal of international human rights standards and of the female population of Afghanistan."[14]

And with a regime as brutal and erratic as the Taliban, any "understanding" was bound to be temporary. The following month the Taliban ordered all private aid groups to gather their workers into a dilapidated building in Kabul, where henceforth they could be more easily controlled. More than two hundred foreigners from thirty-eight aid organizations left Afghanistan in protest, forcing the suspension of three-quarters of international aid to the country.

With Vieira de Mello's backing, large UN agencies such as the World Food Program and the UN Development Program hung on. But security kept deteriorating. On July 13 two local UN staff were abducted in eastern Afghanistan and found hanged a week later. And on August 20 tensions increased when the United States retaliated for al-Qaeda's attacks on the U.S. embassies in Kenya and Tanzania by firing cruise missiles on a terrorist training camp in eastern Afghanistan allegedly housing Osama bin Laden.[15] The following day a French UN employee was shot in the face and an Italian UN military official was fatally shot in the stomach while driving in a UN vehicle in Kabul.

For the next seven months UN agencies remained outside Afghanistan, but Vieira de Mello maintained contact with Taliban leaders. Initially he told them that the UN would not return unless the deaths of UN staff were investigated and punished. But in March 1999, under pressure from donor countries and the aid groups themselves, he said that the Taliban had made a "satisfactory and concerted effort" to investigate the murders, and he claimed that security conditions in the country permitted the UN's gradual return.

Neither he nor powerful governments seemed to appreciate the extremity of the crisis brewing in Afghanistan. He told the Taliban of his fears that bin Laden would stage attacks on UN personnel, but Taliban leaders persuaded him that they had al-Qaeda under control. "We have raised the Osama bin Laden problem with the Taliban leadership," Vieira de Mello told reporters on the day he announced the UN return. He said unconvincingly that they had given him "assurances" that bin Laden was "not above the law" and would "not be allowed to put the lives of international staff of humanitarian agencies in danger."[16] In but one testament to his ability to hear what he wanted to hear, he took them at their word.

"Taking Sides"

Vieira de Mello understood better than most the risks faced by aid workers in the field. Some fifty humanitarians had been killed in 1998, while sixty-four would die in 1999.[17] In almost all of his public appearances, he tried to sound the alarm about the increasing danger to humanitarian personnel. In the new era of warfare, where irregular armed forces were proliferating, aid workers were seen increasingly as bonus targets. "The providers of food are automatically perceived as taking sides," he said. "Anyone helping the victims on one side is bound to be accused by the other side of supporting the enemy." He noted that "for the first time in our history it is more dangerous to be an unarmed humanitarian worker than an armed soldier on peacekeeping duties."[18] Believing the best he could do was to press for laws that might deter attacks, he argued that the new International Criminal Court should punish the targeting of humanitarian personnel as a war crime.[19]

What infuriated him was that at just the time aid workers were assuming ever greater risks, they were taking ever more blame for their ineffectiveness. He defended the work of his colleagues in the field who were not in a position to defend themselves. In 1999 scholar Edward Luttwak published an influential article in *Foreign Affairs* entitled "Give War a Chance," in which he suggested that aid workers and peace-brokers were prolonging wars that would only end permanently if they were "allowed to run their natural course." "Policy elites," Luttwak wrote, "should actively resist the emotional impulse to intervene in other peoples' wars—not because they are indifferent to human suffering but precisely because they care about it."[20]

Vieira de Mello wrote a steaming letter to the editor slamming Luttwak's "simplistic compilation of old arguments and wrong conclusions."[21] He faulted Luttwak for his "uniform picture of war." Since few conflicts tidily confined themselves within national borders, Vieira de Mello argued, turning one's back on violence would often result in wider, messier regional conflicts. In addition, since so many governments and rebel movements benefited from war, they had an incentive to prolong war on their own. They didn't need any help from aid workers. While he acknowledged that humanitarian action could sometimes have perverse consequences, he wrote that "to deny aid altogether is not only unhelpful, it is unthinkable."[22] He noted that he generally valued critical commentary, but he found unhelpful such "oversimplified accounts far removed from the complexities of actual war and blanket statements that lead to quietism."[23]

Of course, after his time in Bosnia and Zaire, Vieira de Mello had his own concerns about humanitarian action and its capacity to do inadvertent harm. But he thought the flawed tendency of aid workers to give aid uncritically and indefinitely was a lesser danger than the tendency of rich countries to turn their backs on humanitarian crises altogether. The biggest flaw in the UN system was that governments came to the UN and paid lip service to the tenets of the UN Charter but were unprepared to do what it took to patrol the global commons. "There are currently more international instruments and mechanisms to control the illicit production and trade of compact discs than there are for small arms," he observed.[24] For as long as countries calculated their self-interest within short time frames, the UN and other humanitarian bodies would be left to manage only the violent symptoms of inequality, rage, and terror.

In early January 1999, a year into his time at Headquarters, Vieira de

Mello nearly quit the United Nations. The *Washington Post* and the *Boston Globe* broke a story alleging that several UN weapons inspectors in Iraq (the team included nine Americans, eight Brits, one Russian, and one Australian) had passed along eavesdropping intelligence to the Clinton administration. The intelligence had made it easier for Washington to bomb targets that it said were connected to Iraq's development of weapons of mass destruction. The scandal underscored just how tangled the webs of intergovernmental and governmental allegiances could become. The inspectors had joined the UN only after working for their national intelligence services. "When we ask for nonproliferation people, where do they come from?" Charles Duelfer, a senior U.S. inspector on the team, was quoted as saying. "The Red Cross doesn't have chemical weapons experts."[25] But the inspectors had been admitted to Iraq only because they operated under the UN—and not the U.S. or British—flag. Inspectors signed loyalty oaths when they joined the UN, promising never to share their findings with their governments or the public.[26] In Iraq on a UN mission of peace, they seemed to have instead facilitated an American war.

Vieira de Mello telephoned Omar Bakhet after midnight on a Friday, two days after the story first broke. "Sergio, you sound drunk," said Bakhet, who had been posted to New York after Rwanda.

"Something terrible has happened," said Vieira de Mello. "Can you meet me in the morning?"

The two men met the next day at a Starbucks in midtown Manhattan. When Vieira de Mello arrived bleary-eyed and unshaven, Bakhet exclaimed, "Sergio, I never thought the day would come where I would be able to say this to you, but you look horrible."

Vieira de Mello ignored his friend and thrust a copy of the *Washington Post* down before him. "This is unacceptable. It will taint the UN everywhere," he said. "I think I have to resign."

Bakhet glanced at the cover story and back at his friend. "You're not actually surprised that the Americans are using the UN as cover, are you?" Bakhet asked.

"Omar, the United Nations is *spying* for the United States," said Vieira de Mello. "Spying! We have completely surrendered our independence, our impartiality, and our neutrality. And without our principles, we have nothing. Nothing!"

Bakhet shook his head and said, "What amazes me, Sergio, is your naïveté."

Vieira de Mello cut him off: "I am not speaking to you naïvely. The minute we become an instrument, the minute that we cover up for governments, we've lost all we've got to offer."

"But, Sergio," Bakhet said, "you of all people know the influence of the United States."

Vieira de Mello interrupted again. "Influence, yes," he said, "but outright servitude, no."

Only after several espressos did he agree to let the weekend pass before drafting his letter of resignation. By the following day he had calmed down and begun debating tamer measures, such as visibly snubbing Richard Butler, the head of the UN inspections team, who was thought to be responsible for the leaks, when he next visited UN Headquarters. Hochschild, his assistant, agreed that some kind of public rebuke of Butler was called for, and was thus taken aback when he saw Vieira de Mello greet Butler on his next visit as if nothing had happened. No matter how great his outrage, Hochschild noted, Vieira de Mello remained as reluctant as ever to make an enemy.

Kosovo: "Not Waging War"

When he lived in the Balkans in the early 1990s, Vieira de Mello had refused even to make an enemy of Serbian president Slobodan Milošević, who, like Saddam Hussein, had tormented his citizens for more than a decade. Milošević had been halted but not deposed by Western military force in Bosnia in 1995. Throughout 1998, Vieira de Mello's first year in New York, Milošević's police and paramilitaries had responded to an insurgency in the southern Serbian province of Kosovo by stepping up their attacks on ethnic Albanians, who made up 90 percent of the population of two million.[*]

By the fall of 1998 a guerrilla force known as the Kosovo Liberation Army (KLA) had also stepped up its attacks on Serb policemen and other

---

[*] The 1974 Yugoslav constitution had given the province of Kosovo self-governing powers comparable to those of Serbia and the country's other five republics. In 1989, however, Milošević stripped the province of its autonomy and put it under Serbia's jurisdiction. For clarity, I will refer to "Kosovo" and "Serbia" as if they were separate geographic entities, when in fact Kosovo was a province within Serbia.

Serb authorities in the hopes of driving them out of the province. The Serbs had retaliated by forcing some 230,000 Kosovar Albanians out of their homes and killing some 700 civilians. In September the UN Security Council passed a resolution demanding that the Serbs cease their attacks on ethnic Albanians and withdraw their forces from Kosovo. The Council also authorized the dispatch of international monitors. But despite the resolution and the presence of the monitors, by December Serb gunmen had resumed burning homes and displacing civilians. On January 15, 1999, Serb paramilitary forces murdered some 45 Kosovar Albanians in the town of Racak. Because NATO had already put its reputation on the line in the region—some 33,000 NATO troops were still patrolling the peace in neighboring Bosnia—Western leaders believed that Serbia's antics were making the alliance look weak, and they began to consider using military force against the Serbs.

In February 1999 diplomats from the United States, Europe, and Russia convened Kosovar and Serb leaders at the French château of Rambouillet and presented a take-it-or-leave-it plan that would have kept Kosovo within Serbia but granted it unprecedented powers of self-governance. It would also have provided for the deployment of a NATO force to deter violence and enforce the deal. After a delay the Kosovar Albanians accepted the plan, but the Serbs walked out of the talks. In the meantime, 40,000 Serbian soldiers, one-third of Serbia's total armed forces, massed in and around Kosovo.

Richard Holbrooke, the Clinton administration's envoy to the Balkans, traveled to Serbia's capital, Belgrade, to inform Milošević that he could either accept the Rambouillet deal or face NATO bombing. When the Serbs made no concessions by March 23, he departed Belgrade. Kofi Annan withdrew UN aid workers from Kosovo the same day. The stage had been set for war—and for the biggest challenge to the UN Charter since the end of the cold war.

On March 24, 1999, NATO began bombing Serbia. NATO secretary-general Javier Solana was insistent that, despite all appearances to the contrary, NATO's action was not especially aggressive. "Let me be clear," he said implausibly as cruise missiles rained down on Serbia, "NATO is not waging war against Yugoslavia."[27]

The UN Security Council had not authorized what NATO was doing. The United States and the U.K. had not introduced a resolution in the council because Russia and China, two of its five permanent members, had made plain their intention to veto it. And according to the UN Charter, the Security Council was the only body empowered to determine whether Milošević's attacks on ethnic Albanians constituted a sufficiently grave "threat to international peace and security" to warrant collective military action. The Council had authorized the U.S.-led Gulf War in 1991, as well as the U.S. feeding-cum-nation-building exercise in Somalia. And it had established the UN "safe areas" in Bosnia and eventually called upon NATO to protect them. Vieira de Mello was a true believer in the Security Council's primacy, which he said carried the "central and unique responsibility" for keeping peace.[28] But suddenly his respect for the Charter had come into conflict with his determination to prevent atrocity.

No country likes to be seen as breaking the law—even law as fuzzy as international law—and U.S. and British officials argued that the Security Council had effectively already licensed the war with a resolution it had passed the previous September. Clinton's national security adviser, Sandy Berger, also invoked the consensus within NATO, saying, "We have 19 members of NATO, all democracies, having authorized this action."[29] But Western officials could not mask the reality that a major military operation was being undertaken without the blessing of the Security Council.[30]

Having gotten to know Milošević five years before, Vieira de Mello was no stranger to the Serbian strongman's brutality. Nor was he opposed, in principle, to the use of force. He was a different man than the civil servant who in Bosnia had dutifully probed Council resolutions like a Talmudic scholar. After Rwanda and Srebrenica he had reluctantly come around to the view that military action on humanitarian grounds, while never desirable, was sometimes necessary. When the UN failed to act, it was not only the victims of massacres who suffered; it was the credibility of the UN as a whole.

Vieira de Mello understood that Russia and China would almost never support military action for humanitarian purposes. As countries that committed grave human rights abuses at home, they had too much to lose themselves. Throughout the 1990s the two countries had regularly invoked sovereignty as grounds for stymieing discussions of government misdeeds. Only when Western powers stood together unequivocally, flexing their collective diplomatic

The Vieira de Mello family on the beach in Beirut, 1955.

Sergio Vieira de Mello and his father, Arnaldo, on the balcony of their home in Rome, undated.

Sergio *(center)* acting in a school play in Rome, 1958.

Sergio holding a soccer ball on the balcony in Rome, undated.

Sergio Vieira de Mello,
Geneva, 1967.

Sergio and his sister,
Sonia Vieira de Mello,
Stuttgart, 1968.

Vieira de Mello, Chittagong Airport, Bangladesh, February 25, 1972.

Vieira de Mello with Olimpio Vaz of FRELIMO, in Nyazonia, Mozambique,
near a camp that was attacked by the Rhodesian army, August 1976.

Annie Vieira de Mello with her and Sergio's sons, Adrien and Laurent, October 1981.

From left to right: Timur Goksel, Vieira de Mello, Brian Urquhart, and General William Callaghan in Lebanon, 1982.

Jamshid Anvar, Vieira de Mello, UN High Commissioner for Refugees Sadako Ogata, and Udo Janz in Battambang, Cambodia, January 1992.

Vieira de Mello with Annie, Adrien, and Laurent, on a ski holiday in Canada, February 1992.

Vieira de Mello in front of the Angkor Wat temple in Cambodia, 1992.

Vieira de Mello watching refugees board buses in Thailand in the first UN repatriation operation in Cambodia, March 30, 1992.

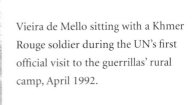

Vieira de Mello sitting with a Khmer Rouge soldier during the UN's first official visit to the guerrillas' rural camp, April 1992.

Lieutenant General Sir Michael Rose *(left)*, Vieira de Mello, and Lieutenant Colonel Simon Shadbolt, formulating the terms of a draft peace agreement for Bosnia on Rose's laptop, Geneva, June 6, 1994.

Vieira de Mello standing with Lieutenant General Sir Michael Rose *(right)*, Yasushi Akashi *(seated, right)*, and Bosnian Serb leaders *(left to right)* Nikola Koljevic, General Ratko Mladić, Momcilo Krajisnik, Radovan Karadžić *(seated)*, and Aleksa Buha in Geneva, June 8, 1994.

Vieira de Mello on a ten-day assessment mission in the former Yugoslavia,
viewing the Zastava car factory on May 19, 1999, in Kragujevac,
Serbia, which was destroyed by NATO bombing.

Vieira de Mello with UN secretary-general Kofi Annan at a
UN Security Council session on Kosovo, June 1999.

Vieira de Mello introducing his successor, Bernard Kouchner, to Lieutenant General Sir Michael Jackson, commander of UN peacekeeping forces in Kosovo, July 15, 1999.

Vieira de Mello with sons Laurent and Adrien in Beijing, April 2000.

Vieira de Mello inspecting peacekeepers in East Timor, January 16, 2002.

Above: Vieira de Mello and his special assistant Fabrizio Hochschild sailing off the coast of East Timor, May 2000.

Left: President Bill Clinton arriving at the airport in Dili for East Timor's independence ceremony, May 19, 2002.

Vieira de Mello embracing Dennis McNamara in East Timor, May 2002.

Vieira de Mello and Carolina Larriera saying good-bye to Domingos Amaral, Vieira de Mello's translator, at the airport in East Timor, May 21, 2002.

Vieira de Mello and Larriera visiting King Sihanouk in Cambodia, June 2002.

Larriera and Vieira de Mello with his mother, Gilda, in her apartment in Rio de Janiero, Christmas Eve, 2002.

On March 5, 2003, Vieira de Mello and his special assistant Jonathan Prentice entering the White House *(left)*, and Vieira de Mello meeting with President George W. Bush *(below)*.

Iranian president Mohammad Khatami greeting Vieira de Mello in Tehran, Iran, July 17, 2003.

Larriera, Vieira de Mello, Prentice, and Gamal Ibrahim running in Baghdad stadium, July 2003.

Vieira de Mello with John Sawers, British representative in Iraq *(left)*, and L. Paul Bremer, U.S. administrator in Iraq *(center)*, at the first gathering of the Iraqi Governing Council, July 13, 2003.

Larriera and Vieira de Mello receiving security training in Baghdad, August 17, 2003.

Laurent, Annie, and Adrien Vieira de Mello in Rio de Janeiro, receiving the Brazilian flag after loading Sergio Vieira de Mello's coffin onto a plane, August 24, 2003.

Memorial service at the Palácio da Cidade, Rio de Janeiro, August 23, 2003. *From left to right:* Gilda *(in profile)* and Sonia Vieira de Mello, UN secretary-general Kofi Annan, and Annie Vieira de Mello.

and financial muscles, did Russia and China come around, as in the Persian Gulf War or in the belated decision to act militarily in Bosnia. But Vieira de Mello knew that occasions would arise when all the Western unity and diplomacy in the world would not change their views. In those circumstances, he was prepared to admit, exceptional emergencies might require a "coalition of the willing" to bypass the paralyzed Council. Ever so rarely, the urgency and legitimacy of the cause could excuse the illegality of the procedures.

But he had not made up his mind whether the circumstances in the former Yugoslavia in March 1999 qualified. If NATO went to war without the Security Council's blessing, he worried other countries would view the UN Charter's provisions as optional. And he made his views known to Nancy Soderberg, the Clinton administration's acting ambassador to the UN. "We have the international machinery to stop the Serbs' abuses," he said. "We just have to give the machinery time to work. Why the rush to bomb?" Soderberg, speaking for the Clinton administration and the Kosovars, countered, "Sergio, Milošević has been killing Albanians for more than a decade. If this is a rush, I'd hate to see what it would look like to take our time."

UN officials at Headquarters were bitterly divided over the war, and many looked to Vieira de Mello, the under-secretary-general for humanitarian affairs, for guidance. But either because he was conflicted or because he did not want to alienate those he did not agree with, he did not give it. He never openly declared whether on balance he opposed or supported the NATO war. "Even with a small group of us over drinks he would make his views appear totally neutral," recalls Rashid Khalikov, a Russian colleague in OCHA.

Vieira de Mello knew one thing: His personal view of NATO's war was irrelevant. To the degree that citizens of the world looked to the UN for comment, they looked to Secretary-General Annan, who had a checkered past when it came to responding to crimes against humanity and genocide. He had been in charge of the UN Department of Peacekeeping Operations during the Rwandan genocide and the Srebrenica massacre, and he had been justly criticized for failing to sound the alarm. Annan felt that the very countries that had turned their backs on the Rwandans and the Bosnians were the ones making him their scapegoat, but he knew that his name would appear in the history books beside the two defining genocidal crimes of the second half of the twentieth century. Since becoming secretary-general in 1997, he had used his pulpit to publicly urge governments to embrace a new "norm of humanitarian intervention" to halt atrocities.

Nonetheless Annan was the primary guardian of the UN rulebook. Since NATO was acting in defiance of that rulebook, the war's critics expected him to decry NATO's military action. But in this, the Security Council's first major crisis on his watch, Annan had two competing fears: Either the United States would come away believing it could do as it chose, or the Russians would be so disgusted with the UN's failure to deter the United States that it would turn away from the institution. The first day of the war Annan thus issued a statement in which he tried to have it both ways. He lamented the use of force but added the following jarring sentence: "It is indeed tragic that diplomacy has failed, but *there are times when the use of force may be legitimate in the pursuit of peace*."[31]

To the delight of the Clinton administration, the *New York Times* headline the day after the launch of the war read "THE SECRETARY-GENERAL OFFERS IMPLICIT ENDORSEMENT OF RAIDS."[32] Sergei Lavrov, Russia's ambassador to the UN, stormed into Annan's office and denounced him for his complicity in the illegal NATO attack. Vieira de Mello too told Hochschild that Annan had gone too far to appease the United States.

As the war progressed, Annan continued to walk a fine line between making clear that the NATO war technically violated the Charter and stressing that atrocities demanded a response. "Unless the Security Council is restored to its preeminent position as the sole source of legitimacy on the use of force, we are on a dangerous path to anarchy," the secretary-general said in one speech. "But equally importantly, unless the Security Council can unite around the aim of confronting massive human rights violations and crimes against humanity on the scale of Kosovo, then we will betray the very ideals that inspired the founding of the United Nations." He continued, "The choice must not be between Council unity and inaction in the face of genocide, as in the case of Rwanda, on the one hand; or Council division, and regional action, as in the case of Kosovo, on the other."[33]

Annan kept speaking out, both denouncing the horrors and asserting the indispensability of the UN. On April 7, two weeks into NATO's war, he delivered a speech at the UN Commission on Human Rights in Geneva in which he said:

When civilians are attacked and massacred because of their ethnicity, as in Kosovo, the world looks to the United Nations to speak up for them. When men, women and children are assaulted and their limbs hacked off, as in Sierra Leone, here again the world looks to the United Nations. When women and girls are denied their right to equality, as in Afghanistan, the world looks to the United Nations to take a stand. . . . We will not, and we cannot accept a situation where people are brutalized behind national boundaries.

Annan closed with a line that Vieira de Mello triple-underlined on his copy of the speech:

For at the end of the twentieth century, one thing is clear: A United Nations that will not stand up for human rights is a United Nations that cannot stand up for itself.[34]

After a few days of NATO bombing, pundits shifted away from debating whether the war was legal to discussing whether its ghastly consequences could be contained. In September 1995, when NATO had finally intervened forcefully in Bosnia, it brought the Bosnian Serbs to heel with remarkable speed. This precedent, as well as NATO's colossal 300–1 superiority in military expenditures, had left U.S. and U.K. planners bullish about the odds of a swift air campaign in Kosovo.[35] On the first day of the war, President Clinton had said that the United States had no intention of deploying ground troops. He expected the Serbs to surrender after just a few days.

But Milošević had other ideas. Within hours of NATO's first attack on March 24, he launched Operation Horseshoe, using prepositioned Serbian police and paramilitary forces to systematically empty Kosovo of ethnic Albanians. Masked gunmen in uniforms turned up in villages and threatened to kill any individual who refused to leave. By March 29, some 4,000 ethnic Albanians were pouring out of Kosovo per hour. In the first week more than 100,000 Kosovars streamed into Albania and 28,000 entered Macedonia, while another 35,000 fled to Montenegro. And in the days ahead they kept coming, by foot, by car, by train, and on tractors.

UNHCR had expected a maximum of 100,000 refugees to spill into neighboring countries, so they were overwhelmed when ten times that number crossed.[36] Sadako Ogata rushed staff to the border who hurried to fly

in extra food stocks, set up tents, and negotiate with neighboring Macedonia, which tried to deny entry to the refugees. But in the early days, when
the petrified Kosovars crossed the border into Macedonia and Albania, they
found almost nobody to welcome them. Indeed, in Macedonia five times
more international journalists awaited the refugees than UNHCR staff.[37]

Based in New York, Vieira de Mello could do little to help the refugees,
beyond hoping that his former colleagues at UNHCR caught up with the
flow. Telegenic and articulate, he took to the airwaves to shift attention from
the UN's lack of preparation to the ongoing suffering of Kosovar Albanians.
"Reports of masked men in uniforms knocking on doors and telling people
to leave or be killed are countless," Vieira de Mello told reporters. "We
are witnessing the emptying of ethnic Albanians from Kosovo."[38] Most of
the refugees reaching Macedonia and Albania were women, children, and the
elderly, he said, which raised "the disturbing question as to the fate of a large
proportion of Kosovar Albanian males within Kosovo."[39] No international
aid workers were present inside Kosovo, and less than four years after the
massacre in Srebrenica, he feared that the absence of men could well mean
the massacre of men.

Although UNHCR's reputation was severely bruised by the early chaos,
its fieldworkers quickly got their footing, amassing enough food and tempo-

The MacNeil/Lehrer NewsHour, *April 28, 1999.*

rary shelter to defuse the emergency. Families in Albania displayed remarkable generosity toward their Kosovar kin, and very few refugees died of disease, exposure, or starvation. The emergency abated. Some 800,000 Kosovar Albanians settled into refugee camps.

Initially, they had reason to fear their exile would be permanent. Clinton's renunciation of ground troops had convinced Milošević that, although his forces were hopelessly outgunned, they could wait out the air attacks until domestic public opinion in NATO countries turned against the war. Events on the battlefield augured well for the Serbs. Serb antiaircraft gunners shot down a U.S. F-117 stealth bomber on March 28. Four days later Serb forces captured three U.S. soldiers near the Macedonia–Yugoslav border. On April 12, NATO struck a passenger train south of Belgrade, killing thirty civilians and forcing Clinton to issue a public apology. Two days later NATO hit a convoy of families in flight, leaving sixty-four dead. On April 23, NATO destroyed the Serbian state television building, killing ten.

The heads of state of the nineteen NATO countries had expected to gather in triumph on April 23–25 in Washington to celebrate NATO's fiftieth birthday. But the alliance's first-ever war cast a pall on the occasion. And the bad news kept coming. On May 2 a U.S. F-16 fighter jet crashed inside Serbia (though its pilot was rescued). Three days later NATO suffered its first fatalities, as two U.S. Army pilots on a training mission in Albania died when their Apache helicopter crashed. On May 7 a NATO cluster bomb aimed at a military airport in Niš went astray and hit a hospital and a fruit and vegetable market, killing fifteen Serbs and wounding seventy.

NATO's lowest point came at 9:46 p.m. on May 7. Relying on an out-of-date map, American pilots fired three cruise missiles at what they thought was a Serbian government building but that proved to be the Chinese embassy. As firemen descended on the scene, a blood-soaked, frantic Chinese cultural affairs adviser appeared on Serbian television, saying, "We haven't found some of my colleagues." More than twenty people in the embassy were wounded, and three were killed. Chinese ambassador Pan Zhanlien stood before the ruins and said, "The People's Republic has been attacked." In Beijing a mob gathered at the U.S. embassy, trapping the ambassador inside. Protesters in the NATO countries of Greece, Italy, and Germany decried the civilian toll of the war.[40] A spokesman for Annan said the secretary-general was "shocked and distressed" at the growing number of deadly NATO mistakes.[41]

BEHIND SERB LINES

NATO's struggles on the battlefield caused the UN's star to shine brighter. The Western allies started to recognize that, while they had the military prowess to inflict severe harm, they would not necessarily succeed in extracting a surrender from Belgrade. For that they would need Serbia's historic backer, Russia, to press for peace. The Russians, who were not quick to forgive NATO for launching the war, attached a condition to their cooperation: The UN (where Moscow had great clout) rather than NATO (from which Moscow was excluded) would play the dominant role in any postwar transition.

Vieira de Mello had his own ideas about how to make the UN relevant again, and they did not entail waiting for the Russians to broker a deal. In a senior staff meeting in early May, as Annan described the criticisms he was getting for not condemning NATO, Vieira de Mello spoke up: "Well, there's one area we can take a stand," he said, "the humanitarian area." "Yes," said Annan, "but what can we do that we are not already doing?" Vieira de Mello answered, "We can get inside Kosovo."

It was a stroke of political genius. He would lead the first international team into Kosovo since NATO bombing had begun forty days before. The UN would place unarmed officials behind the front lines in a province from which Kosovars were fleeing and that NATO ground forces were avoiding. By entering Kosovo, Vieira de Mello thought he could ascertain the fate of the displaced civilians who had not made their way to safety and assess the extent of NATO's collateral damage. The trip would instantly elevate the UN's profile and might even do some good. Annan leaped at the idea, proposing it to the Security Council the following day.

The Russians were elated. Believing Vieira de Mello's mission would aid his Serbian allies, Ambassador Sergei Lavrov told Deputy Secretary of State Strobe Talbott, "It is no accident that Sergio and I have the same name!" Lavrov urged Vieira de Mello to document the severe economic and environmental devastation caused by NATO. U.S. and U.K. officials had the opposite reaction. With new reports of NATO collateral damage surfacing each day, and with no sure victory in sight, NATO planners did not want to have to go out of their way to avoid hitting UN personnel and thus reduce their already-thin list of targets. Because Yugoslav officials on the ground would block the UN's movement, the allies were also concerned that Vieira de Mello would emerge with more horror stories about stray NATO missiles than about Serb brutality. Nancy Soderberg, the acting U.S. ambassador to the UN, called him on May 5 to complain about the mission. "Sergio, this is a stupid idea," she said. "You are playing right into Serb hands." Firmly but gently he pushed back. "Nancy, my dear, I'm afraid this is nonnegotiable," he said. "We are the United Nations, and no country, not even one as powerful as yours, can tell us where we can and cannot go." U.S. officials nixed a planned Council statement welcoming the initiative.[42] The following day the divided Council instead issued a noncommittal statement saying it "took note" of the mission "with interest."[43]

One of the first people Vieira de Mello telephoned after he got approval to assemble a team was his friend Bakhet. They had spent countless hours debating whether there could ever be any such thing as "humanitarian" war. "Omar," he said, "do you want to go to Kosovo so we can study the merits and demerits of humanitarian intervention up close?" Bakhet accepted eagerly. "In a simple sense the activist Sergio preferred to be in the field, to find out what people needed," says Bakhet. "But the activist Sergio also knew that being in the field gave him more credibility in political discussions when he returned to capitals."

Vieira de Mello was exhilarated by the prospect of returning to the center of "the action" and, in so doing, inserting the UN back in the game. At the press briefing where he laid out plans for the trip, he downplayed the dangers. "There is an element of risk in any such mission, and, although we are not irresponsible, I would say that we are used to working in that kind of environment. Unfortunately this is not new to the kind of job that we do."[44] He also waved off U.S. concerns that his team would be duped by the Serbs, saying testily that he would not be the "prisoner of a pre-arranged itinerary." He had not amassed twenty-nine years' experience for nothing, he said: The UN would not be manipulated.[45]

Vieira de Mello pulled together a team of experts on nutrition, health care, child care, sanitation, shelter, and reconstruction, even though he knew that the humanitarians would not be able to conduct detailed assessments on such a short trip under fire. The battle among agencies for a spot on the team was fierce. Louise Arbour, the UN prosecutor at the war crimes tribunal in The Hague, had been trying to send investigators into Kosovo since the massacre in Racak in January. She was enraged that Annan had thrown his weight behind Vieira de Mello's mission but had not made any effort to press for access for tribunal investigators, even though reports were swirling that the Serbs were destroying evidence of their crimes. Arbour telephoned Vieira de Mello and demanded that a member of her staff be permitted to join his delegation. "I can't do that, Louise," he said. "The Serbs would never allow it." "Have you asked them?" she asked. "Have you even tried?" He admitted that he had not. She then called Secretary-General Annan and persuaded him to insist.

Vieira de Mello entrusted Nils Kastberg, a forty-four-year-old Swede who headed UNICEF's emergency programs, to lead an advance mission to the region to lay the groundwork for the trip. Kastberg's first stop was Geneva, where he met two NATO officers from Brussels. They insisted that the UN drive in clearly marked white vehicles, travel only by day, notify Brussels of their precise route forty-eight hours in advance, and never deviate from the preordained plan.

Kastberg spent May 10–12 in Belgrade conducting delicate negotiations with the Serb authorities. The Serbs insisted that the UN travel at all times with a Serb escort and that before visiting Kosovo they first tour Serbian cities that had been bombed by NATO. Each day of negotiations Kastberg kept one eye trained on the clock, as he needed to ensure that he and his colleagues reached their hotel rooms by nightfall, which was when NATO commenced bombing each day. On May 11, as the afternoon negotiations wore on, Kastberg received a call from Arbour. She said that Annan had given her his word that a war crimes investigator would have a spot on the team.

Kastberg dreaded raising the issue with the Serbs, but when an order came from the secretary-general, he had no choice. He asked Serbia's lead negotiator to join him for a walk in the garden, away from the listening devices. "I have something to ask you, and it is going to make you very angry, but after you express your anger I would like to ask you if we can put our heads together and find a solution." The official nodded. When Kastberg explained the new wrinkle, the Serb negotiator erupted in rage. "You know how we feel about this so-called court," he said, referring to the Serb belief that the tribunal was anti-Serb. "Are you trying to humiliate us?!" Kastberg waited him out. "I warned you that it would make you angry," he said. The official

paced back and forth around the garden. It was 4:30 p.m., and Kastberg
needed to resolve the matter. A rumor was circulating that NATO was going
to bomb one of Belgrade's main bridges that day, so the UN team was in a
special hurry to get back to their hotels. Finally the Serb gathered himself and
said quietly, "You know, if anybody heard that there was someone from The
Hague on the mission, not only is that person likely to be attacked, but so is
the entire UN delegation." Kastberg nodded, knowing that the Serb also saw
an opportunity to present the tribunal with evidence of NATO war crimes.
"The only way this will work," Belgrade's negotiator said, "is if the person
assumes a different identity." It was agreed that whoever Arbour nominated
for the team would travel undercover.

Arbour tapped Frank Dutton, a fifty-year-old South African who had
spent a decade investigating apartheid hit squads before joining the UN
court. Dutton flew from The Hague to Geneva, where the UN drew up a
temporary contract making him a "human rights officer" and giving him an
entirely new UN passport, which no longer listed him as an employee of
the tribunal. "We thought we had masterfully disguised his identity," recalls
Kastberg, "until he showed up to leave for the trip with all kinds of cameras
and film and asked me to negotiate the filming of mass graves."

While Dutton joined the UN assessment team eagerly, others felt as
though they had no choice. Kirsten Young was based at UNHCR in Geneva
as executive assistant to Dennis McNamara. A thirty-four-year-old Australian,
Young had been subjected to relentless shelling when she worked in Bosnia
in 1993. In the intervening years she had gotten married, undergone intensive
post-traumatic stress counseling, and finally made her peace with the ghosts
of the Balkans. Yet suddenly McNamara, her mentor, was asking her to return
to the region. As she drove home from her office at UNHCR in Geneva,
Young telephoned her husband, the head of an international NGO. As she
broke the news of her forthcoming trip, she began sobbing so violently that
she had to pull over to the side of the road. The prospect of aerial bombard-
ment terrified her. "Kirsten, you don't have to go," her husband said. "No, I
do, I do," she said. "I have to go. How do I say no to this kind of mission?"
Young remembers the pressure she felt. "The whole humanitarian world is
such a macho cowboy environment," she says. "They all talk about 'having
balls.' You're terrified to say no because then you would be showing you
don't 'have any balls.' Even feminists get sucked into that trap." Young re-

mained jittery until she met up with Vieira de Mello in Geneva a few days later, and her fears abated. "Sergio had this aura of nonchalance and invincibility," she says. "I just resolved not to leave his side."

Annan too was energized by the imminent trip. In a lengthy Q and A moderated by Judy Woodruff on CNN, he said he was tired of hearing criticisms of the UN. "This morning," he said, "when people started talking about the incompetence of UNHCR and others, I did not hear a single person mention the sacrifice these people make and the risks they take."[46] Annan spoke suddenly as if from a position of strength. "I don't think we are going to see NATO setting itself up as a policeman of the world, replacing the United Nations. My own sense, and I may be wrong here, is that after what NATO has gone through in the Balkans, it is going to reassess its own approach. And I think it should."[47] He said countries should not avoid the Security Council. "It's like saying, 'I'm not going to this or that court because I know that things will not go my way. So I'm going to do something else,'" he said. "We cannot lecture everybody about the need for the rule of law and ignore it when it's convenient."[48] At a subsequent press conference Annan said that any apparent loss of relevance for the UN was "a short-term phenomenon because we live in a global and an interdependent world and today we need the UN even more than we did yesterday and the day before that." In words that prophesied the U.S.-led invasion of Iraq in 2003, Annan warned, "Any nation or group of nations that decides to ignore this is setting a precedent and creating a situation that is likely to haunt all of us."[49]

Twelve

INDEPENDENCE IN ACTION

Vieira de Mello believed that the potential political and humanitarian benefits of inserting himself and his hastily assembled UN team into a live war zone vastly outweighed the physical risks. But even as he made his way to the region, the Clinton administration stepped up its criticism of his trip. On May 16, 1999, Secretary-General Annan, who was staying at the home of Queen Beatrix in the Netherlands, received a furious phone call from Thomas Pickering, the under secretary of state for political affairs, who was calling from the United States, where it was 4 a.m. Pickering told Annan that he had just seen Vieira de Mello's itinerary and it was unacceptable. The UN delegation would be in the region for eleven days, but in Kosovo for less than three of those, from Thursday afternoon until Saturday morning. Washington officials remained concerned that the UN team would see the power plants and bridges NATO had hit in Serbia, but that they would not get an accurate picture of the destruction and bloodshed the Serbs had caused in Kosovo. "Milošević is going to get huge propaganda mileage out of this," Pickering said. He advised Annan to cancel the mission unless the Serbs allowed at least three-quarters of it to be spent in Kosovo. Annan refused.

When Annan's special assistant Nader Mousavizadeh tracked down the UN envoy in the lobby of the Sheraton Hotel in Zagreb, Vieira de Mello said he was fed up with American bullying. He had already heard twice from the U.S. mission in New York, once from the U.S. representative in Geneva, and the night before from Pickering himself. He was aware of the danger that, on such a short, restricted trip, he would hand the Serbs a public relations victory, but he expected to bring back useful information. "Enough is enough," he told Mousavizadeh. "I am on a needs-assessment mission. I will do what I have to do to assess needs!"

When he rejoined his assembled team in the hotel lobby, he said, "The Americans are livid. They are refusing to offer us security assurances. Each of you should decide for yourself whether you still want to be a part of this mission. I am going to go ahead, but that should not influence your decision." The very fact that Washington was so hostile to the trip only strengthened the team's sense that they were right to attempt to conduct an independent investigation. Almost all of those gathered had experienced war before, and many thought the risk of being struck by one of NATO's precision-guided munitions was low in comparison to the dangers they had faced in other war zones. None of the team members dropped out.

While Western officials had reasons to be anxious, the Serb authorities should have been concerned as well. Milošević was trying to pretend as though Kosovar Albanians were leaving voluntarily or fleeing NATO air strikes. "Everyone runs away because of the bombing," Milošević told CBS News. "Birds run away, wild animals run away."[1] He urged the public not to believe the deceitful Western media. "I personally saw on CNN at the beginning of this war poor Albanian refugees walking through snow and suffering a lot. You know, it was springtime at the time in Kosovo," he said. "There was no snow. . . . They are paid to lie."[2] He noted that while the Serbs may have occasionally burned "individual houses," their misdeeds did not compare to Vietnam, where "American forces torched villages suspected of hiding Viet Cong."[3]

The reports of the number of Kosovar Albanian men who had gone missing ranged from 10,000 to 100,000.[4] Vieira de Mello believed his team could improve the clarity of the picture. "It's the first time we are able to embark in this kind of way and right in the middle of a war," he told journalists after driving from Zagreb to Belgrade.[5] He said that he hoped to talk to those Kosovar Albanians in hiding who had been unable to escape to a neighboring country. "Many say this mission is madness," he said, but only officials with the UN could reach "those who are in desperate need inside Kosovo."[6]

After driving from Croatia to Serbia, he held meetings with Serb official-dom that were tense and interminable. The Serbs directed their rants against NATO at him personally. "I don't know how he put up with all he heard," says Sarah Uppard, then a forty-three-year-old aid worker with Save the Children. "I would have lost it several dozen times over. But he managed to be firm, patient, and charming at once. He made everybody feel listened to without making even the slightest concession. Even the most aggressive of-ficials found themselves taken in by him." The minister of refugees, Bratislava Morina, was a close friend of Mira Marković, Milošević's wife, and was used to getting her way. She denounced NATO for its "genocide" against Serbs and slammed the UN for failing to prevent the war. Yet by the end of the meeting, she was a different woman. "Sergio had her eating out of his palm," recalls Kirsten Young of UNHCR.

On May 18 his UN team left Belgrade and embarked upon an investiga-tion that would take them almost nineteen hundred miles in eleven days. They traveled in a fleet of ten white Toyota 4Runners, each marked with a large black "UN" logo. Terry Burke, the UN head of security for the mis-sion, brought a separate stack of large black UN decals and plastered one to the roof of each of the cars. "I don't want to get blasted for an error," Burke

Vieira de Mello and Yugoslav minister of refugees
Bratislava Morina, May 1999.

told Vieira de Mello. "If we get hit, I want everyone to know that whoever hit us did so *because* we are the UN." The UN convoy was led and trailed by a Serbian police car. Burke had attempted to draft a getaway contingency plan, but he had just ended up with question marks. "Getaway where? With what?" he had asked himself. "If you run away from the Serb paramilitaries on the main roads, then you end up on the side roads vulnerable to NATO bombers."

The first stop on the UN tour was the Chinese embassy in Belgrade, which had been struck eleven days before. When the UN team reached the ruins of the building, Vieira de Mello shook his head in disbelief at the sight before him: The attack had blown a six-foot-deep crater out of one side of the building and a pair of gaping holes out of the other side. One of the walls seemed to have been peeled off, revealing, like the exposed interior of a dollhouse, the desks, bookshelves, couches, and artwork of the embassy, which, though covered in a thin layer of dust, remained intact. "NATO is precise all right," Vieira de Mello muttered to a colleague. "They just hit precisely the wrong target."

It had not been easy to find drivers willing to transport a UN delegation into a three-way battlefield. UN policemen who worked in neighboring Bosnia had lent themselves to the mission, but this meant that the drivers of the vehicles were not professional drivers and were not from the region. (The full-time drivers in Bosnia were natives of the area and thus could have become targets.) Already two of the UN cars in what had originally been a twelve-vehicle fleet had failed to show after getting lost on the drive up from Sarajevo.

After leaving the Chinese embassy, the driver of Vieira de Mello's lead vehicle suddenly noticed that the rest of the convoy was no longer visible in the rearview mirror. Once their car turned around and drove a mile back up the road, Vieira de Mello saw an overturned UN 4Runner on the horizon. Horrified, he pieced together what had occurred. The route was heavily trafficked because NATO had bombed several of the major roads. A Serb driver had become so transfixed by the sight of ten white UN vehicles speeding toward him on the other side of the road that he did not notice until the last minute that the traffic in front of him had stopped. Instead of ramming the car in front of him, he had swerved into the oncoming traffic, where a Ghanaian

UN policeman was zooming toward him recklessly at close to eighty miles per hour. In order to avoid a head-on collision, the Ghanaian had jerked his car toward the side of the road. As he did, he lost control of the vehicle, which flipped in the air, hit a tree, and landed upside down in a ditch.

Bakhet, who was traveling in the car directly behind the vehicle that crashed, had only looked up in time to see a large white vehicle flying through the air, for seemingly no good reason. Although he had given up smoking, he was so shaken that he asked for a cigarette, then nervously joined in the team's effort to remove the injured UN officials from the wreckage. His cigarette hung precariously out of his mouth as diesel trickled slowly out of the car's tank and out of jerry cans in the trunk.

The men pulled out of the vehicle were Nils Kastberg and Rashid Khalikov, who had led the advance mission to Belgrade the week before. Trembling and pale on the side of the road, Khalikov had multiple fractures in his upper left arm and lower back. He shouted, "My mobile, give me my mobile." He wanted to call his wife. Kastberg was also disabled with multiple fractures to his right foot.

Vieira de Mello rushed between Kastberg and Khalikov. He instructed the Yugoslav security services to call an ambulance and turned to David Chikvaidze, an aide whose job it was to maintain contact with NATO headquarters. "Tell them that we have two men down," he said, "and to go easy on the bombing around Belgrade hospitals."

Nothing seemed to be going according to plan. NATO had refused to guarantee the security of the mission. The Serbs had routed the delegation away from the terra incognita of Kosovo to towns in Serbia proper, where Western journalists were already present in droves. And finally, no sooner had the UN convoy left Belgrade and begun the journey into the countryside than it had been felled by a serious road accident. "I can see the Serbian papers tomorrow," Vieira de Mello quipped. "A photo of one of our cars in the

Vieira de Mello comforts an injured
Nils Kastberg of UNICEF.

ditch, and the caption, 'Beware, the UN has arrived!'" Most team members
had the same reaction as they took in the scene, saying to themselves, out
loud or in their heads, "Classic UN!"

Once Kastberg and Khalikov had been bundled off to the hospital,
Vieira de Mello set about comforting the other team members. Kirsten
Young, who had been ambivalent about joining the UN team to begin
with, was asking herself, "What the hell am I doing here? We have no idea
what we're doing!" As Young remembers, "You fear you are going to get
bombed, but instead of getting bombed, you have a car crash completely
of your own making." Dr. Stéphane Vandam, the WHO representative on
the team, had helped organize the medical evacuation. He too began to
wonder whether they were in over their heads. "We were standing up for
humanitarian values, putting them back in the hands of Kofi Annan, and
taking them away from the politicians," he remembers. "It was a brave mission, but it began then to feel like a very stupid mission." After the accident
Vieira de Mello went out of his way to give off an almost exaggerated air of
confidence. Young recalls, "I was terribly frightened. I didn't trust our drivers, I didn't trust our security guys, and I didn't trust the Serbs or NATO.
Yet every time I looked up and saw Sergio smiling, I thought to myself, 'If
Sergio is here, it'll be okay.' He was a Teflon guy in the sense that nothing
bad seemed to touch him."

The delegation continued onward to the town of Novi Sad, in the
Serbian province of Vojvodina. There they saw the Sloboda (Freedom)
bridge collapsed in the Danube River. It was the second of Novi Sad's three
bridges hit in the early days of the NATO air campaign. Confronted with
the hysteria and rage of Yugoslav authorities and Serb civilians, Vieira de
Mello tried to argue that the UN had not authorized the war and that it
and NATO were distinct entities. His hosts were unpersuaded. After the
UN delegation had concluded a meeting with one Serbian town mayor,
Chikvaidze spotted a poster on the door to the city hall with an image of
a skull capped by a UN helmet, and he asked a burly Serb guard in the
lobby of the building whether he could take the poster with him. The guard
shrugged a grudging acceptance, as if to say, "Everything is now possible
in my country." Vieira de Mello shook his head when he saw the poster.
"That is the predicament the UN is in," he said. "What the Serbs are saying
with that poster is, 'The UN is no better than NATO. Because you didn't

stop NATO from doing this, you are all the same.'" When Vieira de Mello would go to Iraq in 2003, many would similarly blame the UN for failing to stop the U.S.-led invasion.

Vieira de Mello was alternately impressed and horrified by NATO's aim. While he talked to villagers in one southern Serbian city, he heard a whistling sound and looked up to see a cruise missile flying through the sky. "Wow," he exclaimed with boyish wonderment as the missile crashed in the distance. "Thank you, General Electric, for not screwing that one up." Ten miles down the road, the mission encountered the burning ruins of a Serb police station that the missile had struck.

Just before the UN team sat down to a dinner hosted by officials in Niš, Yugoslavia's third-largest city, the Serbian government host presented Vieira de Mello with photographs of the cadaver of a pregnant woman who he claimed had been killed by a NATO strike. The Serb official ended his presentation by circulating pictures of a destroyed fetus. Vieira de Mello was disgusted by the images, but he was just as outraged by the Serbs' willful exploitation of the carnage. A Serbian reporter asked him about the photographs he had seen. "They're deplorable," he said sternly. But he added, "I've told you what I think you need to do to stop that."[7] He knew that once he reached Kosovo, he was likely to find many such gruesome scenes—the victims of Serbian ethnic cleansing.

Throughout the trip he remained concerned about the fates of Kastberg and Khalikov, who were sharing a room in the intensive care unit of Belgrade Central Hospital. In solidarity with the mission, the men had refused to be evacuated back to Geneva and had undergone surgery in Belgrade. Vieira de Mello thus had to worry not only about the safety of the personnel in his convoy but also about them. Nonetheless, he was personally moved by their courage and loyalty, and knowing that they were crestfallen to have been sidelined after planning the trip, he telephoned them nightly in order to keep them in the loop. "He would tell us exactly what the mission had done that day," Khalikov remembers. "He wanted to show us we were still part of the team." Each night when Vieira de Mello checked in with the men, he could hear the crash and thud of bombs landing nearby. "We both knew that if something went wrong, we wouldn't be able to run," recalls Khalikov. "I was lying flat. I couldn't get up. Nils couldn't walk." The men had also been warned upon arrival that a likely NATO target, the ministry of the interior, was located nearby. Although NATO had been given the coordinates of the hospital, the men had seen the wreckage of the Chinese embassy and knew that deadly mistakes were possible. Kastberg assured Vieira de Mello that the morale of the two patients was high. "Between us, we have three legs and three hands," he said, "but we are in the hands of gorgeous nurses!"

Inside Kosovo: "Pretty Revolting"

On May 20 Vieira de Mello's UN convoy finally entered the province of Kosovo, which appeared to have been emptied of ethnic Albanians. He was relieved finally to be on the most important leg of the trip. "I want to be able to move freely," he told a reporter. "I don't want any more speeches."[8] As the UN vehicles trundled into the province, men at the roadside shouted "Serbia! Serbia!" and offered the three-fingered Serbian salute. The UN team was now vulnerable to attack from three sides; armed Serbs, NATO, and the Kosovo Liberation Army (KLA) were all engaged in fighting.

The three UN security officials on the trip were not carrying guns, so the team had no choice but to rely on their police escorts for protection. These Serb "minders" were not about to let UN officials move around as they wished. Several times when Vieira de Mello tried to visit villages off the main roads, they refused, claiming the areas were unsafe. As the convoy progressed, the UN team encountered columns of ethnic Albanians fleeing on tractors or on foot. They saw houses, apartments, and shops that had been systematically burned or looted. Anti-Albanian and pro-Serb slogans had been painted on newly vacated buildings. In some areas 80 percent of the homes had been torched. On two occasions the team members themselves witnessed houses being set ablaze.

As his precious few days in Kosovo raced by, Vieira de Mello grew claustrophobic and started to make unscheduled stops. The Serbs, who were anxious to hide the extent of the ethnic cleansing, tried to stop him. After parking the cars at the edge of one village near Urosevac, he broke away from his posse and strode toward what appeared to be abandoned homes and barns. "Sergio, no!" shouted Young. "They could be booby-trapped!" Others chimed in with similar admonitions. But he plowed ahead, knowing that the more he witnessed with his own eyes, the greater his impact would be when he returned to New York. He found homes littered with clothes, bedding, and household goods. Whoever had left the village had fled hastily, leaving behind livestock, family pets, household electronics, photograph albums, and personal legal effects. In one apartment he saw a full pot of tea on the kitchen table, ready to be consumed. "Silent confirmation," he said.[9]

Young had known Vieira de Mello for more than a decade at UNHCR, and she was aware of his reputation for compromising with governments at the expense of refugee rights. Her boss was Dennis McNamara, Vieira de Mello's frequent foe on policy questions. But the man who was storming into ethnic Albanian homes for proof of war crimes bore little resemblance to the man known as a master diplomat with insufficient regard for human rights. "I had been a protection officer my whole career," she says, "but there I was saying, 'Aw, why is he pushing so hard?' He was far more vigilant about protection than I was."

He seemed to have come full circle. It was as if his regrets over his own neutrality in Bosnia, combined with his self-consciousness over having forced Hutu refugees back to Rwanda, and his disgust over the way NATO governments had paid no heed to the UN Charter, had resurrected in him the uncompromising righteousness that he had not displayed since his days in Lebanon. If he had once believed that his job was to carry out the aggregate will of powerful governments, he now acted as though he believed that promoting UN principles and protecting the UN flag entailed standing firmly for the advancement of human dignity, even if that required acting in defiance of those governments.

Some members of the UN team felt so unsafe that they began trailing him as if he were ensconced in kryptonite. On one occasion when he stopped the convoy and again charged out of his vehicle, a half dozen members of the team hopped out of their cars and followed him. "People were like, 'Where is the champ going?' 'Where is God going?'" recalls Eduardo Arboleda of UNHCR. "They were trailing him like puppy dogs. Until they got halfway down the road and realized he had stopped to take a leak." The embarrassed UN officials returned to their vehicles with their heads down.

In one town in Kosovo a group of children who had been orphaned by a Serb attack ran toward the UN officials, who realized they had almost nothing to offer. "We could pass out chocolate," Vandam recalls. "But we knew we would then be abandoning them. I don't think any of us had ever felt so helpless." As Sarah Uppard entered her vehicle, one of the children grabbed her hand and refused to let it go. "The kids had no idea what would happen after we left," remembers Uppard, "and neither did we. It was heartbreaking."

Vieira de Mello's unexpected stops and his endless follow-up questions in conversation with Kosovar Albanian civilians caused the convoy to fall behind schedule every day. In one instance, when a group of displaced ethnic Albanians emerged from the trees to speak with him, Chikvaidze contacted a NATO liaison officer to inform him of the delay. Speaking through an interpreter, Vieira de Mello asked the refugees when they had fled, how long they had been hiding, where they were finding food, and whether there were Serb or KLA forces in the vicinity. The discussions dragged on, and Chikvaidze received a telephone call from a UN official at Headquarters who himself had just been telephoned by the office of an enraged secretary-general of NATO. "Oh my god, Mr. Chikvaidze," the official exclaimed, "NATO is so pissed off that you're interfering with their work." Chikvaidze, already conscious of the clock, approached Vieira de Mello, who was in his element conversing with the Kosovars. "They're terrified in the operations center, Sergio. The secretary-general of NATO is raging mad—" Vieira de Mello, whose back was to Chikvaidze, wheeled around 180 degrees and burst out: "Fuck the secretary-general of NATO. I'm working here." Chikvaidze was taken aback, as Vieira de Mello rarely let his temper show. "Do you want me to call NATO and pass along that message?" Chikvaidze asked. Vieira de Mello smiled and returned to his task. Every evening at dinner Terry Burke, the team's chief security officer, would plead with him to do a better job sticking to the schedule. "But, Terry, think of what we're achieving!" Vieira de Mello would say, adding, "Sit this man down, he needs another glass of wine."

He was tense on the trip, not so much because of the physical danger but because he knew he needed to bring home fresh evidence of Serbian aggression. If he returned to New York empty-handed, he would miss both an opportunity to raise additional resources to meet humanitarian needs and a chance to remind governments and publics of the UN's unique value. Between the propaganda he had been fed by Serbian officials before he got to

Kosovo and the restrictions the Serbs had imposed on his movements while inside the province, he was not sure he was getting what he needed. Yet despite the pressure and the grimness of the surroundings, he remained playful with his colleagues, treating them to multiple bottles of wine each night. Team members marveled at how he would hold forth at the table tipsily but then, at a designated hour, head upstairs to his room to make his ritual satellite phone calls to New York until the early hours of the morning.

He felt most at ease with his friend Bakhet. The two men did what they had done for more than two decades: They talked about the fate of the UN and bantered about women. Vieira de Mello made repeated references to the beauty of one of the interpreters assigned to him by the Yugoslav foreign ministry. Once when the convoy stopped to interview Kosovo refugees, he summoned Bakhet to him under the guise of discussing highly classified business. When Bakhet asked what was so pressing, he said, "That goddamn minder from the ministry of foreign affairs won't leave me alone with the translator for one minute! Create a decoy, will you?"

The Serbs had their fun as well. Before the mission began, Kastberg had advised team members that, in light of the food shortages in Kosovo, each team member should bring his or her own supplies. Many members of the delegation brought huge suitcases stocked with bread, dried fruit, chocolate, chamomile tea, and toilet paper. At hotels and guesthouses the Serbian authorities made a point of housing the UN delegates on the top floor. Since NATO attacks had disabled the province's electricity grid, the elevators did not work, and the Serbs delighted in watching UN team members hauling their heavy stashes of food up successive flights of stairs. Once the UN staff panted their way to their rooms, the Serb officials typically invited them to the local municipal offices where large feasts had been prepared.

On Saturday, May 22, the team's last full scheduled day in Kosovo, Vieira de Mello was not satisfied with his ability to document life and death behind Serb lines. He instructed Bakhet to take most of the team across the border into Montenegro,* while he and a small group would spend an unplanned

---

*Montenegro and Serbia were close allies, which then jointly made up the "Federal Republic of Yugoslavia."

extra night in Kosovo, making their way to Montenegro a day later than originally scheduled. Young opted for what she called the "cowards' convoy." Uppard initially made the same decision but changed her mind the following morning, as she felt she could trust Vieira de Mello to lead what became known as the "cowboy convoy." Vieira de Mello informed NATO of the split, but it nonetheless very nearly brought disaster. NATO officials had been instructed to look out for a convoy of ten white vehicles, which would be clearly visible from the air. Officials in Brussels did not tell NATO pilots of the change of plan. As a result, he later learned, when the bombers spotted one of the two smaller convoys, they made preparations to strike what they initially assumed was a Serbian military convoy.

On May 24, after gathering additional evidence and testimony during the extra half day in Kosovo, Vieira de Mello's smaller team crossed out of Kosovo into Montenegro.[10] Bakhet's group, which had arrived the previous evening in Podgorica, the Montenegrin capital, erupted into cheers when their colleagues reached the hotel. Vieira de Mello knew how to make an entrance, and he had instructed Bakhet to arrange a press conference to coincide with his arrival. Although he had not seen all he had hoped to see, he expected his findings would have broad media appeal. "Just by being here, we don't have to say, 'There are reports of . . .' We will be able to say, 'We have seen . . .'" he told Bakhet.

Although he had watched his friend in action for close to two decades, Bakhet was impressed. "The usual UN bureaucrat would have waited to have his press conference in Belgrade, or once he was safe and sound in Geneva or New York," he recalls. "But Sergio knew that the impact on the world would be so much greater if he delivered his findings breathlessly just when he had 'escaped' Kosovo." At the media event, Vieira de Mello described the "ghost towns" that his team had encountered. He said the evidence was overwhelming and irrefutable. "Everything indicates that there is an attempt to displace, ethnically cleanse, Kosovo," he said. "In a word, it is pretty revolting."[11]

He was saying nothing new. The mere fact that 800,000 ethnic Albanians had already flooded out of Kosovo was ample proof of Serbian paramilitaries' ethnic cleansing. Yet his presentation of "eyewitness" findings received prominent play in the press. It stripped those who remained skeptical about Serb brutality of the excuse of "hearsay" or "insufficient information." Kastberg and Khalikov, lying in their hospital beds in Belgrade, heard snippets of their boss's press conference on the BBC. Kastberg asked his colleague, "What do you think the Serbs will do to Sergio when he gets back to Belgrade?"

Vieira de Mello knew the risks of returning to the Serbian capital. When his team arrived back on May 26, his first stop was Belgrade Central Hospital, where he checked on his injured colleagues. "Here I was feeling sorry for you, risking kidnapping and NATO bombing for the sake of the UN and the principles of humanitarianism," Vieira de Mello teased. "But look at these nurses! I clearly chose the wrong car to drive in." He then made his way to what he knew would be a difficult meeting with the Serbian authorities. Told he would be meeting with Milošević, Vieira de Mello said to Bakhet in the car ride over, "I don't want to shake hands with that man." Milošević, in fact, did not show. And when the Yugoslav minister of foreign affairs, Zivadin Jovanovic, the country's former ambassador in Angola, greeted him in Portuguese, Vieira de Mello interrupted him in English. "Your Excellency, I would prefer not to tell you what I am going to tell you in Portuguese," he said melodramatically. "It would be an insult to my mother tongue." He proceeded to launch into the most impassioned and rigorous defense of the core UN right to human security and dignity that Bakhet had ever heard. "Sergio was so outspoken and so undiplomatic, and yet so professional," Bakhet recalls. "It was as if the UN Charter was speaking through a person." As the men drove back to their hotel, Bakhet could only shake his head. "You must have a death wish, Sergio," he said.

When the two men walked into the lobby of the Belgrade Hyatt, they saw Zeljko "Arkan" Raznatovic, Serbia's most notorious warlord, who gave them the finger. Deciding it best to remain out of view, they proceeded directly to the elevators. Arkan sat down in the Hyatt bar with his wife, popular Serbian folksinger Ceca, and their two children, who were dressed primly as if for church. Relieved to be out of Kosovo, Kirsten Young was having a drink with several UN team members, and she shuddered when she saw Arkan at the adjacent table.

When Vieira de Mello reached his hotel room, he ordered room service and turned on CNN. There he saw Christiane Amanpour deliver a shocking leaked exclusive: Louise Arbour, the UN war crimes prosecutor in The Hague, had indicted Milošević for war crimes and crimes against humanity. It was the first time a sitting head of state had ever been indicted by an international tribunal. Vieira de Mello was taken aback by the timing of the indictment. Frank Dutton, Arbour's war crimes investigator who had accompanied the mission under cover, had assured him that no indictment would be issued while they were in the region. "Why did they do this now?" Vieira de Mello shouted at Bakhet. "Why not at any other time within the last five or six years? Why not tomorrow? What if we are held hostage here?" Vieira de Mello, the same man who kept a poster of Bosnia's MOST WANTED war crimes suspects on the wall in his office in New York, wanted to see Milošević behind bars. Yet he felt that the security of his mission had been jeopardized, and the UN had revealed itself to be disorganized and dysfunctional. Few of the UN team members slept soundly that night. Vandam of the WHO opted to sleep in his clothes. "I decided that if they were going to kidnap me in the middle of the night, I would prefer not to be taken naked," he recalls.

The UN team was scheduled to drive back to Croatia the following day, but Vieira de Mello pushed forward the time of the UN departure, opting to leave at the crack of dawn. Before leaving, he went to Belgrade Central Hospital and escorted Kastberg and Khalikov to the airport, where they were put on a plane back to New York. He also pulled Dutton aside and asked him for the notes, film, and videotapes he had collected. "The Serbs will be much less likely to search me than you," Vieira de Mello said. The same man who had once befriended war criminals like Ieng Sary and Radovan Karadžić and agreed that his biography might best be entitled *My Friends, the War Criminals* was now doing his part to ensure that Balkan war criminals faced justice. After burying a bounty of evidence beneath his socks and T-shirts, he crossed the border from Serbia into peaceful Croatia and breathed an audible sigh of relief. "You don't think NATO can miss this badly, do you?" he asked Bakhet. Later that day Arbour formally announced Milošević's indictment. The Serbian dictator would be arrested and transferred to The Hague two years later. The leak had proven harmless.

As Vieira de Mello drove with Bakhet into Zagreb, he complained that officials from the Croatian foreign ministry were likely waiting for him at the hotel. "I've had enough of meetings," he said suddenly. "Let's forget the Croats and go get a proper meal." The two men ducked into a restaurant Vieira de Mello knew from his days working for UNPROFOR five years before. They talked about all topics under the sun except Kosovo. When they arrived at the airport to catch their flight to Switzerland, they found a panicked UN staff and irritated Croatian officials. Vieira de Mello beckoned Dutton over to his suitcase, where the war crimes investigator retrieved his evidence.

Team members flew from Zagreb to Zurich, where they stayed at an airport hotel. There Vieira de Mello found a fax awaiting him from his assistant, Fabrizio Hochschild, who had read a wire story describing the UN press conference in Montenegro. Hochschild, who was loyal to Vieira de Mello but also often sharply critical, wrote that his boss's rebuttals of Serbian falsehoods "were courageous and made us all feel proud."[12] UN Headquarters in New York had had a funereal feeling in March, when NATO went to war unilaterally, but Vieira de Mello's mission had lifted spirits. The Security Council may have been bypassed, but by offering the first independent eyewitness proof of the ethnic cleansing, UN officials felt they had proven the organization mattered.

The exhausted UN team members gathered in the hotel garden for drinks and dinner, but their leader retired to his hotel room. As his colleagues released the tension of the previous two weeks with alcohol and laughter, Vieira de Mello stood at his hotel window looking down at the courtyard, clutching a phone to his ear and waving occasionally.

When he returned to Headquarters in New York, he became the first humanitarian official ever to be called to testify before the UN Security Council. On June 2, all eyes were on him, as he had gone where even NATO generals had not dared to go. He began his remarks by commending the Yugoslav health authorities for caring for Kastberg and Khalikov, but then he delved quickly into a detailed discussion of Serb ethnic cleansing. His team, he said, had enjoyed access that "was more than expected, but less than requested."[13] The Serbian authorities had limited the team's movement by citing security concerns that were "often neither understandable, nor convincing." Nonetheless he had seen enough of the province to know that it was a "panorama of empty villages, burned houses, looted shops, wandering livestock, and unattended farms."[14]

Since the bulk of the mission's time had been spent in Serbia, he had plenty to add about the destruction caused by NATO bombing as well. He reported that civilians would be suffering for many years the effects of the environmental damage, psychological trauma, and destruction of essential services, such as electricity, health, communications, and heating. Although his presentation was evenhanded, he had led with a discussion of Serb violence, and it was these comments that captured global news headlines, as he knew they would.

His daredevil mission had not brought radically new information to light, but he had highlighted civilian suffering and reasserted the UN's independent voice. He had shown as much to himself as to anyone that the UN was prepared to stand up for the victims of ethnic cleansing, while also standing up for itself.

Thirteen

VICEROY

In three decades of responding to war and displacement, Vieira de Mello had made a specialty out of understanding governments. Although he never entirely got his way, he had learned to negotiate with them, to extract resources from them, and to manipulate them. His senior colleagues in New York, who themselves were generally veterans of national government service, were usually surprised to learn that he had never himself worked for Brazil. The UN was not a place one could go to get experience running a country. But all that changed, unexpectedly, with the crisis in Kosovo.

ENDING A WAR

When he and his team returned to the United States after their risky assessment mission, NATO's war was still going poorly. Nonetheless, Viktor Chernomyrdin, the former Russian prime minister, and Martti Ahtisaari, the Finnish president, were spearheading peace talks supported by the Clinton administration, and those talks were managing to gather steam. The mothers and wives of Serbian soldiers had begun protesting the casualties the army was suffering, and NATO had begun bombing businesses belonging to Milošević's closest associates. The Serbian leader, who had expected to be able to play Russia off against NATO, found himself boxed in when the UN, NATO, and Russia suddenly began presenting a united front. On Thursday,

June 3, 1999, after seventy-eight days and 12,500 NATO bombing raids, Chernomyrdin and Ahtisaari handed Milošević a "take it or leave it" deal, and he surrendered. That evening NATO officers began negotiating the withdrawal of Serbian police and military forces from Kosovo.

One major question had been left unresolved: After Serb forces departed, who would run Kosovo? Kosovo's ethnic Albanian majority, which had operated its own informal, underground governing structures since the province was stripped of its autonomy in 1989, was eager to take over, but the Russians would not allow it. Serbian officials would have been happy to remain in charge, but that was precisely what the NATO air campaign had been designed to undo.

Vieira de Mello gave numerous media interviews following his return to New York in which he argued that, as an interim measure, the UN (and not NATO) was the organization best suited to running the province. "If the UN were to play that role," he told a large audience at the National Press Club in Washington four days after Milošević's surrender, "I can assure you that it is ready to move, and move fast."[1] But neither he nor Secretary-General Annan expected the UN to be handed such a role. Even though the Russians were lobbying for it, UN officials assumed that the organization would be cut out of the peace much as it had been cut out of the war. Indeed, Vieira de Mello was so confident that others would be given the task of managing Kosovo's fate that, having neglected the rest of the world since March, he made plans to fly to Beijing on June 9, then on to Islamabad, Pakistan, on June 13, to assess regional humanitarian conditions.

But Moscow quickly forced him to change his travel plans. The Clinton administration had bypassed the UN Security Council in the run-up to the war because Russia would have vetoed any U.S. resolution authorizing NATO bombing. Now that the Russians were insisting the UN lead the transition, Washington was prepared to return to the Security Council and invite it to help shape Kosovo's future. On June 10, the Security Council passed Resolution 1244, which amounted to a lowest-common-denominator fudge among powerful countries. It granted Kosovo "substantial autonomy" but not independence, and "meaningful self-administration" but not self-government. Serb police and military units would have to leave Kosovo. But the Security Council countries reiterated their respect for "the sovereignty and territorial integrity of the Federal Republic of Yugoslavia." At an unspecified date down the road (a date that had not yet arrived in late 2007), the province would move out of this halfway house and either legally remain part of Serbia or, more likely, achieve full international recognition as an independent country. Kosovo still needed a government, so the UN would function as an "interim international administration" until the province's final status could be resolved.

Resolution 1244 called on Annan to appoint a Special Representative of the Secretary-General (SRSG) as transitional administrator. This person would oversee civil administration, humanitarian affairs (via UNHCR), reconstruction (via the EU), and institution-building (via the Organization for Security and Cooperation in Europe). This administrator would work in tandem with—but would have no say over—NATO, which would send in 50,000 ground troops in a peacekeeping role to stabilize the province.

UN staff had done no advance planning to lead what, by the look of things, would be both the most ambitious political mission in the organization's history and its highest-profile assignment since the Bosnia and Rwanda debacles. Even though it was unclear whether the UN had the in-house expertise to actually govern anything, Annan embraced the assignment. In the words of one UN staffer, "When the Security Council calls, the Secretariat doesn't bark. It bows its head, puts its tail between its legs, and starts walking."

Annan knew that the UN couldn't afford to fail, and the choice of his special representative was essential. Because the countries on the Security Council had given him no warning, he had not lined up a candidate. On Friday, June 11, he summoned Vieira de Mello to his office on the thirty-eighth floor. "Sergio," he said, "I need you to go back." Although Vieira de Mello was exhausted, he was also delighted. Angolan rebel leader Jonas Savimbi had nixed his appointment as SRSG in 1993; this would mark the first time in his career that he would run his own UN mission. The only catch was that the assignment was temporary. Since Europe would supply the bulk of the funding for Kosovo's rebuilding, Annan felt he needed to find a European to succeed Vieira de Mello as soon as possible.

Assembling a Team

When Vieira de Mello led his eleven-day humanitarian mission into Serbia the previous month, he had been handed a diverse interagency team. But for this vital political mission, he was given the freedom to choose his own staff. He picked a half-dozen trustworthy colleagues who were prepared to leave their lives and families on twenty-four hours' notice. Dozens more UN staff would soon follow, but the nucleus would be key. Helena Fraser, a twenty-seven-year-old British national, had been the Kosovo desk officer in New York. "Can you be ready to leave tomorrow?" Fabrizio Hochschild asked her. "I'm getting married in a month," she said, but then added, "I did go for my last dress fitting earlier today."

Hansjörg Strohmeyer, a thirty-seven-year-old former German judge who had only recently joined Vieira de Mello's office, had worked in Bosnia for three years and knew the Yugoslav legal codes. "I need a lawyer down there," Vieira de Mello told him. Strohmeyer's mother had just flown in from Dortmund that day, and unable to speak English, she would be lost in New York without him. But he eagerly accepted. When he delivered the news to his mother that evening, she burst into tears.

The next day, Saturday, June 12, Fraser, Strohmeyer, and the other young team members raced around New York preparing for the trip. Fraser went to Bloomingdale's with her fiancé to buy light cotton clothing for the mission. As the couple hurriedly piled up purchases, the saleslady asked what the occasion was. "I'm going to Kosovo," Fraser said. The woman looked puzzled. "Where's that?" she asked. "It's in the former Yugoslavia," Fraser answered. "Where's that?" the saleslady followed up. "It's in the Balkans," Fraser said. "Hmmm," the lady said. "Where's that?" "It's in Europe," Fraser replied. The woman's face brightened. "Oh, congratulations," she said. "Have a wonderful trip!"

Strohmeyer had been told that Vieira de Mello's team would likely depart on Sunday. On Saturday morning he dropped off his laundry and swung by the UN to pick up a few relevant books. "Have you picked up your ticket already?" Vieira de Mello's secretary asked. Strohmeyer said he had not. She told him that he could get it from Hochschild at the airport later. "What do you mean 'later'?" he asked. "The flight leaves this afternoon," she said.

"Didn't they tell you?" They had not. Strohmeyer, who had his passport with him, ran back to the Laundromat, stuffed his wet laundry into a bag with his books, and hailed a cab to the airport. His mother would have to fend for herself.

Vieira de Mello barely made the flight himself. Like the others, he had spent the day organizing his life for the trip. But he had also been getting hourly updates from the Balkans, where a new exodus was under way. Thousands of Serbian civilians had suddenly taken to the road, heading for Serbia proper. They had voluntarily piled their belongings atop their cars and wagons in much the same way Kosovar Albanians had recently been forced to do at gunpoint. The Serbs scoffed at Western assurances that NATO forces would protect the Serbs. "How can we believe NATO when they bombed us?" a young Serb student was quoted by the *Washington Post* as asking.[2] Yet while Vieira de Mello was aware of the fears of the Serb minority, he underestimated the longing that some ethnic Albanians felt for revenge.

By the time he reached New York's Kennedy airport, cleared security, and sprinted to his gate, the flight attendants were just about to close the airplane door. Team members who had nervously awaited their boss's arrival, cheered his entrance but groaned at his attire. He was wearing a khaki safari suit that made him look twenty years older and significantly more colonial than he intended.

In Charge at Last

He used the overnight flight to Rome to study Security Council Resolution 1244, which left Kosovo's final status undefined but gave him far more power than Yasushi Akashi had been given in Cambodia. Akashi had supervised Cambodian ministries; in Kosovo Vieira de Mello would have to build and run them. Somehow, with no money, no valid precedents, and no institutions to draw upon, he would have to determine what law should apply in the province and decide how to collect customs and taxes, what kind of passports should be issued, how to kick-start the economy, whether Yugoslav currency should remain in effect, and what on earth to do with the Kosovo Liberation Army (KLA), the ethnic Albanian guerrillas who would be an uncontested armed presence as soon as Serbian police and soldiers had fully withdrawn. Vieira de Mello was the interim administrator. He did not know how long "interim" would last, but he set out to establish a framework for governing the place. His greatest challenge, he knew, would be rapidly mobilizing police, UN staff, and money from New York.

His small UN governing team flew from Rome on to Skopje, Macedonia. When they landed, they proceeded straight to NATO's temporary headquarters, where the force commander, British lieutenant-general Michael Jackson, was garrisoned. Vieira de Mello told Jackson that his team intended to drive north to Kosovo that very day. Jackson advised against it. "The province has not been secured," he said. "We haven't even set up our headquarters yet."

Vieira de Mello told General Jackson that he was aware of the risks of premature entry. But having traveled around Kosovo while NATO was bombing and Serb paramilitary forces were on the loose, he was not about to be deterred now that a peace deal had been struck. Although the UN Security Council had put the UN in charge of the province, he knew that if he did not quickly establish a UN ground presence, NATO and KLA soldiers would fill the vacuum. Jackson wished him luck, and the two men agreed to hold daily meetings in Kosovo so as to coordinate their separate civilian and military chains of command.

Because the mission had been jerry-rigged in a hurry, Vieira de Mello's team needed to beg and borrow supplies from aid groups, governments, and other branches of the UN that were already present in the region. They borrowed two vehicles from a Swedish relief organization, communications equipment from the British government's aid agency, water and fuel from UNHCR, and military rations from NATO. Vieira de Mello felt he was on what he later called "an under-budgeted high school outing."[3]

The trip from the Macedonian border to Pristina, the Kosovo capital, was straightforward; the two vehicles simply had to drive forty miles northward. But the scenes around them were anything but normal. Less than three weeks before, when he had driven a portion of the same road, it had been deserted. Now the streets were lined with cheering Kosovar Albanians who had never quite believed that they would be free of Serb tyranny. Most Kosovars were still outside the country in refugee camps in Macedonia and Albania. Those who flocked to greet the UN convoy were mainly those who had hidden inside the province during the NATO bombing campaign. They made the peace sign, threw flowers into the street, and cheered the British prime minister and U.S. president, chanting, "TO-NY, TO-NY" and "CLIN-TON,

CLIN-TON." "This must have been what it felt like for American troops at the end of the Second World War," Fraser said to a colleague.

Vieira de Mello eyed families walking along the side of the road. They were carrying bundles and appeared to be heading back to their homes. He saw scattered cars piled high with suitcases and appliances. "Once these people start heading home," he noted, "there'll be no stopping them." Yet having toured Kosovo's charred villages, he knew many would return to find only the ashen remains of their past lives.

After around three hours on the road, as the UN convoy ascended the crest of a hill, he instructed his driver to stop the vehicle. He disembarked with the others and eyed the capital city of Pristina below. As he did, he turned back and looked at the cars that his team had appropriated. "This is ridiculous," he said. "We have to show people that it is the United Nations, and not Sweden, that is arriving. Who's got a UN flag?" Somebody produced a royal blue UN flag, around the size of a pillowcase, and tied it to the antenna of Vieira de Mello's lead vehicle. He looked satisfied, even though the enormous decals of the Swedish flag emblazoned on the side of the cars were far more visible to onlookers.

He had been in a hurry to get to Pristina for another, more juvenile reason. Dennis McNamara, who was managing UNHCR's operations in the region, was bringing the first UN relief into Kosovo in nearly three months. McNamara had told Vieira de Mello that he intended to be the first UN official to reach the newly liberated capital. Over their radios the two friends had ribbed and taunted each other constantly throughout the afternoon, but McNamara had gone silent, and Vieira de Mello worried that his friend had won the bet.

McNamara had enjoyed a lengthy head start, having departed Skopje in the morning. But he was traveling in a twenty-three-truck convoy that carried 250 tons of supplies, including bottled water, wheat flour, hygienic kits, blankets, plastic sheeting, and 48,000 Meals Ready to Eat.[4] It took most of the day for his unwieldy convoy to snake its way to the UN warehouse on the outskirts of Pristina. Staffan de Mistura, the Italian who on Vieira de Mello's advice had hired smugglers as "UN consultants" in Bosnia seven years before, was part of McNamara's convoy. He was unaware that they were part of a race, and it never dawned on him that Vieira de Mello, who had been appointed interim administrator only two days before, could have already

reached Kosovo. Yet no sooner had de Mistura disembarked from his truck
at the UN warehouse than he heard a familiar voice. "*Benvenuto,* Staffan!"
Vieira de Mello said.

As Vieira de Mello, McNamara, and de Mistura embraced warmly,* an elderly Serb who was guarding the gate of the UN warehouse began screaming
obscenities and raising his machine gun as if to shoot them if they approached.
The man was visibly drunk and so incoherent that he seemed at once harmless
and dangerous. Vieira de Mello had been informed that the Serbs had burned
down the other large UN warehouse in Kosovo, so he knew the UN needed
to hang on to this one.

"Staffan, I need a drink," he said suddenly to de Mistura.

"What you mean, you need a drink?" the Italian asked. It was broad daylight, and there was work to be done.

"Do you have any slivovitz here?" Vieira de Mello pressed.

De Mistura asked the UN interpreters to see what they could find. A few
minutes later one of the locals approached with a small bottle of the Balkan
spirit. Vieira de Mello approached the angry Serb cautiously and pointed
to the bottle. "I would like to drink some slivovitz with you and talk things
out," he said.

The Serb guard looked skeptical, but the Balkan rules of hospitality required him to accept. The men raised their glasses. "*Živeli,*" Vieira de Mello
toasted to the baffled Serb in his language. De Mistura was not sure whether
he or the Serb guard was in a greater state of shock. But when he saw the
guard rest his gun beside his chair and return the toast, he knew who would
soon win the battle of wills.

Speaking through a UN interpreter, the Serb began explaining the
source of his rage. He had guarded the UN warehouse for almost a year,
and the Serbian government had yet to pay him. His friends and relatives
had already fled Kosovo, but he had remained in order to collect what was
owed to him. Vieira de Mello finished his drink, returned to his vehicle,
and dipped into a tin box that he used to store petty cash. When he handed
the Serb the several hundred dollars he was owed, the guard pocketed the

---

*UN officials present that day still dispute who actually arrived first and won the bet.

money, picked up his gun, and walked away. The warehouse belonged to the UN.

Having secured a home for the UN's humanitarian supplies, Vieira de Mello and the others made their way into town. Pristina was even more deserted than it had been during the war. Most of the Serbs had left, and few ethnic Albanians had yet made it back. As the UN group reached town, they saw that Serb forces were still setting houses aflame. The circumstances reminded him of his arrival in Gorazde five years before. But while in Gorazde the arson had been a sign of the Serbs' invulnerability, this time it was clearly a last gasp by the departing Serbs—a sign of their relative weakness.

In advance of arriving, they had not lined up a place to stay. Randolph Kent, who was part of the group, remembers the chaos and uncertainty that they felt as they drove aimlessly around Pristina. "Have you ever been on the holiday where you arrive and you say, 'Why the hell didn't we book a hotel?' Well, that's what it was like," Kent recalls.

As the team stopped at the side of the road to discuss their plans for the rest of the day, they saw another drunken Serb soldier in a militia uniform staggering up the road. They thought little of it, as the sight was becoming familiar. A few minutes later as they drove up the road, however, they saw the same soldier's body lying facedown. He had been shot—one of four Serbs who were reported killed by the KLA that day.[5] Because it was the Serbs who had maintained order, even if brutal order, their departure was leaving a dangerous vacuum.

Although he had hardly slept on the transatlantic flight, Vieira de Mello was in a familiar hurry to establish the UN presence. He held a press conference downtown at the Grand Hotel. When he was shown the room where the event was to be held, he eyed the podium. "There's a NATO flag there," he told Eduardo Arboleda of UNHCR. "I can't appear before a NATO flag." "But, Sergio, people will concentrate on what you are saying," Arboleda said. "No, I'll offend the Serbs," he replied. "They were just bombed by NATO." Since a UN flag could not be found as a backdrop, Vieira de Mello demanded someone find a light blue sheet, which was procured from housekeeping and hung instead. "For this forlorn group without food, cars, sleeping bags, or a place to stay, to say, 'We're here, and we're the new UN administration!' seemed preposterous," recalls Strohmeyer. "There were ten of us and fifty thousand NATO troops." Yet Vieira de Mello's self-respect, personal and institutional, made him and the other team members believe that they had an essential role to play.

At the press conference he was asked about the likelihood that ethnic Albanians would carry out revenge attacks against Serbs. Although McNamara had urged him to condemn displacements and revenge killings, Vieira de Mello sent an unfortunately passive signal to the inhabitants of the polarized province. Instead of denouncing the spate of attacks on Serbs, he said, "I believe it is unavoidable that there will be security incidents here and there."[6] It was late June before he brought Kosovo's Albanian and Serb leaders together to issue a joint appeal for peace.

After the press conference McNamara led his friend's political team to a four-story house that was owned by a Kosovar acquaintance and had been used by UNHCR staff before the bombing. UNHCR had negotiated with the family, who agreed to move into the basement while the UN took over the main house. It would double as UN residence and UN headquarters until Vieira de Mello's UN transitional administration appropriated a former Serbian government office building for its permanent operations.

Every evening in the hallway outside his bedroom on the top floor, Vieira de Mello would gather his team, which by now included Martin Griffiths, McNamara, Kirsten Young (his assistant), Kent, Hochschild, Fraser, Strohmeyer, and Susan Manual, a spokesperson. Somebody would pull a small bridge table into the center of the landing, and he would plop down a bottle of Johnnie Walker Black Label and several bars of Lindt and Ritter Sport chocolate. While the others dipped deep into the bottle, Vieira de Mello alternated between leading the discussion of the day's events and disappearing into his bedroom to place his calls to New York.

Fraser did not enjoy cohabiting in a virtually all-male house without running water. With their disagreeable stomachs, the smell could be unbearable. Her bedroom housed the highly secure UN code-cable machine, and because of the time difference with New York, the machine rang and churned out classified paper faxes all through the night. At one point Fraser grew so exasperated with the machine's frequent interruptions of her sleep that she unplugged it. When she confessed her crime to Hochschild the following day, he said, "Don't worry about it. When was the last time you saw something important in a classified UN code cable?"

Despite the unhygienic conditions in the house, Vieira de Mello maintained his reputation for elegance with the disheveled members of his staff. One night after he headed out of the house for a meeting, McNamara, who had had a few drinks, broke into his friend's room and raided his suitcases. "I've found him out," he shouted out into the hallway. "Come quick!" The officials in Vieira de Mello's team gathered guiltily beside his bed, where McNamara had laid out the evidence. "This is how he does it, the bastard," McNamara exclaimed. Inside the case were a dozen identical, spotless, crisply starched and ironed blue button-down shirts.

Most of Vieira de Mello's staff were, like him, left-leaning progressives who had been attracted to the UN because of its support for decolonization. They thus found it ironic to be involved themselves in a quasi-colonial governing experiment. They joked about Vieira de Mello's newfound imperial impulses and nicknamed him "Viceroy." But they all felt the tensions inherent in the arrangement. Vieira de Mello himself did not naturally embrace the full range of powers granted to him. He struggled to wrap his mind around the idea that all of the buildings, finances, and companies that had been owned by the Serbian government were now, technically, his. Speeding down Kosovo's main thoroughfare one day, he cautioned Griffiths to slow down, as it would not send the right signal to the Kosovars if the administrator were given a speeding ticket. Griffiths agreed and slowed down. But suddenly he remembered the Hobbesian setting they were in. "Sergio, there's nobody here to arrest us, besides us," he noted. "We're the ones in charge." Vieira de Mello grimaced. "What a truly terrifying thought," he said.

As the administrator, Vieira de Mello found that his responsibilities were enormous. The garbage had been piling up since NATO began bombing in March, and he would have to find some way to pay the collectors. He pleaded with the UN legal adviser's office in New York for permission to spend revenues from state-owned enterprises, such as electric and water utilities, without checking with the authorities in Belgrade. Headquarters was frightfully slow in answering him. "Sergio got almost no guidance on the big issues, and major guidance on tiny issues," recalls Fraser. "He couldn't stand the combination of silence and tinkering."

If the UN rules and regulations had tormented him in his office in New York, they very nearly ruined his efforts to govern Kosovo. The one way he could have won the affection of the ethnic Albanians was to offer them tangible assistance by paying them the state salaries they were owed or by quickly finding funds for them to rebuild their destroyed property. Some 50,000 ethnic Albanian civil servants had not been paid in more than two months, but he could not simply do as he had done for one drunken Serb guard and reach into his tin of petty cash to supply their back pay. Although the Security Council had given the UN mission a $456 million budget, the money came from assessed contributions and thus, as had been true in Cambodia, could be used only to cover the needs of UN employees: staff salaries, vehicles, computers, and air conditioners. If he wanted to pay Kosovars for their labor as security guards, civil servants, road builders, teachers, or garbage collectors, he had to drum up a separate trust fund, to which countries in the UN had no obligation to contribute. The fund didn't really get started until after he left, by which point local frustration with the UN was already high. In Cambodia a government had existed alongside the UN, whereas in Kosovo the UN was the government. This gave it the power to detain and release murderers, to appoint judges, and to fire mayors. Yet UN rules devised decades earlier for vastly less ambitious missions denied him the flexibility to hire and fire UN staff or to disburse funds as he saw fit. "It is like being asked to perform Olympic gymnastics and then being placed in a straitjacket," he later wrote.[7]

On June 16 he returned to one of the villages near Urosevac that he had visited on his assessment trip in May, and he tracked down a woman he had met there who had been forced from her home at gunpoint. "I told you I'd be back," he said to the woman. "I told you I'd look after you." She wept with gratitude but told him that her home had been destroyed and she had nothing to eat. When it came to meeting those vital needs, he had nothing to offer.

Vieira de Mello went out of his way to convey to his staff, to NATO, and to ethnic Albanians and Serbs that everything was proceeding according to a clear and sophisticated plan. But privately he screamed to the heavens about "fucking New York." "We were stragglers," recalls Fabrizio Hochschild. "It was smoke and mirrors. Sergio always managed to look like he was in charge and credible whether he was standing on a tower of marble or a small lump of sand, which is what we were on in Kosovo."

THE POLICING GAP

The biggest failing in the transition, and the one whose consequences would be felt for generations to come, was the absence of law, order, and justice. Vieira de Mello had two problems: an abundance of returning Kosovar Albanian refugees who bore grudges against Serbs who had first oppressed them and then expelled them, and the overnight disappearance of the institutions that had maintained order in the province.

In Cambodia Vieira de Mello and UNHCR had organized most of the refugee returns. But in Kosovo civilians marched back on their own, with no regard for the condition of their homes or for the mines, booby traps, and unexploded NATO ordnance that was scattered throughout the province. Within two weeks of his arrival, some 300,000 Kosovars had spontaneously crossed back into Kosovo, and an additional 50,000 were returning every day. They came as they had left: on foot, by car, or by tractor. In formation they resembled the columns of Hutu refugees that had been forced back to Rwanda in 1996, but while those refugees returned only under the barrel of the gun, in Kosovo the UN would have needed guns to prevent the flood. By June 25 the number of returnees exceeded 650,000. In his first month there more than 130 returning Kosovars were injured by ordnance.[8]

Any UN official who had worked in the aftermath of violence was familiar with the "policing gap" that often opened between the time when one government stepped down and another got its bearings. When an occupier departed, or when security forces were disbanded, criminal elements were usually the prime beneficiaries. Vieira de Mello had believed that NATO troops would be able to prevent most revenge attacks against Serbs. At the National Press Club in Washington in early June, he had said confidently, "Kosovo is a very small province, so 50,000 troops are . . . likely to stem any revenge rampage that might be in the making."[9] Here he proved dead wrong. The skills needed for war fighting varied greatly from those needed for crime prevention. And Kosovo didn't have few police or corrupt police, as Cambodia did; after the Serbs left, it had no police. The Pentagon had suggested that the UN simply "recycle" the KLA as a police force, but this UN officials found laughable, as it was precisely the KLA that had taken to terrorizing

Serb civilians. This left Vieira de Mello's tiny UN mission to confront the most daunting postwar challenge: ending the vicious cycle of violence. It would take an eternity to recruit enough international police to secure the streets. Bernard Miyet, who ran the Department of Peacekeeping Operations in New York, said he could not even recruit a UN police commissioner for Kosovo until he knew the nationality of Vieira de Mello's replacement as special representative. The UN's other hires had to ensure national balance.[10]

The UN had begun recruiting police only on June 10, the day of the unexpected Security Council resolution creating the UN administration. Vieira de Mello pleaded for units with the foreign ministers of the U.K., France, Germany, and Italy who visited Kosovo on June 23. Four days later some thirty-five police arrived from the UN mission in Bosnia, hailing from Argentina, Bulgaria, Canada, Chile, Estonia, Pakistan, Portugal, Romania, and the United States.[11] But they functioned only as advisers to NATO. Since few countries had spare police capacity at home, they had none to siphon off to Kosovo to do real police work. Vieira de Mello requested specialists to combat organized crime, which had flourished in Kosovo even before the war and was now booming. This appeal would not be satisfied until 2001, two years after it was made, by which time Kosovo's crime networks were firmly entrenched.[12]

Vieira de Mello controlled all the functions of Kosovo's new interim government, except he had no say over NATO forces. He urged General Jackson to take initiative, but since NATO had just fought a war against the Serbs, NATO officers continued to view the Serb minority as the threat and not as potential victims. Vieira de Mello understood their view. Some ten thousand ethnic Albanians had been killed in recent months, more than six hundred villages had been razed to the ground, and fresh graves were being unearthed each day. Throughout the country NATO soldiers were discovering eyeglasses, watches, tobacco tins, IDs, and bits of clothing amid piles of bones. Vieira de Mello knew from his own helicopter tours of the province how moving it was to see the results of the Serbs' scorched-earth campaign: acre upon acre of ashen neighborhoods. Still, he thought it was incumbent on NATO to stop the violence. But no matter how many appeals he made, Jackson did not give his troops standing orders to stop looting or arson. As typically happened in UN missions as well, some national contingents in NATO reflexively took civilian protection more seriously than others. While the British battalion intervened regularly to stop ethnic Albanians from assaulting Serbs, German and Italian soldiers tended to remain in their armored personnel carriers, reluctant to carry out foot patrols. An American captain was candid when he told one Serb, "It is better to leave, we can't protect you."[13]

The most isolated forces in Kosovo were the Americans. While most of the other troop-contributing countries occupied factories, warehouses, or abandoned Yugoslav military complexes in urban areas, American planners built a garrison from scratch in an enormous wheat field four miles from the nearest town. The U.S. military hired the contractor Brown & Root to carry out the construction of facilities in the 750 acre complex known as Camp Bondsteel. Hemmed in by nine guard towers and forbidding wire fences, the soldiers slept in prefabricated huts with heating and air-conditioning. More than any other base, Bondsteel would be a preview of the Green Zone fortress that U.S. administrators would set up in Iraq in 2003.

Vieira de Mello did not see how the Americans would possibly be able to protect the Serb minority or win Kosovar hearts and minds if they were holed up so far away from the local community. But he understood that, ever since the deaths of U.S. soldiers in Mogadishu in 1993, the Clinton administration had become driven by "force protection." Secretary of State Madeleine Albright and others who had pushed for the war in Kosovo were concerned that as soon as U.S. troops took casualties, Congress would press for an American exit. As a result, while Vieira de Mello viewed the posture of the U.S. forces as counterproductive, he shrugged it off, deeming it the price of the U.S. participation in, and perhaps even funding for, the Kosovo mission as a whole.

He also made use of the U.S. base to house prisoners on the rare occasions on which NATO made arrests. With the Serbs gone, Kosovo had no justice system.[14] Almost all of the prison staff had fled alongside the Serb military and police. With no place to put Kosovar Albanian looters or thugs, NATO soldiers tended to dump the suspects in tents inside the Western bases.[15] Within two weeks of the start of Vieira de Mello's mission, some two hundred detainees (charged with arson, violent assault, or murder) faced indefinite detention. The UN needed to put in place a body to try them.

On June 30 he appointed nine judges and prosecutors, three of whom were Serbs, to act as a mobile unit to dispense justice throughout Kosovo. By mid-July they had heard the cases of 249 detainees and released 112 of them.[16] The ethnic Albanians criticized the UN for overrepresenting Serbs on the bench. This didn't last long. After just a few days in office, one of the three Serb judges was evicted from his apartment and threatened with death. He fled to Serbia.[17]

The ethnic Albanians' purge of Kosovo's Serb minority, which NATO now estimated was taking fifty Serb lives each week, was not merely revenge. It was a deliberate attempt to affect future negotiations on Kosovo's status. By promising sovereignty to Serbia, autonomy to the Kosovar Albanians, and governing authority to the UN, the Security Council had handed Vieira de Mello and his staff a mandate predicated on fundamental contradictions. The Serbs resented the UN for stripping them of their power and giving the Kosovars rights and privileges they had never had before. The Kosovars resented the UN for taking the place of Serbs in running the place and denying them their independence. It was, Vieira de Mello liked to quip, "an effort to combine motherhood with virginity."[18] And success in Kosovo, like a virgin giving birth, would have required a divine intervention. The Kosovars had chosen not to wait. They had opted instead to alter Kosovo's demographics so as to make it impossible for international mediators to later hand the province back to Serbia. If Kosovar independence required ethnic purity, they appeared prepared to achieve it.

COMBINING MOTHERHOOD AND VIRGINITY

Vieira de Mello could not give Kosovars a timetable for independence because it was not up to him: The countries on the Security Council would decide. But because the UN mission was the face of international ambivalence about Kosovo's statehood, it would be UN officials who would take the blame. The acronym for the UN Interim Administration in Kosovo, UNMIK, sounded like *anmik,* which in Albanian means "enemy."[19] Strohmeyer recalls the progression of Albanian sentiment: "Just before the UN moved in, the Albanians were forced to give the three-finger Serb salute. When the UN arrived, they gave us the peace sign. And then after we'd been there a week, they gave us the middle finger."

Vieira de Mello divided his time battling New York for personnel and office supplies, urging donor countries to contribute funds to Kosovo's economic development, and defusing ethnic Albanian frustration. His most important act as administrator was the creation of a transitional council comprising representatives from the major political, ethnic, and social groups: six Kosovar Albanians, two Serbs, one Bosnian Muslim, and one Turk. The council was to advise the UN on how to govern.

Having fought for independence, KLA soldiers had expected to run the province themselves. Since the KLA had people and money in place all over Kosovo, they were able to commandeer municipal buildings that had been vacated by the Serbs and even issue political regulations and legal edicts. In a direct snub to Vieira de Mello's nascent transitional council, Hashim Thaci, the leader of the KLA, named a twenty-one-member all-Albanian cabinet in early July. Thaci also appointed mayors in twenty-five of the province's twenty-nine municipalities. On July 15 Ibrahim Rugova, the more pacifistic founder of the Kosovo independence movement, returned to the province from exile and declared, "I am the president."[20] Vieira de Mello declared that neither man had any official status until democratic elections could be held.[21] The UN, he insisted, was "the only source of authority in Kosovo."[22]

As frustrated as he was by local intransigence, he was also exhilarated. It stung to know that he would not be the permanent international administrator. The European Union was planning to put up more than half of the annual $1.5 billion needed to run and reconstruct Kosovo, and he awaited word of which European Annan would select for the top job.

French president Jacques Chirac lobbied for France's own Bernard Kouchner, a former French health minister and the founder of Médecins Sans Frontières, one of the most influential humanitarian aid and advocacy organizations.* On July 2 Annan announced Kouchner's appointment.[23]

Vieira de Mello went to the airport to greet Kouchner when he arrived in Kosovo on July 15. He had no doubt about Kouchner's commitment to the former Yugoslavia. The French advocate had helped organize the Barbara Hendricks visit to Sarajevo in 1994 and had been a longtime ally of the Kosovars. The two men were friends, but they had very different styles. Vieira de Mello had often cringed over the years at Kouchner's efforts to promote himself as well as his causes. In 1992 he had groaned audibly when he heard that,

---

*In 2007 French president Nicolas Sarkozy named Kouchner as his foreign minister.

in Somalia, Kouchner had posed for the television cameras wading toward the shore carrying a bag of rice on his back. Now, seven years later, upon seeing Kouchner disembark from his airplane in Pristina, accompanied by a television crew, Vieira de Mello decided to get out of town as quickly as possible.

He had loved serving as interim administrator, as it was his most senior political appointment and it combined so many of the challenges that he had seen tackled in isolation during his career: repatriation of refugees, governance, reconstruction, and law and order. He was truly sorry to leave. But he was proud of what he had achieved in a short time. In addition to setting up the Kosovo Transitional Council and engaging restive Kosovars in a UN-led political process, he had established a warm and cooperative personal relationship with NATO (even if staff within the organizations did not mesh easily), and most remarkably, with scant guidance, he had put in place the basic laws that Kosovo would need to govern itself. "He established the law of the land with no rules and zero advice," Helena Fraser remembers. "And this was 1999, when you couldn't yet Google some recently decolonized nation and find out how they wrote their first laws. He was totally improvising."

He masked his frustration at being big-footed with humor and deference. He brought Kouchner to the former ministry of defense building, where he had set up UN headquarters. While Kouchner's media entourage filmed, Vieira de Mello wore a big smile and pulled out the chair from behind what had been his desk. "Welcome to your office," he said. "You are the boss!" Kouchner planted himself at his new desk, as Vieira de Mello shuffled over to the wall, out of camera range. He teased Kouchner, "Like the Soviet system, you can tell the importance of a man by the number of phones he has." The French diplomat eyed the four phones cluttering the desk before him and fell for the bait, picking up the receiver on one of them. "Do any of them work?" he asked. "No, of course not," Vieira de Mello answered, smiling. "This is Kosovo."

The following day, in his last act, he opened the first meeting of the multiethnic Kosovo Transitional Council, then handed over the chairmanship to his successor. "He couldn't bear playing second fiddle to Kouchner," recalls Strohmeyer. After saying a few quiet good-byes, he slipped off to the airport.

Vieira de Mello's last public statement as administrator was: "Killings, kidnapping, forced expulsions, house burnings, and looting are a daily occurrence. These are criminal acts. They cannot be excused by the suffering that has been inflicted in the past. Kosovo's future must be built on justice, not vengeance."[24] By the time of his departure, only 156 of the 3,100 police requested by the UN had arrived, and some 150,000 Serbs had already fled.[25]

No Quick Fix

Back in New York, where his staff ribbed him as the "proconsul," Vieira de Mello was not in a playful mood. After his two high-profile trips into Kosovo and almost two months in the field, his spirits slumped in the office environment. "How long am I now going to be stuck behind this desk?" he asked Hochschild. An earthquake in Turkey struck within four weeks of his return, requiring him to busy himself raising funds for emergency relief, but his mind drifted to the province he had left.

Before heading to Kosovo, he had promised the cleaning lady in his office at UN Headquarters that he would track down a nephew of hers in the province who was wheelchair-bound. While he had been in the region in June and July, he had made no progress. But back in New York he now pressed McNamara and Young to find the young man. He wrote multiple letters, offering leads on the boy, who was thought to be living as a refugee in Macedonia. "We were trying to do our jobs as systematically and fairly as we could," recalls Young. "But every couple of weeks we would get a note from Sergio asking us to drop everything and help somebody new. For a while it was the nephew of his cleaning lady, but then, once we had helped him, it was somebody else. There was always somebody. It got to the point that we dreaded his phone calls. It was very kind of him, but not very efficient for us."

Vieira de Mello monitored events in Kosovo with the vigilance of a parent who has left his child in a neighbor's care. He devoured reams of cable traffic from the Balkans, and he defended the UN's nation-building experiment and urged skeptics to give the Kosovars and the UN a little more time before they wrote off the possibility of peace. He angrily penned an op-ed for the *International Herald Tribune,* faulting the UN's shortsighted critics who thought it "naïve" to work for coexistence. The violence in Bosnia and Kosovo, he wrote, "pales beside the mutual slaughter that characterized until relatively recently relations between many West European nations." He argued that Kosovo was no more marked by revenge killings than South Africa had been after white rule ended. But observers there had not given up on reconciliation. "No serious commentator suggested, even in private, that blacks and whites were doomed to separation in South Africa, or that partition was inevitable," he wrote. "Why should we apply different criteria to the Balkans? Why should its peoples not be given the time to heal their wounds? Why do we look for quick fixes there?"[26]

He understood where all the pressure was coming from. Rich countries had given $207 per person in response to the 1999 UN Kosovo appeal, as distinct from the $16 per person raised for Sierra Leone.[27] This was a problem in its own right. "Just because these people look like us and are white," he had long complained to staff, "doesn't mean they are more deserving." But the disproportionate spending mattered for another reason: If, with all the resources expended, Kosovo could not be stabilized, donor nations would be reluctant to give money to shore up other trouble spots.

He still hadn't made up his mind as to whether NATO was right to have sidelined the UN Security Council and intervened in Serbia. He believed a precedent had been set. If a powerful country wanted to act and could not get the support of Security Council countries, he knew the country would be just a little more tempted to go it alone. President Clinton spoke before the General Assembly on September 21, 1999, and argued convincingly that when NATO bombed Serbia, it had in fact been defending the interests and values of the UN as well as those of the Kosovars. "NATO's actions followed a clear consensus, expressed in several Security Council resolutions that the atrocities committed by Serb forces were unacceptable," Clinton said. "Had we chosen to do nothing in the face of this brutality, I do not believe we would have strengthened the United Nations. Instead, we would have risked discrediting everything it stands for. By acting as we did, we helped to vindicate the principles and purposes of the UN Charter, to give the UN the opportunity it now has to play the central role in shaping Kosovo's future."[28] Vieira de Mello ended up largely persuaded, as allowing Serbia's atrocities so soon after Rwanda and Srebrenica would have indeed cost the UN. He adopted a formulation common among those who supported NATO's action but were nervous about its implications: The war was illegal (under the procedural rules of the UN Charter) but legitimate (according to the substantive ideals the UN was trying to advance).

Vieira de Mello tried to share the lessons he had learned in Kosovo, most of which related to law and order, with governments and senior UN officials at Headquarters. He proposed the establishment of a roster of pretrained, multinational police, along with judges, lawyers, and prosecutors, who would place themselves on call and who could head into the field on short notice.[29] The success of a mission could be decided in its first month. Providing civilians with security needed not only to be the top priority; it also had to be "the first, second, third, fourth, and fifth priority," he argued. "Unlike other nation-building tasks," he wrote, "law and order cannot wait."[30]

Fourteen

BENEVOLENT DICTATOR

Vieira de Mello did not have long to stew over being big-footed as the UN administrator in Kosovo. At the opposite end of the earth, a humanitarian crisis of potentially catastrophic proportions was unfolding. East Timor, a tiny half-island in the Pacific, was attempting to rid itself of the Indonesian forces that had occupied it since 1975.[1] And after a bloody conflict Vieira de Mello would be given a permanent chance to run his own long-term, complex mission. If he proved himself in Timor, he knew he would also demonstrate that the UN was in fact capable of stabilizing a broken country. If he failed, he also understood, the repercussions would be felt far from the Pacific.

INDEPENDENCE

During the occupation of East Timor from 1975 to 1999, Indonesia's armed forces killed some 200,000 Timorese. But in May 1999, while the world's gaze was fixed upon NATO's war with Serbia, the UN negotiated a deal by which the Indonesians agreed to give East Timor's 800,000 people the chance to vote for independence. Just as Vieira de Mello was returning from Kosovo, six hundred UN officials in East Timor were staging election education seminars, preparing voter lists, and setting up polling stations. They were backed by 800 unarmed UN police and military liaison officers. Even though violence had been escalating all summer, the UN team hoped that the 26,000

Four days ahead of the UN vote, Indonesian police chasing, shooting, and killing
pro-independence supporter Joaquim Bernardino Guterres. These were the first
photographs of Indonesian police actually killing an East Timorese.

Indonesian army and police forces in East Timor would keep their pledge to guarantee security during the vote.

On August 30 the Timorese headed to the polls for the long-awaited vote on independence.[2] UN election observers estimated that more than half the voters were already lined up when the polls opened at 6:30 a.m.[3] Worried about Indonesia's wrath, most went directly from the polling stations to hiding in the hills. Some 98.6 percent of registered Timorese cast ballots.

On September 4, 1999, anxious Timorese gathered around their television sets and radios to hear Ian Martin, the head of the UN election mission, read the results. Many wept joyously when the local radio and television reporters translated Martin's announcement: 78.5 percent of Timorese had voted for independence. "This day will be eternally remembered as the day of national liberation," declared Xanana Gusmão, the Timorese independence leader, who had been jailed in Indonesia since 1992. Domingos Sarmento, a former guerrilla who had also spent time in an Indonesian prison, listened to the news in his Dili home with his family. Upon hearing the results, he and his relatives went outside holding hands, and they kissed the land. "We were kissing something that finally belonged to us," he recalls. "East Timor was a country." But in fact the Indonesians had other plans in mind.

Within an hour of the announcement of the results, the sound of gunfire and screams abruptly halted Timorese celebrations. Black-uniformed pro-

Indonesian militia, backed by the Indonesian army and police, embarked upon a savage looting, cleansing, and killing spree that left at least three-quarters of all property burned or destroyed, most of the population purged from their homes, and more than a thousand Timorese dead.[4] The actions were calculated to destroy East Timor's prospects for survival. Indeed, the gunmen went so far as to pour battery acid into the electrical generators. "We knew the Indonesians were going to do something dramatic," recalls Taur Matan Ruak, then commander of the Timorese guerrilla resistance. "When you kill an animal, its last movement is like a spasm, and it is very strong." In the next fortnight, the marauding militia also butchered sixteen Timorese employed by the UN as election workers.[5] José Ramos-Horta, the longtime face of Timor's movement for independence and corecipient of the 1996 Nobel Peace Prize, helplessly watched events unfold from New York, where he had flown to lobby the Security Council. "I saw on CNN that whole towns were being burned to a crisp, and my family in East Timor was hysterical with fear," he recalls. "I thought that we were about to see the end of East Timor."

Fearing a human cataclysm, Gusmão instructed Timorese rebels to turn the other cheek. "If we strike back," Matan Ruak, the guerrilla commander, told his troops, on Gusmão's instruction, "we will give the international community the excuse they want to call this a civil war, to equate us with the Indonesian militias. We have to stay clean."

On September 5, after an American UN policeman was shot in the stomach, Martin ordered the withdrawal of UN election staff from rural areas. Timorese and international UN workers flocked to the capital, Dili, gathering at the UN base there. They saw that many terrified Timorese with no connection to the UN had taken shelter at a high school that abutted the UN compound. As night fell, a mob of militiamen hacked one man to death in the school yard and then began firing homemade guns—welded pipes packed with nails and gunpowder that were set off with cigarette lighters—at the Timorese, who fled toward the UN compound.

UN security officers guarding the base initially fended off the desperate Timorese. But fearing that the militia were closing in on them, mothers began hurling their children over the concrete wall separating the high school from the UN complex. Other Timorese cut themselves as they forced their way through holes they had sliced into the razor wire fence. As UN staff saw parents begin to follow their children over the wall, they formed an impromptu assembly line, passing the Timorese from one pair of hands to the next, until they were safely inside the UN building. The nighttime images of panic and rescue were broadcast globally. By the end of the evening more than fifteen hundred Timorese had joined foreign journalists and UN Timorese and international staff in the UN compound, where they slept on cardboard and shared dwindling rations. Ramos-Horta's thirty-eight-year-old sister, Aida, and her six children, aged three, five, eight, ten, thirteen, and fourteen, were among those being sheltered. With corpses lining the streets, the sound of gunfire echoing through the night, and bare-chested militiamen brandishing large machetes outside the UN gate, UN staffers feared that the mob would storm the compound.

Vieira de Mello watched events unfold from New York, and still under-secretary-general for humanitarian affairs, he attempted to coordinate the UN's humanitarian response. He herded the heads of the World Food Program, UNHCR, and the major aid groups together to ramp up their emergency aid deliveries. But while the militia were on the loose, he knew it would be very difficult to reach those in greatest need. He believed the crisis was so severe that military intervention, that rare and risky measure, was necessary.

Although the evidence indicated that Indonesian armed forces were committing and abetting the massacres, Western diplomats continued to point to the original referendum agreement in which Indonesia had accepted responsibility for maintaining East Timor's security. When Sandy Berger, the national security adviser to President Clinton, was asked why the United States had not stepped up to try to stop the violence, Berger said, "You know, my daughter has a very messy apartment up in college; maybe I shouldn't intervene to have that cleaned up. I don't think anybody ever articulated a doctrine which said we ought to intervene wherever there's a humanitarian problem."[6] None of the major powers seemed inclined to rescue the Timorese. "Nobody is going to fight their way in," said Robin Cook, the British foreign secretary.[7]

But because it was UN staff who had staged the referendum, it was again the organization rather than the specific countries that constituted it that came under fire. The French newspaper *L'Express* ran a commentary by philosopher André Glucksmann, who called for the abolition of the UN, the "alibi of cynical powers":

> The UN lured the Timorese into an ambush: it offers them a free referendum,
> they vote under its guarantee, it delivers them to the militias' knives . . . Is the
> ability to foresee and to reform inversely proportional to the size of its re-
> sources? 180 nations, a lot of money, a plethora of bureaucrats. . . . A warning
> to the brave people who are counting on it: the UN knows, the UN keeps
> quiet, the UN withdraws.[8]

Le Point, another French newspaper, published an editorial by the prominent philosopher Bernard-Henri Lévy, who invoked Somalia, Rwanda, and Srebrenica as the "other theaters of the UN's shame." He slammed the "slow but sure League-of-Nations-ization of the UN." And he closed the appeal by arguing, "The UN did its time. The time of the UN has passed. We have to finish off this macabre farce which the UN has become."[9]

Vieira de Mello was so incensed by the attacks that he fired off an intemperate response, which *Le Monde* entitled "Retort to Two Intellectual Show-offs." The under-secretary-general denounced the "two prosecutor-philosophers." Although it was "so easy to caricature, to ridicule, to defame" the UN "from the comfort of their Parisian homes," he wrote, their reasoning was an "insult to philosophy" and would do nothing to improve people's lives. He defended the UN referendum, which he noted had the full support of the Timorese. And he wondered why he could not recall Glucksmann and Lévy denouncing Indonesia's occupation of East Timor.[10] Instead of "shooting us in the back" by urging that the UN "rampart against anarchy" be destroyed—"a nonsense philosophically, politically and practically"—Vieira de Mello wrote, the men could do some real good by pressing Western governments to rescue East Timor.[11]

Secretary-General Annan too was defensive, as the associations with Rwanda and Srebrenica were inescapable. He claimed that the Indonesian slaughter was unexpected: "If any of us had an inkling that it was going to be this chaotic, I don't think anyone would have gone forward. We are no fools."[12] When journalists challenged him to account for why the UN had not deployed force to stop the atrocities, he explained that he did not have a protection force of his own. The countries that composed the UN were to blame. "We all talk of the United Nations and the international community," Annan said. "The international community is governments—governments with the capacity and the will to act. The governments have made it clear that it will be too dangerous to go in."[13] When a reporter asked if he was advocating a Kosovo-style intervention, he avoided making a forceful appeal, instead answering with characteristic tentativeness: "I do not think your analogy is completely irrelevant."[14]

An unshaven and frazzled Ramos-Horta shuttled between New York and Washington, invoking Rwanda whenever he could. "It was clear that people in the office of the secretary-general and in the White House were traumatized by Rwanda," he recalls. "So I kept repeating, 'Do you want another Rwanda in Timor? That's what you're going to get if you don't act now.'" Vieira de Mello, who spoke often about the Don Bosco school in Rwanda

The remains of East Timorese homes in the Ermera district, thirty-one miles south of Dili, September 27, 1999.

that the Belgians had abandoned, had the same concern. The Security Council had instructed UN election workers to carry out the referendum. Surely, he thought, the countries on the Council would not again abandon civilians who had trusted them.

When the violence began, the BBC chartered a plane to evacuate journalists, but a few remained and used UN satellite phones to plead for outside help. The pressure on Annan and the countries within the UN mounted. A vast network of religious groups and other grassroots organizations kicked into gear, demanding intervention. On September 7, Annan was informed that the UN had received 60,000 e-mails regarding East Timor, a deluge of concern so great that a separate computer server had to be set up to handle the influx.[15]

UN MUTINY

Martin was worried both about the bloodshed in the country and about the people gathered at the compound. In a reversal of its previous position, Australia agreed to admit Timorese UN staff on the condition that Australian citizens be evacuated from East Timor first and that any Timorese who landed in Darwin, Australia, would not be eligible to apply for longer-term visas.[16]

Martin's bigger problem was the fifteen hundred Timorese civilians with no UN connection who had poured into the compound on September 5 and whom Australia would not take. The militiamen who prowled outside the blue-painted gates seemed poised to attack at any point. Piled into a large auditorium, the displaced Timorese sang songs that the UN had made up for the election, lit candles, and prayed before their small crucifixes and statues of the Virgin Mary.[17] One Timorese woman gave birth to a baby boy inside the compound, and out of gratitude to the UN mission in East Timor, or UNAMET, the woman chose an unusual name for her new son: "Pedro UNAMET."[18]

The UN had a policy of never evacuating civilians, but Martin urged New York to lobby member states to do something to protect all Timorese (UN and non-UN alike) at the compound. Hearing nothing, on the evening of September 8, Martin felt he had no choice but to follow the advice of Alan Mills, the head of UN civilian police, and his security advisers, and recommend to New York that the secretary-general declare a

"Phase V" emergency.* Annan reluctantly accepted the recommendation and ordered the withdrawal of all UN staff. Before Martin had shared the news with UN officials at the compound, most learned of the evacuation from CNN.

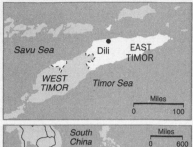

Patrick Burgess, a forty-four-year-old Australian who worked for OCHA, the branch of the UN that Vieira de Mello ran, was horrified by the news of their departure and protested. But Martin explained that the few reliable Indonesian army officers who had been protecting the UN compound had been spotted preparing to leave. This meant that they and the Timorese civilians would soon be left at the mercy of marauding killers. "We can't think only about this mission. If there is a massacre here, it will doom UN missions like this all around the world," Martin told Burgess. "What country is going to send its nationals into harm's way if it can't trust the UN officials in charge to look after them?" Since Burgess spoke Indonesian, Martin asked him to tell the Timorese of the UN decision.[19]

Burgess asked two Canadian colleagues, Geoffrey Robinson, forty-two, and Colin Stewart, thirty-eight, to help him assemble Timorese leaders. "We have been ordered to leave tomorrow morning," Burgess told the Timorese. "It is better we tell you now. The men are obviously going to be a target, but we can cut a hole in the fence tonight and you can make a run for the mountains." Burgess and Robinson wept openly as they stammered their way through an explanation of the logic behind the UN's withdrawal. Sister Esmerelda, a Timorese community activist whom the UN staffers had known for several months, heard them out. "Whatever else may happen," she said,

---

*The UN system uses five escalating security phases to describe the prevailing conditions in a country and the commensurate requirements for staff: Phase I, precautionary; Phase II, restricted movement; Phase III, relocation; Phase IV, program suspension; Phase V, which can be declared only by the secretary-general, evacuation.

"this referendum has removed any doubt that [the] East Timorese wish to be free. For conducting it, we will always be grateful to UNAMET." As she wiped away tears, she continued: "We knew there would be violence after the vote and we hoped that you would stay. And yet, we are not surprised that you plan to leave us now. We are used to being abandoned in our times of greatest need." The UN workers hung their heads in shame. "When you leave tomorrow," Sister Esmeralda went on, "many of us will be massacred, but those of us who survive will continue the struggle to be free." Saying she had to hurry, she shuffled away.[20]

Most Timorese made no attempt to hide their emotions. They grew so panicked that they wailed in agony. Some plotted their escape. A small group began scheming to take hostages. "We must stop the UN from leaving. The bald man cannot leave the compound," said one Timorese man, referring to Martin.[21] UN security staff began preparing to depart, burning UN documents and removing the hard drives from computers.

Throughout the compound groups of UN staff members clustered together to discuss their predicament. Many were sure a Rwanda-style massacre would commence if they withdrew. Some, like Carina Perelli, the head of the UN Electoral Assistance Division, suggested that the staff resign so that nobody would have the authority to order their evacuation. "We were trying not only to save the Timorese," she recalls, "but to save the UN from itself." Rosie Martinez, a Filipina personnel officer, spent the evening on her computer typing up faux UN contracts for Timorese civilians, so that they might pose as UN personnel in the hopes of being evacuated. She would ask each international staff member his or her rank and then proclaim, "Well, you are entitled to two interpreters, a driver, a secretary, and didn't you have a cook in your house?"

Burgess, Robinson, and Stewart sat together. "I can't believe we are doing this," said Robinson. "We *can't* do this," said Stewart. Burgess was nominated to return upstairs and ask Martin to reconsider. "When we leave here tomorrow," he pleaded, "all these people are going to be killed. I don't want to live with that for the rest of my life." Martin agreed but said he had an obligation to protect the UN staff. Burgess challenged him. "We are not in immediate danger, and a lot of staff want to stay." Martin, who had been hearing mainly from his police and security advisers about imminent militia attacks and about staff panic, looked surprised. "How many people feel that way?"

he asked. Burgess guessed fifty or sixty. Martin asked Mark Quarterman, a thirty-nine-year-old American aide, to survey the staff and take down the names of those who were willing to remain. Quarterman returned several hours later with a list of more than eighty volunteers. Martin was persuaded and told New York that he intended to remain with UN staff in Dili until the evacuation of non-UN Timorese civilians could be negotiated. "We had decided to serve the flag," Perelli recalls, "instead of serving the bureaucracy. Sergio always said that serving the flag gave you the power to do what you should do, not just what you were ordered to do."

With reports of hundreds of Timorese already murdered, Vieira de Mello had the feeling of "here we go again." In Bosnia in 1993 and 1994 he, like other UN officials, had understood the major powers to be unwilling to act to stop atrocities and had not pushed the matter. But a central lesson of the calamities of Rwanda and Srebrenica was that UN officials should, at a minimum, be on the record advocating solutions and challenging political constraints instead of simply deferring to them. When large numbers of lives were at stake, the smooth pragmatist had to exercise moral leadership. Doing so, he saw, was its own form of pragmatism.

Although his responsibilities toward East Timor were technically only humanitarian, he took a strong political stand. Just as the UN should not have trusted the Serbs to guarantee the Bosnians' safety in Srebrenica, he argued, the UN could not now trust the Indonesians. Since the UN had already rightly decided to evacuate Timorese UN staff, he endorsed a proposal that was gathering momentum at Headquarters: to send a small Australian contingent to the UN compound to protect the non-UN Timorese who had sought shelter there. "I appreciate there is a high likelihood that this will be unacceptable with the Security Council," he argued in writing. "However, I feel if we wish to avoid being a scapegoat, we should put the onus of rejecting solutions on others."[22] He pressed the point. "If we learned anything in the last five years," he said, "it is that we have to stop telling the Security Council what it wants to know, and instead tell it what it needs to know." He added, "We can't censor ourselves."[23]

Powerful countries were still officially accepting Indonesia's assurances that it would keep its pledge to secure East Timor. But he wrote, "Should we not be skeptical in this regard?"[24] He and his senior colleagues in the UN Secretariat had an obligation to put forth their independent view, which meant pushing for Australian intervention. "For once," he urged in a senior staff meeting, "let's allow the states on the Council to make the wrong decisions instead of saving them the trouble by making the wrong decisions for them."

The two parts of the UN—UN career staff and UN member states—were responding differently. While UN staff were refusing to leave Dili without the Timorese and UN senior staff in New York were pressing Western governments to act, the governments themselves were still resisting sending troops to rescue either the Timorese at the UN compound or the imperiled population as a whole. The Indonesians knew that, so long as the major powers remained uninvolved, control of East Timor would remain theirs. "Don't hector and lecture us," a defiant Indonesian foreign minister Ali Alatas said on CNN. "That doesn't help."[25]

But not all Western countries were alike. Portugal, East Timor's former colonizer, joined the push for intervention. Portuguese prime minister António Guterres telephoned President Clinton and pleaded with him to bring the issue before the Security Council. In Australia, the first UN member state to have recognized the legality of Indonesia's occupation, the political left pressed Prime Minister John Howard to make up for the country's past sins, while conservatives argued that something had to be done to stave off the flood of Timorese refugees who would end up in Australia. In his boldest statement of the crisis, Secretary-General Annan warned that what he called "crimes against humanity" would be punished.[26] On September 9, 1999, on his way out the door to New Zealand for the Asia-Pacific Economic Cooperation summit, Clinton announced that the United States was suspending a $2.5 million military assistance program to Indonesia, as well as $40 million in commercial sales.[27] The IMF suspended a $450 million installment of aid, and the World Bank announced a freeze on its annual $1 billion aid program. The Indonesians, Clinton said, "didn't like the results of the referendum and they're trying to undo it by running people out of the country or into the grave." He continued, "We expect the authorities to live up to their word and their responsibilities. [They] must invite"—Clinton repeated himself for effect—"must invite the international community to assist in restoring security."[28] Hiding in the mountains, Sarmento, the former guerrilla who had celebrated the referendum results, heard Clinton's statement on his shortwave radio and cheered the ultimatum. The Timorese who were gathered in the UN compound jumped up and down, rejoicing at what they hoped was a reprieve.

On September 12, the international economic and diplomatic pressure on Indonesia paid off. President B. J. Habibie announced in both Indonesian and English, "I have decided to invite the international peacekeeping force in order to assist us—together with the Indonesian military, in a cooperative manner—to restore stability to the troubled province."[29]

An outside military intervention would at last occur in East Timor, and the Indonesians would not contest it. After a tense, all-night negotiating session, the Security Council gave its blessing to sending an international force. As had occurred in Kosovo in March, the rescuers would be war fighters, not peacekeepers. After the peacekeeping humiliations of the 1990s, so-called coalitions of the willing or Multinational Forces (MNF), operating totally distinct from the UN bureaucracy, were seen as preferable to UN-led missions. They deployed more quickly, brought more aggressive rules of engagement, and because they were usually led by a single country, operated in more straightforward and disciplined chains of command. In this instance Australia would command an 11,500-troop MNF known as the International Force for East Timor, or INTERFET. Thanks to the pressure of powerful governments and the courage of local UN officials who refused to strand Timorese civilians, East Timor would survive.

At midnight on Monday, September 13, Burgess woke up the Timorese community leaders, including Sister Esmerelda. "You are being evacuated to Darwin, Australia," he said. "You need to be lined up, quiet and ready, in one hour." Although the Australian force had not yet deployed, the Indonesians had clearly relented, and the island had calmed. Beginning as dawn broke, five Australian and one New Zealand Hercules C-130 aircraft undertook the unprecedented evacuation. By 4:30 p.m. on September 14, a total of 1,454 East Timorese (UN and non-UN alike), 74 UN employees, and a remaining British reporter had been pulled out.[30] John Dauth, Australia's deputy secretary of foreign affairs, helped negotiate the passage of the refugees. "Normally, the gut assumption of Australians is that refugees will find the country so fabulous that they will stay on," says Dauth. "But none of us wanted to relive the fall of Saigon, where people who had entrusted their fates to the international community had been left behind."[31]

AN INTERVENTION AND A TRANSITION

The Australian-led force landed on East Timor's shores just five days after the Security Council authorized it. Vieira de Mello recalled that in Cambodia months had elapsed between the Council's approval of the force and the peacekeepers' actual deployment. He applauded the wholly different sense of urgency with which governments were now springing into action. Australia, Canada, the U.K., and the Philippines all contributed personnel, equipment, or intelligence to the Multinational Force. The Indonesian military and paramilitary leaders hightailed it out of East Timor, while the Timorese militia aligned with them fled across the border to Indonesian-run West Timor, where the international force was not permitted to follow them. Within two weeks of the intervention, almost the only signs of the twenty-four-year Indonesian occupation of East Timor were the smoldering ashes, the unburied corpses, and the parting Indonesian messages, graffitied onto the walls of buildings: "SLOWLY BUT SURELY, THIS PLACE WILL FALL APART" and "A FREE EAST TIMOR WILL EAT STONES."[32] Vieira de Mello took the obvious lesson from the force's swift success, which he shared in public remarks a few months later: "Whenever lives of civilians are at risk and a rapid international intervention is necessary, the only effective solution is the establishment of a multinational force."[33] Peacemaking was not a job for lightly armed blue helmets. But it was a job that had to be done, and one that UN officials could use their pulpits to urge be done.

The Timorese had been waiting to govern themselves for more than two decades—in the jungle; in exile in Portugal, Australia, and Mozambique; and under the boot of the Indonesians in Timor itself. Indonesia had released Gusmão, fifty-three, the former rebel leader and head of the independence movement, from its custody on September 7, 1999. Gusmão's poetry and letters from prison, as well as South African president Nelson Mandela's meeting with him in 1997, had made him a national hero and an international cult figure. With Indonesia's abrupt departure from East Timor, the Timorese resistance leaders were in charge by default, but they knew that they would pass through some period of transition en route to full sovereignty—living under a UN administration or governing themselves with UN help. Whatever arrangement was made, all Timorese assumed that Gusmão, the undisputed national leader, would be recognized as the supreme authority in the newly liberated state.

In late September Gusmão, the future president, and Ramos-Horta, the future foreign minister, visited Washington and New York, where heads of state were gathering for the annual launch of the UN General Assembly. Although East Timor was not yet formally a free nation, this was the first time Gusmão could walk among the world's leaders and imagine the Timorese flag flying alongside the flags of the other UN member states. The Timorese delegation was invited to attend a reception hosted by President Clinton at the Metropolitan Museum of Art. Grateful for Clinton's firm stand against Indonesia, Gusmão and Ramos-Horta joined a lengthy receiving line. When the line had hardly moved after half an hour, they made a motion to leave, but a White House staffer commandeered them back into line, assuring them that President Clinton would be very disappointed if he could not personally congratulate them on their hard-won freedom. Back in line, where they would end up waiting almost two hours, they made small talk with the person standing behind them, who just happened to be Hun Sen, the premier of Cambodia. Hun Sen had strong views on one aspect of East Timor's future: UN involvement. He complained that the UN had sent thousands of peacekeepers and bureaucrats to Cambodia, had spent more than $2 billion, and had abruptly left the country after holding elections. He said that international donors now felt that, because they had funded the mammoth UN mission, they had already done their part for Cambodia. "The UN will come with their white cars and their high salaries, and they will run around busily for two or three years," Hun Sen warned. "Then their mandate will expire, they will leave, and you will be left with almost nothing." Gusmão and Ramos-Horta thanked him for his warning and said that they intended to avoid a similar fate.

Gusmão flew back to Dili on October 22, 1999, a free man in his homeland for the first time since his imprisonment in 1992. Thousands of Timorese flocked to the Dili seafront plaza to greet him. "All of us must try to let go of the bad things they have done to us," Gusmão told them. "Tomorrow is ours."[34] With tears in his eyes, and every expectation that his people were only days or weeks away from playing important roles in a new government, he proclaimed, "We knew we would suffer, but we are still here."[35]

But on October 25 the Security Council in New York took decision-making out of Timorese hands and announced, in Resolution 1272, the creation of the UN Transitional Administration in East Timor (UNTAET). The resolution gave "all legislative and executive authority" not to Gusmão but to a foreign UN administrator who would run East Timor for at least fifteen months.[36] Gusmão, who had favored a central UN role but not outright UN rule, was livid. When he first learned of the UN plan several weeks before, he had shouted to his colleagues, "What are they doing? What do these people want?" When he saw the resolution, he was even more steamed. The other Timorese leaders tried to calm him down, but they sympathized. "Imagine a transition in South Africa, where Mandela wasn't given the ultimate authority," says Ramos-Horta. "Imagine if some UN official were given all the power and told it was up to him whether he felt like consulting Mandela or not." Sarmento, the former guerrilla who was also a lawyer, was also taken aback by the UN resolution. He had studied constitutional law, legal theory, and comparative law. "It looked like no legal structure I'd ever seen," he recalls. "I knew that in democracies the powers were supposed to be separated and not clumped together in one man." However, knowing that East Timor lay in ruins and needed outside help, he resigned himself to a period of UN administration.

Secretary-General Annan's top advisers scrambled to assemble the second enormous mission of the year. The UN officials who had helped arrange the referendum believed Annan's planners were shunning them as if they were responsible for the carnage.[37] Ian Martin, who had organized the vote and remained in East Timor afterward, was rarely canvassed for advice. He pleaded with officials in Headquarters to move their planning base to Darwin, Australia, so that Gusmão and other Timorese leaders could be consulted. But New York paid no heed and gave no guidance to Martin, who was told to bide his time until his successor showed up.

Lacking familiarity with Timor itself, UN officials in New York took the plans they had developed for the Kosovo administration and virtually transposed them onto East Timor. UN staff who felt sidelined joked that Security Council Resolution 1272 was a "delete Kosovo, insert East Timor" resolution. Annan asked Lakhdar Brahimi, the former foreign minister of Algeria and UN negotiator in Afghanistan, to become the head of UNTAET. Brahimi declined on the grounds that an international administration was unnecessary now that the Indonesians had left. He also argued that it was wrong to assume that what suited Kosovo would fit East Timor. "I know nothing about either Kosovo or Timor," Brahimi told Annan, "but the one thing I'm absolutely certain of is that they are not the same place." Since most of the UN planners had never visited East Timor, they had no feel for Gusmão's extraordinary popularity and no grasp of the difference between the Kosovo Liberation Army and the Timorese guerrilla force known as FALINTIL.[38]

Even if the UN planning staff in New York had put the most knowledgeable senior people in place, they still would have been overwhelmed. In the wake of Rwanda and Srebrenica the Security Council had stopped turning to the UN for help in peacekeeping or conflict resolution, and the UN staff in the Department of Peacekeeping Operations, never large, had been cut by more than a quarter. But suddenly in 1999 Annan found himself unable to keep up with the demands. At the same time that the peacekeeping planners were setting up the transitional administrations in East Timor and Kosovo, they were also fielding missions to Sierra Leone and the Democratic Republic of the Congo as well as maintaining thirteen preexisting operations.[39] The department was so thinly staffed that it could commit just one professional staff member per operation.[40]

After Brahimi turned down Annan, it was obvious who would become UN administrator. Vieira de Mello was the only UN official who brought fluent Portuguese, extensive experience in Asia, and, after his second stint in Kosovo, the spirited backing of the Clinton administration, which would foot a large portion of the UN bill. He was the UN official best suited to performing tasks as varied as overseeing the drafting of a constitution, planning elections, and facilitating the return of Timorese refugees. There was only one problem: Vieira de Mello already had a job as under-secretary-general for humanitarian affairs.

Annan asked him again to take a leave from UN Headquarters and to become the Special Representative of the Secretary-General in East Timor. Vieira de Mello accepted eagerly. He had been bristling in his desk job in New York since returning from Kosovo in July. He lured those who had worked with him on previous missions to join him for a short stint. "It will only be for six months max," he told them. "We'll be back in New York in time for the summer." In fact, he would stay in East Timor for two and a half years.

He packed up his apartment in New York and on November 8 flew to Geneva in order to see Annie and his sons. Since East Timor was the most inaccessible place imaginable, he knew that he would see his family even less than he had while he had been at Headquarters. Laurent and Adrien were still in university, and he would speak to them by telephone and e-mail them, but while they had liked passing through New York, East Timor was a harder sell.

Instead of resigning his position, which would have allowed a successor to take over, Vieira de Mello went on temporary leave, and his office, filled with his books and mementos, awaited his return. Fabrizio Hochschild was uneasy about his boss having abandoned the newly restructured office. "I tried to make him feel guilty about it," he recalls. "To be honest, I failed."[41]

On his many connecting flights en route to Dili, Vieira de Mello read and reread the all-encompassing Security Council Resolution 1272, which left nothing to the imagination. Even though the text included one vague line on the need for the UN to "consult and cooperate closely with the East Timorese people," his control as administrator was absolute.[42] Before he left, Brahimi ribbed him, "Sergio, instead of you being the dictator and Gusmão your adviser, why don't you make Gusmão the dictator and you be the adviser?" But both men knew that UN civil servants could not reverse Security Council edicts. He had been appointed what he called a "benevolent despot" in a country he had never before even visited. Neither the Timorese nor other international organizations had been given a say in how the country was to be run—or in this case built. Nothing like this had been tried before. And although East Timor's end state was clear—independence—Vieira de Mello would have to pave his own path to that goal. He would complain often that he lacked "an instruction manual."[43]

Although Vieira de Mello knew the Security Council resolution by heart by the time he landed in Dili, it would take him months to grasp the significance of what was missing from the four-page text: a plan for sharing power with the Timorese and for providing them with day-to-day economic and physical security. These gaps would haunt the mission and very nearly cost him, and the UN, a rare success.

Fifteen

HOARDING POWER, HOARDING BLAME

"Year Zero"

As his Red Cross plane landed in the Dili darkness on November 16, 1999, Vieira de Mello had two thoughts. The first was "This time you've got to do it right." He, like all senior UN staff, knew that the UN's reputation for competence had plummeted in the 1990s. His second thought was "How do we do this? We've never done anything this big before."[1] The single-runway airport bore a sign that said, WELCOME TO THE MOST RECENT COUNTRY IN THE WORLD.

He knew that the UN mission had a number of things going for it. In a country that was ethnically homogeneous and 90 percent Catholic, he did not have to worry about curtailing ethnic or sectarian strife of the kind that raged between ethnic Albanians and Serbs in Kosovo. Also, the people were united in their goal of achieving independence. Most of the militiamen and voters who had favored remaining part of Indonesia had fled to West Timor. And Xanana Gusmão, East Timor's de facto leader, himself preached reconciliation and patience. Vieira de Mello noted the absence of the "mortal hatred" he had observed in the Balkans.[2]

An additional factor that distinguished East Timor from Kosovo making the place what he later called "a pretty perfect petri-dish," was that all of the countries on the Security Council were united behind the aims of the UN mission. Russia and China joined Western democracies in welcoming East

Timor's march to independence. And rich countries seemed prepared to give generously to assist in the birth and teething of this new country.

But as he drove from the airport into town and saw the shocking scale of destruction, he could tell that he would need all the help he could get. He peered out at row upon row of houses that had been turned to cinders. Although in New York he had tracked the Indonesian burning and killing campaign and had even argued for a military intervention, the thoroughness and freshness of the onslaught were jarring. "It is shocking to think that all of this *just* happened," he said to his special assistant Fabrizio Hochschild. "Three months ago all these buildings were standing, and now they're gone." In Kosovo schools and hospitals and post offices had been left intact. "It was just a question of figuring out where the hell the key was," he remembered, while in East Timor. "Nothing, literally nothing, was left intact on the ground, except the will of the Timorese."[3]

East Timor had never enjoyed the autonomy that Kosovo had prior to 1989. Under the Indonesians the Timorese had filled primarily low-level jobs. The middle and senior ranks of the civil service would have to be recruited and trained almost from scratch, from a population that was 60 percent illiterate.[4] In Kosovo the UN mission had struggled to reestablish the rule of law in the wake of the Serbs' departure, but the province did not lack for lawyers. In East Timor Vieira de Mello was quickly told that the island was home to only sixty lawyers. Even though he had anticipated that Indonesia's rules and records would need to be thoroughly amended, he had not expected to discover that the Indonesians had systematically burned every record they laid their hands on, including property deeds, tax records, and marriage licenses. The holistic campaign of destruction and the obliteration of the state records reminded him of "Year Zero," the Khmer Rouge's launch of a new society back in 1975.[5]

As UN administrator, he knew that he would have to make a wide range of decisions in a hurry. Airports and ports had to be opened, clean water procured, health care provided, schools resuscitated, a currency created, relations with Indonesia normalized, a constitution drafted, an official language chosen, and tax, customs, and banking systems devised. Policies that normally evolved over hundreds of years would all have to be decided within months of arrival—by him and his team. For decades, he observed, UN advisers had "lectured Governments on how to best go about their business," and the organization now found itself "in the awkward position of being called upon to practice what it has been preaching."[6]

UN officials who had been in East Timor during the bloody referendum felt that Vieira de Mello was going out of his way to distance himself from his predecessors. Tamrat Samuel, a forty-seven-year-old Eritrean who had helped plan the referendum, flew into Dili with him and remained for a month. He warned his boss that the UN officials who had lived through the election trauma were suspicious of the new arrivals. "You have to be concerned about perceptions," Samuel said. "People think 'Sergio's boys' from Kosovo are coming to show them who knows best." Vieira de Mello laughed. "That's silly," he said. "We are here to do this together. There is no such thing as 'my crowd.'" But Samuel stressed that many UN staff believed his team thought, "We are the saviors who have come to fix this mess made by the UN before us."

Vieira de Mello claimed he did not share the view of UN officials in New York who acted as though the bloodshed were somehow the fault of the UN election workers. In fact, he so admired the stand that UN officials in Dili had taken on behalf of the Timorese at the UN compound that he made Carina Perelli, who ran the election division, promise to take him on a tour of the scene. "I want to know every detail of the siege, of who did what and when," he told her. And indeed, when he got to East Timor, the Timorese told him how much they respected the prior UN mission for having carried out the referendum amid the violence and for having refused to abandon the Timorese at the compound. But he did not make a sufficient effort to communicate his respect to those UN election officials he overlapped with in Timor. He was far more concerned about the impression he made on the Timorese than about the one he made on his UN colleagues.

EXPECTATION GAP: POWER SHARING

His first priority was building governing structures. When he worked in Cambodia, he had understood the hallowed local status of Prince Sihanouk and spent months cultivating ties with him. In East Timor he knew his success would hinge on his relationship with Gusmão, who was both the former rebel commander and unquestioned political leader.

The day after Vieira de Mello landed in Dili after traveling for more than twenty-four hours, he made an unusual, and essential, courtesy call. Instead of waiting for Gusmão to pay his respects to him, he made the two-hour trek to the town of Aileu, where the Timorese leader was encamped. The stifling journey along steep, largely unpaved mountain roads gave him his first glimpse of the country he now ruled. Gusmão thought it a welcome gesture. "I had expected to go down to Dili to see him," he recalls. "So I took note when Sergio went out of his way to come find me."

Gusmão told Vieira de Mello that he was pleased the UN had appointed a Brazilian, so that they would be able to communicate with each other in Portuguese, the language of those Timorese who had been educated by Portuguese colonizers before the Indonesian annexation. But he complained that thus far the UN had been doling out humanitarian aid without much local consultation. And he conveyed the concern that had been irking him since his conversation with Hun Sen in New York: East Timor did not want to suffer the "Cambodia trauma." "I know the UN means well," he told the new UN administrator, "but in Cambodia the UN came in, spent millions, and then left a vacuum behind them, which was filled with chaos. How are we to suppose that the same thing won't be done here?" Vieira de Mello smiled graciously. "Well, I served in Cambodia, so I know a few things about that mission," he said. "The UN certainly made mistakes, but there was more than enough blame to go around." Gusmão was not interested in the specifics. "Just promise me you're not going to run Timor like you ran Cambodia," he said. "We don't want you to come and go and for us to be left shaking our heads and saying, 'Was that a storm that just passed through here?'" Vieira de Mello agreed. "I promise we will not repeat Cambodia here." Not repeating Cambodia meant aggressively establishing functioning governing structures that made a concrete and lasting difference to citizens.

He struggled to decide how much preferred status to give to Gusmão. UN officials in New York urged him not to play favorites and to treat Gusmão as the head of one party among many. But it did not take Gallup pollsters or a formal election to confirm Gusmão's hallowed local status.[7] Vieira de Mello appreciated New York's concerns. If he relied on Gusmão to gauge "the will of the people," he would alienate anybody who did not follow Gusmão. Plus, even if doing so meshed with overall Timorese sentiment, it would send the wrong signal to the Timorese about how leaders would be chosen in the new democratic East Timor. In advance of presidential elections, he would try to walk a fine line, respecting Gusmão's de facto authority without formally enshrining it.

In Cambodia Yasushi Akashi's administration had supervised certain ministries, but in East Timor Vieira de Mello and his UN team were asked to run them all themselves. On December 2, 1999, in his most important early ruling, he set up the National Consultative Council (NCC), an advisory body that he hoped would make Timorese feel as though they had a voice in their futures. On its face the council looked reasonable enough. In addition to Vieira de Mello, the NCC included three other UN officials, seven representatives from Gusmão's party, three members of other political groups, and one representative of the Timorese Catholic Church.[8]

But since the Security Council had authorized only the UN administrator to make law, the NCC was merely a sounding board. Vieira de Mello could have passed any measure he wanted, irrespective of Timorese wishes. In practice he issued only regulations that the entire advisory body was willing to support. In the early months of the mission, he issued regulations establishing a banking system, a civil service, and a currency: U.S. dollars.[9]

José Ramos-Horta, East Timor's eventual foreign minister, laughed off the UN's invitation to join the NCC. "I was powerless outside of East Timor for long enough," he told Vieira de Mello. "The last thing I need is to be powerless inside Timor." Gusmão accepted the invitation to serve, but after several meetings, he recalls, "We felt we were being used. We realized we weren't there to help the UN make decisions or to prepare ourselves to run the administration. We were there to put our rubber stamp on Sergio's regulations, to allow the UN to claim to be consulting." Ironically, others felt Vieira de Mello was too deferential to Gusmão, that the country was becoming a "Xanana Republic."[10]

As administrator, he had to find a way simultaneously to offer short-term solutions and to nurture the Timorese capacity to govern themselves in the long term. He repeatedly stressed that the UN was there not to rule, but to prepare the Timorese to do so. But in the meantime UNTAET would have to ensure that tax revenue was collected, the garbage was picked up, and schools were refurbished and run. The UN mission would recruit and train a local

Timorese civil service, but in the meantime the UN itself would supply basic services. Jobless Timorese (some 80 percent of the working-age population) thus saw foreigners staffing their civil service, while they went hungry.

Vieira de Mello knew that the Timorese would not suffer UN rule for long. In a November 27 brainstorming session with staff, he argued, "The current goodwill of the East Timorese toward the mission is an expendable asset. The longer UNTAET stays, the greater the chances that it will be perceived as a competing power." But even though he was sensitive to the danger of stoking Timorese resentment, he was so convinced of the UN's impartiality that he found it impossible to view the UN as a colonial power. He blanched whenever somebody used the word "protectorate" to describe what he and his colleagues were attempting. He saw a UN administration as totally different from a colonial mission run by a single country, and he pointed out that the Security Council had explicitly tasked UNTAET to work itself out of existence. Yet while he was eager to hold elections, the recent referendum had been so traumatic that he suggested delaying the vote by a year or two.[11]

In most sectors international UN staff members were put in charge so as to mentor and train the Timorese and to restore services. Unfortunately for Vieira de Mello, UN staff performed neither task well. Most UN officials did not speak any of the relevant languages (Portuguese, Bahasa Indonesia, or Tetum) and thus had difficulty transferring skills.[12] However, as bloated as the UN bureaucracy in New York was in certain departments, it was sorely lacking staff with actual technical expertise. Because he was unable to recruit from any pre-vetted list of experts, crucial posts remained vacant for months. "Our system for launching operations has sometimes been compared to a volunteer fire department," Secretary-General Annan later wrote. "But that description is far too generous. Every time there is a fire, we must first find fire engines and the funds to run them before we can start dousing the flames."[13] Vieira de Mello complained that he could hire political officers, logisticians, and administrators but could not summon the road engineers, waste managers, tax policy experts, and electrical engineers he needed to make East Timor run. Ian Martin, who watched Vieira de Mello's struggles from afar, recalls, "Suddenly the UN became formally responsible for everything, and yet it had zero capacity for anything." Jonathan Prentice, a political officer in the mission who later replaced Hochschild as Vieira de Mello's special assistant, noted, "We're not a great rent-a-government. In the first few months, we had all these people sent in from New York who could write diplomatic cables, but nobody who could lay electrical cable."[14]

The Timorese, who were already frustrated to have so little governing authority, pounced on the early signs of weakness. "I know many of them have no experience, no expertise, no academic qualifications at all," Ramos-Horta said of the UN staff. "I asked one of them—an American lady—what her qualifications were, and she said only that she had worked in Yosemite National Park."[15] Most hiring decisions were made in New York. And once the internationals had been contracted, Vieira de Mello was largely stuck with them. Although he was running a mission of his own, he did not have the hiring authority to make use of the "box of possibilities" that he had kept in his office for nearly a decade. And even if he enjoyed full say, he would have been hard pressed to persuade the few specialists he knew to move overnight to a malaria-ridden island in the Pacific. He was unsure how he would manage to deliver tangible goods and services to the Timorese.

While some UN officials had difficulty viewing their less-educated Timorese counterparts as partners, others were self-conscious about the mismatch between the UN's huge responsibilities and its staff's inapt experience. Hochschild remembers: "I would get into arguments on what the salary scale for teachers should be, and I'd suddenly hear myself and think, 'What the hell am I talking about? Is this fair to East Timor to let people like me contribute to this debate?'" But Vieira de Mello did his best to remind himself and his staff that "only the Security Council, not I, can divest myself of this ultimate authority."[16]

ADDING INSULT TO INJURY

Vieira de Mello had always been acutely sensitive to symbolism and to what he had long called "national self-esteem." In the early months of the mission he tried not to act like a governor. "Just call me Sergio," he had said to so many Timorese that when his secretaries attempted to set up appointments for their boss, they usually got nowhere when they said they were calling on behalf of "Mr. Vieira de Mello." On several occasions, when his vehicle was stuck in traffic, his Egyptian bodyguard Gamal Ibrahim affixed a siren to the roof of the car. "Gamal, Gamal, what are you doing?!" Vieira de Mello would shout. "Take that thing down. I'd rather be late than act like a king."

Initially he slept in the Hotel Resende, which had neither locks on the doors nor hot water but did have an abundance of cockroaches. On one occasion, fed up with the grief he was getting from Gusmão and Ramos-Horta about the luxuriant lifestyles enjoyed by UN staff, he invited them to his hotel room for drinks. He proudly welcomed them into his suite, escorting them the length of his small bedroom and into his minuscule bathroom. "I want you to see this opulent palace you're all talking about," he told his guests. After four months he was told that a villa along the Savu Sea had been restored for him. But when he saw the eight-bedroom house, he was aghast. "I can't stay here," he said on his first tour of the capacious quarters. He had the house partitioned, keeping two rooms for himself and designating the rest as a guesthouse for international visitors.

He studied the local language, Tetum, scheduling several lessons a week with Domingos Amaral, his translator, and squeezing in practice sessions whenever his schedule offered a window. When Amaral worked as a translator in the UN election mission, he had traveled in the car behind his boss's. But Vieira de Mello surprised him by frequently summoning him to sit beside him. "Domingos, where are you going?" he would protest. "Let's use the journey to practice my Tetum." Dipping into his large collection of hotel note pads, Vieira de Mello used them to jot words and pronunciation keys for himself. Before he gave a speech, he would have Amaral phonetically mark the key words or lines in Tetum, so that he would know where to place the stress. He referred to Amaral as "Professor." "Professor, how do you win the sympathy of the people?" he asked rhetorically. "First, you have to learn the language. Language is the key to a people's culture, and culture is the key to a people's heart. If you force them to speak your language, you will never win their sympathy." As Amaral helped him rehearse whole paragraphs of Tetum, he would whisper, "Don't tell Ramos-Horta or Xanana. It will be our secret."

Local staff members were unaccustomed to being treated with such respect by foreigners. When Vieira de Mello held a barbecue at his house, he made sure Amaral's whole family attended. And as he had done with Lola Urošević, his translator in Sarajevo, he never stopped asking the Timorese how they judged their economic prospects or the UN's performance.

But for all of his sensitivity to symbols, some of his decisions sent the wrong signal to the Timorese. With the havoc wreaked by the Kosovo Liberation Army foremost in his mind, he initially urged the Timorese to disband FALINTIL, the guerrilla army that had been fighting for independence for a quarter of a century. Much as NATO had been tasked with stabilizing Kosovo, he thought that it should be the job of the Australian-led Multinational Force to keep the Timorese secure. He thought that the presence of the FALINTIL guerrillas might intimidate those Timorese who had voted in the referendum to remain a part of Indonesia and who would eventually return to their homes in East Timor. But his early idea met with an uproar, as the rebels were beloved as both the symbol of and the vehicle for the end of Indonesia's occupation. He quickly reversed his decision, instructing the fighters to remain in their barracks, off the streets. Gusmão was angry about this edict as well, complaining that independence fighters should not be "encaged like chickens."[17]

On November 18, tensions over FALINTIL came to a head. The Australian force commander, General Peter Cosgrove, instructed the guerrillas to consolidate some seventeen hundred fighters in a single barracks in Aileu. The soldiers did so in a relatively orderly fashion, but one truck filled with soldiers had a flat tire on its way and decided to stop in Dili for the night. The Australian military got word of their unauthorized presence and confronted them, seizing their knives and guns. When Gusmão was roused from his bed and informed, he was outraged. "The Australians are treating my men like common criminals," he exclaimed. "They came to Timor, they didn't fight a single battle, the militias fled, and now they are walking around with big chests like conquerors. We fought for twenty-four years, and yet they actually think they are superior."

Gusmão's first task was soothing his men. "We played by Indonesian rules for all these years," he said, as much to himself as to his fighters. "We can follow UN rules for a few more months." But then he made a public stand. He drove to Dili with a platoon with weapons and was intercepted by General Cosgrove personally. "I don't speak in the streets," said Gusmão. "I'm on my way to Dili. If you want, feel free to come along." When Cosgrove blocked the road with an Australian armored personnel carrier, Gusmão disembarked. "We are used to walking," he said. He and his men walked the remaining several miles into town, and Cosgrove trailed on foot. Vieira de Mello was scheduled to meet with Gusmão that very morning. When he arrived amid a loud commotion, he exclaimed, "Xanana, what have you done? I thought we were going to meet to discuss our strategic plan!"

UNTAET's symbolic mistakes kept coming. Since the hotels and guesthouses had been burned down along with everything else in East Timor, most arriving UN officials had no place to stay. At the start election officials who had stayed on slept beneath their desks at the UN compound, hanging washing lines between their offices. Unwisely, UN administrative staff arranged for two ships, known as the *Hotel Olympia* and the *Amos W,* to sail to Dili and serve as hotels for those waiting for housing. The $160-per-night rooms in the floating hotels were not grand—the ships were really nothing more than barges topped with four layers of stacked containers—but from the vantage point of the Timorese onshore, the ships looked like luxury liners, especially after a rooftop disco opened on one, blaring music into the night. Timorese nationals were initially barred from dining or sleeping on the ships, which stirred further unrest. Unemployed Timorese milled around the esplanade near the gangplanks, hoping to be hired for the going wage paid by the UN and other international employers: three dollars for a twelve-hour day.[18] The ships would become such a headache for Vieira de Mello that in July 2000 he ordered the nightclub on the ship to be closed at midnight. But by then the damage had long been done.

The Timorese were jobless, homeless, and hungry. They saw few signs that their country was being rebuilt. They did not control their own destinies. And they grew angry. In December 1999 some 7,000 Timorese who were waiting in the scorching heat to be interviewed for 2,000 UN jobs learned that the jobs would go first to those who spoke English. The crowd began throwing rocks, hitting an Australian soldier in the mouth. Then they turned on Timorese who worked for the UN, beating up several and stabbing one. Only when Ramos-Horta arrived on the scene were tempers calmed.[19] The following month, at the first major demonstration against the UN, one of the protesters held up a sign that read, "EAST TIMORESE NEED FOOD AND MEDICINE, NOT HOTELS AND DISCOTHEQUES."[20]

In 2000 the UN moved from its election headquarters at the teacher training compound into the Governor's House, a two-story colonnaded Mediterranean mansion that overlooked the ocean, which had first housed the Portuguese and then the Indonesian colonial powers. Since no other facility that was still standing could accommodate the large UN mission, Vieira de Mello moved into the same second-floor office that months before had housed the unpopular Indonesian governor.

Instead of simply departing their prior headquarters, the UN staff stripped the premises bare. In a highly literal reading of the UN rules laid down by the member states, they removed all "UN property": not only the tables, chairs, and bulbs but also the air conditioners, cables, and wires. "Anything they couldn't take, they broke," recalls Padre Filomeno Jacob, who would later become Timorese education minister. "It was like vandalism." Upon learning of the incident, Vieira de Mello personally delivered certain items back to the Timorese. But it was too late. "That's when we realized we had to look out for ourselves," Jacob says. "We entered the confrontation phase." Gusmão began to refer to the UN presence as the "second occupation."

The protests picked up steam. In February 2000 angry medical students marched in the streets demanding the right to go back to school. One fish merchant came and dumped his raw fish at the doorstep of the UN mission, protesting the lack of electricity, which had deprived him of refrigeration.

Vieira de Mello and Xanana Gusmão.

The Timorese gathered regularly to protest price hikes, and the UN's fourteen hundred local staff staged their own strikes over pay.

The arrival of the UN had raised expectations that, thanks to familiar UN funding strictures, the mission could not deliver. The Security Council had handed UNTAET an ambitious mandate and a generous budget of more than $600 million. But the UN rules still forbade peacekeeping funds from being spent on rebuilding Timorese electricity grids or on paying the salaries of Timorese civil servants. Just as had been true in Cambodia and Kosovo, the UN budget could be spent only on UN facilities and UN salaries. "Something is clearly not right if UNTAET can cost $692 million, whereas the entire budget of East Timor comes to a bit over $59 million," Vieira de Mello declared before the Security Council. "Can it therefore come as a surprise that there is so much criticism of United Nations extravagances, while the Timorese continue to suffer?"[21]

An even more remarkable UN rule held that UN assets could be used only by mission staff. This meant that, although the UN was there to assist in "state-building," owing to liability concerns, the Timorese technically could not be transported on UN helicopters or in UN vehicles. UN staff eventually had more than five hundred vehicles, but Vieira de Mello had to break the rules in order to get a dozen of them released for the top Timorese leaders who would one day be running the country themselves.[22] "This is ridiculous," he exclaimed during one of many arguments with the UN official in charge of administration. "I have the authority to order troops to open fire on militia leaders, but I don't have the authority to give a computer to Xanana Gusmão!" Since New York was thirteen hours behind East Timor, he could rarely get the authorization he needed in a timely fashion. Prentice explains, "There will always be that tension, with headquarters thinking we are all a bunch of Colonel Kurtzes, and the field people thinking, 'These guys who just sit behind their nice desks don't understand anything.'" The rules, Vieira de Mello wrote in a "lessons learned" paper, "make the UN appear arrogant and egotistical in the eyes of those whom we are meant to help."[23] The World Bank administered a $165 million trust fund for East Timor, which was meant to be used for vital reconstruction, but Vieira de Mello had no say on how the budget was disbursed.[24] "We are very focused on the risk of corruption. We don't always recognize that there's a similar risk in delay," recalls Sarah Cliffe, who ran the World Bank program there. "Something is probably not right if we have the same rules for a $500,000 grant as we do for a $400 million loan."

LAW AND ORDER GAP

In every sector there was a debate about how much to rely upon the Timorese and how much international expertise to enlist. "The natural reflex of an international organization is to dump lots of international people into a situation," recalls Hansjörg Strohmeyer, Vieira de Mello's legal adviser who accompanied him to East Timor as well as Kosovo. Strohmeyer instead canvassed the country for lawyers. The Australian-led force dropped leaflets from airplanes, calling for qualified Timorese to contact the UN. And the UN employed a pair of Timorese to drive around Dili on their mopeds to put out the word that lawyers would meet every Friday at 3 p.m. on the steps of the parliament building.

Within a week the UN had identified an initial group of seventeen jurists, and lacking chairs or furniture to sit on, they sat with Strohmeyer on the ground.[25] The educated Timorese generally had only bachelor's degrees from Indonesian universities, but they had what Vieira de Mello called *"une rage de bien faire, de vite faire"*—a rage to do well, to do fast.[26] In a moving ceremony on January 7, 2000, Vieira de Mello handed black robes to eight judges and two prosecutors in the burned-out shell of the courthouse in Dili.[27] Domingos Sarmento, the former FALINTIL guerrilla fighter, was one of the hastily trained Timorese who was given a robe that day. "Mr. Sergio handed me the robe, and I felt like he was handing me the country," he recalls. Sarmento and the other UN-appointed judges took up offices in smoke-blackened chambers in courthouses that the Indonesians had stripped of their doors, windows, and pipes.[28]

With the departure of Indonesian security forces, East Timor desperately needed to deter violent crime. The well-equipped Australian-led Multinational Force had, in January 2000, handed off to a traditional UN peacekeeping force, composed of 8,500 lightly armed blue helmets. This time, unlike in Kosovo, the force commander would report to Vieira de Mello. The UN civilian police were as slow as ever to arrive. Resolution 1272 had authorized the dispatch of some 1,600 officers, but three months into the mission only 400 UN police had turned up.[29] He tried to find a local solution by opening the country's first police training college. The college enrolled fifty Timorese trainees, including eleven women, in a three-month crash course. But no matter how long he served in the UN system, or how many frustrated cables he wrote to New York, Vieira de Mello had made little progress in finding the means to fill the inevitable security void that followed the UN's arrival in vulnerable places.

Because the prisons had been torched and all the prison guards had fled to Indonesian territory, few arrests could be accommodated, and many criminals had to be released in order to make way for new arrivals. In April 2000 Vieira de Mello said, "We cannot fill jails that we don't have." He suggested that community service sentences be given to "people who have not done bodily harm, who do not have blood on their hands."[30] This meant that many lawbreakers were let loose.

The untrained Timorese did their best to learn the law quickly, attending weeklong training courses in Australia. But they were too few and too new to manage the bustling docket. By early 2001 there was a backlog of more than seven hundred cases in the category of serious crimes alone.[31] While Timorese in other parts of the government complained that they had not been given enough power, Timorese judges complained that UNTAET's decision to throw them unprepared into the courtroom had compromised Timorese faith in the rule of law. "We had no idea what we were doing," recalls Sarmento, who would become East Timor's justice minister in 2003. "And it will take the people a long time to recover from seeing all the mistakes we made in the early days."

Vieira de Mello tried to keep the Governor's House as accessible to Timorese as possible. Locals could simply ride their bikes up to the entrance if they wanted to make a complaint or apply for a job. In mid-2000, when the UN chief of administration attempted to fence in the compound with barbed wire, Vieira de Mello went ballistic. "What the hell kind of signal are you trying to send?" he shouted, insisting that the barbed wire and barricades be torn down. "A lot of people said Sergio wasn't security conscious," recalls Gamal Ibrahim, who would spend two years as his bodyguard in East Timor. "But I'm one of the few people who knows: He didn't like to live in ways that other people couldn't." When he headed to the market after work to buy bananas, he teased his bodyguards about their wandering eyes. "Someday I'll be shot by a sniper and you'll be chatting up a girl," he said. Gilda, his eighty-two-year-old mother in Brazil, was so worried about his catching malaria or being targeted by pro-Indonesian forces that he turned his former Geneva cell phone into her "direct line," handing the phone to Ibrahim as he entered high-level meetings. "If my mother calls," he would say, "tell her I'll be out in an hour." In the early months of the mission she called every other day to check on her son.

The security threat posed by pro-Indonesian militia who lived in West Timor was still very real. For the first year of the UN mission, the Timorese were petrified that their killers would return. On one occasion Gusmão and Ramos-Horta told Vieira de Mello that Indonesian loyalists had infiltrated Dili from West Timor and were on the verge of seizing it. They urged him to authorize the police to detain anybody who appeared on their list of suspects. Chastened by his own reluctance to use force in Bosnia, Vieira de Mello was tempted. When Sidney Jones, his senior human rights adviser, raised objections, Ramos-Horta exclaimed, "Human rights? Human rights? That is *Alice in Wonderland*. We have to deal with reality here." Hochschild sensed that Vieira de Mello was leaning toward authorizing unlawful detentions and argued that he was losing touch with his values. Vieira de Mello, who felt like he was under siege from all sides, snapped, "Maybe I should resign and go back to New York." Many Timorese were starting to wish that the entire UN mission would do just that.

STAYING PUT

Vieira de Mello was no fonder of the diplomatic circuit in East Timor than he had been in New York. When informed of meetings with dignitaries, he would curse playfully in e-mail, expressing his distaste for them with mock expletives ("?#!%&X"). As had been true in all of his missions, his closest ties were to his special assistants (Hochschild and later Prentice) and his body-guards (Ibrahim and Alain Chergui, a former French paratrooper). Ibrahim, who had arrived in East Timor in January 2000, had not been there long when Lyn Manuel, Vieira de Mello's Filipina secretary, noticed on a flight manifest that it was Ibrahim's birthday. Standing outside his boss's office, Ibrahim was shocked to hear Vieira de Mello, whom he did not yet know well, shout out, "Well, Lyn, I hear it's somebody's birthday today!" Ibrahim was dragged inside, and Vieira de Mello produced a bottle of his trademark

Johnnie Walker Black Label. Each member of his inner circle toasted Ibrahim with a different drinking device—a Dixie cup, a throwaway plastic coffee cup, and a plastic Coke bottle cut in half.

Just before he had left the United States, Ibrahim had become engaged to Marcia Luar, an Angolan. As the weeks passed, Luar grew suspicious that Ibrahim might be straying with Timorese women. "What are the women there like?" she asked her fiancé. "What do you mean 'women'?" Ibrahim answered. "There's not even any food here!" Luar was unpersuaded. "Who are you working with there?" she asked. "Let me speak to him. He speaks Portuguese, right?" Ibrahim was horrified and told Luar that he worked for the Special Representative of the Secretary-General and under no circumstances could she speak to him.

One day when they were waiting for their helicopter to refuel, Vieira de Mello overheard Ibrahim arguing with Luar. "Give me the phone, Gamal. I'll set her straight." Ibrahim held the phone to his chest. "I made a mistake," he said. "I gave her a ring before coming here." Vieira de Mello grabbed the phone and assured Luar that her fiancé was behaving himself. From that point on, anytime he overheard the couple speaking, he insisted on intervening with what he called a "security briefing." When he realized that their mission together was going to last far longer than six months, Vieira de Mello found a UN job for Luar in East Timor.

Because of the toll his life in the field had taken on his own family, and because his closest friends were his UN colleagues, he always made a point of inquiring after the personal lives of his staff. In February 2000 Strohmeyer, the UNTAET legal adviser, slipped a note under his door at the Hotel Resende requesting that he be released to return to New York. He had gotten married in 1998 and did not think his marriage could survive another year's separation. Vieira de Mello called Strohmeyer into his office and granted his request to return to UN Headquarters. "Look, if you want a marriage to work, you have to be present," he said. "I should know." Strohmeyer, who had expected to have to argue his case, was relieved that his boss was so understanding. But before he departed, Vieira de Mello stopped him. "Before you leave Timor," he said, "there are three projects I'd like you to undertake." Those "three projects," which he ticked off with a straight face, were gargantuan: helping to normalize Timorese relations with Indonesia, negotiate a treaty on oil-revenue sharing, and establish a war crimes court. Strohmeyer did not make much of a dent in any of them, but he remained in East Timor until July 2000. He was divorced by the following year.

Vieira de Mello never imagined that he would stay in East Timor as long as he did. Most of his colleagues assumed he would be appointed to the job of UN High Commissioner for Refugees, a position that Sadako Ogata, his former boss, would vacate at the end of 2000 and one that was more prestigious and powerful than the coordinating job he had held in New York. Although he had tired of refugee work when he was at UNHCR, running an entire UN agency would present ample political and diplomatic challenges, and his two years in New York had made him nostalgic for the tangible assistance offered by UNHCR, which he had previously taken for granted. He knew that the plum jobs in the UN system generally did not go to those who had toiled in the UN ranks. Annan had been a significant exception. But Vieira de Mello had drafted more repatriation agreements, negotiated with more government officials, and led more field missions than any other candidate. Most UN staff in Geneva, New York, and East Timor were sure that the job of UN High Commissioner for Refugees was his for the taking. Popular consensus was that he would serve his time in East Timor and then return to Geneva to assume the refugee crown—a crown many people believed was the penultimate post he would hold before becoming secretary-general.

But two things got in the way of this plan. First, Annan, like his predecessors, looked to fill senior appointments with individuals from countries that would donate significant funds. And second, the very qualities that made Vieira de Mello a shoo-in for the high commissioner's job made governments reluctant to let him leave East Timor. Richard Holbrooke, President Clinton's ambassador to the UN, believed that UN peacekeeping, which was coming off the "triple failure" of Somalia, Bosnia, and Rwanda, had been bent to its breaking point. The East Timor mission had given the UN a rare chance to resurrect itself. In the fall of 2000, as Vieira de Mello's name began circulating for the job of high commissioner, Holbrooke telephoned Annan and urged him to keep "the ultimate go-to guy" in East Timor. "I didn't need any persuading," Annan recalls. "I knew Sergio was too valuable to bring home early." Holbrooke telephoned Vieira de Mello in Dili and said, "I'm sorry to do this to you, but I'm asking Kofi to keep you there. This mission will define the UN for decades. It will show the UN can actually do things right." Vieira de Mello did not betray his disappointment.

"I will do what my brother tells me to do," he said, referring to Annan. In October 2000 Annan asked Ruud Lubbers, the former prime minister of the Netherlands, the third-largest source of UNHCR funding, to become high commissioner for refugees.

Vieira de Mello was less stung by the news of Lubbers's appointment than by the way it was imparted. He learned about it from the news media and then received a formulaic typed letter with Annan's machine-produced signature stamped on the bottom. "Given Sergio's long history in the UN," his special assistant Hochschild recalls, "he obviously thought he merited at least a phone call." Hochschild persuaded his demoralized boss to host a dinner for his closest staff, then told the staff to surprise him by wearing pajamas to the occasion. This amused Vieira de Mello, as did an "Ode" prepared by his British secretary Carole Ray, which read in part:

> Dear Boss, this special evening is designed to make you happy
> 'Cos the news in from New York, of late, has all been rather crappy.
> Though things in the past weeks have not gone quite the way you
>   planned,
> You must admit your office here is beautifully manned.
> We know that living in this place is getting really tough,
> And if you had been asked, you would have said you'd had enough.
> So whilst we all acknowledge the S-G's massive cock-up
> Your loyal team is here to do our best to cheer you up . . .
> You're the only one who knows the dates, the names, the times, the
>   places.
> You recall the dignitaries and, of course, the pretty faces . . .
> Where your team all work their buns off and rarely do get cross,
> But only because Sergio Vieira de Mello is their boss.
> We are glad you are not going, that you're staying here with us.
> So try to make the best of it and stop making a fuss!

In an effort to fend off claustrophobia on the small island, he tried to persuade his friends in Europe and Asia to visit him. "But, Sergio," the American soprano Barbara Hendricks said, "Timor is just not *on the way* to anywhere!" Ever since the mid-1980s, whenever he had been away on a mission, his friend Fabienne Morisset had sent him a diplomatic pouch at the end of each week filled with all five days' hard-copy editions of *Le Monde*. When he reached Dili, he had discouraged her from sending the papers, saying, "It will take six months!" His mother sent him *Veja,* Brazil's equivalent of *Time* magazine, which he read faithfully, no matter how outdated it was when it arrived.

He wrote to his old friend Annick Stevenson (formerly Roulet),* urging her to come to East Timor and to write a story for the French regional daily *Le Progrès* on the elections and the formation of a new government. "I well know that Indonesia and Timor are not the principal preoccupations of readers from Lyon," he wrote, "but you could try to broaden their horizons."[32] Stevenson regretfully relayed her editor's response: "Taking into account the density of news in the world at this time (Middle East, Macedonia, Northern Ireland), it seems difficult to justify sending you there."[33] Vieira de Mello masked his disappointment, exclaiming cheerily, "The answer is not surprising!"[34]

The climate within the UN mission was almost as tense as on the Timorese street. The heat (90 degrees daily, with humidity between 60 and 90 percent) was withering. Most of the UN staffers lived off rice and Indonesian noodles. Those UN staff who worked in the districts, far from Dili, felt particularly cut off, unable to procure desks, computers, or even pens and paper. Following their boss's lead, UN staff worked nineteen-hour days and on weekends. East Timor offered no diversions. The UN was taking the blame for all that was going wrong, and those in Vieira de Mello's inner circle felt they were on the brink of a major failure or at the very least a major outbreak of social unrest. "Normal people reacted in strange ways," recalls Hochschild, "but strange people reacted in outlandish ways."

Vieira de Mello knew the flaws of the UN system intimately. While working in New York, he had kept a cartoon pinned to the wall from the mid-1990s, at the time that Euro Disney was suffering its financial crisis. The cartoon showed Mickey saying to his companion Goofy: "It looks as if the UN is taking over—now it really can't get worse."[35] But understanding those flaws was different from living them. The people of East Timor had high hopes for self-governance and improved living conditions, but Vieira de Mello felt as though he and UNTAET were dashing them daily. "Our

---

*Annick Roulet had gotten married in 1999, and her married name was Stevenson.

vision was we'd administer the place and we'd consult with the Timorese. Then, after elections we'd hand over the keys to the Timorese and be on our way," recalls Prentice. "The Timorese, who had been waiting centuries to govern themselves, understandably had different ideas." And eventually so did Vieira de Mello, who came to see that he would need to bend the UN rules in order to save the mission. The most effective way for him to exercise power in East Timor would be to surrender it.

Sixteen

"A NEW SERGIO"

I f Vieira de Mello revealed an important quality in East Timor, it was not his wisdom so much as his adaptability. As early as the spring of 2000 he felt that his mission, which was seen outside of East Timor as a rare UN success, was on the brink of failure. Physical security was breaking down, the economy was in ruins, and the Timorese had begun to view the UN as a second "occupier." Desperate to recover, he aggressively cracked down on security threats and attempted to give the Timorese a meaningful say in their own affairs. In order to regain momentum, he realized, he would have to pay more attention to Timorese dignity and welfare than to UN rules.

PROVIDING SECURITY FIRST

The greatest fear of the Timorese was that the Indonesian militias would return. While they resented the UN political footprint, they valued the UN military presence. When the peacekeeping troops took over from the Multinational Force, Vieira de Mello made clear there would be no letup in security. The UN force, he warned, would "maintain the highest deterrence and reaction capacity in East Timor, which I would not advise anyone [to] test."[1] Rumors still swirled that the pro-Indonesian militia planned to come back to massacre the population. On July 24, 2000, Private Leonard Manning, a twenty-four-year-old blue helmet from New Zealand, became the first battle casualty of the peacekeeping force when he was shot in the head while out on patrol near the town of Suai, on the border with West Timor. When his body was recovered several hours later, his throat had been slashed and his ears cut off.[2]

The day of the attack Alain Chergui, one of Vieira de Mello's bodyguards, drove to his boss's house. When he arrived at the door, Vieira de Mello skipped his usual pleasantries and said simply, "We are going to Suai." Chergui recalls the transformation. "His face was so serious, so heavy, dour," the French protection officer remembers. "He was not like Sergio." When they arrived in the town where the killing had occurred, Vieira de Mello grilled Manning's colleagues in the Kiwi battalion. "He was obsessed," says Chergui. "He wanted every detail of what Manning had done all day long." He would use the information to argue with New York that the peacekeepers' rules of engagement should be made more aggressive. But he would also use it to soften the blow suffered by Manning's parents, who would be left with a precise picture of the good their son had been doing the day he died. He would make a point of visiting them when he passed through New Zealand on official business.

Vieira de Mello had learned a vital lesson in Bosnia and Zaire. It was essential to signal to armed elements that the UN would not roll over. If the militants smelled weakness, he knew, they would exploit it. Therefore, in the wake of Manning's death, he revised the peacekeepers' rules of engagement to maximize peacekeepers' flexibility to defend themselves and to protect civilians. Previously, peacekeepers had had to wait to be fired upon before they struck back, and they had to fire warning shots before directly targeting anybody. But henceforth the blue helmets would be able to initiate fire at suspected militia without waiting. UN soldiers and police would also be permitted to apprehend suspicious individuals on the basis of minimal evidence. Vieira de Mello authorized large police and military sweeps to drive out the militia and restore public confidence. He later reflected, "We chose not to opt for the usual and classical peacekeeping approach: taking abuse, taking bullets, taking casualties and not responding with enough force, not shooting to kill. The UN had done that before and we weren't going to repeat it here."[3] At a speech in which he congratulated the troops on neutralizing the threat, he presented a bellicose face of the UN. "Let them try again, and they will get the same response," he said.[4]

His favorite part of the job, he made clear, involved managing military affairs. His staff teased him for his seeming delight at attending military parades in the scorching sun. A big believer in such parades ever since he had accompanied Brian Urquhart around southern Lebanon in 1982, he visited with each unit separately and often found occasions to present medals to the soldiers to boost their morale. "A parade may never have been the most important event in Sergio's day," recalls Jonathan Prentice, "but he knew it was likely to be the most important event in a soldier's day."

Neither he nor the peacekeepers had jurisdiction over West Timor, which was part of Indonesia. Nonetheless, UN humanitarian agencies like UNHCR operated there in order to help repatriate some 90,000 East Timorese refugees who had not yet returned home. On September 5, 2000, militia leader Olivio Moruk, one of nineteen men named by the Indonesian attorney general as a key orchestrator of the 1999 massacres and a suspect in the murder of Leonard Manning, was killed in his home village in West Timor. Word of his death spread quickly. The following day a funeral procession of some three thousand people wound its way past the UNHCR compound in the town of Atambua, in Indonesian-controlled West Timor. UNHCR security staff considered evacuating the office, but the local police chief assured them that the demonstration would pass peacefully. Instead, an advance group of thirty to fifty militiamen on motorbikes, armed with a mix of stones, bottles, homemade guns, and semiautomatic weapons, broke off from the march and stormed the UN office. "White people have caused our loss in the referendum," one gunman shouted, "and now they're causing our suffering."[5] The men burned the UNHCR flag and raised the Indonesian flag. As the militia shouted insults nearby, Carlos Caceres, a Puerto Rican UNHCR worker inside the agency compound, responded to an e-mail from a colleague. Caceres wrote:

My next post needs to be in a tropical island without jungle fever and mad warriors. At this very moment, we are barricaded in the office. A militia leader was murdered last night. He was decapitated and had his heart and penis cut out . . . Traffic disappeared and the streets are strangely and ominously quiet. I am glad that a couple of weeks ago we bought rolls and rolls of barbed wire . . .

We sent most of the staff home, rushing to safety. I just heard someone on the radio saying that they are praying for us in the office. The militias are on the way, and I am sure they will do their best to demolish this office. The man killed was the head of one of the most notorious and criminal militia groups of East Timor. These guys act without thinking and can kill a human as easily (and painlessly) as I kill mosquitoes in my room.

You should see this office. Plywood on the windows, staff peering out through openings in the curtains hastily installed a few minutes ago. We are waiting for this enemy, we sit here like bait, unarmed, waiting for a wave to hit. I am glad to be leaving this island for three weeks. I just hope I will be able to leave tomorrow.

Carlos

Minutes after hitting "send," Caceres was brutally hacked to death, along with Samson Aregahegan, an Ethiopian supply officer, and Pero Simundza, a Croatian telecommunications officer.[6] Their bodies were then set aflame in front of the office. Another UNHCR staffer suffered machete wounds to the head. The mob, which then ransacked and torched the UNHCR office, went around town on trucks and motorcycles inspecting private houses and hotels, saying they were looking to "finish" the "white people from UNHCR."[7] With Vieira de Mello's strong support, Secretary-General Annan declared "security Phase V" for West Timor, ordering the withdrawal of all international staff and the suspension of UNHCR operations until security could be established and the guilty brought to justice.

The Indonesian authorities proved uninterested in reining in the militia or rounding up the killers.[8] Conditions in West Timor remained too volatile for the UN to return. While Vieira de Mello knew that a UNHCR presence in West Timor might speed refugee repatriation, he never recommended that the UN resume its operations there because he was never satisfied that it could do so safely. The humanitarian imperative no longer trumped all other concerns.

In East Timor itself he focused on improving the performance of UN police. Although he was a committed multilateralist, he took what for him was the heretical step of deciding that on occasion geographic distribution should be sacrificed in the interest of unit cohesion. "What is more important?" he asked. "That twenty countries each send six policemen, or that the UN police stop crime?" In March 2001 UNTAET began to experiment with new models for UN policing, assigning responsibility for the Bacau district to police from a single country, the Philippines.[9] When UN officials in New York objected because they thought that the new single-nationality units were an affront to the UN ethos, Vieira de Mello successfully defended the move.

In 2001 he persuaded his friend and foil Dennis McNamara to become his deputy. He had talked up the mission and the fun they would have conspiring together once again. But by the time McNamara arrived, Vieira de Mello was drained by the relentless job pressure. His sense of play seemed to have vanished, and even though the two men had clashed often over principle in the past, they had never feuded as they did in East Timor. "Sergio didn't want a number two," McNamara recalls. "He wanted special assistants who were loyal to him above all."

Vieira de Mello made McNamara responsible for cleaning up the UN Serious Crimes Unit, which was meant to pursue those responsible for crimes against humanity. Talk of an international tribunal modeled on those for Rwanda and the former Yugoslavia had quickly faded, as Western states rushed to normalize ties with Indonesia. The serious crimes panel, which consisted of two international judges and one Timorese, would investigate 1,339 murders and indict 391 suspects. Although 55 trials would be eventually held, 303 leading suspects, including the ex-governor of Timor and General Wiranto, the head of the army during the massacres, would live comfortably on the Indonesian mainland and in West Timor.[10]

Vieira de Mello didn't give McNamara support when he needed it. His deputy traveled to Indonesia to press Jakarta to arrest suspected war criminals, but Vieira de Mello backed his chief of staff, Nagalingam Parameswaran, a Malaysian who encouraged the militia leaders to return to East Timor and assured them that they would not be prosecuted. Vieira de Mello believed that if he could persuade the spoilers to reintegrate in East Timor, it would enhance East Timor's prospects for peace. "Sergio, you've become like a bloody politician," McNamara said. "How can you just let the killers go free?" Stability mattered more to Vieira de Mello than immediate justice. Although he personally supported war crimes tribunals, Gusmão and Ramos-Horta were eager to normalize ties with Indonesia, even if that required pardoning those with blood on their hands. In the role he was in, Vieira de Mello believed he should defer to their assessment that the peace of the present should be valued above reckoning for the crimes of the past. McNamara continued to press the prosecutor's office to pursue indictments and arrests. And the clash with Parameswaran grew bitter, with the Malaysian publicly calling McNamara a "racist" and a UN oversight body accusing him of political interference in serious crimes. To McNamara's shock his friend did not speak up for him. Instead Vieira de Mello focused on the overall mission, urging his critics in East Timor and beyond to take a long-term view and not despair. "Regularly," he said, "we hear of aging war criminals from the Second World War being indicted."[11]

FILLING THE POWER-SHARING GAP: TIMORIZATION

The UN Security Council had given Vieira de Mello a mandate to govern East Timor on his own for more than two years. During his first six months he did not challenge this assumption, even as he struggled to manage the colossal responsibilities associated with absolute powers. But in the spring of 2000, with Timorese unrest boiling over, he sent a half-dozen trusted members of his staff on a two-day retreat and asked them to return with proposals for overhauling the mission. He delivered a new set of options to the Timorese at the annual gathering of their resistance movement. "The most acute phase of the emergency is overcome," he told the Timorese leaders. "We hear clearly your concerns that UNTAET fails to communicate or involve the East Timorese sufficiently." He described the two alternative models. "Under the first model UNTAET and myself will continue to be the punching bag," he told the audience, smiling. Under a second "political model" the UN would speed up the "Timorization" process and form a "co-government" in order to "share the punches with you."[12] He would create a mixed cabinet divided evenly between four Timorese and four internationals. "Faced as we were with our own difficulties in the establishment of this mission, we did not, we could not, involve the Timorese at large as much as they were entitled to," Vieira de Mello said. "To the extent that this was due to our omissions or neglect, I assume responsibility and express my regret. It has taken time to understand one another."[13]

Gusmão recalls the sense of relief within his party. "This was the time we started to believe that Sergio was committed to the Timorese," he says. "The Security Council had given him all of the power, but he said, 'No, I need you.'" He approached Vieira de Mello after his speech and said, "I see this is not Cambodia after all."

Vieira de Mello's ties with Timorese officials improved. Ramos-Horta, the unofficial foreign minister, began to tease him for his authoritarian tendencies, referring to him as the "Saddam Hussein of East Timor" or chiding, "Sergio, you have more powers than Suharto ever did. How can you live with yourself?" Vieira de Mello could give as good as he got. He referred to Ramos-Horta as "Gromyko," the eternal Soviet foreign minister. "José, you've been foreign minister of East Timor for twenty-four years. You've never managed a career change or a promotion."

Officials in UN Headquarters had a different reaction: Vieira de Mello was breaking the rules. The Security Council had empowered the UN, and not the Timorese, to run the place before independence. Vieira de Mello scheduled a video conference with New York to defend his power-sharing plan. Without informing Headquarters, he invited the Timorese who were slated to become cabinet members to participate in the discussion. "Sergio knew that he was trying to do something revolutionary in the UN system," recalls Prentice. "And his attitude was, 'If you want to deny the Timorese power, then have the guts to fucking say it to them yourself.'" UN officials in New York muted their concerns, and on July 15, 2000, Vieira de Mello swore in a new mixed cabinet. UN officials would keep control of the police and emergency services, and the political affairs, justice, and finance portfolios. Timorese would take charge of the ministries for internal administration, infrastructure, economic affairs, and social affairs. A few months later Ramos-Horta, who had informally represented East Timor abroad for years, would become the official minister for foreign affairs. For the first time in the UN mission, high-paid foreigners would work under Timorese managers.

Some UN staff in East Timor were even more uneasy with the new arrangement than those in New York. They had not come all the way to East Timor to answer to Timorese, they said. Their contracts said that they worked for the UN secretary-general.[14] Vieira de Mello decided to confront the UN staff members who resisted the changes. He assembled the entire UN staff—some seven hundred people—along with the four new Timorese cabinet ministers, in the auditorium of the parliament building. He spoke from the dais and, pointing to the Timorese sitting in the front row, said, "These are your new bosses." When one UN official objected that there was no provision in the UN Security Council resolution for what UNTAET was doing, he was defiant. "I assume full responsibility," he said. "You either obey, or you can leave."

Vieira de Mello also set out to mend fences with FALINTIL soldiers, who were still holed up in their barracks. The UN supplied $35,000 worth of humanitarian assistance per month until February 2001, when the new army, the Timorese Defense Force, was officially christened. He had stopped viewing FALINTIL through the prism of the KLA and had come to see how central the fighters were—culturally, as well as practically—to Timorese identity and stability.

Timorese leaders were only temporarily appeased by Vieira de Mello's power-sharing initiative. They quickly grew dissatisfied with the pace of the transfer of power.[15] Sure, they were part of a mixed cabinet, but they could not fire UN staff, and the UN senior staff continued to hold their regular executive meetings without them, presenting them with regulations as if they were faits accomplis.

Although he never attacked Vieira de Mello personally, Gusmão slammed UNTAET. The Timorese were supposedly being taught "democracy," he said, but "many of those who teach us never practiced it in their own countries." The UN were preaching reliance on nongovernmental organizations, but "numerous NGOs live off the aid 'business' to poor countries."[16]

Part of what was irking Gusmão was the absence of a "transition timetable."[17] As he remembers it:

The people were asking, How long? How long? How long? It was important psychologically to get a timeframe. If you just say "transition," without giving specifics, ordinary Timorese will say, "Twenty-four years—yes, that was a transition!" They were asking, we were all asking, quite simply, When will the *malaes* [foreigners] go?

Vieira de Mello responded to Gusmão's demands, and in January 2001 he finally laid out a political road map. An eighty-eight-member constituent assembly would be elected in August. This assembly, in turn, would draft and adopt a constitution within ninety days, decide upon the date for presidential elections, and choose the date on which East Timor would become independent. The assembly, duly elected, would decide to sign the constitution in March 2002, hold presidential elections in April, and receive full independence at long last in May.

By mid-September Vieira de Mello had formed a new cabinet, composed only of Timorese. With the deadlines in place, the Timorese were finally confident that they would soon take over, and tensions abated.

A GAP TOO FAR

Vieira de Mello had managed to bend UN rules in order to do what he thought was best for East Timor when it came to security and self-government. But he was never able to redress the greatest source of frustration in East Timor: the UN rules that forbade him from spending money directly on the country. In the economic sphere, these rules ensured that the large UN peacekeeping and political mission managed to distort local economies without being able to contribute to development. Rebuilding the country and revitalizing the economy were tasks left to the UN Development Program, the World Bank, and the International Monetary Fund. Since these agencies and funds worked slowly, the UN mission took the blame for leaving little tangible behind. The economic side of what Gusmão had called the "Cambodia trauma" was in fact being repeated in Timor.

Vieira de Mello fought with New York over taxation policy. In March 2001 he wrote to Headquarters, describing his "Solomon's dilemma." On the one hand, under UN rules UN staff and UN contractors could not be taxed locally. On the other hand, as the head of a government, he needed tax revenue and was sending a bad signal to the Timorese by exempting the richest people on the island from taxes. He argued the case from the Timorese perspective. If the UN paid workers extra to make up the difference in taxes, the added toll on the UN budget would be minor, while the infusion of such revenue into the Timorese budget would make a significant difference.[18] But he was again informed that the rules could not be altered.

Although he knew that the rules were the rules, he urged the Secretariat to try to see if the countries in the UN could be persuaded to change them. "What we spend on spare parts for our vehicles, for example, is the same amount as East Timor is able to spend on justice," he wrote to Headquarters. "We spend on helicopter charters three times what is foreseen in the national budget for education." He proposed that at a minimum after independence

UN member states agree to allow UNTAET to hand over used UN assets to the East Timorese government.[19] Lacking even basic infrastructure and equipment, the Timorese welcomed hand-me-down UN vehicles, generators, computers, and other hardware. After a long struggle Vieira de Mello succeeded in getting permission to donate 11 percent of UN assets—about $8 million worth of equipment—to the new government of East Timor.[20] By claiming that East Timor's ravaged roads were damaging UN vehicles, he also managed to get a portion of his budget used for road repair—a major victory.

The press had little knowledge of his internal struggles and started to make him a target of their attacks. *Tempo,* an Indonesian weekly, published an exposé on the discrepancies between international staff (who earned an average of $7,800 per month) and local staff (who earned only $240). The article inaccurately described Vieira de Mello as the "flamboyant father of three" and as "one of the most diligent partygoers" in Dili. Living off a salary of $15,000 per month, he was said to host "lavish parties teeming with wine and food." Although most of the facts (apart from his salary) were false, the article stung him, as its core observations—for example, the UN spent more on dental care for its peacekeepers ($7 million) than it did on local staff salaries ($5.5 million)—hit home.[21]

Since he was the effective governor of the place, any criticisms of the UN mission were in effect criticisms of his leadership. In early 2001 the Brazilian daily *O Globo* quoted extensively from a letter sent by an anonymous female Brazilian Catholic missionary, referred to only as "A.M." A.M. had described UNTAET as a "job bank for foreigners" who acted like "'pharaohs,' arrogant and authoritarian." UN officials drove air-conditioned SUVs, while the Timorese crowded onto trucks filled with "roosters, pigs, goat kids, bags of rice, vomit, and suffocating heat." The majority of UN officials treated the Timorese as "monkeys," A.M. wrote. "They do not come to serve. They come to command and to be served."[22]

Vieira de Mello stewed over the article for a month, then erupted in writing, denouncing the author. He wrote:

> I am, proudly, a career functionary of the UN, ever since I left university
> 31 years ago. I served—or, according to your informer, I spent delightful
> holidays—in tourist paradises such as Bangladesh, Sudan, Cyprus, Mo-

zambique, Peru, Lebanon, Cambodia, Bosnia, Rwanda, Kosovo and, since November 1999, East Timor . . . I left my position in New York and I came to Dili because I believed in the cause of this suffering people. I accept—in fact, I stimulate—constructive criticism, but I do not allow gratuitous attacks such as yours . . .

It was the UN that kept ablaze the flame of the right to self-determination since Indonesia's invasion of Timor in December 1975. It was our Secretary-General who mediated the agreement of May 5, 1999, that made possible the referendum of August 30, 1999, in which more than 78 percent of the population chose independence. I lead, with humility, this mission, and I take responsibility for all of its errors. We had to improvise and, with scarce resources, to create a government in an environment of desolation . . .

We share the frustration of the people with the slow execution of these projects. If destroying is easy—it took a few days here—constructing a new public administration and civil service takes time. I did not learn to make miracles, and one of the reasons for the delay is the control mechanisms, whose objective is precisely to prevent that which your source affirms to be the norm: corruption . . .

The headline of your article was "White Intervention in East Timor." Intervention, yes! White? There are more Asian, African and Arab people than Europeans in this mission . . . I haven't served the UN for more than three decades to swallow gratuitous effrontery from anybody. To the readers of O Globo I excuse myself for the tone of this reply. It is easy to assail when one does not have knowledge of the facts.[23]

The one fight Vieira de Mello refused to lose with Headquarters was that over securing compensation for families of sixteen UN employees killed during the 1999 referendum. When New York requested their marriage, birth, and death certificates, as well as written proof of employment, he patiently explained by cable that East Timor presented a "very unique case" where all documentation had been destroyed and the UN would have to be flexible and accept witness statements vouching for a staff member's employment and death. "I am sure you will agree that we have a moral obligation to staff members who died in their line of duty," he wrote, "particularly since rampaging militias specifically targeted local staff."[24]

In March 2001 Jean-Marie Guéhenno, head of the Department of Peacekeeping Operations, wrote to Vieira de Mello expressing regret that "our hands are tied." Despite the unusual circumstances surrounding the deaths and the compensation claims, Guéhenno wrote, the department was unable to get the standard requirements waived. More than two decades after he had battled New York for compensation for a Lebanese doctor killed by peacekeepers, Vieira de Mello argued that the UN needed to overhaul its entire approach. "In my long association with UN peacekeeping operations, the issue of the UN's incredibly late payment of compensation to nationals of our host countries [has] always been a source of embarrassment to the Organization," he wrote. "Victims' families are usually very poor, and it is difficult for them to understand how the UN, which is perceived to be wealthy, could not pay compensation within a reasonable amount of time." He informed Guéhenno that he intended to go ahead and "grant a one time lump sum payment of $10,000" to each family. Knowing how to force a response, he advised: "If I do not hear from you by 19 July, I shall direct the Director of Administration to disburse these funds immediately."[25] This cable got New York's attention, and Vieira de Mello's multiyear campaign finally bore fruit. Guéhenno informed him that he had finally persuaded UN administrators to allow the Timorese families to be compensated beginning on August 1, 2001.[26]

Vieira de Mello's fiercest clash with Headquarters came over his handling of petroleum, East Timor's one potentially lucrative source of revenue. In 1989, when Australia had recognized Indonesia's occupation of East Timor, a grateful Indonesia granted Australia generous access to oil resources that lay close to East Timor's shores. Vieira de Mello knew that UNTAET would be considered a failure if it did not manage to persuade the Australians to return what rightfully belonged to the Timorese. Australia's GDP dwarfed any oil revenues the country would receive from the vicinity of East Timor. By contrast, if the UN could secure the oil fields for Timor, they could potentially triple the island's GNP.

The negotiations were tense from the start. Australian diplomats tried to claim that the oil was worth so little that the status quo should be preserved. Sensing that Australia would not give up its claim without a fight, Vieira de Mello decided to preserve his own warm ties with the Australian government by removing himself from the proceedings and appointing as the lead

UN negotiator Peter Galbraith, who had been U.S. ambassador to Croatia in the Balkans and whom he had made UNTAET's minister of political affairs. Galbraith, who could be undiplomatic, threatened to sue Australia at the International Court of Justice if it did not offer the Timorese, in accordance with the law of the sea, all revenues north of the midway point between East Timor and Australia. The Australians complained repeatedly to Vieira de Mello that Galbraith was raising Timorese expectations unreasonably and sabotaging ties between the UN and Australia. They had expected the UN to negotiate the agreement, not to act strictly in the interests of the Timorese. But the Security Council had tasked UNTAET to act as the Timorese government, so mere mediation was not appropriate. Vieira de Mello urged Galbraith to drive the best bargain for the Timorese.

In order to drive that bargain, he, Galbraith, and others in UNTAET pleaded with Headquarters to send a lawyer with expertise in petroleum law. But just as UN Headquarters took two years to respond to pleas for experts in organized crime for Kosovo, it could not quickly call upon specialists for Timor. Yet not long before a deal was to be signed divvying up one portion of the oil proceeds, UN Under-Secretary-General for Political Affairs Kieran Prendergast sent Vieira de Mello a long cable, telling him that he had consulted with an expert on the law of the sea who had said that he was giving too much away. "It will be for East Timor, as an independent nation, to define its national interest," Prendergast wrote. Vieira de Mello was livid. "Sergio decided rightly that the way to be a success was to become more Timorese than the Timorese," recalls Prentice. "So anything that suggested that he hadn't placed their best interests at heart was always going to draw a rather strident response." Vieira de Mello whipped off one of the most blistering cables of his long career, writing:

> Although I read Prendergast's memo on 1 April, I note that it was dated 22 March and was thus, despite appearances, not an April Fool's joke . . . Headquarters was kept fully informed at each and every stage. I would have welcomed any timely advice . . . Why did I not hear previously, either in person, by telephone, or in writing? . . .
>
> I am (I had hoped that this was presumed) fully aware that East Timor will have to live with any decision made much longer and more profoundly

than will we . . . in short, contrary to the impression given, the East Timorese
leadership do have minds of their own and do not simply wait, mutely, for us
to provide poor advice. More frequent contact with the realities of the field—
as I learnt in my career—provide a vital antidote to such misconceptions.

He defended Galbraith's approach to the negotiations and fired back that
New York was being unduly influenced by an adviser to the subsidiary of
an American company called Oceanic, which had a vested interest in the
negotiations. "I have yet to read of an alternative, feasible route that could
have been taken that would have led to a more beneficial outcome," he
wrote. "These gains should not be jeopardized by an eleventh-hour lack of
unity on the part of East Timor and the United Nations, particularly if this
were to become public, which, as we all know, is regrettably a risk within
the United Nations." In a second draft of the cable, Vieira de Mello noted
that while the Timorese had been made aware of his response, "The pique
is mine." And for the final draft he altered the sentence to: "The disappointment, irritation, and pique are mine."[27]

In the end Galbraith secured a deal by which the Timorese and Australians
would create a Joint Petroleum Development Area, from which the Timorese
would receive 90 percent of the revenues and the Australians 10 percent, a
dramatic improvement over the unfair 50-50 split that predated the UN
negotiations. The Bayu-Undan development within this area was thought
to contain gas and oil reserves worth $6 billion to $7 billion, which would
henceforth bring $5 billion in revenue to tiny East Timor.[28] The Galbraith-
led negotiations would quadruple the oil available to East Timor for sale.

On April 24, 2002, East Timor's presidential elections were held. Xanana
Gusmão's opponent said that, even though he expected to lose in a landslide,
he thought it important to show the Timorese that they would have alternatives in elections. The two candidates walked together arm in arm into the
polling station where they cast their votes. In a marked contrast to the August
1999 referendum, only one slight irregularity was reported in the 282 polling stations throughout the country.[29] Gusmão was elected president of East
Timor with 83 percent of the vote. Vieira de Mello told Carlos Valenzuela,
the Colombian who ran the elections for the UN, "Thank you for the most
boring elections of my life." East Timor was less than one month away from
being a fully independent nation.

GETTING A LIFE

Part of the reason Vieira de Mello had time to work nineteen-hour days was that he had no serious romantic attachments tying him down. The job's challenges distracted him from his loneliness. Indeed in February 2000, just two months into the new millennium, he complained memorably to his close friend in Geneva, Fabienne Morisset: "February already and still a bonkless century."

In his isolation Vieira de Mello had settled into a routine in East Timor. He ate a sandwich in the office for lunch, used the Internet and reading packages from friends to keep up with events in the rest of the world, brought work home, dined ascetically on rice and chocolate bars, made his phone calls to New York late at night, and avoided the cocktail circuit. Kosovo had given Vieira de Mello his first taste of being a local celebrity. But as the ruler of East Timor, he was almost as well known as Gusmão. He rarely went out because his unfailing politeness toward the Timorese and toward his UN employees demanded energy and because he cherished the few hours he had to himself. When he served as the best man in the Dili wedding of his special assistant, Fabrizio Hochschild, he ducked out of the after-party early. "I'm so sorry, Fabrizio," he told his close friend. "I just can't take being 'on' anymore. I'm exhausted." He told his friend Morisset of the hollowness he felt despite having finally reached great heights at the UN. "Everything is all swimming along professionally," he said. "But what am I doing with my life? What is all of this for?"

In late 2000 he had met Carolina Larriera, a twenty-seven-year-old willowy, elegant Argentinian who had gone to university in New York and in 1997 had volunteered her way to a Headquarters staff job as a public information officer. In East Timor, her first field posting, she helped dispense World Bank microcredit grants to Timorese businesses. Larriera was drawn to Vieira de Mello's familiar South American charisma, but she had heard about his exploits with women and steered clear. In October 2000, nearly a year into her posting, she briefed him on the microcredit program in advance of a donors' conference he was attending. The pair discussed the problem of finding and retaining qualified Timorese managers. A month later, when she attended a small dinner party at Ramos-Horta's home, Vieira de Mello approached her, and the two drifted into easy conversation. Playing up the traditional rivalry between Brazil and Argentina, he described how his mother had fled Buenos Aires and returned to Rio when she was seven months' pregnant so as to make sure he was born in Brazil.

The pair became romantically involved in January 2001 and conducted their relationship privately. Larriera was concerned that her colleagues would judge her for her involvement with the head of the UN mission. He was not fully invested: He saw other women and concentrated mainly on work, spending many evenings at his home alone, listening to Beethoven or another somber composer and poring over paperwork, while drinking a glass of Black Label. "You can work and be involved in a meaningful relationship. The two are not incompatible," Larriera insisted. "No, I can't," he said.

In September 2001, frustrated by his refusal to prioritize the relationship, she broke it off and stopped taking his phone calls. "This isn't worth it," she told him. "You're not with me, and I want more." He asked her to reconsider, but she was firm. Unless he made a real commitment, she said, they were through.

On September 11, 2001, Vieira de Mello was in Jakarta, Indonesia, meeting with senior Indonesian officials. At the end of the day he said good night to his aides and headed upstairs to his room, where he ordered room service. His cell phone rang, and it was Larriera telling him to turn on the television. The regular CNN broadcast had been interrupted and was showing the flaming World Trade Center towers that he used to view from his apartment in New York. Ibrahim, his bodyguard, knocked loudly on the door. "Mr. Sergio," he shouted, "have you seen what happened?" When Ibrahim entered, his boss was holding his shortwave radio tuned to a French broadcast, as the English CNN broadcast played behind him. He just shook his head, speechless. "There was nothing to say," recalls Ibrahim. "What do you say?"

On October 14, 2001, a month after the terrorist attacks, Vieira de Mello called Larriera and invited her over, saying he needed to talk. When she arrived at his Dili home, the lights were out. She let herself in through the side door and found a row of candles leading her from the doorway to the living room. Sprinkled on the floor were paper hearts that he had cut out of colored construction paper. "From now on, it's the new Sergio!" he said, emerging. Larriera was skeptical. "I have changed," he said. "And I will change. Don't

believe me. Watch me." From that point on, the couple referred to their relationship before his October turnaround as their "prehistory." "History," he
said, "begins today."

Vieira de Mello's closest colleagues at that time were in serious relationships.
Jonathan Prentice, his special assistant, had married his high school sweetheart,
Antonia, and the pair were inseparable. Hochschild, his previous assistant, had
been a determined bachelor, but he and his wife had given birth to a child
soon after their wedding in East Timor. Martin Griffiths, his former deputy
in New York, had gotten divorced and remarried in 1999, naming Vieira de
Mello the godfather of his newborn daughter. Now Vieira de Mello seemed to
want what they had. He wrote to Larriera a week after they got back together,
sounding like a teenager. After sending her *"un besito matinal,"* or morning kiss,
he wrote that he found himself thinking that what they had together was too
good to be true, but he exclaimed, "Fortunately, it *is* true."[30]

He filed for divorce in December 2001. Although he had lived a separate
life from Annie since 1996, she took the news badly. However distant they
had grown, she had never expected him to leave the marriage. But he was determined to go ahead. He wrote to Antonio Carlos Machado, his best friend
in Brazil, that after "various gaffes of mine designed to duck reality," he had
decided that he was deeply in love. Noting that he had no idea how draining
love could be, he wrote that it had nonetheless filled him "with a new and
vital *élan,"* and he was determined "to make the most of what remains of my
life instead of wasting the few years that are left."

Vieira de Mello told Machado that he had what would be an exhausting
six months remaining in East Timor. Afterward he planned to take three
months off "so as to do many of the things I've dreamed of and delayed my
whole life."[31] He crammed a few of those ambitions into his weekends with
Larriera in Timor. He insisted the couple climb Ramelau, Timor's highest
peak. He said he wanted to learn to scuba dive, and they got PADI certified.
He announced he wanted to do the deepest dive in the area, so they plunged
130 feet off the coast of Atauro island.

At Christmastime he did something with Larriera he had done with none
of his other girlfriends: He invited her home to Brazil to meet his mother.
She in turn brought him to Buenos Aires, where she guided him to 1853
Vincente López Street, the house where the Vieira de Mello family had lived
from the time he was twenty days old until he was three.

As his relationship with Larriera intensified, he settled into a reclusive domestic routine. She moved into his home, and they got a dog, Manchinha (Portuguese for Spot). In the early evening after the temperature cooled, they went for long runs along the coast or hiked up a nearby hill to the eighty-eight-foot-tall statue of Christ, which was modeled after the Christ the Redeemer statue above Rio de Janeiro. On the weekends they shopped at the market or continued their scuba-diving adventures with bodyguard Alain Chergui and the Prentices. As the mission began to coast along toward Timorese independence, he and Larriera even took long weekends on the nearby resort island of Bali. He grew giddy as the handover date approached, blasting the Paul McCartney song "Freedom" in their home.

In the week before East Timor's gala independence ceremony, the Timorese leaders held a dinner in honor of their departing governor. Vieira de Mello toasted them and their future as an independent country. But he toasted most dramatically Larriera. "East Timor is special to me for many reasons," he said, "but none more than because this is where I met Carolina. For two years we worked together in the same building in New York and never met. We had to travel to this small island ten thousand miles away in order to find one another."

Vieira de Mello's close friends were stunned by his transformation and by his espousal of monogamy. Many speculated that his fidelity could not last. Others disagreed, suggesting that at the pinnacle of the UN system he had realized he could not carry on relationships outside his marriage. All seemed to agree that Larriera had brought out a relaxed side to him that they had not seen in such abundance before. Morisset recalls long talks with him while he was in East Timor:

> Sergio couldn't accept getting old, getting less handsome. He'd always been preoccupied with his looks, but in later years he became obsessive about his fitness. He wanted to stay a seductive young guy. This was his role. This was his identity. This was what made him famous. And Carolina awakened in him his youth.

As he focused on his future with Larriera, he hoped that Secretary-General Annan would compensate him for having stranded him in Timor for two and a half years. He told Larriera, "He has the obligation to send me to a civilized place, to a decent post."

But as his mission approached its end, Annan did not tell him where he was heading next. When a journalist asked Vieira de Mello his plans, he answered testily: "Regarding my next mission, you will have to address that question to the Secretary-General. I do not know yet."[32] As he boxed up the life he had built in Timor, he exclaimed to McNamara, "Where am I supposed to send my fucking boxes?" He could not understand how senior officials in New York were not more empathetic toward those who slogged away in the field. "Some of those bastards in New York should try this sometime," he said.

Vieira de Mello reflected publicly on where the mission had succeeded and failed. "When I arrived in 1999, I felt like an ambulance driver arriving at the site of a car crash and finding a dismembered body in a state of clinical death," he told reporters in Dili. The UN administration had helped put the territory back on its feet, he said, but with the average Timorese still living on fifty-five cents per day, the transition would be a long one. "You don't change the devastation of 1999 into a Garden of Eden in two and a half years," he said, adding that "we have laid solid bases for the country to live in peace."[33]

The UN had spent $2.2 billion. It had renovated 700 schools, restored 17 rural power stations, trained thousands of teachers, recruited more than 11,000 civil servants for 15,000 posts, established two army battalions, and suited up more than 1,500 police. And Vieira de Mello had learned a valuable lesson about legitimacy: It was performance-based. "The UN cannot presume that it will be seen as legitimate by the local population in question just because in some distant Security Council chamber a piece of paper was produced," he said. "We need to show why we are beneficial to the people on the ground, and we need to show that quickly."[34]

His biggest surprise, he said, was the Timorese "capacity to forgive." "I have never seen it elsewhere," he told a journalist, "and I've seen conflicts." He cited regrets over handing the judiciary to the Timorese too soon and over being hemmed in by rules "too elaborate and too complex for a country that was still coming out of intensive care."[35] "Local people have little time for rules," he wrote later. "They want results."[36] His final verdict? "I felt

*Vieira de Mello presenting Gusmão with a symbolic key
to the Governor's House, May 16, 2002.*

that we had done as much as an unprepared organization could have done."
When he tried to publish a self-critical report on the lessons the UN had
learned, his superiors in New York forbade him from doing so.

On May 18, with President Clinton and other heads of state arriving the
next day for a flag-raising ceremony, he welcomed to East Timor the parents
of Leonard Manning, the New Zealand peacekeeper who had been the first
UN soldier murdered by the militia. He had invited the Manning family to
be his only personal guests at the independence ceremony, and Larriera accompanied them throughout their stay. He spent the eve of independence
in his office, where he stayed up all night at his desk signing letters to the
unheralded individuals who had helped him in East Timor. At the end of
each letter he handwrote two or three sentences of personal thanks. He
wrote to the UN staff, to peacekeepers (past and present), to diplomats, to
the Timorese, and to Indonesians.

The next day, when Secretary-General Annan arrived, Vieira de Mello
approached Annan's assistant Nader Mousavizadeh and pleaded, "You've got
to find me time to speak with him one-on-one. I have to find out where I'm
going next. I don't want to be left hung out to dry." Later he and Annan sat

on the terrace of his home, facing the beach, but Annan offered little clarity. The secretary-general had still not decided where to put him.

Vieira de Mello had written to U2 in the hopes that they would travel to Dili and belt out their song "Beautiful Day" on independence day, but the band's representatives had not responded, and he ended up reaching out to his old friend Barbara Hendricks instead. At midnight on May 19, in a candlelight ceremony, the light blue UN flag was lowered in Dili as Hendricks sang "Oh, Freedom," a Civil War–era slave spiritual. Once the UN flag had come down, the red, yellow, black, and white Timorese flag, long the flag of the Timorese resistance, was raised. Vieira de Mello had made it a point to walk a half-step behind Annan and Gusmão throughout the event, and in the moving ceremony it was Annan who officially handed over sovereignty from the United Nations to the Timorese. The longest posting of Vieira de Mello's career had come to an end. The time he had spent at the edge of the earth, cut off from museums and concerts and friends, sweltering in the equatorial sun, ushering in the first new nation of the twenty-first century, had tested his endurance and his perennial cheeriness.

The following day, as the independence celebrations continued and the Timorese leaders mingled with Clinton and a dozen other heads of state, Vieira de Mello slipped away and went for a run with Larriera—his first without bodyguards in East Timor.

At noon on May 21 Taur Matan Ruak, the former guerrilla leader and head of the Timorese army, arrived at the airport with his colleague Paulo Martins, the head of police. They expected a crowded Timorese send-off for Vieira de Mello. But as Matan Ruak recalls, "We arrived and nobody was there. Then Sergio and Carolina arrived, and then the time started moving, and still nobody came." Matan Ruak was furious at his governmental colleagues for not paying more respect. "Not to say good-bye to Sergio, after all he did for East Timor . . . was to betray him," Matan Ruak says. "The only consolation was that we knew we'd have many more chances to thank him properly."

Matan Ruak embraced Vieira de Mello before he boarded the plane. "Thank you," he said. "You will have friends here forever." Vieira de Mello ascended the steps onto a small jet with Jonathan and Antonia Prentice, and with Larriera.

He had been saying for months that he could hardly wait to toast the end of his mission, and Prentice had brought two bottles of champagne onto the plane. But as Vieira de Mello rested his head against the window, he was flooded with melancholy. He pressed his hand up to the glass, as if to say good-bye. And as the faces of the few Timorese on the tarmac faded into the distance, he turned away from the window, buried his head in Larriera's lap, and sobbed.

Part III

*Vieira de Mello at a UN news conference
in Geneva, December 4, 2002.*

Seventeen

"FEAR IS A BAD ADVISER"

Vieira de Mello's reward for having governed Kosovo and East Timor in close succession was to be appointed to a UN job in the crosshairs of what president George W. Bush was calling the "war on terrorism." In his new incarnation, in a world increasingly polarized over how to manage twenty-first-century economic and security challenges, he would be asked to take sides, which had never been his strong suit.

"Now What the Hell Do I Do?"

Before he was thrown into this thicket, and still unaware of his next job, Vieira de Mello spent several months in Southeast Asia with Carolina Larriera. In the past he had always relaxed well but never long; this was perhaps the first time in his adult life that he felt truly suspended in time and space. Drawing on thirty years of accumulated earned leave, he took Larriera on a trip that started in Bali and wound its way west to West Papua (formerly Irian Jaya), then north to Myanmar, Thailand, Laos, Cambodia, Vietnam, Macau, and Hong Kong. Mostly they traveled incognito, but when they reached Thailand, a surprise official reception, complete with crowns of orchids and a motorcade, awaited them, arranged by his friend General Winai Phattiyakul, the Thai who had commanded UN peacekeepers in East Timor.

The pair spent no more than two nights in any single place, traveling by plane, bus, and rented motorcycle. They shopped for their future home, buying carved doors in Bali, spears and shields in Papua, antique puppets in Thailand, iron Buddhas in Cambodia, and textiles in Laos. Since they were as yet unaware whether they were headed to New York or Geneva, they sent their purchases to Vieira de Mello's apartment in New York, which he had rented out while in East Timor. They scheduled stops along the way so as to be able to watch their home soccer teams play their matches in the 2002 World Cup. They generally remained out of telephone contact while on the road, but when Brazil eliminated the U.K. in the quarterfinals, he could not resist gloating by phone to Jonathan Prentice, his British special assistant. The highlight of the trip came on June 30, when King Sihanouk welcomed his old ally back to the royal palace in Phnom Penh. The two men spoke of Cambodia's prospects and the planned war crimes trials of the Khmer Rouge (which would include Ieng Sary), and Vieira de Mello invited Sihanouk to their wedding. The couple then headed to the Foreign Correspondents Club, which had a wall-to-wall television on which they watched Brazil defeat Germany in the World Cup finals.

The only times Vieira de Mello tensed up on the trip were the rare occasions when he telephoned UN Headquarters to try to determine where he was headed next. "I'm going to call the boss next Monday," he would tell Larriera on a Wednesday. Then on the Friday, he would wake up and say, "Remember, I'm calling the SG on Monday." And when Monday rolled around, he would spend the day mentally preparing for his conversation with Annan. "I never saw Sergio nervous," recalls Larriera, "except for when he was speaking with the SG, or thinking about speaking with him." She would tease him, "Are you biting your fingernails?" "No," he would reply. "I'm biting my cuticles. There's a big difference!" Even though he had known Annan for two decades, he respected the office of the secretary-general so much that he spoke to Annan as formally as he might have to a stranger in the position, never calling him "Kofi" but only "SG."

The couple returned to New York in late July. Larriera reclaimed the UN public information job she had held before East Timor and studied for the GRE so that she could apply to graduate programs in public policy. Vieira de Mello awaited word of his fortune, joking to friends that he was "unemployed" and intended to live off of Larriera. Annan finally decided to offer him the Geneva-based job of UN High Commissioner for Human Rights. Since he was not ready to go back to the field to run another mission so soon, and since there were few alternatives, he felt he had no choice but to accept. On July 22, 2002, the secretary-general announced his appointment. Vieira de Mello had won out over a long list of candidates that included Corazon Aquino, the former president of the Philippines; Surin Pitsuwan, the former Thai foreign minister; and Bronislaw Geremek, the Polish dissident.[1]

Vieira de Mello's predecessor in the job was former Irish president Mary Robinson. Robinson had been outspoken in her criticisms of the Bush administration's human rights abuses in the wake of 9/11. She had slammed President Bush's decision to withhold prisoner-of-war status and Geneva Convention protections from al-Qaeda and Taliban detainees housed in Guantánamo and elsewhere.[2] And she had called on the United States to increase the percentage of its GNP devoted to foreign aid, which had fallen from 0.21 percent in 1990 to 0.10 percent in 1999. Although the United States was the UN's biggest single donor, she had alienated U.S. officials by observing that while each Dane was coughing up $331 per year on aid, each American was giving only $33.[3] Unsurprisingly, the United States refused to support her bid for a second four-year term as high commissioner. Still, she was unrepentant. "Holding back criticism, for whatever political reasons," she said, "takes away the legitimacy of the agenda and the cause."[4]

Although Vieira de Mello had dealt with human suffering and humanitarian law for his entire career, he never saw himself as a "human rights type." He saw human rights advocates as those who named and shamed governments. He saw his strength as working with governments behind the scenes to secure consensus. He did not feel temperamentally suited for a job that required more bluntness than any other in the UN system. But after Robinson, Annan felt that Vieira de Mello's very unsuitability for the human rights commissioner's job made him an ideal candidate to smooth out relations with the United States.

Western diplomats hailed the choice, but human rights groups sounded displeased. Michael Posner, head of the Lawyers Committee for Human Rights, wondered whether the new commissioner would confront the Russians on Chechnya, or the United States on its post-9/11 detentions. "It requires a very strong backbone," Posner said. "Mary Robinson had that."[5]

"My concern," recalls Ken Roth, executive director of Human Rights Watch, "was that Sergio had no record of using public pressure." Roth and others were willing to give him a chance, but they believed his personal ambition would make him reluctant to alienate governments. "Ideally, you'd get somebody who saw becoming high commissioner as the pinnacle of their career, not as a stepping-stone to higher ground, to becoming secretary-general," says Roth.

Naturally, the more senior Vieira de Mello became, the more people were convinced that he was angling for the top job. That summer Prince Zeid Raad Zeid al-Hussein, Jordan's ambassador to the UN, told him that the other ambassadors had begun speaking of him as a serious contender to succeed Annan in 2006. Vieira de Mello waved him off, referring to the tradition by which the position of secretary-general rotated among regional blocs. "Latin America has had its turn," he said. Javier Pérez de Cuéllar, a Peruvian, had given way to Boutros Boutros-Ghali, an Egyptian, who had been replaced by Annan of Ghana. In 2006 it would be Asia's turn in the queue. "But, Sergio," Zeid said playfully, "after all you did for East Timor, don't tell me they haven't made you a citizen. You can be Asia's candidate."*

The raw ambition of his youth seemed to have receded. Partly this was because after spending thirty-three years in the system, he knew too much about its flaws—flaws that would only loom larger if he were to hold the top job. Less than a week before he was to fly to Geneva to take up his new post, he met Larriera in the UN lobby, and the couple walked several blocks up First Avenue together. Suddenly a motorcade belonging to Annan came tearing out of the gates of UN Headquarters. "Do you want to become secretary-general?" she asked. He shrugged. "Carolina, if I were to become secretary-general, there'd be no more Sergio, and no more Sergio and Carolina." He took her hand as they crossed East Forty-eighth Street. "There'd be only that," he said, nodding in the direction of the UN gates as they closed behind the last vehicle in the convoy. As they walked uptown, he explained

---

*The question of whether Vieira de Mello could have become secretary-general ignites great debate even today. Since it was in fact Asia's turn to nominate a secretary-general in 2006, those who believed Vieira de Mello would be appointed assumed that national rivalries in Asia would prevent them from reaching a consensus and that Vieira de Mello would be chosen to break the stalemate. Others thought that, having waited several decades for its turn, Asia would never forfeit the chance to appoint one of its own, and Vieira de Mello would be chosen a decade down the line.

his ambivalence. "When the SG took office, he had a vision, an ambitious reform agenda," he said. "And what became of it? The job of SG took over. The job will always take over. Now there is no more Kofi. No more vision. He is just the SG. And that's what would happen to me." Whatever the drawbacks of becoming secretary-general, though, he had never met a challenge he didn't embrace, and if powerful governments had put his name forward, it seems inconceivable that he would have taken himself out of the running.

He did not see becoming UN High Commissioner for Human Rights as a great career move. Although it was the most senior post he had ever held, it carried little prestige, relative to other jobs he had been eligible for, and the Office of the High Commissioner for Human Rights (OHCHR) had one of the smallest overall budgets of any UN agency ($66 million). It carried out few operations in the field, where he was in his element. Its commissioner would inevitably be attacked, either by governments (if he was critical of them) or by human rights groups (if he was not). And in its decade of existence, the OHCHR had managed to exert scant real-world influence. Powerful governments held it in low regard.

His colleagues in the UN had told him that the ideal high commissioner would combine the skills of a politician, a bureaucrat, and a human rights expert. He was none of these things. He had no independent political base, no patience for bureaucracy, and little human rights background. After the press conference at which Annan announced his appointment, Vieira de Mello rode the elevator up to the twenty-second floor, where he was sharing a borrowed office with Prentice, closed the door behind him, and said, "Now what the hell do I do?" The first thing he did was walk with his aide to the Barnes & Noble near New York University and begin piling up books on the theory and practice of human rights. "Did he ever think he would be the high commissioner for human rights?" says Prentice. "No, not in a month of Sundays."

TIME TO GET SERIOUS

Worn out from the long slog in East Timor, Vieira de Mello and Larriera spent the remainder of the summer in Larriera's studio flat in New York. She worked on the weekends as a volunteer at the Metropolitan Museum of Art, where he picked her up after work. Because UN Headquarters was largely deserted in August, he felt little pressure to make appearances on the diplomatic cocktail circuit.

Whatever headaches lay ahead, Vieira de Mello was relieved to be back in Western civilization after nearly three years in the most remote reaches of Southeast Asia. He was also determined not to let his new job get in the way of his personal life, which had become a priority. He told his friends that, although his divorce proceedings were taking time, he would soon put an end to what he called *"l'hypocrisie du passé,"* the hypocrisy of the past—of his past. Annan had been through a messy divorce two decades before and cautioned, "Be patient and do it right. Once you are living apart, there is no need to force it. For the sake of the children, do it on a civilized basis." Vieira de Mello told Annan that he was glad to be moving back to Geneva so he could finally be near his sons. "It was sort of a guilty feeling," Annan recalls.

Vieira de Mello was boyishly proud of his relationship with Larriera. While in New York, he introduced her to his friend Omar Bakhet. When she got up to go to the restroom, he watched her walk away and said, "I'm totally in love." Bakhet reacted with initial skepticism, as did other friends. "Do you have any idea how many times you've told me this?" he asked. But Vieira de Mello was insistent. "You have to listen to me," he said. "I've had enough of breaking people's hearts. It's time to get serious about these matters." His friend Fabienne Morisset remembers, "Sergio had tired of the contradictions in himself. In his professional life he was working around the clock to try to reduce suffering in the world. Yet in his personal life he knew he had caused pain. He was determined to reconcile both halves of his being."

On September 11, 2002, Vieira de Mello cleared passport control at JFK International Airport. He was on his way to Geneva, where he would finally start his new job. He stopped at an Internet kiosk to mark the dawn of the next stage of his life with Larriera—a life, he wrote to her, "with so many and such dangerous unknowns, where I await for you to accompany me." He thanked her for her support at a time when "I myself know that I haven't been easy to manage," and he promised her reciprocal support in the days ahead.[6]

Larriera was planning to move to Geneva in the spring, when she would take up a job with Martin Griffiths, who had left the UN to run a conflict resolution center in Geneva. She also gained admission to a distance-learning master's degree program tailored for UN officials at the Fletcher School of

Law and Diplomacy in Boston, which she was to begin the following August. Vieira de Mello found it hard to be separated from her. On September 13 he e-mailed her his home, cell, and work phone numbers and instructed her to keep them with her at all times, and even to "hide them in Central Park, in case you get an irrepressible urge to call me while you are running."[7] The same day he wrote to Marcia Luar Ibrahim, the wife of his former bodyguard in East Timor, that he was lonely because *"Não sei mais viver sem a Carolina."*[8] He no longer knew how to live without Carolina.

He rented a tiny one-bedroom apartment in the old town in Geneva, promising Larriera that once she moved to Europe they would splurge on a house somewhere around Lake Geneva. The first time she stuck her head out the window of their temporary quarters, she spotted a plaque on the building diagonal from theirs. It was the former home of Jorge Luis Borges, her favorite writer, who was also from Buenos Aires. On a run one day they then stumbled upon a small walled park tucked into downtown Geneva. It proved to be a cemetery for the town's most prized citizens. The couple entered and found Borges's understated grave, which was so elegant that they returned to take photos of it.

The couple settled into a range of habits to keep them connected despite the four thousand miles that separated them during the week. They shopped online together at Ikea—he from Geneva, she from New York. They declined invitations to go out in the evenings. He told colleagues, "I am not a dinner person," and asked them to accommodate him at lunchtime. Larriera gave him wake-up calls at 1 a.m. New York time, and he did the same, calling her at 1 p.m. Geneva time. They tried to see each other every weekend, with him flying to New York and she to Geneva twice a month. When her mother was diagnosed with kidney cancer, he flew twenty-one hours to Buenos Aires so he could spend the day of the surgery by Larriera's side. The couple generally spoke Spanish together, as his was flawless and she was still mastering Portuguese. But whenever he talked about his feelings for her or about their future, he drifted unselfconsciously into Portuguese. As he had gotten older, he had grown more proudly Brazilian. He ostentatiously checked the manufacturers' labels in shops to see if items were "made in Brazil"; he affixed a bumper sticker of the Brazilian flag to his car in Geneva; and he donned gold and green T-shirts with Brazilian football logos. When he recycled UN paper, he explained it by saying, "These are the trees from my Amazon we are printing on." His relationship with Larriera caused these habits to grow more pronounced, as he told others she had reawakened his roots.

When the couple reached the one-year anniversary of the launch of "history," he marked it with another e-mail to thank her "for standing me for a year" and to express hope that "for the rest of my life it will be like this."[9] Ever since "history" had begun the previous October, he had referred to her in public as "my wife Carolina," and over the summer they had begun wearing gold rings made at Tiffany's. His had the name "Carolina" engraved on the inside, and her matching ring bore the name "Sergio."

But his romantic happiness came at a price. Annie was resisting his efforts to divorce her, failing to show up for court appointments. He was most stung by the criticism he was getting from his sons, who were protective of their mother and refused to meet Larriera. He could not convince them of his sincerity. "I should have done this ten years ago," he told his friend Annick Stevenson. "Maybe it would have been easier on them if they were younger. But I can't delay any longer. I have got to deal with my life." When his sons refused to take his calls, he e-mailed them, proposing a "direct dialogue." He wrote that he did not seek to undermine their loyalty toward their mother but wanted "a chance to explain to you many things so you could maybe understand my mistakes."[10]

In this time of profound personal change, Vieira de Mello became more spiritual. He had long been vehement about his atheism. Once, when he and Larriera attended a mass in East Timor performed by Bishop Felipe Ximenes Belo, everyone else made the sign of the cross, but despite his prominence he kept his hands by his sides, stubbornly staring down at the floor. Afterward she ribbed him about his defiance, but he shook his head. "You know I don't believe in all the bullshit of the Catholic Church," he said. "I can't betray my principles." In his twenties and thirties he had told religious colleagues, "We have to realize God in man." He had shown no signs of moving toward organized religion, but had long observed the superstitions of his native Brazil. "If God is Brazilian," he often said, knocking on wood twice, "I'll be safe."[11]

But Buddhism, which he saw more as a philosophy than a religion, had always intrigued him. Ever since 1989 he had carried with him a silver Buddha given to him by Bakhet. When he felt he needed luck during the Cambodian refugee repatriation launch in 1992, he had lit incense in front of the Buddha statue near the Thai border. Bakhet traveled annually to India on a six-week meditation retreat, and while in the early years of their friendship Vieira de Mello had mocked his friend's interest in "mystical nonsense," his attitude had begun to change. "One of these days I need to sit down with you, Omar," he said. In 1998 Bakhet had given him a large glossy picture book on Buddhism and assumed that he simply filed it away, unread. But when Bakhet visited him in East Timor, he spotted the book lying prominently on the coffee table. When Vieira de Mello disappeared into the shower, Bakhet opened the book and discovered his friend's meticulous scribbles all over the margins.

"When I retire," Vieira de Mello announced one day to his friend Morisset, "I want to be a Buddhist." In the meantime, although he did not have the time to seek formal instruction, he learned what he could. In November, shortly after he moved back to Geneva, he and Larriera visited the British Museum in London, and he e-mailed their guide afterward that he had "developed, jointly with my wife Carolina, a curiosity and eager taste for Buddhist philosophy, art and culture," which he noted was "rather unusual for two Latin Americans." He asked for further clarity on Luohan, whom he understood to be a guide to truth. He asked specifically about Luohan's "effort to transcend mundane repetitiveness (did I get it right?) and attain unity with the world."[12] The guide responded that Luohan had managed to reach a personal nirvana without leaving the earthly world and had therefore reached a level of spirituality somewhere between ordinary man and Buddha. "Sergio's level of consciousness was rising," Morisset recalls, "and this meant he was more in touch with the world's cruelty."

"What Would Victims Expect?"

As he settled into his new life in Geneva, Vieira de Mello tried to get a quick handle on the high commissioner's job. The office seemed mired in an impossible paradox. Without the direct support of governments, he would not get the funds or political cooperation he needed; but if he was seen to be too close to powerful governments, he would lack credibility. He answered his early critics. On September 20, 2002, he declared, "My job will require speaking out.... But it also requires tact and political acumen, as well as the ability to roll up one's sleeves and get down to work to protect human rights away from the spotlights and the microphones."[13] He joked that his preparation for a job that entailed tiptoeing in political minefields came when he ran the Mine Action Center in Cambodia.[14] He admitted to friends that publicly criticizing governments would require the biggest adjustment of his career. "Sergio was aware that his days of being loved by everyone were coming to an end," recalls Prentice.

He began to conceive of his role as that of emergency "first responder." He could swoop into a place where abuses were being carried out and attract a burst of media coverage. At a brainstorming session in New York, Harold Koh, who had been assistant secretary of state for democracy, human rights, and labor in the Clinton administration and had subsequently become dean of Yale Law School, urged him to try to pass the "taxi driver test." "When the driver of the average taxi cab that you hail—whether in Delhi, Rio, Nairobi, Cairo, Paris, Beijing, or New York—asks, 'Aren't you Sergio, the high commissioner?' (placing you on a first-name basis with Saddam, Madonna, and Pelé), you will finally be well on your way to having the independent political base that you will need."[15] The better known Vieira de Mello became, the less dependent he would be upon particular governments.

He would never have found it easy to be office-bound again, but the high commissioner's perch was worse than most offices. As he became acquainted with his new employees, he thought many of them were measuring their impact not by the lives they bettered but by the number of human rights conferences they planned or the number of human rights treaties they invoked. "The place is just infested with fucking lawyers," he told his close associates. He noted that the way to reach those desperate for the UN's help was "certainly not workshops."[16] "If our rules, our debates, this commission and my office's very existence, cannot protect the weak," he declared, "then what value do they have?"[17] His deputy Bertrand Ramcharan suggested the office acquire more space in order to manage the influx of new hires that the new commissioner hoped to make. Vieira de Mello was incredulous: "No, we'll have every office doubled up. The little money we have should be spent on human rights." In a note to Prentice in the margins of his draft human rights strategic plan, he scrawled, "What would victims expect from us, from me?"[18]

Most of the human rights staffers he encountered in Geneva were UN lifers who had rarely ventured into the field.[19] He vowed to make the office more operational. "The majority of people who work at human rights have been here forever. Forever! Ask them whether they have seen one violation of human rights in their professional careers. Most of them will tell you they haven't," he told Philip Gourevitch of *The New Yorker.* "This is a crazy system that kills motivation and that kills the flame."[20] He e-mailed a colleague that bureaucratic life in the UN "demotivated young and capable staff, rewarded dinosaurs who have made their entire careers behind their HQs desks, punished those who believed in mobility, rotation and dared volunteer for field missions and undermined the goals of the UN as a result."[21] He planned to begin systematic rotation of staff from Geneva to the field so that the violations they were trying to curb became more real to them.

As UN High Commissioner for Human Rights, he struggled to distance himself from the UN Commission on Human Rights, which he saw as an embarrassment to the UN and to human rights. The UN Commission on Human Rights, which met for six weeks every March and April in Geneva, was made up of fifty-three states that were elected after being nominated by countries in their regions. Often those elected were themselves flagrant human rights abusers. The year before he arrived, the United States, which had occupied a seat on the commission continuously since 1947, had been denied a seat in a secret vote.[22] The snub was seen as payback for the U.S. failure to pay some $580 million in back dues to the UN, its rejection of the Kyoto environmental pact, its frontal assault on the International Criminal Court, and its decision to expedite the building of a nuclear missile shield. Each year the commission directed several resolutions at Israel's occupation of Palestine, but it had never in its history passed resolutions against China, Syria, or Saudi Arabia. In 2002 the UN Commission on Human Rights had failed to censure Iran, Zimbabwe, and Russia. And in 2003 Gadaffi's Libya was elected to serve as the chair of the upcoming commission.

Vieira de Mello was irked by the natural association people made between him and the commission, the most widely criticized part of the UN. People seemed to expect him as commissioner to be able to influence the body's composition and habits, which he was powerless to do. He tried to be patient with the journalists who constantly grilled him about the human rights abusers who populated the commission. "The UN High Commissioner's office is what I control," he said. "The UN High Commission is an intergovernmental organ comprised of states." He understood why people might be unhappy with the chair of the upcoming commission, but he told critics to "address that question" to the governments that had elected Libya.[23]

Sitting through his first six-week session of the UN Commission on Human Rights proved excruciating. The members defeated a resolution criticizing Zimbabwe and eliminated the position of human rights rapporteur for Sudan. The Palestinian representative charged Israel with "Zionist Nazism."[24] Seeking to preserve his office's integrity and speak his mind, Vieria de Mello ridiculed the ritual "insulting language" that made the commission seem "stuck in an earlier time."[25] "I would suggest to you," he said, "that when a denunciation has become traditional it should perhaps be abandoned or revised." The commission's problem was not that it was "too political," which was to be expected of a body made up of governments. "For some people in this room to accuse others of being political," he said, "is a bit like fish criticizing one another for being wet."[26] The trouble was not politics. The trouble was simply that many countries on the commission had little regard for human rights.

The part of the job that he liked most was philosophical: He was returning to his roots. His speeches before international organizations, human rights groups, and gatherings of dignitaries were sprinkled with references to Arendt, Kant, and Hegel. "What are the fundamental human rights?" he asked. "Are they not the basis for philosophy?"[27] In East Timor he had been responsible for making sure that school textbooks were printed and water pipes were repaired. As high commissioner, he parsed definitions of democracy. He frequently noted democracy's shortcomings: "Democratic rule does not automatically correlate with respect for human rights, nor does its presence necessarily lead to economic and social development."[28] He delighted in promoting his concept of "holistic democracy," which encompassed Franklin Delano Roosevelt's "freedom from fear" and "freedom from want." He faulted those who equated democracy with the casting of ballots, and argued, "Democracy is as much about what happens between elections as it is about what happens during them."[29] He liked to paraphrase Nelson Mandela, saying that people should never be "forced to choose between ballots and bread."[30] Holistic democracy would provide physical and economic security as well as voting rights.

He argued that human rights were the foundation for interstate stability.

He wanted human rights to matter to geopolitics (as he always wanted to be where "the action was"), but he also did not understand why disarmament was a key item on the Security Council checklist while human rights were not. "A regime that can grossly violate the rights of its own people is *ipso facto* a threat to its neighbors and to regional and international peace and security," he insisted.[31] He had viewed some human rights advocates he had clashed with in his career as shrill and absolutist. When they urged him to delay refugee returns to Cambodia, or to avoid negotiating with the Khmer Rouge, Serb nationalists, or the Taliban, he thought they were being unrealistic and often unhelpful. But now he appreciated that even if international humanitarian law, refugee law, and human rights law were politically inconvenient, they were also essential mechanisms for regulating state behavior.[32] He told skeptics that "human rights" was another phrase for rule of law, which they found less controversial "He was impressed and surprised," recalls Prentice. "It was an education for him that his core values—all of his basic instincts and beliefs—were out there in this body of human rights law." "I've been dealing all my life with the effect of human rights violations," he told Edward Mortimer, a senior adviser to Annan in New York. "At last I have a job which deals with the source of the problem." He was fond of quoting the former Afghan ambassador to the United Nations Abdul Rahman Pazhwak, who in 1966 had presided over the General Assembly and said: "If the United Nations could be said to have any ideology, it must be that of human rights."[33]

He had always supported the UN war crimes tribunals for Yugoslavia and Rwanda, but he now had a pulpit from which to lobby on behalf of the International Criminal Court (ICC). He met the objections of those, like senior Bush administration officials, who believed the court would never get off the ground by citing recent historical advances: "Many people said the ad hoc tribunal on the former Yugoslavia and the ad hoc tribunal on Rwanda were jokes. Well, they were not jokes. An international criminal court . . . will come into being . . . and you will see that that will not be a joke . . . The ICC will exist and will operate whether one or the other country joins it or not."[34]

American Exceptionalism

The one country on everybody's mind was the United States. On the ICC and countless other issues, the world's most powerful country had a view different from his own. The high commissioner and his staff occupied the Palais Wilson, a peach-colored manor on a slope overlooking Lake Geneva. The first headquarters of the League of Nations, the building had been named after former U.S. president Woodrow Wilson. Vieira de Mello was unshy about referring to his own "Wilsonian" leanings and reminded visitors of America's founding role in crafting international institutions as a way of convincing them that President Bush's unilateralism was not likely permanent. The Bush administration's disdain for international law was perhaps best reflected in the statements of John Bolton, then under secretary of state for arms control and international security. "It is a big mistake for us to grant any validity to international law even when it may seem in our short-term interest to do so because, over the long term, the goal of those who think that international law really means anything are those who want to constrict the United States," he said.[35] It was Bolton who delighted in being the one to inform Secretary-General Annan that the United States would be "un-signing" the treaty that established the International Criminal Court, which Bolton branded "a product of fuzzy-minded romanticism that is not just naïve but dangerous."[36] "Taking a big bottle of Wite-Out" to President Clinton's signature on the statute, Bolton later boasted, was "the happiest moment in my government service."[37] In 2004 President Bush would name Bolton U.S. ambassador to the UN.

Vieira de Mello knew he would have to figure out a way to work with, through, and around the United States. In his speeches he chipped away at notions of American exceptionalism, arguing that the tendency to violate rights was as universal as the rights themselves. "There does not exist on this earth a paradise for human rights," he said. "It is too tempting to divide the world into zones of light and zones of shadow, but the truth is that we all sail between the two."[38]

He sought to balance respect for a country's right to protect its citizens from terrorist attacks with efforts to make sure that it respected international rules in the process. He thought human rights organizations that condemned Bush at times sounded as though they were defending terrorism. In his public remarks he stressed that it was important to delve into "root causes" but asked, "Are there not justifications for every crime and every atrocity?" He continued, "The sadist has his reasons just like he who is pushed by madness. There were economic motivations for slavery," he said. "We have the right to live without this fear of dying, no matter where, at any moment."[39] He urged his staff to remember to denounce terrorist acts with every bit the fervor with which they criticized human rights violations by states. He did not want to alienate the United States before he had a chance to influence it behind the scenes.

Because he had been in Asia on 9/11, he had not personally experienced the jolt that the attacks delivered to the American psyche. More palpable for him was the terrorist attack that occurred one month into his tenure as high commissioner. On October 12, 2002, several bombs exploded in and near a popular nightclub on the Indonesian island of Bali, where he and Larriera had taken many long weekends. More than two hundred people were killed, many of them Australian youths. After the attack the al-Jazeera network broadcast a statement from Osama bin Laden in which he said he had warned Australia not to send its troops to join in the UN's "despicable effort to separate East Timor" from Indonesia. "It ignored the warning until it woke up to the sounds of explosion in Bali," bin Laden said. He asked why the killing of Muslim civilians in Afghanistan, Chechnya, and Palestine did not outrage Western audiences. "Why should fear, killing, destruction, displacement, orphaning, and widowing continue to be our lot, while security, stability and happiness are your lot?" bin Laden said. "This is unfair. It is time that we get even. You will be killed just as you kill, and will be bombed just as you bomb."[40]

This was the second speech in which bin Laden had used East Timor's liberation from Indonesia as a rallying cry. The previous year, in November 2001, the al-Qaeda leader had delivered a lengthy diatribe against the United Nations, blaming a UN resolution for partitioning Palestine in 1947, attacking UN peacekeepers for standing by when Muslims were murdered in UN safe areas in Bosnia, and accusing "the criminal Kofi Annan" of dividing Indonesia, "the most populous country in the Islamic world." Bin Laden had lumped the UN with U.S. and Israeli interests and said, "Under no circumstances should any Muslim or sane person resort to the United Nations. The United Nations is nothing but a tool of crime."[41]

The Bali bombing sickened Vieira de Mello. He and Larriera were together in Geneva when they heard the news. They spent the afternoon scouring the Internet for a map of Bali that would help them ascertain which nightclub, among the many they had strolled by, had been struck. They were horrified that a place of such tranquillity could have been so brutalized. Two UN soldiers on mission in East Timor (one of whom was Brazilian) were among those killed. One month after the attack, when the Balinese held a ceremony at the scorched site, the couple performed their own private ritual in Geneva, lighting a candle to honor the dead.

His disgust over al-Qaeda's strikes at civilian targets made Vieira de Mello argue even more strenuously that Western countries must obey international law. Even before he took up his post, disturbing evidence of American involvement in torture had been mounting. In January 2002 photographs had been leaked of shackled prisoners in Guantánamo, kneeling and wearing heavy gloves, face masks, and earmuffs, stirring international outrage but little outcry in the United States.[42] In March 2002 U.S. diplomats had been quoted in the *Washington Post* describing the practice of "extraordinary rendition," or sending terrorist suspects to countries such as Egypt, where intelligence agents routinely engaged in torture.[43] And in April the press ran "souvenir photos" taken by U.S. soldiers, of their peers posing beside the blindfolded, shackled, and naked body of John Walker Lindh, the twenty-one-year-old California native who had joined the Taliban. Defense secretary Donald Rumsfeld dismissed what he said were only rumors of mistreatment. "I guess if you ask me when I got up in the morning and we've got people getting killed in the Middle East, and we've got a war going on in Afghanistan, if I'm going to change my schedule and go chasing after the rumors on things like that, it's unlikely."[44]

The evidence of U.S. abuse mounted throughout Vieira de Mello's time in Geneva. In September, just after he left his post as head of the CIA counterterrorism center, Cofer Black testified in a joint House and Senate Select Intelligence Committee hearing: "This is a very highly classified area, but I have to say that all you need to know is there was a 'before 9/11,' and there was an 'after 9/11.' After 9/11 the gloves come off."[45] And in December *Washington Post* reporters Dana Priest and Barton Gellman published a devastating account of the Bush administration's "brass-knuckled quest for information" and their harsh dealings with terror suspects. The lengthy cover story quoted one U.S. official responsible for capturing and transferring suspected terrorists as saying, "If you don't violate someone's human rights some of the time, you probably aren't doing your job."[46] Priest and Gellman quoted another American involved in rendition candidly explaining the virtues of the practice. "We don't kick the [expletive] out of them," the official said. "We send them to other countries so they can kick the [expletive] out of them."[47] Despite these highly public revelations and the harm they could do to America's standing in the Islamic world and elsewhere, senior officials in the Bush administration did not seek to distance themselves from these practices and did not even condemn them until May 2004, when American soldiers, CIA agents, and contractors were found to have systematically tortured Iraqi detainees in the Abu Ghraib prison in Baghdad.

In light of the Bush administration's stated hostility to the UN in general and to human rights treaties specifically, Vieira de Mello knew he would hardly be pushing on an open door when he urged Washington to adhere to international rules. He tried to be politic, using speeches to stress the gravity of the threat posed by terrorist networks. "A brutal attack and an exceptional threat may require an extraordinary and unequivocal response," he said. But, he continued:

> these measures must be taken in transparency, they must be in short duration, and they must take place within the framework of the law. Without that, the terrorists will ultimately win and we will ultimately lose as we would have allowed them to destroy the very foundation of our modern human civilization. I am convinced that it is possible to fight this menace at no cost to our human rights. Protecting your citizens and upholding rights are not incompatible: on the contrary, they must go firmly together lest we lose our bearing.[48]

He believed that international human rights law already gave governments the flexibility they needed to meet exceptional threats. They were free to extend the length of detentions in times of emergency, but if they did so, they had to notify the secretary-general, as Great Britain had done in December 2001.[49]

Although he generally preferred raising his concerns about state practices behind closed doors, torture was an exception. "I have been appalled at the resurgence of debate in certain parts of the world as to whether resort to torture may be justified to tackle terrorism," he said at a regional conference in Islamabad. "It may not. The right to be free from torture was recognized a long time ago by all states. There can be no going back, no matter—I repeat, no matter—how grave the provocation."[50]

Washington had just invented its own legal rules and begun acting as though international law did not exist at all. He urged that the prisoners in Guantánamo be tried or released, and he argued that the denial of rights was "one of the very goals of the terrorists."[51] "We live in fearful times, and fear is a bad adviser," he argued in one of his more memorable lines before the UN Commission on Human Rights. "For when security is defined too narrowly—for example, as nothing more than a state's duty to protect its citizens—then the pursuit of security can lead to the violation of the human rights of those who are outside the circle of the protected."[52]

Vieira de Mello's every public move was scrutinized. In May 2003 Annick Stevenson, who had become a press officer in the office, forwarded him an e-mail from an Arab journalist who complained that he had denounced a Palestinian suicide attack but had not done the same after a recent violent Israeli response. He could not win, and he knew it. He wrote to Stevenson:

> Nonsense of course. I didn't issue a statement on the bombing in Chechnya either . . . so I'm anti-Russian and pro-Chechen terrorists (Muslims by the way). The problem is: either we issue one after every attack or we continue exposing ourselves to this kind of biased interpretation. One thing is sure: as long as Arab (or Jewish) journalists continue to think in this unidimensional way, there will be no peace in the Middle East.[53]

IRAQ

The threat of war elsewhere in the Middle East cast a shadow over Vieira de Mello's tenure as human rights commissioner. On September 12, 2002, his first official day on the job, Secretary-General Annan and President George W. Bush had duked it out in the UN General Assembly Chamber before the world's heads of state. The subject was Iraq. Pointing to the UN-mandated Gulf War that Bush's father had orchestrated, Annan argued, "There is no substitute for the unique legitimacy provided by the United Nations."[54] He staked out a middle ground on the war path, calling for the resumption of weapons inspections but also for Iraq to finally meet its obligations. "If Iraq's defiance continues," Annan warned, "the Security Council must face its responsibilities."[55] Annan wanted peace, but he desperately wanted the Security

Council to take a united position. For that to happen, he knew, Saddam Hussein would have to make visible new concessions.

President Bush had brought his trademark swagger to the podium. As Annan looked on from nearby, Bush dangled the prospect of UN irrelevance before the packed house. "We created the United Nations Security Council, so that, unlike the League of Nations, our deliberations would be more than talk, and our resolutions would be more than wishes," Bush said. "Are Security Council resolutions to be honored and enforced, or cast aside without consequence? Will the United Nations serve the purpose of its founding, or will it be irrelevant?"[56] Bush offered his own definition of adherence with UN principles: It meant siding with the United States against Saddam Hussein.[57]

Part of Vieira de Mello was tempted to support the war in Iraq. He had openly supported the Australian-led intervention in East Timor, and he had eventually come to see NATO's war in Kosovo as justified. He publicly echoed the secretary-general's recognition that states had a right, even a duty, to intervene to end gross violations of human rights. He often invoked the UN member states' "responsibility to protect" citizens who were being murdered or allowed to be murdered by their own governments.* Vieira de Mello was eager to see Saddam Hussein's genocidal regime replaced. He had not joined those UN colleagues who had decried the decade-long American sanctions regime in Iraq. When he was asked in December 2002 what the UN would do to alleviate the toll of the sanctions, he stressed, "Let's not forget that it also takes two to tango," and blamed the Iraqi dictator for failing to get food and medicine to his people.[58] In an op-ed he questioned how the Security Council could be debating weapons of mass destruction in Iraq without considering Saddam Hussein's mass destruction of civilians. What was missing in geopolitics, Vieira de Mello wrote, was "the recognition that flagrant and systematic violations of human rights are frequently the principal cause of global insecurity."[59] States had to move away from

---

*The "Responsibility to Protect" or "R2P" was a concept introduced in December 2001 by the independent Commission on State Sovereignty and Intervention, cochaired by Gareth Evans and Mahmoud Sahoun, and composed of former diplomats, politicians, and public intellectuals. In September 2005, 150 countries in the General Assembly unanimously endorsed the new norm.

"dysfunctional definitions of security" and start recognizing the nexus of security and human rights.

But however much the UN human rights commissioner might have welcomed the removal of Saddam Hussein, the Bush administration was justifying its invasion by arguing that Hussein posed an "imminent threat"—an argument Vieira de Mello found unpersuasive. He also knew how challenging it was to reassemble a country once a regime had been toppled. Even in tiny Kosovo and East Timor this task had proven difficult, and Iraq was an ethnically and religiously heterogeneous country of 27 million people.

Above all, Vieira de Mello was concerned about the precedent an American and British war would set. His loyalty to UN procedures made him deeply uncomfortable with the Bush administration's flouting of the UN Security Council. The divisions over Iraq, he feared, might actually dismantle or render obsolete the UN architecture. He saw similarities between the circumstances in 2003 and those that had existed around the time of NATO's war in Kosovo four years before. But while in 1999 NATO had gone ahead and attacked Serbia over the opposition of China and Russia, on this occasion the United States and the United Kingdom were plowing ahead despite the resistance of every country on the Council except Spain. In the year leading up to the 1999 NATO air strikes, Serbian president Slobodan Milošević had killed some 3,000 Kosovo Albanians and displaced 300,000 others; Saddam Hussein had committed genocide against the Kurds back in 1987–88, but even a tyranny as brutal as his did not seem adequate grounds to undertake something as risky as regime change. Also Vieira de Mello knew that the Clinton administration's foreign policy team had done all it could to try to get the countries on the Security Council to back the NATO war in Kosovo. Then, once the Russians had made plain they would block an authorizing resolution, Washington had launched the bombing campaign while simultaneously maintaining close contact with Kofi Annan. The Bush team, by contrast, seemed to relish thumbing its nose at the UN. Indeed, one senior Bush administration planner told Strobe Talbott, who had been Clinton's deputy secretary of state: "That's the difference between you people and us, Strobe. Your type agonizes, ours seizes opportunities. You see our interests in Iraq and in the UN as in tension with each other; we see an opportunity to kill two birds with one stone."[60] With a war in Iraq, many senior U.S. officials saw a chance both to bring down Saddam Hussein and to weaken the UN. Vieira de Mello was understandably concerned that such an action constituted a far greater repudiation of international rules and of the Security Council's primacy than had Kosovo. In the end, then, though he had become a supporter of humanitarian intervention, he believed that Bush's top advisers were not motivated by a regard for the Iraqis and that an American-British invasion would endanger both the Iraqi people and the United Nations.

Despite his personal view, he again did not speak out. "Why should I?" he told those closest to him. "Nobody is going to listen to me anyway, and it will only interfere with my ability to help the Iraqis down the road." But trying to stop the war and trying to be sure the UN developed a coherent strategy to deal with the war were two different things. He believed that the UN was being altogether too reactive on Iraq. He sent a letter to Annan, also signed by Dennis McNamara (with whom Vieira de Mello was back on good terms) and several other colleagues, in which he offered to gather a group of senior UN officials to formulate a UN strategy regarding the invasion. "It was clear we were going to get hit by a tsunami," recalls one UN official, "and we weren't ready." Annan never responded.

While UN staffers agonized over the consequences of the imminent conflict, President Bush seemed to be utterly convinced of the strategic and moral benefits of dislodging Saddam Hussein. His advisers had arranged meetings for him with Iraqi exiles who favored the war and generally downplayed the potential costs. On January 10, 2003, Kanan Makiya, a Brandeis University professor of Islamic and Middle Eastern studies and distinguished Iraqi exile, told Bush that the invasion would transform the image of the United States in the Middle East. "People will greet the troops with sweets and flowers," Makiya said. Hatem Mukhlis, a Sunni doctor also present at the meeting, generally agreed with Makiya but urged Bush to be sure to keep the Iraqi army intact and stressed the importance of making a strong and humane first impression: "If you don't win their hearts at the start, if they don't get benefits," Mukhlis said, "after two months you could see Mogadishu in Baghdad."[61]

On February 5, 2003, Colin Powell gave his infamous presentation before the UN Security Council, making many worrying claims that would later prove false about Iraq's chemical, biological, and nuclear weapons programs.[62] The corridors of UN Headquarters in New York were abuzz with debate and anticipation. UN staff who had never met before because they worked on disparate geographic or substantive issues were suddenly embroiled in heated discussions about Iraq. The discussions touched upon the latest testimony from Hans Blix, the head of the UN weapons-inspection team; the question of whether the UN team in Iraq running the Oil for Food Program should pull out; the rules in the UN Charter and their suitability to meet twenty-first-century threats (when weapons of mass destruction *could* be used without warning); and the worry that the Security Council or the secretary-general would not survive a steamrolling by two of the UN's founding member states. Secretary-General Annan seemed convinced that if the United States and Great Britain went to war without the approval of the Security Council, the UN would seem irrelevant. But working-level UN officials had never felt more relevant. "The entire world—the weapons inspectors from Iraq, the foreign ministers from the major powers, the top correspondents from the major media—they had all descended upon the United Nations," recalls Oliver Ulich, a midlevel official. "We were the center of the universe. Besides, the only way to become more 'relevant' was to become an accomplice in the war."

Annan chose not to denounce the Iraq invasion. "Do we really think that this war can be avoided or delayed if I speak out?" he asked his colleagues. His special assistant, Nader Mousavizadeh, remembers, "It was like choosing between the plague and cholera. Do you implicitly sign on to the war, or do you set the UN on a collision course with its most influential member?"

A Big Interview?

In March 2003, in a meeting that would alter the course of his life, Vieira de Mello had the opportunity to voice his human rights concerns with President Bush directly. Anthony Banbury, with whom he had worked in Cambodia and Bosnia, had served on the staff of the National Security Council under President Clinton and stayed on after Bush's election. Before leaving his job, Banbury wanted to ensure that the Bush administration saw the most appealing face of the United Nations: that of Vieira de Mello.

Getting on the calendar of the president was next to impossible, especially on the eve of a major U.S.-led war in Iraq. But Banbury prepared a memo for National Security Adviser Condoleezza Rice in which he made the case for Bush to meet Vieira de Mello. "There are some very good people in the UN," Banbury noted. "Sergio is the very best of the best." Banbury also contended that it was in the interest of the White House to be seen engaging with the human rights commissioner. "The United States is taking some hits on human rights lately," he argued. "The U.S. is the leader in the field of human rights. This will give the president a chance to address the criticisms and get our story out." As he recalls, "This was a stretch. The president of the United States doesn't meet with human rights people from the UN. This was the secretary of state's job or his staff's job."[63]

Yet to his and Vieira de Mello's surprise, Rice embraced the idea and placed the meeting on the president's schedule (over the objections of Bush's schedulers). Vieira de Mello, a true believer in the UN, and President Bush, a lifelong UN skeptic, would meet on the afternoon of March 5, 2003.

Vieira de Mello spent the morning meeting with senior officials at the State Department, discussing the role his office could play in the wake of any U.S. invasion, sharing the insights he had gained on war crimes and policing in the Balkans and East Timor. Having feared that the Bush administration would sideline the UN, he was relieved to hear Richard Armitage, the deputy secretary of state, say that he expected the UN to play a prominent role as soon as Saddam Hussein was overthrown. "The sooner that activities can be turned over to respected international actors, the better," Armitage said. "Expect to be hearing from us a lot."[64] When Vieira de Mello noted that sixteen prisoners in Guantánamo had recently attempted suicide, Armitage conceded that the delicate balance between security and liberty had been skewed. "The ends do not justify the means," Armitage said. "The pendulum has swung too far."[65] In other State Department meetings Vieira de Mello was told of the Future of Iraq Project, the elaborate $5 million, eighteen-month-long process by which Iraqi exiles and American experts drafted blueprint laws and institutions to replace Saddam Hussein's after his fall. Vieira de Mello would learn later that Defense Department officials Donald Rumsfeld, Paul Wolfowitz, and Douglas Feith would decide the Iraqis' course. The Future of Iraq Project reports would go unread by the U.S. administrators who followed U.S. troops into Baghdad.

Perhaps because Rice had given Bush a favorable briefing on Vieira de Mello, the president greeted him warmly, shaking his hand vigorously and commenting on how fit he seemed. "You must work out," Bush said. As soon as the two men sat down and began discussing U.S. treatment of detainees, Bush stressed that in wartime exceptional measures were required. "Guantánamo is not a country club, but it should not be," Bush said, insisting that fighting terrorism demanded forcefulness. Vieira de Mello nodded. "I know," he said. "In East Timor I gave UN peacekeepers shoot-to-kill authority to go after the militia." His aide Prentice, was so taken aback that he commented to a UN colleague, "I can't fucking believe this: The UN High Commissioner for Human Rights is showing off about his shoot-to-kill policy!" Prentice understood that his boss's seemingly spontaneous outburst had in fact been deliberate. "Sergio knew exactly what he was doing," he remembers. "He knew that Bush probably presumed him to be a tree-hugger and that this was a quick way to show him otherwise."

Vieira de Mello, who had seemed relaxed even with the Khmer Rouge, sat at the edge of his chair, and his easy smile seemed frozen and forced. But his reflexive charm paid off. He managed not to make the president defensive when he described Guantánamo as a "legal black hole" and warned of possible torture being carried out by Americans in Afghanistan. Khalid Sheikh Mohammed, the suspected mastermind behind the 9/11 attacks, had just been arrested in Pakistan, and he urged Bush to ensure that U.S. interrogators played by legal rules. "He is a killer," Bush said, "but he will be treated humanely."[66] A year later the New York Times reported that the high-level detainee had been in fact systematically subjected to water-boarding and other harsh treatment prohibited by international law.[67]

Vieira de Mello had visited Pakistan in late February. There he had met a man who believed his sons were in Guantánamo but was not sure. Vieira de Mello told Bush of the father's desperation and appealed to him as a parent to alert families to the whereabouts of their relatives. Bush turned to Rice and said, "We need to look into this. It would be terrible not to know where your children are." Nonetheless, the Bush administration would not in fact disclose the identities of the Guantánamo detainees until March 2006. On the issue of torture, Bush was adamant. "Americans won't torture anybody," he said. "I won't allow it." Bush justified the war that the United States would soon launch in Iraq on human rights grounds. "I cannot say how strongly I feel about what Saddam Hussein has done to his own people," Bush said. "Deep in my bosom is a real desire for the freedom of people. The human condition matters to me."[68] Bush also said that in going to war to disarm Iraq, he would be defending the United Nations. "UN words must mean something," he said.[69]

Although Vieira de Mello brought up the thorniest human rights issues of the day, Bush took a visible liking to him. The president was so engaged in the discussion that he doubled the length of the meeting, which had been scheduled to last fifteen minutes. When Bush's secretary came in to tell him it was time for his scheduled call, he waved her away. "Tell Tony I'll call him back," Bush said, referring to the British prime minister. "Sergio was Sergio," recalls Banbury. "The president was so used to people bowing to him that he appreciated Sergio's directness." Another observer recalled, "The courtiers took note that the king was happy." Banbury remembers that U.S. officials came away from the meeting thinking, "This is a reasonable guy we can do business with. He's not going to give us everything we want, but he's a smart guy we can talk to."

In early 2003 the world was so polarized and the debate over the war in Iraq was growing so vitriolic that any inroads Vieira de Mello made with Washington inevitably cost him elsewhere in the UN. Some of his critics began whispering that President Bush had agreed to the meeting only because Vieira de Mello was having an affair with Rice (he was not). At UN Headquarters in New York others speculated that Vieira de Mello had offered Bush a friendly UN face so as to earn himself a job in Iraq after the war—and the top job of UN secretary-general after Annan. "Guys like Sergio don't meet with George Bush," recalls UN spokesman Fred Eckhard. "I could only see it as a big interview." Vieira de Mello laughed off these comments and got back to work, relaying word to the families he had met with in Pakistan that he had passed on their concerns to the president of the United States.

OFF TO WAR

President Bush had insisted that he would return to the UN Security Council for a resolution to authorize an invasion of Iraq. But as the weeks passed, even seemingly reliable allies like Vicente Fox of Mexico and Ricardo Lagos of Chile rejected the president's war plans. Bush did not take these rebuffs as grounds to reexamine his thinking, but rather as proof that the UN was not up to the task of combating rogue regimes. "The UN must mean something," he said. "Remember Rwanda or Kosovo. The UN didn't do its job. And we hope tomorrow the UN will do its job. If not, all of us need to step back and try to figure out how to make the UN work better as we head into the twenty-first century."[70] Vieira de Mello drafted an op-ed in response to these taunts, stressing that the UN's "major crisis" was the fault of the countries in it, not of the organization itself. "When member states make a mess of their own rules or disrupt their own collective political architecture," he wrote, "it is wrong to blame the UN or its Secretary-General."[71]

When Ruud Lubbers, the UN High Commissioner for Refugees, asked him to join in rallying the heads of UN agencies to jointly oppose the war, Vieira de Mello declined. He had come to see the war as inevitable. "When I sat down with Bush, I saw a very relaxed man," he told Lubbers. "This was not a man pondering other options."

Indeed, without an authorizing Security Council resolution, President Bush charged ahead. On March 17, 2003, he issued a forty-eight-hour ultimatum to Saddam Hussein, demanding that he and his sons leave Iraq. The ultimatum expired on March 19 at 8 p.m. EST, and roughly ninety minutes later U.S. and British forces invaded. "My fellow citizens," President Bush declared from the Oval Office, "at this hour, American and Coalition forces are in the early stages of military operations to disarm Iraq, to free its people and to defend the world from grave danger."[72]

In mid-April, by which time Baghdad had already fallen, Vieira de Mello telephoned UN Headquarters and pleaded for guidance. "What is the UN position on the war in Iraq?" he asked. He was scheduled to appear on the notoriously confrontational BBC talk show *HARDtalk* the following day, and he needed the secretary-general and his top advisers to develop a strategy in a hurry. "What message does the UN want to give the public on Iraq?" he asked. "If we don't figure out where we stand, I'm going to get massacred." Even though he received no instructions from New York, he felt he had to go ahead with the interview because the UN couldn't be silent at such a vital time. As he headed into the studio in Geneva, he told Prentice, "Watch this little lamb go to slaughter."

He was smooth but evasive and thus came across as apologetic on behalf of the American invaders. When the interviewer, Tim Sebastian, asked about collateral damage, Vieira de Mello said it was "difficult to avoid civilian casualties." When Sebastian asked him about the looting that had broken out in Baghdad, he said, "It is probably unavoidable after you've kept the lid on those people for so many years." When Sebastian asked him about reports that U.S. Marines were firing on unarmed civilians, he explained, "The problem is that there has also been a lot of deceit on the other side using fighters disguised as civilians." When Sebastian asked him about the Coalition's poor planning, he said, "I'm not sure it was badly planned. I think the planning was to topple that regime and to neutralize its armed forces. . . . I'm sure sooner or later they'll get a grip on that." When Sebastian asked him whether he worried that the rights of detainees in Iraq would be trampled as they had been in Guantánamo, he answered, "I have no reason to presume that they will subject them to the same treatment." And when Sebastian pushed him to answer whether the Iraqis were paying too high a price for freedom, he urged people to recall the twenty-four years of suffering under the prior regime. Sebastian eventually lost patience. "Is the human rights commissioner too scared to speak out against the United States?" he asked.[73]

When Vieira de Mello and Prentice left the studio, they did not discuss the interview. "You could tell from his body language afterward that he knew how terrible it was," Prentice recalls. "I didn't see the point of telling him after the fact that he sucked." At UN Headquarters in New York, the transcript of his appearance on *HARDtalk* was e-mailed from one outraged UN official to another. "With that interview," one UN official remembers, "anyone who had suspicions about what Sergio was after or whether he was sucking up to the Americans got all the proof they needed."

Eighteen

"DON'T ASK WHO STARTED THE FIRE"

A VITAL ROLE?

Once the Coalition invasion began, two questions consumed UN officials: Would Saddam Hussein put up a fight? And would the UN play a postwar political role in Iraq? While the U.S. and British embassies in Baghdad had been closed since 1991, the UN had maintained a continuous base of operations in Iraq since the Gulf War. Before the U.S.-led war more than a thousand expatriates worked in the country, partnering with some three thousand Iraqi staff.*

At Headquarters in New York, UN senior staff had spent months debating whether and how they should be involved in the postwar "peace." Annan feared that Washington's marginalization of the UN over Iraq would detract from the organization's overall global relevance, and this made him eager to find a way to get UN international staff back to Iraq as soon as possible. With his senior advisers he repeatedly stressed, "We have to prove we can do something useful." Mark Malloch Brown, Vieira de Mello's friend from their days together at UNHCR and now the head of the UN Development

---

* The organization's largest program (which later became the most notorious) was the Oil for Food Program. In 1996 the Iraqi government, under severe sanctions, signed a deal with the UN Secretariat allowing Iraq to sell its oil to finance the purchase of food and medicine. All told, the program, which the UN monitored, was used to fund the delivery of some $31 billion worth of humanitarian supplies, while another $8.2 billion remained in the production and delivery pipeline.

Program, agreed, arguing, "For Iraq's sake, for the world's sake, and for the UN's sake, we can't sit this out." As Malloch Brown remembers, "There were lots of tactical conversations about how much of our virginity to lose, but the overwhelming majority of us felt that, if you're the fire brigade, you don't ask who started the fire and whether it is a moral fire before you get involved."

The under-secretaries-general for peacekeeping and political affairs, Jean-Marie Guéhenno and Kieran Prendergast, were more cautious. "It isn't written anywhere in stone that the UN has to be deployed to every crisis," said Guéhenno. Prendergast, who was strongly influenced by his American special assistant, forty-year-old Rick Hooper, argued that it was a mistake to chase "a role for role's sake." Hooper, who had attended the University of Damascus and spoke flawless Arabic, was known in UN circles for his strong views on Middle Eastern politics and for combining operational and strategic thinking. "We should look for the UN's comparative advantage," Hooper urged, "and not simply pick up whatever crumbs are thrown at us."

It seemed likely that Washington would eventually need to involve the UN, because the U.S. welcome would wear thin in Iraq, because a U.S. occupation would harm U.S. standing internationally, or because the United States would not want to foot the bill for Iraq's reconstruction on its own. Vieira de Mello participated in these high-level UN discussions by speakerphone from Geneva. He believed that the Bush administration would turn back to the UN as soon as it achieved its military objectives. He knew better than anybody just how hard it was to manage postwar transitions, and he knew that the United States did not have the in-house expertise necessary to re-integrate the Iraqi military, facilitate the return of refugees, or plan elections. Whenever he was asked whether the Iraq war signaled the end of the UN, he would say of the Americans, "They will come back."[1]

Since late 2002 the British had been pressing the Americans to give the UN a prominent political role after the war. British prime minister Tony Blair, President Bush's most trusted Coalition partner, knew that British voters were unenthusiastic about U.S. plans to run Iraq unilaterally. Polls in the *Daily Telegraph* showed that while British support for the war had risen to a high of 66 percent, only 2 percent of those polled supported the establishment of an American-controlled administration afterward.[2] On April 3, two weeks into the war, British foreign secretary Jack Straw presented Secretary of State Colin Powell with a detailed "day after" occupation plan that envis-

aged the appointment of a powerful UN special envoy.[3] If the UN ran the
show, the plan showed, instead of paying for the occupation, the United States
would be charged just 20 percent of the cost (its share of the UN peacekeeping budget).[4] France and Germany naturally favored the British plan because,
having opposed the war, they were dead set against the idea of leaving the
Americans in charge of Iraq. France had proposed an arrangement like that
after the 1999 Kosovo war, in which NATO had run the military operation and the UN, initially under Vieira de Mello, had overseen the political
administration.[5]

But the Bush administration rejected the British approach. The U.S. attitude was "We aren't going to expend blood and treasure to have *you* decide
who runs Iraq." Bush's top advisers did not think highly of the UN, both
because of the Security Council's refusal to endorse the war and because
they looked down upon the UN's past performances in the Balkans, Rwanda,
Kosovo, and even East Timor, which elsewhere was seen as a success.[6] In a
speech in February 2003, Secretary Rumsfeld had said that the United States
intended to avoid the kind of "nation-building" that the UN did. He faulted
the UN performance in Kosovo. "They issue postage stamps, passports, driver's licenses, and the like," he said, "and decisions made by the local parliament
are invalid without the signatures of the UN administrators."[7] In poverty-
stricken East Timor, he continued, the UN had caused the capital city of
Dili to become "one of the most expensive cities in Asia." Restaurants there
"cater to international workers who have salaries that are some two hundred
times the average local wage," he said. "In the city's main supermarkets prices
are reportedly on a par with London and New York."[8] Rumsfeld seemed to
believe that the United States would simply be able to dislodge Saddam Hussein and walk away without itself getting involved in Iraqi affairs.

In thinking about the war's aftermath, other U.S. officials believed that
they faced a trade-off between legitimacy and control, and they expressed
a clear preference for control. Even Secretary Powell was insistent. "The
Coalition, having taken the political risk and having paid the cost in lives,
must have a leading role," he said.[9] Three weeks into the war, after their third
summit in as many weeks, Bush and Blair could only agree that "the United
Nations has a vital role to play in the reconstruction of Iraq."[10] Neither man
specified what "vital role" meant. When journalists pressed Bush to clarify
the meaning of the phrase, he grew irritated. "Evidently there's some skepti-

cism here in Europe about whether or not I mean what I say," Bush said. "Saddam Hussein clearly knows I mean what I say. And a vital role for the United Nations means a vital role for the United Nations."[11] Paul Wolfowitz was more concrete, saying that the UN would perform humanitarian tasks. "The UN can be an important partner," the deputy secretary of defense said. "But it can't be the managing partner. It can't be in charge."[12]

For all of their differences with Washington, Annan, Vieira de Mello, and other senior UN officials were actually in full agreement with the Bush administration that the UN should not run Iraq. In a March 21 memo, Annan's top advisers argued that the UN should "resist and discourage" notions of a UN transitional administration, which would vastly exceed the UN's capacity. In 2000 Lakhdar Brahimi, the former Algerian foreign minister, had released a highly touted report in which he culled the lessons of UN political and peacekeeping operations of the previous decade and concluded that the UN Secretariat needed to learn to "say no" to unachievable mandates. As Vieira de Mello had experienced firsthand in Bosnia and Kosovo, the UN too often took the fall for the wrongheaded decisions of the countries on the Security Council. When asked by a reporter whether the UN would be willing to run an Iraqi administration similar to those in East Timor and Kosovo, Annan replied, "Iraq is not East Timor and Iraq is not Kosovo. There are trained personnel, there is a reasonably effective civil service, there are engineers and others who can play a role in their own country. . . . Iraqis have to be responsible for their political future, and to control their own natural resources."[13]

As the speculation about the postwar phase began to heat up, Vieira de Mello began to wonder whether he might get pulled into the fray. His job in Geneva was frustrating him. In an e-mail to Peter Galbraith, he noted that he was still struggling to define his role, which was "not easy after three decades of operational, high-adrenaline stuff."[14] He complained to a journalist that a "succession of appointments, of meetings, of trips, deprive me of my freedom."[15] When Fabrizio Hochschild, his special assistant in Kosovo and East Timor, visited him in his plush new office, several times the size of his prior quarters, Hochschild brought his two-year-old son, Adam, who began playing in Vieira de Mello's swirling desk chair. As the two friends got caught up, Adam suddenly began wailing at the top of his lungs. Hochschild did all he could to console him, but the boy cried on as if in agony. The high commissioner quipped, "At least someone knows how I feel."

In March 2003, shortly after he met with Bush, Vieira de Mello traveled to Brussels, where his friend Omar Bakhet was working. Bakhet set up a meeting with Romano Prodi, then president of the European Commission, but in the middle of their discussion, Prodi drifted to sleep. Leaving the meeting, Vieira de Mello erupted. "Fuck, Omar, this is what we are doing with our lives, putting up with this kind of garbage. He wouldn't dare do that if I represented a Western country." Bakhet tried to make light of the incident. "How do you think I feel, Sergio? This is my life here. Normally I bring blankets to meetings." But his friend did not laugh. Bakhet recalls, "I felt like the flame in Sergio was dying slowly inside him."

Still, although office life had never suited him and he felt removed from the "action" on Iraq, Vieira de Mello was committed to finishing what he had started. He was planning a politically delicate trip to Israel and the Palestinian territories for the fall, and he was ready to use the political capital he had amassed in capitals throughout his career to elevate the profile of his office and of human rights. He was also determined to complete his divorce. When his name began to appear in the press as a possible candidate to be UN envoy in Iraq, he played it down. The April 1 edition of *Development News,* a World Bank publication, quoted a London *Times* article saying that the Americans saw him as their candidate. He forwarded the link to Larriera. "Here starts the speculation," he wrote. "I must have serious enemies in the UK for someone to say this of me!"[16] Since he had only just arrived in Geneva to take up the post of human rights commissioner, he did not think Annan would even consider removing him. A few days later he e-mailed Larriera an invitation that had been sent to him from the mayor of Geneva, who on June 7 would be hosting a reception in order to open five hundred bottles of wine. "Some good news," he wrote her. "Let's go!"[17]

On April 9, a U.S. Marine tank helped topple the towering statue of Saddam Hussein in Firdos Square, Baghdad. The mood on the thirty-eighth floor at UN Headquarters, where most people had opposed the war, was not celebratory. One of the few UN officials who had backed the invasion was sickened. "They couldn't step back, even for one day, to rejoice in the end of Saddam's tyranny," the official recalls. The Americans were triumphant. On May 1, 2003, President Bush made his infamous proclamation in front of a MISSION ACCOMPLISHED banner: "Major combat operations in Iraq have ended. In the battle of Iraq, the United States and our allies have prevailed."[18]

At a town hall meeting at a U.S. base in Qatar, an army officer asked Rumsfeld whether he had been "bombarded with apologetic phone calls" from his "doom and gloom" critics. Amid much laughter and applause, Rumsfeld responded: "There were a lot of hand-wringers around, weren't there? You know, during World War II, I think Winston Churchill was talking about the Battle of Britain, and he said, 'Never have so many owed so much to so few.' A humorist in Washington the other day sent me a note paraphrasing that, and he said, 'Never have so many been so wrong about so much.' But I would never say that."[19]

Vieira de Mello hoped that the smugness of American decision-makers would be matched by competence on the ground. Battlefield success did not automatically translate into long-term stability, as the United States was already learning in Afghanistan. He was all too aware of how quickly progress could be reversed. As retired Marine general Anthony Zinni, former head of U.S. Central Command, said later, referring to the swift U.S. success in the initial conventional war in Iraq: "Ohio State beat Slippery Rock sixty-two to nothing. No shit."[20] Whether the American and British invasion would prove a lasting success would turn on whether the Americans could provide physical and economic security for Iraqis. And in this regard Vieira de Mello took note of the fact that nobody he had talked to at the UN, in Europe, or in the Bush administration seemed to be able to answer an essential question: After Saddam was defeated, who would run Iraq?

AMERICAN RULE

Administration officials had initially suggested that an Iraqi interim authority (split between Iraqi exiles and those who had stayed in Iraq and suffered under Saddam) would be chosen as soon as Coalition troops secured the country.[21] After a summit meeting with Prime Minister Blair in April, President Bush said, "I hear a lot of talk here about how we're going to impose this leader or that leader. Forget it. From day one, we have said the Iraqi people are capable of running their own country . . . It is a cynical world that says it's impossible for the Iraqis to run themselves."[22] After his meeting with Bush in March, Vieira de Mello had met with National Security Adviser Rice, who told him that Washington hoped "very soon to identify technocrats who can help run the country." She had insisted that people who

claimed that President Bush intended to appoint a military governor "do
not know what they are taking about," adding, "We have no desire to be in
Iraq longer than necessary."[23] Publicly, she said, "If Afghanistan is any guide,
the people themselves will tell you, well, that person has been a leader."[24] As
late as mid-May the Bush administration still imagined having a transitional
Iraqi government composed of Iraqi exiles and internals in place by the end
of the month.[25]

Jay Garner, a sixty-five-year-old retired U.S. general who was to manage
the civilian side of the U.S. postwar presence, did not arrive in Baghdad until
April 21, twelve days after Baghdad's fall. He was told that, in advance of the
creation of the new Iraqi government, he would preside over twenty-three
ministries—each of which would be headed by an American with Iraqi assistance. These ministries would keep the country running until normalcy
returned. The Americans had ambitious but limited objectives. They wanted
to remove Saddam Hussein and his henchmen and decapitate the Ba'athist
terror apparatus. And in the wake of Saddam's overthrow, they wanted to see
Iraqi institutions up and running "under new management."

When Vieira de Mello was administrator in East Timor, he had taken care
to live unobtrusively and to shun a dignitary's siren. By contrast, Garner traveled around in a GMC Suburban, trailed by a convoy of nine Humvees and
three security vehicles filled with Coalition troops. Garner did try to convey
to Iraqis that they would control their own destiny. Visiting a power station
that had been destroyed by vandals, Garner was asked if he was the new ruler
of Iraq. "The new ruler of Iraq is an Iraqi," the American said without elaborating.[26] Garner was winging it. The only formal plan he had been given was
a twenty-five-page paper, dated April 16, 2003, entitled "A Unified Mission
Plan for Post-Hostilities Iraq." It began: "History will judge the war against
Iraq not by the brilliance of its military execution, but by the effectiveness of
the post-hostilities activities."[27]

The Coalition's "post-hostilities" performance did not begin well. Iraq's
infrastructure was far shoddier than U.S. planners had expected. Compounding matters was that, in the days after the fall of Baghdad, Iraqi gangs had carried out widespread looting, gutting seventeen of the twenty-three ministries,
burning the Iraqi National Library (destroying more than one million books),
stripping hospitals of their equipment and medicines, and smashing and steal-

ing antiquities from the National Museum.[28] Secretary Rumsfeld was widely quoted dismissing the significance of the lootings, saying, "Freedom's untidy, and free people are free to make mistakes and commit crimes and do bad things."[29] But images of the U.S. military in Iraq standing by helplessly—failing to declare martial law or impose a curfew—were beamed throughout Iraq, the region, and the world.[30] The scenes were not different from those Vieira de Mello had seen in Kosovo when NATO soldiers had refused to prevent Kosovar gunmen from looting Serb villages. But the stakes in Iraq, a country of 27 million in the most volatile region in the world, were far higher.

In early May, with chaos afoot, President Bush announced that he was replacing Garner with sixty-one-year-old L. Paul "Jerry" Bremer, who had served as ambassador to the Netherlands, ambassador-at-large for counterterrorism, and, more recently, managing director at Kissinger Associates. Henceforth he would head a newly created body called the Coalition Provisional Authority (CPA).[31] On May 8 John Negroponte, the U.S. ambassador to the UN, and Jeremy Greenstock, the British ambassador there, sent a letter to the Security Council in which they spelled out the responsibilities of the CPA. This was the first written word that UN officials received that the American and British invaders—*and not Iraqis*—were in fact going to govern Iraq and provide for the "responsible administration of the Iraqi financial sector."[32]

Most Iraqis were shocked. "Until the creation of the CPA, we thought we were going to run our own country. That's what the Americans had been telling us," recalls Adnan Pachachi, a leading Iraq exile who had served in the 1960s as Iraqi ambassador to the UN. In April Pachachi had attended two large meetings of returning Iraqi exiles and local Iraqis who believed that they were debating the composition of a new Iraqi government. They were thus blindsided by the Bush administration's decision to make Bremer the effective ruler of the country. On May 19, in response to the indefinite postponement of Iraqi sovereignty, the militant young cleric Moqtada al-Sadr brought some ten thousand protesters to the streets of Baghdad in the largest gathering since the arrival of U.S. forces six weeks before. The crowd denounced Bremer's announcement that Iraqi self-government would be postponed. "No to foreign administration," they chanted. "Yes, yes to Islam."[33]

Bremer swept into Iraq as the anti-Garner. If Garner, with his khakis and golf shirts, was deferential and hesitant, Bremer, dressed in his business suits and combat boots, was firm and swift. If Garner went out of his way to insist that as-yet-unidentified "Iraqis" were in charge, Bremer showed instantly that he was. Only he, "the administrator," had the power to sign laws, which were called "orders."

The success of any U.S. administration in Iraq was handicapped by decisions made before Bremer's time. The Pentagon had decided to attempt to man the "peace" with only 130,000 troops, an impossibility in a country so large. The White House had opted to make the Pentagon the lead agency in the postwar period, thereby sidelining the U.S. government's only intellectual capital on governance, development, and reconstruction: that of the State Department and the U.S. Agency for International Development. And the Iraqi looting rampage that had begun in early April had ravaged basic services and greatly eroded Iraqi confidence in the Coalition.

But Bremer was also the victim of the orders he issued on arrival. On May 16, only four days after he landed in Baghdad, he issued a fateful edict that would change Iraq forever: He banned Saddam Hussein's Ba'ath party and forbade senior party members from participating in public life. While Garner had said he would punish only the leading culprits in the Ba'ath party, Bremer's order targeted the top four levels of the party, whose numbers ranged between 1 million and 2.5 million. The de-Ba'athification order, which was modeled on the de-Nazification process after World War II, was said to have come from the White House.[34] The effect of the measure was immediate. Bureaucrats and technocrats who knew how to operate the ministries of health, transportation, and communications were replaced by "fifth stringers," in the words of Coalition official Stephen Browning, who attempted to run the ministry of health. "Nobody who was left knew anything."[35] While in World War II the Allies had left most German institutions in place, getting rid of only the most culpable Nazis, Iraq's core institutions (schools, hospitals, social services, telecommunications, police, courtrooms) were not merely decapitated and left awaiting senior leadership; they were gutted to the point that they could not meet the daily needs of Iraq's citizens. Low-level Ba'ath party officials were told that they could appeal, but the mechanisms to hear their appeals would not be set up for many months.

A week later Bremer announced his second fatal move: the disbanding of the Iraqi army. More than 400,000 Iraqi soldiers and officers, only some of whom were actually loyal to the previous regime and most of whom had families to support, were let go.[36] Bremer justified the move on the grounds that he was only formalizing a dissolution that had already occurred spontaneously. But in a matter of days the CPA had dissolved the two primary instruments for governing the country. The seeds for Iraq's implosion had been planted.

RETURN TO THE UN

Although security in Iraq had begun to deteriorate, even U.S. critics still saw the Coalition invasion as a military success. None of the calamities that the French, Germans, and Russians had forecast in Iraq had yet materialized. Flush with their victory and eager to cement it by receiving the international blessing denied them before the war, U.S. officials returned to the UN Security Council in New York to try to get a resolution passed that would legitimize U.S. and British rule. One official at the French mission recalls the American attitude: "They said, 'We told you it would take one month to topple Saddam, and we've done as we said.'" European governments had many reasons to want a fresh UN resolution passed in the war's aftermath: They wanted to mend fences with the Americans; to ensure that their companies were not shut out of the postwar reconstruction and oil contracts; to signal their support for a democratic and stable Iraq; to bind the Americans to the Geneva Conventions by forcing them to acknowledge that, under international law, they were technically occupiers (not "liberators"); and to try to give the UN (which they trusted more than they trusted the Americans) a significant role in shaping the new Iraq.

Whatever Europe's aspirations, U.S. diplomats largely dictated the terms of the new Security Council resolution. After three weeks of negotiations the countries that had opposed the war back in March agreed to recognize the United States as the occupying authority in Iraq, which many interpreted as a belated show of UN support for the American and British invasion. While the UN resolution did oblige the occupiers to abide by the Geneva Conventions, the resolution effectively superseded the traditional legal rules

of occupation by giving the Americans and British the right to choose Iraq's
political leadership and transform Iraq's legal, political, and economic structures.[37] It also called on other UN member states to contribute personnel,
equipment, and other resources to the Coalition's effort.

In advance of the resolution's passage, one diplomat noted how radical
the resolution was. "The Security Council would be legitimizing the occupation of the territory and state functions of one member by a group of
other members," he said. "That has never happened before."[38] "Occupation
was a goldmine," recalls a U.S. official. "The UN and the Europeans wanted
us·to accept our responsibilities as occupying powers, and by doing so, we
got things we never thought we'd get through the Council: oil revenues,
day-to-day functioning of ministries, power over the armed forces. We were
thrilled. We hadn't found a way to legally get at Iraqi oil until the UN led
us there. It was a dream come true for the Pentagon. The Europeans didn't
really understand what we were getting out of the resolution. It was only
much later that they went, 'Fuck, we voted for this thing?'"

The one aspect of the resolution that the Europeans could point to as
a U.S. concession was the appointment of a UN Special Representative of
the Secretary-General for Iraq who would play a role in setting up an "Iraqi
interim administration." Still, even this UN envoy was made subservient to
the Coalition. He had none of the powers of Lakhdar Brahimi, the UN envoy
to Afghanistan who had helped select that country's first president. Annan's
advisers were split on whom he should choose to fill the limited role. Several
of them believed that he should send a junior official, a person whose rank
was more commensurate with the minimal responsibilities that the Coalition
seemed willing to offer the UN. "Are the Americans actually going to create
a space for us to play a political role," Under-Secretary-General Prendergast
asked, "or are they intent on doing everything themselves and just appro-
priating the UN decal?" He urged Annan to select an Arabic speaker. "If a
mob comes toward you, and you don't understand what they're saying, you
can't even read the road signs in the place, you're going to be in trouble," he
argued. The British, who still hoped the UN could play a truly vital role in
Iraq, urged Annan to appoint a high-profile UN envoy. Annan told Jeremy
Greenstock, the British ambassador to the UN, that he was considering appointing the former president of Costa Rica. Greenstock shook his head and
advised, "We are really talking about Sergio."

"Sergio Will Fix It"

Greenstock and others close to Annan believed that if the secretary-general did not send somebody of Vieira de Mello's stature, the United States would walk all over the UN. Vieira de Mello was not an Arabic speaker, but he brought enough hands-on technical expertise to compensate. "It is very strongly in the Secretary-General's and the UN's own interest to have as effective and credible a representative as possible," an aide to Annan wrote in an internal memo, "one who can interact authoritatively with the Coalition representatives on the ground, and demonstrate to the broader international community what a UN representative can add to such a process." Although the Americans preferred Vieira de Mello, the aide wrote, this should not deter Annan from appointing him. Rather, the secretary-general should take heed of the fact that from an Iraqi perspective Vieira de Mello was the best man for the job.[39]

Annan was not yet persuaded. He was leaning toward appointing Kamel Morjane, the Arabic-speaking senior UNHCR official who then held the post that Vieira de Mello had once held at UNHCR, that of assistant high commissioner for refugees. But on May 16 Morjane read a *New York Times* story by Elizabeth Becker, who quoted a senior diplomat on the Security Council saying that Vieira de Mello was "the man Washington wants." The two friends met in Geneva's Old Town for Sunday morning coffee, and Morjane told him, "Sergio, be careful. Even if you end up having to go to Iraq, this kind of publicity is not good for you. If the interveners are endorsing you, you will be seen as their tool." Vieira de Mello agreed. "I know," he said. "Kamel, if you are my friend, you will tell everyone you know that I don't want to go."

Vieira de Mello was torn. He took seriously the line in his contract that required him to serve wherever the secretary-general sent him. He also made no secret of missing the action. In Geneva he spent his days restructuring his office, meeting with diplomats, giving speeches on the centrality of human rights, and making recommendations to his small teams in the field. It was a desk job. He felt removed from Iraq, one of the most wrenching geopolitical crises of his lifetime. Although he had long ago stopped admitting his aspiration to become secretary-general, he must have known that his stock would rise significantly if he helped stabilize Iraq. He also knew that he was the best man for a bad mission and could, without arrogance, observe that he had more experience managing postconflict transitions than any other person in the UN system. He could tap these skills to serve the Iraqi people, who had suffered enough.

But for all the obvious appeal, a great deal held him back. He was just settling into his new job, and if he ran off to Iraq, the already-suspicious human rights community would pounce. He had just turned fifty-five and had finally begun to focus on his personal life. On May 16, the same day the Becker story appeared, Annie and he had appeared before a divorce tribunal. A year and a half after he first filed for a legal split, the judge ordered the division of the family property, giving Annie the house in Massongy and requiring Vieira de Mello to pay a substantial monthly stipend.

As the days passed and the countries on the Security Council refined the text of the resolution, Vieira de Mello saw that the odds that he would be summoned were increasing. So he took matters into his own hands: He telephoned Iqbal Riza, Annan's chief of staff. "Iqbal, if my name comes up on lists for Iraq, please take it off," he said. "I can't go to Iraq. I need to finish my divorce. I can't send that signal to the human rights community. And I didn't believe in this war." Riza told him that he understood and would oblige. In Vieira de Mello's mind, the matter was settled. The day of his court appearance, Peter Galbraith, his colleague in East Timor and an expert on the Iraqi Kurds, sent him an e-mail offering to brief him on Iraq, and he wrote back, urging Galbraith not to believe what he read in the press, and stressing, "Hope not to need your briefing."[40] When Steven Erlanger of the *New York Times* inquired, he wrote back, "I can't seriously drop my current (eight-month-old) job and go off on another adventure. Moreover, the mandate, as far as I can tell, does not look right to me."[41]

Riza told Morjane that he was on the short list for the job. Unlike Vieira de Mello, Morjane had close ties to his home government, Tunisia, and owing to the political sensitivities of an Arab national taking up a post in occupied Iraq, he would have to clear any such appointment with his president. "Going to Iraq for the UN would not be like going to Australia or Peru," Morjane recalls. He quietly made arrangements to fly home to see President Zine El Abidine Ben Ali two days later.

On Sunday, May 18, Vieira de Mello went jogging around Lake Geneva with his assistant Jonathan Prentice. After the run, they sat in the grass to stretch, and Prentice urged his boss to face the inevitable, saying, "Sergio, it is going to happen." But Vieira de Mello remained convinced that he would not be asked. "I really don't think it will," he said. "I've made it clear to the secretary-general that I don't want to go." The next day, he had lunch with his secretary, Carole Ray, who asked him to confirm the rumors that he was headed to Baghdad. "Carole, my dear, I've been in this job for eight months. What are the governments that backed me going to think if I bugger off to Iraq? So if you are counting on being part of another mission, forget it." As the two got up to leave the UN cafeteria, however, he conceded, "If the old man tells me that I have to go, then I have no choice."

Initially, when Secretary Powell pressed Annan to appoint Vieira de Mello, the secretary-general declined. "Sergio has a job," Annan said. "And it is an important job which he has just started." But Powell kept calling, and the British too kept up the chorus. Even though Annan was being pressured by the very two countries that had bypassed the Security Council to begin with, he did not feel as though he had many options. "If the U.S. secretary of state comes to say to you, 'We want Mr. Jones,'" says one UN official close to Annan, "your reasons for saying no better be more compelling than 'He has a job' or 'He's tired' or 'He needs to finalize his divorce.'"

Annan today insists that Vieira de Mello changed his mind about going to Iraq. "The Americans had gotten to him," he recalls. But Vieira de Mello's last official word on his possible appointment had been his phone call to Riza requesting that his name be taken off the short list. Contrary to Annan's claim, senior Bush administration officials did not reach out to him directly. He never spoke with the president after their first meeting.[42] Only Kevin Moley, the U.S. ambassador in Geneva, paid him a visit. "It was 'Hey, Sergio, we'd very much like you to do this,'" Moley remembers, "but it wasn't anything more than that." The Bush administration was conscious of the risks of exerting too much pressure. "It's the kiss of death to be the U.S. candidate," says Moley. "If Sergio was to go to Iraq, we wanted him to be seen as legitimate."

On Wednesday, May 21, Vieira de Mello's day at the Palais Wilson was packed with meetings, including a late-afternoon gathering with a dozen interns. One of his senior advisers tried to get him to cancel the session, but he refused. "Don't take them off the agenda," he said. "They work here for free.

They deserve my time." Much as Thomas Jamieson had enjoyed taking him out for long lunches three decades earlier, he now found it relaxing to chat with students and young human rights devotees. When Ray tried to end the meeting after twenty-five minutes, he demurred. "Give me a little more time," he said. Fifteen minutes later, when Ray returned and said Annan wanted to speak to him, he reluctantly rose from the table and walked out with her. "Was that a lie?" he asked. But he was in fact connected to Headquarters, and Annan asked him to fly to New York the next day. Vieira de Mello hung up the phone and turned to Ray. "I think they are going to ask me to Iraq," he said. "Can I count on you to come for three months?"

Having explicitly asked to be taken off the list, something he had never done before in his career, he was frustrated that the UN system had such a thin layer of talent at the top that he was always the one whose life was disrupted. Others, like his Indian colleague Under-Secretary-General Shashi Tharoor, seemed to glide up through the UN ranks without ever serving in a hardship post. "If this is such an important job," he asked Prentice, "why the hell don't they ever send Shashi? Why is it always me?" He telephoned Morjane, who was flying to Tunisia to speak with his president. "Kamel, the SG called me last night. I leave today for New York. If they put pressure on me and I can't refuse, I'll tell them I'll do it for three months and you will succeed me."

On Thursday, May 22, Vieira de Mello flew first class on the daytime flight from Geneva to New York. Before he departed, he and Prentice made calls to the Chinese ambassador to the UN in New York and to Irene Khan, the head of Amnesty International, asking them, in the event that he was named UN envoy to Iraq, to issue statements praising his appointment. He hoped that this would counter any notion that he was an American puppet by making it clear that he had broad support in the international community.

Prentice, who normally flew economy class, received an unexpected upgrade. He and Vieira de Mello spent the flight together in first class drinking champagne, feasting on lobster and fine cheeses, and poking fun at the draft Security Council resolution, which (in a long career of working with lousy mandates) was by far the worst Vieira de Mello had ever seen. "What the fuck does this mean?" he asked, pointing to the clause outlining the special representative's functions. "I have no idea," said Prentice.

While Vieira de Mello was flying, the countries with seats on the Security Council were meeting to vote on the final draft of the resolution. At 9:30 a.m. in New York, diplomats chatted amicably in the Council chamber and stared expectantly at the door, where they hoped the Syrian ambassador would appear. After a forty-minute delay and frequent cell phone calls, the ambassador never showed, and the fourteen other ambassadors voted unanimously in favor of Resolution 1483.[43] Most midlevel UN staff were demoralized by the rush to endorse the U.S. and British occupation. One UN lawyer, Mona Khalil, put a screen saver up on her computer that read: "The UN Charter has left the building." But Annan was personally pleased that the UN was "back in the game" and also relieved the Council had not asked the UN to administer the country. "I have always held that the unity of the Council is the indispensable foundation for effective action to maintain international peace and security," he told reporters after the session. "We should all be gratified that the Council has come together."[44] Calling it a "foot in the door resolution," Mark Malloch Brown, the head of the UN Development Program, seconded Annan's satisfaction. "It's a very good resolution," he said.[45]

The Europeans had swallowed giving the United States and Great Britain virtual control over Iraq's oil revenues, and giving the UN vague and subservient tasks, but they put a positive spin on this occasion. They pointed to some ninety changes made to the original draft resolution as evidence of their influence.[46] "The war that we did not want, and the majority of the Council did not want, has taken place," German ambassador Gunter Pleuger said. "We cannot undo history. We are now in a situation where we have to take action for the sake of the Iraqi people."[47] The French did not think they had the option of opposing it. "We could have abstained from the resolution," recalls one official at the French mission. "But we asked ourselves, what do we get by abstaining? We'll be blamed for being anti-Iraqi and obstructing efforts at reconstruction. And if things go wrong, the United States will scapegoat us and say we obstructed what was necessary. We couldn't give them another opportunity to blame us."

The Bush administration was riding high. It had infuriated its allies, gone to war, dislodged Saddam Hussein, and now gotten the Security Council to bless its occupation. As one U.S. official recalls, "We had staved off divorce or murder, and we had moved back into the house together."

When Iraqis got wind of the contents of the UN resolution, they were crushed. A month before the resolution Shiite militant cleric Moqtada al-Sadr had granted one of his first-ever interviews, to Anthony Shadid of the *Washington Post*. When Shadid had asked al-Sadr whether Americans were occupiers or liberators, al-Sadr had been circumspect: "This is not a question to ask me," he said. "It is a question to ask them. I don't know their intentions. Only God does." But with the passage of Resolution 1483, al-Sadr and millions of other Iraqis had their answer: It was an "occupation"; the UN resolution said so. The Arabic word for occupation, *ihtilal,* carried several damning resonances: the British occupation of Iraq (1915–1932), the Israeli occupation of Lebanon (1978–2000), and the ongoing Israeli occupation of the West Bank and Gaza.

With the passage of the resolution, all that was left to announce was who would be named the Special Representative of the Secretary-General for Iraq. When Vieira de Mello landed in New York, he phoned Larriera, who had been awaiting his arrival in her office at the UN. Together they rehearsed the arguments for not going to Iraq. "Repeat after me, Sergio: 'I can say no. I am the UN High Commissioner for Human Rights, and I've just started,'" Larriera said. He assured her, "I already told Riza to take me off the list. They probably just want to brainstorm about the other candidates." He knew better.

He took a cab directly from Kennedy airport to Larriera's tiny studio apartment on East Sixty-second Street, between First and Second avenues. He showered and then walked the five short blocks to Annan's home. When the meeting began, they discussed the generic functions that the UN envoy in Iraq would have to perform. "He will have to serve as a bridge to the Coalition, but he will also have to distance himself from the Coalition," Annan said. He would have to get out into the countryside and listen to what Iraqis were saying. And he would have to push the Coalition to develop a more transparent timetable for holding elections, drafting a constitution, and handing over full sovereignty to the Iraqis. The two men did not discuss the physical dangers in Iraq because, although looting was occurring, it looked as though Saddam Hussein's Republican Guard forces had been roundly defeated. Iraq seemed more peaceful than Bosnia and Kosovo had been when Vieira de Mello had risked his life as a UN envoy. Annan never asked him directly whether he would go, but after almost an hour of general discussion about the tasks that lay ahead, the secretary-general said, "So when are we going to announce your appointment?"

Gamal Ibrahim, Vieira de Mello's former bodyguard, had not seen him since he became human rights commissioner the previous September. Ibrahim was leaving the UN to get a bite to eat when he spotted Vieira de Mello on the street coming from Annan's home. "Stop the car," Ibrahim told the person he was driving with. "Sergio? What are you doing here?" Vieira de Mello's face brightened. "Gamal!" Ibrahim offered him a lift uptown to Larriera's apartment. "The SG just told me I'm going to Baghdad," Vieira de Mello said. Ibrahim was impressed. "That's good for you, Mr. Sergio, good for your career," he said. "What do you mean, Gamal? I've worked for the UN for thirty-four years. I'm going to retire in two or three years. I've been everywhere. I've done everything. I'm the High Commissioner for Human Rights. What career am I working for? What do I have left to prove?" Ibrahim was taken aback and asked, "So why are you going?" "Can you say no to your boss?" Vieira de Mello said. "I cannot say no to mine." They arrived at Larriera's apartment building. "We'll talk later," he said as he got out of the car. Ibrahim feared he knew what that meant and figured that he would be equally bad at refusing a job he didn't want.

Larriera knew something had gone wrong when Vieira de Mello hadn't called. When she telephoned her apartment from work, he answered. "They put it in such a way that I couldn't say what we had planned I was going to say," he blurted out. "But would you come with me?" She was stunned. "What do you mean?" she said. "They asked you to go to Iraq?"

He had accepted the job on two conditions. First, unlike his posting to East Timor, the Iraq assignment would not be prolonged. Annan had asked Vieira de Mello to serve for six months. Vieira de Mello had said three. And the two men had settled on a four-month term. Vieira de Mello would preside over a UN start-up mission, just as he had done in 1999 in Kosovo, and then he would hand the operation over to a more permanent special representative and return to Geneva to his full-time job as UN High Commissioner for Human Rights. He would not stay a day past his assigned tenure, he told Annan, "no matter what." His second condition was non-negotiable: Larriera would be part of his team.

The couple passed the evening in gloomy resignation. They had spent

months plotting the next phase of their life together in Geneva, and suddenly their plans had been turned upside down. He had persuaded Annan
to postpone the formal announcement so that they could enjoy a weekend
of relative peace. Resolved to make the best of the time they had together
in New York, she suggested that they leave her cramped apartment for a few
hours and get dinner at one of their favorite restaurants. When they entered
L'Absinthe, a brasserie on East Sixty-seventh Street, however, they spotted
a crowd of UN colleagues inside. "No more UN tonight," he said, spiriting
her back outside.

Knowing he would be in high demand, he avoided Headquarters the
next day for fear of being buttonholed. In Tunis his friend Kamel Morjane
was meeting with President Ben Ali, who agreed to support his candidacy.
"I have only one condition," Ben Ali said. "If the secretary-general chooses
you, I will give you a team from my own personal security detail. I will not
let you go alone." Morjane accepted the offer of additional security and
telephoned Riza, who informed him that Annan had already chosen Vieira
de Mello. Morjane's pride was wounded, but he telephoned his friend to
congratulate him. "Prepare yourself," Vieira de Mello said. "I will not stay one
day longer than four months, and you will replace me." Morjane was disappointed. "The only person happy in my house was my wife," he recalls. "But
rationally I thought Sergio was the best man for the job, not only because of
his skills, which were obvious, but also because he was the one UN person
who might be able to influence the United States and the U.K. He'd be able
to find the best space for the UN. There was nobody better than Sergio at
finding that space." Annan had come to the same conclusion. "At the end
of the day everyone was hoping that 1483, with all of its absurdities, would
be salvaged by Sergio himself," recalls one UN official. "That was the whole
plan: Sergio will fix it."

Vieira de Mello telephoned his mother to ensure she did not read about
his latest assignment in the Brazilian press. When she got the news, she was
devastated. "Sergio, stop taking care of the world, and start taking care of
yourself," she said. She had always worried about her son's physical security.
"What if they mistake you for an American?" she asked.[48] He assured her
that they would not and promised that he would fly straight to Rio at the
end of his four-month appointment. She wrote his name on a piece of paper
and placed it inside a Bible.[49]

On Saturday, after stopping into the UN for a few hours of briefings, he met up with Larriera and toured the Metropolitan Museum of Art's exhibit *Art of the First Cities: The Third Millennium B.C. from the Mediterranean to the Indus.* The couple paid particular attention to the architecture, sculpture, jewelry, carvings, and tablets from Iraq. They then went shopping at the Gap for light cotton shirts and khaki slacks.

In the end, Vieira de Mello went to Iraq not primarily because he was auditioning for the position of secretary-general or because he needed an adrenaline hit. He went to Iraq for a far more prosaic reason: The secretary-general of the United Nations had asked him. "People forget this about Sergio," Prentice says. "For a man who had huge vanity, he respected the UN structure. He was remarkably quaint."

On Tuesday, May 27, Vieira de Mello attended a meeting of the Iraq Steering Group, Annan's brain trust on Iraq. He continued to scrutinize Resolution 1483, pleading with his colleagues for clarification. Since they had been in New York during the three-week drafting process, they could better gauge the Council's "original intent." "Can anyone explain this to me?" he asked. Edward Mortimer, Annan's director of communications, recalls, "Each time they tried to explain, I thought to myself, 'If he wasn't confused before, he certainly will be now.'"

Events were moving so quickly that Vieira de Mello had to absorb an enormous amount of new information overnight. He had read about the Coalition's decision to demobilize the Iraqi army, but at the Steering Group meeting he began hearing about the violent consequences of the U.S. edict. Ramiro Lopes da Silva, a fifty-two-year-old Portuguese official who had been the UN humanitarian coordinator for Iraq before the war, had returned to Baghdad with a small team in early May to resume operations and await word of the UN's forthcoming role. On speakerphone he reported that the UN had offered humanitarian assistance to Iraqi soldiers, who were no longer being paid. Louise Fréchette, the deputy secretary-general and chair of the Steering Group, argued that payments to the army were the responsibility of the United States, and the UN should not divert aid from elsewhere in the world to bail out the Americans. In the end UN officials decided the soldiers should be eligible for aid like other Iraqis.

UN staff members were split about Annan's decision to appoint Vieira de Mello. Many were upset that so soon after being steamrollered by the Coalition, the secretary-general would scamper to service U.S. needs by sending his best. They were also disturbed that Vieira de Mello was "America's pick" and speculated that this was little more than a brown-nosing dress rehearsal for his secretary-generalship. "Sergio has been contaminated by the fact that the Americans consecrated him," Prendergast argued to the secretary-general. Others reacted differently. "We were flattered that Bush wanted him," recalls Fred Eckhard, the UN spokesman. "Sergio was one of us. And he wasn't a turncoat. He stood for what we stood for."

The human rights community was not at all split. They immediately voiced their displeasure. Michael Posner, the executive director of the Lawyers Committee for Human Rights, lamented Annan's choice. "It suggests that the human rights job is a part-time job that can be done from Baghdad," he said. "That's not the signal we want to be sending."[50] Like almost everyone who knew Vieira de Mello, human rights advocates were sure that he would stay well beyond four months. The human rights groups jointly approached Annan with a list of possible replacement high commissioners. Vieira de Mello was stung. He felt they had never fully trusted him and were using his Iraq assignment as an excuse to nudge him out.

After Annan publicly announced his appointment on May 27, Vieira de Mello received dozens of e-mails from friends and colleagues around the world. He would later write to a colleague that "I was never entirely convinced if it was congratulations or commiserations I should have been offered."[51] Perhaps none of the e-mails was as stark as that from Mari Alkatiri, the prime minister of East Timor, who recalls writing a two-line note that read: "Sergio, be careful. Iraq is not East Timor." Secretary of State Powell telephoned and told him that the resolution's vagueness offered him an opportunity to give the UN a strong role in Iraq. When Vieira de Mello said that he had every intention of seizing upon the ambiguity, Powell laughed and said, "Well, if you go too far, we'll let you know."[52]

On May 29, the UN's new Iraq envoy sent out a group e-mail to thirteen close friends who had written to him. He thanked them in five languages for their notes and wrote that he was going to Iraq "with mixed feelings." On the one hand he wanted to do what was "best for the UN." But on the other he was "conscious of the many pitfalls, of my own ignorance and of the Security Council's mandate ambiguities" and "sad that my personal life again comes last, yet energized and inspired by Carolina."[53]

Even if he was conflicted about going to Iraq himself, he was pleased that the UN had been summoned. The deployment of the UN mission was proof of America's dependence on the organization. He told a *Wall Street Journal* reporter: "After cursing the UN or calling it irrelevant or comparing it to the League of Nations and stating loud and clear that the United States would pay no attention to the Security Council in the future if it didn't support the United States in its war against Saddam Hussein, the United States very quickly came back, even though they will never admit it, in search for international legitimacy, realizing that they can't really act on their own too long."[54] He continued: "I don't have a crystal ball, but my guess is that the U.S. and the UK will realize that this is too big, that building a democratic Iraq is not simple . . . and as a result they have every interest in encouraging others who are seen to be more impartial, independent, more palatable to join in and help create these new institutions. . . . We will then look back at the war as an interlude that will have lasted two or three months, that was indeed shocking and did shake us a great deal, but nothing more than that: an accident rather than a new pattern . . . and I touch wood when I say that."[55]

Nineteen

"YOU CAN'T HELP PEOPLE FROM A DISTANCE"

Vieira de Mello, bodyguard Gamal Ibrahim (right), and UN spokesman Ahmad Fawzi (left) at the Baghdad airport, June 2, 2003.

"A Team"

Vieira de Mello knew little about Iraq but a lot about helping societies that were emerging from tyranny and conflict. He understood that, on such a short mission, it was even more essential than usual to assemble the best possible team. Before leaving New York, he asked Rick Hooper, the American Arabic-speaking political analyst, and Salman Ahmed, an American who had been Lakhdar Brahimi's aide in Afghanistan, to work with his own special assistant Jonathan Prentice to assemble an "A team." "I want Arabic speakers," he said, "and I want my team members to be with me when I get off the plane." He needed to establish momentum right away.

Among the Arabic speakers he tapped were Nadia Younes, an Egyptian who had been Bernard Kouchner's chief of staff in Kosovo; Jamal Benomar, a Moroccan lawyer who before joining the UN had been jailed for eight years in his country as a human rights activist; Ahmad Fawzi, an Egyptian who had been Brahimi's spokesman during Afghanistan's Bonn Conference; Mona Rishmawi, a Palestinian human rights officer; and Jean-Sélim Kanaan, a French-Egyptian veteran of Kosovo who had a reputation as a master logistician and acute political operator. Among the others he brought, in addition to Prentice and Ahmed, were Fiona Watson, a Scottish political officer who had been working on Iraq issues from New York; Carole Ray, his British secretary in Geneva; and Alain Chergui and Gamal Ibrahim, who had been his bodyguards in East Timor. Because Vieira de Mello offered his friend Dennis McNamara a seat on his plane, McNamara found himself named UNHCR special envoy to Iraq.

Vieira de Mello was not one to take no for an answer. He had made an art form out of teasing, flattering, and pressuring to get what he wanted. When Lyn Manuel, who had been his secretary in New York and East Timor, initially declined his offer, on the grounds that her daughter was getting married, he kept pushing. When she finally accepted, her supervisor in New York refused, but Vieira de Mello got Iqbal Riza, Annan's chief of staff, to overrule him. He believed that UN staff should by definition be readily available to undertake any field mission at any time, in much the same way he was. And he used the same argument with junior and senior staff that he knew Annan would have made to him, had he refused the job: The mission was important for Iraq and for the UN, and their services were indispensable. Vieira de Mello had accepted the job on May 22, 2003, the day Resolution 1483 had been passed. He stopped off in Cyprus for briefings on June 1, and would fly with his team to Baghdad the following day.

He knew that his most important choice would be his political adviser. On the advice of Riza, he met in Cyprus with Ghassan Salamé, a former Lebanese minister of culture and professor of international relations at the prestigious Institut d'études politiques (Sciences Po) in Paris. Salamé had studied the politics and history of Iraq and had long been acquainted with leading Iraqi opposition officials and intellectuals, as well as members of the Ba'ath regime. His book, *Democracy without Democrats,* and his occasional columns in the pan-Arab daily newspaper *al-Hayat* had been banned in Iraq, but his name was known.

At their meeting in Cyprus, Vieira de Mello said: "I don't know much about Iraq. I need to pick your brain on who's who, and how the country is moving." Salamé warned that the influence of Iraq's neighbors was going to increase and not diminish in the coming months, and he said that by deciding to demobilize an army of more than 400,000 soldiers, the Americans had committed "hari kari."[1] After two hours of discussion it was clear that they clicked. Salamé had opposed the war, but he wanted to do what he could to help the UN end the Coalition's occupation.

On the flight from Cyprus to Baghdad on June 2, Vieira de Mello wore a finely tailored gray suit, a crisp starched white shirt, and an emerald green Ferragamo tie ("the color of Islam," he said), given to him on his birthday by Larriera, who was getting her paperwork sorted and would join him on June 15. He had grown very sentimental. In his briefcase he carried the paper hearts that he had cut up in East Timor and sprinkled on the floor on the night they got back together in 2001.

He characteristically used the plane ride to study his only real instructions from the major powers: Resolution 1483. He focused on its provision "stressing the right of the Iraqi people freely to determine their own political future." The resolution did not stipulate what the UN would do to make that happen. After exercising absolute power in East Timor, he was unaccustomed to the helping verbs that defined his functions. In Iraq it would not be up to him to devise laws or political structures; he would "encourage" and "promote" measures to improve Iraqi welfare. This meant that he would make inroads only insofar as the Coalition accepted his advice. "I think I could just as easily 'encourage' progress from Geneva," he joked.

The UN mandate was awkward to say the least. Instead of negotiating with the local government, as UN officials usually did in countries where they deployed, his team would have to negotiate with the invaders, who had dismantled local structures. He knew that a large part of what he was there to do was to stress publicly and repeatedly that the day of Iraqi self-rule was near.

Before the group left Cyprus, Prentice had printed up a dozen copies of the draft statement he would deliver on the tarmac upon landing. On the plane each UN official offered his or her suggested changes, and Vieira de Mello incorporated half a dozen of them. The statement seemed relatively pro forma, and some on the plane were puzzled by his perfectionism. "For a three-minute speech, it seemed excessive to scrutinize and rescrutinize every clause," remembers Fawzi, the spokesman. "But for Sergio it had to be just so." Well practiced at descending into foreign lands, he had long understood what American planners had not adequately grasped before invading Iraq: Outsiders almost never get a second chance to make a first impression.

When the flight touched down in Baghdad, he disembarked from the plane. He had expected a large turnout, as the "return of the UN" was being widely hailed in the region and beyond. But when he stepped into the Baghdad heat, about a dozen journalists were on the tarmac to greet him. UN officials later learned that Paul Bremer had held his own press conference a short time before their arrival. After all of the intensity of the previous weeks, when the UN officials got off the plane and saw so few journalists, one recalls, "It felt like a bust." As he disembarked, Vieira de Mello called Larriera in New York and insisted she turn on the television to watch his first press conference.

He spoke as meticulously as he dressed. He tucked his prepared text into his breast pocket and gave the appearance of speaking off the cuff: "The day when Iraqis govern themselves must come quickly," he declared. "In the coming days, I intend to listen intensively to what the Iraqi people have to say."[2]

But when it came to reaching out to "the Iraqi people," he was unsure where to start. He asked Prentice to pester Salamé, who was back in Paris, and to call him every day, sometimes several times a day. Vieira de Mello too would call. "Where are you?" he would ask. "Why aren't you here?" Salamé explained that he could not simply zip off to Baghdad for a month. He was not a career UN civil servant who was accustomed to routinely disappearing on a moment's notice. Vieira de Mello was unforgiving: "I need you. Iraq needs you." Salamé succumbed to his new boss's charm, but then the UN administrators failed him. "People keep calling me from all over the UN system," he complained to Vieira de Mello. "Each of them has told me that they know I am going to Baghdad and need my details. But for all of the phone calls, I still don't have an airplane ticket!" "Welcome to the UN," said Vieira de Mello.

Salamé ended up arriving in Baghdad on June 9, exactly one week after the rest of the A team. It did not take long for the two men, who would become inseparable, to begin bantering. "Ghassan, straighten your tie," Vieira de Mello would rib his unkempt adviser before their high-level meetings. Salamé smoked two cigars each day, and his new boss urged him to stop. "You don't want to die young like my father," he said. One month into the mission Salamé, whom Vieira de Mello had nicknamed "the *wazir*," or minister, made motions to depart. "Of course you're not thinking of leaving," Vieira de Mello said. "The universities in Paris don't start until October, so we will leave together, *wazir*."

One vital source of experience in the country was the UN humanitarian coordinator in Iraq, Ramiro Lopes da Silva. Lopes da Silva had lived in Baghdad from 2002 until just before the Coalition invasion, and he had led the first UN mission back to Iraq on May 1. He had been a member of Vieira de Mello's ten-day assessment mission in Kosovo in 1999, and as native Portuguese-speakers, they shared a cultural bond. There was so much work to be done that the labor could be divided naturally between humanitarian and reconstruction tasks, which Lopes da Silva managed, and political tasks, which Vieira de Mello oversaw. Lopes da Silva would continue coordinating the work of the humanitarian agencies and would develop a plan for liquidating the Oil for Food Program.[3] Vieira de Mello, who preferred high politics to "grocery delivery," would work with the Coalition to try to speed the end of the occupation. He had somehow to earn the trust of the Iraqis and develop a strong working relationship with the Coalition. He knew that suspicious Iraqis, who were angry about a spike in violent crime and the seeming permanence of American rule, would not necessarily see these tasks as complementary.

PLAYING IN THEIR GARDEN

When Vieira de Mello arrived in East Timor in 1999, the Timorese had been hugely grateful to the UN for having staged the referendum on independence. But when he landed in Iraq, he knew that Saddam Hussein had demonized the UN weapons inspectors and the Oil for Food Program. The inspectors were cast as meddling agents of Washington. And the Oil for Food officials, although technically offering humanitarian succor to needy citizens, were symbols of the UN sanctions that had crippled the Iraqi economy. He was aware that he was inheriting the sins of his predecessors. For all of the disadvantages of having a past in Iraq, however, there were also advantages. While the Coalition continued to rely disproportionately on Iraqi exiles for intelligence, the UN had three thousand Iraqi staff members who had remained enmeshed in the country even during the invasion. He thought he would have an easier time than Bremer in getting a read on the Iraqi street. Unlike in East Timor, he did not have to scrounge up offices, computers, vehicles, or translators. He and his team moved into offices in the Canal Hotel, a white, three-story former hotel training college that had been converted into UN headquarters in the 1980s. Trimmed with the UN's trademark light blue paint, and located in the eastern suburbs of Baghdad, the site was well known to Iraqis.

He set out to make the Canal familiar to the Americans as well. On June 3, his first full day in Baghdad, he ventured to the four-and-a-half-square-mile fortified district along the Tigris that had already become known as the Green Zone. When the U.S. Army's Third Infantry Division fought its way into downtown Baghdad, it had chosen Saddam Hussein's seat of power as the Coalition's own and converted the modern Ba'ath party headquarters, the National Assembly, and the 258-room Republican Palace into the Coalition's offices.[4] Concrete blast walls and rolls of concertina razor wire were erected around the eight-mile perimeter, and sandbagged U.S. machine-gun posts warded off intruders.

As U.S. soldiers inspected the badges of officials in the UN convoy, Vieira de Mello observed the long, wending line of Iraqis queuing up outside the American barricades to apply for work and to register complaints. Before they were allowed to enter, they were patted down, some roughly. He shook his head. "There go the hearts and minds," he muttered to Prentice.

There was much that was off-putting about the Green Zone. During the evening Americans danced in the disco of the Rashid Hotel, where Hussein's son Uday had once held vicious court, and gift shops would soon sell T-shirts depicting Uncle Sam daring insurgents to BRING IT ON![5] Several thousand internationals (mainly Americans but including some British, Australians, Dutch, Japanese, Poles, and Spanish who were part of the Coalition) shuttled among former Iraqi government buildings adorned with murals of Babylonian glory. They strolled along boulevards lined with eucalyptus and palm trees, wearing safari vests, combat boots, and cargo pants. And they slept in prefabricated housing containers. Their phones carried New York (914) area codes, meaning that when the Iraqi phone system was restored, reaching an Iraqi would carry the price of an overseas call.[6] The manicured lawns and sparse traffic inside the Green Zone presented a study in contrasts with the congested chaos of the unpoliced urban gridlock outside the walls. Even Coalition staff had begun to refer to their island of residence and work as "The Bubble."[7] In a phone conversation with Bernard Kouchner, his successor in administering Kosovo, Vieira de Mello would marvel at the Americans' insulation in the Green Zone. "You know the way they are," he told Kouchner. "It is just like Camp Bondsteel in Kosovo. They have created their own wooden town. They stay in their barracks. They leave in armored cars. They wear flak jackets. They barely go out and when they do they return as quickly as possible."

When Vieira de Mello and his UN team entered the palace where Bremer had set up shop, they saw clean-scrubbed Americans emerging from offices marked for various ministries. This was the first time he really comprehended that the Coalition considered itself the actual government of Iraq. Not wanting to alienate Bremer from the start, he mainly listened, holding back his own views. He had expected to hear the details of Bremer's plan for devolving power, but he quickly realized that Coalition officials had no such plan. They were improvising.

Bremer's top American adviser was Ryan Crocker, the Arabist whom Vieira de Mello had befriended in Beirut in 1982. "Sergio is as good as it gets not only in the UN, but in international diplomacy," Crocker had told Bremer before their first meeting. "He is the personification of what the UN could be and should be but rarely is." Bremer would make up his own mind. "He didn't take my word for it," Crocker recalls. "He had to see for himself."

Bremer explained that he saw phase one of the transition as the uprooting of the old regime and the establishment of law and order and basic services. "We expect to turn the corner in the next month or so," he said, seemingly unaware that the wholesale evisceration of the old regime that he had undertaken was at odds with the establishment of law and order. They would then proceed to phase two, which included economic reconstruction, job creation, and the formation of democratic bodies. On the all-important political side, Bremer said, he intended to appoint a group of Iraqis to a constitutional conference, where they would draft a new constitution that would be submitted to Iraqis for a referendum. Vieira de Mello winced at the idea that the constitution would be drafted before general elections were held, as it would thus seem like an illegitimate American charter. Bremer said that he would also appoint a "consultative committee" composed of representatives from all religious, political, and social backgrounds. This committee in turn would appoint Iraqi technocrats to the different ministries to work with the American and British ministers in charge.[8] Bremer was impressed with what he saw of Vieira de Mello. "The Iraqis were concerned, and we were concerned, about whether the UN would play a helpful role or not," the American remembers. "The thing that pleased me is that Sergio said he wouldn't work against us and he wouldn't stand off. He wanted to work with us."

This didn't sit well with some of Vieira de Mello's own staff. After the meeting in the Green Zone, he returned to the Canal Hotel to discuss the UN's options with his staff. Benomar, one of his political advisers, insisted that the Coalition was in violation of Resolution 1483 because it had taken over the governing functions of Iraq. He urged Vieira de Mello to press for the immediate creation of an Iraqi government. Marwan Ali, a Palestinian UN political aide who had attended university in Iraq, complained about the vagueness of the Security Council resolution, which offered no guidance on how the UN should interact with either the Americans or the Iraqis. "It's constructive vagueness," Vieira de Mello attempted. "There's no such thing as constructive vagueness in Iraq," Ali countered. "It's just vague vagueness." Most members of the team recognized that the CPA had established facts on the ground that the UN would not be able to alter. The majority felt that the only way the UN could make a meaningful difference in Iraq would be not to denounce the Coalition but to persuade it to alter its approach. Vieira de Mello sided with the pragmatists. "We can't just sit at the Canal Hotel and do nothing," he said. "You can't help people from a distance."

In his meetings with American and British officials, he never focused on whether the Coalition should have been in Iraq in the first place. "Sergio didn't bother himself with whether the war was right or wrong," says Prentice. "The war was a fact. The occupation was a fact. You've got two choices when you have those facts: Either you can try to help the Iraqi people out of the mess and urge a swift end to the occupation. Or you can take the moral high ground and turn your back on it." Throughout his career Vieira de Mello had often spoken of the importance of "black boxing" intentions. "By taking the Americans at their word, and then making them abide by those words," he told colleagues, "you can create leverage." This was what he had done with the Khmer Rouge in Cambodia and with the Serbs in Bosnia. It was also what the UN had done with Indonesia when Jakarta had agreed to a referendum in East Timor and then been forced to stand by the results.

On his third night in Baghdad, Vieira de Mello had dinner with John Sawers, the British diplomat who served as Bremer's deputy. Since it was still a relatively calm time, the two men sat out on the terrace in the open air, eating steaks and drinking Iraqi beer late into the evening. Vieira de Mello's adult experience in the Islamic world had been confined to his tours of Sudan in 1973–74 and Lebanon in 1981–83. He spoke fluent English, French, Italian, Portuguese, and Spanish and mediocre Tetum (the Timorese dialect), but he spoke hardly a word of Arabic. Sawers noted Vieira de Mello's self-consciousness about his linguistic handicap. "Here was one of the greatest linguists in the history of the UN system," recalls Sawers, "and he could barely say hello and good-bye in Arabic. He was not pleased."

Vieira de Mello knew that most UN officials who had amassed Middle East experience had also acquired baggage. He consoled himself that as an outsider he might bring fresh eyes to the country's challenges. His main asset wasn't his Iraq-specific knowledge, but his problem-solving experience and his war-tested ability to charm thugs. Carina Perelli, the head of the UN Electoral Assistance Division, called him an *"encantador de serpientes,"* a mesmerizing charmer of even the most poisonous snakes. While dining with Sawers, Vieira de Mello offered a comparative perspective, speaking at length about what he took to be the lesson of East Timor. "The Timorese were okay with the UN in charge for a certain, brief period of time, but at a certain point we had to switch to a support role," he said. "You'll have to do the same." In the early weeks of his time in Iraq, when Vieira de Mello had a suggestion to make, he would forward it to Sawers. "If Bremer thinks these are British ideas rather than UN ideas," he liked to say, "they are far more likely to be accepted!" Sawers suggested that the UN co-locate with the Americans and the British in the Green Zone. But Vieira de Mello dismissed the idea, saying, "My instincts are to keep a degree of distance from the Coalition. And that will require some physical distance."

Nadia Younes, his chief of staff, managed the UN's day-to-day ties with the Coalition. At the first large meeting between midlevel U.S. and UN officials in the Green Zone, Younes passed around copies of UN Resolution 1483, and the group went over the text line by line. The Americans looked flummoxed. "What does 'encourage' mean?" a U.S. official asked. "We don't know," Younes replied. "You wrote the thing!" Her colleague Benomar remembers, "The CPA made it clear that it expected the UN to issue a press release from time to time applauding the Coalition's efforts. They would do everything and we would clap." It would take many more meetings for Coalition officials to see the UN role as anything more than either cosmetic or confrontational. For Bremer the resolution was useful because it made clear that there was only one ruler of Iraq: "We were the occupying authority. We were the sovereign. Under international law you are either sovereign or you are not. It's like being pregnant. Under 1483 the role that Sergio and the UN could play was limited. They were there to help us."

While Vieira de Mello soon managed to win Bremer's respect (if never his full trust), other U.S. officials remained suspicious of the UN. In late June Vieira de Mello was stopped at a Coalition checkpoint on the airport road. Alain Chergui, who was part of his team of bodyguards, told a U.S. soldier that under international rules UN vehicles were not to be checked. The young soldier refused to let the UN convoy pass. "Do you know who is in the car?" Chergui said, frustrated. "No, and I don't care," the soldier replied. Chergui called Patrick Kennedy, Bremer's chief of staff, who agreed to intervene. But Chergui got nowhere when he told the soldier who was on the line. "Is he civilian?" the soldier asked. Chergui nodded. "Then I don't give a shit." When Ibrahim, Vieira de Mello's more hot-tempered bodyguard, began to pick a fight with another one of the Coalition soldiers, the special representative finally stepped out of the car and placed a call to Bremer, who reached somebody in the military chain of command, who eventually ordered the convoy through. On subsequent occasions when the UN bodyguards (several of whom were French and thus believed the Americans were deliberately hostile) ended up in quarrels, Chergui told his colleagues

to muzzle their fury. "You have to stay cool, or we will impair Sergio's job
for silly reasons," he said. "The Americans don't want us here to begin with.
We are playing in their garden."

The mistrust was mutual. Almost all UN staff had opposed the U.S.-led
invasion. They thought that the Coalition staff, who were vetted by Rumsfeld's office at the Pentagon, were frighteningly young and inexperienced.
Most were Republicans, and many dreamed aloud of turning Iraq into a
free market laboratory. A growing number had adopted Bremer's dress code,
trudging around in khakis, blue blazers, and desert combat boots. While two-
thirds of Vieira de Mello's closest advisers spoke Arabic, very few in Bremer's
senior circle did.[9]

Jeff Davie, a colonel in the Australian Defense Forces who served as Vieira
de Mello's military adviser, experienced this mutual suspicion firsthand. When
Davie first reached Baghdad, his suitcases carrying his regular Australian military uniform lagged behind, and he wore civilian clothes. UN officials embraced him, as he provided invaluable insight into the Coalition, of which
Australia was a member. But ten days into his posting, his Australian khakis
arrived, and he began wearing them to work, along with his blue beret. UN
staff were horrified. "Suddenly they saw a Coalition soldier emerging out of
the office next to Sergio's. I looked like a fifth columnist," he recalls. "They
couldn't believe Sergio would hire somebody like me." The reception was
no warmer over in the Green Zone. He remembers, "The Coalition said,
'You're wearing a blue beret; we can't trust you,' and the UN staff said, 'You're
wearing a Coalition uniform; we can't trust you.'"

LAW AND ORDER GAP

Looking back, it is almost impossible to recall the brief period, between early
April and late June 2003, when Iraq was a relatively peaceful place. The two
months after Saddam Hussein's statue was pulled to the ground by American
soldiers brought some joyous scenes of Iraqis celebrating the toppling of the
tyrant and some traumatic scenes in which families located the remains of
missing relatives. But mainly those two months brought creeping uncertainty
and shock that the Coalition wasn't more organized.

The Baghdad that Vieira de Mello and his team entered was nowhere near
as dangerous as Khmer Rouge territory in 1992, besieged Sarajevo in 1993,

or war-torn Kosovo in May 1999. The Iraqis that Vieira de Mello met were worried about theft, unemployment, lack of electricity, and the indignity of a foreign occupation, but they were not worried about an imminent civil war or suicide bomb attacks. A nascent insurgency was afoot, but it was Coalition forces who were being targeted, and it initially seemed as though the attacks were a last gasp by the prior regime. In a few short months the attacks on "soft targets" in Baghdad would grow so frequent that the city outside the small Green Zone would become known as the Red Zone. But that was not the Iraq of June 2003.

Typically the head of a UN mission (here, Vieira de Mello) automatically assumed the role of "designated security official" and bore the ultimate responsibility for staff safety. But since Lopes da Silva already carried the title from having run the UN humanitarian mission before the war, and since Vieira de Mello would be on the road constantly and was to remain in Iraq only until September 30, Lopes da Silva retained the security reins. "I'm here for four months," Vieira de Mello told his colleague. "Don't try to get me involved in that!"

The biggest concern preoccupying Iraqis and internationals alike was crime, which was not unusual after the fall of a regime.[10] Vieira de Mello and Lopes da Silva were worried that UN staff would be robbed or accidentally caught near Coalition personnel who came under fire. "Our biggest fear was 'wrong place, wrong time' incidents," Lopes da Silva remembers.

While Lopes da Silva offered the last word on security within the mission, Robert Adolph, an ex–U.S. Marine, was day-to-day security coordinator. One of Adolph's first tasks was to find secure accommodation for UN staff in Baghdad, which proved difficult. Most hotels seemed infiltrated with shady characters from the past regime or woefully exposed. The first batch of UN arrivals had slept under their desks at the Canal and then moved out into a "tent city" in the field adjoining UN headquarters. On May 28 Adolph had announced that UN staff were permitted to leave the Canal premises and take up rooms in one of a dozen hotels that his team had cleared. It was assumed that UN staff would live in hotels only temporarily. Once security improved and crime subsided, the staff would likely rent their own private apartments or houses as they had in other UN missions.

Vieira de Mello was given a suite on one of the top floors of the Sheraton Hotel, where the elevators rarely worked, and he felt vulnerable. "How would

I make it down all these stairs if the hotel were hit?" he asked Chergui, his bodyguard. "It is insecure and insecurable," Chergui said. Vieira de Mello insisted that he be moved to the less trafficked Cedar Hotel, which he was in late June.[11]

In Saddam Hussein's day Iraq had been virtually crime free, and the UN base at the Canal Hotel, guarded by Iraqi diplomatic police, had been safe. When Lopes da Silva returned to his old office on May 1, he had found the Iraqi guards gone and U.S. troops from the Second Armored Cavalry Regiment using the Canal as their command headquarters. He was told that back in April, in the wake of the U.S. takeover, local looters had pounced on the then-deserted Canal and begun ransacking it, stealing cars, desks, computers, air conditioners, and all else they could pilfer. U.S. soldiers had ended up taking over the hotel because a group of Iraqi UN staff had emerged from hiding and hailed them to come and stop the rampage. With the return of the UN's humanitarian and Oil for Food Program staff in May and the arrival of Vieira de Mello's small political team in June, the American presence had been reduced to a light shield around the perimeter of the compound. Unarmed Iraqis manned the front gates. Iraqis entered and exited all day, meeting UN staff in the cafeteria for tea and coffee. It was as easy to enter as the U.S. embassy in Beirut had been two decades before. As was the case with most halfhearted security measures, the UN guards inconvenienced without deterring or impeding.

Veteran security officers were concerned that if a bomb aimed at Coalition forces went off nearby, it might shatter some of the Canal Hotel's many glass windows. Indeed, five days before Vieira de Mello's arrival, Coalition forces near the Canal had exploded ordnance that broke several. When a building survey revealed that some 1,260 square meters of the Canal's outer glass was exposed, the UN Security Management Team (SMT) resolved to cover up the windows with blast-resistant film. But because it was not clear which administrative budget should cover the expense, the matter was deferred.[12] Lopes da Silva and Adolph also found that the perimeter fencing around the complex had numerous breaches and ordered the construction of a wall to enclose the Canal. The wall would be thirteen feet high with spiking on top. But because elaborate UN rules required an open bidding process, it would take six weeks to award the construction contract.[13]

Iraq's law-and-order problem grew more severe by the day. Because of his de-Ba'athification and demobilization decrees, Bremer had alienated the very Iraqi forces that might have maintained security. Because Secretary Rumsfeld had sent in too few U.S. troops to control Iraq's borders and blanket the country, foreign insurgents passed easily in and out of Iraq from Iran and Syria. And because of the absence of support in the UN Security Council for the war, other UN member states did not chip in postwar stability forces or civilian police in the way they had done for the peacekeeping missions in Cambodia, Bosnia, Kosovo, and East Timor. The ministries that kept Iraqi garbage collected, buses running, and electricity intact were now run by American and British citizens who neither spoke Arabic nor had ever managed such tasks in the United States or the U.K. And the unemployed Iraqi ex–army officers, who had been assured by Jay Garner that they would retain their jobs, felt betrayed by the Coalition. Since the Coalition had no Iraqi security partner, it had to build a brand-new security force from scratch. And now it had a new concern: The soldiers in the old army had kept their guns.

Vieira de Mello urged Bremer to scale back the de-Ba'athification edict and to meet the needs of the Iraqi army veterans. He reminded the U.S. administrator that all over the world UN officials had amassed experience setting up programs to reintegrate demobilized soldiers. Most promisingly, in one meeting he told Bremer that the top adviser to Javier Solana, the secretary-general of the European Union, had written to the UN to make an as-yet-informal offer of Spanish civil guards, Italian carabinieri, and French gendarmerie. Instead of eagerly seizing the opportunity, which might have lightened the U.S. load, Bremer said that if the Europeans wanted to contribute police, they would have to place them at the disposal of the Coalition.[14]

Each time Vieira de Mello visited Bremer in the Green Zone, it had grown more fortified. Sandbags piled up around the outer entrance, and the lines of Iraqis attempting to get inside twisted farther into the distance. At the Canal Hotel, by contrast, Iraqis could just walk up to the guard booth and request entry. If somebody inside vouched for the visitor, he or she was ushered inside and steered to the appropriate UN staffer, who would hear his or her complaint or request. Iraq was a country riddled by grievances, past and present. Once it became known that the UN (unlike the CPA) would not

A former Iraqi soldier outside the Green Zone, June 18, 2003.
A U.S. military spokesman confirmed that U.S. soldiers
killed two Iraqis during the demonstration.

turn Iraqi petitioners away, ousted Ba'ath party members, demobilized officers, and relatives of those detained by Coalition forces began gathering at
the Canal gate in the hopes of securing redress.

On June 18 some two thousand former Iraqi officers gathered outside the
Green Zone to protest the disbanding of the army. While the protest raged,
a small group of officers peeled off and made their way to the Canal Hotel
in the hopes of convincing Vieira de Mello to help them get reinstated. He
promised he would serve as an intermediary with Bremer. But Bremer rejected Vieira de Mello's appeals, and when Salamé relayed the news to the
officers, they turned and walked away from the Canal. "There go the future
insurgents," Benomar said to Salamé, who nodded. "Yes," he said. "I see bullets in their eyes."

LEARNING TOUR

In order to be of actual use to Bremer and to Iraq, Vieira de Mello felt he
needed to learn a lot in a hurry. In his early weeks he deliberately refrained
from speaking to the media. When he finally gave his first major press conference on June 24, 2003, he explained, "You may have noticed that over
the past three weeks I have been rather quiet. That is because I have been

listening, traveling, and learning." Mortified that Bremer had ordered de-Ba'athification and demobilization after spending so little time in Iraq, Vieira de Mello was determined to look before he leaped. When he set out to learn, he did not learn on the fly. He developed a game plan that would enable him to glean the needs and interests of the Iraqis systematically. "Okay, who am I meeting today?" he would ask his staff in the morning. They had divided Iraqi society into categories: political parties, professional associations, non-governmental organizations, human rights groups, lawyers, judges, women's groups, and religious groups. Once he had made his way through the list of Baghdad contacts, he announced, "Okay, now I'm heading out to the regions." Influential Iraqis were identified in Basra, Mosul, Erbil, Sulaimaniya, Hilla, and Najaf. "Bremer didn't have time to talk to people," Salamé recalls. "Because Resolution 1483 gave the UN no real tasks, we had all the time in the world to listen."

At the time Vieira de Mello launched his learning tour, the Americans had little contact with Iraq's religious leaders. His political officers believed that the UN could valuably contribute to stability if they could enlist the support of the powerful clerics, especially Shiite cleric Ayatollah Ali al-Sistani. Salamé sent out feelers through Dr. Aquila al-Hashimi, a powerful Shiite Muslim in Baghdad who spoke fluent French and English and seemed likely to be named Iraq's first ambassador to the UN. When she confirmed that her uncle, an influential cleric in Najaf, was willing to help arrange a meeting with al-Sistani, Vieira de Mello knew he had scored a coup. "Ya'llah!" he exclaimed.

The politics of the June 28 trip were complex. "There are three forces in Najaf," Salamé said, "the pope, Sistani; the black sheep, Moqtada al-Sadr; and the politician, Mohammed Baqir al-Hakim. Ideally we would make three trips to Najaf." Even Vieira de Mello had his limits, and he couldn't imagine driving the two and a half hours there and back on three separate occasions. "Okay, we'll meet with all three," he said, "but we'll have lunch with none of them." They dined with al-Hashimi's uncle, Sheikh Mohammed al-Faridhi, who had organized the visit.

After meeting briefly with al-Faridhi at his home in Najaf, the delegation headed into a meeting that Vieira de Mello knew would be the most important of his time in Iraq. Al-Sistani brought a political agenda to the meeting that surprised his UN visitors. In a soft voice hardly more audible than a whisper, al-Sistani said the Americans had no business privatizing state-owned enterprises, as that was the job of a sovereign government. And he wanted the UN to act more autonomously from the Coalition. He said the organization should condemn a recent U.S. helicopter attack at the Syrian-Iraqi border. Vieira de Mello promised to look into the incident.

The most important part of the discussion concerned the future Iraqi constitution. Al-Sistani said that he was planning to issue a fatwa that said that only Iraqis could write the founding charter. This was directed at Noah Feldman, the Arabic-speaking professor of constitutional and Islamic law at New York University who was said to be drafting Iraq's constitution for the Coalition. *"Samahet al Sayyid,"* Vieira de Mello said, using the Arabic expression for "your eminence," which he had rehearsed on the drive from Baghdad, "I understand you want the constitution written by Iraqis—" Al-Sistani cut him off. "I didn't say the constitution should be written by Iraqis," the cleric said sharply, clutching the hand of Marwan Ali, who was translating. "I said it should be written by *elected* Iraqis." Vieira de Mello nodded and said that he had learned the same lesson in East Timor.

Without realizing the significance of what he had said, Vieira de Mello had set himself up in direct opposition to the Coalition, which planned to appoint a committee of its own to draft the constitution. In one respect, his instinct to stand up to Bremer was the right one, as the Coalition was paying too little heed to just how discredited any U.S.-picked drafters of the constitution would be. But with his casual statement, the UN special representative had also implicitly raised expectations that elections could be held quickly, which was technically impossible. Al-Sistani would frequently refer to his meeting with Vieira de Mello when he insisted that only the decisions of elected Iraqis should be recognized as law. Bremer would be incensed. "It would take us months to undo the damage that Sergio did in that one meeting," he recalls.

After meeting with Sistani, Vieira de Mello was shown the sacred shrine where Imam Ali was buried. "I want to go into the mausoleum," he said to Salamé, who shook his head, explaining that a bloody confrontation had occurred there a few weeks before. With the same enthusiasm with which he had snapped photos of the Khmer Rouge, Vieira de Mello pleaded, "No, Ghassan, we must. I may not get back here again." Salamé asked al-Faridhi whether they might enter the mosque's outer mausoleum, but Vieira de

Mello pressed, "I want to go inside." Salamé recalls al-Faridhi turning white with panic and begging them to leave quietly. A large group of Iraqis was gathering around the mysterious assemblage of foreigners. Some had begun murmuring to one another, "What are the foreigners doing here?" "Out now, Sergio," Salamé said, firmly. "Why?" he asked. "Out now," Salamé said. "Sergio was discovering the world of Iraq," recalls a member of his UN team. "From an intellectual point of view, he wanted to see everything, and sometimes he was oblivious to the political sensitivities."

The UN team enjoyed a relatively relaxed lunch with al-Fahridi, then proceeded to their meeting with Moqtada al-Sadr, the twenty-something radical who was amassing a large and violent following and whom Bremer was shunning. When Vieira de Mello entered, al-Sadr sat on the ground chain-smoking, along with two of his religious aides. Vieira de Mello offered his usual introduction, describing the UN's impartiality and expressing hope that the organization could help end the occupation that he knew al-Sadr opposed. Al-Sadr looked at him listlessly, refusing to respond. When the Iraqi finally spoke, he made plain that he knew nothing about the UN. "Can Muslim countries be members of the UN?" he asked. When Salamé said yes, he asked for examples, and Salamé told him his own country had been a founding member of the UN. Again al-Sadr lapsed into silence. After several more unsatisfying and awkward exchanges, the UN delegation got up to leave.

In their final meeting in Najaf, the UN officials met with Mohammed Baqir al-Hakim. In the 1960s al-Hakim and Mohammed Baqir al-Sadr, the father-in-law of Moqtada, had founded the modern Shiite Islamic political movement in Iraq. When Mohammed Baqir al-Sadr was executed in 1980, al-Hakim fled to Iran and formed the Supreme Council for the Islamic Revolution in Iraq (SCIRI). He returned to Iraq in May 2003 and was denounced by Moqtada, who did not believe that he had a claim to Shiite political leadership.[15] This meeting went far better, as al-Hakim was warm and personable. He explained Iraqi impatience with the Coalition by analogizing Iraq's occupation to a cat that a man acquired in order to free his house of mice. "He got a cat, which got rid of the mouse," al-Hakim said. But then, unfortunately, "the cat wouldn't leave."[16]

On their drive back to Baghdad, Salamé congratulated Vieira de Mello on an impressive day establishing the UN's distinct credentials, and he told him that their meeting with al-Sistani could prove important. "You know you made a big statement there," he said, referring to his endorsement of al-Sistani's electoral ground rule. Vieira de Mello punched Salamé playfully and resorted to what was becoming his favorite quip: "You know, Ghassan, I don't want to become a Bremello!"

Three days after the meeting al-Sistani issued his fatwa saying he would not recognize the legitimacy of any constitution that was not written by an elected Iraqi assembly. He also said that the UN had agreed with him. Bremer asked Vieira de Mello to refute the cleric's claim as a misrepresentation of the UN position, but he refused, hoping that perhaps the Coalition would at least speed its election planning. In a note to a UN colleague soon thereafter, he sounded upbeat: "I feel confident that the UN will truly, as opposed to rhetorically, be able to play its 'vital role' in Iraq."[17]

POWER SHARING AND LEGITIMACY

Over the years he had found that Americans tended not to appreciate the importance of legitimacy. He saw the toll the U.S. occupation was taking on Iraqi morale. "You need to be sure to accommodate Iraqi pride and Iraqi trauma," he told Sawers.[18] Iraqi patience would last longer, he stressed, if people received tangible, material dividends from the Coalition. But the Americans and British were not offering impressive returns. Jean-Sélim Kanaan, one of Vieira de Mello's political aides, wrote letters to his wife, Laura Dolci-Kanaan, a UN official in Geneva, in which he reflected on the Americans he was encountering in the Green Zone:

> To see young fresh Americans sent from their virgin suburbs playing the sorcerer's apprentices on questions as significant as the systems of pension, the national distribution networks of wages or the ministerial reorganization . . . is somewhat surreal . . .
>
> We pass from the doors on which panels were quickly posted that announce triumphantly: "Minister of Health," "Minister of Transportation." Behind the door, one often finds seated a good American . . . He is the minister. It doesn't matter that within five meters from there the revolt thunders and that he has practically no contact with the men and women in his ministry of supervision.
>
> But how could he? As soon as he wants to take three steps, he must be

escorted by two overflowing vehicles of soldiers armed up to their teeth and often very nervous. He crosses the city without really seeing it . . . Iraq today is an occupied country, and poorly occupied."[19]

Kanaan, whose father was Egyptian and mother was French, had been able to read and write Arabic since he was a child, but he had never mastered spoken Arabic. He had been thrilled to earn a spot on the A team, but in his phone calls home he described his mounting horror at American unpreparedness. "In the UN we've screwed up a lot of times," Kanaan told his wife. "But for all of our mistakes in Bosnia and Kosovo, we were never *this* bad. The Americans had no plan. Absolutely no plan!"

Vieira de Mello shared Kanaan's horror at the Coalition's blunders, but he also saw that the Americans' lack of experience and competence created an opening for the UN. His team had genuine insight to offer on how to develop a power-sharing plan. "Iraqis need to know that they will get tangible, executive authority at the end of this first phase," Vieira de Mello told Coalition officials.[20]

The UN had a wealth of experience with elections, constitutions, and timetables for transitions. In their weekly meetings Vieira de Mello urged Bremer to begin planning for elections, which would take close to a year to organize. He appealed to him to present the Iraqi people with a transparent timeline that spelled out the process by which they would come to control their destinies. In East Timor he had come to regret his original failure to offer such a road map. He e-mailed Carina Perelli of the UN Electoral Assistance Division in New York and told her that he was pushing Bremer to launch a voter-registration drive, which would be "a tangible demonstration of intent by the CPA that its rhetoric about handing over sovereignty to a representative Iraqi government as soon as possible actually has substance."[21]

Seeing elections as a wedge into larger political influence for the UN, he asked Perelli to come to Baghdad to conduct a feasibility study. Most of the e-mail, which was copied to a variety of UN officials, was written in formal English, but knowing Perelli was in South America awaiting the birth of her niece, Vieira de Mello signed off in Spanish: *"No me vengas con el cuento de que tenías vacaciones programadas en Montevideo: yo tenía planeado pasar tres semanas en Rio . . . !"* (Don't come to me with the story of how you had time off planned in Montevideo: I had planned to spend three weeks in Rio . . . !) As was his wont, he followed up often to be sure Perelli would come quickly. "It will be a breezy 50 degrees (Celsius!) [122 Fahrenheit] or higher in Baghdad by the time you come," he wrote, "so you will need to wrap up warm."[22]

Bremer's political plans raised a wide assortment of red flags with Vieira de Mello. He remembered the hostility that his creation of a nonexecutive, consultative body had engendered in East Timor, which was a relatively homogeneous society in comparison to Iraq. If Bremer gave the Iraqis on his new advisory council titles without responsibilities, they would be seen as American puppets. If Bremer handpicked the members of the new body, the same could be true. Decisions of whom to include and exclude would have unforeseen consequences, and foreigners were never well placed to anticipate them. On the other hand, Vieira de Mello appreciated Bremer's predicament. Since it would take at least a year for Iraq to prepare for an election, and since the Security Council had put the Americans (and not the UN) in charge, Bremer saw it as his job to appoint some kind of Iraqi body quickly.

Vieira de Mello offered a range of suggestions. He urged Bremer to rename his "consultative committee" the Iraqi "provisional government." Bremer refused, but he eventually came around to the idea that Iraqis should not be relegated to the role of mere "advisers." Vieira de Mello convinced Bremer that "council" carried a more authoritative air than "committee." But that was not enough. "We need to signal executive powers," the UN special representative said. Salamé, the only native Arabic speaker in the room, leaped in. "We should put *hukm* in the name," Salamé said. In Arabic *hukuma* meant "government," which would give the impression that the body would have power of its own. "As soon as I heard it," Crocker recalls, "I thought, 'How come we didn't think of it ourselves?'" It was settled: The new body would be called *majlis al-hukm,* which was translated into English as "Governing Council."

Bremer sometimes changed his mind after consulting with Washington, and UN officials were not sure that the new name would stick. But at their next meeting with the CPA, Bremer began by asking, "When are we going to inaugurate the"—he pulled a slip of paper from his pocket and continued—"the *majlis al-hukm?*" Salamé winked at Vieira de Mello.

The functions of the Governing Council remained undefined. Vieira de Mello knew that the more independent governing responsibilities the new body exercised, the more the Iraqis would respect it. He urged Bremer to give it the power to manage foreign affairs, finance, security, and the constitutional process. He insisted that the Iraqis on the council be allowed to designate "ministers" and, crucially, that the council be given the power to approve the budget. But he knew he had to be careful about overreaching. "Resolution 1483 gave the UN almost no scope for maneuver," recalls Salamé. "At any time the CPA could have told us, 'You are trespassing,' and they would have been right."

Deciding just who belonged on the twenty-five-member council was no easy task. Vieira de Mello, who had spent the previous six weeks building his Rolodex, served as an intermediary between Bremer and Iraqi political, religious, and civic leaders. He pushed Bremer to allow the secretary-general of the Communist Party, Hamid Majeed Mousa, to be included. He urged that Bremer take special care to maximize Sunni membership. Aquila al-Hashimi, who had helped to arrange Vieira de Mello's meetings in Najaf, made the cut, becoming one of just three women on the council. And he was pleased by Bremer's appointment of Abdul Aziz al-Hakim of SCIRI, despite al-Hakim's links to Iran. Only high-level Ba'athists were excluded.

Vieira de Mello felt proud of his contributions to the Governing Council. In a cable back to UN Headquarters in early July, he wrote that "Bremer was at pains to state that our thinking had been influential on his recalibrations." He noted that the CPA demonstrated a "growing understanding" that the "aspirations and frustrations of Iraqis need to be dealt with by greater empathy and accommodation and that the UN has a useful role to play in this regard."[23] Vieira de Mello saw it as a victory that only nine of the twenty-five Iraqi members of the body were exiles. But from the Iraqi perspective, six of the thirteen Shiite representatives and three of the five Sunnis were exiles, and neither the inclusion of five Kurdish representatives who had lived in northern Iraq under Saddam nor the addition of Turkmen or Christian representatives appeased the Sunni population.[24] Vieira de Mello hailed the fact that the Governing Council had the power to appoint interim ministers and propose policies, but Iraqis saw that Bremer was left with the authority to veto any of the new body's decisions.

The UN staff were split again, this time on whether to embrace this new body. Vieira de Mello argued that, despite its manifest imperfections, the Governing Council was the "only game in town."[25] "We have to take the leap of faith," he said. At last Iraq would have a recognized body, and the UN would be able to offer its services to it rather than to the Americans. "This is only a start," he insisted. "But it is a necessary start in the same way the first mixed cabinet in East Timor was a start."

He attended the inauguration of the council on July 13, 2003. The members of the Governing Council acted as though they had not been appointed by the Coalition but had simply congealed into a body on their own. In a carefully staged visual the council summoned Bremer, Sawers, Crocker, and Vieira de Mello and "self-proclaimed themselves." Vieira de Mello was the only non–Iraqi asked to speak at the ceremony. Wearing a pale blue tie to remind the audience of the organization he represented, he began and closed his remarks in Arabic: *"Usharifuni, an akouna ma'akum al-yaom. Wa urahhib bitashkeel majlis al-hokum."* Although he knew few words, he pronounced them effortlessly: "It is an honor to be with you today. And I welcome the formation of the Governing Council." He hailed the gathering as the first major step toward the return of Iraqi sovereignty, and he pledged ongoing UN support. "We are here, in whatever form you wish, for as long as you want us," he told the beaming council members.[26] Crocker watched him admiringly. "He was wrapping the blue flag around what we were trying to do politically. I thought it was an act of real political courage. It was also an act of unbelievable physical courage, although we didn't see it at the time."

Vieira de Mello knew that some on his staff would have preferred for him to avoid any association with the Coalition. He continued to have heated exchanges with Marwan Ali, his political aide. "Sergio, don't you see, you're not changing the Americans. You are helping the Americans." But Vieira de Mello believed he was making progress and that Bremer could still go either way. The two men were getting along well. They were both handsome, charismatic, hyperachieving workaholics who knew how to take charge. Although Bremer had close ties to the neoconservatives, who were known for their anti–UN fervor, Vieira de Mello believed that Bremer was cut from a different cloth because he spoke French, Dutch, and Norwegian. This gift for languages testified to a curiosity and a breadth of perspective that he did not often find among Americans. "I've been giving Bremer advice on how to manage the hurt pride of the Iraqis," he told Jonathan Steele of the *Guardian.* "There's been a gradual change in him. Everything I'm telling you, he buys." Although Vieira de Mello had resisted his appointment to Iraq, he found the first two months of the mission exhilarating. He felt as though he was actually making inroads with the Coalition and with the Iraqis, and he naturally loved being at the center of what felt like the geopolitical universe. In an e-mail he asked Peter Galbraith why he intended to spend just a single day in Baghdad, noting that the Iraqi capital was where things were "happening . . . good and bad."[27]

Occasionally, though, he grew frustrated over Bremer's mixed messages. He complained about the "5 p.m. syndrome," where, he said, "I have my Bremer till 5 p.m. [or 9 a.m. D.C. time], and after 5 p.m. Washington has its Bremer."[28] But because of his own experience being micromanaged by UN Headquarters, he sympathized with the "long screwdriver" that Bremer fought off from his higher-ups in the United States. "Bremer will succeed if he makes himself Iraq's man in Washington rather than Washington's man in Iraq," he told the *Washington Post*'s Rajiv Chandrasekaran over a drink. He had saved the UN mission in East Timor only by coming to that realization himself.

In conversations with visitors at this time, he swung between two extremes. On the one hand he acknowledged that the UN was a "minor player" on the scene and confessed embarrassment at its "total lack of authority." He frequently reminded visitors: "The UN is not in charge here. The Coalition is." But he also stressed, perhaps to convince himself, that the United Nations would not be "a rubber-stamping organization for whatever the military occupiers decide," and he insisted that many Iraqis saw the UN as the guardian and promoter of Iraqi sovereignty.[29] He believed that the UN role would expand over time, and he expected it would be the United Nations that would help organize the country's first free elections. He was convinced that no other body could meet twenty-first-century challenges. "Iraq is a test for both the United States and for the UN," he said in an interview with a French journalist in Baghdad. "The world has become too complex for only one country, whatever its might, to determine the future or the destiny of humanity. The United States will realize that it is in its interest to exert its power through this multilateral filter that gives it credibility, acceptability and legitimacy. The era of empire is finished."[30] While he was correct that the United States would eventually need the UN in Iraq, he was wrong in thinking that Washington was close to recognizing this.

On July 21, he flew to New York, where he briefed the Security Council the following day. Defending the Governing Council's representativeness, he stressed, "What the Council needs at present is not expressions of doubt; it is not skepticism, it is not criticism, that is too easy. What it needs is Iraqi support [and] . . . the support of neighboring countries."[31] Resolution 1483 had given the UN almost no formal authority, but he genuinely believed that his small political mission had made a tangible difference. "Can you believe we stretched our marginal mandate as far as we did?" he asked Salamé.

Despite his optimism, one thing worried him: the deteriorating security climate. "The United Nations presence in Iraq remains vulnerable to any who would seek to target our organization," he said in his remarks before the Security Council. "Our security continues to rely significantly on the reputation of the United Nations, our ability to demonstrate, meaningfully, that we are in Iraq to assist its people." Two days before his testimony an Iraqi driver with the UN-affiliated International Organization for Migration (IOM) had died in Mosul when he swerved into a bus in an effort to evade the gunfire coming from a passing car. And on the very day Vieira de Mello testified, a Sri Lankan with the International Committee of the Red Cross had been killed south of Baghdad. Vieira de Mello mentioned both attacks in his testimony and stressed that the Coalition bore responsibility for security. As he wound down his remarks, a woman in the gallery shouted out her criticism of the Governing Council. "This is not a legitimate body," she yelled, "and you know that!" In the press briefing afterward, a reporter asked Vieira de Mello to elaborate on his security concerns. He said that the Shiite south and mainly Kurdish north were peaceful. "What you have is a triangle, Baghdad, the north and the west, that are particularly dangerous and risky for Coalition forces. And more recently I'm afraid for internationals as well." [32] These were Vieira de Mello's last words on the record before returning to Iraq.

Twenty

REBUFFED

*The first gathering of the Iraqi Governing Council
in Baghdad, July 13, 2003.*

"Like a Victorian Parlor Maid"

After Vieira de Mello helped Bremer with the formation of the Governing Council, his influence diminished and his renowned political instincts let him down. The Coalition had relied on him in late June because he brought expertise on political transitions and because he had familiarity and credibility with a variety of Iraqi political and religious forces. But paradoxically, by serving as a talent spotter, he had made himself dispensable. Once Bremer was able to work directly with the Governing Council, he had less need for a UN intermediary. Similarly, prominent Iraqis who had previously used Vieira de Mello to convey their views to Bremer found it easier to negotiate directly with the Americans.

Vieira de Mello was sad to see Ryan Crocker and British ambassador John Sawers leave Baghdad at the end of July. Bremer was surrounding himself with advisers who seemed more hostile to the UN. Vieira de Mello told one visitor that "the more neocon side of Jerry's personality" was emerging.[1]

While in New York, after briefing the Security Council, he had turned up in the office of his colleague Kieran Prendergast and plopped down on Prendergast's couch. "My god," he had said, "I need a drink." He and Prendergast were not friends, but the two men had worked together more closely while he was in Iraq than they had before. Prendergast produced a bottle of Mongolian vodka with golden flecks inside that an aide had brought back from a recent trip. "That looks awful," Vieira de Mello said, "but it will do." After taking several swigs of the spirit, he said that the Americans and Iraqis were already showing signs of losing interest in UN help. Then sure enough, as soon as he got back to Baghdad, the Iraqis on the Governing Council began prevaricating and delaying when he tried to meet with them. They told him that he was welcome to join them after an upcoming lunch with Bremer, while coffee was being served. "He was like a Victorian parlor maid," recalls Prendergast. "Seduced and discarded."

Vieira de Mello had hoped the Iraqis on the Governing Council would rise to the occasion and actually govern by exercising the limited authority they had been given. But they were doing the opposite, spending most of their time squabbling. He suggested the council would be better off if it were funded by the UN (rather than the United States and the U.K.) and if it received assistance from UN technical advisers. But Iraqi council members were not interested. He wrote to Headquarters that their behavior did "not indicate a particular willingness for compromise."[2] They seemed woefully out of touch with ordinary Iraqis and were operating, he complained, "in a kind of cocoon."[3]

But if the choice was between absolute U.S. rule and flawed Iraqi rule, Vieira de Mello would take the Governing Council. To persuade Iraq's neighbors to give the council "the benefit of the doubt," he went on a whirlwind tour of the region. On a trip to Turkey, he met with the Turkish and Indian foreign ministers. He visited Crown Prince Abdullah in Saudi Arabia. More than three years before the Iraq Study Group (chaired by James Baker and Lee Hamilton) would urge the Bush administration to enlist Iraq's neighbors, he tried to do so, flying to Damascus and Tehran to meet with President Bashar al-Assad and President Mohammad Khatami. In Amman he met with the foreign ministers of Egypt and Jordan. And in Egypt he met with Amr Moussa, the secretary-general of the Arab League.

Vieira de Mello knew he was a more palatable salesman than any American and than certain members of the Governing Council itself. Nonetheless he had to be careful not to come across as a handmaiden to the occupation. When Arab journalists quizzed him as to whether the UN was there as "just a cover to the American invasion," his temper flared: "The UN, its secretary-general, and the SRSG [Special Representative of the Secretary-General] are no tool and no cover for anyone. We are an independent organization. Secretary-General Kofi Annan and myself are independent from anyone. So do not suggest for any second that we are there supporting the United States or the Coalition."[4] He rejected the charge that the Governing Council had been "handpicked" by the Americans. In fact, he insisted, the council was "as representative an institution of governance as one could imagine in the Iraq of today." Those Arab governments that faulted the Governing Council because it had not been elected, he wrote in a draft op-ed he hoped to publish in the region, "should be prepared to promote the same principle in their domestic constituencies."[5] He convinced himself that he was making progress, as several Arab governments said that they were prepared to support the council if the occupiers really let it govern.

His sales tour alarmed his staff in Baghdad and friends around the world who read about it. An August 2003 Gallup poll found that three-quarters of Iraqis thought that the policies of the Governing Council were "mostly determined" by the United States and the U.K., while only 16 percent deemed the body "fairly independent."[6] "Here you had Sergio in public saying, 'I helped create this Governing Council. I support this Governing Council,'" recalls Ramiro Lopes da Silva, his deputy in Baghdad. "And then the Governing Council did not really attempt to represent the concerns of the Iraqi population, as the members were probably more concerned with themselves. How did that make the UN look?" Timur Goksel, who was still spokesman for the UN in Lebanon some two decades after he had worked with Vieira de Mello in Naqoura, was shocked to hear Vieira de Mello's defense of the council on Arab television. "I thought maybe he felt a bit too secure in Iraq," Goksel recalls. "I thought something was going wrong. He dressed like an administrator. He talked like an administrator. He looked like one of them." Goksel sent an e-mail to his friend urging him to break away from the formal structures and do as they had done in Lebanon. "Go to the coffee shops, Sergio," he recalls writing. "Reach out to the men with the guns." Omar Bakhet got in touch with Vieira de Mello to deliver the same message. Bakhet appealed to him to "stop trying to carve out a political role for yourself. No one in the Middle East is innocent."

But Vieira de Mello had invested too much to give up on the nascent council. Despite the evidence he saw daily, he told himself it would eventually succeed. "I wouldn't be touring countries in the region trying to sell the Governing Council if I didn't believe what I'm saying," he told *The New Yorker's* George Packer. "The last thing I need and the organization needs is to be marketing the interests of the United States."[7]

But the Iraqi political landscape was changing in ways that he did not appreciate. Moqtada al-Sadr and other militants were gaining clout because they were delivering social services and physical security that the Coalition was not. While Vieira de Mello was selling the council in July, al-Sadr had taken to demanding its dissolution. He said that the Hawza, or the Shiite religious authority, should run Iraq, and on July 25 he gathered tens of thousands of Shiites in Najaf to show his strength and urge an end of the occupation. "The Iraqi Governing Council was set up by the Americans, and it must be disbanded," al-Sadr told his followers.[8]

Vieira de Mello knew that in the three key areas where the Coalition was foundering—power sharing, policing, and economic development—the UN had made grave mistakes but had amassed unique expertise. Yet, to his amazement, the Coalition seemed uninterested in tapping it. On the law-and-order side, he liked to repeat what he had learned through years of frustration: "Soldiers make bad policemen." Although the UN had trained local policemen in Cambodia, Bosnia, Kosovo, and East Timor, the Coalition did not request its assistance. Instead, the CPA gave a $50 million contract to DynCorp International, which was originally supposed to send six thousand trainers, but which eventually set just five hundred. One police chief from North Carolina, Jon Villanova, was given a staff of forty to train twenty thousand Iraqi policemen.[9] Electricity, water, and other utilities operated intermittently at best, lagging far behind public expectations. Vieira de Mello reminded Bremer that much of Kosovo and all of East Timor had been burned to the ground when the UN arrived, but the UN administrations had eventually managed to mobilize the resources needed for recovery. Still, Bremer seemed unreceptive to UN advice. "We could have helped," Vieira de Mello told Packer in August. "We still can," he said. "There's still time."[10]

The one issue on which Vieira de Mello and Bremer clashed heatedly was the rights of detainees in U.S. custody. In Cambodia, Congo, and East Timor, Vieira de Mello had feuded with his friend Dennis McNamara over human rights issues. But in Iraq he behaved like the UN High Commissioner for Human Rights that he had reluctantly become. He talked constantly of "bringing the high commissioner's post to the field." He behaved as though he had acquired a new pride in, and perhaps a new understanding of, his Geneva job, as he saw that violations of human rights were the cornerstone of all that had been wrong with Saddam Hussein's reign and all that *could* go wrong under the Coalition. "The moment we landed in Iraq," recalls Mona Rishmawi, a UN human rights adviser, "he was a different man." "Some people think that human rights are the UN's soft underbelly," he told aides. "But Iraqis know that human rights conditions will make or break Iraq."

On July 15, 2003, he and Bremer were scheduled to discuss detainees. Sawers had counseled him to raise any concerns about excessive use of U.S. military force or prison conditions, not by criticizing but instead by asking Bremer, "How will you deal with criticisms?"[11] It was the only meeting in the Green Zone from which Bremer insisted on barring Prentice and Salamé. Vieira de Mello inquired about the conditions of the thousands of prisoners at the Baghdad airport who were crammed into inhumane facilities. He stressed the importance of creating a database for Iraqis in detention, and just as he had done with President Bush in March, he asked that family members and lawyers be granted access to the detainees. He urged that the detention period be reduced from twenty-one days to seventy-two hours, that status review be instituted, and that something like a public defender system be created.

"I'm not accusing your soldiers of abuse," he told Bremer. "I'm saying you don't have the checks and balances in place to guard against abuse." Bremer said he undertood the UN position but felt that it was being unjustly biased by "the Palestinian on your staff." He was referring to Rishmawi, who carried a Jordanian passport but was of Palestinian descent and at recent international gatherings had been critical of U.S. detention practices. Vieira de Mello defended Rishmawi, who accompanied him to the meeting and was waiting outside. He argued that the Coalition was harming its own cause with its reckless approach to detainee issues. Nearly a year passed before the Abu Ghraib scandal broke, forcing Bremer to address Rishmawi's criticisms on the merits. Vieira de Mello was the first international official to warn Bremer of the potential for grave abuse and national embarrassment.

At a subsequent meeting with Bremer he brought with him a local newspaper clipping that carried a photo of Iraqis who had been hooded in U.S. detention. "This is incredible," he said, but Bremer looked confused. "What's wrong with hooding?" he asked. Knowing that Coalition commander General Ricardo Sanchez and Bremer frequently clashed over their interlocking responsibilities, Vieira de Mello raised detainee practices with Sanchez as well, requesting that the UN be given the right to inspect U.S. prison facilities. Sanchez said he thought such external monitoring unnecessary. "My troops are among the best in the world," he said. "I want to maintain these standards. I am proud of my troops, and I intend to remain proud of them."

Throughout his career Vieira de Mello had always liked to be liked. On the issue of detainees, he conveyed all of his complaints to the Americans in private, at no time speaking out publicly. When he pushed for a visit to the Abu Ghraib prison, which the Coalition had renovated and reopened on August 4, he asked Bremer to accompany him. The morning of the visit, he presented Bremer with a cartoon he had cut out of the *International Herald Tribune*. The cartoon, *The Wizard of Id*, depicted the king who lived in isolation from his people, inspecting conditions in the dungeon. Entering the dungeon, the king was escorted by a guard into the dining area, where he was shown the types of "swill" from which prisoners could choose: "swill," "fat-free swill," "vegetarian swill," and "kosher swill." The guard explained: "The human rights people are coming in the morning." Vieira de Mello convinced himself that his private pressure was paying dividends. He told reporters that a central data bank for detainees was in the works, showers had been built for four hundred of the Iraqis detained in sweltering tents, proper prison buildings would soon replace the tents, and the number of juvenile detainees in Baghdad had dropped from 172 to 30. But however much he hoped for progress, he could not get either Bremer or Sanchez to prioritize the fate of detainees.

The one area on which the Coalition proved amenable to UN help was elections. Vieira de Mello persuaded Carina Perelli, one of his favorite people from UN Headquarters in New York, to lead a delegation to Iraq on August 1. Perelli (a brash, chain-smoking, heavyset ex-revolutionary) and Vieira de Mello (an immaculate, health-obsessed company man) were an unlikely pair. But they had come to respect and even adore each other while managing East Timor's elections. In Baghdad they completed each other's sentences in the office and bantered to ease the tension. "I need a quickie with you," Vieira de Mello would say if he saw Perelli in the hallway when he wanted to discuss the election lists. "At my age, I don't do quickies anymore," she would answer.

Perelli and her team spent almost three weeks touring Iraq so as to be able to assess whether the UN Electoral Assistance Division could reasonably contribute. Just before leaving Baghdad in mid-August, she drove with Vieira de Mello to the Green Zone for a meeting with Bremer. On the drive there her friend urged her to be straight. "Bremer still sees elections as a technical matter and not a wholly political one," Vieira de Mello said. "You have to educate him like you educated me . . . The problem with you election people," he continued, smiling, "is that you are an acquired taste."

In the meeting Bremer presented his plan: The unelected Governing Council would draft an electoral law, and the Iraqis would ratify the law in a referendum. Perelli disagreed vehemently with the sequencing the Coalition had in mind. "You have to be very careful with referendums in transitions," she said. "They become public opinion polls, which, on the basis of my conversations with Iraqis, is not in your interest."*

---

*Iraq's elections were held in January 2005, and the constitutional drafting committee was appointed by the elected parliament. Their draft constitution entered into effect after it was approved by a majority in all but two of Iraq's provinces.

She left the meeting optimistic that the Coalition would request UN assistance. Vieira de Mello liked to quote Yassir Arafat saying, "Give me a square kilometer, and I'll control the country." As Perelli recalls, "We saw we had a window. We knew it was not the front door." The challenge for the UN would be to figure out how to open the window. Vieira de Mello assured her that he would pull the plug on UN electoral assistance if she came to believe the Americans were sacrificing core principles. Perelli had a different worry: Vieira de Mello, her chief ally in the UN, would be leaving Baghdad in six weeks' time, and she would be stuck on her own. "If you abandon me," she said, "I'll have to deal not only with Bremer but also with whatever jerk they replace you with. I can handle the Americans, but I can't handle both." He assured her that he would stand up for her from Geneva. "I've got to get out of here," he said. "This place is getting to me, and I want to start my life with Carolina."

In previous missions he had helped offset flagging staff morale by making himself available after hours for drinks with close staff. But in Baghdad he socialized only rarely. Larriera had arrived in mid-June, toting the items he had asked her to bring: large stashes of chocolate, his Sony portable stereo, a Discman for his runs, a Brazilian music CD collection, a James Bond Gold DVD collection that she had given him for Christmas, photographs from East Timor, and, for good luck, two small iron Buddha statues that they had bought together in Thailand. He held two wine and cheese parties in his office at the Canal, but he typically hurried home to the drab oasis that he and Larriera had established in their suite at the Cedar Hotel. She was working as an economics officer with the mission, but also preparing to start a master's program in August. "You study," he would say when they reached the hotel. "I'll cook!" And so he did. Before leaving the Canal, the couple would pick up aluminum trays of leftover lunchtime food at the cafeteria, and he would heat them up on a tiny electric burner. Or he would prepare breaded veal, steaks, and potato omelets of his own. The staff grumbled that he was reclusive. Salamé pushed him at least to go out for Friday lunches. But on one occasion when he thought he was having lunch with Salamé alone, he arrived at the restaurant and found a table filled with UN staff. He waited out the meal stiffly and later instructed Salamé, "Next time tell me who's coming to lunch." Once Salamé phoned to tell him that he had tracked down an Iraqi book of photographs for him and was leaving it at the hotel reception desk. "No," Vieira de Mello said, "come up and have a scotch." Salamé's room abutted Vieira de Mello's, yet this was the only occasion that he was invited inside.

Now a War Zone

The violence was getting worse, and it was wearing everybody out. Soon after Vieira de Mello arrived in June, the insurgents began experimenting with improvised explosive devices (IEDs). Initially they left IEDs on the road at night so as to trap U.S. convoys on patrol. But as the weeks had passed, the attacks grew more sophisticated. The bombs were better disguised and more powerful, and were often followed by gunmen shooting from hideouts nearby. The attacks on Coalition forces increased daily. Some 117 attacks occurred in May, 307 in June, and 451 in July.[12] FBI agents had originally come to Iraq to interrogate senior Iraqi detainees at Camp Cropper near Baghdad International Airport. But in the second week of July, FBI agents in Iraq put in a request to headquarters for post-blast bomb gear, such as gloves and swabbing material. None of this equipment had been sent before because the Bush administration had not anticipated the kind of resistance the Coalition was encountering.

Vieira de Mello occupied a spacious third-floor corner office at the back of the Canal Hotel that combined a relaxed living room alcove, a desk area, and a boardroom table to accommodate larger meetings. The windows on one wall looked out onto a seven-foot-wide gravel access road that turned off Canal Road, a main thoroughfare. Across the access road he could see a hospital for patients with spinal injuries. Farther down the road, diagonal from Vieira de Mello's office, was an Iraqi catering school and the newly established Coalition Civil-Military Operations Center, occupied by two dozen American civil affairs officers attached to the Second Armored Cavalry Regiment. The Americans had erected huge sandbags and a ten-foot-high steel gate laced with barbed wire around their quarters. They had also posted guards on the roof of the Canal itself to man a twenty-four-hour, 360-degree observation post.

The access road that ran behind the Canal Hotel was open to public traffic. UN security officials and U.S. military officers with the Second Armored Cavalry Regiment worked to close off the road, which ran very close to the back of the hotel, but senior UN staff were concerned that if the UN began disrupting traffic or blocking the road to the catering school or the spinal hospital, they would alienate Iraqis as the Americans had done when they sealed off the Green Zone.

Rishmawi, the human rights officer, occupied an office on the back side of the building near Vieira de Mello's. Her desk was positioned such that she had her back up against the window. She found herself worrying that a gunman would position himself atop the neighboring spinal hospital and fire at the back of her head. In late June, when another office opened up down the hall, she leaped for it. Vieira de Mello pretended that he was hurt. "How could you strand me here?" he said. "Aren't you going to miss the view?" "You see a view," she answered. "All I see is snipers." Yet she felt foolish for moving.

The security team based at the Canal was small, never exceeding a half-dozen UN officials. So many UN agencies were jockeying to send staff to Iraq that the team spent more time processing travel requests from New York and Geneva than they did securing UN staff who were already in Iraq. On June 18 Robert Adolph sent Ramiro Lopes da Silva an e-mail complaining of the deluge. "The overwhelming majority of UN staff that are in Iraq should not be here," Adolph wrote disapprovingly. "The volume of security clearance requests has been staggering. . . . Tired people tend to make more mistakes. Given the current security context, we dare not permit those mistakes to be made."[13]

The person who was the most vigilant about Vieira de Mello's personal security was Alain Chergui, the fifty-year-old former French special forces officer who had guarded him in East Timor. In early June Chergui had joined Vieira de Mello in Cyprus and asked Paul Aghadjanian, the UN mission's chief administrative officer, where he could find the container of security equipment and instructions sent from New York. Aghadjanian had said he knew of no such container. "I was expecting weaponry, ammunition, ballistic vests, night-vision goggles, helmets, trauma kits, GPS, all the equipment mandatory for such a mission," Chergui remembers. "Plus a map and some notes and and and and . . ." Their first day in Iraq, Adolph had delivered a security briefing to Vieira de Mello and his team that Chergui found condescending. "He said things like 'Don't fuck with a guy with a gun,'" he remembers. "I thought, 'What do they think you should do when there's a guy with a gun?'"

Chergui had worked for the UN in Iraq back in 1998. Even in a Baghdad that was then tyrannical but orderly, he had labored for six months to get waist-high cement barriers erected outside the Canal so that arriving vehicles would be funneled through a chute to a checkpoint. When he had arrived back at the Canal with Vieira de Mello on June 2, he had been stunned to discover that, in a much more deadly environment, only forty-three Iraqi national staff and thirty-eight U.S. soldiers were manning the gates of the premises. "Of the American soldiers, some have to eat, some have to rest, some have to do paperwork," he said to himself. "How many are actually offering perimeter security?" Then he spotted the concrete barriers he had installed five years before. They were propped up parallel to the perimeter fence, unused.

Chergui was part of Vieira de Mello's nine-member close protection team. Each member was given only a 9mm pistol. These guns were appropriate for manning the entrance to the UN compound in Geneva but were totally unsuited to a war zone. Chergui pleaded with New York for submachine guns. Seven weeks into his time in Baghdad, the guns finally arrived: hand-me-downs from the UN civilian police in Bosnia. He was relieved, but when he opened the box, he was stunned to see that three of the seven guns lacked the pins required to fire. "It's like giving somebody the present of a pen without ink," he says.

When Chergui saw Vieira de Mello's corner office, he was aghast. Looking out the office window, he could peer into the nearby spinal hospital and see a mosque in the distance. Concerned mainly about snipers, he asked the head of the close protection team to look into moving the office. But when he presented the idea to Vieira de Mello, his boss vetoed the move. The Canal was overcrowded with staff, and he said he did not want to ask his staff to bear risks that he would not.

Later in the month two of Vieira de Mello's other French bodyguards took security matters into their own hands, borrowing several AK-47s from the French embassy. Since the UN in New York would never have approved these weapons, Vieira de Mello had personally given the go-ahead. In the morning as they left the hotel, he would often ask whether "Santa Claus" (his nickname for the guns) was joining them. One day while Perelli was in the car, Gaby Pichon, a French bodyguard, confessed to his boss, "We need training." Vieira de Mello teased, "Just hand the gun to Carina—she'll show you how to use it."

While UN security officials grew alarmed about the escalating violence, U.S. officials sounded oddly unworried. Secretary of State Donald Rumsfeld was asked why he was reluctant to characterize the Iraqi rebellion as a "guerrilla war." "I guess the reason I don't use the phrase 'guerrilla war,'" he said, "is because there isn't one."[14] The resistance was coming from "dead-enders" who would be quashed.[15] In Baghdad, U.S. officials all sang from the same hymnbook. Paul Bremer told *The New Yorker*'s Jon Lee Anderson on August 7, "More people get killed in New York every night than get killed in Baghdad."[16]

Though fewer than a dozen attacks occurred each day—a relatively small number when compared to 2007, when there would be 163 daily attacks by insurgents and militia—UN officials understood that circumstances had changed.[17] The UN's June Threat Assessment, dated June 29 and written by Adolph, noted: "To date there have been no direct assaults on UN staff or facilities, but it is the consensus of the UN-Iraq Security Team that it is only a matter of time."[18] In a June 30 meeting of UN officials with security responsibilities, Kevin Kennedy, a former U.S. Marine who worked on logistics and humanitarian affairs, told staff, "The situation has changed. This is now a war zone." Kennedy ordered three bomb shelters to be built for some two hundred people.[19] When a World Food Program warehouse and IOM office in Mosul were hit with grenades, Vieira de Mello sent a note to Bremer on July 6 that attached a rough translation of a leaflet "against religious enemies" that had been distributed around a nearby mosque prior to the attack.[20]

Kennedy and Vieira de Mello discussed the deluge of staff that UN agencies were irresponsibly sending to Iraq. Whatever the political pressures and funding opportunities, they needed to stay away until the risks abated. "People are coming to Baghdad and treating it like they're making a trip to Geneva," Kennedy said. A few days later, as the two men waited together at Baghdad airport for a flight out, they watched a motley crew of foreigners working for the UN and other humanitarian agencies emerge from a plane. "What the hell are all these people doing here?" Vieira de Mello asked. He dubbed the inessential personnel who flocked to the city "the tourists."

At a meeting of the UN Security Management Team in Baghdad on July 12, UN security staff updated attendees on the status of previous security recommendations. Adolph's notes on the meeting read as follows:

> Cease the influx of incoming staff . . .
> NOT ACHIEVED
>
> Reduce the numbers of staff . . .
> NOT ACHIEVED[21]

As the attacks on the Coalition continued, UN security officers tried to curtail the mobility of UN staff. Curfews were imposed, and travel without a two-vehicle escort was forbidden.

At a UN press briefing in Baghdad on July 24, Salim Lone, a spokesman at the mission, took note of the string of four recent attacks against international staff. "Certainly we can no longer call these isolated incidents, not at all," he told the press. UN staff were "easy, soft targets," and it was "so easy to pick on us." His comments were picked up in the international media, and Fred Eckhard, the chief UN spokesman in New York, sent a note to Shashi Tharoor, the head of public information, recommending that Lone be barred from speaking to the press in the future. Eckhard wrote that Lone had "contradicted [the official] position that attacks on UN workers were isolated incidents."[22] When Lone received his dressing-down, he responded with fury and demanded an apology. He described as "laughable" Eckhard's notion that attacks were isolated:

> I guess you will want us to hold on to that line even when we are bunkered down in [the] Canal Hotel or hightailing it out of Iraq to implement our rapid reaction plan. Which could happen any day. MANY think this should be implemented automatically if there is one more fatal attack on a UN staff/vehicle. Some actually say we should be evacuated. Do you know what the security situation here is like and the conditions we now work under are, especially after the two attacks and the two UN deaths and a third near fatality that occurred two days before the briefing? Do you know how many UN missions are being conducted in an active combat zone undergoing guerrilla warfare?[23]

Vieira de Mello with Shiite clerics in Hillah.

But Lone was inexperienced in conflict settings. More seasoned UN staff in Iraq saw the recent flurry of incidents differently.* Because several of the attacks had occurred in the vicinity of IOM offices or personnel, many UN staff believed the IOM was being targeted because it had effectively made itself part of the Coalition. The IOM was not a UN agency, but it used UN vehicles, and it had gotten involved (despite having assured Vieira de Mello that it would not) in two highly sensitive initiatives sponsored by the Coalition: resolving property disputes in Kurdish areas, and helping reintegrate demobilized Iraqi soldiers. Vieira de Mello was enraged by the IOM's double-dealing, but he resisted his colleagues' calls to sever UN links to the organization. Lopes da Silva remembers, "It was part of Sergio's personality to work things out. That was Sergio—he would keep trying, keep trying, rather than cut them loose."

By the end of July at least four hundred UN international staffers were in

---

*By coincidence, the person in charge of all of UN security, a sixty-year-old Burmese named Tun Myat, was named to the post after serving as humanitarian coordinator in Iraq from 2000 to 2002. Because of his perceived special knowledge of Iraq, those on the Steering Group who had never visited the country or the region almost never challenged him.

Baghdad alone, and their safety was looked out for by some twenty professional security staff, who were responsible for the entire country.[24] Very few
incoming UN officials attended the mandatory security briefings, and almost
none of the heads of agencies insisted they do so. The UN security team's
threat assessment, written July 25, said: "Direct assaults on clearly identified
UN staff and facilities are all but a certainty."[25]

By August Vieira de Mello had grown unusually irritable. Whenever he
left the country and traveled along the airport road, American security contractors stopped his UN car and attempted to search it. He continued to
refuse to grant the Coalition this right. "The bastards need to learn to respect
the UN flag," he said. He staged acts of civil disobedience reminiscent of the
actions he had taken as a thirty-four-year-old political officer in Lebanon.
With the 120-degree summer heat blaring down on his convoy, he often sat,
arms folded and fuming, for more than an hour until the contractors agreed
to allow his UN vehicle to pass.

When he ducked out of Iraq to attend a World Economic Forum meeting
in Amman, Jordan, prominent foreign ministers besieged him with requests
for meetings, but as he scanned the roster of renowned attendees, the only
name that caused him to light up was that of Brazilian novelist Paulo Coehlo.
"Look!" he exclaimed to his aide Salman Ahmed. "Do you think there's any
chance I could get a meeting with him?" When he returned to Baghdad, he
told colleagues that his private meeting with Coehlo had been the highlight
of his trip. When the novelist Mario Vargas Llosa passed through Baghdad,
Vieira de Mello cleared out his schedule to spend time with him. After Vargas Llosa had left, Vieira de Mello immediately wrote to André Simões, his
nephew and godson in Brazil, and asked him to send the Portuguese translation of The Way to Paradise by mail as soon as he could.[26] He wanted to read
about anything except Iraq. The reading care packages from his mother and
friends came as they had throughout his career, and he devoured them.

But with his UN staff, he tried to keep up appearances. His staff watched
him carefully. "Whenever his face would change," Marwan Ali recalls, "we
would wonder what was happening." His reports back to New York concentrated on what had been achieved, not on what was being denied. He
worried about his team. The hotels lacked electricity and running water, and
the heat was unbearable. He signed off his e-mails "with warmest (literally
and figuratively) personal regards." When Larriera told him that one mem-

ber of his team had picked up a cold in the scorching heat, he corrected her: "No, Carolina, she doesn't have a cold. She's breaking down because the stress is too high." He insisted that Prentice take a week off to join his wife for a celebration of their first wedding anniversary. Rick Hooper, the Arabic-speaking political officer who worked on Iraq in New York as Under-Secretary-General Prendergast's special assistant, flew to Baghdad to replace him. Hooper had long argued that Annan should have declared the Coalition invasion illegal (which the secretary-general would not do until an interview with the BBC in September 2004).

Jean-Sélim Kanaan, the French-Egyptian political officer, left Iraq in July so that he could be with his wife, Laura Dolci-Kanaan, in Geneva when she gave birth to their first child. In his last letter before departing Baghdad, he wrote that the Coalition had taken the UN colors and "trailed them in mud."

> I have to say that I am secretly awaiting the moment when the United Nations finally finds a role that is our own . . . What an extraordinary moment that will be—one where we will be able to give the order to a [U.S.] soldier to lower his weapon and to keep silent. And no longer having to undergo this public humiliation of the body searches in the streets, despite our UN badges, despite our diplomatic status . . . It appears to me more and more evident that the United States is going to come begging for the aid of the rest of the world to face this titanic task. The quagmire becomes stickier each day . . . But we must be careful in this game, as there are twenty-eight million players who no longer find this funny at all. And God knows how much harm angry people can do.[27]

As the security concerns of UN staff multiplied, each team member expressed different fears. Carole Ray, Vieira de Mello's secretary, hated traffic jams because she feared an angry mob. Shawbo Taher, an Iraqi Kurd who worked as Salamé's assistant, felt most frightened in her hotel at night. The hotel was not guarded, and the rooms had large glass windows that looters or assailants could easily break through. A sense of doom pervaded. In late July Bob Turner, a UN humanitarian official, remarked to Kevin Kennedy, "It isn't a question of if we get hit. It is a question of how we get hit and where we get hit."

Although Vieira de Mello urged others to take breaks, he did not feel he could do the same. "Sergio was very conscious of his role as the leader of the mission, setting the tone for everyone else," recalls Larriera. "He knew he couldn't be seen to be breaking down in front of his staff." In all the time he was in Iraq, he took only one day off, stealing twenty-four hours with Larriera in Jordan. Desperate for a break, he arrived in Amman at 2 a.m. on July 18, and they drove to Petra at 8 a.m. the following morning. In other postings he had been able to exercise freely, but in Baghdad he was restricted to jogging fifteen laps in a stadium that was heavily guarded by the Americans. "You know, Sergio, I will not die by bullet here in Iraq," Ibrahim, his bodyguard, said, running in the Baghdad heat with Larriera, Prentice, and Vieira de Mello. "But I will definitely die of heat exhaustion." Vieira de Mello also attempted nightly workouts inside the hotel, jogging up and down the stairs. But the security deterioration increasingly confined his movements to the route between the Cedar Hotel and the Canal Hotel.

In previous missions his frustrations with UN Headquarters—the delayed responses, the administrative hassles, the seeming obliviousness of bean counters and ambassadors alike to the field staff's daily trials—had exasperated him. But in Iraq they infuriated him. Salamé wondered aloud how Vieira de Mello could have remained in the system. "The UN is a residual institution," Salamé said. "When nobody wants to deal with an issue, it is left to the UN." Vieira de Mello was initially defensive. "No, it is not residual," he said. "In terms of productivity," Salamé persisted, "it is not a zero, it is less than a zero." Vieira de Mello snapped, "Listen, Ghassan, the UN is unable to attract the best. None of the member states will give the UN their best. And on the rare occasion that the UN happens to find the best, it doesn't have the slightest idea how to keep them. If the UN ever succeeds, it is by accident." He gave Salamé some advice: "If you ever join the UN, I have just one rule for you: Spend as little time as possible in New York."

Increasingly claustrophobic in Iraq, he tried to focus on the personal life that awaited him once he left. He received word from the tribunal in France that his divorce would be completed in October. His relations with his sons had improved. Laurent had received his engineering degree in Lausanne, and they had celebrated together before he left Geneva. His relationship with Adrien had taken longer to heal, but they had begun to correspond again. By good fortune Adrien happened to be in New York with his girlfriend and her parents when Vieira de Mello briefed the Security Council in July, so they had gone out for dinner at a steak house. Still, he hoped to build closer ties to them. He e-mailed them that it was "very hot and very difficult" in Baghdad and urged, "Please keep writing to me."

Vieira de Mello knew from Bosnia how difficult it was to persuade Western countries to share intelligence with the UN. But in other missions the UN was at least able to rely on its own peacekeepers and police, or on local authorities, for assistance; in Iraq the Coalition was the only available source of intelligence, early warning, and security. Vieira de Mello's Australian military adviser, Jeff Davie, found the Americans' tight-lipped posture exasperating. "If I hadn't been wearing a blue beret," Davie says, "my access would have been entirely different." Davie was not allowed to enter the Coalition's operations room or review its intelligence assessments. Vieira de Mello pushed General Sanchez for more cooperation. He even offered to send over Prentice. "Intelligence will not go beyond these four eyes," Vieira de Mello said, "and Jonathan is a Brit. He's one of you!" Sanchez demurred. On July 14 Lopes da Silva sent the CPA a letter requesting that the UN formally post a security liaison officer with the Coalition, but the appeal was ignored.[28] In Vieira de Mello's meetings with General Sanchez, he pleaded for more access to information. "I'm security blind," he told the U.S. commander. "I don't have any idea what's going on." On July 24, when he met with several senior Coalition military officers, the group discussed improving U.S. knowledge of UN locations, establishing a "9-1-1 number" for incidents, and streamlining a process for assessing and circulating threats to the UN.[29] But security cooperation between the UN and the Coalition remained ad hoc and inadequate.

Many within the UN would have been upset if the relationship had grown closer. In August Vieira de Mello prepared for a trip to northern Iraq. In testimony to his increased concern about security, he asked Davie to review his itinerary. "I already have the approval of my security team," he said, "but have a look at this and let me know what you think." Davie brought the schedule to the Green Zone and ran the locations by an accessible U.S. intelligence officer. When Nadia Younes, Vieira de Mello's chief of staff, learned that Davie had done so, she was very upset. "How could you have told the Coalition where Sergio was going?" she said. "We don't want to run our plans by them."

The platoon of U.S. soldiers who offered light perimeter security for
the Canal complex had been given UN radios so they could communicate
with UN security officers, but they were not authorized to search incoming vehicles or personnel. They could use the UN cafeteria and the Internet
facilities, but they were forbidden to bring their weapons inside.[30] But most
U.S. soldiers simply shielded their pistols as they entered, putting them in the
back of their waistbands. The U.S. platoon that milled around the perimeter
manned a pair of 50-caliber-machine-gun posts on the roof of the hotel.
They were wedged in between the large water tanks and not visible from the
ground. But on July 23, when Saddam Hussein's two sons, Uday and Qusay,
were killed by U.S. troops, gunfire erupted throughout the capital and several
shots hit the building. The soldiers from the Second Armored Cavalry Regiment on the roof fired back, and a mini-firefight ensued.

By August the UN was torn between needing the Americans for security
and believing that the American presence, which was increasingly despised
by Iraqis, undermined its security. "The Coalition and the UN were like two
tango dancers, locked in an embrace, but determined to stay at arm's length
from one another," Davie recalls. Baghdad was far more dangerous than it had
been in June, but the number of U.S. troops offering light security outside
the Canal did not increase.

Lopes da Silva, who chaired the UN security meetings, was overwhelmed
by his manifold humanitarian tasks. He did not convene the meetings regularly or keep careful records. The security staff never did contingency planning for a bomb attack. And Tun Myat, who ran UN security in New York,
did not press Lopes da Silva to comply with regulations.

In late July and early August UN security officials invited several private
security firms to the Canal to pitch their services. But the process of hiring
them would be torturously slow. Even the security improvements to the
Canal Hotel facilities ordered back in May had not yet been undertaken.
On June 15 the windows in Vieira de Mello's office had been treated with
sun-resistant ultraviolet sheeting but not with professional blast-resistant film.
The solution was understood to be temporary. In late June, after a shooting
incident near the Canal resurrected concern over the Canal's windows, an
official from the World Food Program offered to fund the procurement and
installation of the film, but inexplicably the chief administrative officer, Paul
Aghadjanian, turned the offer down, claiming that he had already started

the tendering process.[31] Aghadjanian had his hands full wrapping up the Oil for Food Program, and security follow-through was never his priority. Because he opted to finance the film installation using petty cash, he instructed the engineer who began coating the windows in mid-July not to exceed the $200 petty cash ceiling.[32] Nearly three months after the need for blast-proofing the windows had been identified, only Vieira de Mello's office and the cafeteria had been fitted with shoddy film. The rest of the UN's office windows remained exposed.

Meanwhile the new wall that was being erected to separate the Canal from its neighbors was being built right up alongside the UN building itself, leaving no real buffer between the UN complex and the outside world. The wall would be thirteen feet high around much of the compound, but beneath Vieira de Mello's office and several of those next to his, it would reach just seven feet. The builders said they would try to finish the wall by September.

Soft Target

The first dramatic sign that Americans were not the only target of the ever-evolving insurgency came on August 7. At 11 a.m. a minivan pulled up outside the gate of the Jordanian embassy, where Iraqis were lining up for visas. The driver got out of the vehicle, crossed the median, and got into another vehicle, which drove off.[33] Minutes later the deserted minivan exploded, killing seventeen Iraqis, including five police officers. In the wake of the attack a group of Iraqi men ran into the embassy wreckage and emerged carrying portraits of the former King Hussein of Jordan, which they ripped into bits and threw into the flames. "We don't need you, Jordan!" one man shouted in Arabic, as he tore up a Jordanian flag.[34]

The force of the blast was so great that a Mercedes parked next to the detonating vehicle was blown onto the roof of a nearby three-story building. A group of children in a nearby house who were watching the Cartoon Network on satellite television emerged into the street when they heard the explosion, only to watch men and women in flames running around helplessly while they burned to death. Scattered body parts, including a severed head, lay by the side of the road.[35] No group claimed responsibility for the attack.

The attack on the Jordanian embassy was unprecedented. It was the single deadliest attack in Baghdad to date and the first prominent attack on a "soft target." Prior to this bomb the insurgents had primarily targeted U.S. military personnel and Iraqis working with them. In UN security and policy meetings the incident was hotly debated. Was this a turning point? Were internationals now seen as fair game? Or was this attack somebody's private vendetta against Jordan? Salamé, who joined in a UN press briefing after the attack, was asked why the UN had condemned this attack but not others. "Well, this attack appears to be a new kind of attack," Salamé said. "This is a new form of violence. This is an attack on civilians, and I don't see who can really applaud this kind of unjustified and unacceptable act of terror."[36]

Davie, Vieira de Mello's military adviser, asked his contacts at the Coalition to share their forensic and intelligence assessments of the bomb, which they promised to do. The FBI, which had only just received the requested bomb-blast equipment, quickly determined the type of bomb used and the way it was detonated. Davie checked back with the Coalition and was told that the intelligence assessment was still in the works. Davie did not find the delay surprising, as the CPA seemed to have limited insight into the nascent insurgency. What Davie did not know was that the FBI intelligence had yielded two utterly conflicting theories.

One theory held that Saddam Hussein's enemies had struck the Jordanian embassy because Jordan had recently granted asylum to Hussein's two daughters and their nine children. The daughters had not gone gently into the night. They had appeared on CNN and al-Arabiya shortly after arriving in Amman and praised their father, calling him "tender, very loving."[37] The attack could have been payback against those who had aided the family of the Iraqi dictator.

Another view held that Saddam Hussein loyalists had struck the embassy because Jordan had taken the side of the United States in the 1991 Gulf War and had allowed some two thousand U.S. Special Forces to enter Iraq from Jordanian bases during the recent invasion.[38] Jordan had also been the only Arab state to send troops to join the U.S. effort in Afghanistan. In the preceding several weeks Saddam Hussein had released four broadcasts, delivered in the style of presidential statements, urging citizens to become "a loaded rifle in the face of the invading foreigner."[39] Jordan could have been targeted as an ally of the invaders. As one U.S. analyst involved in the investigation recalls,

"You had incredibly high-powered analytic work being done, in which dia-metrically opposite conclusions were drawn."

Vieira de Mello phoned his old friend Prince Zeid Raad Zeid al-Hussein, Jordan's ambassador to the United Nations, who offered a third theory. "We can't be sure," said Zeid. "But the rent-a-mob aspect makes it look like Cha-labi's people." In 1992 Jordan had convicted Iraqi exile Ahmed Chalabi in absentia and sentenced him to twenty-two years in prison for financial mis-conduct. The very day of the bomb, Chalabi's daughter had published an op-ed in the *Wall Street Journal* defending her father and attacking Jordan's "servile complicity with Saddam."[40] Both Vieira de Mello and Prince Zeid thought it suspicious that, with the Jordanian embassy still smoldering, a group of Iraqis had ignored the injured, entered the compound, and extracted not valuables but portraits of King Hussein, so as to rip them up ostenta-tiously on television.

The theory that got the least traction was the one that would prove most likely. August 7 was the fifth anniversary of the al-Qaeda attacks on the U.S. embassies in Kenya and Tanzania, which killed 224 people. The CPA floated the possibility that behind the Jordanian embassy strike was Ansar al-Islam (Supporters of Islam), a Kurdish terrorist group with ties to al-Qaeda, which was reported to have had a small presence in northern Iraq before the war. General Sanchez said publicly that an al-Qaeda presence in Iraq was "clearly a possibility," but the Americans then had minimal evidence of their infiltration. The al-Qaeda theory got minimal play.[41] Vieira de Mello told the secretary-general he was not yet sure the attack was a turning point. "It just depends on who did it and why," he told Annan. "This incident alone doesn't give us enough to go on." The Bush administration downplayed the event. Larry Di Rita, the Pentagon's chief spokesman, said the attack was part of an inevitable "ebb and flow" in violence.[42] General Sanchez said the 37,000 U.S. troops in Baghdad would not assume responsibility for guarding embassies. "This is the Iraqi police's responsibility," he said.[43] Secretary of State Powell said, "Maybe what you want to do is stand back a little bit more and let Iraqis" take over more protection tasks.[44] But in Iraq Thomas Fuentes, the American who headed the FBI team, cabled headquarters and requested they send him ex-perienced bomb-blast experts. He expected more attacks on civilian targets.

As Mona Rishmawi was leaving her hotel on the morning of August 12, she saw a stash of leaflets scattered on the ground before her. On inspection she saw that the leaflets bore Osama bin Laden's picture. Rishmawi thought, "Baghdad and al-Qaeda—these two things don't match. What a bizarre joke. What are these people doing?" Since President Bush had partly predicated the war on a link between Saddam Hussein and September 11, she wondered whether the Americans had planted the leaflets to justify the invasion. The same day the UN daily security incident summary noted, "The [Coalition Forces] received intelligence reports that hundreds of Islamic militants who fled the country during the war have returned and are planning to conduct major terrorist attacks."[45]

On August 12, 2003, Salim Lone, the UN public affairs officer, sent an e-mail to Vieira de Mello describing the mounting fear in the mission after the Jordanian embassy attack. The following day he provided his boss with a list of questions that he might be asked at that day's press conference, the first he would give in more than six weeks. Among them was: "Is the UN worried it is one of the soft targets?"[46] Lone urged security team members to tell the U.S. soldiers to leave. Chergui, who felt the violence escalating, thought Lone's idea irresponsible. "Don't come here and say they should go," he said. "We don't have anyone else, and if something happens, we will immediately blame the U.S. for not being there."

Salamé moved freely around Baghdad without concern for the security protocols. But on August 13 a Lebanese journalist brought him small slips of paper that he had found at the scene of an explosion in the commercial Karada district. The papers were colored sky blue, and each was the size of a business card. They had been thrown from a car like confetti after the explosion. "Al-Qaeda" was written on them in Arabic. Salamé was as puzzled as Rishmawi. He went straight to Vieira de Mello. "This is the first time I've seen anything like this," he said. "It could be fake, but it looks serious." Vieira de Mello showed the papers to his trusted bodyguard Chergui. "Where were these found?" Chergui asked. The three men discussed the papers for a few minutes but didn't know what to conclude, beyond that they should keep an eye out for further signs of foreign infiltration. It was their first serious conversation about a possible al-Qaeda presence in Iraq. Up to that point the insurgency was widely assumed to be fueled by Iraqis who had been close to Saddam Hussein or who were contesting the American occupation. Chergui was supposed to go on leave the next day, but he told his boss that he would prefer to postpone his departure. The two men were so close that Vieira de

Mello maintained an e-mail correspondence with Chergui's wife, Martine. On August 7 he had e-mailed her asking whether she felt lonely without her husband. Claiming sole responsibility for Chergui's absence, Vieira de Mello noted that, while Chergui was doing an excellent job, "You have an equal right to him."[47] He insisted that Chergui take leave as he had planned.

The UN staff was split between those who expected an attack on the UN and those who could not imagine it. All agreed that security was spinning out of control. "I come from the most violent part of the world," Marwan Ali recalls, "and I, even I, couldn't believe that in two or three months things could deteriorate as badly as they had, even though the whole time I was saying things would deteriorate badly." Most UN staff also agreed that the UN had an image problem throughout the country. Vieira de Mello had come to realize that Resolution 1483, which legitimated the occupation, had been one more factor eroding the UN's shaky standing. "I think we must be honest to ourselves and recognize there exists, in the minds of many Iraqis, mixed feelings about the record of the United Nations here," Vieira de Mello told a reporter. "And you can't expect them to make these fine distinctions between mandates given to the Secretary-General by the Security Council and the role of the Secretariat per se. They lump this all together as any public opinion would do."[48]

Bob Turner began chairing a UN advocacy group aimed at improving the UN reputation. "We thought that the negative impression of the UN was going to have a security impact," he recalls. "We'd be safer if we could improve the standing of the UN." A few days later a UN staffer in Mosul prepared a paper proposing a UN outreach campaign. "In view of the increased incidents targeting certain UN agencies and NGOs," the paper said, it was time for the UN to use print, radio, and TV and to network with prominent Iraqi figures to publicize the UN's humanitarian services and to gain citizens' "trust." In attempting to "feed" images to the media, the staffer warned against the "static image of the UN shot in studio" and recommended images that show "we are out there dirtying our hands to serve the population."[49]

But Vieira de Mello was sure that, whatever the UN's sins, Iraqis still saw the organization as preferable to the Coalition. Iraqis he met told him that they hoped for a stronger, not a weaker, UN role. "They see the UN as an independent, reliable, good faith partner," he assured visitors. "They know the UN has no hidden agenda." He added, "They see clearly in the United

Nations an independent and impartial player that is the only source of international legitimacy."[50] When he had briefed the Security Council in New York, he said that the Iraqi people "unanimously call including those who are critical, even resentful, over what they perceive to be the United Nations' past record in their country—for an energetic, center-stage role for the organization."[51] But the trouble with this attitude was that he never disaggregated the "they." And the Iraqi people were increasingly at odds with one another. More important, the Islamic radicals, who he did not yet know had infiltrated the country, had an agenda all their own.

Unusual for him, Vieira de Mello was beginning to feel personally vulnerable. He discussed moving offices with Chergui but feared it would panic staff. "I'd better leave that to my successor," he said. Chergui decided to look for another space in the building where he could bring his boss in the event of an attack. After rummaging through the Canal, he identified a small storage space filled with folding chairs and tables just off the conference room on the lower level. He resolved to bring Vieira de Mello there in an emergency.

Throughout Baghdad, Coalition forces were getting ever jumpier. On August 12 the Pentagon released its official report effectively exonerating the U.S. military for the April shelling of the Palestine Hotel in Baghdad, which had killed two journalists and injured three others.[52] This followed an incident on July 27 when U.S. troops had killed at least three Iraqis who crossed a military cordon; another on August 8 in which they fatally shot five more Iraqis, including an eight-year-old girl, at a newly erected checkpoint; and a third on August 9, when Coalition soldiers killed two Iraqi policemen whom they mistook for criminals.[53] On August 17 Mazen Dana, a forty-three-year-old veteran Palestinian cameraman with Reuters, had received U.S. permission to film the Abu Ghraib prison, which the day before had been the scene of a mortar attack that killed six Iraqis and wounded fifty-nine. U.S. troops outside the prison, perhaps mistaking his television camera with its white microphone for a rocket-propelled-grenade launcher, fired several shots at close range. Dana's camera recorded a tank heading toward him, the crack of six shots in quick succession, and the tumult of his camera falling to the ground.[54] Dana was killed on the spot. Vieira de Mello knew that the time for quiet diplomacy with the Americans had passed; he would have to speak out.

Although Dana was the twelfth journalist killed since the start of the war, this shooting had struck a particular nerve at the UN because it seemed to reflect a larger trend. Wearing the hat of human rights commissioner, Vieira de Mello knew that as attacks on U.S. soldiers increased, the Americans would become increasingly jittery and prone to shoot civilians. "In previous positions, I always condemned attacks on journalists," he wrote in an e-mail to senior staff. "Should I not do it here as well?" His aides responded quickly, agreeing that the attack should be denounced, but expressing concern about the implications of condemning an "accidental" attack on a journalist when the UN had not publicly faulted the Coalition when it had killed Iraqi civilians.

Younes, his Egyptian chief of staff, urged her boss to couch the condemnation of Dana's killing in a statement that "deplored in general the increasing number of civilian deaths and injuries occurring in the past few weeks," but she noted, "We have to weigh the effect your statements, if you start reacting to all violence, will have on Bremer and Co."[55] But having concluded that his private admonitions to Bremer were falling on deaf ears and that his access to the Coalition had already shriveled up, Vieira de Mello authorized his press officer to draft a press release condemning the incident.

Younes was one of the most outspoken members of Vieira de Mello's team. As an Arabic speaker, she had a better sense of the swelling anger toward the Coalition than most of her international colleagues, whose primary exposure to Iraqis came in shuttling to and from their hotels. The previous week she had received a phone call from UN Headquarters in New York. Lamin Sise, Annan's Gambian legal adviser, told her that she had been promoted to assistant secretary-general. She had been elated, not least because the job would get her out of Baghdad. But she quickly realized that as the chief of staff she was expected to facilitate the handover between Vieira de Mello and his as-yet-unnamed successor. This wouldn't do. On Friday, August 15, she called Sise in a panic. She could not wait two months to leave. "Lamin," she said, "I need to get out. The history of this country is very bloody. This place is on fire." She telephoned twice more in order to press the point. Sise promised to try to expedite the hiring of her replacement.

Vieira de Mello did not have that option and focused on salvaging the mission. Unable to control security, he reflected on the source of the insurgency, which was an increasingly malignant occupation. He assumed that the way to improve security was to work even harder to get the Coalition to give up power. "Who would like to see his country occupied?" he asked a Brazilian journalist. "I would not like to see foreign tanks in Copacabana." Coalition troops had to have "more sensitivity and respect for the culture of the population," he said.[56] The dignity of Iraqis was being trampled. Their "pride," he told visitors, was "today deeply hurt." He rattled off the catalog of harms that would have wounded anybody: They had lived under a barbarous regime; they had been killed by the hundreds of thousands in the war with Iran; their army had invaded Kuwait and then been swiftly dislodged, at the cost of thousands of lives; they had suffered years of devastating sanctions and isolation; their government had been overthrown by outsiders; and now, in "one of the most humiliating periods in the history of these people," they had almost no say on how they were being ruled, and nobody had presented them with a road map to their liberation. Even in his remarks before the Security Council in late July, Vieira de Mello had urged diplomats to stop speaking of Iraq as the sum of its past afflictions. "Iraq is something other than a past repressive regime, it is something other than a pariah state," he said. "It is not simply the scene of conflict, deprivation and abuse."[57]

The Americans had to stop talking about "nation-building," he said, as "Iraq has five thousand years of history." The Iraqis had "more to teach us about building nations," he told a British interviewer, than the United States or UN had to teach them. Iraqis were fed up with being treated like a failed state. He told another visitor that the Iraqis complained to him that the Americans "keep referring to Rwanda." "Why the hell do they refer to Rwanda?" they asked him. "This is not Rwanda!"[58] Vieira de Mello believed that additional Coalition troops should have been sent in the immediate aftermath of their ground victory in April. But now he argued that "saturating Iraq with foreign troops" would only exacerbate the humiliation and rage experienced by Iraqis. Instead, applying a lesson from East Timor, he pressed for a transparent timetable, "a calendar with dates."[59] Just as Gusmão had taught him in East Timor, people had to be given a concrete road map so they could see how and when they would gain control of their own destinies.

Vieira de Mello began drafting an op-ed on the occupation. "In the short time I have been in Iraq, and witnessed the reality of occupation," he wrote, "I have come to question whether such a state of affairs can ever truly be legitimate. Certainly, occupation can be legally supported. Occupation can also certainly be carried out benignly, grounded in nothing but good intentions. But morally and practically, I doubt it can ever be legitimate: its time, if it ever had one, has passed." He urged the Coalition to "aim openly and effectively at their own disappearance."[60]

On Sunday, August 17, he gave a long interview with the Brazilian journalist Jamil Chade of *O Estado de São Paulo*. Asked if he feared the UN might be targeted by terrorists, he said, "I don't think so." Although in-house he had urged the launching of a national advocacy campaign to improve the UN's reputation, he knew his mother, Gilda, would read the interview in Rio de Janeiro, and he said, "The local population respects the United Nations, which is not what they feel toward the occupation forces. They view us as an independent and friendly organization and know we are here to help them." He said he had few personal concerns for his safety. "I don't know exactly why, but I believe I have been in more risky situations. Here in Baghdad, I don't feel in danger as in other places where I worked for the UN."[61]

Yet for all his attempts to maintain a brave face, he had soured on the mission so much that he was biding his time. The Iraqis on the Governing Council had initially told him that a UN representative would be housed with them, but they reversed this decision. His ties with Bremer were growing more tense. A few days after he had shared a relatively uneventful lunch with Ayatollah Hussein Ismail al-Sadr, a moderate cousin of the young Shiite militant, an enraged Bremer had telephoned him and accused him of "inciting the Iraqis to ask for democracy." Bristling at the reprimand, Vieira de Mello asked his aide Marwan Ali, who had attended the lunch, whether he could remember what he had said. "Nothing inflammatory," Ali said. "It was just the usual blah blah blah about democracy." Vieira de Mello understood Bremer's concerns about the time it would take to organize an election, but he thought that if Bremer started to find democracy inconvenient, the U.S.-led mission was doomed.

The Coalition was straying further from the rapid handover of power that Vieira de Mello had proposed. At the same time Moqtada al-Sadr was gaining power, and the more the Coalition tried to crush him, the stronger he became. "The last thing we should do is ostracize him," Vieira de Mello told Jonathan Steele of the *Guardian*. "It's always useful to have an *enfant terrible* if you can control him." If Bremer had a timeline in mind for ending the occupation, he was keeping it to himself. Vieira de Mello told journalists what he had told Bremer from the start: "Iraqis are completely in the dark. They've got to know when this will come to an end."

With the staff he had brought from Geneva, he began discussing the restructuring of the high commissioner's office. He also began doing things he had never done in other, supposedly more dangerous missions, such as signing off his e-mails by urging friends to "please pray for us." Coming from an avowed atheist, these e-mails struck people as strange. The day before he spoke with the Brazilian journalist, he had accompanied his bodyguards to a shooting range, where he received training in how to fire a gun and how to maneuver his vehicle in a hazardous situation.

The weekend of August 16 and 17 was not a good one. Insurgents blew up the pipeline transporting oil to Turkey and destroyed a water main in northern Baghdad, cutting off water to nearly half a million people.[62] The only boost to the morale of Vieira de Mello and his team was the return of Jean-Sélim Kanaan, who arrived at the Canal Hotel the afternoon of Monday, August 18, toting cigars, champagne, and photos of his newborn son, then three and a half weeks old.

Vieira de Mello knew he needed to do what Kanaan had done: get out of Iraq. He asked Larriera if she could join him the following weekend for a break. But she told him that she could not skip an upcoming human rights workshop. She said his presence too was essential. "I just need one day off," he told her. But she could not very well duck out of the workshop at his request.

Desperate for an exit strategy, he asked his secretary back in Geneva to book his and Larriera's flights to Brazil, where he would see his mother and have surgery on his right eye, which had started to droop downward a full quarter-century after the Paris police had hit him with their truncheons in May 1968. On the afternoon of Monday, August 18, his airline tickets arrived from Geneva, dated September 30, 2003, his last day in Iraq. Vieira de Mello brought the tickets back to the Cedar Hotel and held them up before Larriera. "I need to think about the future, so I don't lose my mind in the present," he said. The tickets were proof that he and Larriera would actually escape Baghdad. When he bumped into Salamé in the hotel, he said he needed to sit down with him to discuss the tour of the Middle East he and Larriera were planning for later in the fall. He wanted to return to Alexandria, which he had visited with his father, and Lebanon, where he had lived as a boy and as a young UN official.

Annan telephoned the same day, asking him to meet him in Europe to update him on his recent consultations with Iraq's Arab neighbors. "Don't forget," Vieira de Mello said, "you promised me. I'm going to spend a month with my mother in Brazil after I'm done here." Annan replied, "Don't worry, you've more than earned it. Take the month."

Twenty-one

AUGUST 19, 2003

On Tuesday, August 19, Vieira de Mello and Larriera had breakfast at their hotel. When Mona Rishmawi, Vieira de Mello's human rights adviser, joined them, they discussed the UN's future in Iraq. In his first two months in Baghdad he had spoken of bringing the job of UN High Commissioner for Human Rights to Iraq. Beginning in August, though, he had grown anxious to get back to Geneva to bring field wisdom back to the high commissioner's job. "In his mind he had already traveled," recalls Rishmawi. When he returned to his post, he planned to expand a team of human rights monitors that had set up a foothold in Iraq but were having marginal impact. Over breakfast he gave the green light for Rishmawi and Larriera to go ahead with a human rights workshop the following Saturday, where the UN would help train Iraqis in human rights fact-finding and humanitarian and human rights law. He thought the workshop might be one more way for the UN to differentiate itself from the Coalition.

Most days it took twenty minutes to travel from their hotel to UN headquarters. But the traffic on the roads that day was far lighter than usual, and they reached the Canal Hotel in ten minutes. The unarmed Iraqi security guards checked the badges of those in the UN convoy, scanned the bottom of the vehicle with metal detectors, and waved the familiar faces inside the gate.

Gil Loescher and Arthur Helton, American refugee experts studying the humanitarian effect of the war for the e-magazine *OpenDemocracy.net,* were just landing in Baghdad. Loescher, a fifty-eight-year-old Oxford University researcher, had flown to Amman, Jordan, from London. Helton, a fifty-four-year-old St. Louis–born lawyer based at the Council of Foreign Relations in New York, had met up with him there. And the pair had taken an uneventful flight from Amman to Baghdad.

Loescher and Helton had known Vieira de Mello a long time. Back in the 1980s they had criticized the UN's Comprehensive Plan of Action, which he had helped negotiate and which had helped stop the hemorrhaging of Vietnamese boat people but had also given rise to human rights abuses. Loescher had argued that Vieira de Mello had deferred to the interests of states instead of upholding the rights of refugees. Helton had felt that the screening procedures designed to keep Vietnamese boat people out of neighboring countries had been unduly harsh. But they had not come to Iraq to rehash old disagreements. They were there to carry out a two-week field assessment.

Vieira de Mello had welcomed news of their visit. He wasn't normally much for "assessments." Too often, he thought, they were carried out by inexperienced individuals who took only cursory sweeps of a place and then boasted about the hardships they had endured "in the field" at ensuing dinner parties. Most studies offered generic or grandiose prescriptions without offering any concrete proposals for mobilizing political will among indifferent or unwilling implementing actors. Such recommendations generally went unread or unheeded. In this case, though, he welcomed an independent review of the Coalition's performance. He had plenty of ideas as to how things ought to be done differently, and he knew that if the recommendations came from two Americans, they would gain more traction in Washington than anything that came from the UN.

From the moment they disembarked from the airplane, Loescher and Helton felt uneasy in Baghdad. Even though the men were not UN staff, a UN vehicle came to the airport to pick them up. Here they were fortunate, as UN rides had grown scarce in recent weeks. Mounting attacks on Coalition personnel had caused the UN to tighten its security regulations and require two-vehicle convoys. The airport road, which was known as Ambush Alley, was notoriously dangerous. The two men were relieved to reach the downtown, where, with the exception of the attack on the Jordanian embassy, civilians had not yet been deliberately attacked.

They traveled straight from the airport to the Green Zone, where they met with Paul Bremer, who gave them a full hour of his time. He presented a rosy picture. "There are a few security issues," he said, "but we are getting everything under control."

The two men were not scheduled to meet with Vieira de Mello until 4 p.m., so they used the gap in the schedule to drop their bags off at their hotel. Vieira de Mello's secretary had made them a reservation in a hotel that was considered secure. When they arrived at the front desk, however, the receptionist told them she had no reservation on file. The UN driver took them to another hotel, but when they went up to their rooms, they discovered the doors had no locks. The men decided to find a different hotel after they returned from their meeting at the Canal Hotel.

Over at UN headquarters it had been a routine day. Larriera spent the morning away from the Canal, visiting the leading human rights, women's rights, and legal organizations in Baghdad, in order to extend personal invitations to them to attend the Saturday human rights workshop. Bob Turner, the humanitarian official, chaired a communications strategy session on "UN messages to the Iraqi people" at 10:30 a.m. Khaled Mansour, a spokesman for the UN World Food Program, presented a paper on how to improve the UN's standing. "The main goal," he wrote, "is to present a UN distinct from the U.S.-led coalition as subtly as possible."[1] In their dealing with Iraqis, Mansour argued, UN officials had to emphasize their desire "to ensure the earliest possible end of occupation."[2]

Marwan Ali, the Palestinian political officer, also felt the rage of Iraqis mounting. He had been pressing Vieira de Mello to criticize the Coalition for a recent attack in the Sunni triangle that had killed an eight-year-old boy and his mother. His boss had approved the statement the previous day. "I've done all I can do to influence the Americans behind the scenes," he had told Ali. "I have to start speaking out." Ali was relieved. This would be the first-ever public UN condemnation of a Coalition human rights violation. Finally, he thought, the UN would begin to carve out an identity truly distinct from the Coalition. He hoped it wasn't too late.

At 1:30 p.m. Vieira de Mello was scheduled to meet with Bremer and a U.S. congressional delegation in the Green Zone. Alain Chergui, the head of his close protection team, had gone on leave five days before, along with

Jonathan Prentice, his assistant, and Ray, his secretary. Gaby Pichon, another French bodyguard, prepared the three-vehicle convoy, which lined up at the entrance to the building. But he soon got word that the flight of a group of American senators and representatives, including Harold Ford, Jr., Lindsey Graham, Kay Bailey Hutchinson, and John McCain, had been delayed.[3]

At 2 p.m. Vieira de Mello ran into Marwan Ali in the hall and inquired about whether the critical statement had been issued. He knew Ali was heading away on leave and asked where he was going. Ali said he was flying to Amman the next day. "Try to come back refreshed," Vieira de Mello said, adding, "Don't do anything to get yourself arrested by the Israelis!"

At 3 p.m. he met with a pair of senior International Monetary Fund (IMF) officials visiting from Washington, Scott Brown and Lorenzo Perez. Larriera, who was responsible for liaising with financial institutions, also attended. It was the most senior IMF delegation in Iraq in more than three decades. Vieira de Mello offered his advice on working with Bremer, warning Perez to walk a very fine line and to engage in such a way that Bremer felt ownership over the IMF initiatives (or else he would block them) but that Iraqis also saw the IMF programs as independent. When the meeting ended at 4 p.m., Larriera walked out with the visitors. As she exited, Vieira de Mello beckoned her back toward him, but she motioned that she needed to catch another meeting that would soon be ending. He gave her a playful hangdog look. As she raced down the stairs to catch the last few minutes of the NGO coordination meeting, she heard a woman from the International Committee of the Red Cross (ICRC) deliver a panicked report that somebody had spotted people taking down the numbers of all car license plates leaving the ICRC compound. Larriera believed the alarm serious enough to telephone Vieira de Mello, who was just about to start his next meeting. *"En serio?"* he asked in Portuguese. "Really?" He said his meeting with Loescher and Helton was about to start, but he wanted to discuss the details later.

Benon Sevan, an under-secretary-general of the UN and the longtime head of the UN's Oil for Food Program (who in January 2007 would be indicted in a New York federal court on charges of bribery and conspiracy to commit wire fraud), happened to be visiting Baghdad to help liquidate the program. He was preparing for a 4 p.m. meeting with a visiting WHO delegation on the construction of hospitals in northern Iraq. His meeting was to take place in the office directly beneath Vieira de Mello's.

Shortly before 4 p.m. Sevan poked his head into Lopes da Silva's office and said he'd prefer to meet there instead. "Your secretary makes good coffee, I like looking at your goldfish," he said, "and I want to smoke a cigar." Lopes da Silva's office had a balcony with sliding doors, ideal for a smoker.

When Loescher and Helton arrived at the Canal Hotel for their meeting with Vieira de Mello, they passed easily through security at the front gate and were ushered up two flights of stairs. Pichon, Vieira de Mello's bodyguard, escorted the two guests from the hallway on the third floor through the small office outside Vieira de Mello's, where his two secretaries were at their desks. Ranillo Buenaventura, a forty-seven-year-old Filipino, was subbing for Ray. Lyn Manuel, the fifty-four-year-old Filipina and eighteen-year UN veteran who had served with Vieira de Mello in East Timor, seated the guests around a knee-high glass table in the alcove near the window that looked out on the access road and the spinal hospital.

Vieira de Mello greeted his guests with warm handshakes. Younes joined the meeting, as did Fiona Watson, the Scottish political officer, who was a last-minute addition. Watson had just returned the day before from New York, where she had attended a budget-based management training program. She had been selected for Vieira de Mello's A team because she had worked in Kosovo but also because in February she had helped the secretary-general pull together a strategic plan weighing the options for a UN postwar role in Iraq. She used to joke that the best-laid plans often led to the lousiest mandates.

Vieira de Mello sat closest to the window, next to Younes, on a black leather sofa. Loescher and Helton sat directly opposite them, with Loescher nearest the window. Watson sat on a chair at the end of the table facing the wall and window. Pichon and Manuel returned to their offices. It was 4:27 p.m.

Rick Hooper, one of Marwan Ali's closest friends, was in Baghdad subbing for Prentice. Ali stopped into Hooper's temporary office, which abutted Vieira de Mello's, and reminded him that they were supposed to be interviewing an Iraqi lawyer who had been hired by the UN as a driver but who they both felt could be put to better use. "Give me fifteen minutes," Hooper said. "I just need to finish one thing first." Ali, who was leaving Baghdad the following day, shook his head. "I've got to buy gifts for my children before the curfew," he said. Hooper, who had known Ali's children since they were born, said, "Okay, I'll do this afterward. Be right there."

Just as Ali was leaving Hooper's office and Vieira de Mello was getting reacquainted with Loescher and Helton, a Kamash flatbed truck was driving along Canal Road, a multilane thoroughfare divided by a fetid canal. Kamash trucks were Russian-made and had been purchased in bulk in 2002 by Saddam Hussein's government for use in mining, agriculture, and irrigation. These flatbeds looked similar to the commercial trucks that were becoming ubiquitous around town now that reconstruction had finally begun picking up. This truck had a brown cab and an orange base. At 4:27 p.m. the driver made a right turn onto the narrow, unguarded access road that ran along the back of the Canal Hotel complex. Nobody paid much attention to the truck's turn or to its load.

Most flatbed trucks in the vicinity of the Canal Hotel carried building supplies to fortify the wall around UN headquarters or to renovate offices in nearby buildings. But this truck wasn't carrying cement or building tools. All that was visible on its bed was a metal casing that resembled the shell of an air-conditioner unit. Underneath the casing, though, was a cone-shaped bomb the size of a large man, which had been bundled up in 120mm and 130mm artillery shells, 60mm mortars, and hand grenades. All together some one thousand pounds of explosives were heading toward the Canal Hotel.

The truck didn't have far to go. It drove at high speed a hundred yards down the access road, past the edge of a UN parking facility.[4] It sprayed gravel that hit the ground-floor windows and startled UN staffers.[5] When the driver reached the Canal Hotel, he turned the vehicle toward the unfinished brick wall that ran alongside the back of the building, two stories beneath the unsuspecting occupants of Vieira de Mello's office.

After Pichon left his boss's office, he crossed the hallway and reentered the small office for close protection officers. Just as he sat down, an enormous blast ejected him from his chair and carried him through the air. He landed fifteen feet from his desk, next to the elevator at the end of the corridor. Everything went black. Loescher, who sat across from Vieira de Mello, saw not darkness but light—the bright and sudden glare of "a million flashbulbs."

Larriera was sitting in her small third-floor office at the top of the staircase.

When she first arrived in Iraq in mid-June, she had occupied a desk beneath a tiny grated window. But because she had been visible to anyone who came up the stairs, dozens of people stopped to ask her for directions. Larriera had tired of feeling like the third-floor receptionist, and Vieira de Mello had helped her prop her desk against the wall, out of visual range of people in the hall. This move saved her life. She heard a deafening popping sound and in the same instant saw the steel grate that covered her window go flying the length of the office, along with shards of glass. Ripped from its hinges, the metal door over her left shoulder crashed down into the center of the office. The suction from the blast also caused the door to the adjoining office, that of Rishmawi, to fly open. Rishmawi stood up slowly and looked in Larriera's direction. Larriera spotted a tiny cut in the center of her colleague's forehead, from which blood began to trickle slowly.

Jeff Davie, Vieira de Mello's military adviser, who had been lent to the UN from Australia, had spent the afternoon escorting a pair of UN aviation advisers around Baghdad airport. The meetings had run longer than he had expected, partly because the experts had stopped to pose for pictures at the airport. Davie had finally freed himself of his guests and was hurrying back to the Canal Hotel for a meeting with Younes.

Davie was several minutes from the Canal when his UN vehicle trembled from the force of a shock wave. When he looked to the side, he saw an enormous gray plume of smoke emerging from the area around the Canal. He called Colonel Rand Vollmer, the Coalition's chief of operations, on his cell phone. "There was a large explosion at the hotel," Davie said. "It's bad. Call in a medevac now." Vollmer immediately called the medical brigade evacuation number, and a dozen Black Hawk rescue helicopters marked with white crosses were deployed to the scene.

When the bomber struck, Bremer was in the Green Zone meeting with the congressional delegation that had arrived late. The palace shook with the force of the distant blast. One of his aides passed him a yellow slip of paper: "There has been an explosion at the Canal Hotel. We are attempting to raise people on the telephone there." Ten minutes later the aide handed him a second note: "The situation looks very bad." When the Jordanian embassy was bombed twelve days before, Bremer's chief of staff, Patrick Kennedy, had served as the liaison between the Jordanians and the U.S. military. Now

Kennedy excused himself from the meeting, called his deputy Dennis Sabal, a Marine colonel, gathered radios and a pair of cell phones, and headed to the Canal. Sabal had already seen footage of the burning UN base on CNN. He had an unusual CV in that he was the person called to manage the aftermath of the U.S. embassy bombing in Kenya, which had killed 212 people, including 12 Americans. Then, on 9/11, he had been in the Pentagon watching television coverage of the burning Twin Towers when it too was hit, and he had helped set up a morgue for the deceased. Because of these attacks, which had a common perpetrator, he had a sudden epiphany in Iraq that others would not have for many weeks: "Al-Qaeda is here," he thought. "The minute I saw on CNN, 'UN attacked,'" he recalls, "that was when the switch went on: Al-Qaeda had come to Iraq."

Sergeant William von Zehle, a fifty-two-year-old retired fireman from Wilton, Connecticut, who was in Iraq as an army civil affairs officer, was sitting at his computer in the U.S. military building across the narrow lane that ran alongside the Canal. The explosion, which he thought was just outside his window, threw him to the ground. He saw an intense orange light and felt a sharp pain in his right thigh. His windows had shattered, and he had been stabbed by a four-inch piece of glass. He yanked the glass, which was like a knife blade, out of his leg and tried to scrape a piece of shrapnel from his arm. He looked at the clock on his desk, which had stopped. It was 4:28.

When von Zehle made his way to the roof of his building, he saw that the neighboring Canal Hotel was on fire. He radioed his commander and got permission to head in the direction of the attack. As he moved along the access road connecting his office building and the UN headquarters, he broke into a covered rush, cocking his AK-47 and alternating dashes with a colleague. As the pair approached the scene of the explosion, they saw that almost all of the UN's navy blue vehicles with orange lettering that had been in the parking lot were ablaze. For the first time in Iraq, von Zehle thought his firefighting experience would be of use. "This had become a fire rescue," he remembers. "I needed cranes, floodlights, shoring equipment."

After a long day of patrols Captain Vance Kuhner, a U.S. reservist in charge of a military police unit, had returned to his base, a collection of tents beside Saddam Hussein's Martyr's Monument, a little under a mile from the Canal. After ordering his men to unload their Humvees, Kuhner was walking toward the barracks for a shower and a bite to eat. As he passed the cement volleyball court where children were playing, he was knocked to his knees by the explosion behind him. He got up quickly, turned around, and saw the dark gray cloud in the distance. "Get back in the vehicles," he shouted to his men. "Someone's been hit." He assumed that a Coalition helicopter or plane had gone down, or that a U.S. convoy had been ambushed. "I need every medic I have," he radioed his commander. Andre Valentine, a firefighter paramedic, loaded up four Humvees with six medics. "Follow the smoke," Valentine told the driver of his Humvee.

In her small office adjoined to Vieira de Mello's, Lyn Manuel was confused. A few seconds before the explosion she had turned her head away from her boss's door in order to make a phone call. And almost as soon as she picked up the receiver, she had gone blind in both eyes. She thought that an electric wire had fallen from the ceiling and that she had been electrocuted. Panicked, she began crying out to her office mate, Ranillo Buenaventura. "Rannie, Rannie," she shouted, "help me." But when he ignored her cries, she thought perhaps he had slipped out of the office without her notice. Manuel started to call out again but quickly stopped herself. She was afraid her cries would disturb Vieira de Mello's meeting.

Larriera had been miraculously untouched by flying debris in her office, but like Manuel, she was in a state of shock. Having seen Rishmawi stand up, she darted out of her office and began navigating her way along the pitch-black hallway toward Vieira de Mello, who she knew would be worried about her. Because of the power outage and the dust clouds, she couldn't see down the hall, but she half-expected to bump into him as she walked. She called out his name softly: "Sergio. I'm here, Sergio . . . Are you there?" The building was still shaking from the force of the blast, and she could smell what she thought might be gunpowder.

Manuel, who still could not see, made her way out of her office in the hopes of finding help elsewhere in the building. If she had turned right instead of left, she might have fallen into a three-story pit of burning concrete, metal, and furniture. Instead she groped her way through her doorway and toward the staircase, which was in the opposite direction from the source of the explosion. In all likelihood Manuel, who was hugging one wall, passed Larriera, who was sliding along the opposite wall, but neither was aware of the other's presence.

Larriera had a firm destination in mind. She wanted to reach the private side door to Vieira de Mello's office—a door that only she had permission to enter. But as she continued along the wall, she saw that at the end of the corridor the lights appeared to have come back on. She was so disoriented that she wondered if she had died and was approaching the gates of heaven. Then, her reason flitting in and out, she thought that maybe the generator had kicked in and the building's electricity had been restored. But then she realized in horror that the light she was seeing was not artificial light but Baghdad's afternoon sunshine. The corridor ended abruptly and, where there had once been a floor and a ceiling, now only clouds and sunshine were visible above. Unable to grasp what had occurred, she turned around mechanically, retraced her steps, and attempted to enter Vieira de Mello's office via the office of his secretaries, Manuel and Buenaventura.

The scene in their shared office was ghastly. The doors were off their hinges. Glass and debris littered the floor and desks. Papers were strewn everywhere. The air conditioners and computer screens had exploded. And a large white bookshelf had toppled onto Buenaventura's desk. Buenaventura himself had been projected onto Manuel's desk. He was lying in the fetal position, his eyes were fluttering, and part of his face was missing. Larriera, still uncomprehending, quickly moved into the next office, the last small room before Vieira de Mello's. There she saw that Hooper, who was wearing a red and white checkered shirt, had pulled his swivel office chair around to the side of his desk to be closer to a person visiting him. He was leaning over in that chair, and his spine seemed unnaturally extended. The visitor, whom Larriera could not identify, turned out to be Jean-Sélim Kanaan, the French-Egyptian political officer who had returned to Baghdad the previous evening after spending a month in Geneva with his newborn son. Kanaan, who had slipped into the office just after Ali left Hooper, sat with his legs crossed in a chair. Both men were sitting in stillness and were covered in white dust. They appeared to have been crushed by beams that had fallen from the collapsed ceiling.

At the sight of these casualties, the scale of the devastation struck Larriera for the first time. She stopped calling out to Vieira de Mello softly and began screaming, "SERGIO!" But the passage in front of her was blocked by the beams and rubble piled high, and he did not answer. She turned around, exited into the corridor, and resumed her previous effort to find Vieira de

Mello's office side door. This time, when the corridor ended, she looked more carefully into the pit of rubble below. There, for the first time, she saw movement. A man covered in dust was lying on his back thirty feet below, and miraculously, he was blinking and waving his arms like a snow angel. The person below seemed too tall to be Vieira de Mello, but she thought he might be down there as well. She considered jumping into the mangled rubble, but the drop was so high that she thought she might kill both herself and the injured man. She sprinted down the corridor away from the destruction in search of Ronnie Stokes, the head of administration. Less than a minute had passed since the explosion.

The floors and beams beneath Vieira de Mello's office had exploded upward and then crashed down. Thus his third-floor office had effectively become the first floor. The ceiling of his office and the roof of the Canal had remained largely intact, but they had collapsed diagonally. Anybody who had been on the southwest side of the building at the time of the explosion lay beneath couches, desks, computers, air conditioners, large slabs of glass from the shattered windows, and beams and concrete from the walls of the building itself.

Manuel was still blinded. As she staggered toward the stairs on the third floor, she bumped into Pichon, who had regained consciousness. He told her to get out of the building and ran past her into the office Larriera had just vacated. He came to the same devastating realization that Larriera had just reached. "There is nothing here," he said to himself.

Ghassan Salamé, Vieira de Mello's Lebanese political adviser, had been in his office meeting with the brother of the first former regime official the Coalition had arrested. Salamé rushed from his office to the third floor, where he joined Pichon. When he shouted out to his boss, he heard nothing back, but at the base of the rubble viewed from the corridor, he saw what Larriera had seen: a man whose entire body was covered in white dust except for his eyes, which seemed to be blinking furiously. The man waved. Salamé thought that it was Vieira de Mello. *"Courage, Sergio, nous venons te sauver!"* he shouted. "Let's get to him from the back of the building," he said to Pichon.

As Larriera rushed away from the wreckage in search of the head of administration, she saw Rishmawi, who was bleeding badly. "I can't see," Rishmawi cried. "I think I lost my eye." Larriera escorted her down a flight of stairs, which were shaking and covered in dust, glass, blood, shoes, pieces of clothing, and office paper. On the second floor Rishmawi's husband, Andrew Clapham, a legal consultant with the mission, emerged from his office, and the couple was reunited. Larriera sprinted back up the stairs. "I need to find Sergio," she said. "Don't, Carolina!" Rishmawi shouted. "The building is going to collapse!"

Manuel still didn't know what was happening. She tried to feel her way down the corridor, and as she did, she felt the crunch of unnatural debris beneath her feet. She had begun hearing screams and commands ringing throughout the building, which meant that she was not the only one who had been hurt. She wiped one of her eyes and was able to make out Marwan Ali, who was running in her direction in search of his friend Rick Hooper. She called out to him. "Marwan!" He looked at her blankly, as if he didn't recognize her. "Marwan, it's me, Lyn," she said. His face contorted in horror. "Lyn, my god," he shouted. "Noooooo." He was horrified by the sight of her. For the first time Manuel became truly frightened.

Ali picked up Manuel in his arms and carried her down the two flights of stairs to the front entrance of the Canal Hotel. He laid her down on the cement just outside and made a motion to head back inside. She cried out to him. "No, Marwan, the pavement is too hot!" she said. The cement had gathered the day's heat and was some 160 degrees. With her one functional eye she looked down at her legs and realized she was barefoot. Her shoes had been blown off her feet. She called out again to Ali, but he had disappeared back inside the building, where many others were trapped.

Scores of UN officials spilled out of the Canal, passing Manuel on the ground. Many were bleeding profusely from cuts caused by flying glass. Two people had pieces of steel rebar protruding from them, one from his head, another through his shoulder. The aluminum office doors had been converted into stretchers.

Kuhner, the army reservist from New York in charge of the 812th Military Police, had 9/11 on his mind. He was worried about the New York police officers and firemen on his team. Two of them had already broken down. As they rushed toward the building, they had stopped suddenly. One walked back the way he had come. "I'm sorry, captain," he had said. "I can't." He was having a flashback to the World Trade Center, where he had lost close friends when the buildings collapsed. The Canal too looked as if it was on the verge of imploding. Kuhner, who had no rescue experience himself, deduced the obvious: Given the size of the slabs of rubble, those trapped underneath would remain pinned there unless engineering and fire rescue equipment could be found.

Ramiro Lopes da Silva, Vieira de Mello's deputy, was the UN official responsible for security. He had a piece of glass stuck in his forehead but was fully conscious. Benon Sevan's desire to smoke a cigar during their 4 p.m. meeting had kept Lopes da Silva away from the side of the building where the blast occurred. He was a longtime humanitarian field worker and not a security expert, but he remembered from UN security briefings that in the event of an explosion outside, UN staff was supposed to move to a large enclosed blue-tiled courtyard. "We were always told, 'Move in, don't move out.' Because out was where we thought any explosion would be. When the explosion happened inside," he remembers, "we had no plan. We were lost. We didn't know what to do. If we had ever thought that such an attack could occur, and if we had planned to respond to such level of emergency, the UN would not have been in Baghdad." He joined other UN staff ducking under collapsed beams to exit the building, climbing over the fallen masonry in the corridor, and holding hands as they made their way down the staircase.

After exiting the Canal Hotel, Lopes da Silva walked around 250 feet to Tent City, where he and other UN staff had lived temporarily in early

May, before the Canal reopened. The tents now acquired unexpected functions. One of the tents was converted into a first-aid facility, while another contained a satellite phone on a small table, which became what passed for a UN communications center. Lopes da Silva called Tun Myat, the head of UN security at New York Headquarters, to share information and receive guidance. "Initially," he remembers, "nothing clicked in me about my colleagues on the third floor, about Sergio." He assumed that the explosion had injured many but not killed anybody. Around fifteen minutes after the blast, Rishmawi approached him. "Sergio is in the building. What are you doing for Sergio?" Lopes da Silva looked confused, and she grew agitated. "Ramiro, we are in the presence of the greatest army in the world, this is what *they do*. Call Bremer!" Lopes da Silva left Tent City and returned to the Canal building, venturing around the back to the scene of the explosion for the first time. He saw U.S. soldiers beginning to gather at the site. He knew that the UN had neither the equipment nor the expertise for rescue and recovery efforts, and he assumed, not unreasonably, that the Coalition would have made plans to respond to large-scale attacks on civilian targets. Even though Vieira de Mello was clearly out of commission, Lopes da Silva did not consider himself in charge of the bomb scene. After just a few minutes at the back of the Canal, he returned to Tent City and resumed discussions with New York.

Back in New York, Tun Myat was not the first to learn of the attack. At 8:32 a.m. (4:32 p.m. Baghdad time) Kevin Kennedy, the former U.S. Marine and senior humanitarian official who had only left Baghdad on July 28, got out of the elevator on the thirty-sixth floor in New York and saw that he had a message on his cell phone. Bob Turner had called him just after the attack. "Car bomb, car bomb, Canal Hotel, Canal Hotel," Turner had shouted into Kennedy's voice mailbox. Kennedy called the UN operations room, but they had not yet heard about any bomb. Kennedy next called the thirty-eighth floor so that the secretary-general, who was on vacation with his wife on a small island off the coast of Finland, could be informed. He then sprinted the length of the corridor to find an office with a television set. CNN was showing nothing on the attack, so Kennedy hoped Turner's message might have overstated the case. But at 9:01 a.m., thirty-three minutes after the blast, Kennedy's face sank as CNN broadcast a "breaking news" item from Baghdad. UN headquarters in Iraq had been struck by a car bomb.

Information was spotty. Within minutes of the attack, U.S. soldiers from the Second Armored Cavalry Regiment had begun to cordon off the hotel, preventing CNN's correspondent, Jane Arraf, from reaching the complex. But CNN did have a crew on the scene who at the time of the blast had been filming a press conference on the UN's de-mining efforts. For the next three hours, as UN staff in Geneva and New York awaited word of their friends and colleagues, Arraf and her CNN colleague Wolf Blitzer became the relayers of bad news.

In her first commentary, at 9:01 a.m. New York time (5:01 p.m. Baghdad time), Arraf described the Canal's shattered facade and the Black Hawk medical helicopters circling the building. She explained, inaccurately, that the UN had "beefed up security considerably, particularly in anticipation that someone might try to set off a car bomb." But "still it was a UN building, and they really did not want to send the message that it was either an armed camp or part of the U.S. military."

Arraf did not speculate on casualties, but within half an hour Duraid Isa Mohammed, a CNN translator and producer inside the U.S. cordon, spoke by telephone to CNN and reported that five helicopters had already evacu-ated casualties from the site. As he spoke, he said he was seeing stretchers carrying two victims from the building. The U.S. military, he observed, were "not answering any questions to the relatives of those local employees who came over to the scene by now and started asking questions about them. I see many women crying around here, trying to find their sons or husbands."[6] With word of stretchers and distraught families, UN officials glued to their televisions around the world knew that this was no small attack. At around 9:30 a.m. New York time, CNN reported for the first time that Vieira de Mello had been "badly hurt."[7]

Jeff Davie had done what those who worked closest to Vieira de Mello had done: gone looking for his boss. When the traffic on Canal Road stalled, he had leaped out of the vehicle, ran to the building, and sprinted up the stairs to the third floor. He found Stokes and Buddy Tillett, a supply officer, inspecting the offices to see who had been wounded. In one third-floor office Davie found Henrik Kolstrup, a fifty-two-year-old Dane who was in charge of the UN Development Program in Iraq. Kolstrup was alive but covered in glass wounds. As he writhed in pain on the floor, he was cutting himself further on the broken glass. Davie hastily wrapped Kolstrup's wounded upper body. Stokes and Tillett arrived with a stretcher and carried Kolstrup down the stairs to the wounded area. Davie continued on toward Vieira de Mello's office. Kolstrup was contorting so badly that he almost fell off the stretcher and down the gap in the stairwell.[8]

When Davie made his way to Vieira de Mello's office, he looked down through a collapsed part of the office wall and spotted below the same person Larriera, Pichon, and Salamé had seen lying faceup in the rubble and covered in dust. The man, who Davie did not think was his boss, appeared to be lying on a portion of Vieira de Mello's office floor, which had now become the ground floor. Davie noted that while the damage caused by the attack was colossal, many of the floors and ceilings, including the flat roof of the building, had at least fallen in large slabs, pancake style, creating voids. A narrow tunnel, no wider than three feet in diameter at the top and at least thirty feet deep, separated Davie from the man below. Davie assumed Vieira de Mello was lying in the heap somewhere near this man, and he hurried down the stairs to try to find another point of entry.

Normally, in order to reach the rear of the Canal Hotel, Davie would have needed to exit through the front entrance and walk the entire width and depth of the building. But this time, at the base of the Canal Hotel staircase, he tried to turn right into those offices that had stood beneath Vieira de Mello's. He was able to enter a cavity the size of a small room. But as he tried to move through the room, he was stopped by what appeared to be the roof of the first floor. He exited the cavity, which was pitch dark, and found a better path through the rubble of two partially intact offices. The walls and windows of these offices had been so thoroughly vaporized by the attack that he was able to walk through them to the outside rear of the building, where the truck had detonated. He was staggered by the destruction before him.

After leaving Rishmawi, Larriera had headed back upstairs to the third floor, but she felt helpless. She had watched UN staffers Stokes and Tillett open up a supply closet and remove what appeared to be the building's only two stretchers. She went back down the stairs and caught up with Rishmawi again at the entrance to the Canal. "Have you seen him?!" she asked desperately. An Iraqi security guard approached them and said that he had seen the UN head of mission walking out of the building. Even though Larriera had left Vieira de Mello's office ten minutes before the blast and spoken with him just two minutes before it, and though it would not have been like him to walk away from such mayhem, the Iraqi sounded so authoritative that she clung to the hope, imagining that perhaps he had taken charge of the rescue from outside the building. An American soldier trying to clear the scene approached Larriera with authority. "Ma'am," he told her mechanically, "you've got to take care of yourself. We'll take care of the rescue."

Standing at the building entrance, she spotted a bulldozer moving across the parking lot, past the burned-out armored car that she and Vieira de Mello had driven to work in that morning, and toward the back of the building. She ran toward the bulldozer. As she did so, she spotted Stokes, who had carried Kolstrup downstairs and was standing at the entrance to the building. "Where is Sergio?" she cried out to him as she ran. "He is alive," he shouted back. "He has been found." "But where is he?" she yelled. Stokes pointed to the enormous pile of rubble at the corner of the building. "Over there," Stokes said. "He is trapped in the rubble."

Andre Valentine, the New York firefighter and EMT, had been one of the first U.S. medics to arrive at the scene, reaching the Canal around fifteen minutes after he heard the explosion. U.S. soldiers were already beginning to establish a security perimeter, but Valentine recalls, "We didn't know who was involved or if the bad guys were still inside." Accustomed to responding to emergencies in the United States, where a command post is established rapidly, Valentine was frustrated by the chaos. A few cool-headed U.S. personnel and UN officials had set up a treatment triage area in a grassy patch at the Canal entrance, but most UN staffers were milling about unhelpfully. "Don't worry about calling the United Nations in New York City to tell them you got blown up," Valentine said, infuriated by UN officials on their cell phones who were getting in his way. "It's pretty obvious by now. Put the damn phone in your pocket. Stop smoking. I could use your help." He grew so enraged that he instructed the U.S. soldiers around him to forbid anybody who wasn't a medic from entering the three-hundred-foot perimeter treatment area. "I want you to shoot to kill anybody other than a four-star general who comes through here," said Valentine. The other medics looked at him, unsure if he was serious.

Lyn Manuel had not moved. She lay propped up outside the building entrance, as dozens of her hysterical colleagues streamed past her. She tried to get the attention of someone with a cell phone so she could call her husband in Queens, New York. That year her brother had been killed in a hunting accident, and her father had died of a heart attack, and Manuel worried that her mother's aging heart would not withstand the news of an attack on UN headquarters. But no matter how hard she tried, Manuel was unable to get the attention of those around her. People who looked at her quickly turned their heads away. "I am not good," she cried out to Shawbo Taher, the Iraqi Kurd who was Salamé's assistant. "I am not good," she repeated. Taher tried to reassure her: "No, Lyn, you are good. Nothing is wrong with you. It's just small injuries." But as Taher recalls, "Her face was a piece of meat, a piece of bloody red meat." The Americans were ordering anybody who could move of their own accord to evacuate the area. There was still a chance that the building would collapse. Manuel, who was still losing blood, began to lose consciousness. As she did, she took note of the scene around her. She was surrounded by bodies, beige and lifeless.

Lieutenant Colonel John Curran, who oversaw the medical evacuation, did a remarkable job. He had put his men through elaborate planning drills, rehearsing an evacuation from the Canal and scoping the neighborhood for locations where helicopters could land in the event of an emergency. Thanks to his foresight and the performance of his regiment support squadron, the injured (including Manuel) were rushed from the staging area to trucks and helicopters, then flown to U.S. medical facilities. Although many would die that day, nobody would die because of the tardiness of evacuation.

Ralf Embro, an EMT colleague of Valentine's in the 812th Military Police unit, helped manage the shuttling of bodies between the treatment area and the helicopter landing area. Embro helped load the injured onto military trucks and helicopters. Over the next three hours, the trucks and helicopters shuttled some 150 wounded to more than a dozen U.S. military and Iraqi hospitals around the Baghdad area, then onward to more sophisticated facilities in Amman and Kuwait City.

Jeff Davie, Ghassam Salamé, and Gaby Pichon had each taken a different route to the rear of the building, where the bomber had struck. They had each stood up on the third floor and stared into the pit of human and material debris and concluded that, if their boss was alive, he would have to be reached from below and not from above.

Davie began prying at the rubble from the spot in the rear of the

Canal that he thought approximated where Vieira de Mello would have been holding his meeting. Almost as soon as he pulled some of the lighter concrete away and created a slight gap, he heard a voice that sounded like the one he was looking for. Davie squeezed up to his waist between what appeared to be a slab of the roof and a slab of the third floor, and he shouted out to the person who had made noise. Miraculously, Vieira de Mello answered, this time clearly. "Jeff, my legs," he said. More than half an hour had elapsed since Davie arrived at the hotel.

Vieira de Mello, whom Davie couldn't see but could now hear, was conscious and lucid. But while he knew his legs had been injured, he could not describe his physical predicament. Pinned beneath the rubble, he could neither see nor feel his legs. After a minute or two Davie removed himself from the gap and shouted out to Pichon, who was digging through the rubble some thirty feet away. "Sergio is alive!" Davie said. "But he's trapped between the floors."

Davie climbed on the rubble and spotted a twenty-inch gap between two slabs of concrete. From here, he saw the same man who had waved at him when he had been up on the third floor. Davie reached through the debris to hold his hand and spoke with him through the gap. The man said he had lost at least part of one of his legs. He said his name was Gil. It was Gil Loescher, the refugee expert who had flown in from Amman that morning. Davie told Loescher that he would go and find help.

As he raced around the Canal Hotel, Davie grabbed the first U.S. soldier he could find. It was William von Zehle, the Connecticut fireman, who was helping Valentine, Embro, and the others with medical triage in the staging area. "We've got people trapped," Davie said. He escorted von Zehle around the building to the mound of rubble where Loescher was buried. Davie told the soldier that the only way to reach Loescher was likely from the shaft on the third floor. He did not think the same was true of Vieira de Mello, who sounded far enough away—at least ten feet—to require his own separate rescue effort. After taking Loescher's pulse, von Zehle quickly left the rubble pile and made his way from the rear to the front entrance of the building, where he hoped to reach Loescher.

Annie Vieira de Mello and her two sons, Laurent and Adrien, had not yet received word of the attack. They had spent a hot afternoon at the Personnaz family lake home in France, where she and Vieira de Mello had vacationed so often when their sons were young. As they returned to shore and moored the boat, Annie saw her sister-in-law's mother rushing toward the dock. "There's been an attack!" she screamed. "Something has happened to Sergio!" Annie rushed past her and raced in her car to Massongy. Laurent and Adrien followed in the car behind. They frantically turned the radio dial in the hopes of receiving news but could confirm only that the UN headquarters in Baghdad had been attacked. When they reached their home, they turned on the television and saw the monstrous pile of rubble under which their father was buried. The crawl at the bottom of the screen gave them hope. It said their father was injured in the explosion, but that he had been given water.

After leaving Loescher in von Zehle's care, Davie hustled back to the gap where he had spoken to Vieira de Mello. But in the short time he had been away, the opening he had cleared had half-filled with mud. Mud was not something Davie expected to find in parched Baghdad, but he saw that Iraqi concrete was made of cement on the outside and clay on the inside. The bomb blast had shredded the concrete and caused the water pipes to burst, so the clay and the water were blending together, forcing the survivors and rescuers to worry about mud slides and suffocation as well as further structural collapses. Vieira de Mello's voice had grown faint. "Jeff, I can't breathe," he said. Davie, slowed by the narrowness of the space, began removing the mud and rubble from the hole. After around ten minutes, Vieira de Mello's voice became clearer. "I can breathe," he said. "I can see light."

Davie emerged again from the gap. The Americans brought small shovels, around a foot long, which were almost useless in prying away slabs of the wall and ceiling. But most soldiers were preoccupied with security, which, unlike rescue, was what they had been trained for. Colonel Mark Calvert, a squadron commander in the Second Armored Cavalry Regiment, put in place an impenetrable cordon around the building. The security he established around the site, using 450 men, was airtight. What was missing were professional rescue workers and equipment, which were what Vieira de Mello and others trapped needed. "We came to the fight with what we had," recalls Calvert. "But were the tools adequate for the fight? No way. We just weren't trained or equipped to rescue people after that kind of attack."

For around an hour Pichon joined Davie in attempting to clear rubble from the gap. Davie continued to speak with Vieira de Mello, mainly to keep him conscious and to try to pinpoint his location. "I am facing a large flat object," Vieira de Mello said. "It's dark," he said. "My head and one arm are free." He asked for water, but Davie could not reach him to provide it. Vieira de Mello repeated, "Jeff, my legs," many times. He also asked constantly about the members of his team. "Jeff, the others . . . where are they . . . who is treating them?" he asked. "Where is Carolina? . . . Where are Gaby and the others? Please look for them. Please don't leave them . . . don't pull out."[9]

William von Zehle had been an EMT since 1975. He knew from past rescue missions that the best way, and often the only way, to extract trapped people from collapsed buildings was from the inside. After briefly speaking with Loescher at the rear of the building, he had gone inside and arrived at the edge of the collapse on the third floor. Overlooking the pit of rubble, he felt as though he were standing on a balcony of a motel. He had a radio, but it didn't get reception, so he used his cell phone to telephone Scott Hill, his commander. "Tell my wife and kids I love them because I might not be coming back," he said. Hill was taken aback. "Roger that," he said. Von Zehle took off his flak jacket and prepared to enter the shaft.

He used the rebar rods poking out of the shattered concrete as hand grips to lower himself down. The rubble was so unstable that as he leaned against the debris, it frequently gave way beneath or beside him. He knew that one of the gravest risks to those trapped below was that, in his attempt to reach them, he would unleash a mini-avalanche, killing them all.

After von Zehle had ventured down around fifteen feet, the hole widened slightly. When he reached Loescher at the base of the shaft, he saw another man to Loescher's right and his own left. This man had his back to the center of the shaft. He was lying on his right side. His right arm seemed to be pointing downward, as if he had been attempting to break his fall. His legs were buried in debris, and he seemed to be boxed in between two slabs of concrete. One slab faced him, while another slab lay several inches above him. Are you okay?" von Zehle shouted. "I'm alive," the man said. "I'm Bill," von Zehle said. "What's your name?" "I'm Sergio," he said.

Although Vieira de Mello had not been visible from the top of the shaft on the third floor, he was so close to Loescher that the two men could nearly have touched hands. Vieira de Mello had been carrying on scattered conversations with his rescuers on the outside, but it had taken a tremendous strain to be heard. Now able to speak more easily to von Zehle, he asked if anybody had been killed. Von Zehle said yes but did not know who or how many. "I'm not going to get out of here, am I?" Vieira de Mello asked. "Don't worry," the rescuer assured him. "You have my word: We'll get you guys both out."

Von Zehle knew the predicament of both men was dire, but he had managed more severe rescues in the past. He telephoned his superior officer on his cell phone again. "I need rope, lighting, morphine, reinforcing rods and four-by-fours to hold the debris up, and screw jacks," he said. In his four months in Baghdad he had tried to help get the fire department up and running. He knew firsthand that the department did not have the supplies he needed. "I hope the army engineering folks have them," he said to himself.

The attack had occurred in the sector of Baghdad under the control of the Second Armored Cavalry Regiment (ACR). But the ACR consisted mainly of war fighters and had only one company of light engineers. As a result, after the attack it turned to the First Armored Division's engineering battalions, based out at Baghdad International Airport, which operated heavy engineering equipment. These combat engineers were in Iraq to build base camps, bunkers, roads, airfields, and bridges. But the equipment they used for construction could also be used for rescue and recovery operations. The 1457th Engineering Battalion, based out of Utah, which had wheeled rather than tracked engineering equipment and which prided itself in serving as the army's 9-1-1 unit, had been designated as emergency first responder in Iraq.

True to form, when the attack on the UN occurred, Major John Hansen, the operations officer with the 1457th Engineering Battalion, dispatched two separate contingents to the scene. One group, with the 671st Bridge Company, had spent the day bolting and extending a portable Maybe Johnson bridge across a river that was a ten-minute drive from the Canal Hotel. Hansen directed half of the men at the bridge, around fifteen soldiers, to UN headquarters to assist with the rescue. He told them to bring with them the heavy equipment they had been using to push the bridge across the river. The bridge company arrived around an hour after the explosion, but they were directed toward securing and clearing the outer perimeter of the Canal complex, not toward assisting the ongoing rescue efforts. They used a backhoe (a tractor with a large bucket on the front) to clear out the UN's SUVs, which were burning and smoldering and which had been scattered widely by the blast.

Hansen had also instructed a platoon of combat engineers at their airport base to saddle up and make their way to the scene of the explosion. This took time, as the platoon did not have designated equipment sets ready to go. The gear they packed included suits and gas masks to ward off nuclear, biological, or chemical fumes; pioneer kits, which contained axes, pickaxes, saws, ropes, round-mouthed shovels, square-mouthed shovels, crowbars, rigging devices, and hand tools; a half-dozen dump trucks; a tracked vehicle with one big arm known as a hydraulic excavator, so big it had to be moved on a flatbed truck; and several small emplacement excavators, which were lightweight all-wheel-drive high-mobility vehicles with digging arms, chain saws, jackhammers, and a hydraulic rock drill attached to a hose. The 1457th combat engineers did not arrive with this equipment at the Canal Hotel until approximately three hours after the blast, and even then they were not directed either to the rear of the building or inside, where their mobile equipment might have been of use.

Von Zehle needed more than equipment. He also needed help. At six feet two and 180 pounds, he was too big to maneuver in the space between Loescher and Vieira de Mello. He had been able to put an IV in Loescher's right arm. But Vieira de Mello was not nearly as exposed, and all he could do was to try to pull the rubble away by hand and prop up a few heavier slabs of concrete to stabilize the debris around him.

Von Zehle asked Vieira de Mello whether he could move his toes. He said he could. "How about your fingers?" He could. "What day of the week is it?" "Tuesday," he answered. Von Zehle was satisfied that he was lucid and could be rescued. "Is Carolina okay?" he asked. "Is she your wife?" von Zehle asked. Vieira de Mello grunted yes. Von Zehle was surprised and thought, "I don't think his wife is here with him in Baghdad." But Vieira de Mello did not seem delirious. "I didn't know who this man was," recalls von Zehle, "but it was obvious he was somebody who was a take-charge kind of guy." He had many questions. "How bad is the explosion?" he asked. "How many people are hurt?" Because Vieira de Mello never mentioned who he was, von Zehle learned only later that he had been treating the UN head of mission.

Around thirty minutes after von Zehle had descended into the hole, three faces appeared in the light at the top of the shaft. "Can we help you?" one asked. Von Zehle wasn't achieving much with his solo digging, but he worried that well-intentioned soldiers lacking search-and-rescue experience would only make matters worse. "Any of you have any training in this?" he asked. Two of the men shook their heads, but one said the words he had been waiting to hear. "I'm a firefighter paramedic from New York City," the man said. Von Zehle eyed the five-foot-seven, 150-pound man above. It was Andre Valentine, the medic who had been running triage at the entrance to the Canal. "I'm too big," said von Zehle. "Get down here."

At the top of the shaft on the third floor, Valentine took off his flak jacket, laid down his weapon, and put on his gloves. Having already treated the injured downstairs, he was almost out of supplies. All that he had left in his medical kit were three IVs, two vials of morphine, and five bandages. Von Zehle pulled himself out of the pit, and the two exchanged biographical notes. "Well, at least two people in Baghdad have done this type of work before," Valentine said. Looking down into the dark rubble tunnel below, he said, half-joking, "We should be just fine now." Von Zehle nodded. "What I wouldn't do for the right equipment right about now," he said. It was around 5:30 p.m., more than an hour since the attack. Davie tried to keep Vieira de Mello informed about the progress of the rescue. A U.S. Army medical sergeant named Eric Hartman arrived. "Eric is an expert in this type of recovery," Davie told him. "He has an expert team and engineering equipment." Vieira de Mello placed his hope in this new-found expertise. He said he could hear Hartman and called back to him several times, "Eric, can you hear me?" Hartman could not hear him, perhaps because he was turned in the opposite direction or because the noise at the site had grown too loud with the arrival of the helicopters above. "Sergio, we are trying to find a way to you from two directions," Davie said. Vieira de Mello responded simply, "Jeff, please hurry."

When Larriera approached the back of the building, Vieira de Mello's bodyguards and U.S. soldiers at the base of the rubble attempted to keep her away, roughly grabbing her by the arms and trying to deposit her back behind the cordon rope. She was stunned to see how few people were digging in the rubble itself. Most of the soldiers had their backs to the rubble and were more focused on keeping people away from the crime scene than on extracting those trapped within the pile. Larriera begged the U.S. soldiers manhandling her to start digging. "Let's use the mangled metal lying around," she tried. "Or what about your helmets?" As she bent over at the base of the enormous pile, she dug pathetically with her hands. "I thought maybe if I was digging, even if I looked like a fool, they would get the idea," she recalls. But the soldiers were following orders and continued to face away from the Canal Hotel. Several cameramen filmed the rescue, and she pleaded with them to join in. "Please help," she shouted. "Don't film! Help!"

The closest thing to civilian leadership on the scene came from Patrick Kennedy, Bremer's chief of staff, who had arrived with Colonel Sabal forty-five minutes after the bomb struck. As they entered the area, Iraqi civil defense corps guards were trying to get in, but the U.S. soldiers who had erected the cordon were trying to keep them back. "I've got to get them in," Kennedy told Sabal. "We trained them. We can't just leave them out there. This is their country." Kennedy succeeded in clearing their entry and then ran into Captain Kuhner. "Captain, what do you need?" Kuhner told him: "I need a backhoe, shoring materials to prop up the building, a C truck with a jackhammer on one end, cranes, earth-moving equipment." Kennedy said he would do what he could. He radioed Bremer's military aides and requested further assistance.

Kuhner had already sent a group of military police into town to commandeer Iraqi fire brigades. And to his delight, at around 6 p.m., ninety minutes
after the blast, two gleaming red fire engines pulled into the Canal complex.
Kuhner and a sergeant raced toward them. When they tugged at the hatches,
however, they realized that the storage cabins were bolted shut. And the vehicles had arrived with drivers but without firemen. When Kuhner asked the
driver of one of the fire engines where the keys were, the driver shrugged.
"Somebody find me bolt-cutters," Kuhner ordered. When the bolt-cutters
arrived, he and the sergeant hustled to opposite sides of the fire truck and
sliced through the iron locks. The hatches swung open. But when Kuhner
looked inside, all he saw were the legs of his colleague on the other side. The
equipment—sledgehammers, ladders of various lengths, Sheetrock pullers,
crowbars, rappelling rope, and backboards to transport the injured—was missing. "Where the hell is everything?" he raged at the Iraqi driver. The driver
shrugged. *"Ali baba,"* he said, using the derogatory Iraqi phrase for "thief." In
yet another consequence of the Iraqi looting spree, the *ali baba* had run away
with the fire department's gear.

Back in Geneva, Jonathan Prentice, fresh off the celebration of his wedding anniversary in Beirut, had gone for a run in the morning and stopped
in town for a haircut. As he walked home, he dropped by the security hut
at his regular place of employment, the Palais Wilson, home of the Office of
the UN High Commissioner for Human Rights. The security guards looked
at him like they were seeing a ghost. "What are you doing here?" one asked.
"I'm on holiday," he said cheerily. "Haven't you heard?" a guard said. "There's
been a bomb at the Canal." Prentice's stomach dropped, but he quickly assured himself that this was an incident like other incidents. He scrambled
inside the palais and joined his colleagues who were crowded around a television in Vieira de Mello's office on the top floor. When CNN showed the
size of the rubble pile that used to be Vieira de Mello's office, Prentice gasped.
He telephoned a friend at UN Headquarters in New York every half hour
for what was left of the day.

Alain Chergui, Vieira de Mello's trusted bodyguard who had left Iraq
on August 14 with Prentice and Ray, was in Bali. The Iraqi dry cleaners
had stained some of his clothes, so he spent the afternoon shopping. He
returned to his hotel and turned on the television, where he saw news of

the attack and glimpsed the back of his colleague Pichon's bald head. He desperately telephoned the close protection team members in Baghdad. He reached a Swedish bodyguard and attempted to take charge from Bali. "We're going to need blood," Chergui said. "He'll need a transfusion." The Swede sounded as though he had lost hope. "We can't get blood here," he said. "It'll be too late."

With the bomb Salim Lone suddenly became the television face of the UN mission. In his multiple appearances on CNN, Lone, whose head was bandaged, delivered unpolished, flustered comments. He often seemed to be talking more to himself than to his interlocutors. "It is quite unspeakable to attack those who are unarmed. You know, we are not protected. We are easy targets. We knew that from the beginning, but we came nevertheless, knowing there was a risk, but every one of us wanted to come and help the people of Iraq, who have suffered for so long. And what a way to pay us back."[10]

An hour later Lone appeared on CNN again: "There are also some wonderful Iraqis who died here today, so it just wasn't us," he said, noting that the UN death count had already reached thirteen. "It is such a devastating experience to be so hated, when all you're trying to do is help. I mean, every one of them who died was here as a humanitarian." The only note of optimism he sounded concerned the efforts being made to rescue Vieira de Mello. "It's just been agonizing. We're just making every effort to pull him out, and we have not been able to do it so far. But we think we have made some very good progress, and he might soon be removed from the rubble."[11] Rumors were flying among survivors, U.S. soldiers were offering speculative words of reassurance, and Lone was repeating the hopeful words on CNN.

A frustrated Captain Kuhner had nothing to show for his attempt to requisition Iraqi fire rescue equipment. He moved back to the rear of the building and made himself the primary barrier between Larriera and the pile. She thought that if Kuhner understood who was under the rubble, he might get U.S. soldiers to do more. "Sergio Vieira de Mello, the SRSG, is buried right under there," she said. Kuhner stared back blankly. "The Special Representative of the Secretary-General of the UN is buried there," she tried. Again Kuhner was unmoved. "The UN boss is buried there," she said "Kofi Annan's envoy, the equivalent of General Sanchez." Kuhner urged Larriera to go to Tent City with the other survivors. "You are only going to make it more difficult for us," he told her. Larriera would not be dissuaded. "No, I'm not going," she said. "You can't make me." The more patronizing the soldiers were with her, the more she had to struggle to maintain her calm.

Over Kuhner's shoulder Larriera saw that Davie, Pichon, and Salamé seemed to have found a way to communicate with Vieira de Mello from a hole on top of one pile of rubble. She feigned an intention go back to Tent City, which caused Kuhner to relax his grip, and then she broke free and managed to tear past him. He pursued her but was weighted down by his heavy armor.

At the rear of the building Vieira de Mello seemed to be able to hear people through two separate crevices between the concrete slabs. The first was fifteen feet up the rubble, where Davie had held Loescher's hand. The second point of entry was about fifteen feet to the right and slightly lower, near the right rear corner of the building. It was there that Larriera saw Davie, Pichon, and Salamé apparently speaking to Vieira de Mello. They could not reach him, but when Davie squeezed into the crevice up to his waist, he could see one of his boss's arms. Vieira de Mello's voice was able to carry through the crevice to where they were. He could hear and be heard. In Davie's judgment, if the UN and U.S. officials could just lift the outside collapsed slab a few inches or pull rubble away from this gap, they could reach him.

In order to speak with Vieira de Mello, which Larriera was determined to do, she needed to scale the rubble. Once she escaped Kuhner's grip, she still met resistance from her UN colleagues. Pichon, who was lower down in the rubble than Salamé and Davie, tried to wave her away, but she persisted. "What would you do if it was your wife under there?" she asked. Salamé, above, said, "Carolina, you'll cause the rubble to collapse on top of Sergio." But she would not be deterred. "You're much heavier than I am, Ghassan," she shouted. She climbed the rubble quickly, terrified that the U.S. soldiers would try to pull her down from behind. In so doing, her sandals got stuck in the mud, and she felt her skirt get caught on a piece of steel rebar. She kept moving up the rubble and grimaced as the back of her skirt tore off, leaving her underwear exposed from behind.

She stared up at one final steep flat block of concrete between her and Salamé. She cried up for help, and he extended his hand, pulling her up to where he was crouched on the pile. For the next five minutes she squatted down atop the rubble and poked her head inside the gap. "Sergio, are you there? It's me," she said in Spanish. "Carolina, I am so happy . . . you are okay," he answered, relieved by his first confirmation that she had survived. "How are you feeling?" she asked. "My legs, they are hurting. Carolina, help me," he answered. "Be still, my love," she replied. "I am going to get you out of there." But realizing that a far more industrial rescue effort was needed and feeling as though she was the only one possessed with frantic urgency, she told him that she had to leave temporarily to get proper help. "I am coming back very soon," she said. *"Volve rápido, te amo,"* he replied. "Come back quickly, I love you."

Soon after news of the blast hit London, the BBC posted a discussion page, "Baghdad UN Blast: What Future for the UN?" A diverse range of comments went up, slamming the U.S. occupation, lamenting the silence of moderate Muslims, and deploring the attack. The tenth comment on the site came from Argentina:

My sister was in the building, she works for the UN, her name is CAROLINA LARRIERA. PLEASE, any notice you have about her, send a mail. Someone notice me that she appears in the BBC TV broadcast. THANK YOU.

Pablo Larriera, Argentina

A UN staffer in Kosovo quickly posted a message, informing Larriera's thirty-two-year-old brother that she was safe. "Apparently," the UN official wrote, "she was seen on television trying to enter the site after the bomb had exploded."[12]

With Kofi Annan and his deputy Louise Fréchette on vacation and absent from New York, Iqbal Riza, the secretary-general's chief of staff, was the most senior UN official at Headquarters. He did not make calls to Secretary Powell, National Security Adviser Rice, or any other senior U.S. official to expedite the rescue because, from CNN, it looked, in his words, "as if all that could be done was being done." But it was left to UN spokesman Fred Eckhard to interface with the press. At 12:01 p.m. in New York he read Annan's first statement on the attack, from Finland. The secretary-general denounced the "act of unprovoked and murderous violence against men and women who went to Iraq for one purpose only—to help the Iraqi people." Pressed by reporters to say what implication the attack would have for the UN, Eckhard said he had few doubts that "we're going to stay the course."[13] Responding to charges that the UN had been lax with its security, he said, "The security is the responsibility of the Coalition partners. We depend on the host country for our security wherever we work in the world."[14]

The chaos at the Canal Hotel on August 19 stemmed in part from the novelty of the occasion. Only one large attack on a civilian target had occurred before in Iraq, and that was just twelve days before, the August 7 attack on the Jordanian embassy. But the bulk of the confusion was the result of multiple, dueling command structures and improper planning that gave rise to insufficient capacity. Wherever the United Nations set up operations around the world, it depended on local authorities for emergency services. If the UN Headquarters in New York City were hit, New York firemen and police would rush to the scene and FBI officers would investigate. In Baghdad, just as the UN had relied upon U.S. and Iraqi forces for protection, so too the UN now relied upon both for rescue.

But when it came to rescue in Iraq, it was unclear just who constituted the "local authorities." Were they American or Iraqi? The Coalition had become the "provisional authority," and it was an American civilian, not an Iraqi fireman, who actually ran the Iraqi fire department. U.S. soldiers at the Canal did not know what equipment the Iraqi fire department had, where the equipment was located, or who had the authority to summon it. If Americans were in charge, should U.S. civilians or military officers command the scene? Again, had the attack occurred in the United States, the division between civilian and military responders would have been clear. Even when the Pentagon was struck on September 11, 2001, it was the Arlington, Virginia, fire chief who served as the on-site commander for ten days. Even the most senior Defense Department officials technically answered to him. But in Iraq, while it was civil affairs officers who had rescue experience, they didn't have the rank to issue instructions to their superior officers. "There was no one evidently in charge," recalls Patrick Kennedy, Bremer's chief of staff, who himself lacked any line authority over the U.S. military.

So the UN wasn't in charge, the Iraqi fire department wasn't in charge, and the U.S. Army tried to be in charge, but, in Valentine's words, "they hadn't dealt with a blown-up building before. They didn't know what to do." For Valentine and von Zehle, two of the few men on the scene who had experience undertaking rescue missions, descending into the shaft was something of a relief. At least they would henceforth be masters of their own destinies.

Desperate to do anything she could to help her fiancé and stunned by the lack of urgency and the primitive state of the rescue, Larriera left the rubble and went to Tent City to beg for help. She tried to get the UN's most senior officials involved. The highest-ranking UN official at the Canal that day, apart from Vieira de Mello, was under-secretary-general Benon Sevan, who was visiting from New York. But Sevan did not return to the Canal once he reached Tent City. As Larriera prodded him to take charge, he refused even to make eye contact with her. Lopes da Silva, Vieira de Mello's deputy, seemed to be constantly on the phone to New York. He had paid just one visit to the rear of the building. Bob Adolph, the head of security, also was in Tent City. "Who is in charge?" Larriera pleaded, begging one of the men responsible for security to go to the back of the hotel. "The soldiers there have no idea who is under the rubble! Sergio is dying!" Both men attempted to assure Larriera that the maximum was being done. "We're trying to get him out, Carolina," Lopes da Silva said. "You have to calm down." As she chased after him, he turned his back, saying, "The Americans are in charge."

Having failed to get help in Tent City, Larriera attempted to make her way once again to the rear of the Canal. But by this time the army had established an inner cordon of soldiers, sandbags, and trucks, preventing UN officials and nonspecialist U.S. soldiers from reaching the back of the building. Larriera paced the length of the inner cordon, pleading with U.S. soldiers to let her pass, but she was blocked. Although she had promised Vieira de Mello she would return, she could not do so.

Bremer might have helped streamline the multiple lines of command, but he did not arrive at the Canal Hotel until dusk. Since Eckhard had taken a swipe at the security provided by the United States, Bremer asked Kennedy and Sabal to find out what protection U.S. forces had offered. Sabal wrote Bremer's query in his notebook: "How do we answer the question of why we were unable to provide security?" Sabal scribbled next to it: "Lack of troops." While at the Canal, Bremer spoke to the media. "My dear friend

Sergio is somewhere back there," he said. "It may well be that he was the target of this attack." From Bremer's remarks, it was clear he believed that pro-Saddam loyalists were responsible. "These people are not content with having killed thousands of people before," he said. "They just want to keep killing and killing and killing. And they won't have their way."[15] He was sure that, despite the attack, the UN would stay. "I'm absolutely certain that the United Nations, instead of cutting and running, will stand and stay firm, as indeed the Coalition will."[16]

Back in the United States, President Bush was on vacation at his ranch in Crawford, Texas. So many journalists were away that New York *Newsday* columnist Jimmy Breslin called August 19 a day when "a congressman could commit homicide and not make the news."[17] Bush received word of the attack while playing golf. Initially he kept playing, but after an hour he returned to his ranch and issued a statement at 7:05 p.m. Baghdad time. "The Iraqi people face a challenge, and they face a choice," the president said. "The terrorists want to return to the days of torture chambers and mass graves. The Iraqis who want peace and freedom must reject them and fight terror."[18]

The UN lacked any in-house capacity to determine who had carried out the attack or to bring the plotters to justice. But the FBI response in the immediate aftermath of the attack was impressive. When the bomber struck, Thomas Fuentes, who ran the FBI unit in Iraq, was at Baghdad airport, and he used GPS to guide him and a team of agents to the blast. Within an hour of the explosion nearly two dozen agents had descended on the crime scene to begin sifting through the rubble to gather evidence. This was the first attack in which U.S. civilians had been among those targeted, so the FBI's jurisdiction was uncontested.

When Fuentes arrived, Iraqis were crowding around the army's outer cordon rope, calling out the names of loved ones who worked in the building. Iraqi teenagers had come with coolers to sell Pepsis to the crowd.[19] The spinal hospital, which was on the opposite side of the access road from the Canal, had also been badly damaged by the blast. Ten of its patients had been injured, and the others, many of whom were survivors of Iraq's three wars, were petrified. Some were trapped for more than an hour under the collapsed roof, while others, who were barely dressed, were rolled outside in their wheelchairs and left sitting, carrying their catheter bags, in the scorching sun.[20]

On the day and evening of the nineteenth, the FBI analysts avoided the rear of the Canal, where rescue efforts were proceeding, and instead fanned out in a lot beside the spinal hospital. Three hundred feet from the point of impact, the lot was layered with a wide variety of debris: shards of metal from the bomber's truck, rubble from the cement walls, and multiple body parts belonging to the driver himself. Fuentes's team included one experienced bomb-blast expert, who was in the country to help investigate the Jordanian embassy attack, and he offered on-site training to the others so they could efficiently assemble the forensic clues. The explosion had sent pieces of evidence in hundreds of directions, and they would eventually be retrieved from a five-square-mile area. In but one testament to the scale of the strike, the crater from the explosion, which was around three and a half feet in diameter and around five feet deep, could have easily fit a Volkswagen.

Valentine, the New York medic, had an even bigger crater to navigate. "Keep your eyes closed, folks," he said as he rappelled downward into the shaft. He was worried about the cascading debris. "I'm coming down!" Loescher answered him, saying, "Good, I need your help." But Vieira de Mello was silent. In his twenty-eight-year career the American EMT had dealt with multiple collapsed buildings and had once extricated a woman trapped under a crane in New York City. But although he had already served eleven months in Afghanistan and four months in Iraq, this was his first wartime civilian rescue effort.

EMTs are trained to follow their ABCs—they focus on Airways, Breathing, and Circulation—and to stop massive bleeding. They consider themselves only the first line of defense in medical rescue: They deal with these basics and move on. "I know my job," Valentine says. "I am supposed to do meatball surgery on the casualties and wait for the cavalry to come in behind me with the real equipment and the real specialists." As he made his way down this Baghdad shaft, though, Valentine knew nobody was pulling up his rear.

Valentine reached Loescher around 5:45 p.m. He was lying at a 45-degree angle with his head lower than his feet, which had helped to maintain his circulation. Valentine used IV fluid to wipe away the plaster dust from Loescher's face and tried to keep his patient conscious by asking about his family. "Are you married, Gil?" he asked. "How many kids?" Loescher said he had two daughters, and Valentine said he had six children. "We'll get you out of here so you can dance with your wife very soon," the EMT said. "But

I'll be in a cast," Loescher said. "You've never danced on crutches before?" Valentine asked.

When Ralf Embro returned to the triage area outside the Canal Hotel entrance after loading casualties onto trucks and helicopters, he entered the building and shouted, "Are there any eight-twelve medics up here?" When he reached the third floor, one U.S. soldier screamed back, "Yeah, there's a medic here, but he's down the shaft." Embro peered into the hole, and Valentine shouted up, "I need to get the rubble off the casualties. We need to get a pulley system going."

Embro was at a loss. He had neither pulleys nor anything in which to put the rubble. He scrambled around the dark offices of the third floor and returned carrying a curtain, a curtain drawstring, and a woman's large straw handbag. "This is all we got," he said. He tied the curtain rope around the handbag and lowered it down past von Zehle, who was perched halfway down the shaft, to Valentine. Using his bare hands, Valentine cleared loose rubble and deposited no more than half a dozen chunks of concrete at once into the handbag, which Embro and two U.S. army privates hauled upward. The curtain, a makeshift stretcher, would prove useful only if Loescher or Vieira de Mello could be dislodged. As Embro and the others hauled the rocks upward, they held on to beams that quaked. Embro worried that Valentine and von Zehle would end up trapped like those they were aiming to save.

Loescher's legs appeared to have been crushed below the knees by the ceiling of Vieira de Mello's office. Valentine reached into Loescher's pocket and took out a passport. He placed it inside the handbag with the rubble. From that point on the assembly line of U.S. soldiers knew the name of the man they were attempting to help. They also knew he was an American. "Gil, stay awake," Valentine said repeatedly. "We're going to get you out of there."

Vieira de Mello was four feet to the right of Loescher but trapped in a separate pocket. His right leg remained buried in rubble, along with his right arm, which was extended downward into the debris. Whereas Valentine was able to squat to treat Loescher, he could access Vieira de Mello only if he lay on his stomach and stretched his left arm into the tight space above Vieira de Mello's head. By lying on his belly, the medic was able to shine a flashlight down to Vieira de Mello's legs, which were partially submerged and bleeding. He was also able to tie a bandage around his left arm and find a vein for an IV on the first try. He inserted the IV and hung a bag of fluid on a steel rebar rod that was poking out of a piece of hanging concrete. "Get me out of here," Vieira de Mello said in a clipped tone.

The attempted extraction was torturously slow. Valentine was the only soldier who was compact enough to fit at the bottom of the shaft. He crawled between the two men, trying to keep both of them talking, offering morphine or fluid where he could, but mainly stalling while he attempted to dig the rubble out from under and on top of them. Valentine spent most of his time working on Loescher. He was pessimistic about Vieira de Mello, whose right arm was lodged in such thick debris that he didn't see how he could extricate it. He began thinking about severing the arm, but he wouldn't have the space to do that, or to move Vieira de Mello into the base of the shaft, until he had removed Loescher, who lay in his path. When Valentine removed rubble around Vieira de Mello, the only place he could put it was in the cavity where Loescher was lying. "I had a plan. I had to get Gil out first, then I would have someplace to put the rubble, and I could try to move Sergio to where Gil was," Valentine says.

In their brief interactions, though, Vieira de Mello grew irritated by Valentine. "Are you a Christian?" the medic asked. Vieira de Mello said he was not. "Do you believe in the Lord Our Savior?" Valentine continued. He again grunted no. "We're in a tough situation here," Valentine said. "We should pray to God together."

Vieira de Mello was having none of it. "I don't want to pray," he said. "If God was who you say he is, he wouldn't have left me here."

"God has reasons for everything he does," Valentine insisted.

"Fuck God," Vieira de Mello said. "Please just get me out."[21]

While Valentine, von Zehle, and Embro manned their own minirescue from the inside, their efforts were hampered by the efforts of well-meaning rescuers on the outside of the building. Because nobody had taken overall command of the rescue effort, good Samaritans in the U.S. military and the UN were largely free to make up rescue tactics as they went along. Valentine and von Zehle were grateful to the medics on the outside who passed IV bags, bandages, morphine, and bottled water through the external cracks to the two rescuers. But they wished the others would clear out. They had almost managed to remove the rubble from Loescher's torso when somebody working from outside removed a slab that sent broken cement tumbling down on top of Loescher. The unburial would have to begin again. "The army was doing what to it seemed logical," recalls von Zehle. "Common sense would tell you, if somebody is underneath a pile of stuff, you start pulling that stuff off the pile." But what was logical wasn't helpful. Valentine, who was short-tempered on the best of days, was furious. "Tell them to stop messing around," he bellowed up the shaft. "Are they morons?" He needed professional equipment, not amateur assistance. "We knew we had a time problem. Every rescue has a golden hour," recalls von Zehle. "And we were getting well beyond the golden hour."

The FBI agents outside also had a golden hour. They had to gather forensic evidence before the crime scene became contaminated. And unlike Valentine and von Zehle, the FBI officials were making terrific progress. At 6 p.m., half an hour after the FBI team arrived on the crime scene, the bomb-blast specialist approached lead agent Fuentes, holding a ten-inch-long, three-inch-wide, and two-inch-thick shard of twisted metal in the shape of a banana peel. "I know what kind of bomb it was," the analyst said. Fuentes stared at the slender strip of metal incredulously. He was not a forensic expert and was amazed that such a small piece of metal could yield such a sizable clue. "It was a 1970s Soviet-made aerial bomb," the analyst said.

The evidentiary bounty would only grow. Within minutes another FBI agent approached Fuentes. This one was holding the axle of the truck and part of the door, which was engraved with the vehicle identification number. The next morning a CNN journalist would phone to say that a large hunk of metal the size of a desk had landed at a military checkpoint across Canal Road, nearly a mile from the scene of the explosion. It took three agents and a pickup truck to retrieve the metal, which contained the license plate of the truck. Rounding out the clues, an FBI analyst would present Fuentes with the left hand of the bomber. The hand, which had been severed at the wrist, was still clutching part of the truck's steering wheel and had been found on the roof of the U.S. civil-military operations building where von Zehle worked.

Fuentes thought the investigation was in unusually good shape: He had a range of witnesses who had seen the truck turn onto the service road; he had the make of the bomb and the vehicle identification number; and he had the means to fingerprint the bomber. He used a volunteer team of some one hundred soldiers to gather the grenades, mortars, and smaller explosive devices that had been strapped to the aerial bomb. The plotters had attached hundreds of munitions, but they had failed to add the necessary fuses, and almost all of the ordnance ended up in the FBI's six-foot-high pile.

Inside the shaft von Zehle had turned himself into a human beam. Halfway down the vertical tunnel, he had wedged his head up against one side of the passage and jammed his butt up against the other. This shielded Loescher and Valentine from any rubble that fell from above. Serving as a middleman on a slow assembly line of rubble removal, he continued to hope that engineering equipment would arrive. Large machinery was always cumbersome to work with and usually proved more useful for recovery of the deceased than for rescue of the living. But in this instance, since slabs of the roof and floor had fallen virtually intact, von Zehle thought holes could conceivably be drilled into the top slab, bolts could be inserted, and a crane might be able to pull an entire slab upward. Von Zehle knew the risks of using such equipment. While removing a large slab could free a person pinned below, doing so might also cause debris to shift, endangering both the survivors and the rescuers, who would need to remain in the shaft so as to stabilize the two injured men. Von Zehle also knew that sometimes collapse victims stayed alive only *because* the weight of the rubble on top of them slowed internal bleeding. He worried that rapidly removing the concrete around Loescher and Vieira de Mello might counterintuitively expedite their demise. In the United States during building collapse emergencies, rescuers would weigh these risks, relying heavily upon building plans and on structural engineers who by glancing at a site could determine which maneuvers would minimize the risk of further collapse. Here, von Zehle knew, no such layouts or building specialists were available. Nonetheless, as he helped inch the woman's handbag up to the third floor, he hoped the assembly line would soon begin moving in the opposite direction, supplying at least the light materials and tools that would be indispensable for rescue.

But it didn't. What Valentine and von Zehle most needed, the 1457th Engineering Battalion did not bring to Iraq: lumber. With just a few four-by-four planks or even simple plywood, they could have stabilized the shaft and become more aggressive in their removal of the rubble beneath and above the two injured men. As it was, with nothing to shore up the walls, they had to proceed gingerly. Because the U.S. Army had never responded to a car bombing of this scale nor attempted excavation in a collapsed building, it had not made stockpiling wood a priority. In Iraq, where there were almost no forests and where builders relied on cement and concrete for construction, wood was almost impossible to come by. Only as it got dark, around 7 p.m., did Major Hansen, the head of operations for the 1457th, dispatch a small quantity of the scarce lumber from Baghdad airport to the Canal. "We didn't know what we were getting into," says Hansen. "Rescue and recovery from a crumbled building is its own specialty. It is not something we had ever done. We did everything we could think of to help, but at the end of the day we were combat engineers, not EMTs or firefighters." The two American medics had trouble fathoming that even basic lumber was beyond their reach.

The other items that the men needed, but which they did not really expect to receive, were the spreaders and cutters that would have allowed them to saw through rebar and I-beams inside the shaft. But while this equipment is standard issue with the Federal Emergency Management Agency and many fire departments in the United States, the army did not issue it to units in Iraq. The closest substitutes in the army stocks were gas torches, but these torches, which did not arrive at the Canal until long after dark, relied on external gas sources. Their extension cords would not have reached the base of the shaft. As a result, while the U.S. military possessed state-of-the-art war-fighting equipment, from the time of the blast at 4:28 p.m. to the time the rescue effort was terminated after dark, the most powerful military in the history of mankind was forced to rely for rescue on brute force, a curtain rope, and a woman's handbag.

Valentine knew he was running out of time and that the cavalry was not coming. He had stabilized Loescher but needed to extract him from the hole in order to get him medical care. He was afraid that even if he managed to move the wall covering Loescher's legs, the whole building would collapse on top of them. He decided he had no choice but to cut Loescher out of the rubble. "Gil, I have a question for you, and I want you to consider it carefully," he said. "Are you prepared to allow me to amputate your legs?" Loescher, who was still conscious, did not hesitate. "Just get me out of here," he said. "I want to see my family."

Valentine had the consent of his patient, but he did not have a surgical instrument. He called up the shaft, and the GIs went scavenging around the Canal Hotel. In a few minutes they returned with a rusty carpenter's saw and passed it down the shaft in the handbag. Valentine shrugged. This would have to do. A U.S. Army surgeon appeared at the top of the shaft, and Valentine asked his permission to begin cutting. "Do what you have to do to get him out," the surgeon said. Valentine injected Loescher with ten milligrams of morphine, tied two bandages like tourniquets below his knees, and began using his scissors and saw to remove what was left of Loescher's lower legs, above the ankles. Loescher fell into such a state of shock that he did not cry out in pain. After Valentine removed Loescher's two feet, he worked with von Zehle to pry the injured man free.

Jeff Davie and Gaby Pichon were unaware that rescuers inside were so close to their boss. They continued to take turns from the right outside rear of the building, trying to dig a crevice large enough to reach Vieira de Mello. The heat was dangerous. Around ninety minutes into the attempted rescue Davie had fainted, and Pichon had pulled him out of the gap and taken over. Pichon worked furiously in the hole, but the heat quickly got to him as well, and a U.S. soldier replaced him. Davie went to get water, and when he returned ten minutes later, he asked the soldier if he was still able to speak with Vieira de Mello, and the soldier said no. It was close to 7 p.m.

The gap that Davie and Pichon had attempted to widen had seemed promising. Yet more than two hours after the explosion, they had little to show for themselves but false starts. The final demoralizing blow came when they began digging into a corner of the collapsed roof, only to realize that the "hole" that they had worked to expose at the bottom of the collapsed corner was nothing more than a hole in the insulation of one of the ceiling walls. A further four inches of concrete lay below it. They were exhausted and had run out of ideas. Davie turned to Pichon and said what neither man had been willing to admit before: "There is no way to reach Sergio from outside without lifting the roof."[22]

Inside the shaft, Valentine had not given up. As the minutes ticked by, Vieira de Mello was growing less responsive. "I need you to work with me, Sergio. I need you to stay awake," Valentine said, nudging him and pinching him back to consciousness. "I'm going to die, aren't I?" Vieira de Mello asked. Valentine didn't have a good answer. For all the digging, the UN head of mission remained in the identical position he had landed in after the blast. Around 7 p.m. Vieira de Mello stopped initiating conversations but was still able to answer lucidly when spoken to. When Valentine asked, "Sergio, Sergio, are you okay?" he answered yes or no. But by around 7:30 p.m., Vieira de Mello was responding only to painful stimuli, and his breathing was growing more labored. "You could tell he was going into shock," von Zehle recalls.

Since Annie, Laurent, and Adrien returned to their home in Mossongy, the telephone had been ringing constantly. Annie answered hoping for news, but each time it was close friends and relatives rather than somebody in Iraq who knew something. When she telephoned UN Headquarters in New York, the officials she spoke with were watching the same broadcast on CNN and offered no additional information or grounds for hope.

Xanana Gusmão, East Timor's president and Vieira de Mello's close friend, turned on CNN just before he and his wife, Kirsty, went to bed in Dili. The UN blast was the top story. Initially the reports had been encouraging. The special representative had been injured, they were told, but he was being given water. He would be rescued. But as Gusmão sat transfixed by the CNN coverage over the next three hours, he grew agitated. He spotted Larriera on the television screen attempting to evade U.S. soldiers. "It's Carolina!" Gusmão exclaimed. He began screaming at the television screen, "Let her through!" He saw a handful of men digging with their hands in the rubble. "Where are the goddamn bulldozers? Where are the saws?" he asked as he paced in front of the television. His wife was similarly flabbergasted by the primitive rescue effort. The pair stayed up watching, hoping. Gusmão continued yelling, but his anger turned to desperation. "Where are the Americans? Why aren't they coming?!" he pleaded. He watched a muscular bald man motioning helplessly for extra help. It was Pichon. But as the minutes ticked by, Gusmão began to weep. "They're not going to save him," he said. "They're going to let Sergio die."

In fact, the rescuers in the shaft were making progress. Having amputated Loescher's feet and wrestled him free, Valentine and von Zehle loaded him onto the curtain stretcher that Embro had devised. As the men at the top of the shaft pulled, he and von Zehle pushed from below. After 8 p.m. Loescher reached the third floor, with Valentine behind him. Valentine pulled himself out and lay down next to the stretcher, exhausted. He had been in the hole for almost three hours. "We're up, Gil," he said. Somehow Loescher retained partial consciousness. "Thank you," he said. None of the medics placed high odds on Loescher's survival, but they knew that if he could reach the U.S. Army hospital in Landstuhl, Germany, he would receive top-of-the-line medical care.

Embro helped carry Loescher on a litter to an ambulance, which drove around the rear of the building, where it met up with a Black Hawk helicopter. It was only then that Embro saw the site of the explosion. "Holy shit," he said out loud. After placing Loescher in the care of others, he headed back toward the entrance of the Canal Hotel to assist in Vieira de Mello's rescue. But as he entered, he bumped into Valentine, who was carrying his medical bag, dripping with sweat and covered in blood. "The other person didn't make it," he said.

Larriera had spent the first hour after the bomb scrambling between the third floor and the rubble pile at the rear of the building. She had then rushed to Tent City and unsuccessfully tried to persuade senior UN officials to assert themselves in the rescue effort. Since U.S. soldiers had blocked her attempt to get back to the Canal, she had sat down on the ground as close as she could get, beside a telephone on a plastic lawn chair. Someone told her to man the phone.

A stream of medics, U.S. soldiers, and UN officials walked past Larriera, but none paid her any attention. At around 8 p.m. an American officer passed her en route to the rear of the building. Larriera blocked his passage, and he promised he would find out how Vieira de Mello was faring. Soon after he left, a Red Cross ambulance blared by her and past the inner cordon to the Canal building. The American returned. "I have good news," he said. "Your man has been rescued." He pointed upward. "You see that helicopter," he said. Larriera's heart leaped as she eyed the Black Hawk medical helicopter in the sky. "He's in there." But the man said he also had bad news. "We had to amputate his legs," he said. She sighed in relief. "As long as he is alive," she said, "I don't care about his legs." But something in her gut told her the man was not credible. "How do you know that was Sergio?" she asked. "I was told by the rescuers," he said.

Jeff Davie had refused to give up. Having exhausted all options from the outside rear of the building, he decided at last to head back to the third floor. He expected to find it cluttered with rescue personnel but instead found it vacated. A flashlight was lying at the entrance to the shaft, and Davie picked it up and shone it down upon the spot where the man who had identified himself as "Gil" had been lying. Loescher was gone, but Davie saw that the back of another person had become visible. He crawled into the shaft and quickly discerned it was Vieira de Mello. The removal of rubble and the extraction of Loescher had exposed a small pocket adjacent to the shaft where Loescher had lain.

Davie faced the back of Vieira de Mello's head. He lay close to the concrete roof, which was what Davie had not been able to penetrate from the outside. A triangle had formed between the roof, the floor of Vieira de Mello's office, and the black leather sofa, which had partly cushioned his fall and stopped the sliding rubble from crushing his back and head. "Sergio!" Davie shouted. "Sergio!!" There was no answer.

A group of U.S. soldiers called out from above and shone their flashlights down. One of them, a U.S. Army engineer lieutenant colonel, scaled downward and joined Davie's effort to remove rubble. It was this U.S. engineer who first reached around Vieira de Mello's neck, where he found no pulse. Davie, who had been working nonstop for four hours to rescue his boss, slumped in despair. He suddenly felt very tired.

Every day for the previous week General Michael Rose, the controversial British general who had commanded UNPROFOR in Bosnia, had been meaning to send Vieira de Mello an e-mail commending his recent outspokenness against the occupation. Finally, during the evening of August 19, he headed up to his study to write the note he'd been formulating in his head. "You're taking the absolutely correct position," he remembers writing. "If the Coalition continues to overuse force, they'll cause more and more Iraqis to join the resistance. Hang on in there." As Rose wrapped up the e-mail, his wife, Angela, called up the stairs. "Did you send that e-mail to Sergio?" she asked. "No, I'm just typing it up now," he answered. "Don't bother," she said.

Recovering Vieira de Mello's body remained a risky task, as the rubble continued to shift. Davie and the U.S. engineer removed some electric cabling that was blocking the way. They tied a rope around his waist, and the soldiers on the top floor pulled so that he was finally yanked from the protected triangle abutting the shaft. This was the first time Davie was able to see Vieira de Mello's body. His legs were lacerated. His left sleeve was torn and his left hand was covered in blood. Improbably, he had been lying on a part of the UN flag that had hung in his office. He was pulled up to the third floor and placed on a stretcher. It was around 9 p.m.

Ghassan Salamé was asked to identify Vieira de Mello's body. He headed up the stairs and pulled back the sheet. Vieira de Mello looked calm. The only visible sign of trauma were small specks of blood on his bronze face. He was driven to the morgue at a U.S. base near the airport, where around fifteen bodies were already lying inside the U.S. Army tent.

At 2:24 a.m. East Timor time (9:24 p.m. Baghdad time, 2:24 p.m. Brazil time, 1:24 p.m. New York time), CNN correspondent Michael Okwu said, "We understand, Kyra, from the UN spokesman's office, that Sergio Vieira de Mello has, in fact, passed away. We understand that this was given to us just moments ago—Mr. Vieira de Mello, of course, a fifty-five-year-old veteran, a Brazilian diplomat who was highly respected here at the United Nations." Adrien, Laurent, and Annie Vieira de Mello saw this announcement before they heard from anybody at UN Headquarters.

Not long afterward, Wolf Blitzer turned to the camera and told his viewers that it was their turn to weigh in on the story. "Our Web question of the day is: 'Is Iraq becoming a quagmire for the U.S.?' We'll have results later in this broadcast."

In Rio de Janeiro, Vieira de Mello's eighty-five-year-old mother, Gilda, was confused. People who lived in her apartment building, family members, and close friends had been arriving at her apartment all day. Complete strangers were even gathering outside on the street. Afraid all summer that her son would be confused for an American, she had increased her dosage of antianxiety medication. André Simões, Vieira de Mello's nephew and godson; Antonio Carlos Machado, his closest childhood friend; and Dr. Antonio Vieira de Mello, his closest cousin, broke the news. When she let out screams, Dr. Vieira de Mello administered sedatives.

At the Canal Hotel, Larriera was still awaiting news. Around 9 p.m., fifteen minutes after the U.S. officer told her Vieira de Mello had been helicoptered to a hospital, she overheard Lopes da Silva say to somebody else, "Sergio is dead." She began screaming and rushed toward him. "Tell me it's not true," Larriera pleaded. Lopes da Silva turned toward her and said, "He's gone."

Larriera refused to leave the Canal Hotel until she saw his body, but at 11 p.m. she was informed that it had already been transported to the American morgue. She was taken to a private home rented by UN officials and given a sedative. At the crack of dawn the next morning, she demanded to be brought to him. When her colleagues refused, she left the house and began walking in what she thought was the right direction. A UN official quickly caught up with her and drove her to her hotel, where she was told by Ronnie Stokes, the head of administration, that she and other survivors were being evacuated. Back in the room that she and Vieira de Mello had shared for more than two months, she packed up eight pieces of luggage and retrieved a suit he had had specially tailored in Thailand on their trip, as well as the green tie she had given him for his birthday.

Pichon and another of Vieira de Mello's bodyguards, Romain Baron, who had checked himself out of an Italian hospital despite suffering a bad shrapnel wound to the shoulder, took the suit to the morgue. There they washed their boss's body and ripped the back of the suit in half so as to be able to dress him. Baron placed a rosary in his hand. The two bodyguards then said goodbye. Vieira de Mello looked elegant to the end.

In the end Salamé helped arrange for Larriera to go to the morgue. When she arrived, she ran inside, only to find Vieira de Mello lying on the table. It was then, gazing down at the lifeless body, that his death sank in. "His body was there," she recalls. "But Sergio was gone." The suit suddenly looked too big on him. He was wearing his gold engagement ring, which had "Carolina" inscribed on the back, and the gold chain he had worn for many years, with a golden "C" he had taken from her necklace and worn as a pendant. The blast had somehow stripped him of his silver necklace and silver dog tags, which had borne his name, his birth date, and an engraved UN flag.

From his first day in Iraq he had kept on his nightstand an e-mail that Larriera had sent him, urging him to keep faith in himself while there. "While Iraq is a deviation from our goal of permanently establishing ourselves and our life," she had written him, "nothing will separate us again. We are one, and we will walk on this road of life together." On this day, their last together, she folded up the e-mail, which she had retrieved from their room at the Cedar, and placed it in his pocket. "I will always love you, Sergio," she said, sobbing. Before she left, she was given a small U.S. Army bag with Vieira de Mello's possessions: bloody dollar bills, Chapstick, a bloody handkerchief, and the engagement ring they had taken off his finger.

The same day, by coincidence, East Timorese officials were holding a ceremony to rebury those who had died in the war of independence against

Indonesia. They had gathered more than six hundred skeletons in Waimori, a four-hour drive from Dili. Some twenty thousand mourners and dignitaries stood solemnly to pay their respects to the fallen guerrillas. Xanana Gusmão stepped up on the stage to make his remarks. He informed the audience that Sergio Vieira de Mello had been killed by a bomb in Iraq. The audience gasped. When Bishop Felipe Ximenes Belo read the long list of names of martyred Timorese, he added one more: that of Sergio Vieira de Mello.

President Xanana Gusmão (right) and Prime Minister
Mari Alkatiri (left) in East Timor.

Twenty-two

POSTMORTEM

RETURNING TO THE CANAL

The night of August 19 the UN officials who had survived the Canal Hotel bombing gathered in their Baghdad hotels. Many were so paralyzed by shock that they had not yet cried. But when they walked into the hotels where they slept and saw colleagues whose fates they had not known, the events of the day hit them and they wilted. Often it was only when they reached their rooms and looked in the mirror that they realized they were covered in blood. In many cases the blood was not their own. Information on the dead and injured was hard to come by, but surviving staff were under the impression that anybody who had been in, near, or under Vieira de Mello's office on the third floor had not made it.

Hearsay competed with facts all night, but the list of the known dead and gravely wounded was long. Many of the deceased had been killed instantly, and their families were notified. For others, like Lyn Manuel, Vieira de Mello's Filipina secretary, and Nadia Younes, his Egyptian chief of staff, rumors of sightings persisted well into the evening. Finally both the Manuel family in Queens and the Younes family in Cairo were notified that neither woman had survived the blast.

Those listed as killed, in addition to Sergio Vieira de Mello, the UN Special Representative of the Secretary-General, were:

United Nations

Reham al-Farra, 29, Jordan, spokesperson

Emaad Ahmed Salman al-Jobory, 45, Iraq, electrician

Raid Shaker Mustafa al-Mahdawi, 32, Iraq, electrician

Leen Assad al-Qadi, 32, Iraq, information assistant

Ranillo Buenaventura, 47, Philippines, secretary

Rick Hooper, 40, United States, political officer

Reza Hosseini, 43, Iran, humanitarian affairs officer

Ihssan Taha Husain, 26, Iraq, driver

Jean-Sélim Kanaan, 33, Egypt/France, political officer

Christopher Klein-Beekman, 32, Canada, program coordinator for United
    Nations Children Fund (UNICEF)

Marilyn "Lyn" Manuel, 53, Philippines, secretary

Martha Teas, 47, United States, manager of the UN Humanitarian Information
    Center

Basim Mahmood Utaiwi, 40, Iraq, security guard

Fiona Watson, 35, United Kingdom, political affairs officer

Nadia Younes, 57, Egypt, chief of staff

Others

Saad Hermiz Abona, 45, Iraq, Canal Hotel cafeteria worker

Omar Kahtan Mohamed al-Orfali, 34, Iraq, driver/interpreter, Christian
    Children's Fund

Gillian Clark, 48, Canada, child protection worker, Christian Children's Fund

Arthur Helton, 54, United States, director of peace and conflict studies at the
    Council on Foreign Relations

Manuel Martín-Oar Fernández-Heredia, 56, Spain, assistant to the Spanish
    special ambassador to Iraq

Khidir Saleem Sahir, Iraq, driver

Alya Ahmad Sousa, 54, Iraq, consultant to the World Bank Iraq team

Secretary-General Annan was not known for allowing people to get close
to him, but he spoke of Vieira de Mello and Younes as if they were excep-
tions. He had known Vieira de Mello since their days together in UNHCR
in the 1980s, and Younes had been his chief of protocol for three years in

New York. As he stopped briefly at Stockholm's airport en route back to New York, he was less diplomatic than usual. "We had hoped that by now the Coalition forces would have secured the environment for us to be able to carry on . . . economic reconstruction [and] institution building," Annan said. "That has not happened." Ever careful, though, he added, "Some mistakes may have been made, some wrong assumptions may have been made, but that does not excuse nor justify the kind of senseless violence that we are seeing in Iraq today."

Annan did not consider pulling the UN out. "The least we owe them is to ensure that their deaths have not been in vain," he said. "We will persevere." The UN had operated in Iraq for more than twelve years without being attacked. "It's essential work," he said. "We are not going to be intimidated."[1] Annan's line echoed that of U.S. officials in Iraq and Washington.

On August 21 Kevin Kennedy, the former U.S. Marine and UN problemsolver, landed back at Baghdad airport in Iraq. Although he had lost Vieira de Mello and several other close UN colleagues, he knew that he was in a more stable psychological state than those who had actually lived through the attack, who were in no condition to manage arranging the evacuation of the wounded and the deceased.

Kennedy walked across the tarmac, where some fifty shell-shocked UN personnel were gathered in advance of being evacuated to Jordan. Carolina Larriera approached him, frantic. "I'm not getting on the plane to Amman," she said. "They are making me leave. I want to go on the plane with Sergio." The Brazilian government had dispatched an air force 707 to Baghdad to collect his body. Kennedy had been told that Annie would be on the Brazilian plane. He called Lopes da Silva. "Carolina wants to fly with Sergio," he said. "What the hell do we do?" Lopes da Silva was decisive. "Get her on that plane to Amman," he said. "Get her out of here." Kennedy assured Larriera that she would be able to meet the Brazilian plane in Amman, and she was steered onto the UN plane with the other bomb survivors.

Most of the families of the deceased had begun making burial arrangements. Lyn Manuel's grief-stricken family in Woodhaven, Queens, was no exception. Manuel's husband of thirty-four years and her three children had already held a private memorial service at their home and were awaiting the return of Manuel's body for the funeral. At 3 a.m. on August 21, two days after the bombing, Eric and Vanessa, Manuel's two youngest children, aged twenty-five and twenty-nine, were sitting in their living room telling stories about their mother. The phone rang, and Eric answered it. The line was filled with static. Eric's heart stopped. "Hello," the voice said. "Hello, Eric. It's Mom." "What?" he said. "It's Mom," she answered. "Eric, it's Mom." Seeing the look on her brother's face, Vanessa ran upstairs and picked up the other phone. Lyn Manuel, whom UN officials in Iraq had listed among the dead on August 19, was calling from a U.S. Army clinic outside Baghdad. She had regained consciousness next to a patient with a cell phone. Manuel panicked when she heard the voice of her daughter, who lived in Hawaii and had not planned a trip to Queens. "Is everybody okay?" Manuel asked. Her son and daughter assured her that everything was fine and did not tell her about the mix-up. Instead, they wished her a happy fifty-fourth birthday and told her they loved her. After hanging up, they collapsed in sobs of joy.

As the bomb survivors prepared to fly out of Baghdad, an FBI team established a kind of checkout procedure by which UN staff left their names and contact details. Many of the UN officials questioned were hostile to the FBI, which they saw as yet another offshoot of the U.S. occupation, but most agreed to make themselves available for future questioning. The FBI inquired particularly about the UN's Iraqi staff, and two Iraqis who worked for the UN were detained and interviewed repeatedly in the days that followed. The United Nations did little to keep survivors and family members informed of the progress of the investigation, beyond setting up a confidential Web site and a Listserv (iraqinvestigation@ohchr.org) through Vieira de Mello's office in Geneva. The site was barely used.

On August 22, the day after Larriera and other survivors were shepherded out of Baghdad, the Brazilian government's 707 arrived to collect Vieira de Mello's casket. The plane would then make its way to Geneva, where it would collect Annie, Laurent, Adrien, and their guests, en route to Brazil. William von Zehle, the Connecticut fireman who had kept Vieira de Mello company in the shaft during his last hours, had written a letter to Annan in which he described fragments of what Vieira de Mello told him under the rubble. Von Zehle distinctly recalled the dying UN official saying, "Don't let them pull the mission out."

On the tarmac at the coffin ceremony, Benon Sevan, the highest-ranking UN official on the scene, quoted from von Zehle's letter in urging a continued UN presence:

Sergio was fully committed to the United Nations until his last breath. Even under the most extreme pain, pinned down under the rubble of his office, he said . . . "Don't let them pull the mission out." . . .

Our beloved Sergio . . . Bowing before you at this very difficult hour, I assure you that no heinous act of terrorism will deter us from carrying out the noble tasks entrusted to us in the service of the United Nations. We will resume our activities as of tomorrow and continue your legacy.[2]

Those closest to Vieira de Mello were skeptical that, having so soured on the ineffectual UN mission, he would have made such an appeal. But Annan and the press henceforth made frequent reference to his alleged last wishes. "His dying wish was that the United Nations mission there should not be pulled out," Annan declared. "Let us respect that. Let Sergio, who has given his life in that cause, find a fitting memorial in a free and sovereign Iraq."[3]

The media tried to provoke Annan into blaming the Bush administration for going to war in the first place, but the secretary-general remained politic. "We all know the military action was taken in defiance of the Council's position," he said. "Lots of people in this building, including myself, were against the war, as you know, but I think we need to put that behind us. That is something for historians and political scientists to debate." The UN's focus needed to be on the future, as "a chaotic Iraq is not in anyone's interests—not in the interest of the Iraqis, not in the interests of the region, and not in the interest of a single member of this organization."[4]

Vieira de Mello's family was divided over where he should be buried. A cosmopolitan, he had not lived in Brazil since he was a boy, but his pride in his nationality had intensified over the years. His mother, Gilda, was desperate for him to return home. Annie proposed that he be buried in her family's plot in a cemetery near Massongy. In the end the Swiss government extended an invitation for him to lie in rest at Geneva's exclusive Cimetière des Rois, or Cemetery of the Kings, the small, elegant gated cemetery where Argentine writer Jorge Luis Borges was buried and which, eerily, Vieira de Mello and Larriera had visited twice that spring. André Simões, his thirty-seven-year-old nephew, explained the decision to a Brazilian journalist: "His sons said that, as their father was always absent, at least now they would be near him." Simões's voice faltered. "It is understandable."[5]

Carolina Larriera did not manage to reach Vieira de Mello before he was

buried. After traveling to Amman, she attempted to get a connecting flight
to Rio de Janeiro in time for the memorial service. But officials in New
York were worried that if she and Annie converged, there would be an ugly
scene. With a cold formalism that was excessive even by the standards of a
gargantuan bureaucracy, they told Larriera that staff rules dictated that the
UN would pay only for her to return to her home country of Argentina. She
would have to make her own way to Brazil. Larriera flew from Amman to
Paris to Buenos Aires and on to Rio de Janeiro, but by the time she arrived
in Rio five days after the bombing, still in the torn and bloody skirt she had
been wearing the day of the attack, her partner's casket was gone. The Brazilian 707 had left for Geneva earlier in the day.

Thomas Fuentes, the head of the FBI's Iraq team, had gathered a wealth
of evidence at the crime scene. In the World Trade Center bombing of 1993
and the Oklahoma City bombing of 1995, the vehicle identification number
had led the FBI to the terrorists. In Baghdad the FBI had that number, as
well as the license plate number and the hand of the bomber.[6] But for all of
the encouraging early clues, the investigation quickly stalled. Because Muslim
burials typically occur within twenty-four hours of death, Iraq did not have

*Left to right: Gilda Vieira de Mello, Carolina Larriera, Renata and
André Simões, and Sonia Vieira de Mello at a memorial mass in
Rio de Janeiro seven days after the Canal Hotel attack.*

refrigerated morgues. The only facility available to store the UN's deceased and the body parts of the bomber had been the air-conditioned morgue at the U.S. base near Baghdad International Airport. But even in the American morgue the temperature often reached 100 degrees because of electricity shortages and overcrowding. As a result, the hand of the bomber, which had seemed a promising source of fingerprints, had begun to decompose. Hoping to preserve it, Fuentes got permission to have it flown back to the United States with the three deceased Americans. But by the time the hand reached the FBI laboratory in Quantico, Virginia, the forensic analysts were able to retrieve only partial fingerprints. And the FBI analysts later learned that Saddam Hussein's Iraq had never created a fingerprint data bank. Thus, Fuentes had no Iraqi records with which to compare the bomber's markings. Equally frustrating, he established that the Kamash truck had been made in Russia and purchased by the Iraqi government, probably back in 2001. But despite having its manufacturing and license plate numbers, the FBI was unable to find the vehicle records kept by the Iraqi government—they were presumed to have been looted.

UN senior staff in New York left the criminal investigation to the FBI and focused on the future of the UN in Iraq. Heated debates commenced about what had become known as the UN's "perception problem," the Iraqi belief that the UN was a stooge of the Coalition. Before any long-term decisions would be made, senior staff agreed on the necessity, in the words of one Iraq Steering Group debate, "to reduce the size of the 'UN target.'"[7] International staff who had survived the bomb were required to take fourteen days of leave, and most would not be sent back.* The four thousand Iraqi nationals who served the UN were also granted leave, though they were instructed to take it inside Iraq.[8]

Ghassan Salamé flew to New York, his first trip back since he had accompanied Vieira de Mello to brief the Security Council in July. He told the secretary-general and other senior UN staff that the UN was caught in a catch-22: "If we do not accept increased protection from the CPA, we would be reckless," he argued. "But if we accept their security, we will reinforce the perception that we are 'hand in glove' with the CPA."[9] The most vocal

---

*By September 23, there would be forty-nine internationals in Baghdad and forty-seven in northern Iraq.

advocate of withdrawing all UN staff was Kieran Prendergast, the head of the Department of Political Affairs, who was devastated by the death of Rick Hooper. He did not believe that the UN was doing enough good to justify its continued presence in Iraq. "The UN has not been able to establish a differentiated brand," he argued. "If a fortress is required to ensure security, why be there?"[10] He urged his colleagues to ask a simple question of the mission the UN was undertaking in Iraq: "Is it worth risking the life of one individual?"[11] Staying, he argued, was nothing more than "a suicidal mission."[12] The downsized UN team that remained in Iraq did little beyond concentrate on securing themselves. Most staff were especially frightened in their hotels at night, and some, Lopes da Silva wrote to UN Headquarters, "were displaying signs of irrational behavior, including requests to carry firearms."[13]

The UN posted twenty-six additional security staff to Baghdad, a dramatic expansion of the tiny squad that had been overwhelmed all summer. Coalition intelligence officers, who had tended to shun UN requests for information on the insurgency prior to the bomb, were suddenly forthcoming. On September 1 they warned the UN that they had intelligence that three heavy sewage trucks had disappeared and one of them might be used to target the UN between September 5 and 10.[14] On September 2 a report

UN staff in Baghdad at a prayer memorial, August 30, 2003.

from Erbil, in northern Iraq, said that two vehicles marked UN-HABITAT were missing and might have been stolen and packed with explosives.[15] Later UN officials picked up a rumor in Baghdad that U.S. forces were the ones who had attacked the Canal Hotel so as to drive the UN from Iraq and, in the words of one UN Iraqi staffer, "keep government to themselves."[16] Although no evidence surfaced to bolster this theory, the Bush administration's well-established hostility to the UN made it a popular one in the Middle East and in Vieira de Mello's native Brazil.

Since the Canal Hotel had been reduced to rubble, Lopes da Silva, Kennedy, and others scouted Baghdad for other properties. The Coalition again offered to house UN staff inside the Green Zone, but Kennedy declined. He and Lopes da Silva soon concluded that it would be easier to fortify the Canal complex and consolidate UN staff there than to find a new, safe space. The Canal was, Kennedy said, "the best solution in a worst case scenario."[17]

Containers where UN staff would now work and sleep were flown in from Kuwait and set up on the Canal grounds near the ruins of the hotel. UN staff began to refer to the Canal complex as "Fort Knox." The Coalition replaced the antiaircraft platoon outside the premises with a reinforced U.S. rifle company. But because UN staff remained concerned about the signal such a partnership sent, the UN went back to reviewing bids from private security firms that might guard the vulnerable premises.[18]

All of the security precautions that had not been taken—or that had been taken halfheartedly—before August 19 now got full attention. UN security officials in Iraq kept a constant watch on the mission's staff lists, gathering not only names but blood types, contact details, radio call signs, and cell phone numbers. They created an inventory of available resources: radio and communication equipment; protected vehicles; flak jackets; helmets; Mylar plastic film for the windows; and ballistic blankets that could shield doors, windows, and people. The security staff went about setting up emergency medical facilities, a security operations room, and new external wall barriers at the Canal. They expanded the number of bunkers meant to shelter staff during mortar attacks and pasted luminescent arrows on the ground between the containers to guide staff to the exits in the event that an attack caused darkness or occurred at night.[19] Kennedy urged his bosses in New York to appeal to UN member states to replace the lumbering UN transport planes that were so vulnerable to ground fire with military aircraft that could detect and neutralize surface-to-air-missiles.[20] In the meantime the UN varied its flight times and stopped publishing its timetable. It also repainted part of its fleet of vehicles from navy and orange back to plain white and removed the UN decals.[21]

As the weeks passed, and as insurgents unleashed a wave of fresh attacks against a broad range of Iraqi and international targets, it became clear that the attack on the Canal Hotel had marked a turning point in Iraq's history. Colonel Mark Calvert, the squadron commander who set up the security cordon on August 19, recalls, "We had a lot of NGO support up until that time, people flooding in wanting to help, bringing capabilities that combat forces don't have. When that bombing took place, it had a devastating impact on reconstruction and development, which was exactly what the terrorists wanted." Security unraveled for civilians everywhere. On August 29 a car bomb outside the Imam Ali Mosque in Najaf killed ninety-five people, mostly Shiite pilgrims.

On September 2, acting on advice from the Security Management Team in Baghdad, Tun Myat, who ran the UN security department in New York, recommended that the UN in Iraq move to Phase V, the highest security level, and withdraw all its international staff from Baghdad.[22] Secretary-General Annan, the only UN official with the authority to order an evacuation of staff, rejected the recommendation, saying it would send the wrong signal to terrorists. On September 13 a ninety-minute gun battle erupted outside the perimeter of the Canal Hotel complex. The staff felt intensely vulnerable, but Annan remained determined to show the UN flag. "We didn't stay in Iraq to do anything," recalls one UN official. "We stayed in Iraq to show we were staying."[23]

Senior UN staff in New York were naturally caught up in a blame game that intensified with time. All-knowing analysts in the United States, Europe, and the Middle East pointed to the ominous warning signs that Vieira de Mello and other UN officials missed. The consensus view was that the UN had been naïve in viewing itself as untouchable and in failing to appreciate just how hated the organization was in Iraq, owing to sanctions, weapons inspections, and (thanks to Vieira de Mello's high-profile intermediary role) its association with the Governing Council. Just as people had speculated as to what the Jordanian government had done to earn the ire of the August 7 attackers, everybody seemed to have a theory as to why the UN had been so savagely struck.

UN officials in New York walked around like zombies for a month and then gathered on September 19 for a large commemoration in the giant General Assembly hall. Annan spoke of his "irreplaceable, inimitable, unforgettable friends." "When we lost them, our Organization also suffered another loss, of a different kind: a loss of innocence for the United Nations," he said. "We, who have tried from the beginning to serve those targeted by violence and destruction, have become a target ourselves."[24] The August 19 attack, many noted, was the UN's "9/11."

The day of the memorial service, the UN flag at the Canal Hotel was raised to full mast for the first time since the attack. UN staff in Baghdad were impatient for guidance from headquarters and warned New York: "If the UN is to remain in Iraq, and particularly if it is to re-engage in political affairs, the Organization must assume that it will be the victim of more attacks."[25]

At 9 a.m. on September 20 Aquila al-Hashimi, the Shiite Muslim who had helped arrange Vieira de Mello's meeting with al-Sistani and one of three women on the Governing Council, was ambushed by nine gunmen on a residential street two blocks from her home in western Baghdad. Guarded only by her brothers, who did not wield weapons, she was shot in her abdomen and died five days later. It was the first assassination of a member of Iraq's Governing Council. Prior to her murder, Iraqi politicians were not given Coalition bodyguards or police escorts, disproportionately endangering independents on the council who did not have their own militias.[26]

The insurgents were not finished with the UN. On September 22 at 8:04 a.m., a man driving a small gray Opel sedan approached the back gate of the Canal compound, where he was told by Iraqi guards that he would have to park in the dirt lot across the street, where Iraqi UN staff and the guards themselves parked. In accordance with the UN's post–August 19 heightened security screening procedures, an Iraqi guard approached the Opel and asked the driver to open his trunk. When he did, the driver detonated two sets of explosives—one in the trunk and one that he was wearing as a belt. The blast blew the car in half, killing the Iraqi guard and the bomber instantly and injuring nineteen others. Iraqi guards complained that they were wearing bull's-eyes, being forced to guard buildings without training, weapons, or flak jackets, while well-fortified American soldiers avoided such hazards. "We are just like human shields for the Americans," said Haider Mansour al-Saadi, twenty-two, a guard who received shrapnel wounds to his hand and leg in the blast.[27]

The attack that killed Vieira de Mello and twenty-one others the month before had occurred at the end of the day. Amid the frenetic focus on rescue and identification, the UN Security Management Team in Baghdad had not had the chance to recommend a full staff withdrawal before Annan had announced that the UN was staying. But this second attack on the UN occurred in the morning, Iraq time. By the time senior staff in New York reached their offices, the security team had already cabled New York with the "unanimous recommendation" that the secretary-general declare Phase V for all of Iraq.[28] Aware that local staff were often forgotten in New York, the security staff stressed that "the security and safety of national and international staff members must be considered on par."[29]

Annan, however, ignored the advice of his Iraq team and that of his senior staff (all but one of whom voted to evacuate Iraq), and again rejected the recommendation to pull out. The staff in Baghdad were incredulous.

The insurgent attacks on soft targets (which only began with the bombs at the Jordanian embassy and the UN) continued. On September 25 the hotel housing the staff of NBC News was hit, a sign that the media had become a target. Two days later three projectile rockets were fired at the Rashid Hotel inside the Green Zone. This marked the first time a civilian target inside the Green Zone had been hit. On October 9 a Spanish diplomat was assassinated. On October 12 the Baghdad Hotel, which housed American contractors and Governing Council members, was bombed, killing eight and wounding thirty-eight. On October 14 the Turkish embassy was struck. On October 26 the Rashid Hotel, where U.S. deputy secretary of defense Paul Wolfowitz was staying at the time, was hit again, killing one and wounding fifteen. And on October 27, the first day of Ramadan, in a devastating coordinated assault, four bombs were detonated simultaneously, including one at the Baghdad headquarters of the International Committee of the Red Cross, which killed thirty-four and wounded two hundred. Three days later, after the Red Cross announced it was leaving, Annan finally declared Phase V, and all UN international staff were at last withdrawn from Baghdad.

The secretary-general launched two investigations into staff safety and

security surrounding the Canal Hotel attacks. The first, chaired by former
Finnish president Martti Ahtisaari, produced a short report nine weeks after
August 19. The second, chaired by Gerald Walzer, the former deputy high
commissioner for refugees who had been the one to give Vieira de Mello
a flak jacket as his going-away present from UNHCR, yielded a 150-page
report, with six volumes of supporting documents, and was delivered to
Annan on March 3, 2004. After receiving the Walzer report, which described
the UN security system as "dysfunctional," the secretary-general called for
the resignation of Tun Myat, the UN security coordinator, who complied.
Additionally, the UN took disciplinary action against Paul Aghadjanian, the
chief administrative officer, and Pa Momodou Sinyan, the building manager,
who had failed to ensure that the windows were coated with Mylar or that
the concrete wall was completed. Since Lopes da Silva had been the designated security official, Annan demoted him, stripping him of his assistant
secretary-general rank and barring him from taking UN posts with security
functions.[30] Louise Fréchette, the deputy secretary-general who had chaired
the Iraq Steering Group in New York where security was discussed, offered
her resignation to Annan, but he refused it.

UN staff and bomb survivors felt let down by the secretary-general. At no
time did he delve into the UN's more fundamental failings on Iraq—failings
that had far broader implications for the future of the organization than the
absence of blast-proof plastic sheeting for the windows. Why had Annan so
eagerly accepted the Security Council's summons to go to Iraq? Why did he
send his finest staff to enforce an almost nonexistent mandate? Why, after the
attack, had he chosen to keep UN staff in harm's way, even though they were
not performing vital tasks? What would it take for the UN secretary-general,
in fact, to learn to say no to powerful countries?

Friends and family of those attacked on August 19 speculated that Annan
found the Iraq experience so searing that he could not face it. Many thought
he and Fréchette had staged a phony resignation scene even though they had
no intention of instituting accountability at the highest levels. Some were
furious that Annan himself did not step down. They blamed him for allowing junior staff to take the fall for what were above all leadership failures. "If
you were in the room with Kofi Annan, with Iqbal Riza [his chief of staff],
and with Tun Myat," notes one UN official, "you wouldn't see Tun Myat as
responsible for anything."

And the heavyweight countries on the Security Council seemed to care no more about UN staff in the aftermath of the bomb than they had in May when they sent the UN to Iraq in the first place. When Rafiq Hariri, the former Lebanese prime minister, was murdered in February 2005, the UN Security Council leaped to commission an investigation into his murder that cost around $50 million per year. But when it came to the murder of UN staff, the Security Council seemed indifferent. As the violence in Iraq escalated, the memory of the UN attack faded.

SURVIVORS

Gil Loescher, the only person who survived the meeting in Vieira de Mello's office, was flown to Landstuhl, Germany, and given a 25 percent chance of making it. Building upon Andre Valentine's primitive but lifesaving sawing procedure, the doctors in Germany amputated both of Loescher's legs above the knee. On September 2 Loescher regained enough consciousness to begin mouthing words and asking about the pain in his legs. But only in late September, more than a month after the attack, did he realize he had been permanently handicapped. "Now, I have no knees, right?" he asked his daughter.

For more than a year after the attack, tiny shards of glass would work themselves free from his skin.[31] His face was badly scarred, and he initially had no use of his right hand, but he made remarkable progress, reacquiring the use of his hand and mastering computer-assisted prosthetic legs. He returned to the book he had been writing on protracted refugee crises, and in 2006 he managed to travel to the northern Thai border to interview Burmese refugees. In one of the camps, he made a special point of trying to visit an out-of-the-way care center for disabled refugees run by Handicap International. But after wheeling himself across the camp, he found that the facility had been built atop a steep mud bank that his wheelchair could not ascend. Resigned to turning back, he suddenly saw five Burmese faces peering down at him from the top of the bank. The Burmese, each of whom had a wooden prosthetic leg, made their way down the bank, raised Loescher's wheelchair onto their shoulders, and carried him up the hill.

Loescher divides his existence into his "first life" and his "second life." He says that on occasions when he is tempted to feel sorry for himself, he thinks about all that was lost on August 19, including his close friend Arthur Helton. He also thinks about refugees. "My whole career I have been visiting refugee camps, and without realizing it, I was getting tutorials about resilience. If they can bounce back, I certainly can." He says he has his blue periods, but he does not ascribe those to his injuries. "There is plenty to feel blue about in the world," he says.

While Loescher lives with the visible scars of the attack, Vieira de Mello's bodyguards endure the ghosts of August 19. Gaby Pichon, the French close protection officer who was just twenty feet away from his boss when the bomber struck, says his dreams are haunted by his failure to save the man entrusted to him. "Why him and not me?" he says. "I have flashbacks. It is not like a TV that you can turn off. I don't have a remote control." Gamal Ibrahim, the Egyptian who guarded Vieira de Mello in East Timor and for the first two months in Iraq, removed himself from the UN's close protection roster after the bomb and transferred to the canine unit. "I never want to get close to anybody I'm protecting again," he says. "Working with a dog is fine for me." Alain Chergui, who on Vieira de Mello's insistence had taken leave five days before the bomb, is convinced he would have found a way to save his boss. He cannot forgive himself for being absent when it mattered most, for Vieira de Mello, for the UN, and for the world. "If I weren't married," he says, "I would probably be dead now. I would have shot myself maybe. Protecting Sergio was what I was there to do; it was all I was there to do."

Lyn Manuel, fifty-eight, is back living in Queens and working at UN Headquarters. She has undergone four plastic surgeries on her face and five on her injured left eye, and her recovery is nothing short of miraculous. But, because she has lost vision in the left eye, and her good eye has begun to falter, she plans to retire in 2008. She knows that, for many UN officials, she is a walking reminder of the dead.

Jonathan Prentice and Carole Ray, Vieira de Mello's special assistant and secretary, who had gone on leave with Chergui just days before the bomb, live with the knowledge that their replacements, Rick Hooper and Ranillo Buenaventura, died at desks that they normally occupied. After their boss's death, they remained at the Office of the High Commissioner for Human Rights in Geneva partly as a way of staying close to his memory. "I'm not sailing quite so close to the sun as I did when I rode Sergio's coat tails,"

Prentice says. "But maybe that's not as important as I once thought it was, or as Sergio thought it was."

Two of Vieira de Mello's closest friends in the UN, Omar Bakhet and Dennis McNamara, had been outspoken, unconventional staff members throughout their tenures with the organization. On many occasions when they got into trouble with their higher-ups, Vieira de Mello had intervened on their behalf. The year after the Canal attack, Bakhet left the UN, and today he advises the African Union on how to restructure itself. McNamara, who had achieved the rank of assistant secretary-general, retired in 2007 and currently works as a consultant on how to protect civilians in African conflict areas. Although they had sparred constantly, McNamara and Vieira de Mello had worked together in Geneva, Cambodia, Congo, Kosovo, East Timor, and Iraq. "Had things gone differently," he says, "Sergio and I would surely have ended up in some other godforsaken place together." Fabrizio Hochschild, Vieira de Mello's special assistant in Geneva, New York, Kosovo, and East Timor, shared his mentor's taste for working in the field, but he also tried to do what his boss and friend had never managed: put family first. The father of three children, Hochschild returned to Geneva from Tanzania after the Baghdad bomb and became director of operations for Louise Arbour, Vieira de Mello's successor as UN High Commissioner for Human Rights. He took periodic trips to the world's hot spots but tried to remain close to home, even learning how to become a manager.

Martin Griffiths, who became Vieira de Mello's friend late in life, had left the UN in 2000 to run the Henry Dunant Center for Humanitarian Dialogue in Geneva, where he serves as a mediator among war combatants. Glad to be free of the shackles of UN red tape and politicking, he believes Vieira de Mello was himself on a path toward reconciling his personal and professional ambitions. "Sergio had devoted his life to the ideals and organization of the UN. And the countries in it had failed and disappointed him just as much as they had enriched and glorified him," Griffiths observes. "The thing about Sergio was his youth. He still wanted what youth wants. He was getting more and more impatient about the half-measures he had. His tragedy was not his death—that was our tragedy. His tragedy was that he never finally arrived at that state of equilibrium that adults call happiness."

Annie Vieira de Mello, who still lives in Massongy, remains very close to her sons, Laurent and Adrien. Both in their late twenties, the two men have deliberately eschewed the public spotlight. Laurent works as an engineer in Zurich, while Adrien, who graduated with a degree in geography, works in construction and building design in Geneva. With all that has been written and broadcast about their father, they have gained a deeper understanding of why he was so often absent during their childhoods.

Carolina Larriera is the only person who both survived the bomb and lost a loved one. Afflicted by a severe case of post-traumatic stress syndrome, she left the United Nations and moved to Rio de Janeiro. There she and Vieira de Mello's mother, Gilda, attempted to raise his profile in Brazil, a country that has become acquainted with him only in death. They also pushed the UN to investigate the attack and the failed rescue effort. Larriera spoke with the FBI, tracked down William von Zehle, and along with Timorese foreign minister José Ramos-Horta, visited Gil Loescher in the U.K., but she made little headway.

In early 2004, after she and Gilda collected a bagful of sand from Vieira de Mello's favorite spot on Ipanema beach in Rio, she flew to Geneva, where she visited the cemetery they had discovered together, and she sprinkled the Brazilian sand upon his grave. Later that year she reenrolled in the master's degree program at the Fletcher School, which she had been slated to start the month of the attack. In 2006, after graduating from Fletcher, she began teaching international relations at Pontificia Universidade Cátolica in Rio, and the following year she took a job running the Latin American office of an organization that lobbies for access to medicines for the poor.

Gilda Vieira de Mello, who was eighty-five at the time of the attack, remains mentally alert, physically fit, and feisty. She had long declared herself too old to fly, but in 2004 she made an exception, taking one last foreign trip to Geneva to attend the ceremony commemorating the one-year anniversary of the Canal Hotel attack. She remains in deep mourning, her apartment a virtual shrine to her deceased son. She and Larriera see each other almost every day. They blame George W. Bush for the Iraq war, and blame Kofi Annan for sending Vieira de Mello to Iraq. On New Year's Eve 2006 they drank a bottle of champagne to toast the end of Annan's term as secretary-general.

The Canal Hotel stands vacant in Baghdad. The building is distinguished by the fading blue and white paint on the arches and the gaping three-story black hole in its side. Under significant pressure from the Bush administration, Annan reestablished a UN presence in Iraq a year after the attack. In July 2004 Ashraf Jehangir Qazi, a Pakistani diplomat, was named special representative. Since the desire to maintain the appearance of independence had long been trumped by security concerns, Qazi lived and worked holed up in the Green Zone, protected now by a small contingent of UN soldiers from Fiji.[32] He and his team offered political and humanitarian advice to the Iraqi government when they could, but their role was marginal. Where once Iraqis who worked for the UN eschewed any connection with the Coalition, today they avoid association with the UN as well, working undercover. In November 2007 Vieira de Mello's friend Staffan de Mistura replaced Qazi in the thankless job. "I agreed for one reason, for one man," de Mistura says. "I don't know anybody who can walk in the shadow of Sergio. But maybe we can all surprise ourselves and achieve something by trying."

Most of the survivors of the attack and the family members of the deceased went several years without learning the identity of the perpetrators. Only in 2006 did some happen to learn from the media that in January 2005 one Awraz Abd Al Aziz Mahmoud Sa'eed, known as al-Kurdi, had confessed to helping plan the attack for Abu Mussab al-Zarqawi, al-Qaeda's leader in Iraq. In July 2006 a small UN delegation made its way from Baghdad's Green Zone to the U.S. detention facility at Camp Cropper, where al-Kurdi was detained. He had been arrested for involvement in another attack and then confessed to his role in the UN bombing.

In a three-hour interview the UN officials were persuaded that al-Kurdi, thirty-four years old at the time of the attack, was not lying. The father of two, he had been imprisoned for joining the rebellion against Saddam Hussein after the Gulf War in 1991. He had been released in 1995 in one of Saddam's amnesties. He had joined al-Zarqawi's group in 2002 and served as a driver to al-Zarqawi, who had also lived at his home for four months. Later promoted to become "General Prince for Martyrs," al-Kurdi said that in August 2003 al-Zarqawi had instructed him to plan attacks on both the Jordanian embassy and the UN headquarters in Baghdad. At that time al-Zarqawi's network was so poorly understood by U.S. intelligence operatives that he and al-Kurdi had no trouble meeting daily. Later, for security reasons, their meetings would have to be scaled back to once a month.

Al-Kurdi had personally surveyed the premises in advance of the bomb.

He had tried several times to enter the UN complex, using a false ID and posing as a UN job seeker, but he had been blocked. He had gotten inside the neighboring spinal hospital with a false identification and surveyed the short distance between the unfinished brick wall and the Canal building. He said that he told al-Zarqawi that there was "only one place where we can get through." It was via the narrow access road that ran beneath Vieira de Mello's office.

Al-Kurdi did not personally know that the UN envoy kept his office in the most vulnerable part of the building, above the unfinished wall, but he knew that the UN boss was the target. He had placed the odds of success at only 50 percent "because the truck, going toward the building, could be noticed and even one bullet could have killed the driver." He said his group had moral concerns. "We realized that this could of course cause damages to the hospital itself and this would damage the reputation of our organization and would backfire on us," al-Kurdi said. "We were even hesitant to do it."

On August 18, at al-Kurdi's house in Ramadi, al-Zarqawi had explained to the designated bomber, Abu Farid al-Massri, the reasons for targeting the UN. Al-Zarqawi told him that al-Qaeda's decision-making council had ordered the strike because a UN senior official was housed there who, in al-Kurdi's words, was "the person behind the separation of East Timor from Indonesia and who was also the reason for the division of Bosnia and Herzegovina." Al-Zarqawi spent the entire night with the bomber, while al-Kurdi and his children slept in the next room. Al-Zarqawi personally helped load the bomb onto the truck. Disappointed by the force of the Jordanian attack, he had been the one to decide to attach mortars and the plastic explosive C4 to the TNT.

Originally al-Kurdi was scheduled to leave Ramadi at 6 a.m. for a 9 a.m. attack, but he received a telephone call before departing, delaying the strike until the afternoon. He drove the truck to the neighborhood of the Canal Hotel and arrived around noon. The bomber was driven separately and met up with al-Kurdi at the Canal at 3:30 p.m. Al-Massri had chosen to set off the detonation device manually instead of having it detonated remotely. Al-Kurdi reminded him of how to use it and pointed out the access road and the target.

After parting ways with al-Massri, al-Kurdi waited across the street for ten minutes, and then, after seeing the truck explode, he melted into the crowd and returned to his home in Ramadi. He had been instructed not to leave the area until he heard the sound of the explosion. When he arrived at his house, however, his coconspirators were angry with him for not staying long enough to be able to report the results. But they later learned from the media that Vieira de Mello had in fact been killed. The UN questioners asked al-Kurdi if he and al-Zarqawi considered the operation a success. "The purpose of the attack was to send the message and [it was] not like a military operation that is a victorious or failing operation," he said. "But with the death of Sergio, we believed that the message has been fully sent and if Sergio had not died then half of the message would have been sent."[33]

When al-Kurdi elaborated on the motives behind the attack, he said that he had his own view as to why the UN in general and Vieira de Mello in particular were appropriate targets:

> For me personally as an Iraqi, I believe that the resolutions of the UN were not just and a lot of harm has been caused to the Iraqi people for thirteen years, like hunger and diseases. Actually, the [UN] sanctions were on the Iraqi people and not on the government . . . Secondly, a lot of Islamic countries have been through injustices and various occupations and foreign troops using the UN resolutions . . . against Muslim people under the name of the UN. Maybe the UN is not the one issuing these resolutions, but there are super powers using the UN. Crimes are committed in Islamic countries and so we wanted to send the message to this organization . . . The compromise can be before the fight, but not after the fight, and if the UN wanted to rescue the people, it should have intervened before the catastrophe [took] place . . . A lot of families and children have been killed.

Al-Kurdi pleaded not guilty in the Iraqi court. He explained his reasoning: "Maybe during some of the operations innocent civilians were killed, but we didn't intend or mean to kill any child, and if it happened by mistake we asked God for mercy and forgiveness." The insurgency was fully justified, he said:

> My country is occupied, and I didn't go [to] any other country to fight . . . My country has been occupied by foreign troops without any international legitimacy, and the people have been killed, and my religion says that I should

fight. Even the Christians and the Seculars say that when your country is occupied you have to fight the occupier, and that's not only in the Muslim countries but also in the Christian areas like Vietnam, Somalia, and Haiti. Where the countries are occupied, it is legitimate to resist the occupier. There is no religion or international norms or traditions whether Eastern or Western or anybody who is supporting the occupation of my country from either a religious or an intellectual point of view. The ones who cooperate with the occupier should receive the same treatment that the occupier receives . . . As far as I'm concerned, I'm innocent. I didn't kill any people from the street. I didn't steal money from any house . . . There are thousands of Iraqis who are in Abu Ghraib jail or other jails of the occupation without charge for two or three years and nobody can help, and you are telling me that you don't want them to attack the UN or the Red Cross or others . . . When the Americans came, they stepped on our heads with their shoes so what do you expect us to do? Death is more honorable than life . . . You can ask the regular people about this, and now even the people they are wishing that the days of Saddam would come back.[34]

On July 3, 2007, as U.S. troops in Iraq prepared to take time away from the bloody civil war in order to mark American Independence Day, the Iraqi government hanged al-Kurdi. In the few wire stories that covered his execution, journalists referred to several of the high-profile attacks he had helped to orchestrate. None saw fit to mention his involvement in the attack on the United Nations.

EPILOGUE

By the time Sergio Vieira de Mello went to Iraq, he knew too much. He knew that governments were prone to define their national interests in the short term and to neglect the common good. He knew that dangerous armed groups were feeding off of individual and collective humiliation and growing in strength and number. He knew that they were often more nimble and more adaptive than the states that opposed them. And he knew that the UN, the multinational organization that he believed had to step up to meet transnational security, socioeconomic, environmental, and health concerns, had a knack for "killing the flame"—the flame of idealism that motivated some to strive to combat injustice and that inspired the vulnerable to believe that help would soon come.

Vieira de Mello made mistakes and delivered few unvarnished successes that could be guaranteed to last (the world being too complex for guarantees). Nonetheless, as long as he was around—treating the most intractable conflicts as if peace were one phone call away, eschewing diplomatic hierarchy in the frantic pursuit of solutions, and remaining unflappable, impeccable, and seemingly untouchable while the shells rained down around him—a flame continued to flicker somewhere.

He is now gone. But what are we to take from what he saw, what he learned, what we lost? Where, in other words, do we go from here?

While many have responded to today's divisions and insecurities with ideology, Vieira de Mello's life steers us away from one-size-fits-all doctrine

to a principled, flexible pragmatism that can adapt to meet diffuse and un-
predictable challenges.

A BROKEN SYSTEM

In the aftermath of the bomb at the Canal Hotel, Secretary-General Kofi
Annan attempted to convey just how irreplaceable Vieira de Mello had become and just how severe the loss would be for the world. "I had only one
Sergio," he said simply.[1] He knew nobody who had Vieira de Mello's linguistic skills, cultural breadth, critical mind, political savvy, humanitarian commitments, and world-weary wisdom. "Sergio," as he was known to heads of
state and refugees around the world, had long ago surpassed the legend of his
mentor Thomas Jamieson. Confronted by crises, he had often asked, "What
would Jamie do?" And henceforth generations of diplomats and humanitarians will likely ask, "What would Sergio do?"

Vieira de Mello began each mission by trying to "get real": to see the
world as it was rather than as he might have liked it to be. Today getting
real means recognizing that the most pressing threats on the horizon are
transnational and thus cannot be tackled by a single country. But getting real
also requires acknowledging that the international system is polarized and
slow, just when we need cooperation and urgent action. Vieira de Mello
was a UN man to his core, determined to "show the UN flag" whenever he
arrived in a war-torn area. Throughout his career UN successes—in spurring decolonization, helping refugees return to their homes, persuading
militants to engage in political processes, sponsoring elections, and ushering
in independence—filled him with a seemingly guileless pride. The UN remained the embodiment of the "world's conscience" for him because it was
the place where governments assembled to enshrine their legal and moral
commitments. It was the home of the international rules that, if followed,
would breed greater peace and security. But by the time of his death he was
deeply worried that the system he had joined thirty-four years before was
not up to the task of dealing with the barbarism and lawlessness of the times.
"I am the first person to recognize that the UN leaves a lot to be desired,"
he acknowledged.[2] He conceded that the "transition from the ideal to the
real is often extremely long, hard, costly, and cruel."[3]

He knew that the organization he cherished was at once an actor in its own right and simply a building, no better or worse than the collective will of the countries that constituted it. The UN-the-actor needed to be reformed. Twentieth-century rules were no match for twenty-first-century crises. Mediocrity and corruption among UN personnel had to be weeded out, but accountability could not simply mean additional paperwork or micromanaging from Headquarters, as it usually did. UN civil servants had to become more self-critical and introspective, accepting what had taken Vieira de Mello years to learn: that they are agents of change themselves and not simply the servants of powerful governments.

His clashes with Dennis McNamara arose because, in his friend's view, "Sergio sided with power." He had sided with governments in helping organize the forced return of the Vietnamese and Rwandan refugees, and he had been so mute about Serbian atrocities that he had earned the nickname "Serbio." Once he moved to UN Headquarters in New York, however, while he was always careful to gauge the prevailing winds, he was less prone to simply defer to them. He stood up more frequently for the rights and needs of civilians, defying the wishes of the United States to lead an assessment mission into Kosovo under the cover of NATO bombing and arguing forcefully, when the pro-Indonesian militia began burning down East Timor, that UN officials in the country could not abandon the desperate Timorese, no matter what UN member states were saying. "For once," he argued to his senior colleagues, "let's allow the states on the [Security] Council to make the wrong decisions instead of saving them the trouble by making the wrong decisions for them." When he himself governed East Timor, he played by UN rules at the start. But governments had written those rules for an era of peacekeeping when UN troops interpositioned themselves as a "thin blue line" between two sides that had agreed to a cease-fire. The regulations were woefully ill suited for multifaceted missions in countries still racked by internal violence or where the UN had to rebuild whole institutions from scratch. When he realized that he was losing the support of the Timorese, he changed course, taking the revolutionary step of appointing Timorese to supervise their UN underlings. He chose his battles. He seemed to have an uncanny sense of how to bend UN rules to their breaking point without gaining a reputation for insubordination.

But there was only so much one UN civil servant could do. Whether the UN could help "humanize history," as he put it, would not turn on whether

UN bureaucrats became more self-critical or how loudly they howled about an injustice. If the UN was to become a truly constructive, stabilizing twenty-first-century player, as it had to be, the *governments* in the building would have to change their preferences and their behavior. This would mean throwing their weight behind tasks the UN performed well—by supporting the work of the specialized humanitarian field agencies such as UNHCR, vastly improving the logistic and strategic support for UN peacekeeping missions, and making use of the UN's convening powers to deepen and broaden the rules governing international and internal state practices on such vital concerns as climate change and terrorism. But it would also mean being selective, and not asking the UN to do too much, or to perform tasks that could better be performed by regional organizations, nongovernmental organizations, philanthropic foundations, or new quasi-governmental operational entities like the Global Fund for AIDS, Tuberculosis, and Malaria or the International Criminal Court (ICC) (both of which governments deliberately set up outside the UN system).

Vieira de Mello saw that frustrated countries were increasingly working around UN gridlock and assembling in smaller bodies according to geography or shared interests. Believing there were more than enough deadly challenges to go around, he generally treated security and development initiatives outside the UN not as competitors, but as partners. But he was irritated by what he saw as a tendency to romanticize such initiatives, whose success would turn on some of the very same member states that had proven unreliable in the UN. Whatever the precise shape or composition of an international grouping, he argued, if the countries inside these bodies didn't change, many of the UN's weaknesses—diplomatic gridlock, bureaucratic red tape, or insufficient political will—would undermine their performance. In his view, there was no silver bullet or reform "fix" on the horizon. There was only the messy, thankless work of trying to change states' perceptions of their interests. When countries like the United States began speaking of bypassing the UN—and building a new, more amicable "community of democracies"—he understood the appeal. After all, the UN itself was initially founded as a club for like-minded countries. But in the long run he did not see how global threats could be tackled without engaging undemocratic states or rogue nations. Since all of the looming challenges crossed borders, states would have to cooperate and burden-share, and the United Nations remained the only international institution that gathered representatives from all countries in one place.

Vieira de Mello knew from his own journey that when the countries on the Security Council were united and determined to enforce peace and security, his peacemaking or state-building missions stood far higher odds of bringing results. If powerful countries were divided or, as often happened, if their attention wandered, the belligerents and spoilers took heed. "The UN is an instrument, a frame, an engine," he noted. It would be "as dynamic, as conciliatory, as innovative, as successful" as governments "wish it, allow it, make it be."[4] But just how dynamic or successful *did* they wish it to be?

The UN did not create global divisions among rich and poor, secular and religious, urban and rural, modern and traditional. But because the UN is the only global meeting place, those tensions play themselves out in its decision-making chambers. Today, almost five years after Vieira de Mello's death, just when consensus is most needed, the Security Council is more divided than it has been since the end of the cold war. China, which rarely asserted itself at the UN during most of Vieira de Mello's career, is "coming out" economically and geopolitically. While many Western leaders hail the erosion of sovereignty in a globalized world, China clings to it, contending that others have no business meddling in its or anybody else's domestic affairs.

China is not alone. The so-called petro-authoritarian countries, led by Russia, have rolled back their democratic domestic gains and begun leveraging their natural resources to bully their neighbors. European powers still seem confused about how to make use of their newfound collective weight. And the United States, because of its war in Iraq, its disavowal of international legal constraints, and the abuses carried out in its counterterrorism efforts, commands little respect around the world and has increasing difficulty summoning support in international settings. The erosion of U.S. influence, combined with the new assertiveness of countries that do not see their own interests as advanced by improving the living conditions of others, means that UN negotiations on security and human rights issues are commonly yielding even greater theatrics and stalemates than in Vieira de Mello's day.

Vieira de Mello was exasperated by the fact that the UN's loudest critics were politicians from the very countries that had assigned the UN impossible tasks and then starved it of resources or refused to loan it topflight personnel. "I'd like to see them try it!" he would exclaim, when some simpleminded jab reached him in a remote outpost. In the last few years of his life he pushed back, trying to draw the attention of the media and the public to their own governments. Early in his career, working in Sudan, Cyprus, and Mozambique, he had taken satisfaction from the fact that his agency could put up tents, feed refugees, and remind governments of their humanitarian obligations. Later, in Bosnia and Rwanda too, he acted on the UN's humanitarian imperative, helping ensure that hundreds of thousands of victims received food and shelter. But after the massacres in those countries he began speaking out against governments that were using humanitarian aid to avoid dealing with the deeper political and economic causes of violence and death. He likened aid workers to ambulance drivers and complained that they were being treated as though they alone should prevent road deaths. "Little is done to ensure the proper state of the roads, control drunken driving, introduce speed limits, and enforce safety standards," he argued.[5] The aid groups and UN actors who stepped in to offer succor, he noted, "distract attention and divert responsibility from those who are in a position to bring about change: political actors."[6]

Again and again for Vieira de Mello, political actors were the key. He saw that the UN's inadequacies, which were many, were those of the world. Instead of relying on "the UN" to change the countries of the world, he believed, the countries of the world would have to change in order to transform the UN. But at the time of his death, global insecurity was causing those countries to dig in and finger-point rather than to compromise and pool their resources to tackle common problems. He wondered what it would take for a truly *United* Nations to emerge. "Given the intransigence of human stupidity," he said, "maybe we have to wait for an extra-planetary threat, like in the science fiction films, for the United Nations to finally realize their mission." He hoped that it would not take an external threat to concentrate the minds of citizens and their leaders, but he found it alarming that contemporary dangers were not "rational imperatives" sufficient to galvanize unity or real commitments.[7]

FIXING THE SYSTEM

In Western countries today transnational threats could serve as the uniting forces that Vieira de Mello thought were necessary. But while these mortal concerns have begun to reorient governments toward international institutions, thus far they have mostly raised alarms without prompting changes in individual or state behavior.

He once said, "The future is to be invented." With the seeming rise in irrationality and rage in an increasingly interconnected world, a better future might be invented if citizens and governments took heed of the key lessons of Vieira de Mello's long career:

- Legitimacy matters, and it comes both from legal authority or consent and from competent performance.
- Spoilers, rogue states, and nonstate militants must be engaged, if only so they can be sized up and neutralized.
- Fearful people must be made more secure.
- Dignity is the cornerstone of order.
- We outsiders must bring humility and patience to our dealings in foreign lands.

Legitimacy

Vieira de Mello knew that maintaining legitimacy was essential. When countries intervened abroad without the UN's blessing, they were usually greeted with suspicion and outright hostility, whereas a UN mission was more often perceived as being sent by the world, which gave it a longer grace period. But he saw that many other factors shaped perceptions of legitimacy. Did an operation do more good than harm? Did the foreigners play by international rules? Did they observe cultural norms? Were they there to live well or do good? Were they accountable for their performance? Did the local people welcome what was being done? Were they even asked?

Vieira de Mello learned that competence was essential. Legitimacy was performance-based. And neither the UN nor individual governments had nearly enough in-house expertise to perform reliably and earn local respect. When he launched his governing missions in Kosovo and East Timor, he cried out to New York to create a standby roster of technocrats who were experts on customs, agriculture, immigration, communications, banking, health, roads and ports, drugs and crime, and fiscal policy. The generalists whom the UN system dispatched might have been sound political analysts, but few of them had any actual governing expertise, which undermined the UN's standing in the eyes of both the Kosovars and the Timorese. "Until we can get the right people on board quickly, and if necessary, throw them overboard just as quickly," he argued, "then we will continue to founder."[8] Nothing killed legitimacy like a failure to deliver results. "The UN cannot presume that it will be seen as legitimate by the local population in question just because in some distant Security Council chamber a piece of paper was produced," he wrote. "We need to show why we are beneficial to the people on the ground and we need to show that quickly."[9] The same was true of governments, NGOs, and individuals acting outside the UN. Legitimacy would turn on being seen to play by the rules and by bringing concrete improvements, which would require acute cultural sensitivity and tangible skills.

Engage All Kinds

Early on in his career Vieira de Mello was stridently outspoken about his principles. When he joined the UN in 1969, he was fond of reciting Marxist political tracts and bashing the "imperialists" who he thought were running roughshod across the planet. When he saw American cars driving down the streets of Geneva, he made the motion of hurling stones at them. When he heard American accents, he mimicked them. Even as a thirty-four-year-old political officer in southern Lebanon, he was so outspoken in his criticism of the Israeli invasion that one of his superiors thought him a "prima donna and crybaby." But it was in Lebanon that he learned that using words like "unacceptable" or denouncing injustice brought few returns. He resolved instead to find ways to appeal to the interests of diverse stakeholders.

In the years ahead he would never view the United States as a trusted friend, but he would come to see it as a necessary partner. American policies were too often carried out arrogantly, he believed, and with an eye to domestic political audiences. Still, when it came to humanitarian affairs, peacekeeping, and diplomacy, he knew that he and the UN needed U.S. money, leverage, and leadership. And as he amassed experience in the UN, he realized that however unreliable Washington was, it also shouldered substantial global financial, humanitarian, and security responsibilities that other countries would not. So he became masterful at appealing to U.S. government officials in their language. Even when his objectives were purely idealistic, his means could be ruthlessly pragmatic, which made him an unusual breed.

Vieira de Mello's pragmatism also entailed a willingness to engage with "evil." As a lifelong student of philosophy, he had long pored over the classic texts on the nature of evil. As he began to encounter perpetrators of atrocity and warmongers in the world, the theoretical categories struck him as incomplete. They didn't seem to leave space for slippage, for the family man who (usually gradually) rationalizes becoming a butcher. It was that descent that preoccupied him. Where had the Khmer Rouge gone wrong? Was there a moment, one moment, when they stood at a fork in the road and chose their apocalyptic path? If he or somebody could diagnose how and why individuals and groups became militant, he seemed to believe, peacemakers would have better odds of putting the genie back in the bottle. If outsiders were to return refugees home or negotiate peace deals, they would have to understand the wrongdoers. He saw Washington's habit of lumping diverse nonstate groups like Hamas, al-Qaeda, the Taliban, and Hezbollah together with countries such as Iran and Syria as not simply intellectually unsophisticated, but strategically counterproductive and even deadly.

His highly practical mantra of "talking to everyone" caused him lapses in judgment. Sharing French wine with Ieng Sary may have kept the Khmer Rouge engaged in Cambodia's peace process longer than they were otherwise inclined, but it also led him to pay too little attention to the atrocities they had committed. In Bosnia his sometimes obsequious deference to Serb leaders Radovan Karadžić and Slobodan Milošević brought few concessions at all. As he brought Karadžić the latest edition of *The New York Review of Books* or scoured the shops of Belgrade for the perfect gift for Milošević, he lost sight of the fact that he had grown silent on matters of principle and oblivious to the ways extremists were exploiting his determined neutrality to advance their own ends.

But he grew on the job. The massacre in Srebrenica and the genocide in Rwanda seemed to jar him out of an earlier credulousness. For the rest of his career, although he still engaged with thugs and killers, he was less prone to appease his interlocutors. He did not always raise their past sins, but he never forgot them. After his 1999 trip through the ethnically cleansed villages of Kosovo, Vieira de Mello refused to speak Portuguese with the Serbian foreign minister and firmly condemned Serb arson and deportation, while also remaining in dialogue long enough to argue that Serbia had to halt its offensive. If his ever-evolving approach could be summed up, then, it would be: Talk to rogues, attempt to understand what makes them tick, extract concessions from them whenever possible, but remain clear about who they are and what they have done, as well as what you stand for. Past sins mattered not just intrinsically but because they were predictive of future behavior. "Think of how hard it is for any of us to change," he told me once. "Why do we expect it to be easier for a war criminal?"

Law and Security First

In the aftermath of September 11, Vieira de Mello heard Western leaders talk a great deal about the importance of promoting universal values. In 2002, when he read Bush's National Security Strategy doctrine, he noted eleven references to liberty and forty-five mentions of freedom. Vieira de Mello naturally favored the promotion of liberty and freedom, but he believed that fixing the international system would entail advancing one freedom above others: freedom from fear. "Security is the first priority," he liked to say, "and the second priority, and the third priority, and the fourth priority." He could have gone on. The best-laid plans for weak states—returning refugees, promoting human rights, restoring infrastructure, fortifying health and educational facilities, or holding elections—would amount to little if citizens did not feel safe in their own homes and on their own streets. Indeed, he saw elections in the developing world often bring hard-liners to power precisely because fearful citizens voted not for who would govern best but for extremists who stoked fears and then promised to offer safety. And again and again he watched as promising postwar transitions collapsed because of a failure to fill the security void.

In December 1991 he deployed to Phnom Penh, Cambodia, and found a war-ravaged city filled with giddy Cambodians who expected that the imminent arrival of a sizable UN peacekeeping force would enforce the recent peace agreements. Instead, he watched in horror as the weeks slipped by. By the time the blue helmets turned up, political assaults were already rampant and much of the momentum of the peace negotiations had been lost.

Nothing frustrated him more than people's tendency to repeat their mistakes. "I sometimes wonder if those of us engaged in peacekeeping are the human equivalents of goldfish," he once said. "These animals are said to have memories that last in the region of two seconds. Now, for them that means life swimming around and around in a bowl will not be interminably dull. When it applies to us the impact is greater and far more serious."[10] He liked to quote the old adage "Experience is what allows us to repeat our mistakes, only with more finesse."[11] What may have been a forgivable security gap in Cambodia, then, was far less forgivable a full decade after the fall of the Berlin Wall. In June 1999, the same day he shared the jubilation of returning Kosovar Albanian refugees who lined the streets to cheer their NATO liberators, he saw a man who had just been murdered in broad daylight. Within a week Kosovar Albanian gangs had chased away tens of thousands of Serbs. And although fifty thousand victorious NATO troops patrolled the province, they were soldiers trained to fight wars, not to police tight-knit communities. By the time of Vieira de Mello's departure a short five weeks after NATO's entry, the sense of triumph had been spoiled by the tit-for-tat attacks carried out by ethnic Albanian vigilantes. By the time international police had deployed in any sizable numbers, more than a third of Kosovo's Serb population had fled or been ethnically cleansed. Any hope of coexistence had evaporated.

In circumstances where the major powers sent in UN peacekeepers and staff, Vieira de Mello had grown used to halfheartedness from the major powers. After all, no single country's national interests were sufficiently at stake for it to take responsibility for filling the law-and-order void. But since the United States had argued that U.S. interests were mortally at stake in the run-up to the war in Iraq in 2003, he expected the most powerful military in the world to bring careful planning and hefty resources to bear. He didn't support the war, but he never imagined that U.S. planners would think so little about the peace. Surely, he thought, they had watched as UN peacekeepers foundered in their "morning after" efforts to maintain order in the 1990s. Surely the Coalition would take precautions to stave off the kind of chaos that could be far deadlier than anything a regular army could unleash. Surely they would understand that establishing human security was a prerequisite to achieving other aims. Surely . . .

Vieira de Mello did not live to see Iraq descend into the bloody sectarian nightmare it has become. Nor did he live to see the disastrous effect the war in Iraq would have on other regions of the world or on the enforcement of UN principles. Vieira de Mello had once been a vocal opponent of using force for humanitarian purposes, but he had reluctantly come to believe that international military or police action, while undesirable, was sometimes required. He worried that granting this exception would benefit opportunistic countries motivated by other interests who would invoke the cause of civilian protection as a way to justify their ulterior designs. But he also believed that idealists like himself, who had relied faithfully on the power of reason alone, had let victims down. UN peacekeepers should not themselves wage war, but they needed to be prepared to draw distinctions between victims and aggressors. Moreover, in order for UN diplomacy to be effective or UN rules to be respected, they needed to be able to "project credible force" to protect themselves and to prevent large-scale attacks on civilians.

In 2000 he had embraced a new norm first put forth by an independent commission: the "responsibility to protect." The first responsibility to protect individuals from violence fell to those individuals' government, but when that government proved unable (in a failing state) or unwilling (in a repressive state) to offer such protection, then the responsibility vested upward to the international community, which had a duty to mobilize the means to stop mass murder. Getting governments to agree to the concept in the abstract, he knew, was the easy part. While every country in the UN would endorse the notion of a "responsibility to protect," very few would actually prove willing to exercise the responsibility. They wanted civilians to be protected, but they weren't prepared to put their own soldiers or police in harm's way to do the protecting. Unarmed relief workers who worked for NGOs were more likely to enter violent areas than were national militaries. What was true while Vieira de Mello was alive is even more true today, as the specter of Iraq hangs over public discussions of foreign engagement, deterring peacekeeping and state-building elsewhere in the world. And for all the talk of globalized threats, very few countries seem prepared to act on Vieira de Mello's warning that "there is no longer such a thing as distant crisis."[12]

One way Vieira de Mello looked out for physical security was to support international tribunals aimed at ending impunity and removing from the streets those responsible for war crimes and crimes against humanity. When he worked strictly as a humanitarian, he had questioned whether legal accountability didn't simply make perpetrators more determined to fight on. But his view changed in the mid-1990s. The same Vieira de Mello who had tried to convince *Washington Post* correspondent John Pomfret that countries should just put their pasts behind them and "learn to forget" became a vocal advocate of remembering and punishing. He kept a poster of the most wanted UN war crimes suspects from the former Yugoslavia and Rwanda on his office wall in Geneva and then New York. And after his May 1999 daredevil trip into Kosovo, he insisted on stuffing investigator Frank Dutton's war crimes evidence in his suitcase in order to ensure that it made it back to The Hague. It was in the Balkans and in the refugee camps of Congo that he acquired his belief that pursuing justice would not lessen the odds of peace, but would, in the long term, advance them. Milošević, the man responsible for the Bosnian war, was treated like a dignitary in 1995 in order to bring the war to an end. But that same Milošević had not lost his taste for ethnic cleansing and massacres, and in 1999 he spearheaded another Serbian offensive in Kosovo. He would stop destabilizing the region only when he was incapacitated. In Africa, as Vieira de Mello walked through the camps where *génocidaires* were sharpening their knives for future battle, he saw that determined killers would continue to wreak havoc if they were left at large. "It's a false dichotomy, this peace and justice thing," he told his colleagues. "No peace is going to last if impunity reigns." He was not an absolutist. He knew that indictments could sometimes be destabilizing and had to be carefully sequenced, but what mattered was that questions of accountability be addressed with the immediate and long-term interests of victims in mind. Although he was well aware of the Bush administration's contempt for the International Criminal Court, the normally diplomatic Vieira de Melllo was so committed to the court that he made a point of defending it in his only meeting with President Bush.

Dignity Is the Point

Vieira de Mello's relationship with human rights evolved in much the same way that his view of justice did, but it took longer. While to the naked eye human rights and humanitarianism seem like versions of a single theme, in disaster zones they were often seen to be rivals. Aid workers who denounced human rights abuses were often denied access to those in need, so they kept quiet in order to keep abusive governments and gunmen from expelling them. At UNHCR, when Vieira de Mello tried to advance the overall, long-term welfare of refugees as a class, he at times proved willing to cut corners on individual rights.

But when he took up his position as UN High Commissioner for Human Rights, he started seeing human rights as the vehicle to calm interstate relations. Human rights and international law were under siege from all sides and he started to see that if order was to be preserved globally, international rules would have to become more binding on state and nonstate actors alike. His greatest appreciation of the relevance of human rights to high politics came in Iraq. During the occupation, he stressed repeatedly, the Coalition would have to go out of its way to respect and protect Iraqi human rights; that meant changing its detention policies and checkpoint rules of engagement and also respecting local customs. Whether Iraq transformed itself into a stable state would depend not on its oil resources but on whether Iraqis were able to live with dignity. "I could see him changing every day he was in Baghdad," recalls Mona Rishmawi, UN human rights officer in Iraq. "Human rights were no longer abstract principles on a page; they were the indispensable bedrocks of a society's survival." Vieira de Mello wrestled with the trade-offs inherent in achieving respect for human rights. He saw Iraqis living the tension between liberty and equality, as rich Iraqi exiles used the new freedoms to line their pockets. He saw the dangers that self-determination posed to women's and minorities' rights. But whatever the trade-offs, human rights could not be treated as afterthoughts; they had to be central to Iraqi, Coalition, and regional planning. No realistic strategy for stabilizing Iraq or any traumatized country could exclude them.

Although Vieira de Mello became an explicit advocate for human rights late in his career, he had lobbied on behalf of human beings for decades. After his death the quality of his that was most often hailed was his regard for individuals. His colleagues took note of how surprisingly rare it was, even in the world of humanitarianism, to find an official who actually looked out for human beings, one by one, as he or she encountered them. In Lebanon Vieira de Mello paid frequent visits to the relatives of Lebanese wounded or killed by UN fire; in Cambodia he learned the country's history from UN drivers and translators who had survived the slaughter, and he personally oversaw the resettlement of several hundred Christian Montagnards, unwanted by Vietnam and Cambodia, to North Carolina, where they live to this day; in Bosnia he refused to wear a flak jacket because Sarajevan civilians enjoyed no such luxury, and he helped organize the underground "train" to get civilians out of the besieged Bosnian capital; in Azerbaijan he circled back to find the elderly peasant woman who wished to become a cloud, listening to her as if she held the key to world peace; in Kosovo he insisted on tracking down the Albanian nephew of his cleaning lady, following up with incessant phone calls and faxes to UN staff in Macedonia; in East Timor he invited the parents of Leonard Manning, the first UN peacekeeper killed there, to attend the country's independence ceremony; and even in Iraq he found time to wire money to the Timorese woman who had cleaned his house so that she might pay for her children's education. In a thirty-four-year career, he made a trademark of "Sergio letters," a virtual library of thousands of handwritten letters of greeting, thanks, or commendation, penned to friends and colleagues around the world. He treated junior staff, local staff, and local citizens with respect. He understood that he had the single-handed power to enhance their sense of dignity, and this was a power he used often.

He thought the international system would be far more effective and humane if it too focused on dignity—the dignity of individuals, of communities, and of whole nations. But to enhance dignity, he knew, outside actors had to do something they did not do naturally: probe deeply into the societies they were working in. He was acutely conscious of the fact that the future of the places he worked belonged to the individuals who lived there. Well-meaning foreigners could bring money, political leverage, or technical expertise, but they were there to support local leaders and processes and to build local capacity. He sometimes did this badly, overrelying on his close staff or on local favorites. But wherever he went, he tested his assumptions and sought diverse feedback. He insisted on walking around besieged Sarajevo in order to gain a read on the Bosnian "street." In Congo he knew he would be a less persuasive advocate for a multinational military force if he hadn't himself talked to the refugees there, so he slipped across the Rwandan border undercover. In East Timor he insisted that the UN director of administration take down the barbed wire around the Governor's House so that the Timorese would be able to approach and share their complaints. When Timorese representatives told him that they were fed up with working for UN officials who had simply taken the place of Indonesians as their overlords, he listened and changed course, hemorrhaging power as quickly as the UN Security Council would allow him. In Iraq, to his ultimate peril, he opened up the Canal Hotel, dubbing it the "anti–Green Zone" and inviting Iraqis to come and register human rights abuses (past and present) and simply to check their e-mails. If UN officials were to isolate themselves as the Americans were doing, he argued, they would alienate the very citizens they were there to help. And if the Americans didn't become more sensitive to the dignity they were trampling during their occupation, they would fail.

He offered advice to others who tried state-building: "Be humble," he told a conference of diplomats and humanitarians in 2002. "Admit your mistakes and your failures as soon as you identify them, and try and learn from them obviously. Be frank and honest with the people you are there to help because only then will you stand a true chance of succeeding, and of your achievements being acknowledged by them, which is more important than the international community."[13] He valued learning languages because they enabled him to connect with people on their terms. It was a sign of respect for their traditions as well as a window into their psyches. He tried to learn Tetum in East Timor and was self-conscious that he did not know Arabic while in Iraq. He thought understanding a nation's history, pride, and trauma was more important than knowing its literacy rates or trading prospects. He paid careful attention to symbolism. "How many wars could have been avoided by taking care not to create international treaties on the foundation of mistrust and of contempt for nations' sense of self-esteem?" he asked.[14] He came to believe that, whatever their inexperience, Kosovars, Timorese, and Iraqis would be better off governing themselves and learning on the job than getting talked down to by foreigners.

Complexity, Humility, and Patience

In their attempts to prevent conflict, spur economic development, or shore up failing states, Vieira de Mello saw, outsiders had their work cut out for them. Notwithstanding billions of dollars' worth of investments, none of the places where he worked over the years are fully stable places today. Sudan and Iraq are still marred by savage violence, while Lebanon and Congo remain dysfunctional, fragmented states that suffer waves of deadly fighting. Cambodia is booming economically, but Hun Sen remains in power, intimidating his opposition. Bosnia has not seen fighting since NATO intervened militarily in 1995, but it has lost the spirit of multiethnicity that Vieira de Mello so prized, and its two most high-profile war criminals, Radovan Karadžić and Ratko Mladić, remain at large. When it comes to Kosovo, the countries on the Security Council are still divided over whether it should attain full independence, and the interethnic tensions contained since 1999 seem likely to explode if a peaceful resolution is not soon found. East Timor has remained free of Indonesian control, but widespread unemployment and stalled development have resulted in violent riots, causing 150,000 people to flee their homes and requiring the Security Council to redeploy 1,600 international police. The turmoil caused the UN's critics to point out that even a rare UN success story had faltered.

Vieira de Mello read UN situation reports and cables, as well as wire stories, from all over the world in order to keep up with events in the places he had once worked. He was crestfallen whenever he saw that hard won progress had been reversed. But he consoled himself by recalling just how broken the places had been to begin with. The roads were not simply unpaved, and the electricity not simply sporadic. In many cases the entire fabric of society had been obliterated, creating indescribably complex problems that international actors would not ameliorate easily—or quickly. Thus the impatient philosopher-humanitarian became more sanguine later in his career, recognizing that anybody who entered a war-torn society had to do so with humility and patience. "We all tend to measure and judge history in the light of our own existence," he said in one speech. "We have to adopt a more long-term perspective. History is not in a hurry."[15] There might not be early or visible returns on outside investments. Elections might produce ugly outcomes. Corrupt officials might impede reconstruction. Civil unrest might taint the advent of democracy. But whenever donor governments or his own UN staff were tempted to give up in exasperation, he would urge them to ask "Compared to what?" "We know how bad things are today," he would say, "but we should remind ourselves how bad things have been in the past, and how much worse things can get." Frustrations tended to boil over when the gap was too great between the expectations of locals and donor governments on the one hand, and the grim, slow-paced sputtering improvements in battered societies on the other. He saw half of his job as "expectation management."

When Vieira de Mello landed in Iraq in June 2003, it was probably already too late to save the country from the savagery of its internal fissures and from the blunders made by its occupiers. But if there was any person who—drawing upon the wisdom amassed in a lifetime of trial and error—might have found a way to build common cause among foes, or at least to mitigate human suffering, it was he. But for him to have been helpful, the Americans in Iraq would have had to acknowledge that they needed help. They did not.

When he joined the UN back in 1969, similarly, it was probably already too late to save the organization from the interstate rivalries that, in different forms, had cursed the institution from the start. But if there was anyone who could have wrung from the UN whatever reform and promise it could muster, it was he. But if he was to have fixed the UN, the leading member states within it, and especially the United States, would have had to truly wish to see its transformation.

When President George W. Bush declared repeatedly in 2001 and 2002, "Either you are with us or you are against us," he was wrong. Hundreds of millions of citizens of the world may not have been *with* the United States as such, but they were not against America either. Yet, like much of Bush's rhetoric, this description of an imagined dichotomy quickly spawned policies that gave rise to a real one. Bush's self-fulfilling doctrine ensured that those who were treated as enemies of the United States became enemies of the United States. And the terrorists too embraced this totalizing logic. In their summons to jihad, they said, in effect, "If you are not with us in our struggle against the United States, you are against us, and we will destroy you."

Vieira de Mello was born in 1948, just as the post–World War II order was taking shape. He died in 2003, just as the battle lines in the twenty-first century's first major struggle were being drawn. His end could not have been more tragic. Just when he was poised to be most useful—to the United States, to Iraq, to the world—he was killed. And on August 19, after the bomb went off, as he was pinned in the rubble, he found himself in the same impossibly vulnerable position as those whose fates he had championed during his career. When he realized he had miraculously survived the blast, he must have expected that professional soldiers from the most sophisticated military in history would find a way to extract him from the debris. But as his life seeped slowly out of him, there must have been a moment—hopefully not a long one—when he realized he was every bit as helpless in his time of need as millions of victims had been before him. He died under the Canal Hotel's rubble—buried beneath the weight of the United Nations itself.

ACKNOWLEDGMENTS

In one sense, this book was easier to write than the last one. Of the some four-hundred people I contacted for interviews, people who knew Sergio—even those who had only met him once—were left with such strong feelings about him that they generally rushed to share their recollections. No matter where they were around the world, I rarely had to write or phone twice to set up a meeting or a call. Many of the interviews gave way to long phone calls, which in turn gave rise to long meals, which occasionally gave rise to what I hope will be lifelong friendships. Even though Sergio himself never got the chance to make full use of his "box of possibilities" to create a lasting UN "A team," I had the privilege of spending time with the remarkable people he attracted and often mentored. My research was also greatly facilitated by officials at UNHCR in Geneva and at the Department of Peacekeeping Operations in New York who granted me access to their classified files. It was easier than it should have been to walk in the shoes of a man who could no longer offer guidance.

From a personal standpoint, though, this book posed greater challenges than its predecessor. When I wrote *"A Problem from Hell,"* I was a law student, a part-time journalist, and an adjunct lecturer at Harvard's John F. Kennedy School of Government. While my friends, family, and I had high hopes for that book, most of us had low expectations. The advantage of writing a book nobody was waiting for was that I had few competing professional opportunities or concerns. Because of the surprisingly warm reception to *"A Problem from Hell,"* though, writing *Chasing the Flame* proved more difficult. I researched and wrote the book while teaching full-time at the Kennedy School, working with my colleagues to try to build a permanent antigenocide constituency, and, since 2005, offering whatever help I could to Barack Obama, the person whose rigor and compassion bear the closest resemblance to Sergio's that I have ever seen. Since I compressed what could have been a decadelong book project into four years, something had to give, and unfortunately, what gave was what is most important to me: my time with friends and family. So I would like here to acknowledge those who have supported me through this long slog, themselves overlooking a solipsism that I seem disturbingly prone to during these all-consuming ventures.

First, I must thank those who aided the creation of this book. There would be no book at all if not for Cullen Murphy, who, while still the editor of the *Atlantic Monthly,* proposed that I write a magazine profile of Sergio. Every book's quality turns on the inventiveness or significance of the question behind it, and Cullen is the person who chose a question I would not have come up with on my own. My friends Philip Gourevitch and George Packer launched me by donating the transcripts of lengthy interviews they conducted with Sergio shortly before he died. A remarkable number of people offered to read drafts, perhaps unaware that I would take them up on their offers and inflict a messy manuscript on them. Those who suffered most were the early readers, who pretended to overlook the grave flaws in substance and style, engaging critically with every paragraph as if I were just a few snappier transitions away from completion: Jamshid Anvar; Omar Bakhet; Nader Mousavizadeh; Carina Perelli; Carole Ray; Strobe Talbott; Oliver Ulich; my stalwart life policy advisers Richard Holbrooke and Jonathan Moore (who, along with his wife, Katie, introduced me to Sergio back in 1994); novelist Nick Papandreaou, who stages an essential return for every painful book cycle; Chuck Cohen, who never leaves; and my wild and brilliant aunt and uncle in Waterville, Ireland: Patricia and Derry Gibson. Salman Ahmed, Jeff Davie, Helena Fraser, Peter Galbraith, James Lynch, Jon Randal, and Ghassan Salamé reviewed parts of the book for accuracy. Others commented critically on more developed but still ugly full drafts: John Gomperts, Richard Goodwin, Michael Ignatieff, Georgeanne Macguire, Fabienne Morisset, Cullen Murphy, Izumi Nakamitsu-Lennartsson, Laura Pitter, John Schumann, and Diederik Vanhoogstraten. Jonathan Prentice and Fabrizio Hochschild were transatlantic partners in this endeavor, offering intense feedback as well as vital friendship. I tried to take to heart every comment, but any remaining mistakes or oversights are my own. In Brazil Antonio Vieira de Mello, André Simões, Sonia Vieira de Mello, and the epic Gilda Vieira de Mello took a generous leap of faith in inviting me into their close-knit family, sharing memories, letters, and photos. Despite the rawness of the loss and the pain of recalling Iraq, Carolina Larriera did the same, contributing invaluably to my understanding of the man and his mission. Leon Wieseltier stepped in, as he always does, to provide advice when it mattered most. My colleague Sarah Sewall at the Carr Center for Human Rights Policy offered constant moral support and creative push-back. She then salvaged the book's final months, loaning me the indefatigable Meghan Frederico to join me in the all-nighters needed to fact-check an unwieldy tome.

Robin Trangsrud arranged my travel and provided support for my courses. Daniel Camos-i-Duarella drew on his French, Spanish, and Portuguese to help me get to the bottom of mysteries that had persisted into the book's final days. And Sarah Stanlick and Nahreen Ghazarian (thanks to Swanee Hunt) arrived at the center in time to help shepherd the book through publication.

Michel Thieren, a medical doctor with the World Health Organization, deserves singular thanks. After he read *"A Problem from Hell,"* he e-mailed me, a stranger, and announced that he intended to find the book a French publisher. After he spent two years unsuccessfully hawking the book door-to-door in France, he asked to see *Chasing the Flame* in its roughest state and delivered sixty pages of intensive micro and macro comments. Moreover, he tracked down Sergio's professors at the Sorbonne, sneaked me into the UN antechambers so that I could photocopy documents leaked to me by others, and delivered cheering phone calls and e-mails, tracking every deadline as if it were his own.

Six months after starting the book I met Terry George, the director of *Hotel Rwanda.* When I tried to persuade Terry to make a movie about Raphael Lemkin, the coiner of the word "genocide," his eyes glazed over. But as soon as I mentioned this project, he lit up. I have no doubt that Terry will make a superb film out of Sergio's life, but in the meantime I have been blessed to have him as a collaborator. Moviemakers are notorious for ruining books, but my long conversations with Terry have improved this one. Whenever I found myself heading down some East Timorese garden path, it was Terry who would pull me back. "But what is the universal story here, the tale that does not depend on time or place?" he would ask. "Think about it this way: 'Once upon a time, there was a kingdom. And in that kingdom, there was a good, flawed knight named Sergio. He had a sword, and he had a shield . . .'" I also benefitted from talking with Greg Barker, the acclaimed documentary filmmaker, who is making a documentary about the Canal Hotel attack on August 19, 2003. Meredith Blake, who did so much to make *An Inconvenient Truth* inconveniently relevant for so many, has taken on the difficult task of determining how to maximize the social impact of these endeavors (see www.sergiovdm.com). She is backed by Randy Newcomb and the incomparable Pam Omidyar, who is doing more than anybody else I know—in Sergio's words—to "invent the future."

Team Obama's John Favreau, Mark Lippert, Dennis McDonough, and Ben Rhodes offered daily infusions of conviction and banter while Obama himself always found a way to supply impeccably timed moral support despite having a few other things on his plate.

I am blessed to have close friends whom I see and talk to less than I would like, but whose voices roam about in my head regardless: Amy Bach, Steven Bourke, Allan Buchman, Holly Burkhalter, Gillian Caldwell, Greg Carr, Chuck Cohen, Lenor Cohen, Emma Daly, Joy DeMenil, Sharon Dolovich, Mano Felciano, Debbie Fine, Jody Freeman, Danna Harman, Oren Harman, Michele Horgan, George Timothy Horry, Anna Husarska, Peter Jukes, Kate Lowenstein, Martha Minow, Jonathan Moore, Charlotte Morgan, Julian Mulvey, Azar Nafisi, Luis Moreno Ocampo, David Pressman, Lee Siegel, Alexis Sinduhije, Stacy Sullivan, Jim Tipton, Zain Verjee, and Miro Weinberger. Curt Wood, my neighbor and friend, kept my house from falling down while I was away and occasionally when I was working obliviously inside. Cass Sunstein stepped in to offer improbable care, delivering what amounted to the clutch ninth-inning, game-seven RBI. One baritone voice will stay with me forever: that of the late, great David Halberstam, who ordered me to banish lunch and to remember that we have the greatest job on earth.

They say it's a bad idea to mix friendship and business, but I don't know what I would do if my editor, Vanessa Mobley, and my agent, Sarah Chalfant, were not also dear friends. They are the best in their respective businesses and they make my work better, while also enduring one impossibly demanding writer. In the final stretch Lindsay Whalen and Bruce Giffords at The Penguin Press demonstrated infinite patience as they worked overtime to get every precious detail correct. Thanks also to David Remnick and Daniel Zalewski at *The New Yorker*, who launched Sergio by showcasing his Iraq experience.

At the heart of my A team is my former assistant Hillary Schrenell. Hillary was a recent college graduate when she joined the Carr Center as an intern in 2003. Over the following four years she morphed into a scrupulous administrator, a relentless researcher, a photo finder, a merciless editor, and a true friend. I have never known anyone else who cares more than I do about finding the unfindable source, who agonizes over word choices as if the future of the planet depended on linguistic precision, and whose ruthless perfectionism forced me to get my game up on these pages in order to withstand her gleaming scalpel and satisfy her loving eye. I'm not sure I know anybody else who combines such exceptional intellect with such unrelenting conscientiousness. The world needs more Hillarys.

And then there are the friends who kept me daily company: Doris Kearns Goodwin and Richard Goodwin, standard-setting historians and beloved confidantes; David Rohde and Elizabeth Rubin, brave and indefatigable reporters who care enough about their friendships to nurture them from Kandahar; Sayres Rudy, who understands everything, always; Michal Safdie and Moshe Safdie, who have altogether changed what my eyes see in the world; and Elliot Thomson, the wonder twin who has taught me to savor the trajectory of even the pitches we throw straight into the dirt.

Back in 1993 in the Balkans, Laura Pitter patiently introduced this novice reporter to the concept of the "nut graph," and she has offered me a most un-complicated friendship since. A public defender in the Bronx, she infuses those who know her with calmness and goodness. And John Prendergast, a friend whom I can hardly believe I've only known since 2004, lived and breathed this book with me, calling every single day at midnight, insisting on speaking when all I wanted to do was turn off the phones, and making me feel unequivocally accompanied throughout. As the telephone bills from Darfur, the Philippines, Uganda, and countless other places attest, geography was no barrier for long wending discussions on the Royals' "resurgent" farm system, the aims of the lat-est *janjaweed* offensive, or, inevitably, the most deeply personal subjects of life and love. It is no exaggeration to say that every time I might have been daunted by a reportorial, geopolitical, or personal minefield before me, John shrugged, picked me up on his shoulders, and carried me through to the other side.

The book is dedicated to three people: Mort Abramowitz, Frederick Zollo, and Stephen Power. Mort and Fred are two people who, despite all they have seen, retain a capacity for incredulity over hackneyed thinking and unjust acts. Both thought this book a lousy idea—"Samantha, Sergio worked for the *United Nations,*" Fred would say. "What did he achieve exactly?" Mort, who never saw Sergio at his best, was simply puzzled by all my fuss. But their skepticism was rooted in such high standards, and such unyielding support for me, that they helped move me eventually, belatedly, to understand the point of the book and, in many ways, the point of my career. And Stephen Power, my brother, has done what many of us pledge to do and few of us manage: change his life. Indeed, the depth of his self-scrutiny and transformation is staggering.

Of course, as anybody who knows me is aware, every word I write is im-plicitly dedicated to my parents, Edmund Bourke and Vera Delaney. Just as they did on my first book, they again read every word of every draft, managing to act as though each read were a revelation. I believe it was printing out the sixth draft of what was then an eight-hundred-page book that finished off the third of their "Sergio printers." Their commitment to the project was so thorough that they actually hid chapters from each other—behind cereal boxes, under couch cushions, and in sock drawers—so as to be the first to give feedback. Eddie called most mornings to refer me to books he thought might offer insight. And when I didn't leap, he'd buy and read the books so as to sharpen the point. His openness to new ideas and personal growth are a wonder. As for my mother, she might as well have written this book for all the emotion she invested in the last four years. It can't be easy on her to internalize my struggles as if they are her own, but her verbatim renditions of Jon Stewart monologues, exuberant Off-Broadway theater discoveries, obligatory anti–A-Rod updates, and simple cheer made every hard day seem a whole lot softer. Eddie and Mum continue to present a model of how to aspire to be in the world—insatiably curious, unfailingly sincere, and constantly on the lookout for the chance to fall over laughing. I'm so very lucky.

NOTES

I conducted more than four hundred interviews with Sergio Vieira de Mello's colleagues, friends, and family members, many of whom shared their letters and e-mails. To protect confidentiality, I have not listed my own interviews in the endnotes but have cited any material I received from others. I owe a special thanks to UNHCR in Geneva and the UN Department of Peacekeeping Operations in New York, which generously granted me access to internal files that had not previously been reviewed by scholars or journalists. In the end I was able to peruse more than ten thousand pages of classified cables and internal memos, along with Vieira de Mello's own handwritten notes from his missions.

INTRODUCTION
1. Dick Cheney, interview by Tim Russert, *Meet the Press,* March 16, 2003.
2. Bernard-Henri Lévy quoted in Roger Cohen, "A Balkan Gyre of War, Spinning Onto Film," *New York Times,* March 12, 1995 sec. 2, p.1.
3. Paolo Lembo, "Lest We Forget: The UN in Iraq—Sergio Vieira de Mello (1948–2003)," *Azerbaijan International* 11, no. 3 (Autumn 2003).

CHAPTER 1. DISPLACED
1. Ambassador Lincoln Gordon, Top Secret Cable, March 29, 1964, U.S. State Department, www.gwu.edu/~nsarchiv/NSAEBB/NSAEBB118/bz02.pdf.
2. "Brazil: The Military Republic, 1964–85," in Rex A. Hudson, ed., *Brazil: A Country Study* (Washington, D.C.: Federal Research Division, Library of Congress, 1998), p. 80.
3. "The Post-Vargas Republic, 1954–64," ibid., p. 78.
4. Bahia would later be home to such Brazilian cultural icons as singers Caetano Veloso and Gilberto Gil and the novelist Jorge Amado. It had the most racially diverse population and some of the most fertile soil in Brazil.
5. Arnaldo Vieira de Mello, *Bolivar, o Brasil e os nossos vizinhos do Prata* (Bolivar, Brazil, and Our Neighbors in the Southern Cone) (Rio de Janeiro, 1963).
6. Far fewer died in Brazil than in Argentina, where more than thirty thousand people were "disappeared."
7. When Tarcilo left parliament, the daily *Jornal do Brasil* called him "the greatest Brazilian parliamentarian since 1930." *Perfis parlamentares* 29, pp. 55–58, Camara dos Deputados, Centro de Documentação e Informação, Coordenação de Publicacões, Brasilia, 1985.
8. Sergio Vieira de Mello (hereinafter SVDM), "*Sentido da Palavra Fraternidade*" (Sense of the Word Fraternity) in *Pensamiento e Memória* (Thought and Memory) (São Paulo: Editora da Universidade de São Paulo, 2004), pp. 231–32.
9. SVDM, "*Un Chaos salutaire*" (A Healthy Chaos), *Combat,* May 18–19, 1968.

10. Ibid.

11. SVDM to a girlfriend who prefers to remain anonymous, March 2, 1969.

12. SVDM to anonymous, March 12, 1969.

13. SVDM to anonymous, May 19, 1969.

14. SVDM to anonymous, June 23, 1969.

15. "'Jamie': A Man of Action," UNHCR no. 1, March 1974.

16. SVDM to anonymous, July 11, 1970.

17. "'Jamie': A Man of Action."

18. Ibid. Gil Loescher, *The UNHCR and World Politics: A Perilous Path* (New York: Oxford University Press, 2002), p. 157. Bangladesh's independence was declared in March 1971 and was recognized by Pakistan in December.

19. "Quotes from the Press Conference," UNHCR no. 1, July 1972. The press conference took place on July 6, 1972, at the Palais des Nations.

20. Arnaldo Vieira de Mello, *Os Corsários na guerras do Brasil e o dramático batismo de fogo de Garibaldi* (The Privateers in the Wars of Brazil and the Dramatic Baptism of Fire of Garibaldi) (Sialul, 1992).

21. Robert Misrahi, interview by Michel Thieren, June 7, 2007.

22. SVDM, "La rôle de la philosophie dans la société contemporaine" (The Role of Philosophy in Contemporary Society) (Panthéon-Sorbonne, 1974).

CHAPTER 2. "I WILL NEVER USE THE WORD 'UNACCEPTABLE' AGAIN"

1. Sources differ on the number of fatalities brought about by the Israeli invasion. A *Newsweek* account estimated that 1,000 Palestinian and Lebanese civilians were killed, along with 18 Israeli soldiers and some 250 PLO guerrillas. Raymond Carroll et al., "Operation Cease-fire," *Newsweek,* April 3, 1978, p. 39.

2. The first round of the Lebanese civil war, which ran from April 1975 to October 1976, left the central government without control of southern Lebanon. When Syrian troops making up an Arab Deterrent Force tried to deploy there, Israel objected. After the Israeli invasion in 1978, Lebanese government officials complained that Israel's obstructionism had denied Lebanon the means to neutralize Palestinian forces in the south.

3. "A Mission for the U.N.," *Washington Post,* March 19, 1978, p. C6.

4. The first UN military missions were observer missions rather than what would become known as peacekeeping deployments. In 1948, after Israel went to war with Palestinian fighters and Arab armies, the Security Council voted to send twenty-one monitors to supervise the truce. In 2007 the UN Truce Supervision Organization (UNTSO) still kept 152 observers in the Sinai. Similarly, after fighting broke out in 1947 between India and Pakistan over the disputed province of Kashmir, the Security Council established a commission to monitor the India-Pakistan cease-fire, a role that the United Nations Military Observer Group in India and Pakistan (UNMOGIP) performs to this day. The United Nations Emergency Force (UNEF) was established in 1956 in the Suez region of Egypt, when the General Assembly held its first-ever Emergency Special Session after the British-French-Israeli invasion of Egypt, which had been precipitated by Egypt's nationalization of the Suez Canal. Under UNEF's

supervision, the U.K. and France withdrew from the region within two months and Israeli forces withdrew within five months. The cease-fire held for ten years until 1967, when UNEF was withdrawn at the request of the Egyptian government.

5. Five missions began after that in the Congo in the 1960s. In West New Guinea (1962–63) peacekeepers monitored the cease-fire during the transition of West Irian from Dutch rule to Indonesian rule; in Yemen (1963–64) they supervised Saudi Arabia and Egypt's disengagement from Yemen's civil war; in Cyprus (1964–present) they helped prevent further conflict between Greek and Turkish Cypriots; in the Dominican Republic (1965–66) they monitored the situation following the outbreak of civil war; in India/Pakistan (1965–66) they supervised the India/Pakistan cease-fire outside of Kashmir.

6. In 1978 some 1,200 blue helmets were stationed on the Golan Heights, and 2,300 remained deployed in Cyprus.

7. James Mackinlay, *The Peacekeepers* (London: Unwin Hyman, 1989), pp. 56, 66.

8. H. McCoubrey and N. D. White, *The Blue Helmets* (New York: UN Department of Public Information, 1996), p. 94.

9. David B. Ottaway, "Lebanon Is Alarmed by Increasing Israeli Activity in Its South," *Washington Post,* October 26, 1980, p. A25.

10. In 1981 a *Washington Post* reporter recounted an exchange in which an Israeli liaison officer complained that Nigerian soldiers guarding checkpoints did not speak Arabic, Hebrew, or English. As a result, the Israelis claimed, when PLO guerrillas approached the checkpoints, the Nigerians did not conduct thorough inspections. "All they ask is, 'You have boom-boom?' If the answer is no, they let them go," an Israeli soldier said. The *Post* reporter followed up by asking the Nigerian soldier on duty if he spoke English. "We're from a former British colony," the Nigerian said in a British accent. "Of course we speak English." William Claiborne, "Israeli Army Warns of Clashes Between UNIFIL, Haddad Militia," *Washington Post,* April 2, 1981, p. A16.

11. Woerlee Naq to Erskine/Aimé, Most Immediate Code Cable, February 12, 1982, no. FILTSO 351 NAQ 503.

12. When he visited Beirut in February 1982, Urquhart listened to the British ambassador to Lebanon insist (with what Urquhart later described as "the air of complete authority which only simpletons and autocrats enjoy") that the only solution to the Lebanon problem was for UNIFIL to "fight its way to the border." Urquhart noted drily that it was a shame that the British themselves had not seen fit to contribute troops to UNIFIL. Brian Urquhart, *A Life in Peace and War* (New York: Norton, 1991), p. 336.

13. Mackinlay, *Peacekeepers,* p. 61.

14. Urquhart, *A Life in Peace and War,* p. 293.

15. Ibid.

16. Woerlee to Urquhart, Code Cable, February 17, 1982, no. NAQ 542.

17. Woerlee to Urquhart, Code Cable, February 18, 1982, no. NAQ 561.

18. Urquhart to Callaghan, Code Cable, April 10, 1982, no. NYQ 1009 UNTSO 680.

19. Urquhart, *A Life in Peace and War,* p. 373.

20. Callaghan to Urquhart, Code Cable, June 8, 1982, no. NAQ 2045.

21. Andersen to Husa, March 10, 1982, "Medical Facilities," no. NAQ 807.

22. Arafat in fact despised Abu Nidal, who is reported to have staged the assassination to

cause maximum damage to the PLO. Argov, who was shot in the head, survived but was left partially blind and paralyzed for the rest of his life. He died in 2003, having spent the final twenty-one years of his life in a Jerusalem hospital.

23. Callaghan to Urquhart, Code Cable, June 6, 1982, no. NAQ 2016 FILTSO 1261.

24. Ibid.

25. Ibid.

26. "Report of the Secretary-General on the United Nations Interim Force in Lebanon," June 11, 1982.

27. From June to September some 17,825 were estimated to have been killed in Lebanon as a whole, with 5,515 killed in Beirut and its suburbs. Jay Ross, "War Casualties Put at 48,000 in Lebanon," *Washington Post,* September 3, 1982, p. A22.

28. David Ottaway, "Arafat Charges UN Force Failed to Resist Israelis," *Washington Post,* June 9, 1982, p. A18.

29. Urquhart to Callaghan, Code Cable, June 7, 1982, no. NAQ 1600.

30. Callaghan to Urquhart, Code Cable, June 8, 1982, no. NAQ 2045.

31. Callaghan to Urquhart, Code Cable, June 14, 1982, no. NAQ 2141.

32. Timour Goksel, interview by Jean Krasno, Yale-UN Oral History, March 17, 1998.

33. The Lebanese naturally opposed the Israeli invasion, but they supported the continuation of UNIFIL. If the UN remained, it at least signaled the world's intention to bring about an Israeli withdrawal and a return of Lebanese sovereignty. Indeed, when the UNIFIL mandate came up for renewal before the Security Council, Lebanese *mukhtars* (village mayors) wrote to the secretary-general to request an extension. McCoubrey and White, *Blue Helmets,* p. 103.

34. Callaghan to Urquhart, Code Cable, July 29, 1982, no. NAQ 2564.

35. Robert Misrahi, interview by Michel Thieren, June 7, 2007.

36. Ibid.

37. Many Palestinians who lived in Lebanon resided in camps like Sabra and Shatila, dating back to the 1948 Arab-Israeli War.

38. Urquhart, *A Life in Peace and War,* p. 346.

39. Henry Kamm, "Arafat Demands Three Nations Return Peace Force to Beirut," *New York Times,* September 17, 1982, p. A6.

40. In response to public outcry over the massacre in Israel and abroad, Prime Minister Menachem Begin established an investigative commission in late September. Headed by Supreme Court Justice Yitzhak Kahan, the commission issued its findings in February 1983, blaming the massacre on the Christian Phalangist forces that carried it out but faulting Defense Minister Ariel Sharon and Chief of Staff Lieutenant General Rafael Eitan for approving the Phalangists' entry into the camps, for not preventing the massacre, and for not stopping it once it was under way. Prime Minister Begin dismissed Sharon, who the Kahan commission found bore "personal responsibility," but Eitan remained in his job.

41. Ronald Reagan, "Address to the Nation Announcing the Formation of a New Multinational Force in Lebanon," September 20, 1982.

42. Troop contributors to UNIFIL saw the decision by the major powers not to send a beefed-up UNIFIL to Beirut as a snub and a further blow to the UN's reputation in the region. Callaghan wrote to UN Headquarters in New York that Nigeria had decided to withdraw its troops from UNIFIL because it did not want to be seen as

assisting the Israeli occupation and also because the creation of the non–UN Multinational Force was "an outright blow to UN peace-keeping concept and can only be construed as humiliating for the UNIFIL contributors." Callaghan to Urquhart, Code Cable, December 28, 1982, no. NAQ 4123.

43. Brian Urquhart, "A Brief Trip to the Middle East 5–11 January 1983," confidential UNIFIL files.

44. Ibid. Urquhart was scathing of others as well. He wrote that U.S. forces in Beirut "have never been seen to go out on patrol except once on a heavily publicized patrol through east Beirut, which is much safer than New York City . . . What a posture for the marines, and how humiliating for them it must be. I did not see a single American military sailor, airman, marine or soldier in or around Beirut the whole time I was there. They stay in camp."

45. A clan spokesman denounced UNIFIL, saying that the UN had come to bring peace but had taken to killing Lebanese. He insisted that all "colored UNIFIL personnel" be relieved of their checkpoint duties. UNIFIL was in such a vulnerable position that Callaghan felt he had no choice but to comply and quickly replaced the Fijians at volatile checkpoints with members of the largely Caucasian Dutch, Irish, and French platoons. Callaghan to Urquhart, Code Cable, March 31, 1983, no. NAQ 915 FILTSO 763.

46. Urquhart to Callaghan, Code Cable, June 3, 1983, no. NYQ 1219.

47. Thomas L. Friedman, "Peacekeepers Become Another Warring Faction," *New York Times,* October 23, 1983, sec. 4, p. 1.

48. Thomas L. Friedman, "Marines Release Diagram on Blast," *New York Times,* October 28, 1983, p. A1.

49. Thomas L. Friedman, "Beirut Death Toll at 161 Americans; French Casualties Rise in Bombings; Reagan Insists Marines Will Remain; Buildings Blasted," *New York Times,* October 24, 1983, p. A1; Friedman, "Marines Release Diagram."

50. Less than two minutes after the attack on the Marine compound, as French soldiers gathered at the windows of their compound to see what had caused the ruckus, a second car bomber smashed into their eight-story building, killing fifty-eight French paratroopers. Ten days later in southern Lebanon a young man in a green Chevrolet truck laden with some eight hundred pounds of explosives crashed through the main gates of the Israeli military intelligence headquarters just south of Tyre. The suicide bomb killed twenty-eight Israeli soldiers and security personnel, as well as thirty-two Arabs, most of whom were being held in detention cells. Terence Smith, "At Least 29 Die as Truck Bomb Rips Israeli Post in Lebanon," *New York Times,* November 5, 1983, sec. 1, p. 1; Herbert H. Denton, "Bomb in Tyre Kills 39; Israeli Planes Retaliate, Strike PLO Near Beirut," *Washington Post,* November 5, 1993, p. A1.

51. Ronald Reagan, "Remarks to Reporters on the Death of American and French Military Personnel in Beirut, Lebanon," October 23, 1983.

52. Ronald Reagan, "Remarks and a Question-and-Answer Session with Regional Editors and Broadcasters on the Situation in Lebanon," October 24, 1983.

53. Steven Strasser et al., "The Marine Massacre," *Newsweek,* October 31, 1983, p. 20.

54. Ronald Reagan, "Address to the Nation on Events in Lebanon and Grenada," October 27, 1983.

55. Even before the attack on the Marine barracks, a *New York Times*–CBS poll found that three-quarters of respondents supported a withdrawal of U.S. troops from Lebanon if they remained unable to stabilize the country, while more Americans (47 percent) disapproved of Reagan's handling of foreign policy than approved (38 percent). David Shribman, "Foreign Policy Costing Reagan Public Support," *New York Times,* September 30, 1983, p. A1.

56. Ronald Reagan, President's News Conference, April 4, 1984.

57. Donald Rumsfeld, "Take the Fight to the Terrorists," *Washington Post,* October 26, 2003, p. B7; "Donald H. Rumsfeld Holds Defense Department News Briefing," October 23, 2003, online at www.defenselink.mil/transcripts/2003/tr20031212-secdef0986.html.

58. "Donald Rumsfeld Delivers Remarks at the National Conference of State Legislatures," December 12, 2003 online at www.defenselink.mil/transcripts/2003/tr20031212-secdef0986.html.

CHAPTER 3. BLOOD RUNNING BLUE

1. SVDM, interview by Philip Gourevitch, November 22, 2002.

2. Jean-Pierre Hocké succeeded the previous high commissioner, Poul Hartling, a seventy-two-year-old Dane who had served for seven years.

3. UNHCR racked up a deficit of $7 million in 1988 and $40 million by 1989.

4. "Hocké Says Resignation Was His Decision," Associated Press, October 27, 1989.

5. "Démission de M J-P Hocké: Bon organisateur mais trop autoritaire," *Le Monde,* October 28, 1989.

6. Anthony Goodman, "UN Aide Says He Was 'Stabbed' Over Refugee Job," Reuters, November 14, 1990.

7. Paul Lewis, "2 Camps in the Search for U.N. Refugee Chief," *New York Times,* November 18, 1990, sec. 1, p. 6.

8. "General Assembly President's Remarks at Conclusion of General Debate," press release, October 14, 1988.

9. Lawyers Committee for Human Rights, *Inhumane Deterrence: The Treatment of Vietnamese Boat People in Hong Kong* (1989), p. 8.

10. In the immediate wake of the war, those who fled Vietnam had generally been people implicated by their ties to the Americans and their South Vietnamese allies. Others had fled Communist "re-education" or military conscription.

11. President Carter had agreed to take in an astonishing 168,000 Vietnamese, Laotians, and Cambodians per year. France, Canada, Australia, the United Kingdom, and others followed suit. But these numbers had dropped precipitously.

12. Malaysia had already adopted a policy of "redirection"—giving the Vietnamese boats, life jackets, a compass, and maps and urging them to make their way to Indonesia. Arthur Helton, "The Comprehensive Plan of Action for Indo-Chinese Refugees: An Experiment in Refugee Protection and Control," *New York Law School Journal of Human Rights* 8, part 1 (1990–1991).

13. Pierre Jambor, the UNHCR representative to Thailand, first raised the screening idea back in 1986, but the human rights lawyers at UNHCR were slow to embrace it.

14. See Sten Bronee, "The History of the Comprehensive Plan of Action," *International Journal of Refugee Law* 5, no. 4 (1993), pp. 534–43.

15. *New York Times,* June 14, 1989, p. A26.
16. W. Courtland Robinson, *Terms of Refuge: The Indochinese Exodus and the International Response* (London: Zed Books, 1998), p. 208.
17. Helton, "The Comprehensive Plan of Action for Indo-Chinese Refugees."
18. W. Courtland Robinson, "The Comprehensive Plan of Action for Indochinese Refugees, 1989–1997: Sharing the Burden and Passing the Buck," *Journal of Refugee Studies* 17, no. 3 (2004), p. 323.
19. Robinson, *Terms of Refuge,* p. 217.
20. Overall, about 28 percent of Vietnamese asylum-seekers were successful in gaining refugee status. Robinson, "Comprehensive Plan of Action," pp. 323, 328. Hong Kong officials were the most reluctant to grant asylum, finding only 20 percent of Vietnamese applicants to have a well-founded fear of persecution. Alexander Betts, *Comprehensive Plans of Action* (Geneva: Evaluation and Policy Analysis Unit, Working Paper No. 120, 2006), p. 37.
21. Betts, *Comprehensive Plans of Action,* p. 40.
22. More than a million Kurds and other Iraqis had fled to Iran. Another 450,000 headed toward Turkey, which refused to admit them. Stranded in the inhospitable, freezing mountain ranges south of the Turkish border, between 500 and 2,000 Kurds were thought to be dying daily.
23. The United States, the U.K., France, and Turkey were the big players, but in the end, thirteen nations participated directly in the Combined Task Force and the material support came from a total of thirty countries. The Security Council also declared a no-fly zone to prevent Saddam Hussein from using his bombers to strafe civilians huddled in the mountains.
24. SVDM, *Civitas Maxima: Origines, fondements et portée philosophique et pratique du concept de supranationalité,* thèse pour le Doctorat d'État ès Lettres et Sciences Humaines, Université de Paris I (Panthéon-Sorbonne), Paris, April 1985.
25. This and all subsequent quotes from the speech are from SVDM, "Philosophical History and Real History: The Relevance of Kant's Political Thought in Current Times," Geneva International Peace Research Institute, December 4, 1991.
26. SVDM, interview by *De Frente Com Gabi,* Sistema Brasileiro de Televisão (SBT), 2002.

CHAPTER 4. HITTING THE GROUND RUNNING
1. Vieira de Mello knew Yasushi Akashi only by his CV. Akashi had begun his career in the Japanese foreign service and in 1979 had left to join the staff of the UN Secretariat, where he spent thirteen years. Prior to being named Special Representative of the Secretary-General in Cambodia, Akashi had run the UN Department of Public Information and the more obscure UN Department of Disarmament Affairs.
2. Philip Shenon, "Norodom Sihanouk: The Prince of Survivors," *New York Times,* October 25, 1991, p. 6.
3. The Paris agreement left the power of the Supreme National Council (SNC) ambiguous. It was established as "the unique legitimate body and source of authority in Cambodia in which, throughout the transitional period, national sovereignty and unity are enshrined." But in Paris the SNC also agreed to delegate to the UN "all powers necessary to ensure the implementation of this Agreement." When it came

to the UN relationship with the named ministries of defense, foreign affairs, finance, public security, and information, the agreement assigned UNTAC only the task of exercising "such control as is necessary to ensure [their] strict neutrality," leaving Akashi and the local actors great discretion in deciding the extent of UN interference, supervision, and executive action. See www.usip.org/library/pa/cambodia/agree_comppol_10231991.html.

4. Sihanouk to SVDM, January 23, 1993.

5. Planning was so chaotic that General John Sanderson, the commander of the UN force, was shown a UN Security Council statement that listed him as commander of the UN force that was then deploying to Bosnia.

6. Nate Thayer, "Plunder of the State," *Far Eastern Economic Review,* January 9, 1992, p. 11.

7. Rodney Tasker and Nate Thayer, "Tactics of Silence," *Far Eastern Economic Review,* December 12, 1991, p. 10.

8. Ibid., pp. 10–11.

9. Nate Thayer, "Murderous Instincts," *Far Eastern Economic Review,* February 6, 1992, p. 13.

10. UN reports warned that returnees would have likely "lost part of their 'peasants memory'" and would not be able to fend for themselves. UNHCR Absorption Capacity Survey, January 1990, p. 15, quoted in W. Courtland Robinson, *"Something Like Home Again": The Repatriation of Cambodian Refugees* (Washington, D.C.: U.S. Committee for Refugees, 1994), p. 13.

11. William Branigin, "U.N. Starts Cambodian Repatriation," *Washington Post,* March 31, 1992, p. A1.

12. Ron Moreau, "The Perilous Road Home," *Newsweek,* April 13, 1992, p. 37.

13. Jarat Chopra, "United Nations Authority in Cambodia," Watson Institute for International Studies Occasional Paper no. 15, 1994, p. 57.

14. UNHCR, "Cambodia: Land Identification for Settlement of Returnees, November 4–December 17, 1991," PTSS Mission Report 91/33, p. 12, quoted in Robinson, *"Something Like Home Again,"* p. 19.

15. Robinson, *"Something Like Home Again,"* p. 13.

16. In 1991 there were 30,000 Cambodian amputees within the country and an additional 5,000 to 6,000 residing in Thai border camps. "Land Mines in Cambodia: The Coward's War," *Asia Watch,* September 1991.

17. Mats Berdal and Michael Liefer, "Cambodia," in James Mayall, ed., *The New Interventionism 1991–1994: United Nations Experience in Cambodia, Former Yugoslavia and Somalia* (New York: Cambridge University Press, 1996), p. 48.

18. Clearing one mine cost between $300 and $1,000, including the cost of training deminers. John Ryle, "The Invisible Enemy," *New Yorker,* November 29, 1993, p. 126.

19. Cambodia's local politics had also been invisible from the skies. As UNHCR representatives traveled the countryside, they realized that while Hun Sen had boasted of the abundance of land his government would cede to the refugees, autonomous provincial and district officials had their own ideas. Many had begun privatizing the land in their districts in order to make a financial killing before the UN attempted to give it away for free.

20. Nicholas Cumming-Bruce, "UN Struggles to Meet Pledge to Refugees," *Guardian*, May 6, 1992, p. 11.

21. Robinson, "*Something Like Home Again,*" p. 66.

22. Cumming-Bruce, "UN Struggles."

23. SVDM to Sadako Ogata, March 21, 1992.

24. William Branigin, "Cambodians Launching Offensive; Khmer Rouge Cited as Endangering U.N. Peace Operation," *Washington Post*, March 30, 1992, p. A1.

25. Nate Thayer, "Phnom Penh Launches Offensive as Cease-Fire Efforts Stall," Associated Press, March 29, 1992. The UN Charter authorizes two forms of military intervention. In the first, which falls under Chapter 6, a host government invites UN blue helmets to perform a consensual set of tasks. In such a mission the troops are supposed to use force only in self-defense. The other type of UN intervention force, which falls under Chapter 7 of the Charter, can be deployed even without the parties' consent; it permits blue helmets to "make" peace and not simply keep it. Cambodia was a Chapter 6 deployment.

26. Bruce Wallace, "Death Returns to the Killing Fields," *Maclean's*, March 1, 1993, p. 32.

27. Prior to UNTAC, the UN's most ambitious peacekeeping mission had been the UN Transitional Assistance Group in Namibia. There the UN policing component was seen as a success. But Namibia had begun with a much stronger, more professional indigenous police corps, and English was spoken throughout the country, making it easier for English-speaking police to help local forces carry out police work.

28. SVDM, Statement at Site 2, March 30, 1992.

29. Teresa Poole, "Cambodians Take Road Back to the Future," *Independent*, March 28, 1992, p. 14.

30. Yuli Ismartono, "Refugees Head Home to Uncertainty and Strife," Inter Press Service, March 31, 1992; Branigin, "U.N. Starts Cambodian Repatriation."

31. Philip Shenon, "Peppered with Mines, Awash in Civil War, It Still Is Home for Cambodians," *New York Times*, March 30, 1992, p. A3.

32. SVDM, Statement at the Sisophon reception center, March 30, 1992.

33. Teresa Poole, "Cambodians Begin New Life," *Independent*, March 31, 1992, p. 16.

CHAPTER 5. "BLACK BOXING"

1. SVDM, "Philosophical History and Real History: The Relevance of Kant's Political Thought in Current Times," Geneva International Peace Research Institute, December 4, 1991.

2. UN Security Council, second progress report of the secretary-general on UNTAC, September 21, 1992, para. 29, p. 7.

3. SVDM to Sadako Ogata, "Visit to Party of Democratic Kampuchea (PDK) Zone—6 to 8 April 1992," April 12, 1992.

4. SVDM to Ogata and Jamshid Anvar, "Report on Visit to Area Controlled by the Party of Democratic Kampuchea (PDK), 6–8 April 1992," April 10, 1992.

5. Tiziano Terzani, "An Indecent Peace," *Far Eastern Economic Review*, June 25, 1992, p. 21.

6. Bruce Wallace, "Death Returns to the Killing Fields," *Maclean's*, March 1, 1993, p. 32.

7. Yasushi Akashi to Tetsuo Miyabara, U.S. General Accounting Office, I-32, August 5,

1993, pp. 1–2, cited in Janet E. Heininger, *Peacekeeping in Transition: The United Nations in Cambodia* (New York: The Twentieth Century Fund Press, 1994), p. 72.

8. Mats Berdal and Michael Liefer, "Cambodia," in James Mayall, ed., *The New Interventionism 1991–1994: United Nations Experience in Cambodia, Former Yugoslavia and Somalia* (New York: Cambridge University Press, 1996), p. 42; John Sanderson, "UNTAC: Successes and Failures," in Hugh Smith, ed., *International Peacekeeping: Building on the Cambodian Experience* (Canberra: Australian Defence Studies Centre, 1994), p. 132.

9. Nayan Chanda, "UN Divisions," *Far Eastern Economic Review,* July 23, 1992, p. 9.

10. SVDM, Reginald Austin, and Dennis McNamara to Akashi, strictly confidential memo, June 15, 1992.

11. SVDM, strictly confidential draft discussion paper on Contingency Repatriation Strategy, July 28, 1992.

12. Jean-Claude Pomonti, "Selon un expert français les capacités militaires des Khmers rouges sont surestimées" (According to a French Expert, the Military Capabilities of the Khmer Rouge Are Overestimated), *Le Monde,* August 22, 1992.

13. SVDM to Christophe Peschoux and Jahanshah Assadi, handwritten note on clipping, September 13, 1992.

14. SVDM to Son Sen, September 3, 1992.

15. SVDM to Ogata and Warren Blatter, "Visit to DK Zone, 30 Sept–1 Oct."

16. Ibid.

17. SVDM, interview by James S. Sutterlin, May 5, 1998, Yale-UN Oral History, p. 26.

18. W. Courtland Robinson, *"Something Like Home Again": The Repatriation of Cambodian Refugees* (Washington, D.C.: U.S. Committee for Refugees, 1994), p. 34.

19. Ibid., p. 37. Robinson, a critic of UNHCR's failure to disclose all the facts to the returnees, notes: "Good information is both touchstone and cornerstone of safe and voluntary repatriation."

20. Philip Shenon, "Call of Land Lures Refugees to Khmer Rouge Zone," *New York Times,* January 31, 1993.

21. Vieira de Mello also bucked the will of the Security Council. In July 1992, when the Khmer Rouge refused to disarm, the Security Council passed a resolution requesting that the secretary-general ensure that "international assistance to the rehabilitation and reconstruction of Cambodia from now on only benefits the parties which are fulfilling their obligations under the Paris agreement and cooperating fully with UNTAC." UN Security Council Resolution 766, quoted in Robinson, *"Something Like Home Again,"* p. 33.

22. Ibid., p. 35.

23. Shenon, "Call of Land."

CHAPTER 6. WHITE CAR SYNDROME

1. Nate Thayer and Susumu Awanohara, "Cambodia Takes a Bath," *Far Eastern Economic Review,* October 15, 1992, p. 56.

2. E.V.K. Fitzgerald, "The Economic Dimension of the Peace Process in Cambodia," in Peter Utting, ed., *Between Hope and Insecurity: The Social Consequences of the Cambodian Peace Process* (Geneva: UNRISD Report, 1994), p. 44.

3. Ibid., p. 55.

4. In 1992 and 1993, 65 percent of all UN food aid in Cambodia went to returnees, though they made up just 4 percent of the population. W. Courtland Robinson, *"Something Like Home Again": The Repatriation of Cambodian Refugees* (Washington, D.C.: U.S. Committee for Refugees, 1994), p. 59.

5. William Branigin, "Missteps on the Path to Peace; Problems Mount and Budgets Soar," *Washington Post,* September 22, 1992, p. A1.

6. The United States, which had made the largest commitment in Tokyo, had only delivered $14 million of its pledged $135 million. Japan, the second-largest donor, had coughed up just $9 million. Report of the Secretary-General on the Implementation of Security Council Resolution 722 (1992), February 13, 1993, para. 31, p. 8.

7. Philip Shenon, "Most Cambodians See Nothing of Aid," *New York Times,* February 21, 1993, sec. 1, p. 10.

8. Jarat Chopra, "United Nations Authority in Cambodia," Watson Institute for International Studies Occasional Paper no. 15, 1994, p. 65.

9. When a UN spokesman was asked whether the entire Bulgarian force could be withdrawn, he acknowledged that they "behave in a manner that makes all of us blush," but said they could not be repatriated because "it would be a terrible insult" to Bulgaria. William Branigin, "Tarnishing the U.N.'s Image in Cambodia; Bulgarians Chided for Monkey Business," *Washington Post,* October 29, 1993, p. A33.

10. A health ministry study found that 77 percent of Cambodians did not know what a condom was. William Branigin, "Key Phases of UN Peace Operation in Cambodia Seen Breaking Down," *Washington Post,* October 4, 1992, p. A33.

11. Report on Public Perceptions of UNTAC in the City of Phnom Penh, Information/Education Division Analysis Report, September 18, 1992, p. 102.

12. "French U.N. Army Commander Orders Brothels Removed," Agence France-Presse, November 1, 1992.

13. Terry McCarthy, "Hot Tempers Rise on the Seamier Side," *Independent,* October 19, 1992, p. 12.

14. As on the military side, the quality of UN police varied. Singapore, for instance, sent a designated unit of seventy-five police who had been prescreened for the mission. They had ten years' police experience and arrived on the heels of a special eight-week training course, where they were taught intercultural communication and lectured in Cambodian history. Janet E. Heininger, *Peacekeeping in Transition: The United Nations in Cambodia* (New York: The Twentieth Century Fund Press, 1994), p. 80.

15. Nayan Chanda, "Cambodia: I Want to Retake Power," *Far Eastern Economic Review,* February 4, 1993, p. 20.

16. Ibid.

17. Ibid., p. 28.

18. Nate Thayer, "Cambodia: Legal Weapon," *Far Eastern Economic Review,* January 21, 1993; "Khmer Rouge Release 21, but Take 46 More Peacekeepers Captive," Agence France-Presse, December 17, 1992.

19. Chopra, "United Nations Authority in Cambodia," p. 27.

20. SVDM to Marrack Goulding, "Our Recent Conversations," February 12, 1993.

21. *Indochina Digest,* March 12, 1993, quoted in Chopra, "United Nations Authority in Cambodia," p. 42.

22. William Branigin, "Montagnards End Fight Against Hanoi," *Washington Post,* October 11, 1992, p. A46.

23. Nate Thayer, "The Forgotten Army," *Far Eastern Economic Review,* September 10, 1992, p. 18.

24. Colonel Y-Pen Ayun to SVDM, handwritten "DECLARATION, September 28, 1992."

25. SVDM to Lionel Rosenblatt, October 10, 1992.

26. SVDM to UNHCR headquarters, "Chronology of Events," October 1992.

27. Robinson, *"Something Like Home Again,"* p. 63.

28. Ron Moreau, "Cambodia: 'This Is My Home,'" *Newsweek,* February 22, 1993, p. 38.

29. SVDM, interview by James S. Sutterlin, May 5, 1998, Yale-UN Oral History, p. 15.

30. Robinson, *"Something Like Home Again,"* p. 46.

31. SVDM, "Refugee Repatriation and Reintegration in Cambodia," *The UNTAC: Debriefing and Lessons, Report and Recommendations of the International Conference, Singapore, August 1994* (London: Kluwer Law International, 1995), p. 151.

32. SVDM to Ogata, "On visit of secretary-general to Cambodia, April 18–20, 1992," May 6, 1992.

33. Nicholas Cumming-Bruce, "Sixth UN Victim Shot Dead in Cambodia," *Guardian,* April 9, 1993, p. 11. The fallout from the incident underscored the fragility of many UN member states' relationship with UN peacekeeping. In Japan the murder kicked off a debate that had been intensifying throughout the month. The constitution of Japan, the second-largest donor to the United Nations, "renounced war as a sovereign right of the nation and the threat or use of force as a means of settling international disputes." In 1992 the Japanese parliament passed an international peacekeeping law that allowed six hundred Japanese soldiers and police to join UNTAC. But these troops served as engineers, road builders, and police, and according to law, they would have to be withdrawn if full-fledged war erupted. Some members of Parliament suggested that day had come.

34. "Angola: UN Secretary General's Envoy Margaret Antsee Reportedly to Be Replaced," BBC News, May 11, 1993.

35. "Angola: UN to Appoint New Special Envoy Soon," Inter Press Service.

36. "Angola Peace Parley Resumes," Agence France-Presse, May 14, 1993.

37. "Angola: UN to Appoint New Special Envoy Soon," Inter Press Service. The person chosen in Vieira de Mello's stead was former Malian foreign minister Alioune Blondin Beye, who arrived in June. Beye died in a plane crash in 1998 as he shuttled between African capitals in pursuit of a settlement.

38. Chopra, "United Nations Authority in Cambodia," p. 49.

39. "Akashi Declares Campaign a Success Despite Violence," Agence France-Presse, May 20, 1992.

40. The official budget was $1.6 billion. But if one adds the pledged rehabilitation and repatriation assistance and off-budget costs, the amount came to $2.5–$2.8 billion. Michael W. Doyle, *UN Peacekeeping in Cambodia: UNTAC's Civil Mandate* (Boulder, CO: Lynne Reinner Publishers, 1995), p. 29.

41. SVDM, interview by Sutterlin, p. 25.

42. SVDM to Courtland Robinson, August 9, 1993.

43. SVDM, draft proposal, "Deceit and Estrangement: The Aborted Relationship Between the KR and the Cambodian Peace Process (1989–1993)."

44. SVDM to Ogata, "Clearance to Engage in a Research Project Related to My Cambodia Experience," September 20, 1993.

45. Christine Dodson to A. Henning, "Mr. Vieira de Mello: Request for Clearance to Engage in a Research Project," October 29, 1993.

46. Lisa Coulombe to SVDM, June 23, 1992.

47. John Burns, "Sarajevans Jeer as U.N. Leader Urges Restraint," *New York Times*, January 1, 1993, p. A1.

48. George Gordon-Lennox and Annick Stevenson, *Sergio Vieira de Mello: An Exceptional Man* (Geneva: Éditions du Tricorne, 2004), p. 67.

49. In December 1992 the first Bush administration sent 28,000 troops to Somalia to participate in a feeding mission. In May 1993 the Americans departed, handing off peacekeeping tasks to a smaller UN force. The largely non-American successor force was authorized at 28,000 troops, but only 16,000 troops deployed. The larger U.S. mission had deployed only in southern and central Somalia, while the smaller UN force was mandated to secure the whole country. After the June 1993 massacre of twenty-five Pakistani blue helmets, Clinton sent 400 Army Rangers and 130 Delta Forces to Somalia and offered a $25,000 reward for the capture of Somali warlord Mohammed Farah Aideed.

50. Bill Clinton, news conference, October 14, 1993.

CHAPTER 7. "SANDWICHES AT THE GATES"

1. In addition to France's 3,096 troops, the U.K.'s 2,281, and Spain's 1,219, other troop contributors on June 1, 1993, included Canada (1,043), Belgium (100), Denmark (186), and Norway (35). The United States fielded 290 troops at a field hospital in Croatia. The main contributors to the UNPROFOR force in Croatia were Argentina (895), Belgium (702), Canada (1,222), Czech Republic (503), Denmark (975), Finland (296), France (2,239), Jordan (918), Kenya (935), Nepal (897), Netherlands (925), Poland (973), Russia (842), Slovakia (404), and the U.K. (250).

2. Five nations flew regularly: the United States, 4,597 flights; France, 2,133; the U.K., 1,902; Canada, 1,860; and Germany, 1,279. Tom Squitieri, "History's Longest Airlift Ends with Food Delivery to Sarajevo," *USA Today*, January 10, 1996, p. 4A. While many UN planes had been hit, a Serb surface-to-air missile had only once brought down a lumbering C-130 and its crew. A small piece of the wreckage from that plane, which crashed in September 1992, killing four Italian crew members, lay in High Commissioner Ogata's office in Geneva. It sat atop a torn piece of one of the blankets that the plane had been carrying. Sadako Ogata, *The Turbulent Decade* (New York: Norton, 2005), p. 62.

3. George Gordon-Lennox and Annick Stevenson, *Sergio Vieira de Mello: An Exceptional Man* (Geneva: Éditions du Tricorne, 2004), p. 70.

4. Bill Clinton, Address to the Nation, October 7, 1993.

5. Bill Clinton, Remarks and an Exchange with Reporters Prior to a Meeting with Members of Congress, October 19, 1993.

6. Ruth Marcus and John Lancaster, "U.S. Pulls Rangers Out of Somalia; Officials Send Conciliatory Signals to Aideed," *Washington Post,* October 20, 1993, p. A1.

7. John Lancaster, "Mission Incomplete, Rangers Pack Up; Missteps, Heavy Casualties Marked Futile Hunt in Mogadishu," *Washington Post,* October 21, 1993, p. A1.

8. William Shawcross, "The UN Murderers Must Never Be Allowed to Achieve Their Aim," *Daily Telegraph,* August 22, 2003, p. 18.

9. Steven A. Holmes, "Word of Bosnian's Killing Cuts Clinton Briefing Short," *New York Times,* January 9, 1993, sec. 1, p. 1.

10. Paul Alexander, "Renowned Soprano Headlines Concert of Peace," Associated Press, December 31, 1993.

11. Boutros-Ghali liked to quote the White Queen in Lewis Carroll's *Through the Looking-Glass,* arguing that the Security Council had asked UN forces to do "six impossible things before breakfast." He wrote, "By helping to evacuate populations threatened by terror or death by advancing forces, the United Nations could be said to be helping ethnic cleansing. And by trying to negotiate cease-fires, the United Nations could be helping to seal the results of the acquisition of territory by force." Boutros Boutros-Ghali, *Unvanquished: A U.S.-U.N. Saga* (New York: Random House, 1999), pp. 86–87.

12. Bernard Henri-Lévy, quoted in Roger Cohen "A Balkan Gyre of War, Spinning Onto Film," *New York Times,* March 12, 1995, sec. 2, p. 1.

13. Milan Jelovac, "Hrvatska ne može biti cipar" (Croatia Cannot Be Like Cyprus), *Danas,* June 21, 1994, pp. 7–9.

14. Ibid.

15. "Oproštajna posjeta Serda di mela kód Dr. Harisa Silajdažić" (A Farewell Visit of SVDM with Dr. Haris Silajdžić), *Oslobodjenje,* February 3, 1994.

16. "In Bosnia's Bog," *Economist,* April 23, 1994, p. 16.

17. Tony Smith, "New British Commander of UN Troops Pledges New, Tougher Aid Approach," Associated Press Worldstream, February 2, 1994.

18. Ibid.

19. Boutros-Ghali, *Unvanquished,* p. 141.

20. Michael Rose, *Fighting for Peace: Lessons from Bosnia* (New York: Warner Books, 1998), p. 35.

21. Ibid., p. 37.

22. Ibid., p. 241.

23. Rose told Bosnian prime minister Haris Silajdžić that he had been misquoted and that he had actually said that he did not want to develop a "siege *mentality*" in Sarajevo. As Rose later noted, Silajdžić "had chosen to sign up to the lie, probably on the grounds that he did not yet know if I would turn out to be helpful to the Bosnians or not." Ibid., p. 42.

24. SVDM and Viktor Andreev to Akashi, "Security of Civil Affairs Staff in BH," January 26, 1994, no. D-SRSG-SAR-0061.

25. "Civil War Between Good and Evil, Say Bosnian Officials," CNN News, February 5, 1994.

26. John Kifner, "Mourners Fear Gunners Even at Burials," *New York Times,* February 8, 1994, p. A15.

27. Paul Adams, "Mortar Attack in Sarajevo Kills at Least 60," *All Things Considered,* February 5, 1994.

28. SVDM, interview by *De Frente Com Gabi,* Sistema Brasileiro de Televisão (SBT), 2002.
29. Rose, *Fighting for Peace,* p. 47.
30. "Serb Leader Claims No Responsibility in Shelling," CNN News, February 5, 1994.
31. "Reciprocal Blame in Mortar Attack on Sarajevo Market," CNN News, February 6, 1994.
32. Mark Heinrich and Robert Block, "Sarajevo Atrocity Turns Market into Bloodbath," *Independent,* February 6, 1994, p. 1.
33. Roger Cohen, "NATO Gives Serbs a 10-Day Deadline to Withdraw Guns," *New York Times,* February 10, 1994, p. A1.
34. *Irish Times,* February 8, 1994, p. A1.
35. In 1997 NATO and Russia would create the NATO-Russia Permanent Joint Council, giving Russia a formal tie with the alliance. The agreement that produced the joint council acknowledged the shared security goals of Russia and NATO and, with the tensions over Bosnia very much in mind, described the new body as "the principal venue of consultation between NATO and Russia in times of crisis or for any other situation affecting peace and stability."
36. Boutros-Ghali, *Unvanquished,* p. 142.
37. Akashi to Annan, "Use of Air Power," February 15, 1994, no. CCZ 229. Vieira de Mello was tasked with talking "wobbling" countries out of bombing the Serbs. He coauthored a paper for the British government that U.K. officials later said helped persuade Foreign Secretary Malcolm Rifkind to continue to stand up to the Americans and resist the temptation to bomb. "It always amused me," Rose later wrote, "that some of the most compelling arguments in the 'UK Eyes Only' paper had been drafted by a Brazilian diplomat." Rose, *Fighting for Peace,* p. 64.
38. Rose, *Fighting for Peace,* p. 62.
39. A key turning point came on February 17 when, on British urging, Russia presented the Serbs with an option for retreating without losing face: The Serbs would withdraw as NATO had demanded, but four hundred Russian troops stationed in Croatia would take their place around Sarajevo. On February 20, with Karadžić among them, Serb crowds flooded the streets to shake hands with their arriving Slavic Russian "brothers," who gave the three-fingered Serb salute. Rose later admitted that "our common determination not to allow air strikes placed me in some kind of unholy alliance with the Russians against NATO." Ibid., p. 88.
40. Ibid., p. 89.
41. Trevor Huggins, "Weather Could Prevent Full Control of Some Weapons," Agence France-Presse, February 20, 1994.
42. *Nightline,* ABC News, February 21, 1994.
43. Akashi to Secretary-General, "Situation in Sarajevo," February 20, 1994, no. CCZ 263.
44. "Tenuous Peace Reigns in Sarajevo after Deadline Passage," CNN News, February 20, 1994.
45. SVDM to Akashi, "Meetings with President Izetbegović, Ministers Ljubijankic and Muratović," February 21, 1994.
46. Alija Izetbegović, Summary of Statement for Bosnia and Herzégovina Television, February 21, 1994.

47. Laura Silber and Allan Little, *Yugoslavia: Death of a Nation* (New York: Penguin Books, 1997), p. 318.

48. In the immediate aftermath of the NATO ultimatum, Washington brokered a landmark deal between Bosnian and Croat forces, bringing an end to some of the most vicious fighting and ethnic cleansing of the war. And on February 28, when four Serb Galeb jets bombed a Bosnian factory, violating a UN no-fly zone, two U.S. F-16s acting for NATO shot them down. Peace *enforcement,* rather than merely peacekeeping, appeared to be the wave of the future.

49. David B. Ottaway, "Sarajevo Exit Route to Open; Muslims, Serbs Sign Access Pact," *Washington Post,* March 18, 1994, p. A1.

50. SVDM, interview by *De Frente Com Gabi,* 2002.

51. All told, on the first day, forty-one people crossed the bridge, nine people traveled by bus into central Bosnia, fifteen Bosnians crossed the airport, and ninety Serbs ventured between their two suburbs. Chuck Sudetic, "Siege of Sarajevo Lifts Briefly as 83 Leave the City," *New York Times,* March 24, 1994, p. A5.

52. David B. Ottaway, "Routes out of Sarajevo Are Opened; A Few Risk Dangers to Reunite with Kin," *Washington Post,* March 24, 1994, p. A21.

53. Emma Daly, "'I Think the Dark Days Are Almost Over,'" *Independent,* March 23, 1994, p. 1.

CHAPTER 8. "SERBIO"

1. UN Joint Commission Officers Reporting, on Gorazde Pocket, April 6–7, 1994.

2. Chuck Sudetic, "Serbs Propose Bosnia Cease-Fire as They Pound Enclave," *New York Times,* April 7, 1994, p. A3.

3. Michael Rose, *Fighting for Peace: Lessons from Bosnia* (New York: Warner Books, 1998), p. 156.

4. Vladislav Guerassev to SVDM, "Reactions to Gorazde Events: View from Belgrade," Most Immediate Code Cable, April 11, 1994.

5. Chuck Sudetic, *Blood and Vengeance: One Family's Story of the War in Bosnia* (New York: Penguin, 1999), p. 233.

6. Jonathan Randal, "Bosnian Serbs Seize, Harass UN Troops," *Washington Post,* April 15, 1994, p. A1.

7. Michael R. Gordon, "Conflict in the Balkans: The Bluff That Failed; Serbs Around Gorazde Are Undeterred by NATO's Policy of Limited Air Strikes," *New York Times,* April 19, 1994.

8. Douglas Jehl, "Clinton Is Telling Serbs That NATO and UN Are Neutral," *New York Times,* April 15, 1994, p. A8.

9. Roger Cohen, "Conflict in the Balkans: United Nations; U.N.'s Bosnia Dilemma: Press Serbs or Pull Out?" *New York Times,* April 17, 1994, p. A12; Viktor Andreev to SVDM (drafted by Harland), "Weekly BH Political Assessment (#62)," Restricted Cable, April 16, 1994.

10. Christopher Bellamy, "Rose Fears 'Tragedy' as Serbs Take Gorazde," *Independent,* April 19, 1994, p. 9.

11. Ruth Marcus, "NATO Powers Consider Expanding Bosnia Role," *Washington Post,* April 19, 1994, p. A1.

12. Muhamed Sacirbey, Security Council Open Debate, April 21, 1994.

13. UN official (anonymous), handwritten notes on the meeting, May 18, 1994.

14. Guerassev to SVDM, "Aftermath of Gorazde: View from Belgrade," Most Immediate Code Cable, April 18, 1994.

15. Chuck Sudetic, "Serbian Soldiers Seize Guns Held by UN, Then Return Most," *New York Times,* April 20, 1994, p. A13.

16. Laura Silber and Bruce Clark, "City Where the Dead Are Lucky: UN Aid Group Describes the 'Living Hell' of Gorazde," *Financial Times,* April 23, 1994, p. 2; Peter Jennings (reporter) and David Gelber (producer), *No Peace to Keep,* ABC News, 1995.

17. Jonathan Randal, "Serb Forces Rain Fire on Gorazde," *Washington Post,* April 19, 1994, p. A10.

18. Srecko Latal, "U.N. Says Little Left to Do, 'Catastrophe' Awaits Gorazde," Associated Press Worldstream, April 18, 1994.

19. Michael Specter, "Yeltsin Warns Bosnian Serbs to Stop Assault on Gorazde," *New York Times,* April 20, 1994, p. A12.

20. Michael Specter, "Moscow Withdraws Its Objections to NATO Strikes Near Gorazde," *New York Times,* April 24, 1994, p. A13.

21. Rick Atkinson, "NATO Has Plan for Massive Air Strikes Against Bosnian Serb Forces," *Washington Post,* April 25, 1994, p. A14.

22. Shitakha to Akashi, "Meeting in Belgrade with Bosnian Serb Civil and Military Authorities, 22 April 94," April 23, 1994, no. Z630.

23. Rose, *Fighting for Peace*, p. 176.

24. Sudetic, *Blood and Vengeance,* p. 234.

25. UN Military Observer, Gorazde to UNMO HQ, Situation Report, April 23, 1994.

26. Ian Traynor, "The Inscrutable Face of a Man Who Said No to NATO," *Guardian,* April 25, 1994, p. 9.

27. Rose, *Fighting for Peace,* p. 179.

28. Roger Cohen, "U.N. and Bosnians at Odds on Serb Pullout," *New York Times,* April 28, 1994, p. A10.

29. Jonathan Randal, "Bosnian Serbs Meet Weapons Deadline," *Washington Post,* April 27, 1994, p. A25.

30. Milan Jelovac, "Hrvatska ne može biti cipar" (Croatia Cannot Be Like Cyprus)," *Danas,* June 21, 1994, pp. 7–9.

31. Akashi to Secretary-General Boutros Boutros-Ghali, April 27, 1994, no. Z646.

32. Roger Cohen, "Man in the Middle Calls on Confucius," *New York Times,* April 26, 1994, p. A6.

33. Paul Lewis, "Serbs Complying with NATO Demand on Arms Pullouts; U.N. Mediator Rebuked," *New York Times,* April 27, 1994, p. A6. Albright said: "The position of my government on the deployment of U.S. ground troops to Bosnia is well known. We believe that this position is correct and consistent with our national interest. If Mr. Akashi believed that we should become involved on the ground, he should have made that view known to U.S. officials. He should not, however, have publicly insulted my president."

34. Jonathan Randal, "U.N., in Double Reverse, Again Blocks Serb Tanks; Muslims Call Akashi Partner in Aggression," *Washington Post,* May 7, 1994, p. A12.

35. Robert Dole, "Lift Bosnia Arms Embargo," press release, May 10, 1994.

36. Akashi to Annan, "HCA's Meetings with PM Silajdžić and Dr. Karadžić on 7 May in Vienna and Pale Respectively, and with President Izetbegović on 8 May in Sarajevo," Immediate Code Cable, May 8, 1994.

37. Akashi to Karadžić, May 10, 1994.

38. Dr. Jovan Zametica to Akashi, May 10, 1994.

39. John Pomfret, "Serbs Move Guns from Gorazde—Possibly for a New Offensive," *Washington Post,* April 28, 1994, p. A20.

40. UN official (anonymous), handwritten notes, May 10, 1994.

41. "U.S. Troops in UN Peacekeeping," *New York Times,* April 25, 1994, p. A14.

42. Roger Cohen, "U.N. and Bosnians at Odds on Serb Pullout," *New York Times,* April 28, 1994, p. A10.

43. Chris Stephen, "A Sheriff Being Driven Out of Town," *Guardian,* April 30, 1994, p. 24.

44. Boutros-Ghali, Report of the Secretary General Pursuant to Resolution 908, United Nations Security Council, September 17, 1994.

45. "UN Official Predicts Progress on Sarajevo Demilitarization," Agence France-Presse, September 8, 1994.

46. Ibid.

47. Akashi to Annan, "Bosnia and Herzegovina—HCA Meetings with Authorities in Pale and Sarajevo," September 26, 1994, no. Z-1473.

48. Milan Jelovac, "O planu za hrvatsku znam koliko i Globus" (I Know as Much as Globus About a Plan for Croatia), *Danas,* November 1, 1994, pp. 8, 9, 11.

CHAPTER 9. IN RETROSPECT

1. Sadako Ogata to Kofi Annan, August 23, 1994.

2. Claire Messina and Oleg Shamshur, "Conference Reports: Regional Conference to Address the Problems of Refugees, Displaced Persons, Other Forms of Involuntary Displacement, and Returnees in the Countries of the Commonwealth of Independent States and Relevant Neighboring Countries," *International Migration Review* 31, no. 2 (1997), p. 464. Holly Cartner of Human Rights Watch said the draft program of action had "no teeth, no mechanisms for accountability," and she described the meeting as "a serious abdication of responsibility and the squandering of a valuable opportunity." See "Human Rights Group Faults U.N. Conference on CIS Refugees," Deutsche Presse Agentur, May 30, 1996.

3. Paolo Lembo, "Lest We Forget: The UN in Iraq—Sergio Vieira de Mello (1948–2003)" *Azerbaijan International* 11, no. 3 (Autumn 2003).

4. SVDM, "Humanitarian Aspects of Peacekeeping," in Daniel Warner, ed., *New Dimensions of Peacekeeping* (New York: Springer, 1995), p. 142.

5. SVDM, "The Evolution of UN Humanitarian Operations," in Stuarte Gordon, ed., *Aspects of Peacekeeping* (London: Frank Cass, 2000), p. 124.

6. David Rieff, *Slaughterhouse: Bosnia and the Failure of the West* (New York: Touchstone 1996), p. 203.

7. SVDM, interview with Philip Gourevitch, November 22, 2002.

8. Adrian Brown, "Serbs Expel 3,000 Civilians from Fallen Srebrenica," Agence France-Presse, July 12, 1995.

9. Report of the UN Panel on Peace Operations (Brahimi Report), August 21, 2000,

p. ix. The report continues: "In some cases, local parties consist not of moral equals but of obvious aggressors and victims, and peacekeepers may not only be operationally justified in using force but morally compelled to do so . . . Impartiality is not the same as neutrality or equal treatment of all parties in all cases for all time, which can amount to a policy of appeasement" (part II, E, 50).

10. Tom Squitieri, "History's Longest Airlift Ends with Food Delivery to Sarajevo," *USA Today*, January 10, 1996, p. A4.

11. The Berlin airlift ran from June 26, 1948, through September 30, 1949. Its 277,000 flights delivered 2.3 million tons of cargo, and sixty-five pilots were killed.

12. UNHCR also delivered some 950,000 tons of food via land convoys, which reached some 2.7 million beneficiaries. Sadako Ogata, *The Turbulent Decade* (New York: Norton, 2005), p. 330.

CHAPTER 10. DAMNED IF YOU DO

1. The Goma area was home to six impromptu "camps" containing 850,000 refugees; the Bukavu area contained twenty-eight camps with 290,000 refugees; and the Uvira area housed twenty-five camps with 250,000 refugees.

2. Fiona Terry, *Condemned to Repeat?: The Paradox of Humanitarian Action* (Ithaca, NY: Cornell University Press, 2002), pp. 8–10.

3. Keith B. Richburg, "U.N. Report Urges Foreign Forces to Protect Rwandans," *Washington Post,* November 18, 1994, p. A1. The refugee leaders urged patience, pointing to their RPF (mainly Tutsi) foes who had been in exile for thirty years but had eventually reclaimed power in Rwanda by force of arms.

4. The Goma camps were about 1 mile from the border; Kibumba was 1.5 miles away; Bukavu was along the border; Mugunga was about 16 miles away; Camp Benaco in Tanzania was around 6 miles away.

5. Vieira de Mello was in fact interested in Mozambique and Sudan, the two countries where he had worked as a young UNHCR field officer.

6. Some 5,800 UN peacekeepers were present in Rwanda, but the Security Council expressly prohibited the blue helmets from helping out in Zaire. UN rules prohibited them from crossing an international border. Kofi Annan, the head of the Department of Peacekeeping Operations, suggested hiring a private security firm called DSL, but Ogata did not think she could persuade the United States, Japan, or other rich countries to pay the fee of $250 million for two years. Sadako Ogata, *The Turbulent Decade* (New York: Norton, 2005), pp. 203–4.

7. John Pomfret, "Aid Dilemma: Keeping It from the Oppressors; U.N., Charities Find Crises Make Them Tools of War," *Washington Post,* September 23, 1997, p. A1.

8. SVDM to Ogata, "My Mission to Eastern Zaire: 29 to 31 July 1996," August 6, 1996, no. AHC/96/0231.

9. Sadako Ogata, "End of Year Statement to Staff," December 14, 1994, online at www.unhcr.org/admin/ADMIN/3ae68fcb30.html.

10. Ray Wilkinson, "The Heart of Darkness," *Refugees* 110 (December 1, 1997), p. 9.

11. Back in December 1935, the League of Nations high commissioner for German refugees, James G. McDonald, resigned to protest international inaction to aid the

flight of Jewish refugees. McDonald, who had been appointed in 1933, stepped down after Hitler's Germany passed the Nuremberg Laws. Gil Loescher, *Beyond Charity: International Cooperation and the Global Refugee Crisis* (Oxford: Oxford University Press, 1996), pp. 42–44.

12. Reuters, "Zairean Security Force Enters Rwandan Refugee Camps," Agence France-Presse, February 12, 1995; "Zairians Begin a U.N. Mission for Rwandans," *New York Times*, February 13, 1995, p. A6.

13. CZSC, the acronym for the Zairean force, comes from the French Contingent Zairois pour la Sécurité des Camps.

14. Reuters, "Zairians Begin a U.N. Mission for Rwandans."

15. "U.N. Official Praises Refugee Action Plan," Deutsche Presse Agentur, February 19, 1995.

16. One U.S. government source estimated that in a single camp the Hutu authorities' appropriation and resale of humanitarian aid generated an additional $6 million a year for arms purchases. Pomfret, "Aid Dilemma." A month before Vieira de Mello's arrival, UNHCR had attempted to register the inhabitants of the camps, but the Hutu militants had spread the rumor that the ink used for registration would cause sterility or death. The propaganda worked: at least 700,000 refugees boycotted the registration, which then made it easy for camp leaders to continue to inflate the numbers so as to divert excess rations to their gunmen. See "UN Locates Missing Hutus," *Financial Times*, November 22, 1996, p. 4.

17. Joel Boutroue, *Missed Opportunities: The Role of the International Community in the Return of the Rwandan Refugees from Eastern Zaire, July 1994–December 1996* (Cambridge, MA: MIT, June 1998), p. 70.

18. SVDM to Ogata, "My Mission to Eastern Zaire: 29 to 31 July 1996."

19. Kurt Mills, "Refugee Return from Zaire to Rwanda: The Role of UNHCR," in Howard Adelman and Govind C. Rao, eds., *War and Peace in Zaire-Congo: Analyzing and Evaluating Intervention, 1996–1997* (Africa World Press, 2004).

20. Boutroue, *Missed Opportunities*, p. 75.

21. UNHCR, *Refugee Camp Security in the Great Lakes Region*, April 1997, no. EVAL/01/97, pp. 12–13, 25.

22. Buchizya Mseteka, "Rwanda Says It Seeks Orderly Return of Refugees," Reuters, August 23, 1996.

23. Xinhua News Agency, "62 Dead in Sweep Against Rwandan Rebels," July 14, 1996.

24. SVDM to Ogata, "My Mission to Eastern Zaire: 29 to 31 July 1996."

25. Elif Kaban, "Rwanda Strongman Blasts Zaire, Wants Refugees Home," Reuters, April 6, 1996.

26. Mahmoud Mamdani, "Why Rwanda Admitted to Its Role in Zaire," *Weekly Mail and Guardian (South Africa),* August 8, 1997.

27. SVDM to Ogata, "My Mission to Eastern Zaire: 29 to 31 July 1996."

28. Chris McGreal, "Rwanda Warns of Looming War; Kigali's Forces Cross into Zaire in Retaliation for Border Shelling," *Guardian,* October 31, 1996. Kagame defended Rwanda's raid across the border and said there was "no question" that his army would press on. "If you slap me in the face," he said, "when I hit back I may not hit in the face. I may hit somewhere else."

29. "Another Congo Crisis," *Africa Confidential* 39, no. 16 (August 7, 1998).

30. Stephen Buckley, "Rwandans Strike Town Inside Zaire; Officer Tells of Raid 'To Destabilize Them,'" *Washington Post,* October 31, 1996, p. A26.

31. Amnesty International, "Hidden from Scrutiny: Human Rights Abuses in Eastern Zaire," December 19, 1996.

32. "Une Situation humanitaire désespérées s'installe dans l'est du Zaire" (Eastern Zaire Faces Desperate Humanitarian Situation), *Le Monde,* October 30, 1996.

33. From 1978 to 1981 Chrétien had served as Canada's ambassador to the Great Lakes countries, jointly accredited to Zaire, Rwanda, and the Congo Republic.

34. Jimmy Burns and Frances Williams, "Refugees' Agency Lost in Wilderness of Bungling and Waste," *Financial Times,* July 29, 1998, p. 7.

35. SVDM to Benon Sevan, November 12, 1996, no. AHC/GL/006.

36. Tony Smith, "Rwandan Hutu Refugees Dare to Go Home; World Cannot Decide How to Help," Associated Press, November 9, 1996.

37. Jim Wolf, "Africa-Bound U.S. Troops Will Not Disarm Factions," Reuters, November 14, 1996.

38. Jessen-Petersen to Ogata, "Situation in Eastern Zaire," November 14, 1996.

39. Luis Arreaga to A. Mahiga, "Redefining the Role of a Multinational Force," November 21, 1996.

40. SVDM to Akashi, Ogata, and Chrétien, "Situation in Burundi—Visit to Bujumbura, 6–7 December 1996," December 9, 1996. Vieira de Mello met with Colonel Firmin Siuzoyiheba, who was expelling Burundians, who were pouring into Tanzania.

41. George Gordon-Lennox and Annick Stevenson, *Sergio Vieira de Mello: An Exceptional Man* (Geneva: Editions du Tricorne, 2004), p. 85.

42. SVDM to Akashi, Ogata, and Chrétien, "Meeting with General M. Baril—Entebbe, 27 November 1996," November 27, 1996.

43. In the two years since the genocide, very little repatriation had occurred. Only 6,427 Hutu refugees returned to Rwanda from Tanzania in 1995, and half that number went home in 1996. UNHCR, *The State of the World's Refugees 2000: Fifty Years of Humanitarian Action* (New York: Oxford University Press, 2001), p. 265.

44. Raymond Bonner, "U.N. Shift on Rwandans a Bow to 'New Realities,'" *New York Times,* December 21, 1996, sec. 1, p. 7.

45. Annie Thomas, "Abandoned Refugee Camp Is Ghost Town," Agence France-Presse, December 18, 1996.

46. Sokiri to SVDM, "Return of Refugees from Tanzania," November 27, 1996.

47. SVDM, "The Humanitarian Situation in the Great Lakes," speaking notes for statement to standing committee of executive committee, January 30, 1997, EXCOM 1 August 1994–December 1997; cited in UNHCR, *State of the World's Refugees 2000,* p. 265.

48. Earlier in the year McNamara had unveiled a new agency doctrine of "imposed return" by which UNHCR would approve sending refugees back against their will "to less than optimal conditions in their home country," provided that UNHCR could monitor conditions. He said UNHCR was forced to approve such returns because host countries no longer wanted the refugees and donors no longer wanted to pay for them. Ben Barber, "Refugees May Be Sent Home," *Washington Times,* April 22, 1996, p. A14.

49. Beginning in the 1960s refugees from Burundi, the Democratic Republic of Congo, Malawi, Mozambique, Rwanda, Somalia, South Africa, Uganda, and Zimbabwe flocked to Tanzania to benefit from its generous asylum policy. The government offered refugees land for settlement, integration into local communities, and occasionally extended citizenship. In 1983 Tanzania's president Julius Nyerere received UNHCR's Nansen Medal for his country's excellent refugee record. Hania Zlotnik, "International Migration 1965–96: An Overview," *Population and Development Review* 24, no. 3 (September 1998), pp. 429–68.

50. SVDM to Ogata and Akashi, "Meetings in Dar, 29–30 November 1996," December 1, 1996, no. AHC/GL//026.

51. Ibid.

52. "Message to all Rwandese Refugees in Tanzania from the Government of the United Republic of Tanzania and the Office of the United Nations High Commissioner for Refugees," *International Journal of Refugee Law* 9 (1997), pp. 328–29. Vieira de Mello said publicly, "We believe that the conditions in Rwanda have evolved in a positive and encouraging manner, so that the refugees can return in safety and dignity." Raymond Bonner, "U.N. Shift on Rwandans Bow to 'New Realities,'" *New York Times,* December 21, 1996.

53. Chris Tomlinson, "400,000 Rwandans Leave Refugee Camps to Hide in Game Park," Associated Press, December 13, 1996.

54. Karin Davies, "Confronted by Tanzanian Soldiers, Rwandan Refugees Head Back," Associated Press, December 14, 1996.

55. Ibid.

56. Christian Parayre, "Rwandan Refugees Crossing from Tanzania at 10,000 an Hour," Agence France-Presse, December 16, 1996.

57. Matti Huuhtanen, "Tanzania Sends More Refugees Home to Rwanda," Associated Press, December 16, 1996.

58. Karin Davies, "Tanzania Sends Rwandan Refugees Home," Associated Press, December 16, 1996.

59. Sokiri to Chefike and Mahiga, "Preliminary Report on the Role of the Army and Police in the Repatriation of Rwandese Refugees from Karagwe and Ngara Districts," December 30, 1996.

60. Karin Davies, "Tanzania Police and Soldiers Herd Reluctant Refugees and Hutu Extremists Toward the Border with Rwanda," Associated Press Worldstream, December 19, 1996.

61. Christian Parayre, "Rwandan Hutus Press Homewards Despite Fears Over Unfair Trials," Agence France-Presse, December 28, 1996. With the returns the Rwandan population was thought to have increased by 20 percent.

62. UNHCR, note for the file, January 10, 1997 (author unknown).

63. Ibid.; Arthur C. Helton, "The State of the World's Refugees: Fifty Years of Humanitarian Action," *International Journal of Refugee Law* 13, no. 1/2, p. 273.

64. Bonner, "U.N. Shift on Rwandans"; "Africa: Human Rights Developments," *Human Rights Watch World Report,* 1998.

65. SVDM to Jessen-Petersen, "Meetings with Kabila and Senior AFDL Officials, Lubumbashi, 13 May 97," May 13, 1997.

66. Mobutu had changed the name from Congo to Zaire in 1971, as a way of stamping out Western influence.

67. Judith Matloff, "Taking Zaire Easier Than Ruling the New 'Congo,'" *Christian Science Monitor,* May 19, 1997, p. 1.

68. UNHCR, *State of the World's Refugees 1997: A Humanitarian Agenda* (Oxford: Oxford University Press, 1997), p. 23.

69. John Pomfret, "Rwandans Led Revolt in Congo; Defense Minister Says Arms, Troops Supplied for Anti-Mobutu Drive," *Washington Post,* July 9, 1997, p. A1.

70. SVDM, speaking notes, EXCOM Standing Committee, January 30, 1997, "The Humanitarian Situation in the Great Lakes Region."

71. SVDM, "The Evolution of UN Humanitarian Operations," in Stuarte Gordon, ed., *Aspects of Peacekeeping* (London: Frank Cass, 2000), p. 121.

72. SVDM, "The Impact of the External Environment and Responsibilities of External Actors," ICRC Conference, March 28, 1998.

73. U.S. opposition to Boutros-Ghali stemmed largely from the fact that, in a presidential election year, the Republicans had so criticized him that Clinton, who had never had an easy time with him, came out against him. Secretary of State Warren Christopher notified Boutros-Ghali in May of the U.S. intention to veto his reelection. When Boutros-Ghali asked for the reasons, Christopher refused to tell him, saying he did not want to harm their friendship. Boutros-Ghali reportedly said, "You are a lawyer. Won't you represent my case to the president?" But Christopher answered, "I am the president's lawyer." Global Policy, "Secretary-General Elections 1996," Chronology, www.globalpolicy.org/secgen/pastsg/e196chro.htm. In mid-September 1996 Boutros-Ghali had arrived at a lunch at the UN after a vacation and declared, "It is great to be back from vacation. Frankly, I get bored on vacation. It's much more fun to be at work here blocking reform, flying my black helicopters, imposing global taxes, demoralizing my staff." Barbara Crossette, "With Little Fanfare and Facing Crisis, U.N. Starts a New Year," *New York Times,* September 18, 1996, p. A9.

74. In 1999 Mark Malloch Brown, a Brit, would become the first non-American appointed to run the UN Development Program.

75. In November 2006 Margaret Chan would be appointed the head of the World Health Organization, the first Chinese to head a UN agency.

76. Thomas G. Weiss, "Civilian-Military Interactions and Ongoing UN Reforms: DHA's Past and OCHA's Remaining Challenges," in Jim Whitman, ed., *Peacekeeping and the UN Agencies* (London: Frank Cass, 1999), p. 56.

77. See www.shashitharoor.com.

CHAPTER 11. "GIVING WAR A CHANCE"

1. Since 1994 the United States had made only token payments to the UN. When House Republicans blocked repayment, they foiled the effort that Bill Richardson, U.S. ambassador to the UN, was making at the UN to get U.S. dues reduced from 25 to 22 percent of the overall total. "The Congress has sent me into a battle to lower our dues scales without even a slingshot," Richardson said. John Goshko, "U.S. Refusal to Pay Debt Alarms UN," *Washington Post,* November 15, 1997, p. A1.

2. Kofi Annan, press conference at United Nations Headquarters, November 14, 1997, online at www.un.org/News/Press/docs/1997/19971114.SGSM6393.html.

3. Ibid. The United States called off the planned missile strikes when the government of Iraq offered unconditional cooperation.

4. Kofi Annan, Statement to the Special Meeting of the General Assembly on Reform, July 16, 1997.

5. Prior to joining the UN, Kieran Prendergast had served as British ambassador in Turkey, British high commissioner to Kenya, and British high commissioner to Zimbabwe.

6. SVDM, "OCHA: Visions, Priorities and Needs," Geneva, Palais des Nations, June 8, 1998.

7. Ibid.

8. UN Department of Public Information, "Episode 708," *UN World Chronicle,* April 21, 1998.

9. Geir Moulson, "U.N. Official. Afghan Rivals' 'War Games' Endanger Aid," Associated Press Worldstream, February 26, 1998.

10. Thalif Deen, "U.N. Restricts Aid to Saving Lives," Inter Press Service, July 22, 1998. Only Pakistan, Saudi Arabia, and the United Arab Emirates recognized the Taliban as the legitimate rulers of Afghanistan.

11. "Taliban Places Restrictions on Foreign Muslim Women Working for UN," Associated Press Worldstream, March 13, 1998.

12. Luisa Ballin, "Nous posons des conditions à p'aide aux talibans" (We Are Setting Conditions for Aid to the Taliban), *La Croix,* March 2, 1998, p. 7.

13. Ibid.

14. Physicians for Human Rights, "Medical Group Condemns UN Agreement with Taliban," June 1998.

15. The Clinton administration carried out the attack on Afghanistan the same day as its infamous cruise missile strike on the Al Shifa pharmaceutical plant in Sudan.

16. Farhan Haq, "U.N. Staff to Return to Afghanistan," Inter Press Service, March 12, 1999; "No U.S., British Nationals Among UN Staff in Afghanistan," Agence France-Presse, March 18, 1999.

17. Dennis King, "Paying the Ultimate Price: Analysis of the Death of Humanitarian Aid Workers (1997–2001)," January 2002, www.reliefweb.int/symposium/payingultimateprice97-10.html. There are no statistics on the number of humanitarian workers worldwide and no common reporting procedures on injuries or deaths.

18. Conrad N. Hilton Foundation, *Conference Report on Humanitarian Challenges in the New Millennium: Where Are We Headed?,* September 29, 1998, p. 14.

19. "UN Official Condemns Attacking of Humanitarian Vehicles in Angola," Xinhua News Agency, May 22, 1998.

20. Edward Luttwak, "Give War a Chance," *Foreign Affairs* 78, no. 4 (July–August 1999).

21. SVDM, "Enough Is Enough," *Foreign Affairs* 79, no. 1 (January–February 2000).

22. Ibid.

23. Ibid.

24. SVDM, "War and Politics: The Humanitarian Deceit," 1998, unpublished.

25. Barbara Crossette, "Reports of Spying Dim Outlook for Inspections," *New York Times,* January 8, 1999, p. A8.

26. Colum Lynch, "U.S. Used UN to Spy on Iraq, Aides Say," *Boston Globe,* January 6, 1999, p. A1.

27. Javier Solana, press statement, March 23, 1999, online at www.nato.int/docu/pr/1999/p99-040e.htm.

28. SVDM, "Promoting Peace and Security: Humanitarian Activities Relevant to the Security Council," Address to an Open Session of the Security Council, January 21, 1999.

29. Sandy Berger, Special White House Briefing on Kosovo and NATO Air Operations, March 25, 1999. Berger said: "We always prefer to operate pursuant to a UN resolution. But we've also always taken the position that NATO has the authority, in situations it considers to be threats to the stability and security of its area, to act by consensus, without explicit UN authority. And that is the case here as well."

30. The Security Council authorized the Korean War in June 1950, while the Soviet Union was boycotting the Council. Later that summer, when the Soviets returned and began vetoing U.S.-sponsored resolutions on Korea, the United States introduced the Uniting for Peace resolution in the General Assembly (also known as the Acheson Plan, after then–secretary of state Dean Acheson), which held that if the Security Council permanent members could not reach consensus and failed to exercise their "primary responsibility" for maintaining international peace and security, the responsibility would pass to the General Assembly, where two-thirds of the members present would need to authorize action. Since Korea, the Uniting for Peace resolution has been used to call the General Assembly into special session ten times, not always to bypass the Soviet veto. Following the British-French invasion of Egypt in 1956, Security Council resolutions calling for cease-fires were vetoed by France and the U.K.; an emergency session held under the Uniting for Peace resolution passed a U.S. resolution, leading to the withdrawal of France and the U.K. less than a week later. See Michael Ratner and Jules Lobel, "A UN Alternative to War: 'Uniting for Peace,'" *Jurist,* February 10, 2003.

31. Kofi Annan, "Statement Regarding NATO Airstrikes of Serbian Military Targets," March 24, 1999.

32. Judith Miller, "The Secretary-General Offers Implicit Endorsement of Raids," *New York Times,* March 25, 1999, p. A13.

33. Kofi Annan, "The Effectiveness of the International Rule of Law in Maintaining International Peace and Security," May 18, 1999, www.un.org/law/cod/sixth/54/english/hague.htm.

34. Kofi Annan, "A United Nations That Will Not Stand Up for Human Rights Is a United Nations That Cannot Stand Up for Itself," Address to the Commission on Human Rights, April 7, 1999.

35. Ivo Daalder and Michael O'Hanlon, *Winning Ugly: NATO's War to Save Kosovo* (Washington, D.C.: Brookings Institution, 2001), p. 140.

36. UNHCR, "Comments to British House of Commons Report on the Kosovo Humanitarian Crisis," undated.

37. Peter Capella, "UN Agency Failed to Meet Refugee Crisis, Says Report," *Guardian,* February 12, 2000, p. 17. See also David Rieff, "The Agency That Has Had a Bad War," *Guardian,* June 10, 1999, p. 19.

38. Farhan Haq, "U.N. Pushes for Access to Refugees," Inter Press Service, April 5, 1999.

39. Edith M. Lederer, "Divided Council Manages to Express Concern Over Kosovo Refugees," Associated Press Worldstream, April 5, 1999.

40. Blaine Harden, "A Long Struggle That Led Serb Leader to Back Down," New York Times, June 6, 1999, p. 1.

41. "Secretary General Shocked and Distressed by Bombing of Civilian Buildings in Yugoslavia, Including Chinese Embassy," press release, May 10, 1999.

42. Nicole Winfield, "Annan Asks Yugoslavia to Accept UN Humanitarian Team," Associated Press Worldstream, May 4, 1999.

43. "NATO Raids Go On as Hopes Rise for Negotiated End to Kosovo Conflict," Agence France-Presse, May 7, 1999.

44. SVDM, Press Briefing, May 7, 1999.

45. Ibid.

46. CNN World Report Forum, Morning Q&A Session, May 7, 1999.

47. Ibid.

48. Ibid.

49. Kofi Annan, Press Conference, May 14, 1999.

CHAPTER 12. INDEPENDENCE IN ACTION

1. Slobodan Milošević, interview by CBS News, April 22, 1999, online at www.serbia-info.com/news/1999-04/25/11279.html.

2. Ibid.

3. Slobodan Milošević, interview by Arnaud de Borchgrave, UPI, April 30, 1999.

4. William Cohen and Henry Hugh Shelton, appearing on Face the Nation, May 16, 1999.

5. Candice Hughes, "NATO Pounds Kosovo; Serbs Complain Troop Withdrawal Obstructed," Associated Press, May 16, 1999.

6. "UN Team Arrives to Study Kosovars' Plight," New York Times, May 18, 1999, p. A10; "UN Team to Spend 2–3 Days in Kosovo," Associated Press Worldstream, May 17, 1999.

7. Candice Hughes, "UN Team Tries to Steer Neutral Course in Question of Who Is Suffering More," Associated Press Worldstream, May 20, 1999.

8. "UN Aid Team in Kosovo," Guardian, May 21, 1999.

9. Candice Hughes, "Silent Kosovo Bears Witness to the Ethnic Conflict," Associated Press, May 21, 1999.

10. Although the two republics were then jointly part of the Federal Republic of Yugoslavia, Montenegro did not share Serbia's war aims. Blessed by a scenic coastline and superior economic prospects, some 55.5 percent of Montenegrins voted for independence in 2006, clearing the European Union threshold, and the country became the 192nd member of the UN on June 28, 2006.

11. "'Enough Evidence of Ethnic Cleansing' in Kosovo," Agence France-Presse, May 24, 1999.

12. Fabrizio Hochschild to SVDM, May 26, 1999.

13. SVDM, Briefing to the Security Council on the UN Inter-Agency Needs Assessment Mission to the Federal Republic of Yugoslavia, June 2, 1999.

14. Ibid.

CHAPTER 13. VICEROY

1. SVDM, "Humanitarian Needs in Kosovo and Yugoslavia," National Press Club, June 7, 1999.

2. Michael Dobbs, "NATO Occupies Tense Kosovo Capital; British Troops Confront Russians at Pristina Airport," *Washington Post,* June 13, 1999, p. A1.

3. SVDM, "How Not to Run a Country: Lessons for the UN from Kosovo and East Timor," 2000, unpublished.

4. Donna Bryson, "Aid Workers Follow Troops to Kosovo," Associated Press, June 13, 1999.

5. "UN Civilian Administrator Arrives in Pristina," Agence France-Presse, June 13, 1999.

6. Ibid.

7. SVDM, "How Not to Run a Country."

8. UN Interim Administration in Kosovo, "Chronology," online at www.un.org/peace/kosovo/news/kos30day.htm.

9. SVDM, "Humanitarian Needs."

10. Ian Johnstone, "Note on the Kosovo Mission Planning Meeting at United Nations Headquarters, New York, on 9 June 1999 at 5:15 p.m.," June 12, 1999.

11. "UN Interim Administration Mission in Kosovo (UNMIK), Fact Sheet, June 12, 1999, online at www.ess.uwe.ac.uk/Kosovo/Kosovo-Closure14.htm.

12. Fabrizio Hochschild, "'It Is Better to Leave, We Can't Protect You': Flight in the First Months of United Nations Transitional Administrations in Kosovo and East Timor," *Journal of Refugee Studies* 17, no. 3 (September 2004), pp. 286–300.

13. Ibid.

14. Before the NATO war, ethnic Albanians constituted just 30 of the 756 judges and prosecutors in Kosovo. Report of the Secretary-General on the UN Interim Administration Mission in Kosovo, July 12, 1999, p. 14.

15. Only on July 4 did Vieira de Mello use his governing authority to issue a legal order retroactively authorizing NATO troops to detain suspects.

16. Hansjörg Strohmeyer, "Collapse and Reconstruction of a Judicial System: The United Nations Missions in Kosovo and East Timor," *American Journal of International Law* 95, no.1 (January 2001), p. 53.

17. Ibid., p. 52.

18. SVDM, "How Not to Run a Country."

19. Simon Chesterman, *You, the People: The United Nations, Transitional Administration, and State-Building* (Oxford and New York: Oxford University Press, 2004), p. 11.

20. Colleen Barry, "Rugova Returns to Kosovo from Wartime Exile," Associated Press, July 15, 1999.

21. Kosovo has held four elections since 1999: municipal elections in 2000 and 2003, and national assembly elections in 2001 and 2004. These elections were conducted under international supervision. The Organization for Security and Cooperation in Europe and other observing groups found the elections generally fair and free.

22. Niko Price, "Competing Governments in Kosovo Raise Questions about Future," Associated Press, July 4, 1999.

23. In a nod to Washington, Annan also announced that James "Jock" Covey, a former

U.S. diplomat who had served in the White House, would serve as Kouchner's principal deputy.

24. "UN Kosovo Mission Appeals for End to Attacks on Minorities," July 14, 1999.

25. John Ruggie, "Press Briefing on Kosovo," July 21, 1999, online at www.un.org/news/briefings/docs/1999/19990721.RUGGIE.html.

26. SVDM, "Resist the Apartheid Temptation in the Balkans," *International Herald Tribune,* August 25, 1999, p. 26.

27. Fiona Terry, *Condemned to Repeat?: The Paradox of Humanitarian Action* (Ithaca, NY: Cornell University Press, 2002), p. 23.

28. Bill Clinton, Remarks to the 54th Session of the United Nations General Assembly, September 21, 1999.

29. Hochschild, "'It Is Better to Leave, We Can't Protect You,'" p. 295.

30. SVDM, "How Not to Run a Country."

CHAPTER 14. BENEVOLENT DICTATOR

1. The day before the Indonesian invasion U.S. president Gerald Ford and Secretary of State Henry Kissinger met in Jakarta with President Suharto. The notes on the Ford-Kissinger-Suharto discussion (online at www.gwu.edu/~nsarchiv/NSAEBB/NSAEBB62/doc4.pdf) reveal that the United States openly approved of the plan to invade. Suharto said, "We want your understanding if we deem it necessary to take rapid or drastic action." And Ford consented, saying, "We will understand and will not press you on the issue." Kissinger expressed some misgivings about the possible U.S. public reaction and cautioned: "We understand your problem and the need to move quickly, but I am only saying that it would be better if it were done after we returned [to the United States]."

2. The Timorese were asked to vote yes to one of the two following statements: "Do you ACCEPT the proposed special autonomy for East Timor within the Unitary State of the Republic of Indonesia?" or "Do you REJECT the proposed special autonomy for East Timor, leading to East Timor's separation from Indonesia?"

3. Ian Martin, "The Popular Consultation and the United Nations Mission in East Timor—First Reflections," in James J. Fox and Dionisio Babo Soares, eds., *Out of the Ashes: Destruction and Reconstruction of East Timor* (Canberra: Australian National University Press, 2003), p. 133.

4. Some 230,000 fled or were deported to refugee camps in Indonesia-controlled West Timor, and several hundred thousand more were internally displaced.

5. Ian Martin, "Commission for Reception, Truth and Reconciliation in East Timor," Public Hearing, March 15–17, 2004.

6. Sandy Berger, "Special White House Briefing, Subject: President Clinton's Trip to APEC Meeting in New Zealand," September 8, 1999.

7. Rupert Cornwell, "East Timor in Turmoil," *Independent* (London), September 6, 1999, p. 3.

8. André Glucksmann, "Impardonnable ONU" (Unpardonable UN), *L'Express,* September 23, 1999.

9. "Le bloc-notes de Bernard-Henri Lévy" (Bernard-Henri Lévy's Note Pad), *Le Point,* September 24, 1999.

10. SVDM, "Réplique a deux intellectuals cabotins" (Retort to Two Intellectual Show-offs), *Le Monde,* October 17, 1999.

11. Ibid.

12. Kofi Annan, Press Conference, New York, September 10, 1999.

13. Ibid.

14. Ibid.

15. Geoffrey Robinson, "'If You Leave Us, We Will Die,'" *Dissent,* Winter 2002, p. 97.

16. On September 9, the Australian government announced that individuals fleeing East Timor would be able to apply for special humanitarian visas upon arrival in Australia (rather than before entry). The humanitarian stay visas were for those who had "been, or will likely be, displaced from their place of residence" and were a more general version of a special visa category that the Australian government had established for Kosovar refugees the previous April. The visas were expected to last no longer than three months, and the Australian immigration minister told ABC radio: "It's not intended to be used in a large number of cases." "Government Change to Humanitarian Visa Arrangements," Australian Associated Press, September 1999.

17. Seth Mydans, "Cry from Besieged City: Don't Forget East Timor," *New York Times,* September 12, 1999, p. A14.

18. Manfred Becker (director), *The Siege,* Telefilm, Canada, 2004.

19. Officially, the language is known as Bahasa Indonesia. East Timor itself is known in Tetum as Timor Lorosa'e, in Portuguese as Timor-Leste, and in Indonesian as Timor Timur.

20. Robinson, "'If You Leave Us,'" p. 94.

21. Becker, *The Siege.*

22. SVDM, "Note for Mr. Prendergast: Re: IDPs in UN Compound," September 9, 1999.

23. Ibid.

24. Ibid.

25. Michael Carey, "UNAMET's Final Humiliation," ABC Australia, September 9, 1999.

26. Kofi Annan, Press Conference, New York, September 10, 1999.

27. Keith Richburg, "Indonesia Softening on Peacekeepers," *Washington Post,* September 12, 1999, p. A1.

28. Bill Clinton, Press Conference on East Timor, Washington, D.C., September 9, 1999.

29. Seth Mydans, "Indonesia Invites a UN Force to Timor," *New York Times,* September 13, 1999, p. A1.

30. Doug Struck, "'The Militias Will Eat Your Crying Babies'; Terrified Refugees Describe Harrowing Escape from Dili," *Washington Post,* September 16, 1999, p. A17.

31. On April 30, 1975, as the United States withdrew from captured Saigon, desperate Vietnamese gathered at the U.S. embassy and other points across the city. Over the previous two weeks, 50,000 South Vietnamese who had supported the United States in the war had been evacuated along with 6,000 Americans. Upon learning that the North Vietnamese would overtake Saigon at daybreak, Secretary of State Henry Kissinger and President Gerald Ford ordered U.S. helicopters to evacuate the embassy in the middle of the night. After discovering that 129 U.S. Marines had been left behind, they sent another helicopter back, now in daylight. As the helicopter ascended, around 400 Vietnamese who had been promised evacuation were abandoned below. Marines tossed tear gas grenades down among the Vietnamese.

32. Seth Mydans, "Refugees Are Joyful in a Dili of Ashes," *New York Times,* September 21, 1999, p. A10.

33. SVDM, Speaking Notes, "Handing Over Ceremony with General Cosgrove," February 23, 2000. He continued, "Had a force like INTERFET been deployed in the spring of 1994 to Rwanda, hundreds of thousands of lives would have been saved."

34. Laura King, "Thousands Cheer East Timor Leader," Associated Press, October 22, 1999.

35. Terry McCarthy and Jason Tedjasukmana, "The Cult of Gusmão," *Time Europe,* March 20, 2000, p. 30.

36. UN Security Council Resolution 1272, October 25, 1999.

37. Francesc Vendrell, the senior UN envoy who had miraculously persuaded the Indonesians to allow the referendum and had been working on East Timor since 1976, was told not to meddle and was treated at UN Headquarters, in the words of one UN official, "like a common criminal."

38. FALINTIL is the Forças Armadas da Libertação Nacional de Timor-Leste (the Armed Forces for the National Liberation of Timor-Leste).

39. Conflict Security and Development Group, King's College, London, "A Review of Peace Operations: A Case for Change, East Timor," March 10, 2003, pp. 18–21.

40. The ratio of professional staff members to operation has since risen to two or three per operation. But the ratio of professional staff in Headquarters to UN personnel in the field remains around 1:149. UN General Assembly, Administrative and Budgetary Committee, "Introductory Remarks by the Under-Secretary-General for the Department of Management," *Comprehensive Report on Strengthening the Capacity of the Organization to Manage and Sustain Peace Operations,* June 5, 2007.

41. Only in December 2000, thirteen months after Vieira de Mello departed, did a near-mutiny in the office convince Annan to formally replace Vieira de Mello with Kenzo Oshima, a career Japanese diplomat.

42. UN Security Council Resolution 1272. Jarat Chopra has helpfully described four categories of transitional authority: assistance, where the state was still intact and functioning, and the UN gave technical advice but exerted no direct authority over a government; control, as in Cambodia, where the UN sent transitional personnel to exercise "direct control" over certain governing functions; partnership, as in Namibia, where the UN and South Africa initially collaborated; and outright governorship, as in East Timor, where the UN exercised direct governmental authority. Jarat Chopra, "Introducing Peace Maintenance," *Global Governance* 4 (January–March 1998), p. 7.

43. SVDM, Address to National Council, June 28, 2001.

CHAPTER 15. HOARDING POWER, HOARDING BLAME

1. Rajiv Chandrasekaran, "Saved from Ruin: The Reincarnation of East Timor; U.N. Handing Over Sovereignty After Nation-Building Effort," *Washington Post,* May 19, 2002, p. A1.

2. SVDM, "The Future of UN State-Building," International Peace Academy conference, October 18–19, 2002, www.ipacademy.org/pdfs/YOU-THE-PEOPLE.pdf.

3. Ibid.

4. World Bank, "Report of the Joint Assessment Mission to East Timor," December 8, 1999, online at http://pascal.iseg.utl.pt/~cesa/jamsummarytablefinal.pdf.

5. SVDM, Speech at the University of Sydney, June 13, 2001.

6. SVDM, "How Not to Run a Country: Lessons for the UN from Kosovo and East Timor," 2000, unpublished.

7. Indeed, the flag of Gusmão's resistance party, which would become the flag of East Timor, had appeared on referendum ballots as the symbol of the vote for independence.

8. The seven seats corresponded to the seven pro-independence parties within the National Congress for the Reconstruction of East Timor (CNRT), the coalition of resistance parties led by Gusmão.

9. James Traub, "Inventing East Timor," *Foreign Affairs,* vol. 79, no. 4 (July–August 2000), p. 82.

10. Abilio Araujo, "To Be or Not to Be a X(B)anana Republic," *Jakarta Post,* January 26, 2001.

11. SVDM, "Notes from November 27 Brainstorming Session with Hedi Annabi," December 2, 1999.

12. Although most Timorese political leaders spoke Portuguese, ordinary Timorese rarely did. The prevalent language was Tetum, but the Timorese leaders deemed Portuguese a more versatile language for Timorese youths and successfully urged Vieira de Mello to make it the country's official language.

13. Millennium Report of the Secretary-General of the UN, April 3, 2000, p. 224.

14. Chandrasekaran, "Saved from Ruin," p. A1.

15. Mark Riley, "Time for the UN to Go," *Sydney Morning Herald,* May 24, 2000.

16. SVDM to Paul Grossrieder (director-general of the International Committee of the Red Cross), February 18, 2002, in response to a harshly critical essay by Jarat Chopra, who had resigned from UNTAET.

17. Some of the Timorese leaders, like Ramos-Horta, had favored disbanding the armed forces altogether. They cited the model of Costa Rica, which had ushered in a new era by eliminating the army after a 1948 peace agreement ended the country's civil war.

18. Carmel Egan and Paul Toohey, "Timor Riviera Meets Hell's Kitchen," *Weekend Australian,* January 15, 2000, p. 11.

19. "East Timor Out of the Woods? Not Quite," *Straits Times* (Singapore), February 12, 2000.

20. Ibid.

21. SVDM, "The Situation in East Timor," presentation to the Security Council, June 27, 2000.

22. SVDM, "How Not to Run a Country."

23. Ibid.

24. The Trust Fund for East Timor (TFET) was established at the December 1999 Tokyo Donors Meeting. By June 15, 2000, a total of about $165 million had been pledged to the TFET: by Portugal ($50 million), the European Commission ($48.7 million), Japan ($28 million), and the United States ($0.5 million). Of this sum only $41.4 million had been received and a mere $2.6 million distributed. TFET, Update no. 1, August 2000, online at http://siteresources.worldbank.org/INTTIMORLESTE/Resources/TFET+Update1.pdf.

25. Hansjörg Strohmeyer, "Collapse and Reconstruction of a Judicial System: The UN Missions in Kosovo and East Timor," *American Journal of International Law* 95, no. 1 (January 2000).

26. SVDM, interview by Fabien Curto Millet, "East Timor: The Building of a Nation," November 2001, on Millet's Web site at Oxford University, http://users.ox.ac.uk/~ball1024/sergioVDM_interview.pdf.

27. Hansjörg Strohmeyer, "Making Multilateral Interventions Work: The U.N. and the Creation of Transitional Justice Systems in Kosovo and East Timor," *Fletcher Forum of World Affairs Journal* (Summer 2001), pp. 107–24.

28. Strohmeyer, "Collapse and Reconstruction."

29. Two years later, in February 2002, the UN police had only 299 vehicles for more than 1,400 officers. Conflict Security and Development group, King's College, London, "A Review of Peace Operations: A Case for Change, East Timor," March 10, 2003, p. 75.

30. SVDM, Press Conference, April 5, 2000. This proved an ongoing problem, as rich countries proved characteristically reluctant to fund prisons.

31. UNTAET Human Rights Report, March 2001, cited in Joel C. Beauvais, "Benevolent Despotism: A Critique of U.N. State-Building in East Timor," *International Law and Politics* 33 (2001), p. 1155.

32. SVDM to Annick Stevenson, August 12, 2001.

33. Stevenson to SVDM, August 13, 2001.

34. SVDM to Stevenson, August 17, 2001.

35. Fabrizio Hochschild, "'It Is Better to Leave, We Can't Protect You': Flight in the First Months of United Nations Transitional Administrations in Kosovo and East Timor," *Journal of Refugee Studies* 17, no. 3 (September 2004), pp. 286–300.

CHAPTER 16. "A NEW SERGIO"

1. SVDM, Speaking Notes, Handing Over Ceremony with General Cosgrove, February 23, 2000.

2. Manning was New Zealand's first battle casualty since 1971. On August 10, 2001, Private Devi Ram Jaishi, twenty-six, of Nepal, was shot in the same area when militiamen attacked his unit. Jaishi died from his injuries while being evacuated to Dili for treatment. Four others (three soldiers and one civilian) were injured. Eugene Bingham, "Ambush on a Timor Jungle Trail," *New Zealand Herald*, September 7, 2002.

3. Rajiv Chandrasekaran, "Saved from Ruin: The Reincarnation of East Timor; U.N. Handing Over Sovereignty After Nation-Building Effort," *Washington Post*, May 19, 2002, p. A1.

4. "UN Confident: East Timor Border Secure," Deutsche Presse Agentur, May 18, 2002.

5. Lakhan Mehrotra to SVDM, January 11, 2001.

6. "Three UNHCR Staff Killed in West Timor," UN News Service, September 6, 2000; Tom McCawley, "Four UN Staff Killed in East Timor Riots," *Financial Times*, September 7, 2000, p. 6. The UNHCR inspector general's report after the murders found that the militia "saw UNHCR not as an impartial humanitarian organization but as indistinguishable from the UN and the international military force (INTERFET)

perceived as having stolen East Timor from Indonesia." The report found that the head of office and field security officer in Atambua made a "serious error of judgment in not insisting on evacuation." Inspector General's Office, UNHCR, "Report of the Inquiry into the Deaths of Three UNCHR Staff Members in Atambua, Indonesia, on 6 September 2000," December 8, 2000, para. 10.

7. Inspector general's report, para. 67.

8. In May 2001, after an Indonesian prosecutor charged six gunmen with the mild charge of "assault," the suspects received sentences of between ten and twenty months. Before the murders, some 170,000 East Timorese refugees had left West Timor and returned home, with UNHCR's assistance, but after the attack and the UN evacuation, only 29,000 did so. Conflict Security and Development Group, King's College, London, "A Review of Peace Operations: A Case for Change, East Timor," March 10, 2003, note 157.

9. King's College, "Review of Peace Operations," p. 78.

10. "Report of the Secretary-General on Justice and Reconciliation for Timor-Leste," July 26, 2006.

11. SVDM, Address to National Council, June 28, 2001.

12. "UN Mission in East Timor Suggests Power Sharing Arrangements," *UNTAET News,* May 30, 2000. SVDM briefed the Security Council on June 27, 2000.

13. SVDM, "Remarks at First Session of the National Congress for the Reconstruction of East Timor," transcript, August 21, 2000.

14. Some objected on the opposite grounds. The thirteen UN district administrators unanimously objected, complaining that the Timorese were not actually being brought into the process, and that the half-measure smacked of "tokenism." Mark Dodd, "UN Peace Mission at War with Itself," *Sydney Morning Herald,* May 13, 2000, p. 19.

15. In December 2000 the Timorese held less than 10 percent of all management positions, only three out of thirteen district administrator positions, and six deputy district administrator positions. Joel C. Beuvais, "Benevolent Despotism, a Critique of UN State-Building in East Timor," *International Law and Politics* 33, no. 101 (December 12, 2001), p. 1144.

16. Simon Chesterman, "East Timor in Transition," *International Peacekeeping* (Spring 2002), p. 70.

17. "East Timor: Transition Calendar Is Priority—Xanana Gusmão," *Lusa News,* August 23, 2000.

18. SVDM to Jean-Marie Guéhenno, "Taxation of Profits from UN Contracts," March 26, 2001.

19. SVDM to Guéhenno, "Transfer of UN Assets," November 25, 2000.

20. The UN financial regulations generally require equipment in good condition to be sent to other UN missions, to be placed on reserve for future UN missions, or to be sold to other UN agencies, NGOs, or governments. As UNTAET wrapped up in 2002, the total inventory value of its assets was $72.4 million. In accordance with UN mission liquidation procedures, 79 percent of these assets were redeployed to other peacekeeping missions (including the East Timor follow-on mission) or to the UN Logistics Base in Brindisi, Italy, for temporary storage. But $8.1 million in assets

were unusually donated (in the words of the secretary-general's report) because, in light of East Timor's wholesale destruction, "removal or withdrawal of all UNTAET assets from the country will have a catastrophic effect on the functioning of the Government after independence." "Report of the Secretary-General: Financing of the United Nations Transitional Administration in East Timor," March 27, 2002. When the small follow-on UN mission in East Timor departed in May 2005, it donated a whopping 41 percent of its assets (worth $23 million) to the Timorese government.

21. "Dollars Flowing from Passports," *Tempo* magazine, October 30–November 5, 2001.
22. Frei Betto, "Intervenção branca no Timor Leste" (White Intervention in East Timor), *O Globo*, February 16, 2001.
23. SVDM, "Difamacao e crime" (Defamation Is a Crime), *O Globo,* April 9, 2001.
24. SVDM to Bernard Miyet, "Local Staff Members Who Died While Serving UN-AMET," September 20, 2000.
25. SVDM to Guéhenno, "Payment of Compensation to Next of Kin of UNAMET Staff Killed in 99," July 6, 2001.
26. Guéhenno to SVDM, "Payment of Compensation in Respect of UNAMET SSA Contractors Killed in 99," July 18, 2001.
27. SVDM to Guéhenno, Kieran Prendergast, "Timor Sea," April 2, 2002.
28. An even larger field, Greater Sunrise, which was thought to hold $10 billion in revenue, was only partially in the joint area, and negotiations on it were deferred until 2003. Galbraith's team (which was by then working directly for the new East Timorese government) secured a 50-50 split of revenues in an area that would have originally gone 91 percent to the Australians.
29. Joanne Collins, "Former Guerrilla Hero Set for Landslide Win in East Timor Presidential Election," *Scotsman*, April 15, 2002, p. 11.
30. SVDM to Carolina Larriera, October 22, 2001.
31. SVDM to Antonio Carlos Machado, November 19, 2001.
32. SVDM, Press Conference, April 13, 2002, online at www.un.org/peace/etimor/DB/transcript.pdf.
33. "UN Official: Timor Prospects Good," Associated Press Online, May 18, 2002.
34. SVDM, "The Future of UN State-building," International Peace Academy Conference, October 18–19, 2002, www.ipacademy.org/pdfs/YOU_THE_PEOPLE.pdf.
35. Bronwyn Curran, "We Will Not Abandon Our Baby, UN East Timor Envoy Promises," Agence France-Presse, May 17, 2002.
36. SVDM, "How Not to Run a Country: Lessons for the UN from Kosovo and East Timor," 2000, unpublished.

CHAPTER 17. "FEAR IS A BAD ADVISER"

1. Carola Hoyos, "UN Appoints Human Rights Chief," *Financial Times,* July 23, 2002.
2. In October 2001 Mary Robinson had called for a suspension of U.S. bombing in Afghanistan so that aid workers could reach starving civilians. Later, noting correctly that the Pentagon seemed uncurious about the extent and source of civilian casualties, she said, "I can't accept that one causes 'collateral damage' in villages and doesn't even ask about the number and names of the dead." She added later, "In my view, people

are not collateral damage. They are people." Sameer Ahmed, "An Interview with Mary Robinson: U.S. Policy and UN Ethics," *Stanford Daily News,* February 14, 2003. See also "UN Critical of U.S. Action in Afghanistan," Associated Press, March 6, 2002.

3. Mary Robinson, "Protecting Human Rights: The United States, the United Nations, and the World," John F. Kennedy Library and Foundation: Responding to Terrorism Series, January 6, 2002.

4. "The Global Politics of Human Rights," interview with Mary Robinson, *Politic* [Yale University], December 7, 2002.

5. Colum Lynch, "UN Human Rights Commissioner Named," *Washington Post,* July 23, 2002, p. A12.

6. SVDM to Carolina Larriera, September 10, 2002.

7. SVDM to Larriera, September 13, 2002.

8. SVDM to Marcia Luar Ibrahim, September 13, 2002.

9. SVDM to Larriera, October 12, 2002.

10. SVDM to Adrien and Laurent Vieira de Mello, November 5, 2002.

11. François d'Alançon, "Rencontre avec Sergio Vieira de Mello, Pompier de l'ONU" (Conversation with Sergio Vieira de Mello, Firefighter of the United Nations), *La Croix,* June 21, 2003.

12. SVDM to guide at the British Museum, November 15, 2002.

13. SVDM, Statement by the UN High Commissioner for Human Rights, September 20, 2002.

14. Christopher Pratner, "UN's Vieira de Mello Sees U.S. Constitution as Human Rights Model," BBC Monitoring International Reports (from Vienna's *Der Standard* online), May 11, 2003.

15. Harold Hongju Koh, "A Job Description for the UN High Commissioner for Human Rights," *Columbia Human Rights Law Review* (Summer 2004), p. 493. The article was based on the paper Koh delivered at a conference at Columbia in February 2003.

16. SVDM, "Five Questions for the Human Rights Field," *Sur: International Journal on Human Rights,* 2004, p. 170.

17. SVDM, Statement to the Informal Meeting of the Commission on Human Rights, September 24, 2002.

18. SVDM, Human Rights "Manifesto," Office of the High Commissioner for Human Rights, undated.

19. Some 270 people held permanent contracts in Geneva, while another 190 staffers were based in twenty countries around the world.

20. SVDM, interview with Philip Gourevitch, November 22, 2002.

21. SVDM to Catherine Bertini, November 15, 2002.

22. The United States had been assured of forty-three votes of support, but only twenty-nine nations ended up backing its membership. France, Austria, and Sweden were elected from the U.S. regional grouping. They joined Cuba, Libya, Saudi Arabia, Sudan, and Syria—five of the ten countries rated "worst of the worst" in Freedom House's annual survey of political rights and civil liberties.

23. SVDM, Press Conference on "The New HCHR," Geneva, September 20, 2002.

24. "Commission on Human Rights Takes Up Debate on Situation in Occupied Arab Territories, Including Palestine," UN Press Release, March 27, 2003.

25. SVDM, Closing Statement to UN Commission on Human Rights, April 25, 2003.
26. Ibid.
27. D'Alançon, "Recontre avec Sergio Vieira de Mello."
28. SVDM, "World Civilization: Barking Up the Wrong Tree?" Third Annual BP World Civilization Lecture, British Museum, November 11, 2002.
29. SVDM, "Holistic Democracy: The Human Rights Content of Legitimate Governance," Seminar on the Interdependence between Democracy and Human Rights, Geneva, November 25, 2002.
30. Ibid. He offered a variety of models for democratic consultation "from the village council to the *diwaniya*, from the *loya jirga* to the circle of elders."
31. *Human Rights Features* no. 6 (April 22–25, 2003), p. 60.
32. SVDM, Q and A, September–October 2002, Office of the High Commissioner for Human Rights.
33. SVDM, Statement to the 59th Session of the UN Commission on Human Rights, March 21, 2003.
34. SVDM, interview on *BBC Talking Point*, December 8, 2002.
35. James P. Lucier, "Just What Is a War Criminal?," *Insight*, August 2, 1999, p. 13.
36. John R. Bolton, "Why an International Criminal Court Won't Work," *Wall Street Journal*, March 30, 1998, p. A19.
37. "Wite-Out" quote is from John R. Bolton, Address to the Federalist Society's 2003 National Lawyers Convention, November 13, 2003, online at www.fed-soc.org/pdf/bolton.pdf. The "happiest moment" quote is from Glenn Kessler and Colum Lynch, "Critic of U.N. Named Envoy; Bush's Choice of Bolton Is a Surprise; Democrats Plan to Contest Nomination," *Washington Post,* March 8, 2005, p. A1. Bolton's most memorable summation of his exasperation with international institutions came in 2005 in a speech at Yale University, in which he declared, "Why shouldn't we pay for what we want, instead of paying a bill for what we get?" Richard Low, "Bolton's Undiplomatic Unilateralism," *Yale Daily News,* October 6, 2005.
38. SVDM, Statement to the Opening of the 59th Session of the UN Commission on Human Rights, March 17, 2003.
39. Ibid.
40. "Bin Laden's message," broadcast by al-Jazeera, November 12, 2002, online at http://news.bbc.co.uk/2/hi/middle_east/2455845.stm.
41. "Bin Laden Rails against Crusaders and UN," November 3, 2001, online at http://news.bbc.co.uk/1/hi/world/monitoring/media_reports/1636782.stm.
42. Ben Russell, "Straw Joins Row Over 'Torture Pictures,'" *Independent*, January 21, 2002, p. 1.
43. Rajiv Chandrasekaran and Peter Finn, "U.S. Behind Secret Transfer of Terror Suspects," *Washington Post,* March 11, 2002, p. A1.
44. Donald Rumsfeld, "Stakeout at the Pentagon," April 12, 2003, online at www.defenselink.mil/transcripts/transcript.aspx?transcriptid=3401.
45. Committee on Select Intelligence, "Statement of Cofer Black, Former Chief, Counterterrorism Center," Investigation of September 11 Intelligence Failures, Hearing, September 26, 2002.
46. Dana Priest and Barton Gellman, "U.S. Decries Abuse but Defends Interrogations:

'Stress and Duress' Tactics Used on Terrorism Suspects Held in Secret Overseas Facilities," *Washington Post*, December 26, 2002, p. A1. Beginning in the mid-1990s, the Clinton administration also rendered suspects to third countries. The CIA has defended rendition by claiming that access to American due process would force intelligence agents, or enable suspected terrorists, to disclose CIA sources and methods. Initially, Egypt (the second-largest recipient of U.S. aid, behind Israel) was the principal destination of rendered suspects. But after the bombings of U.S. embassies in Kenya and Tanzania in 1998, the Clinton administration began sending suspects to other countries as well. Jane Mayer, "Outsourcing Torture," *New Yorker*, February 14, 2005, p. 106.

47. Priest and Gellman, "U.S. Decries Abuse."

48. SVDM, Statement to Informal Meeting of the UN Commission on Human Rights, September 24, 2002.

49. Human Rights Watch, "Indefinite Detention Without Trial in the United Kingdom Under Part 4 of the Anti-Terrorism, Crime and Security Act 2001," June 24, 2004, online at http://hrw.org/backgrounder/eca/uk/3.htm#_ftn18. Even in times of emergency, human rights law did not permit governments to opt out of the fundamental right to life or right to be free of cruel or degrading punishment.

50. SVDM, Statement of the Eleventh Workshop on Regional Cooperation for the Promotion and Protection of Human Rights in the Asia-Pacific Region, Islamabad, February 25–27, 2003. He urged the countries in the UN General Assembly to add a new instrument to the books, the Optional Protocol to the Convention Against Torture, which would have instituted a system of regular independent inspections of detention facilities in order to guard against torture. SVDM, Address to the Third Committee of the General Assembly, November 4, 2002.

51. SVDM, Q and A, September–October 2002; SVDM, Address to the Third Committee of the General Assembly, November 4, 2002.

52. SVDM, Statement to the Opening of the 59th Session of the Commission on Human Rights, March 17, 2003.

53. SVDM to Annick Stevenson, May 21, 2003.

54. Kofi Annan, "When Force Is Considered, There Is No Substitute for Legitimacy Provided by United Nations," Address to the United Nations General Assembly, September 12, 2002, online at www.un.org/News/Press/docs/2002/SGSM8378.doc.htm.

55. Ibid.

56. George W. Bush, Remarks to the United Nations General Assembly, September 12, 2002, online at www.whitehouse.gov/news/releases/2002/09/20020912-1.html.

57. For Annan's reflections on this sequence, see Philip Gourevitch, "The Optimist," *New Yorker*, March 3, 2003, p. 55.

58. SVDM, interview on *BBC Talking Points*, December 8, 2002.

59. SVDM, "Equipe da ONU fará avaliaçâo da segurança em Bagdád" (Making the UN Function in Baghdad), *O Estado de São Paulo*, June 1, 2003.

60. Strobe Talbott, *The Great Experiment: From Tribes to Global Nation* (New York: Simon & Schuster, 2008), p. 364.

61. George Packer, *The Assassins' Gate: America in Iraq* (New York: Farrar, Straus & Giroux, 2006), p. 95.

62. Colin Powell, Address to UN Security Council, February 5, 2003, online at www.whitehouse.gov/news/releases/2003/02/20030205-1.html.

63. The only UN official, apart from the secretary-general, who had met with Bush was the head of the World Food Program, James Morris, but he was a Republican-backed U.S. political appointee, while Vieira de Mello was a lifelong UN civil servant from Brazil.

64. Notes on the Armitage–SVDM meeting, March 5, 2003.

65. Ibid.

66. Notes on the Bush–SVDM meeting, March 5, 2003.

67. James Risen et al., "Harsh C.I.A. Methods Cited in Top Qaeda Interrogations," *New York Times*, May 13, 2004, p. A1.

68. Notes on the Bush–SVDM meeting, March 5, 2003.

69. Ibid. Vieira de Mello also raised the plight of the Palestinians. Bush said that he was the only president to have said there should be two states. (In fact, President Clinton was the first to endorse a two-state solution, which he did in January 2001, shortly before Bush took office.) Bush said that the Palestinians needed a better deal. "Blame Israel last not first for the condition of the Palestinian people," he said.

70. "President Bush: Monday 'Moment of Truth' for World in Iraq," White House press release, March 16, 2003.

71. SVDM, "Making the UN Function."

72. President Bush, Address to the Nation, March 19, 2003, www.whitehouse.gov/news/releases/2003/03/20030319-17.html. The initial invasion was carried out by 250,000 troops from the United States; 45,000 from the U.K.; and 2,000 from Australia. Poland (200), Albania (70), and Romania (278) all provided troops in noncombat roles. Just before the invasion, Colin Powell announced that the Coalition of the Willing consisted of 30 countries: Afghanistan, Albania, Australia, Azerbaijan, Bulgaria, Colombia, the Czech Republic, Denmark, El Salvador, Eritrea, Estonia, Ethiopia, Georgia, Hungary, Italy, Japan, Latvia, Lithuania, Macedonia, the Netherlands, Nicaragua, the Philippines, Poland, Romania, Slovakia, South Korea, Spain, Turkey, the United Kingdom, and Uzbekistan. An additional 15 anonymous countries provided assistance but did not want to declare support. See http://news.bbc.co.uk/2/hi/americas/2862343.stm. On March 27, 2003, the White House announced a list of forty-nine members. Among these were six that were unarmed (or without formal armies): Palau, Costa Rica, Iceland, the Marshall Islands, Micronesia, and the Solomon Islands. See Dana Milbank, "Many Willing, but Only a Few Are Able," *Washington Post*, March 25, 2003, p. A7.

73. SVDM, interview by Tim Sebastian, *HARDtalk*, BBC, April 14, 2003.

CHAPTER 18. "DON'T ASK WHO STARTED THE FIRE"

1. SVDM, unpublished interview by Bill Spindle, *Wall Street Journal*, posted online at www.unmikonline.org/pres/2003/wire/Aug/imm250803pm.htm.

2. YouGov Survey Results, "Iraq War Track Part 9, prepared for the *Daily Telegraph* and ITV News," April 6, 2003, online at www.yougov.com/archives/pdf/tem030101005.pdf.

3. Colum Lynch, "Britain Offers Plan for U.N.'s Postwar Role," *Washington Post*, April 5, 2003, p. A28.

4. James Blitz, "Blair Faces Challenge of Getting Consensus on UN Role," *Financial Times*, March 21, 2003, p. 9.

5. Ibid.

6. U.S. officials were satisfied with the UN's performance in Afghanistan, where in December 2001 Lakhdar Brahimi had chaired the Bonn conference, which resulted in the appointment of Hamid Karzai as president of Afghanistan. Secretary Rumsfeld applauded General Tommy Franks for keeping "the coalition footprint modest" and for allowing local leaders to arrive at local solutions. "Over time," Rumsfeld said, Afghans would be able to "take full responsibility for their security and stability rather than having to depend on foreign forces." Donald Rumsfeld, "Beyond Nation Building," Speech at Intrepid Sea-Air-Space Museum, New York City, February 14, 2003.

7. Ibid.

8. Ibid.

9. Don Melvin, "Bush, Blair Weigh Next Steps; U.N. Role in Iraq May Divide Allies," *Atlanta Journal-Constitution*, April 8, 2003, p. A3.

10. George W. Bush and Tony Blair, "Joint Statement on Iraq's Future," April 8, 2003.

11. "President Bush Meets with Prime Minister Blair in Northern Ireland," White House Press Release, April 8, 2003.

12. Eric Schmitt and Steven R. Weisman, "US to Recruit Iraqi Civilians to Interim Posts," *New York Times*, April 11, 2003, p. A1.

13. Office of the Spokesperson of the Secretary-General, "UN Secretary-General's Press Encounter Upon Arrival at UNHQ," April 7, 2003.

14. SVDM to Peter Galbraith, December 21, 2002.

15. SVDM, interview by Philip Gourevitch, November 22, 2002.

16. SVDM to Carolina Larreira, April 1, 2003. The original article, the first to mention Vieira de Mello in the context of Iraq, was Philip Webster, James Bone, Rosemary Bennett, and Greg Hurst, "Coalition to Stay in Charge for Task of Rebuilding," *Times* (London), March 27, 2003, p. 10.

17. SVDM to Larriera, April 3, 2003.

18. "President Bush Announces Major Combat Operations in Iraq Have Ended," White House Press Release, May 1, 2003.

19. Donald Rumsfeld and General Tommy Franks, Remarks at a Town Hall Meeting with Troops, Doha, Qatar, April 28, 2003.

20. Anthony Zinni, Remarks to the Marine Corps Association and U.S. Naval Institute Forum 2003, Arlington, Virginia, September 4, 2003.

21. Steven R. Weisman and Felicity Barringer, "Against France and Russia, Washington Tries to Curb U.N. Role in Postwar Iraq," *New York Times*, March 27, 2003, p. B10.

22. "President Bush Meets with Prime Minister Blair."

23. Notes on the Rice-SVDM meeting, March 5, 2003.

24. Dr. Condoleezza Rice, Remarks on President Bush–PM Blair Meeting, April 8, 2003.

25. "US Will Ask UN to Back Control by Allies in Iraq," *New York Times*, May 9, 2003, p. A1.

26. Pool Report of Garner's Trip to Baghdad, April 21, 2003, online at www.hq.usace .army.mil/history/enduring_freedom_saved_articles/Garner_powerstation.htm.

27. George Packer, *The Assassins' Gate: America in Iraq* (New York: Farrar, Straus & Giroux, 2006), p. 130.

28. UNESCO estimates that some 150,000 objects were lost or stolen.

29. Donald Rumsfeld and General Richard Myers, U.S. Department of Defense News Briefing, April 11, 2003.

30. The Coalition Provisional Authority would eventually estimate that the looting damage was worth $12 billion. The exiles (the biggest backer of the Coalition's invasion) later blamed the looting on the State Department's refusal to train an army of Iraqi exiles to make up the inaugural security forces (seventy-two Iraqis received training). Packer, *Assassins' Gate*, p. 139.

31. In the weeks prior to the announcement, the Pentagon had been proceeding with plans to deploy a senior civilian administrator, and Rumsfeld had been winnowing a list of names. But Garner expected the person to deploy sometime in August. Bremer's deployment was rushed forward because of chaos on the ground and Garner's inability to manage it. Powell seems to have welcomed the appointment of Bremer, who had been a career State Department official, but Bremer reported directly to Rumsfeld.

32. John Negroponte and Jeremy Greenstock, "Letter from the Permanent Representation of the UK and the US to the UN addressed to the President of the Security Council," May 8, 2003, online at www.globalpolicy.org/security/issues/iraq/document/2003/0608usukletter.htm.

33. Anthony Shadid, "Shiites Denounce Occupation," *Washington Post*, May 19, 2003, p. A1.

34. CPA Order no. 1 de-Ba'athified in two ways: (1) "Senior party members" (the top four levels) were removed from their positions and banned from future employment in the public sector. They were also evaluated for criminal conduct. (2) In the top three rungs of the public sector, those determined to be full members of the Ba'ath party (including two junior ranks) were removed from their jobs. This included all individuals who held jobs "in the top three layers of management in every national government ministry, affiliated corporations and other government institutions (e.g., universities and hospitals)." In January 2004, in an effort to systematize the process, a de-Ba'athification commission was established under Ahmed Chalabi. Some thirty thousand Ba'athists had already lost their jobs. The fourth-highest leadership echelons would be allowed to contest their dismissals if they did not commit crimes and if they had advanced up the ranks of the party by dint of their professional achievements. When Chalabi was asked whether the new body would facilitate reconciliation, however, he dismissed the idea, saying that "reconciliation is an inappropriate term." "Who will reconcile with whom?" he asked. "Will those buried in mass graves reconcile with those who killed them?" Sam Dagher, "Iraq Governing Council Details Plan to Root Out Ba'ath Members," Agence France-Presse, January 11, 2004.

35. Dan Senor, speaking for Bremer in August 2004, said, "The Shia could have been an enormous stumbling block to the Coalition if they had been uncooperative. If we had held back on de-Ba'athification, some have argued that the Sunni insurgency would not have been as bad, but, in the complete picture, the fact that this meant so much to the Shia was crucial." John Lee Anderson, "Out on the Street," *New Yorker*, November 15, 2004, pp. 73, 78.

36. Paul Hughes, Garner's chief of staff, who had promised the Iraqi soldiers jobs and salaries, later told *The New Yorker*'s George Packer: "From the Iraqi viewpoint, that simple action took away the one symbol of sovereignty the Iraqi people still had." Packer, *Assassins' Gate*, p. 192.

37. It was hard to reconcile the Coalition's commitment to rebuild and reform Iraq with the terms of the 1949 Fourth Geneva Convention, which assumes that any occupation will be purely temporary and that the occupier will not impose any particular form of government, or change the status of public officials/judges or penal laws. The 1907 Hague Convention also notes that the laws in force in the country must be respected. So Council Resolution 1483, by encouraging the occupying powers to help create "conditions in which the Iraqi people can freely determine their own political future," seemed to contradict these provisions of humanitarian law.

38. Felicity Barringer, "UN Vote on Iraq Authorization Is Due Next Week, US Says," *New York Times*, May 15, 2003, p. A24.

39. UN source, "Note to Mr. Riza: Special Coordinator for Iraq," May 9, 2003.

40. SVDM to Galbraith, May 16, 2003.

41. Steven Erlanger, "I Should Always Believe Journalists," *New York Times*, August 24, 2004.

42. In 2007 multiple letters were exchanged in the *London Review of Books* over whether Vieira de Mello met with Bush a second time. Tariq Ali wrote that Under-Secretary-General Shashi Tharoor had told him of a second meeting, a comment Tharoor denied making. In fact Tharoor made the same claim to me, but he was repeating hearsay and had no knowledge of Vieira de Mello's movements. Only one meeting between the two men took place: on March 5, 2003, two and a half months before Vieira de Mello would be appointed as UN special representative in Iraq.

43. Felicity Barringer, "Security Council Almost Unanimously Approves Broad Mandate for Allies in Iraq," *New York Times*, May 23, 2003, p. A12.

44. Ibid. Several months after the August 19, 2003 attack on UN headquarters in Baghdad, when the UN was being pressed to return to Baghdad, Annan would say, "Bad resolutions kill people."

45. Ibid.

46. Colum Lynch, "France, Russia Back Lifting of Iraq Sanctions," *Washington Post*, May 22, 2003, p. A1; Felicity Barringer, "US Wins Support to End Sanctions Imposed on Iraq," *New York Times*, May 22, 2003, p. A1.

47. Barringer, "Security Council Almost Unanimously Approves."

48. Marcelo Musa Cavalleri, "Um brasileiro em busca, du paz" (A Brazilian in Search of Peace), *Época*, August 2003.

49. Liana Melo and Rita Moraes, "Com a mesma intensidade que trabalhava, o diplomata reconstruía a vida afetiva" (With the Same Intensity with Which He Worked, the Diplomat Reconstructed His Personal Life), *Istoe*, August 27, 2003.

50. Colum Lynch, "Diplomat Will Oversee UN's Iraq Operations," *Washington Post*, May 24, 2003, p. A18.

51. SVDM to Jane Holl Lute, July 8, 2003.

52. SVDM, interview by Spindle.

53. SVDM to Machado et al., May 29, 2003.

54. SVDM, interview by Spindle.
55. Ibid.

CHAPTER 19. "YOU CAN'T HELP PEOPLE FROM A DISTANCE"
1. Notes on the meeting, June 1, 2003.
2. SVDM, airport statement, June 2, 2003.
3. The same Security Council resolution that had authorized the Coalition occupation and created the post of UN Special Representative of the Secretary-General for Iraq had also provided for the end of civilian sanctions and the resumption of oil exports (the revenue from which would be deposited directly into a Development Fund for Iraq). It also mandated the termination of the Oil for Food Program within six months. (The program was officially closed November 21, 2003.) In January 2004 an Iraqi newspaper published a list of 270 people from 40 countries who had profited from the illicit sale of Iraqi oil during the Oil for Food Program, and in April the U.S. General Accounting Office reported that "the former Iraqi regime attained $10.1 billion in illegal revenue" from the program. The UN, the U.S. Senate, and the Iraqi government launched inquiries, which led to the resignation and ultimate indictment of Benon Sevan, the former head of the program. The report by independent investigator Paul Volcker, released in September 2005, faulted Secretary-General Kofi Annan for a conflict of interest involving his son Kojo (who was employed by a beneficiary of the program) and for the UN's mismanagement of the Oil for Food Program. Annan would later call the whole affair "deeply embarrassing."
4. William Langewiesche, "Welcome to the Green Zone," Atlantic Monthly, November 2004, p. 64.
5. Ibid., p. 88. The T-shirts were a takeoff on President Bush's July 2003 taunts to those who might attack U.S. forces in Iraq. "My answer is, bring them on," Bush said. "We've got the force necessary to deal with the security situation." Press Q&A, July 2, 2003.
6. Langewiesche, "Green Zone," p. 64.
7. Ibid., p. 62.
8. Iraq Steering Group meeting minutes, June 3, 2003.
9. See Rajiv Chandrasekaran, Imperial Life in the Emerald City (New York: Knopf, 2006).
10. A May 28, 2003, memo from the UN security staff in Iraq described the security situation as "post war" with "looting, car-jacking, street robbery, shootings and other crimes . . . widespread and common in cities and along main routes." Report of the Security in Iraq Accountability Panel, March 3, 2004, online at www.un.org/Name/dh/iraq/SIAP-report.pdf (hereafter Walzer report), p. 22.
11. Because visitors could pass freely in and out of the Cedar as well, the security staff began looking for a private house that would offer Vieira de Mello both the communications facilities and the enhanced security he needed. The going rate for the one house they found was $12,000 per month, which he deemed too steep.
12. Walzer report, p. 17.
13. Procurement in peacekeeping and political missions was no easy matter. Each field mission was required to establish a local committee on contracts to review and recommend contract awards. This committee had to be composed of four staffers from the mission: a legal adviser, the chief of finance section, the chief of general services, and the chief

of transport services. Field missions were not permitted to award contracts worth more than $75,000 without approval by the chief administrative officer and the local committee on contracts. Field missions could not award contracts worth more than $200,000 without their approval, plus that of the Headquarters committee on contracts.

14. SVDM to Kieran Prendergast, "Meeting with Ambassadors Bremer and Sawers," June 5, 2003, CZX 03.

15. Al-Hakim would be assassinated on August 29, 2003, in a wave of violence against Shia clerics in Najaf that was thought to have been carried out by al-Qaeda's Abu Mussab al-Zarqawi. Al-Hakim's brother, Abdul Aziz al-Hakim, who was already a member of the Governing Council, would then assume the leadership of SCIRI, which was the largest party in the United Iraqi Alliance coalition and won the most seats in the Iraqi parliament in the December 2005 elections.

16. Bill Spindle, "Identity Crisis," *Wall Street Journal,* August 21, 2003.

17. SVDM to Joseph Vernon Reed, July 5, 2003.

18. Notes on the meeting with John Sawers, June 5, 2003.

19. Letters dated early June and June 25, 2003, published in Bernard Kouchner, *Les Guerriers de la paix: du Kosovo à l'Irak* (Paris: Éditions Grasset & Fasquelle, 2004), p. 423.

20. Notes on the Sawers meeting, June 5, 2003.

21. SVDM to Carina Perelli, June 26, 2003.

22. SVDM to Perelli, July 1, 2003.

23. SVDM to Prendergast, "Meetings with Ambassadors Bremer and Sawers: Comprehensive Update on Political Process," July 1, 2003.

24. Among those polled, 92 percent welcomed lawyers and judges and 75 percent welcomed Iraqi clerics, but only 36 percent welcomed formerly exiled politicians. Office of Research, Opinion Analysis, U.S. State Department, October 21, 2003.

25. SVDM, internal UN draft, August 17, 2003.

26. SVDM, remarks, July 13, 2003.

27. SVDM to Peter Galbraith, July 4, 2003.

28. SVDM, interview by George Packer, August 13, 2003.

29. SVDM, interview by Tim Sebastian, *HARDtalk,* BBC, April 14, 2003.

30. François d'Alançon, "Recontre avec Sergio Vieira de Mello, Le Pompier de l'ONU," (Conversation with Sergio Vieira de Mello, Firefighter of the United Nations), *La Croix,* June 21, 2003.

31. SVDM, remarks to the press at presentation of secretary-general's report, July 22, 2003.

32. Ibid.

CHAPTER 20. REBUFFED

1. SVDM, interview by George Packer, August 13, 2003.

2. SVDM, UN draft, August 17, 2003.

3. SVDM, interview by Packer.

4. UN News Center, "Transcript of Press Conference by Sergio Vieria de Mello, Special Representative of the Secretary-General for Iraq in Cairo," August 9, 2003.

5. SVDM, draft op-ed, August 2003.

6. Office of Research, Opinion Analysis, U.S. State Department, October 21, 2003.

7. SVDM, interview with Packer.

8. Anthony Shadid, *Night Draws Near: Iraq's People in the Shadow of America's War* (New York: Henry Holt, 2005), pp. 258–59

9. DynCorp was given the contract for field training sometime in June 2003. In a 2006 interview with David Rohde, Bremer blamed the contractors for the CPA's failure to ensure that the country was policed: "DynCorp was not producing anybody. We were doing the best we could." Michael Moss and David Rohde, "Misjudgments Marred U.S. Plans for Iraqi Police," *New York Times*, May 21, 2006.

10. SVDM, interview with Packer.

11. Notes on the meeting with John Sawers, June 18, 2003.

12. Report of the Independent Panel on the Safety and Security of UN Personnel in Iraq, online at www.un.org/news/dh/iraq/safety-security-un-personnel-iraq.pdf, p.13 (hereinafter Ahtisaari report).

13. Robert Adolph to Ramiro Lopes da Silva, June 18, 2003.

14. Donald Rumsfeld and General Richard Myers, U.S. Defense Department News Briefing, June 30, 2003.

15. "Donald H. Rumsfeld Holds Defense Department News Briefing with Jay Garner," U.S. Department of Defense, June 18, 2003.

16. Jon Lee Anderson, "Out on the Street," *New Yorker*, November 15, 2004, p. 74.

17. Brookings Institution, "Iraq Index: Number of Attacks by Insurgents and Militias," updated July 20, 2007.

18. Adolph to Lopes da Silva, Security Management Team, and UNSECOORD, Threat Assessment, June 29, 2003.

19. Kevin Kennedy to UN Headquarters September 4, 2003.

20. SVDM to Bremer and Sawers, July 6, 2003.

21. Robert Adolph, Chronology of Events (in possession of author).

22. Fred Eckhard to Shashi Tharoor, "Iraq Briefings," July 25, 2003.

23. Salim Lone to Eckhard, August 12, 2003.

24. Ahtisaari report, p. 10.

25. Adolph, Chronology.

26. SVDM to André Simões, July 1, 2003

27. Jean-Sélim Kanaan, July 1, 2003, published in Bernard Kouchner, *Les Guerriers de la paix: du Kosovo à l'Irak* (Paris: Éditions Grasset & Fasquelle, 2004), pp. 436–38.

28. Ahtisaari report, p. 17.

29. SVDM to Kieran Prendergast, July 24, 2003.

30. Report of the Security in Iraq Accountability Panel, March 3, 2004, online at www .un.org/news/dh/iraq/SIAP-report.pdf, p.13.

31. Ibid., p. 18.

32. Ibid.

33. Robert F. Worth and John Tierney, "FBI Teams Sent to Investigate Bomb Attack on Embassy," *New York Times*, August 9, 2003, p. A6.

34. Vivienne Walt, "Jordanians Ask: Why Us?; Analysts Disagree on Reasons Behind Embassy Bombing," *Houston Chronicle*, August 8, 2003, p. A21.

35. Justin Huggler, "A Mercedes Was on a Roof, Blown by the Force of the Blast," *Independent*, August 8, 2003, p. 2.

36. Office of the SRSG, weekly press briefing, August 7, 2003.

37. Helen Kennedy, "Daughters Talk of a 'Loving Dad,'" *Daily News,* August 2, 2003, p. 3.

38. Initially Jordan denied that U.S. forces were planning on going to Iraq. They were "not participating in this war," Marwan Muasher, Jordan's foreign minister, said. They were there only to train Jordanian soldiers and defend Jordan against Iraqi missile attack. Ian Cobain and Stephen Farrell, "Israeli Special Forces Join 'Secret Front' in Jordan," *Times* (London), March 17, 2003, p. 13.

39. Anthony Shadid, "Attacks Intensify in Western Iraq; Foreigners Suspected in Eight Assaults," *Washington Post,* August 2, 2003, p. A12.

40. Tamara Chalabi, "Jordan Slandered My Father at Saddam's Behest," *Wall Street Journal,* August 7, 2003, p. A10.

41. Dexter Filkins and Robert F. Worth, "11 Die in Baghdad as Car Bomb Hits Jordanian Embassy," *New York Times,* August 9, 2003, p. A1.

42. Rajiv Chandrasekaran, "Car Bomb Kills 11 in Baghdad," *Washington Post,* August 8, 2003, p. A1.

43. Filkins and Worth, "11 Die in Baghdad."

44. Thom Shanker, "Iraqis to Keep Responsibility for Guarding Embassies," *Washington Post,* August 9, 2003, p. A7.

45. Adolph, Chronology.

46. Salim Lone to SVDM, August 13, 2003.

47. SVDM to Martine Chergui, August 7, 2003.

48. SVDM, interview by IRIN news service July 14, 2003.

49. Office of the UN Humanitarian Coordinator in Iraq (UNOCHI) Centre Region, "Draft Paper on the UN Outreach Campaign in Mosul," circulated August 17, 2003.

50. SVDM, interview by IRIN.

51. SVDM, remarks to Security Council before presentation of secretary-general's report, July 22, 2003.

52. The Committee to Protect Journalists found the shelling to be unintentional but avoidable. It faulted senior U.S. officers who knew journalists stayed at the hotel but did not properly convey this knowledge to the tank commander who fired. Eventually the U.S. military investigation into journalist Mazen Dana's death would reach the same conclusion. The death was "regrettable," but the soldier who had shot Dana had "acted within the rules of engagement." Committee to Protect Journalists, "Iraq: CPJ Dismayed by US Investigation into Killing of Reuters Cameraman," September 22, 2003.

53. Anthony Shadid, "US Military Probes Cameraman's Death," *Washington Post,* August 19, 2003, p. A15.

54. Ibid.

55. Younes to SVDM, August 18, 2003.

56. Jamil Chade, "Ocupação e humilihante, diz Vieria de Mello" (Occupation and Humiliation, Says Vieira de Mello), *O Estado de São Paulo,* August 18, 2003.

57. SVDM, remarks to Security Council before presentation of secretary-general's report, July 22, 2003.

58. SVDM, interview with Packer.

59. Chade, "Ocupação e humilihante."
60. SVDM, draft op-ed, August 2003.
61. Chade, "Ocupação e humilihante."
62. Joshua Hammer, "I Saw Many Dying," Newsweek Web exclusive, August 19, 2003.

CHAPTER 21. AUGUST 19, 2003
  1. Khaled Mansour to UN officials, August 19, 2003, 8:01 a.m.
  2. Mansour to Veronique Taveau, August 19, 2003, 8:14 a.m.
  3. The congressional delegation was composed of Maria Cantwell (D-WA), Harold Ford, Jr. (D-TN), Lindsey Graham (R-SC), Kay Bailey Hutchinson (R-TX), Jim Kolbe (R-AZ), John McCain (R-AZ), and John Sununu (R-NH).
  4. Report of the Independent Panel on the Safety and Security of UN Personnel in Iraq, online at www.un.org/news/dh/iraq/safety-security-un-personnel-iraq.pdf, p. 14.
  5. Ibid.
  6. "Blast at UN Headquarters in Baghdad," CNN Breaking News, August 19, 2003, 9:01 a.m. ET.
  7. Ibid.
  8. Jeff Davie, "Search for the SRSG," internal written account, September 11, 2003.
  9. Ibid.
 10. Salim Lone, "Discussion with UN Baghdad Spokesman," CNN, August 19, 2003, 11:45 a.m. ET.
 11. Salim Lone, "Interview with Spokesman for UN Special Envoy Sergio Vieira de Mello," CNN, August 19, 2003, 1:00 p.m. ET.
 12. "Baghdad UN Blast: What Future for the UN," BBC News, last updated August 25, 2003, online at http://news.bbc.co.uk/2/hi/taking_point/3179795.stm.
 13. "Huge Explosion at U.N. Headquarters in Baghdad," CNN Breaking News, August 19, 2003, 12:01 p.m. ET.
 14. Fred Eckhard, "United Nations Briefing Re: Bombing on U.N. Compound in Baghdad, Iraq," UN Headquarters, August 19, 2003.
 15. "Huge Explosion at UN Headquarters in Baghdad," CNN Breaking News, August 19, 2003, 12:03 p.m. ET.
 16. Ibid.
 17. Jimmy Breslin, "Dying over Something That Never Was," Newsday, August 22, 2003.
 18. "Huge Explosion at UN Headquarters in Baghdad," CNN Breaking News, August 19, 2003, 12:03 p.m. ET.
 19. Larry Kaplow, "At a Soft Target, UN and Iraqis United by Shock," Cox News Service, August 19, 2003.
 20. Jamie Wilson, "Baghdad Bombing: They Came to Bring Relief from War. Now They Are Asking: Why Us?" Guardian, August 20, 2003, p. 3.
 21. Several of Vieira de Mello's friends and family members dispute whether the UN envoy would have lashed out in this way. Although he was an atheist, they say, he was also superstitious. In addition, he was in a highly vulnerable position, dependent on the efforts of his devout rescuer. I have relied upon Valentine, the only witness

to the scene, who is adamant that the exchange proceeded as I have described. Assuming Valentine's memory serves him, the outburst can best be ascribed to the pain Vieira de Mello was in, as well as his anger over what he likely saw as unacceptable proselytizing.
22. Davie, "Search for the SRSG."

CHAPTER 22. POSTMORTEM
1. Secretary-General Kofi Annan, Press Conference at Arlanda Airport, Stockholm, August 20, 2003, online at www.un.org/apps/sg/offthecuff.asp?nid=466.
2. "UN Envoy Sergio Vieira de Mello Begins Final Journey Home," August 22, 2003, www.un.org/apps/news/storyAr.asp?NewsID=8048&Cr=xxxx&Cr1=#.
3. Kofi Annan, "Secretary-General Mourns Loss of 'Dear Friend' Sergio Vieira de Mello, Memorial Service in Rio de Janeiro," August 23, 2003, online at www.un.org/News/Press/docs/2003/sgsm8829.doc.htm. Vieira de Mello's "dying wish," which quickly entered popular lore, was not mentioned in the press before Sevan's tarmac speech on August 22. The following day the *Washington Post* published an article with the headline: " 'Don't Let Them Pull the U.N. Out of Iraq'; Envoy's Final Words Related by Army Sergeant Who Tried to Free Him."
4. Kofi Annan, "Secretary-General's Press Encounter with the Ambassadors of Malaysia, Cuba and South Africa Regarding the Attack on the United Nations in Baghdad," August 22, 2003.
5. Liana Melo and Rita Moraes, "Energia e paixão Com a mesma intensidade que trabalhava, o diplomata reconstruía a vida afetiva" (Energy and Passion: With the Same Intensity with Which He Worked, the Diplomat Reconstructed His Personal Life), *Istoe,* August 27, 2003.
6. On August 21 the FBI also got a confession of sorts. A previously unknown group, the Armed Vanguards of the Second Mohammed Army, claimed responsibility. "We say it proudly that we did not hesitate for one moment to kill crusader blood," said the group. In a typewritten statement in Arabic sent to the Dubai-based satellite TV channel al-Arabiya, they pledged "to continue fighting every foreigner [in Iraq] and to carry out similar operations." Brian Whitaker, "Mystery Group Says It Planted Baghdad Bomb," *Guardian,* August 22, 2003. Suspicion also fell upon Mullah Omar, the head of the Taliban, who on August 11 had told the Arab media that the "enemies of Islam" were not only the United States, the U.K., and Jews, but also "the UN and other international organizations." Lopes da Silva to UN Headquarters, August 28, 2003. The Associated Press reported on the contents of the two-page message from Mullah Omar, written in Pashtu, which said: "Oh Muslims, know the enemies of your religion—the Jews and Christians. America, Britain, the UN and all Western aid groups are the greatest enemies of Islam and humanity." Kathy Gannon, "Reclusive Taliban Leader Calls International Aid Groups 'Enemy of Islam,'" Associated Press, August 12, 2003.
7. Iraq Steering Group meeting, August 22, 2003.
8. Ramiro Lopes da Silva to UN Headquarters, August 27, 2003. Among the 4,233 Iraqi staff, 2,830 worked in the northern governorates, 157 in central Iraq, 935 in

Baghdad, and 311 in southern Iraq. Kevin Kennedy to UN Headquarters, September 23, 2003.

9. Iraq Steering Group meeting, August 25, 2003.

10. Ibid.

11. Iraq Steering Group meeting, August 28, 2003.

12. Iraq Steering Group meeting, September 11, 2003.

13. Lopes da Silva to UN Headquarters, August 25, 2003. On August 24 UN security reviewed the ten hotels being used by UN staff and required staff to leave five of them. Iraq Steering Group meeting, August 25, 2003.

14. Lopes da Silva to UN Headquarters, September 1, 2003.

15. Lopes da Silva to UN Headquarters, September 2, 2003.

16. Kevin Kennedy to UN Headquarters, September 10, 2003.

17. Iraq Steering Group meeting, September 8, 2003.

18. Kennedy to UN Headquarters, September 3, 5, and 11, 2003.

19. Kennedy to UN Headquarters, September 5, 2003.

20. Kennedy to UN Headquarters, September 7 and 8, 2003.

21. Kennedy to UN Headquarters, September 16, 2003.

22. Report of the Independent Panel on the Safety and Security of UN Personnel in Iraq, online at www.un.org/news/dh/iraq/safety-security-un-personnel-iraq.pdf (hereinafter Ahtisaari report).

23. Kevin Kennedy was the rare UN official who agreed with Annan. Afraid of stranding Iraqi staff, he wrote to New York: "The UN should only leave if a direct, sustained threat, indicative of an organized campaign against United Nations personnel, premises or programmes, was established." Kennedy to UN Headquarters, September 11, 2003.

24. "Secretary-General Kofi Annan's Remarks to the Memorial Ceremony in Honour of Colleagues Killed in the Bombing of the United Nations Mission in Baghdad," September 19, 2003.

25. Internal UN Discussion Draft, Planning Assumptions, September 19, 2003.

26. Rajiv Chandrasekaran and Anthony Shadid, "Gunmen Injure U.S. Appointed Iraqi Official," Washington Post, September 21, 2003, p. A1.

27. David Filipov, "Rebuilding Iraq: New Strains after Iraq Blast; UN to Reconsider Staffing Levels," Boston Globe, September 23, 2003, p. A1.

28. Kevin Kennedy, "Baghdad Update #3: SMT Recommendations," September 22, 2003. On the suggestion of Kevin Kennedy, the SMT included a caveat that if the secretary-general deemed it necessary, a small voluntary presence of international staff could be maintained in Baghdad to provide leadership to national staff, to liaise with the CPA and the Governing Council, and to continue beefing up security at the Canal Hotel. SMT, "For Consideration of the Steering Group on Iraq, Concept of Operations for a Core Presence in Baghdad, 22 September 2003." In a follow-up memo on September 24, Kennedy elaborated on the functions of this core presence. "A UN international presence, regardless of size, is more than mere symbolism; it indicates visible commitment and involvement. Ongoing discussions of a future role for the organization will be affected if the UN withdraws all international staff from Iraq and even a small presence can perform a critical role." The abandonment of national staff weighed on

him: "National Officers, regardless of experience and rank, will not get the same access or reaction from the Coalition, should assistance be required on an urgent basis." In addition "a complete departure of international staff may have a direct impact on the continued deliverance of NGO programmes." Kennedy also noted the UN's experience with reconstruction and the assistance UN officials were giving civilian contractors and Coalition engineers. "If all internationals leave, that work, for the most part, will cease, making a larger re-entry more difficult." The proposed core team included nineteen UN officials. "Concept of Operations for Core International Presence in Iraq," September 25, 2003.

29. Kennedy, "Baghdad Update #3."

30. In April 2004 Lopes da Silva was named country director of the World Food Program operation in Sudan.

31. Gil Loescher, online diary, www.caringbridge.org/pa/gilloescher.

32. Annan's report to the Security Council in August 2004 said that the security of UN staff would be the "overarching guiding principle" for all UN activities in Iraq. In December 2004 Annan announced the creation at Headquarters of the UN Department of Safety and Security, for which the General Assembly added $53.6 million to the UN's regular budget. The Department of Safety and Security would have 383 posts, 134 of them temporary. See www.un.org/News/Press/docs/2005/dsgsm242.doc.htm.

33. Al-Kurdi said he had also been involved in the September 22 attack, dropping off the car used by the bomber. He was involved in a November 12, 2003, attack on the Italian police headquarters in Nasiriyah, killing nineteen Italians, the first Italian casualties in the Iraq war and the worst single loss of life for Italy since World War II. Twenty Italians were wounded. At least eight Iraqis were killed, and more than fifty wounded. He also owned up to the assassination of Izziden Salim, the former president of the Iraqi Governing Council. Al-Kurdi was arrested on January 15, 2005, and testified on March 30 before the Iraqi Central Criminal Court.

34. All quotes in the confession taken from Ashraf Jehengir Qazi to Ibrahim Gambari, "Meeting with Awraz Abd Al Aziz Mahmoud Sa'eed, aka Al Kurdi," Code Cable CZX-251, July 3, 2006.

EPILOGUE

1. Felicity Barringer, "UN Chief Says New Force in Iraq Can Be Led by U.S.," *New York Times*, August 23, 2003, p. A2. "We have played a vital role," Annan said. "But we did because of that personality. Because of Sergio being who he is. The next time around, the mandates have to be very clear and well-defined. I cannot rely on personalities. I had only one Sergio."

2. SVDM, "The World's Conscience: The UN Facing the Irrational in History," inaugural lecture at the Graduate Institute of International Studies, Geneva, November 2, 2000, p. 11.

3. Ibid., p. 6.

4. SVDM, "Global Governance and the UN," address to annual meeting of Trilateral Commission, Tokyo, 2000.

5. SVDM, "War and Politics: The Humanitarian Deceit," written 1998, unpublished, p. 2.

6. Ibid., p. 4.

7. SVDM, "The World's Conscience," p. 11.

8. SVDM, "The Future of UN State-Building," International Peace Academy conference, October 18–19, 2002, www.ipacademy.org/pdfs/YOU_THE_PEOPLE.pdf.

9. Ibid.

10. Ibid.

11. Ibid.

12. SVDM, "War and Politics," p. 10.

13. SVDM, "Challenges in Peacekeeping: Past, Present and Future," New York, October 29, 2002.

14. SVDM, "Philosophical History and Real History. The Relevance of Kant's Political Thought in Current Times," Geneva International Peace Research Institute, December 4, 1991.

15. SVDM, "The World's Conscience," p. 11.

LIST OF INTERVIEWS

(excluding sources who asked not to be named)

Hamid Abdeljabar
Mort Abramowitz
Robert Adolph
Enrique Aguilar
Rafeeuddin Ahmed
Salman Ahmed
Jean-Claude Aimé
Yasushi Akashi
Marwan Ali
Mari Alkatiri
John Almstrom
Domingos Amaral
Viktor Andreev
Hedi Annabi
Kofi Annan
Jamshid Anvar
Eduardo Arboleda
Louise Arbour
Ghassan Arnaout
Kofi Asomani
Jahanshah Assadi
Reginald Austin
Øivind Baekken
Omar Bakhet
Anthony Banbury
Maurice Baril
Romain Baron
Mark Baskin
Afsane Bassir-Pour
Elizabeth Becker
Jamal Benomar
Catherine Bertini
Nick Birnback

Anne-Wilhelm Bjeleveld
Barbara Bodine
Mieke Bos
Joel Boutroue
Lakhdar Brahimi
Rony Brauman
L. Paul Bremer
Sten Bronee
Scott Brown
Thomas Bryant
Patrick Burgess
Terry Burke
Adam Bye
Dawn Calabia
William Callaghan
Mark Calvert
Luciano Cappelletti
Fiorella Cappelli
Tim Carney
Chris Carpenter
J. Carter
Alexander "Sacha" Casella
Heidi Cervantes
Rajiv Chandrasekaran
Edwin Chaplin
Alain Chergui
David Chikvaidze
Raymond Chrétien
Christa Christensen
Sarah Cliffe
Pierre Coat
Dan Conway
Hans Correll

Nick Costello
Ryan Crocker
Jacques Cuénod
Mark Cutts
Guillermo Dacuhna
Nici Dahrendorf
Flavio da Silveira
John Dauth
Leon Davico
Jeff Davie
Graham Day
Virendra Dayal
Josette Delhomme
Daisy Dell
Staffan de Mistura
Chefike Desalegn
Leandro Despouy
Giuseppe de Vincentis
Eugene Dewey
Robert Dillon
Antonio Carlos Diegues
  Santana
Laura Dolci-Kanaan
Pat Dray
Frank Dutton
Fred Eckhard
Kai Eide
Jan Eliasson
Ralf Embro
Maria Therese Emery
Steve Erlanger
Gareth Evans
Caroll Faubert

Ahmad Fawzi
Alan Fellows
Sylvana Foa
François Fouinat
Helena Fraser
Louise Fréchette
Bill French
Thomas Fuentes
Don Gagliano
Peter Galbraith
Ejup Ganic
Timur Goksel
George Gordon-Lennox
Filippo Grandi
Jeremy Greenstock
Martin Griffiths
Robin Groves
Stuart Groves
Jean-Marie Guéhenno
Vladislav Guerassev
Iain Guest
Xanana Gusmão
Francisco Guterres
Richard Haass
David Haeri
Raymond Hall
Jean Halpérin
Don Hamilton
Josh Hammer
John Hansen
David Harland
Eric Hartman
Ingrid Hayden
Barbara Hendricks
Gavin Hewitt
Fabrizio Hochschild
Nicole Hochschild
Jean-Pierre Hocké
Richard Holbrooke
Dwaine Holland
Larry Hollingworth

Franz-Josef Homann-
  Herimberg
Raymond Hunston
Zeid Raad Zeid al-
  Hussein
Gamal Ibrahim
Filomeno Jacob
Pierre Jambor
David Jamieson
Kris Janowski
Udo Janz
Carmela Javier
Søren Jessen-Petersen
Sidney Jones
Nils Kastberg
Kevin Kennedy
Patrick Kennedy
Randolph Kent
Rashid Khalikov
Irene Khan
Charles Kirudja
Lennart Kotsalainen
Bernard Kouchner
Robert Kroon
Andreas Kuhn
Vance Kuhner
Nina Lahoud
David Lambo
Carolina Larriera
Romano Lasker
Jean-David Levitte
Gil Loescher
Salvatore Lombardo
Salim Lone
Ramiro Lopes da Silva
Damien Loras
Shep Lowman
Ruud Lubbers
James Lynch
John MacInnis
Caroline McAskie

Dennis McNamara
Antonio Carlos
  Machado
Scott Malcomson
Mark Malloch Brown
David Malone
Richard Manlove
Marilyn "Lyn" Manuel
David Marshall
Harriet Martin
Ian Martin
Armando Martinez
  Valdes
Kati Marton
Amor Masovic
Brad May
José Marie Mendiluce
Claire Messina
Robert Misrahi
  (interview conducted
  by Michel Thieren)
Pervez Mita
Hiroko Miyamura
Darko Mocibob
Kevin Molcy
Michael Moller
Jonathan Moore
Katie Moore
Luis Moreno Ocampo
Fabienne Morisset
Kamel Morjane
Nicholas Morris
Edward Mortimer
Ross Mountain
Nader Mousavizadeh
Sue Munch
Hasan Muratović
Thant Myint-U
Basilio do Nascimento
Izumi Nakamitsu-
  Lennartsson

Elisabeth Naucler
Aryeh Neier
Simon Niersz
Norah Niland
Ingrid Nordstrom-Ho
Sadako Ogata
Tadhg O'Neill
Robert Orr
Adnan Pachachi
George Packer
Maria Christina Penna
Agio Pereira
Carina Perelli
Genevieve Personnaz
Michel Personnaz
Ana Pessoa
Gaby Pichon
Paulo Sérgio Pinheiro
John Pomfret
Jean-Claude Pomonti
Heidi Postlewait
Antonia Potter
Kieran Prendergast
Jonathan Prentice
Ashraf Jehangir Qazi
Mark Quarterman
Bertrand Ramcharan
José Ramos-Horta
Carole Ray
Ron Redmond
Kathleen Reen
Grover Joseph Rees
David Richmond
Mona Rishmawi
Paul Risley
Iqbal Riza
Courtland Robinson
Geoffrey Robinson
Michael Rose
Lionel Rosenblatt
Ken Roth

Stanley Roth
Taur Matan Ruak
John Ruggie
John Russell
Dennis Sabal
Joe Sacco
Ghassan Salamé
Tamrat Samuel
Samir Sanbar
John Sanderson
Domingos Marie
  Sarmento
Micheline Saunders
John Sawers
Eric Schwartz
Simon Shadbolt
Anthony Shadid
Nadine Shamounki
Haris Silajdžić
André Simões
Renata Simões
Lamin Sise
Sichan Siv
Brad Smith
Richard Smyser
Bernabe Barreto Soares
Nancy Soderberg
Andrew Sokiri
George Soros
Andre Soubirou
Douglas Stafford
Max Stahl
Jonathan Steele
Donald Steinberg
Annick Stevenson
Colin Stewart
Pat Stogran
Ronnie Stokes
Thorvald Stoltenberg
Carl Strock
Hansjörg Strohmeyer

Paul Stromberg
Athar Sultan-Khan
Zoreh Tabatabai
Julia Taft
Shawbo Taher
Jeanetta Terry-Short
Shashi Tharoor
Nate Thayer
Andrew Thomson
Cedric Thornberry
Daniel Toole
Danilo Turk
Bob Turner
Jack Turner
Charlie Twining
Oliver Ulich
Sarah Uppard
Lola Urošević
Brian Urquhart
Andre Valentine
Olivier Van Bunnen
Stéphane Vandam
Wibo van de Line
Robert Van Leeuwen
Fransesc Vendrell
David Veness
Annie Vieira de Mello
Antonio Vieira de Mello
Gilda Vieira de Mello
Sonia Vieira de Mello
Jeff "Rand" Vollmer
William von Zehle
Gerald Walzer
Brad Ward
Judtya Wasowska
Pat White
Michael Williams
Guy Willoughby
David Wilmhurst
James Wolfensohn
Kirsten Young

PHOTOGRAPH CREDITS

INSERT IMAGES

Pages 1–4, all: Courtesy of Gilda Vieira de Mello

Page 5, top: Courtesy of Gilda Vieira de Mello; bottom: Courtesy of Timur Goskel

Page 6, top: Sylvana Foa, courtesy of Jamshid Anvar; bottom: Courtesy of Gilda Vieira de Mello

Page 7, all: Courtesy of Mieke Bos

Page 8, all: Courtesy of Michael Rose

Page 9, top: AP Images/Srdjan Suki; bottom: UN/DPI Photo

Page 10, top: AP Images/Ruth Fremson; bottom: Courtesy of Gilda Vieira de Mello

Page 11, top: Commonwealth of Australia; bottom left: Edy Purnomo/Getty Images; bottom right: Nicole Hochschild

Page 12, top: Courtesy of Dennis McNamara; middle: UN/DPI Photo; bottom: Courtesy of Carolina Larriera

Page 13, top left: Courtesy of Jonathan Prentice; top right: Courtesy of Gilda Vieira de Mello; bottom: White House Photo by Eric Draper

Page 14, top: AP Images/Vahid Salemi; bottom: Courtesy of Carolina Larriera

Page 15, top: Stan Honda/Getty Images; bottom: Courtesy of Carolina Larriera

Page 16, top: AP Images/Victor R. Caivano; bottom: Vania Laranjeira

INDEX

Page numbers in *italics* refer to illustrations. "SVDM" refers to Sergio Vieira de Mello.